With Jesus Leading the Way
A Memoir

By Norma Christmas Bobbett

*For Jim and Cindy Dudley,
May God bless you both. Thank you for your love for Africa.
Norma Bobbett*

Copyright © 2018 Norma Christmas Bobbett
All rights reserved.
ISBN:978-1719522717

Contents

Acknowledgments iii
Acronyms and Abbreviations iv
Introduction 7
Chapter 1: Beginnings 11
Chapter 2: Early Paths 25
Chapter 3: High School and College Years 32
Chapter 4: Heath's Story 45
Chapter 5: Each for the Other, and Both for the Lord 53
Chapter 6: A Mission Board and Pre-Field Ministry 69
Chapter 7: In France for French Language Study 85
Chapter 8: Finally in Niger 102
Chapter 9: The First Year in Gaya 115
Chapter 10: Finishing Our First Term in Gaya 146
Chapter 11: First Furlough 190
Chapter 12: Second Term in Gaya 203
Chapter 13: Continuing Our Second Term 229
Chapter 14: Second Furlough 243
Chapter 15: Third Term in Niamey 253
Chapter 16: Third Furlough 296
Chapter 17: Fourth Term in Niger 302
Chapter 18: Fourth Furlough 339
Chapter 19: Fifth Term in Niger 343
Chapter 20: Sixth Term in Dosso 359
Chapter 21: Fifth Furlough 368
Chapter 22: Seventh Term in Dosso 375
Chapter 23: Extended Furlough 394
Chapter 24: Zarma Bible Translation and Revision 408
Chapter 25: Seventh Furlough 429

Chapter 26: Eighth Term in Niger 434
Chapter 27: Answered Prayer and Continued Ministry 463
Chapter 28: Final Months in Niger 477
Chapter 29: First Years Back in the States 484
Chapter 30: Work's End or Second Wind? 490
Chapter 31: International Students and Short-Term Ministries 506
Chapter 32: Bénin, Québec, and Haiti 519
Chapter 33: Hebron Dedication, Québec, Niger, Italy, Lebanon 537
Chapter 34: He's Been Faithful to Me 554
Epilogue 570
Final Tributes 572
Some of Norma's Favorite Quotes 574
Appendix 576

Acknowledgments

A heartfelt thanks to our daughter Rebecca Ahlgrim
who worked so hard going through albums, envelopes, and drawers
to find the pictures included in our memoirs.
She spent hours and hours assisting with the editing process.
The best we could have ever done would have been a page or two
of black-and-white pictures, but she has done a marvelous job
of finding and using all these pictures.

A special thanks to our son Jonathan Bobbett for providing
the financial resources for this project. This memoir would have
been impossible without his support.

Thank you to our friends Laura Cerbus and Teresa Clark
for editing, proofing, and polishing my writing.

Acronyms and Abbreviations

BBC – Baptist Bible College in Clarks Summit, Pennsylvania
EBM – Evangelical Baptist Mission
ICA – Ivory Coast Academy High School in Bouaké, Ivory Coast
UEEB – Union des Eglises Evangélique Baptiste du Niger, EBM's first African missionary society
MK – missionary kid
PCV – Peace Corps volunteer
SIM – Sudan Interior Mission (now called Serving In Mission)

AFRICA

Norma Bobbett

Introduction

*Each day, God is writing new things upon our hearts,
and our years are the chapters that record His faithfulness.*
— Roy Lessin

I thank the Lord for my wonderful, godly husband, Heath, who has always been a source of blessing and encouragement to me. Also, I am so grateful for granting me the privilege of being a mother. Rebecca, Jonathan, Alan, Nathan, and Mariama are an indescribable joy to me. I love them more than words can convey.

It was never my intention that my written memoirs from my journals and our prayer letters would become a *book*. I wanted to print them for our children and our descendants, praying they would see what a wonderful and faithful God we serve.

Just as Paul wrote in Acts about his call to Macedonia, our call to Niger was very real. Heath and I were thankful that we could go out with Jesus leading the way (Mark 10:32). In many ways we were like Abraham because we went out not knowing what the land and people would be like. There were no pre-field visits then or short-term assignments. We took our two little ones and went with only the assurance that this was where God was leading us. That was all we needed. How faithful our Lord was to us! His calling is indeed His enabling. We can say confidently with Paul that "He who calls you is faithful, who also will do it." (I Thessalonians 5:24).

Sometimes we were more naïve than brave; we surely were green and had so much to learn. However, the Lord helped us walk that unknown path as His disciples because we had the promises of His Word. He said He would never leave us or forsake us. We never felt afraid of our friends and neighbors there – African hospitality and camaraderie is unparalleled. Over the years, we learned far more from our African friends than we were ever able to teach them. The godly lives of our African brothers and sisters in Christ were a testimony and challenge to us. Even those we met all along the way who were not believers amazed us with their warm kindness, their friendship, their hospitality, and their willingness to share their meager possessions with us.

But I did fear African diseases, especially for my children. Even so, the verses "Be strong and of good courage, do not fear nor be afraid of them; for the Lord your God, He is the One who goes with you. He will not leave you nor forsake you" (Deuteronomy 31:6) and "I'm convinced that nothing can separate us from God's love in Christ Jesus our Lord." (Romans 8:38-39) gave us a firm foundation.

Sometimes others speak of missionaries and the great sacrifices they have made, putting us on a pedestal that we do not deserve. Serving as missionaries in Africa was a unique privilege that our Lord and Savior granted to us. If we had our lives to live over, we would say yes to Him again and follow His leading. It was a life full of adventure with God walking every path with us.

Sadly, many years before we arrived, Islam had swept across West Africa, converting many "by the sword." By the time we put our feet on Nigerien soil, several generations had followed this religion and its false teachings about the Lord Jesus Christ. We did not see abundant conversions as we worked there. Believers suffer ostracism by their families with threats of harm or even death. However, we saw that each one who became a believer in Jesus Christ was a beautiful trophy of God's grace. God bound our hearts together in love for each other.

We bless God for allowing us the great honor to bring them the Good News of Jesus Christ. Those who came to know Him rejoiced knowing that beyond their struggles and hardships there was heaven and that God had made a way for all of us to have our sins forgiven. We had the privilege of planting the seed of the Word of God. Often the soil was rocky and hard, not allowing the seed to germinate, take root, and grow. But there was also the good soil that God had prepared for some from every tribe and nation to hear the truth about Jesus, repent of their sins, and have their names written in heaven.

Lord, going out "with Jesus leading the way," You raised up our support, You blessed us with children, You sustained us during the difficult work among Muslims, You saw us through the painful years of our children's illnesses in Niger. You were always there with me and for me. Father, the pages of my journals could not begin to hold my writing of how marvelous, how wonderful You are!

It is my desire in writing these memoirs that God will be glorified. I want our children and our children's children to see how wonderful He is, how He loves and cares for His own, and how He still is working wonders all around us every day. The greatest joy is when the Holy Spirit works in an individual's heart, bringing that person to repentance and saving faith in Jesus Christ. May I never get over the wonder of it all – "Just to think that Jesus loves me!"

Jesus Led Me All the Way
Lyrics by John W. Peterson

Someday life's journey will be o'er,
And I shall reach that distant shore;
I'll sing while entering Heaven's door,
"Jesus led me all the way."
Jesus led me all the way,
Led me step by step each day;
I will tell the saints and angels as I lay my burdens down,
"Jesus led me all the way."

Chapter 1
Beginnings
October 1933

I was the fourth child born into the home of Eppy Carl Christmas and Lena Elizabeth Goodman Christmas. It was October 5, 1933, and I was literally born into their home because at that time babies weren't born in hospitals. Mother told me that Dr. Beck stopped by our house on Little York Road in Dayton, Ohio, in the morning to check on her. (At that time and for a great portion of my early life, doctors made house calls for illnesses and for delivering babies!) Although Mother felt no contractions, Dr. Beck said, "It looks like I will be back this evening to deliver a baby here." And he was right! Mother sent my siblings, Evelyn Marie (age fourteen), Carl David (almost age twelve), and Melvin Lee (age seven) to a neighbor's home until after the birth. Another neighbor was there to help mother and bathe me.

After the delivery, Dad said that when Dr. Beck emerged from the bedroom he announced, "Well Carl, you have another dishwasher!" I smile as I think about how today's feminists would react to such a statement. Evelyn expressed her joy in finally having a baby sister in a poem she wrote for me:

Little Sister
By Evelyn Christmas

> 'Twas on a bright October morn,
> When I, with eyes alight
> Looked upon a newborn
> And left my heart abide.
>
> Her eyes were like twin cups of dew
> Her skin like a fair, fair rose.

Her hands were soft and new,
But best of all was her funny little nose.

What does a little sister mean to me?
Not just a thing to cuddle and coo.
Not a baby that's new,
But a dream of what she'll be
When she gets as old as me.

Norma is her name,
But we call her "Teachy."
No sweeter thing to us has come,
Since the coming of our Teachy.

She is ours! What a thought!
It makes the world seem brighter.
And let us always be caught
In the web that holds us closer to her and tighter.

Melvin (whom we always called Mickey) had been the baby in the family for seven years, so he was not happy about having his place taken by a baby sister. He had recently seen a movie starring the very homely Wallace Beery, so his first words when he saw my red and wrinkled face were, "Humph! She looks like Wallace Beery!" The family never forgot the laughter he caused with that statement.

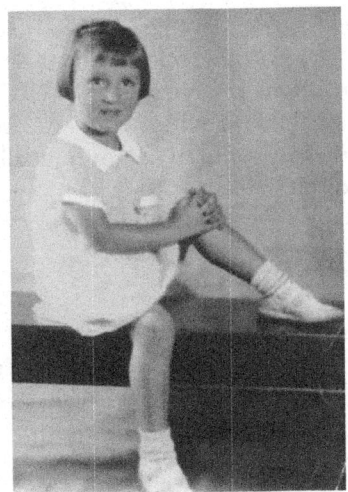

I was born during the Great Depression, and although we were poor, we didn't realize it. Dad worked hard to support his family, but sadly, for years he had a very cruel supervisor who held him back from advancement and a better salary. This boss was so disliked by all the employees that on the day that he retired, no one would sit with him at lunch. Dad's new supervisor was named John Bersuda, and he began to advance Dad continually. When questioned by higher authorities about the rapid advancements, John said, "Eppy is a wounded WWI veteran, having served in the war, but he has been mercilessly held back for years. The work he produces has merited advancement for a very long time, but he was held back by my predecessor." No more questions were asked.

Our house was quite small. One room was a combination living room and dining room, and there was a small kitchen. There were two small bedrooms when he first bought the house. Later Dad built on a small bathroom and another bedroom. I don't know when our indoor bathroom was built, although I do remember the outhouse in our backyard and my mother standing me on a chair in her bedroom to give me a sponge bath. Because our house was on the side of a hill, we had a walk-out basement. Seeking the coolness of the basement on hot and muggy days, Mom cooked and we all ate our meals down there. Mom did all her canning of fruits and vegetables – provided by Dad's large garden and many fruit trees, many times boiling the filled jars into the wee hours of the morning. Preparing the fruits and vegetables for canning was a family project as we sat around seeding the cherries, snapping beans, and so forth. Dad would buy bushels of peaches to can. To this day I can't find any kind of commercially canned or frozen peaches that taste as good as Mom's home-canned ones. She lined up her home-canned jars on basement shelves, and we enjoyed them all winter.

Our home was heated by a coal stove in the middle of the dining and living area. The bedrooms were cold in the winter, especially the back one where Carl and Mickey slept under piles of blankets. On winter mornings we could see our breath in there. My bedroom was closest to the dining and living area, and sometimes Mom and Dad allowed me to leave the door open to warm my bedroom but not for long. My bedroom was the only place for our upright piano. Mom faithfully sent me for piano lessons, and I could open the door to warm my room when I practiced. I had a bedroom all my own for most of my life after Evelyn graduated with honors from Butler High School in 1937 and left home to find work.

We had a four-party line telephone. When the phone rang, each of the parties had a particular ring. One long ring was ours, the other party liners had two short or one short, one long ring, and so forth. Often some folks listened in on other conversations.

We also had a well and a septic tank. There was only cold water in the kitchen and bathroom, but for the Saturday night baths, Mom lit a fire in the basement heater, so we could take hot baths. There was also a small space heater in the bathroom. During the week we took sponge baths in the sink with cold water. Mom also had to heat water for washing dishes. We had a kerosene stove in the kitchen with big wick burners. She was constantly trimming and working with those burner wicks to keep them from smoking and making her wallpaper and ceiling discolored.

We also had an ice box. The ice man delivered a big block of ice a couple of times a week, picking up the block with huge tongs and carrying it into our kitchen on his shoulder. My friends and I often stood at the

back of his truck hoping he would chip off a little ice for us to suck on for a treat. He was kind and managed to find some chips most of the time. The milkman stopped several times a week with milk in returnable glass bottles. In those days milk settled, and the cream was at the top. There were cardboard stoppers or lids on the milk bottles. On extremely cold days, if you didn't hurry out to bring the milk in, the cream froze, popped the lid, and expanded about an inch above the bottle.

The bakery truck also stopped a couple of times a week. The baker had all kinds of goody-filled drawers that he pulled out in the back of his truck. Mom usually just bought bread, although sometimes she gave in to the pleas of us children for cupcakes or pies if she didn't have some of her homemade ones in the house.

We didn't have fast food when I was growing up. All the food was slow cooked by our mothers, and we ate it at home. When Dad got home from work, we sat down together at the kitchen table to eat. My brother Mickey was the only one of us four children who had a bicycle. Our big sister Evelyn bought it for him, and sometimes he let me ride on it. We never had a television in our home, though when I, the youngest child, was in college, Dad did buy his first black and white television. I was in college before I tasted my first "pizza pie." There were few places where you could buy this novelty, and it wasn't delivered.

All newspapers were delivered by paper boys, and all boys had a job as paperboy sometime in their growing up years. Daily papers cost four cents, and the paperboy made one cent profit on each paper.

My mom washed the clothes on Mondays with an old wringer washer and rinse tubs. She hung the clothes on the line outside to dry or on lines strung up in the basement in the winter. She starched some of the clothes. Using a pop bottle with a stopper that had a bunch of holes in it, she sprinkled the dried clothes with water and rolled them up tightly then spent many hours the next day ironing them to perfection. There were no steam irons then. My grandchildren probably don't even know what a sprinkling bottle is!

The first day of school was always the day after Labor Day. I can remember Mom taking me to be registered for first grade in 1939. There was a doctor who checked each child over at the school registration. He remarked that I was underweight at forty-two pounds, so she told him about my serious illness in the preceding months: at the age of five, I had almost died from whooping cough and pneumonia.

All twelve grades of Butler School were in the same building on Route 40 in Vandalia, Ohio. When I was in first grade, Mickey was in seventh grade, and Carl was a senior. It was a public school, and each morning the first thing that occurred was reading the Bible, then all of us children recited the Lord's Prayer together.

I attended Butler School for all twelve grades and rode a school bus to and from school all those years. I remember well one first grade instance when I embarrassed Carl. On the bus that morning, another student gave me a small branch of pussy willows. They were so soft and furry. I was playing with them as Miss Rule, my first-grade teacher, was teaching class. I experimented by putting one in each ear to see if my "ear plugs" would keep me from hearing her. Pushing them farther and farther in, I soon realized I couldn't get them out and I panicked! I told dear Miss Rule what I had done. She tried to extract them, but they were too far in! I was taken to the principal's office, and Carl was called down there from his twelfth-grade class to hear about it. I must have embarrassed him, but he was my big brother and didn't say anything. Our family doctor, Dr. Smith, came and pulled them out. I imagine all of them were rolling their eyes at this silly thing I had done. I wonder if my parents ever got a bill from Dr. Smith. Probably not.

Me at (age 9) with big brother Carl and two younger cousins, Connie and James Goodman.

When school was out for summer vacation, I went barefoot from May until September, only putting on shoes for Sunday school (and boy did they hurt). We had our several acres of property to roam on, as well as neighbors' fields and wooded areas. We spent the summer days in the fields, playing, climbing trees, and playing games with neighbor kids, such as Mother May I; Hide and Seek; Red Rover; and Kick the Can. Dad built a nice little outdoor fireplace and picnic area on the back of our property where we could have weenie and marshmallow roasts and fun around a campfire with our friends. By the end of summer, we were as brown as could be, healthy and content. We had never heard of television but managed to entertain ourselves all day long having fun. We could be gone all day in these activities, only coming home when we got hungry. Mom never worried about us or feared for our safety as long as we were home by dark.

The following came from the internet, and I have added a few observations of my own. It well describes my childhood:

"While carrying their babies, our mothers took aspirin, ate blue cheese dressing and tuna from a can, and didn't get tested for diabetes. Then after that trauma, we were put to sleep on our tummies in baby cribs covered with bright colored lead-based paints. We had no childproof lids on medicine bottles, doors, or cabinets, and when we rode our bikes, we had no helmets (not to mention the risks my brothers took hitchhiking into town from our home in the country!).

As infants and children, we rode in cars with no car seats, booster seats, seat belts, or air bags. Riding in the back of a pickup on a warm day was always a special treat. We drank water from the garden hose and *not* from a bottle. We shared one soft drink from one bottle with four friends, and *no one* actually died from this. We ate cupcakes, white bread, and real butter and drank Kool-Aid made with sugar, but we weren't overweight because *we were always outside playing*. We left home in the morning and played all day, as long as we were back at home before darkness fell. No one was able to reach us all day, but we were okay. We spent hours with our wagons, riding down the hill in our yard. There were no brakes, but after running into the bushes a few times or turning over, we learned to solve the problem. We did not have television, PlayStations, Nintendo, Xboxes, no video games at all. No 150 channels on cable, no video movies or DVDs, no surround sound or CDs, no cell phones, no personal computers, no internet or chat rooms. *We had friends*, and we went outside and found them! We fell out of trees, got cut, broke bones and teeth, and there were no lawsuits from these accidents. Boys were given BB guns for their tenth birthdays, we made up games with sticks and tennis balls, and although we were told it would happen, we did not put out anyone's eyes. We rode bikes or walked to a friend's house, stood outside calling our friend's name loudly. If his mom answered the call, we asked, "Can ____ come out and play?" There were no Little League games to compete in. We changed from our school clothes into our play clothes when we got home from school, went to a nearby field, chose our teams from our neighborhood friends to play ball until it got too dark to see. If you were the last one chosen for a team, you had to learn to deal with disappointment. Imagine that! The idea of a parent bailing us out if we broke the law was unheard of. They actually sided with the law!

If we got in trouble at school and were paddled, we knew if our parents found out we would be paddled again at home. We respected our teachers, and so did our parents. All the mothers in the neighborhood were addressed as Mrs. ____ and never by first names because we respected adults. We grew up as kids before the lawyers and government regulated so much of our lives "for our own good".

I don't remember which birthday it was that Dad's surprise gift to me was his making a huge, wide rope swing in one of the trees in the back part of our yard. This gift from my dad to me meant so much, and I will remember it all my life. There was room for me alone or for a playmate to join me on the swing. It went so high and was a great delight to all of us for many years. Sometimes we wound it around and around and sat in the swing as it unraveled, making us dissolve into laughter when we got off, staggering with dizziness.

We knew all our neighbors along Little York Road for perhaps a mile in each direction. Many women loved to come and talk to my mother and pour out their hearts to her. Mom kept a spotless house, but she always made it homey and warm too. She was known for her warm hospitality, and my teenaged friends loved her.

I must mention one neighbor specifically, Mrs. Karns, because with Jesus leading the way, she was the one who exposed me to the Gospel. Mrs. Karns was a member of the Church of the Brethren. Her husband, Marley, was an alcoholic. She started an adult Bible study in her home and always had a children's Bible class in the kitchen while the adults met in her front room. She enticed us neighborhood children to come because she always had a piece of candy for each of us who met in her kitchen. We really looked forward to that candy treat, and it drew us in. We learned stories from the Bible, and one week there was even a "real live missionary" who spoke! While the adults in the front room were being taught the Word and the way of salvation, we children were hearing good Bible teaching in the kitchen. Mrs. Karns suffered from severe rheumatism, so after a few years, at her doctor's recommendation, they moved to a drier climate in Arizona. Her godly influence was missed in our neighborhood.

This may be the only picture I have of my mom, my sister Evelyn, and me together. While my mother never learned how to drive, she got around well on trolleys and buses. Every Thursday was Mom's day out. She walked up to the four corners of Murlin Heights, caught a Greyhound bus into the city, spent the day shopping at the department stores and five-and-ten stores, had lunch (that often included her favorite – cherry pie) at a counter of the five-and-ten, then took an electric-powered city trolley out to North Dayton to finish her day shopping at a supermarket. On his way home from work, Dad picked up Mom and the groceries. Mom, at times, complained how expensive groceries were getting – "Eight dollars for only four paper bags of groceries!"

She sometimes talked of getting a job, but Dad never wanted her to. He said, "I will provide for my family. You don't have to get a job." We children realized in later years what a blessing it was to always have our mother at home when we returned from school, play, or work.

My Mom

My mother, Lena Elizabeth (Johnston) Goodman, was born in Kentucky, close to the Ohio border, but grew up near Portsmouth, Ohio, and had one full sister, Pearl. Their father's name was Charles Johnston, but we don't know much about him. When Lena was about three years old and Pearl was one year old, their mother, Mary Alice Robbins, married Henry Goodman. Pearl and Lena later had six half sisters and brothers.

We were a close family, and there were lots of visits with aunts, uncles, and cousins as we grew up. Both my mother and my Aunt Pearl spoke very highly of their stepfather and said he was good to them.

My mother was a sweet girl who had great love and respect for her mother, who was a fine Christian woman. My mom had a hard life. She was able to finish eighth grade (considered a good education at that time), then left home at that tender age to earn her own way in life, working as a housekeeper and nanny.

My grandmother Mary Alice died before I was born, so I only knew Grandpa Henry Goodman. He was always so good to me, and I felt like he was my "real" maternal grandpa too. He had later married a nice lady named Velvia who owned a general store on Wilson Run Road near Chillicothe, Ohio. There was no electricity on their property. They also had a hand gasoline pump out front of the general store for people who were buying gas. Grandpa Goodman was a farmer, but he helped Velvia with the store and selling gas.

I have wonderful childhood memories of spending summer days with my cousins on Wilson Run Road and of family reunions at Grandpa and Velvia's house. Besides not having electricity in their house, there also was no indoor plumbing. Their outhouse was located close to the small creek that ran behind their house. This outhouse (or privy) was unique. It was wallpapered and was also a two-seater. Compared to other outhouses we knew, we thought this one was truly special! Old newspapers or catalogs were used for TP. They worked well and were economical; toilet paper and other paper products were not abundant and were considered a luxury. In summertime we didn't mind lingering in the outhouse to look at the catalog or newspapers, but in winter we didn't linger! It was extremely cold when you had to bare your bottom sitting on the wooden seat!

At Grandpa and Velvia's house, water was pumped from the well just outside the kitchen. A bucket of drinking water was kept in the kitchen. We all used the same dipper to drink from and never seemed to get sick from one another's germs. There was a long porch that went across the front of their house and around one side. The tables almost groaned under the heavy weight of all the delicious homecooked foods for our reunions. After everyone had eaten, Grandpa always called us into their living room for a time of hymn singing, and Velvia would play the old pump organ. Grandpa

Goodman had never been to school and couldn't read. However, he had a sharp mind and had all the hymn numbers memorized. He would say, "Let's sing 'The Old Rugged Cross' on page eighty-seven." He liked to ask Bible questions to both children and adults, then challenge us with his answers. He also enjoyed telling you where to find his references in the Bible, though he couldn't read it himself. Jesus was leading the way for me even back then as I saw Grandpa and Velvia and their devotion to the Lord. We always sang one of his favorites, "I'll Fly Away:"

I'll Fly Away
Lyrics by Albert E. Brumley

Some glad morning, when this life is o'er, I'll fly away
To that land on God's celestial shore, I'll fly away.
I'll fly away, O glory! I'll fly away.
When I die, hallelujah by and by, I'll fly away!

Whenever I hear this song, I think of Grandpa Goodman. How wonderful it will be to see him again in heaven!

My Dad

My father, Eppy Carl Christmas, was born March 20, 1896, in a log cabin in Clinton County, Tennessee. That day was his mother Lucretia Pritchard Christmas' eighteenth birthday. His father was Arthur Christmas. A couple of years later, Estella Christmas was born into the family. When Eppy was five years old, his father died of typhoid fever. Eppy also became ill with the typhoid and wasn't expected to live, but by God's grace he did recover. God had a plan for his future which included bringing him to Christ before he died.

Sometime after Eppy's father died, my widowed grandmother married Houck Viles. They had eight more children. Grandpa Houck was a sweet and kind man, and I always felt like he was my flesh and blood grandpa, too. My Grandma Lucretia could be a little spitfire sometimes, but he always remained calm and steady. Their last daughter, Neota, was born when Grandma Lucretia was forty-seven!

Dad was a self-made man. He quit school after third grade in Tennessee. His family was so poor that he had no shoes to wear to school, and the other children taunted him. At the age of nine or ten, he began to work and help the family. He first rode the train from Harriman to Knoxville as a news butch, selling newspapers, candy, and gum. He learned some clever tricks to boost his sales income. If someone bought a paper, read it, and then tossed it aside, he carefully folded it to sell again. He

With Jesus Leading the Way

wasn't above approaching couples, so he could challenge (read: shame) the young man into buying this or that for the pretty girl he was with.

He held various jobs during his teenage years, but at about age twenty, he and a couple of friends decided to make their way from Tennessee to Dayton, Ohio, in search of a job. He ended up working as a short-order cook at a restaurant near a factory. Because of this job, when World War I broke out and he enlisted in the army, he was given a position as army cook.

Dad served in World War I and was seriously wounded in Belgium. He was evacuated to a hospital in London, England. He found it ironic that he served in World War I, "the war to end all wars," but twenty-some years later, his son, Carl David Christmas, served in the army during World War II and was hospitalized in the same London hospital that Dad was. Carl was there for a tonsillectomy, though, and not for being wounded.

Dad and his double cousin Dave Christmas grew up together in Tennessee. (Their fathers were brothers who married sisters.) Dave and Dad remained close buddies and fishing partners all their lives. Dave established The Christmas Lumber Company in Harriman, Tennessee.

Dad and Dave entertained us (and themselves) recounting all their adventures as young boys, going to school and playing together. They were typical young mischievous boys. They laughed so hard remembering their childhood escapades. We loved hearing them each tell what the other did.

21

My father met my mother at a carnival while he was a World War I soldier stationed in Chillicothe, Ohio. Dad said he and his buddy were watching The Whip amusement ride when he looked across the area to see Lena and her cousin also watching the ride. Mom was only seventeen years old, and he was twenty-one. Attracted by her beauty, he told his buddy, "That's the girl I'm going to marry!"

Like many wartime romances, their courtship was short. They were married at the Chillicothe courthouse on October 6, 1917. Right after the wedding, he was shipped out to Montgomery, Alabama. He sent for Mom to come by train after he found an apartment off base. When he was deployed overseas, he asked Mom to go to Harriman, Tennessee, to live with his mother and stepfather until his return. She had never met her feisty mother-in-law before.

One day, Dad's name appeared on a posted list in Harriman of soldiers who had died in the war. His mother refused to believe it and disputed this report about her son. Later word came through that she was right; he had been wounded in Belgium and evacuated to England, but he was not dead.

In Belgium, Dad's left leg was severely wounded. As a result, he carried pieces of shrapnel at various places in his body the rest of his life. After his army discharge, he and Mom went to Dayton to live. Evelyn was born in Dayton on March 5, 1919, and Carl was born twenty-one months later on December 13, 1921. On Christmas Day 1923 as the family was returning by motorcycle and sidecar from celebrating at Grandma Lucretia and Houck Viles' home in Dayton to our home in Murlin Heights, a drunk man in a car came weaving toward them. Dad knew he was going to hit them, so he turned so he would be hit first and not the sidecar where Mom and the children were. This time his war-wounded leg was crushed.

Mom and the children were thrown out, she (unconscious) and baby Carl landed in a yard. Evelyn, wrapped securely in a blanket because of the cold, was lying on the road next to Dad. Dad did not lose consciousness and was able to signal with his arm when he saw another car approaching in the dark. That car stopped just inches from Evelyn's head! Dad was

With Jesus Leading the Way

rushed to the hospital, leaving a trail of blood down the hall as they wheeled him to surgery.

Once they had put him under the anesthesia, the doctor realized the only way he could save his life was to amputate his leg. The call went out to family for blood transfusions for Dad. Houck presented himself and said, "Take all my blood if it will save Eppy." That was the love that Houck had for his stepson. He was such a good man.

Dad told us how terrible it was to wake up in a hospital bed and realize your leg was no longer there. He wondered how he could ever work or care for his family and was sinking into depression. He said he could never forget a nurse who came in and talked to him, saying, "Mr. Christmas, you don't look like a quitter to me. You are going to be all right. We'll get an artificial leg for you, and you will be up walking and able to carry on your life with your family." She put new determination and courage into his heart. Bless her! She was right too.

I was grown, married, and had four children of my own before I knew Dad lost his leg on Christmas Day. He was never bitter about it. He could have made our Christmas Days sad by telling us about what happened to him and the bad memories. He never did that. Christmas was always special and a happy occasion for our family. He was determined that, even with an artificial leg, he would work to support his family. He worked at McCook Field, which later was named Wright Field and later Wright-Patterson Air Force Base. He was a master machinist. When I think of the painful eight hours (or more during the war) that he stood working at his station, I wonder how he ever did it. Some veterans just pitied themselves and went to stay at a VA center, leaving their families to fend for themselves.

Each weekday he left home before daylight to pick up a full load of riders who helped pay for gas expenses. So many times he came home so exhausted yet was loving and cheerful. Mom always had supper ready at 4:30 when he got home.

In the summertime after supper, he went out to sit in our backyard to either practice his casting arm (for fishing) or to watch the purple martin birds soaring around and going into the large apartment-like birdhouse he made for them. It was more like a bird hotel as it had many compartments. Many of our neighbor children came to sit, enjoy his company, and visit too. What wonderful memories of a dad who, though he worked hard, long hours, had time to spend with us and our friends.

When darkness fell, Dad went into the house to listen to the radio for a while then went to bed early for his early rising the next day. Mom always got up to fix breakfast for him. Because of his physical disability, in wintertime she was the one who had to bring buckets of coal up from the basement with kindling to get the stove going again to heat the house. When Carl and Mickey were home, they chopped kindling and carried coal for her too. Mother was a hard worker, having to do many things for Dad because of his amputated leg. After we all left for school or work, she worked to make our home neat and spotless.

Dad's sense of humor made him fun to be with. He loved to laugh and repeat jokes – and laugh as hard the tenth time he told a joke as he did the first time! He loved to play little tricks on us kids. We knew we were deeply loved by our mom and dad.

Chapter 2
Early Paths: Preparing My Heart for His Working and Bringing Me to Himself
1933 to 1944

> *When I stand before the throne*
> *Dressed in beauty not my own;*
> *When I see Thee as Thou art,*
> *Love Thee with un-sinning heart;*
> *Then, Lord, shall I fully know –*
> *Not till then – how much I owe.*

Attributed to Charles Spurgeon

It is a blessing to look back and see that God, in His love, was working and guiding all along the way in my life, even though I did not know it. That is why I chose the title, *With Jesus Leading the Way*, from Mark 10:32 for the story of my life.

Dad's mother, Lucretia Pritchet Christmas, went to a church in Tennessee that was very radical. Her church was known in that area as "The Holy Rollers" because they often did actually jump, fall on the floor, and roll around "when they got the Holy Ghost." Grandma Lucretia would "backslide" from time to time and then "get saved again" when she went back to church. She claimed to have the gift of tongues and would sometimes go into a type of trance. My dad saw the shallowness of this, so he wasn't a church attendee. He told me that when "The Holy Rollers" held their revival meetings, it was like a circus. Dad and his young friends set up a stand outside to sell soft drinks and refreshments to the people and check out the pretty girls!

Dad began smoking when he was in his early teens and became a chain smoker as an adult. He also liked to drink alcohol. Saturday night was when he liked to get together with friends to play cards and drink. He always supported his family, but he also got drunk at these weekend parties. He never was a mean drunk, and Mom was thankful for that. She laughingly told about one occasion when he came home drunk, went to bed, and kept saying, "Just throw the dirt over me!"

Often after a night of drinking, carousing, and cards, Dad's friends would ask Dad to drop them off at a church for confession. Dad didn't understand why they went to confession knowing that the next weekend they would go out and do the very same things. He reasoned that he was just as good as they were without going to church. I loved my daddy so much, so one day when my Sunday school paper showed a cartoon of a man struggling with snakes around him labeled "cigarettes," it scared me. I questioned him, "Daddy, are those snakes going to get you?" He assured me that they weren't and that I shouldn't worry.

My mother was brought up in churches that preached the way of eternal life, and she believed in the Lord Jesus Christ as her Savior when she was a young girl. However, she hadn't grown a lot in her faith, and at that time, it seemed that churches did not teach girls that they were not to be unequally yoked to unbelievers in marriage. She prayed for Dad's salvation for more than twenty years. Was God hearing her prayers and working, even though there was no evidence that He was? The answer is an emphatic "Yes!"

Mother wanted her children to be in church. We lived out in the country, and she didn't drive. So, she walked with us about a half mile to the Murlin Heights Congregational Christian Church. We attended Sunday school and morning service and were in the church programs. A kindly old man was the pastor. Sad to say, we never were taught that we were sinners in need of salvation. We learned that we would go to heaven if we were good. Mother knew something wasn't right about the church when one of the ladies said in a business meeting, "We need to take all the songs about the blood of Christ out of our hymn books. That is barbaric!"

Outside of church, Mom listened faithfully to a fifteen-minute radio program at 6:30 a.m. every weekday. Dr. William Taylor, a pastor in Dayton, preached from the Word of God and made the way of salvation very clear. Mom knew this was the kind of preaching she had heard as a child. She began to grow in the Lord. She also listened to a program called Cadle Tabernacle each day at 7:00 a.m., coming from Indianapolis. Every morning when she awakened me for school, I heard Mrs. Cadle singing their theme song:

> Ere you left your room this morning,
> Did you think to pray
> In the name of Christ your Savior?
> Did you ask for loving favor
> As a shield today?
>
> O, how praying rests the weary!
> Prayer will turn the night to day.
> So when life seems dark and dreary,
> Don't forget to pray.

With Jesus Leading the Way

Morning after morning, I heard that song, and I heard Dr. Cadle's Gospel message. Also, when I was small, Mom or one of my siblings would read me a Bible story every night before I went to bed.

My mother taught me to always say my prayers before I went to sleep. In 1939 when I was just six years old, Dad and his friends were often talking of the situations building in Europe, and I heard Dad say, "I fought in World War I, and that was supposed to be 'the war that ended all wars,' but I am afraid things in Europe are leading toward another world war." Often adults don't realize little ears are listening and being frightened by their conversations. So each night as I knelt at my bedroom window looking down over our peaceful backyard with its fruit trees, grape arbor, garden, play and picnic areas and up at the beautiful stars in the heavens, I ended my nightly prayers with, "And God, if the bad people are going to start a war again, please make Indians come behind the trees and shoot all the bad people!" So much for a six-year-old's reasoning.

The Lord didn't abandon us to the situation of not really hearing the Bible preached. Despite attending a church that did not preach the Word and having a father who wasn't a Christian, God was working behind the scenes to bring us to the Savior.

The impending war was on our minds, but we had no idea that a personal tragedy was on the horizon for our family in 1939 and 1940. When I was seven years old and Evelyn was twenty-one, she became very ill with kidney problems and was hospitalized. Mom called Dr. William Taylor, whom she listened to early mornings on the radio. She called to ask for prayer for her daughter Evelyn. Pastor Taylor said he most certainly would pray for

Evelyn and asked which hospital she was in, so he could go and visit her. As Dr. Taylor explained the way of salvation to her, she opened her heart and received Jesus Christ as her personal Savior.

She was so happy to know her sins were forgiven. She told Mom and Dad, "If I had died before, I would have gone to hell, but now I know that I am God's child, forgiven, and I know I will go to heaven when I die."

For a time, Evelyn got better and was able to come home, but she was weak and unable to work. My mother said that one day as she was taking care of Evelyn, she sensed the Lord saying to her, "Do all you can for Evelyn because you won't have her much longer."

In the summer of 1941, the Lord took her home to heaven. Mom and Dad were devastated to lose their firstborn beloved daughter at the tender age of twenty-one. I don't think my mother ever got over it.

At that time, bodies were seldom kept at the funeral home until burial. After the morticians prepared the body, it was brought to the family home. This is where visitors came to pay their respects and offer their condolences to the family. My bedroom was emptied out to make room for the casket and abundant flowers – Evelyn had a lot of friends.

This is my sister, Evelyn (age 20), and my brother Carl (age 19). The picture must have been taken about a year before she died.

Someone always stayed up all night with the body during the three days before the funeral. I don't know if Dad ever slept those nights as he sat with her. I remember going into the room when no one was there and, on tiptoe, looking at my beautiful sister. She looked like she was just asleep. I put my hand under the netting to touch her hand but was surprised to find it cold and unyielding, so I never did that again.

At her funeral Dr. Taylor preached a great funeral message, making the way of eternal salvation very clear. A few days later after the funeral, Dr. and Mrs. Taylor came out to talk to Dad about his spiritual condition. No one knew they were coming, but the Lord had arranged that appointment so that Dad was all alone that evening, sitting on our porch glider with his head in his hands in great sorrow and grieving over losing Evelyn. Dr. and Mrs. Taylor sat down, one on each side of him, and put their arms around him. Ever so gently, Dr. Taylor said, "Mr. Christmas, you can see your daughter again. We know where she is. Won't you open your heart to believe in Jesus Christ's death for you and receive His salvation tonight?" They continued to talk to Dad, but he kept replying, "I'm not ready yet." Finally, they asked to have prayer with him before they left. Dad later related that they hadn't been gone for more than five minutes before he opened his heart, repented of his sins, and was born into God's family! Hallelujah!

There is a story about a shepherd who had a sheep that wouldn't follow him; however, he knew just what to do. When he picked up that sheep's little lamb and carried it, the mother sheep began to follow the shepherd. The Lord took Evelyn into His arms and carried her to heaven so that Dad would follow. God made it very clear to my dad that believers were to "come out from the world and be separate." This is his testimony from his biography:

"When He saved me, the Lord completely took away my desire for liquor! The men at the shop where I worked couldn't understand it. We often went on fishing trips to the wilds of Michigan (Upper Peninsula). They were a cursing, drinking bunch of men. On our next trip, they tried to tempt me in every way, waving their bottles of booze under my nose saying, 'Just smell that! You know you want some.' One day, I decided to stay at the cabin and fish off the little dock while the rest went out in the boat to fish. When they returned they said, 'Now we know you are telling the truth. We thought you stayed behind to drink while we were gone, but now we see you didn't!' They had marked their whiskey bottles without my knowing it, to see if I was sneaking a drink when they were out!

"When they got sober again, I told them I could wade in liquor up to my knees and not desire it because of what God had done for me! That was the last trip I took with them. I had been so miserable with that crowd that my wife asked me if I was sick when I got home because of the look on my face. I told her I wasn't sick, but that I felt whipped by the Lord for continuing with that old crowd."

Dad, Mom, Mickey, and I all went into the baptismal waters together to be baptized and become members of Haynes Street Baptist Church. I can't recall anyone really dealing with me about my salvation, although one lady asked me just before we were baptized, "You have believed in Jesus as your Savior, haven't you?" I was only seven and didn't know what to answer but "Yes." Yet no one had really explained things to me.

World War II

In 1942 my brother Carl left his job at National Cash Register in Dayton and joined the army's air force division. Carl served both in the Atlantic war theater and in the South Pacific as an aircraft gunner mechanic repairing and maintaining aircraft engines. Under "battles and campaigns" on his honorable discharge papers he is listed as having taken part in the "Air Offensive Japan; Eastern Mandates; Western Pacific; ground combat."

Some of the stories Carl told were hair-raising, and some were comical. From our mother's teachings, he believed there were guardian angels watching over him because he could have been killed several times by grenades that exploded near him and bullets that whizzed by. He was blessed in having a praying mother and dad.

My brother Mickey volunteered to join the army but was very disappointed that he was turned down because of his flat feet. They said he wouldn't be able to endure long marches in the army. Later when he became a postman and walked all day, we laughed about the reason the army turned him down!

Nearly every family in America was affected by WWII. Patriotism ran high, and our military men were honored and admired. We were so proud of Carl in his uniform, as he bravely faced whatever was before him.

Many women began working in factories to supply needed items for the war effort. Each family was issued rationing stamps. According to the number of people in your family, you had a specific number of stamps for rationed meat, gasoline, sugar, and even shoes. The speed limit was thirty-five miles an hour, and it was extremely difficult to get new tires for your car.

When Carl was home on military leave, he met Carol Brown in Atlantic City and fell in love with her. They were married on March 15, 1945, in Mississippi, with neither of their families in attendance. It was war time, men were shipping out to the front, and many were marrying after short courtships. Carl never seemed to grow in the Lord and years later, after attending liberal churches, even doubted the Word of God as being inspired and written by God through men.

Through the years, our family cried out to the Lord for Carol and Carl's spiritual conditions. I always thought of the song "Will the Circle Be Unbroken?" which speaks of loved ones in a family who weren't saved. After I eventually came to Christ at the age of fourteen, everyone in our immediate family circle, except Carl, had been born again and was redeemed for eternity.

After my Dad was saved, our lives changed drastically. Now that he was a follower of Jesus Christ, he drove our family into Dayton to attend Haynes Street Baptist Church. He sat eagerly under the preaching of God's Word, drinking it in Sunday after

Sunday. We began to have Bible readings and prayer in our home as a family. Dad also became an active witness to his relatives, friends, and those he worked with. It was hard for him when his cousin Bill, a thirty-second degree Mason, rejected his witness, held up his Masonic ring, and said, "This is my ticket to heaven!"

Although Dad was able to give up alcoholic drinks right away, he thought he could never give up smoking. He had been smoking since he was a young teenager and now, at age forty-five, was very addicted. The Lord had a special way of taking care of this too in His time.

One Sunday afternoon, Dad ran out of cigarettes and was getting frantic for a smoke. He was looking through our ashtrays to find some butts to smoke, but there weren't enough. He decided to send Mickey, then about fifteen, up to Holthouse Grocery to buy some for him. There were no restrictions in those days for teenagers to buy cigarettes. After a while, Mickey came back and said, "Dad, the grocery was closed. The only place to buy cigarettes was at the saloon across the street, and I didn't want to go in there." To this day I can hear the next words of my dad. He said, "That's fine, Son. I'm glad you didn't go into that saloon. I'll just quit!" And by the grace of God, he did!

After a few months of not smoking, Dad's chronic hacking cough disappeared. He said it was so good to wake up in the morning with clear lungs and not have to cough and cough to clear out his respiratory passageways.

As I think about the way that the Lord brought our family to Him, the love and perseverance of my mother stands out to me. What love she had for her husband and her children! How faithfully she served us and prayed for us, and how she loved God's Word and faithfully studied it daily. With Jesus leading the way, she followed with her whole heart.

Chapter 3
High School and College Years
1945 to 1955

God in the Morning
By Ralph Spaulding Cushman

I met God in the morning
When my day was at its best,
And His presence came like sunrise,
Like a glory in my breast.

All day long the Presence lingered,
All day long He stayed with me,
And we sailed in perfect calmness
O'er a very troubled sea.

Other ships were blown and battered,
Other ships were sore distressed,
But the winds that seemed to drive them
Brought to us a peace and rest.

Then I thought of other mornings,
With a keen remorse of mind,
When I too had loosed the moorings,
With the Presence left behind.

So I think I know the secret,
Learned from many a troubled way:
You must seek Him in the morning
If you want Him through the day!

By the time I was in high school, Mom was in her late forties and suffered with migraine headaches. She called them "sick headaches." Her suffering was great. The pain caused nausea, and she would have to lie down in a darkened room until she felt better. Maybe menopause brought on the migraines. I don't know, but I know they intensified during that time. She also went through severe hot flashes.

Sometimes I look back on my teenage years and remember how self-centered and thoughtless I was during those years by talking back to her. Like a lot of teenagers, I thought I knew everything and that my parents

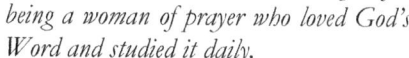

were so backwards and out of date. Years later, I apologized to Mom. You know what? She didn't even remember how awful I had been. What love! She told me she was so sad that because of her migraines, she felt she had neglected me. She said some mornings she was so sick that she couldn't prepare my breakfast and wasn't even aware of my leaving on the school bus. I never remember going without breakfast, so she must have been in such pain as she prepared that she forgot.

Mom, you are up there in heaven now. I hope you know how much I love you and thank God for you. You went home to heaven the first year I was in Africa (1960), and I didn't get to care for you and tell you goodbye. All my life, you are still alive in my dreams, and you are still being such a wonderful mother in them! Thank you for being a woman of prayer who loved God's Word and studied it daily.

As I mentioned previously, I was baptized at age seven. But as I became a teenager, I was very attracted to the world, and it became evident that I didn't really know Jesus as my Savior. I didn't want to go to church anymore, so I made excuses on Sundays. Dad was firm and made me go every Sunday anyway. I thought he was so stubborn and mean! Oh, but God was in that firmness of my dad. He kept me under the sound of the Gospel week after week. With Jesus leading the way. God began to work in my heart, showing me that I was not ready to meet Him and was not really a Christian.

Although Mickey was saved and baptized when he was about fifteen, by age twenty-one he was not walking with the Lord either. At this point, I was a freshman at Butler High School. Mickey and I were both under great conviction, although we didn't realize at the time what the other was going through. My Lord was so patient in dealing with each of us over a period of weeks and months.

One Wednesday night, Mickey surprised us by saying he was going to go to the prayer meeting at our church in Dayton. God was dealing with him about his spiritual condition, and that night he rededicated his life to his Savior. On the way home, he took his cigarettes out of his pocket and said, "Lord, you'll have to take care of this" as he threw his cigarettes away and abandoned smoking. He also stopped drinking. He walked into the house that night with tears in his eyes and told Mom and me what had happened.

I was under such heavy conviction that I went into my bedroom, knelt by my bedside, and prayed, "God be merciful to me, a sinner, and save me for Jesus' sake." I repented of my sins and gave myself totally to my Redeemer. What joy and peace flooded my soul! The song "At the Cross" by Isaac Watts well describes the night Jesus became my personal Savior:

> Was it for crimes that I have done
> He groaned upon the tree?
> Amazing pity! Grace unknown!
> And love beyond degree.
> At the cross, at the cross
> Where I first saw the light
> And the burden of my heart rolled away –
> It was there by faith I received my sight,
> And now I am happy all the day!

Mickey and I began attending the young people's meetings on Sunday evenings before evening service as well as their home fellowships on Friday evenings. There were probably about thirty in our group. On Friday nights we sang, gave testimonies, enjoyed a Bible study, then had games and snacks. These times became the highlight of our week.

I began to miss these youth meetings on Friday nights when there were football games. I had been playing the trumpet in the school band since eighth grade. It was a good experience for me, but I decided to quit. I didn't enjoy playing trumpet. Also, I missed our youth activities.

Rev. James T. Jeremiah was called to be our pastor in 1950 after our previous pastor's moral failure. His wife, Mrs. Ruby Jeremiah, was my

Sunday school teacher. What a precious lady and mentor she was for me! Brother Jeremiah kept his church youth busy with youth meetings, visitation to newcomers or strangers to our church, and visitations to the county old folks' home – all this in addition to the regular church services and prayer meetings on Sundays and Wednesdays. Brother Jeremiah also got us busy holding street meetings in various places around Dayton. Later daughter churches were planted in many of these same locations.

I was about fifteen years old when Carson Fremont, home from Wheaton College, spoke and challenged us for missions. I remember going forward to kneel and say, "Lord, wherever you want me to serve you, I will go." Pastor and Mrs. Jeremiah had been giving me a lot of missionary biographies to read. I was very impressed by Jonathan and Rosalind Goforth and thought I could serve in China, although by then it was a closed field.

However, a few nights later as I knelt to pray by my bedside before retiring, the Lord in a very real way impressed upon my heart that He wanted me to serve Him in Africa someday. That was not in my plans! (Someone has said, "If you want to make God laugh, tell Him your plans!") I struggled and did not want to yield to this call. I wanted to talk God out of it!

How stubborn my heart was, and how patient the Lord was with my young Christian heart! After many tears, I said, "Lord, if you really are calling me to Africa, don't let me go to sleep now." It was very late. I was very tired, and I thought I would, as usual, be asleep a couple minutes after my head was on the pillow. With Jesus leading the way, I could not sleep at all, and my pillow became drenched in tears.

Once again, I crawled out of bed, got on my knees, and said, "Lord if you are really calling me to Africa, then show me by verses in Your Word as I randomly open my Bible!" My Bible fell open to Matthew 28, "Go ye therefore, and teach all nations..." More tears! Again, I closed my Bible and asked for confirmation of His call by the verses it would fall open to. My Bible opened to Isaiah 6, "Whom shall I send, and who will go for us...Here am I; send me." I knew God was speaking to me and confirming my call, but I asked for one more random opening – and this time, my Bible opened at "Unless you see signs and wonders, you will not believe!" The Lord had been patient with my baby Christian type of requests for leading, but now He let me know that was enough! At that moment, I yielded to my Lord and told Him I would go to Africa at his bidding. Again, His peace flooded my soul! I went to bed and slept like a baby.

I haven't told a lot of people about this experience because I never wanted anyone to think they had to have a similar one. The Lord was just so gracious to me as a young believer, and He confirmed my call in this way. As a young Christian, I used that random opening of my Bible for leading, but as I grew in Christ, I realized that we believers have the witness of God's Holy Spirit in our hearts, and He directs us by giving us His peace as we follow His leadings according to His Word.

Soon after this, I told my dad that God had called me to Africa, and I planned to go as a missionary. I think I scared him! I was his only living daughter. He said, "You are too young to know that!" Although he was opposed to the idea then, he later was so proud that I followed the Lord's leading to Africa.

I was preoccupied with my own experience and assurance of His call to Africa, and I never thought of what my mother was going through until one day she emerged from her bedroom and time of prayer with tear-filled eyes to tell me, "I didn't want you to go to Africa, and the Lord had to bring me to the place where I now say, 'Lord, my daughter is Yours. I yield her to You and want Your will in her life.'" It was very difficult for her when we left for Africa, but I knew she was upholding us in prayer daily.

My mother was a woman of prayer, and she loved to study her Bible. She lifted us children up in her prayers constantly. I saved a little poem that she wrote out and sent me when I was a college student and it has meant much to me through the years:

To Norma from Mother

I know within my heart God answers prayer
Because today I heard that still small voice,
And felt a sense of peace and comfort, where
Before was all confusing doubt and noise.
I asked in humbleness that He might grant
A special blessing to some ones I love.
And what I asked with faith unhesitant,
Was poured that selfsame hour from Heaven above.
By G.B. Wilson

During my high school years, it seemed that my whole life revolved around Emmanuel Baptist Church and our youth activities. The Lord used our church in wonderful ways. We saw many come to know Christ as their Savior, and a great number of the youth were called on to full-time service. A large number of missionaries and pastors went forth from our church.

Soon after I really came to know Christ as my Savior and was rebaptized, a high school girl named Barbara Gephart moved to Dayton and began attending our church and we became best friends. She was a wonderful friend to me, and we were together as often as we could be, especially at youth activities. When something was funny to us, we often giggled and laughed ourselves to tears! Once something or someone in the church service struck us as funny as we were up in the choir loft. The more we tried to suppress our laughter, the more hilarious it became. We had to slip out of the choir during prayer and go downstairs to get control of ourselves!

After Barbara graduated from her high school, she began nurses' training at Miami Valley Hospital. I had met several Christian student nurses who also attended Emmanuel, and decided I wanted to become a nurse too, but Pastor Jeremiah urged me to get Bible training first.

I graduated from Butler High School in Vandalia, Ohio, in May 1951 at the age of seventeen. I had been on the honor roll from time to time during my school years and even made that list for graduation. It was many years later that I realized that any honors I received were because of the intelligence Mom and Dad passed on to me.

Bible College

My interest in missions was intense. To this day, my favorite reading is biographies, especially missionary biographies. Pastor and Mrs. Jeremiah urged me strongly to go to Baptist Bible Seminary in Johnson City, New York. In later years, the college relocated to a lovely campus in Clarks Summit, Pennsylvania, and became Baptist Bible College, now called Clarks Summit University.)

With Jesus leading the way, I was obedient to His instructions, and BBS accepted me for the fall of 1951. The Lord was also sending several students from Emmanuel to BBS. Some of the guys had cars, so when vacation times came, we all chipped in on gas for the long trip and crowded into their cars to go to and from school. Sometimes we went by train.

Although I had worked at part-time jobs during my high school years and had some money saved for Bible college, it wasn't nearly enough. I had worked at a dry-cleaning establishment, at McCroy's five-and-ten store, as a nurse's aide at Miami Valley Hospital, and as a babysitter. I needed a good paying job after graduation in 1951 and was hired as a typist-clerk at Wright Patterson Air Force Base. Every job I had prepared me for my future, and I look back now with gratitude for what I learned. My boss at Wright-Pat liked me and thought I had potential to be trained for higher positions, so at the end of the summer of 1951, she offered to send me for training to be promoted. I pondered and prayed over this. Did the Lord want me to stay and work longer at Wright-Patterson, or was this a temptation from the devil to keep me from going off to Bible college? Reluctantly, I resigned at the end of summer but with joy too because I knew this is what the Lord wanted in my life. My boss was very disappointed and couldn't understand why I would choose Bible college over a promotion.

At BBS, dormitory space for girls was limited to one house, Springsteed Hall. By the time I got my application in, the hall was full, so I was assigned to room and board at a widow's home. Hilda Porritt was a working single mother, very efficient, and kind to her boarders.

Before going to BBS in New York, I had never been away from home, except for short stays in the summer with my cousins down on Wilson Run Road near Chillicothe, Ohio. My homesickness was intense during those first months at college. I missed my family and my home terribly! Long distance telephone calls were expensive, so unless there was an emergency, calls were only made on rare occasions. However, Mom had told me I could call home after one month away. As I dialed that familiar number, I began to get choked up, so that when my mother said, "Hello," I burst into tears and couldn't talk! Mom kept saying, "Are you all right?" I could barely say "Yes" because I was sobbing! My poor mother! She kept saying, "You'll be fine. It's okay."

It was doubtful that we Emmanuel students could go home for the long Thanksgiving weekend because it involved many miles to be traveled in those days. However, one of the students who had a car decided if we all chipped in for gas, we could do it! We left after classes and drove all night. Oh, the joy that morning to pull up in front of our little home on Little York Road again. I ran to the kitchen door because I could see my mother inside standing at the sink, and I couldn't wait to be in her arms. She said it was a good thing the door wasn't locked, or I would have ripped it off at the hinges! After that, my homesickness began to subside because I knew in only one month I would be home again for Christmas vacation.

At the beginning of my sophomore year, Jean Fisher and I were in the overcrowded Springsteed Hall dormitory. The new BBS three-storied building was being constructed right behind Springsteed. It would house a cafeteria, lounge, classrooms, and offices while the third floor would be an added girl's dormitory. Jean's and my temporary room was actually just an alcove in the second story hall in Springsteed, screened off for a little privacy.

This was my first experience living in a dormitory, and it was very educational as well as being a time of fun with lively girls from all over the States. It is great for learning how to live and get along with others. Our dorm mother, dear Mrs. Murphy, was a very prim little lady with a wonderful figure who wore a lot of princess-style dresses. She really was a lovely person. As she checked meal tickets in the dining hall, she would comment on how a girl was dressed, if she needed to lose weight, and so forth. I always cringed wondering when she would say something to me about my clothes or weight, but she never did. I don't know why, but I think she really liked me, and she always had a smile for me! We were all surprised when she gave advice to another girl who was very pretty and quiet but was never asked out on a date. One day Mrs. Murphy told her, "You need to flirt more!" How about that shocking advice from prim Mrs. Murphy!

I made lifelong friendships at BBS. Jean (who had finished nurses' training at Miami Valley Hospital in Dayton) and I were sometimes instigators of mischief! One night we were giggling and being noisy during hours reserved for quiet and study. When we heard Mrs. Murphy coming up the stairs to see who was making the noise, we jumped into the hall closet (in various stages of getting undressed for bed) and were quiet until she made her rounds and returned to her apartment downstairs. That was when we discovered that there was no door latch on the inside of the closet! The girls in the room on the other side of the closet were puzzled at first when they heard soft voices coming through their wall saying, "We're locked in the hall closet. Please come and open up for us!" There was lots more giggling, but we kept the noise down lest Mrs. Murphy come upstairs again!

Dress codes were strict. We had to wear dresses or blouses and skirts to classes and even to our places of employment in the afternoons. Also, wearing nylon stockings was a must! These were in the days before pantyhose had become popular, so we also had girdles or garter belts with the rubber fasteners to hold up our stockings or roll-down garter bands that cut off your leg circulation. Makeup was not only frowned upon, but if you wore lipstick, the dean of women or your dorm mother would call you in for a talk! We didn't know this was a form of legalism. Every female student had to abide by these rules, so we didn't feel alone.

Did we girls have ways of bypassing the rules sometimes? Yes, we did! We also wore saddle shoes with cotton anklets and ballerina skirts. Nylons, at that time, had a seam up the back and you had to be careful to keep your seams straight. Nylons were expensive, especially on college girls' budgets. Since very little of our nylon seams showed between our ankle socks and our ballerina skirts, some girls would draw seams on the backs of their legs for going to work or for running out for snacks during the evening. We even had the audacity to roll up our pajama legs, draw the seams on, put on our long coats, and run quickly to the grocery stores!

It was a great day when the new BBS building, Thompson Hall, was finally completed, and we could move into our new third-floor dormitory. Jean and I moved into the dorm with our new roommate, Carol Williams. Carol's dad, Dr. Arthur Williams, was a pastor near Cleveland who was later called to teach at Cedarville College. Doc Williams was another godly man, greatly used of the Lord in teaching and pastoring.

Jean and I were not morning people. When we got up, we were pretty silent as we got ready for classes, only speaking if necessary. Now the Lord put Carol in our room! She woke up bright and happy like a ray of sunshine, jumping out of bed to exclaim with a big smile, "Good morning! How are you this beautiful day?" Jean and I often looked at her with a jaundiced eye, only to mumble, "Fine."

Years later, when we were home on furlough and I was speaking at a ladies missionary fellowship in the church Carol and her family attended, I told that story. Carol's preteen daughter said, "Mom! What happened to you? You aren't like that now in the mornings!" Age and children do change our outlook on the day!

For my senior year, I left the dorm and lived at Dr. and Mrs. Mead Armstrong's home about five blocks from school. I took classes from Dr. Armstrong during my years at school. He was such a kind man and a good teacher. I lived on the third floor of the Armstrong's' home with four other girls, including Cora Morgan from Vermont, my sweetest and closest friend at BBS. Cora loved Jesus, and she was a person who never had a bad mood! She was the maid of honor at my wedding and is still my close friend, though many miles now separate us.

Each year, every student at BBS had to be involved in some type of service outreach. I was in choir my first year. We had a great time on choir tour for one or two weeks. On that tour in New York, I saw the Atlantic Ocean for the first time. Fellow choir member took us to Jones Beach late at night. It was quite a thrill for this Midwestern girl to see the ocean for the first time!

Other service outreaches I did during my school years were teaching in Sunday school and participating in Friday and Saturday night street meetings. We gathered for prayer and then went out to Binghamton, Endicott, Owego, and other places. Our student group gathered on a street corner to sing, and then one of the guys would preach. We also had Gospel tracts to hand out. We had many opportunities to engage people in one-on-one conversations. I was thankful for the street meeting experiences my pastor in Ohio had already involved our high school youth group in.

BBS was still a small school at that time, and meals were served family style in Springsteed Dining Room. This was before the new BBS building was built with a cafeteria. We students lined up at the doors and then filed in to eat. Probably our cook had a limited budget to spend for food, and perhaps that was coupled with her not being the greatest cook, but that's the way it was. At the end of the week, she often took all the leftovers from the past week, ground them up together and served the resulting (revolting) concoction as ragout. It was horrible! The guys said it smelled like wet dog gravy! When the dining room doors opened, and that odor wafted out, all students who could afford to turned around and headed across the street to Nick's Restaurant for a hot dog or hamburger! There were many empty chairs at the table when the cook's ragout was served!

I always had part-time jobs during my college years. Once I worked for a printing firm, collating mimeographed or printed pages to make instructional manuals for offices and factories. Another time I worked in McCroy's, the nearby five-and-ten store, at the notions counter. But mostly I worked for Jewish ladies in Binghamton, cleaning their homes. The pay was pathetic, but it was good experience, and I learned much. I worked often for an attorney's wife. I don't think she did any cleaning from week to week. The house was always a mess when I arrived – beds unmade, dust bunnies everywhere, and a kitchen sink piled high with dishes. It gave me a great sense of accomplishment when I worked there to leave an apartment cleaned and spotless four hours later!

The Bernsteins had a parakeet they claimed had quite a vocabulary, but it just sounded like gibberish to me. My ears weren't attuned to his voice. What a delightful surprise I had as I dusted the base of his cage one day and heard him say ever so clearly, "Give me a kiss, baby!" After that I could make out his sentences! When allowed out of his cage, he loved to walk up and down the length of their dining room buffet in front of the long mirror, looking at himself. Cute!

Every summer vacation, when I returned to Ohio for three months, I had to find full-time work to save for my schooling. In those days, a student could work and almost pay his college expenses. I don't remember what my room and board was, but I do remember that tuition was $45 per semester! My dear mom also helped me all she could, and I was able to graduate debt free.

During the summer of 1952, I worked at Gallagher's Drug Store in Dayton, Ohio. For the summer of 1953, I was employed as a full-time secretary to my pastor, James T. Jeremiah, at Emmanuel Baptist Church. These were all great learning experiences.

Construction was going on at that time for a new auditorium at Emmanuel Baptist Church on Terry Street. There were a lot of construction men who came to the secretary's office for various things. In retrospect, I know one, a Catholic married man, was guilty of sexual harassment. We didn't know what that was back then or how to combat it as we do today. He always made comments with innuendos or double entendres, and he made me very uncomfortable. I was always glad when he left my office. He met his match one day, though, when he said something to Lucille Becraft, who along with her husband, Paul, was the church custodian. Lucille was always well dressed, with her hair fixed perfectly when she left her home. She and Paul were very much in love, and she cared about how she looked for her husband. As she walked into the office one day, the harasser said, "Oh, how nice you look! Did you get all dressed up for me?" Wow! Lucille replied, "Absolutely not! Who do you think you are, talking to me like that? I don't get dressed up for you or any other man except my husband! You'd better not ask me such a question again!" Good for Lucille! The harasser looked embarrassed and quietly left!

During the summer of 1954, between my junior and senior years at BBS, employment was almost impossible to find. I put my application in at so many different places but to no avail. Finally, I got a one-month job in telemarketing at a meat locker/butcher's establishment. My boss had a phone book with addresses and phone numbers listed by street. My work was to call from one house to the next down the street, trying to get appointments for his salesmen to go to homes to demonstrate all the advantages of owning your own Deepfreeze and having it filled periodically with fresh meat and frozen foods from the butcher's business. I got so tired of hearing my voice repeat the same message all day, over and over. It was the least favorite of all the jobs I've had in my life! I was glad when the month was over. Even though my boss tried to talk me into staying another month, I declined!

In January 1953, my mother was hospitalized for a second time because of her anemia. The doctors had to give her blood transfusions to bring up her blood count. This time, they built her up because she had been in menopause for quite a few years and was hemorrhaging at the time of her monthly periods. Once her blood was built up, the doctor planned to do a complete hysterectomy. I was needed at home to care for her. So, sad as it was, I thought I would probably drop out of school and not come back.

I wanted to tell Dr. Paul Jackson, BBS president, about this. This godly man made it a priority to learn every freshman's name each school year, so he could greet us by name in the halls. I got an appointment late in the afternoon but waited for a long time while he counseled the students ahead of me. He was a man who never appeared hurried or made you feel he had other important things to do. He gave you the feeling you were the most important thing in his life at the time he talked to you. His counsel was, "Norma, I know you need to go home for a while and care for your mother. This is important. I know you will miss some classes too. But you know God has brought you here. Please don't quit school. Come back when your mother is better and capable of getting along without you." It was good counsel, and I was able to go home to help Mom as she got out of the hospital and returned after a few weeks to resume my studies.

During my years at BBS, fears of going to Africa alone as a single person overwhelmed me at times. I had dated different fellows in high school and college and was proposed to by three of them. However, I knew the answer had to be no because none of these young men were headed toward Africa where the Lord had called me.

I tried to reason (read: argue) with the Lord that I could be a good church secretary and help others go to the mission field, but I was too afraid to go as a single person. Once again, the Lord dealt so tenderly and graciously with me until the day I finally went into the prayer room in our dormitory, knelt, and surrendered. I remember saying, "Lord, You will help me, guide me, and be sufficient for me. If you want me to go to the mission field as a single woman, I will be obedient and go single!" That was such a hard decision. Later it was evident He didn't want me to go to Africa single, but He did want me to be willing! What a joy and relief it was when I surrendered in obedience to Him! "Lord, yes, to whatever You have for me!" He is so good, and submissive obedience is glorious for His child!

I have nothing but admiration for girls who go out to the mission field single. They are a choice breed and are greatly used of the Lord. It has been our joy to work with many of them and to see their dedication to His service. There is a special difficulty having unmarried women working in Muslim countries though. Muslims, especially Arabs, consider women to be chattel, only good for having children and serving their husbands. In Niger, since men can have as many as four wives, there are husbands enough for every girl. Unless a girl is insane, a husband will be found for her. Once when one of our single ladies went calling with me in the village, the people were very curious about this woman in her forties. Did she have children? Was she married? Why not?! I tried to explain to them that she had given her life to God for His service, but they just couldn't comprehend that and felt very sorry for her because she had no husband and no children. I'm not sure how single missionary ladies who knew the language handled these questions that were surely asked of them. It must have been very difficult.

With Jesus leading the way, my years at church and in Bible College were blessed. The people and the experiences the Lord brought into my life encouraged me in my calling toward Africa. I can think of so many, many men and women who faithfully followed the Lord into missions, the pastorate, teaching, and all kinds of Christian education. Lifelong friends were made. What a privilege it is to have known them!

My greatest blessing of all was meeting my future husband at Baptist Bible Seminary!

Chapter 4
Heath's Story
1930 to 1955

I was born in Syracuse, New York, on October 9, 1930. I was born in a hospital, whereas my two older sisters, Shirley and Jane, were born at home. I was the third and last child of Lena Esther Heath and George Edward Bobbett. I was named George Heath Bobbett, but since George was my father's first name as well as my Grandfather Heath's first name, it was evidently decided that I would be called by my middle name. (This has always been fine with me except that I am now also known as George as far as Medicare and social security is concerned.)

I was born during the Depression years, but my father worked for what we used to call a creamery where the farmers brought their milk each day to be pasteurized and where buttermilk and cheese were also made. So even during those economically difficult years, he had steady employment and usually worked seven days a week because the farmers needed to bring their milk each day.

My earliest memory is me lying in my crib and my sisters standing beside it. Evidently, they had been liberally shaking powder all over me, and it must have caused me to have difficulty breathing. Otherwise that would not have been so deeply impressed upon my brain. They deny to this day that they were guilty of that. At any rate, my mother thankfully came to my rescue.

We lived in the beautiful upstate Finger Lakes area of New York near the village of Skaneateles, not far from Syracuse. Up until my sixth-grade year, we lived a couple of miles outside of town, and I went to a small one-room elementary schoolhouse for the first five years of my schooling. During our recess periods, we sometimes went to nearby woods and climbed the small cliffs there. We also played Dodgeball in those days! Horrors! Today they have outlawed that violent game lest someone get hurt!

Norma Bobbett

We had a cistern in our basement where we caught rainwater for household use and a well with a pump outside in the yard for drinking water. We also had the mandatory outhouse because we had no indoor plumbing.

We always had a dog. These were usually pointers or setters because my father liked to hunt. Most years he also went to the Adirondacks with some of his friends to hunt deer, so we grew up enjoying venison meat when they were successful.

We did not have a lot of toys in those frugal days, but one time my father made me a small V-shaped plow out of wood, and I had a great time pushing it all over to make paths for us during the winter months.

We had especially hard winters when we were growing up, which made for a lot of nice opportunities to go skiing or sledding. One time I was walking down our dirt road in front of our house and the snow must have been a good twelve feet high on each side of the road. I remember thinking, "If a snowplow comes along now, he will never see me, and I will get run over." However, I made it home safely – or I would not now be writing this short biography!

In those days I was not getting very good marks in school, and someone decided that I should have my eyes examined. They discovered that I could not even see the blackboard and that I did indeed need glasses. I was also given exercises to do, like covering one eye and reading with the other to strengthen it, and it did help.

We moved from the country into the actual town of Skaneateles when I was ready to enter the sixth grade. Now that I was wearing glasses, I began to get A's in most of my classes and continued to do so up through my high school years. So I guess their diagnosis was correct. At our new house in town, we enjoyed indoor plumbing.

Skaneateles Lake was just a short walk from our house, and we enjoyed swimming there in the summertime. As I got older, I also worked for my Uncle Bill Snook, driving the tractor while he and his son, Warren, loaded hay on a wagon. Then I would lead the horse as it pulled the rope attached to a huge fork to lift the hay up into the barn. They also owned a piece of lakefront property where we swam and had picnics.

I did not excel enough in sports to make the school teams but did enjoy playing basketball in the upstairs of a neighbor's barn as well as impromptu games of softball with the neighborhood kids.

Our parents worked hard, and I did not spend a lot of time with my father while growing up. I do remember playing catch with him, and one summer our whole family enjoyed a fishing trip up in Canada. Speaking of working hard, I, along with many young boys, had a paper route and had to get up about 5:00 in the morning to cover my route before school began. In my teens, I also began working after school and on Saturdays as a clerk-in the A&P store in town. Back in those days, people came in with a list, and it was up to the clerk to go find the item on the shelf and bring it back to the customer at the counter. We also had to do the addition of the prices ourselves with pencil and paper to tell the customers what they owed.

In my later teen years, I also took up smoking and drank some alcohol. Years later, when I got right with the Lord, I had to go back and confess to that same store manager that I had often stolen packs of cigarettes, and I began reimbursing the store for what I had taken.

One of the highlights of my growing up years was going to visit my mother's parents in Amber, New York. They owned what was called Heath's Grove located on Otisco Lake. This was a large piece of property with hundreds of feet of lakefront. There were cottages built there that people rented during the summer (very spartan by today's standards). Their land also included a large ball diamond, a refreshment stand where we could buy ice cream and snacks (and that included a small dining area), and an icehouse where ice cut from the frozen lake during the winter months was stored in sawdust and sold to people for their ice boxes (the forerunner of the modern-day refrigerator). There was also a large dance hall where square dances were held on Saturday nights. Every birthday, Grandpa Heath would show up to square dance and did so even up into his eighties.

Grandma Heath was really the business woman of the family, and after some years, they began charging cars that drove into the Grove for swimming and recreation. It was just a small sum, regardless of the number of occupants. I think the fee was perhaps 25 cents per, at least at first. Of course, being family meant that this was all free to us. So this was a frequent weekend destination for us, as well as for their other children and grandchildren.

My Grandma Heath was a godly woman. I and others never remember her having a bad word to say about anyone. Grandpa Heath died in his eighty-fifth year, and in a matter of just twelve days thereafter, Grandma Heath herself suddenly went to be with the Lord at age seventy-four. The property was then split up among their four children (Lena, Warren, Ted, and Emma Heath) and much of it sold off. However, even today you can find Heath's Grove listed on maps, though it no longer really exists.

Grandma Heath was originally of the Kinney family, and her family ancestry has been traced back to a Sir Thomas Kinney of England who was born in 1624. Interestingly, her father, Warren Kinney, was born in 1804, and after his first wife died childless, he married again in 1877 at age seventy-three. His second wife was a young twenty-two-year-old Miss Annabel that had cared for his ailing wife before her death! They had three children, a girl and two boys. Sadly, both boys died at young ages of diphtheria, and only my Grandmother Ruby survived. So unless that unusual marriage had taken place, our family would not be here today.

I would say that I grew up in a nominal Christian home. My mother saw to it that we took a bus on Sunday into town where we attended the First Baptist Church. If we could not get to church for some reason, especially in winter when we really had lots of snow, she made sure we had a little service of our own. I vaguely remember leading songs, along with my two older sisters, as we had a time of worship together. My mother told me many years later that she had prayed I would be a preacher someday. I owe much to her for her love, prayers, and support over the years.

After our family moved into town, it was easier to get to church because it was within walking distance. In those days, they used to give out Sunday school pins for perfect attendance, and I earned a seven-year pin for perfect attendance. But during all those years, I never remember anyone ever dealing with me on a one-to-one basis about my soul.

Some special meetings were held in our church during that time, resulting in my two older sisters wanting to be baptized. As the tagalong younger brother, I thought that was a good idea as well. But it is not that easy to become a member of a Baptist church. We had to first meet with the deacons. I remember sitting in that meeting along with the other candidates when the deacons began asking each person to share their testimony of how they came to know Christ. For the first time in my life, I realized that I had no testimony to give. However, having attended Sunday school for all those years, I figured out something to say. I don't remember my exact words, but evidently, they were sufficient to convince the deacons that I knew the Lord, so I was baptized and thus became an unregenerate church member.

Then, when I was fourteen years old our pastor encouraged the young people to go to Bible camp. I think we collected papers and did a few other things to help with expenses, and off I went with a few others from our church to the Canandaigua Bible Conference Grounds for a week of camp.

I went as a young carefree teenager, never realizing that I was there by divine appointment. One night at the conclusion of his message, the speaker said, "If Jesus Christ was standing here asking you to come to Him, you would not refuse. I am standing here in Christ's place asking you to come." He also encouraged us if we were not sure we were saved to make sure. I did not respond publicly, but that night, lying on my cot in my cabin, I opened my heart and trusted Christ as my Savior.

I Am His and He Is Mine
Lyrics by Wade Robinson

Heaven above is softer blue,
Earth around is sweeter green:
Something lives in every hue
Christless eyes have never seen!

I can still remember the sense of the lifting of the burden of sin and the entrance of the sweet peace of God into my heart. I remember getting up the next day and seeing the world with new eyes. The sky had never been bluer or the grass greener than it was that morning. There really is truth in that hymn. And I saw it that day! Praise the Lord!

I love this statement by Warren Wiersbe: "As far as God the Father is concerned, I was saved when He chose me before the foundation of the world. As far as God the Son is concerned, I was saved when He died for me on the cross. As far as God the Holy Spirit is concerned, I was saved one night in May of 1945 when I gave my heart to Christ." For me it was in August of 1945 – and you can put your own name and date in there and praise the Lord with me for your salvation, if you also have trusted Christ as your Savior.

The next night at the Bible camp, I was once again standing during the closing hymn as the invitation was being given, this time to dedicate our lives to Jesus Christ. Once again, I made no outward decision, but standing there I clearly heard the voice of God in my soul saying to me one word – Africa! I don't know who the preacher was that week, but I am looking forward to looking him up in heaven and telling him how God used him in my life. Maybe the Lord will give many of us an experience like that.

Shortly after arriving home from camp, everyone celebrated a joyous V-J Day as it was called, which signaled the end of World War II. After I came home from camp, and not having an especially active youth group at our church, I just lived the life of a typical teenager of the 1940s. However, God kept bringing that call back to my mind and heart. I sometimes read my Sunday school paper (called *Power*) during the morning service, and at times there was an article about Africa. I remember one time being in the dentist's office and opening a magazine, and there was an article about Africa. God wasn't allowing me to forget His calling in my life.

But by the time I graduated from high school, I was pretty immersed in the world and was not sure what I wanted to do with my life. My brother-in-law Homer was attending Syracuse University, so I decided I would do the same.

I enrolled in the college of business administration and was there for two years, but I realized that I did not want to be an accountant. Again, the Lord kept reminding me from time to time of that call to Africa. What to do? In my human wisdom I said to myself, "I know what I will do. I will enroll in a course in religion here at the university, and maybe the Lord will speak to me."

Well, I was spoken to all right, but not by the Lord! The professor told us that the miracles Christ was said to have performed were not really miracles at all. When that boy took out his lunch, everyone else took theirs out as well, so they all had something to eat. When Christ died on the cross, He did not rise physically from the grave. It was a spiritual resurrection.

I thank God for my pastor, Lloyd Crosby. I talked with him about what I was being taught, and he said to me, "You go back and ask your professor how you can bury a spirit?" I thought that was a good answer. I remember writing one paper that came back with red marks all over it as he questioned what I wrote. In spite of all I was taught in that class, I thank God that it never shook my faith. I believe it was because of the grounding in the Word I received all those years as a young person attending church and Sunday school.

I was a typical university student living in the world, but finally the Lord began to get through to me. I shared with my pastor my salvation experience and call at Canandaigua, which I had never personally told him before. He told me about the school he attended to prepare for the ministry, Baptist Bible Seminary in Johnson City, New York. Then he said to me, "If you will straighten up, I will recommend you." When I told my university professor, he said. "Well, the first thing they will do there is have a prayer meeting for you." He meant that derogatorily, but that was exactly what I needed!

During my high school years, my father changed jobs and began attending church with us. In fact, I remember there were times when we both took up the offering together. Shortly after that, however, he became involved with another woman.

That was a difficult time for our family, and it culminated in my mother and father divorcing, but the Lord brought us through it. That precipitated our moving away from Skaneateles to Elmira, New York, where my sister Jane and her husband, Homer Ludington, were living. It was a hard experience, but I believe that had that not happened, I probably would not have gone off to Bible school and into the Lord's work. I rarely saw my father after that. Norma and our children may have seen him once or twice. One time, while I was in seminary, we did arrange to meet, and I had the opportunity to present the Gospel and witness to him. He did not respond to my tearful invitation but said he would think about it. He also said, "I did not think you would turn out like this," which is not what a son hopes to hear from his father. My sisters did keep in closer contact with him than I did. He died when we were overseas, but my sisters who saw him on his deathbed do believe, in talking with him, that he had repented. I trust it was real. Only heaven will reveal whether it was so.

When we moved to Elmira, our Skaneateles pastor recommended we attend Birchwood Baptist Tabernacle where Clyde Truax was pastor. The first time I attended a service, I did not like it! I felt the presence of the Lord there, and I was not yet right with Him! In the years to come, Pastor Truax became like a father to me, and I will always be grateful for his godly input into my life. I was, by the way, rebaptized by him since I was not really saved when I was originally baptized in Skaneateles.

I sent off my application to Baptist Bible Seminary. I have often wondered what Pastor Crosby told them when he sent my recommendation, but I was accepted and began my freshman year in the fall of 1950. Seminary is where I truly gave me heart and life to the Lord and began to grow in Him.

As I think back over my life, I believe my testimony can be expressed in these words of the Apostle Paul found in Acts 26:19 where he declared before King Agrippa, "I was not disobedient to the heavenly vision." When I think of all that I would have missed had I been disobedient, I just thank God for His faithfulness. I heard someone say once, "I thank God for being faithful enough to me to make me faithful to Him." It was because of His faithfulness that we were faithful to His call and have been enabled to serve Him. To Him be all the glory!

By God's grace, my desire as expressed in my life verses in Philippians 3:10-14 continues to be "that I may know him, and the power of his resurrection, and the fellowship of his sufferings, being made conformable unto his death; if by any means I might attain unto the resurrection of the dead. Not as though I had already attained, either were already perfect: but I follow after, if that I may apprehend that for which also I am apprehended of Christ Jesus. Brethren, I count not myself to have apprehended: but this one thing I do, forgetting those things which are behind, and reaching forth unto those things which are before, I press toward the mark for the prize of the high calling of God in Christ Jesus."

Heath Bobbett, 2014

Chapter 5
Each for the Other, and Both for the Lord
1953 to 1956

On my knees in our prayer room at Thompson Hall girls dormitory, I had ended my struggle of trying to talk the Lord out of sending me to Africa as a single woman. The fear of going alone was still there, but now I had yielded it to my Savior, telling Him that I would be obedient and would accept the fact that He would enable me to go alone.

How foolish we are to fight, argue, struggle with, or resist the Lord. He is God, and we are not. There is no way we can win those battles! I remember reading about a well-known former president of Moody Bible Institute. On his deathbed, semi-comatose, he was heard to say over and over, "Yes Lord." One of his attendants said, "All of his life he has been saying yes to the Lord." What a testimony!

While the Lord had been working in me to save me and call me to Africa, I was not the only one He was working in. A young man named George Heath Bobbett had come to BBS a year ahead of me in the fall of 1950. Heath, as he was known, truly gave his heart and life to the Lord and began to grow in Him while at BBS. And – wonderfully for me! – God brought us together for His service.

As students together at BBS, our paths crossed in various places – in the dining hall, in chapel, and other places. The first time I saw Heath, he was sitting in the Springsteed Hall dining room with the girl he was dating. He must have been about twenty-two years old, and I was nineteen. I didn't think much about this couple, only that they both were so good looking. Heath already had flecks of gray in his hair. He was so handsome! Not long after that, I heard that he was no longer dating her. We had prayer bands at school that met at different times to pray for various mission fields. I was in the Africa prayer band, and I remember seeing Heath there too. He says that was the first time he ever really noticed me.

During my sophomore year, I learned something that made me think differently about him. One night another girl and I were in our suite's bathroom, chatting while we both worked on our pin curls – twisting our hair into pins before we went to bed. She was going on and on about this guy she had a crush on. It was Heath Bobbett. I was listening politely, not really much interested, until she made this statement: "There is only one thing that bothers me. Heath is sure God has called him to Africa, and I don't have any calling or interest in Africa." My heart was stirred, and I immediately wondered if I could ever be the one he would go to Africa with! I came back to earth with the thought that no, he probably didn't even know who I was and would never ask me out on a date.

After hearing that he definitely was called to serve in Africa, I began to notice him much more often – in the halls, at chapel, playing basketball, and so forth. I also rode in his car with others involved in street meetings. Our eyes often met, and I must admit my heart began to love him even then. That year Heath was a "middler" in the five-year Bachelor of Theology program. This meant we were both scheduled to graduate in 1955. I began to think maybe it was my imagination that we were attracted to each other when our eyes and smiles met. Soon school was out, and I headed with the other Emmanuel students back home to Ohio.

The summer of 1953, I began dating a young man from my home church in Dayton. He was fresh out of military service where he had gotten his life straightened out and was determined to live for Christ. He was headed to BBS as a freshman that fall. We dated steadily all summer, mostly going to all our church activities together. I had given up on Heath as a lost cause, thinking I was mistaken and that he wasn't interested in me. At the same time, it looked as though God was calling Larry to the pastorate or youth ministry and not to Africa.

During that summer, the Lord had taken Heath in a new direction. There was a group starting a new church near Watkins Glen, New York, (Waneta Lake). They had been meeting around a radio each week, listening to Pastor Clyde Truax preach at the morning service at Elmira Heights Birchwood Baptist Tabernacle. After a while, they contacted Pastor Truax to ask if he could suggest someone they might call to become their pastor. Pastor Truax recommended Heath be their student pastor, and they called him to come. That summer, Heath stayed in different homes of members of the congregation and worked as full-time pastor until school began again in the fall. For the next two years, every weekend he drove the eighty miles to the church they named Waneta Lake Baptist Chapel.

Our junior year began in September 1953, and Larry came that year to BBS as a freshman. Heath said he was going to be obedient to the Lord and ask me out, but then he couldn't because I was going with Larry! God allows wonderful little twists and turns in our lives, later revealing that He was working all the time to bring us onto the path He had planned for us. I was disappointed when Heath didn't ask me out that previous spring, and now he was disappointed that fall because I was dating someone else.

With Jesus Leading the Way

In spite of our failures and straying off of His chosen path, He brings us back after we have learned some of His lessons along the way.

Larry was a fine young man, and God had so evidently worked in his life when he was in the military to bring him back into a right relationship with Christ after years of running from the Lord. However, I started to be convicted that I shouldn't be dating him because he wasn't called to Africa. I had promised the Lord I would go, even if I had to go as a single woman.

A couple of months later, as Heath was studying in his dorm room, his roommate informed him, "Guess who broke up? Larry and Norma!" And once again, the meeting of eyes and smiles began between Heath and me. The attraction was strong. We talked in the halls, walked to classes together, sat in the lounge and visited, and so forth. Our first real date was going to a street meeting together.

BBS had no campus at that time. Classes and chapel were held in the large First Baptist Church on the corner of Main and Baldwin Streets. However, the wealthy Johnson family, who lived in a beautiful home on the main street almost across from First Baptist, welcomed all BBS students to walk in their beautiful gardens, maintained by special gardeners. There were pathways and terraces. We couldn't have had a more beautiful campus! The Endicott-Johnson families were very prominent at that time with their shoe factories in the area. Mrs. Johnson said she enjoyed watching the students walking in her gardens. She said in the fall, when classes began, she saw groups of girls or groups of fellows together, but by springtime, it was mostly couples walking in the gardens!

At Thanksgiving break of my junior year, my roommate, Cora Morgan, invited Ruth Berkhout and me to go home with her to Rutland, Vermont. Cora's parents lived on a farm and had lots of woodland for hunting and lumbering. We had so much fun enjoying her parents' warm hospitality. Cora's mom was very quiet and hospitable. Her dad, friendly but reserved, was not a Christian. We rode a sled up into the woods to cut down and drag back a Christmas tree and pulled in a deer Cora's brother had shot.

Cora's dad had shown no interest in the things of God nor made any pretense of being or becoming a Christian, but Cora believed with all her heart that God had heard her prayers and that her dad would be saved. She told me, "If I receive word one day that my dad has suddenly died in an accident, I believe with all my heart he would have accepted Christ as his Savior the moment before he died and that I would see him again in heaven!" What faith! And what a blessed challenge she was to me, not only in her faith for her dad's salvation but in every aspect of her life.

Many years later Cora told me the rest of the story. After Cora and her siblings had married and left home, her dad retired from farming but continued to live on the old homeplace. He was agreeable to Cora's mom having Bible studies with him in their home. That summer, they studied the book of John and discussed it, but he still wasn't saved – until he woke up in the middle of the night in November and realized in his heart, "It is true!" At that moment, he believed and was born again! He began to write to his four children and told them what had happened. Then on Christmas morning when they were all together and finished opening their gifts, Mr. Morgan said, "For many years I have not felt like I was a part of this family. All of you were Christians, and I was not. I want to ask each of you to forgive me if you can. If you cannot forgive me, at least I know that God has forgiven me!" Of course, the family rushed to put their arms around him and to tell him there was nothing to forgive. They were just rejoicing that he was now a follower of the Lord Jesus Christ. It was about two years later when the Lord took Mr. Morgan home to heaven at the age of sixty-seven.

Every Sunday, Heath left early in the morning, spent the whole day at Waneta Lake Baptist Chapel preaching both morning and evening, and then drove the eighty miles back to BBS late on Sunday night. He felt that he should never take a girl up to the chapel with him until he knew she was the one whom he would marry. What respect could his congregation have for a pastor who brought different girls along that he was dating? Since both Heath and I had been in dating relationships before and had to break up knowing it was not God's will, we wanted to pray much and be absolutely sure that it was God who had brought us together.

Finally, on January 8, 1954 (my spiritual birthday!), he asked me to go for a walk with him after supper. It was a cold evening, but we didn't notice! He asked me to go to Waneta Lake Chapel with him the next Sunday. We had to have special permission from BBS for my going up to the chapel with Heath every Sunday because by the time we got home on Sunday evenings, it was past curfew time.

Waneta Lake Chapel met in an old one-room schoolhouse that had been nicely fixed up with theater-type seats. Since there was only one room, the adults met there for Sunday school, and some of the children's classes met outside in good weather or in someone's car during cold weather. During Heath's senior year, Tom and Ada Utter gave a corner of their farm property to the church, and the men began to build their own church building.

We often spent our Sundays with dear friends Clarence and Velma Knapp and their children at their beautiful farmhouse near PennYan, New York. Clarence owned a small two-passenger airplane at their farm, using their pasture for take-offs and landings. I'll never forget the Sunday he wanted to take me up in the plane. I was so nervous and fearful at takeoff but relaxed and enjoyed the scenery below of hilly farmland and the view of nearby Keuka Lake. Just as I was becoming calm, it was time to land. As we came down toward the pasture, Clarence said, "Now landing is the hardest part of flying." Gulp!

It was around the time of my first airplane ride that Heath and I exchanged our high school class rings. This was the common practice back then and meant we were "going steady" and were not dating anyone else. He wore my ring on his little finger, and I wore his on my ring finger, with lots of tape around the inside of the ring to make it fit. In a sense, these were pre-engagement rings.

On March 17, 1954, Heath asked me to be his wife, and I said "Yes!" We were secretly engaged but could not be formally engaged until our senior year at BBS, without special faculty permission. That year Heath took me to the senior banquet. I remember I wore a pretty yellow formal dress.

When our junior year ended, Heath and I faced the summer apart. I went back to Ohio, and he moved up to Bradford, New York, for the summer to be full-time pastor at Waneta Lake Baptist Chapel. Telephone calls were very expensive, so there were only two times that we were able to have a short conversation. However, we wrote letters to each other daily, and that was a good thing. We still have our love letters. You really get to know things about each other through writing that you might not otherwise learn.

We were looking forward to the end of August when Heath and his mother planned to drive out to Ohio for a week to meet my family. What a reunion! During that visit, Heath got to meet everyone except my dad.

Dad had retired in 1954 after thirty-three years (counting his years of military service in WWI) from Wright Field. He had builders frame the new home he was building on wooded property on Watts Bar Dam (Lake) near Rockwood, Tennessee. When Heath came, Dad was actually in Tennessee finishing all of the interior of the new home. Our home on Little York Road would be sold before the next summer so he and Mom could take up residence in Tennessee.

Mom was very unhappy about the upcoming move to Tennessee. It was so hard for her at age fifty-four to leave her home, church, and friends to start over. But Dad couldn't afford to maintain two homes, and he was hoping to get away from the ice and snow of Ohio in retirement. Besides, he could then indulge in his favorite hobby (fishing) any day he wanted to! It was really a beautiful though secluded location and was an ideal vacation spot for their children and grandchildren to visit. He built a dock and a small boathouse. We could swim, fish, relax, and visit the nearby Smoky Mountains. Mom had no choice about moving there, but she was so lonely and missed Ohio greatly.

She had been having some problems remembering some words for a while, but she remembered all events and was good at laughing at herself when she couldn't come up with simple words sometimes. When these things happened, Mom laughed along with the rest of us. I wonder now if all of this was related to her severe anemia or if perhaps she was having some TIAs because her high blood pressure was off the charts.

The week when Heath came to my home in August 1954 was very busy and went quickly. Heath attended Emmanuel with me and endured being looked over by the folks there. (They all approved, as far as I know!) He spoke at one of our youth group's street meetings in Tipp City where one man received Jesus Christ as his Savior. The Dayton Air Show at Vandalia was that week too, so we enjoyed all the aerial performances. We both got sunburns because it was a blistering hot day.

Our love was growing daily, and we marveled at God's goodness in bringing our paths together in His perfect timing. Both of us had become believers at age fourteen and both of us knew God was calling us to serve Him someday in Africa. We had lots of long talks late at night and planned to announce our engagement as soon as we were back at BBS in September. We also planned the date and place of our wedding the next summer – June 16, 1955, at Emmanuel in Dayton.

At one point during the visit, Heath's mother asked Mom how far we lived outside of Dayton. My mother, true to Daytonian practice, measured our distance from Dayton by our distance from the courthouse, which was in the exact center of the city. But when she replied, "Seven miles from the courthouse," Heath began to laugh. He assumed she was making a joke, hinting that we needed to go to the courthouse for a marriage license!

Engagement, Graduation, and Wedding

By mid-September 1954, classes began again at BBS. On September 15, Heath drove me up toward Lone Tree Hill with a beautiful view looking down at the lights of Johnson City. There he officially proposed, giving me a beautiful solitaire diamond. The date was inscribed inside the band. Inside our wedding bands, we had engraved Psalm 34:3, "O magnify the Lord with me, and let us exalt His name together."

It was about 11:00 that night when I returned to Dr. and Mrs. Armstrong's home and climbed to the large third-floor attic room that I shared with four roommates. My idea was not to announce that Heath had given me a ring but to just wait and see when my roommates noticed it. However, they were busy talking, doing homework, getting showers, and preparing for bed, so they didn't even look my way. I could stand it no longer! When I announced that Heath had given me a diamond, all the girls jumped up to see it.

Heath's mother, had moved to Johnson City and was working in the kitchen, so Heath and several of his friends then lived with her. It helped her pay her rent, and for the men it was cheaper than living in the dorms. In those days, a wise and frugal student could pretty well pay his or her own way through Bible college by working full-time in the summer and part-time during the school year. What a blessing it was for us to graduate debt free.

I was looking for my wedding dress and had always dreamed of having one with a hoop skirt underneath. One day, I saw "my" dress on a rack of gowns that had been reduced 50 percent. The original price of $110 had been reduced to $55. I wanted it so badly, but that was a lot of money in those days. The year earlier, Pearl Smith had found her wedding dress there with a long cathedral train. Because the yoke was an ugly tan netting, it never sold, so that dress had been reduced from $110 to $10! Pearl persuaded my roommate, Jean Fisher, to remove the tan netting of the yoke and put a satin yoke in. I thought that if I prayed and the Lord wanted me to have "my" dress, it would be reduced to $10 like Pearl's. That is when my dear roommate, Cora Morgan, gave me a lecture. She said, "Norma, God is just as able to supply $55 as He is $10! If you believe that is the dress you should have, put it in layaway and pay it off as the Lord enables you!" She was so right! I was able to pay it off in a few months, with my mom chipping in to help me.

A vivid memory has always stayed with me from the day Cora and I were shopping in Binghamton for my wedding dress. As we walked the streets and shopped, I was so happy that God had brought Heath into my life in His time and that we had His assurance that it was His will for us to be married. I thought of how awful it would be to be engaged and eventually married out of God's will. I was so thankful too that the Lord had kept both of us from any premarital sex with others or with each other so that we could marry in purity.

Our senior year was so busy it seemed to literally fly by. To graduate, each student had to have an oral exam by a panel of professors. We had to defend our beliefs with Scripture. Besides that, there were final exams, papers to write, and so forth. Heath qualified for the honor society early in his seminary days. I finally made it into the honor society my senior year.

Graduation was in June. It was sad for me that none of my family came, but the anticipation of our soon-coming wedding kept me in a happy, excited state. I think my family just felt that it was so far, "way out there in New York," that they couldn't make the trip.

With Jesus Leading the Way

We graduated on June 6, and our wedding was ten days later. Heath got to meet my dad the day before our wedding! He had written to Dad and asked permission to marry me, but Dad had not responded, so he then called to ask. Dad loved Heath from the first time he saw him and always called him Son.

Pastor Jeremiah performed the ceremony. Emmanuel's new pastor, Nile Fisher, assisted. I carried an orchid on a white Bible. For "something old" I had a pretty, seventy-five-year-old handkerchief given to me by Margie Carmen. My "something new" was my gown, "something borrowed" was Joy Cutherbertson's wedding veil, and "something blue" was my garter! Harold Engle, our soloist, sang "Always" and "Because" which were the popular wedding songs at that time.

My dad, always the jokester, said to Heath at the reception, "Congratulations, old man! I thought I'd never get rid of her!" and we all laughed. He said he was afraid I would be an LOPH (Left on Papa's Hands)! A lot of Dad's good humor and enjoying good jokes rubbed off on me!

Our plans were to spend our first night in a Dayton motel then head south to Kentucky, visiting Mammoth Caves. They were awesome. (We returned there on our forty-fifth wedding anniversary and had a great time again exploring the caves.) After Mammoth Caves, we drove on to Chattanooga, Tennessee, to see Lookout Mountain. We were there on a Sunday, so we visited the very large Highland Park Baptist

Church where Pastor Lee Roberson ministered. It was Cradle Roll Sunday, so 300 babies and toddlers, carried by their parents, walked across the platform in the morning service! Next, we drove through the Smoky Mountains, visiting a Cherokee village. We ended up at Mom and Dad's new home on Watts Bar Dam for the final part of our week's honeymoon. Dad and Mom still were visiting up in Ohio for a couple of days, so we had the house to ourselves until they came back. Their house on the lake was very nice, and we could swim, take a ride in Dad's boat, or go fishing. Mom was still having a hard time adjusting to the isolation and leaving her friends and church behind in Ohio.

Waneta Lake Baptist Chapel

When we arrived back in Ohio, we packed our car full of all our wedding gifts and headed to Bradford, New York, thinking we could move into our apartment (half of an old house) that our landlady had promised to have ready for us by then. But it wasn't ready! Dear Margie and Charlie Carmen welcomed us to live at their lovely farmhouse for the first month of our marriage.

I learned so much from this precious couple. Charlie's father had been spending his winters in DeLand, Florida, then came back to the farm for the summers. After being a widower for several years, he had married a rather aristocratic woman from Kentucky. The elderly Mrs. Carmen could be opinionated and bossy. Dearest Margie quietly put up with her and her sharp tongue. Just once in a while I could see Margie's eyes well up with tears, but she never retaliated. She and Charlie were undoubtedly much relieved when the elderly Carmens headed back to Florida for the winters. Grandpa Carmen, though in his nineties, still insisted on going out to the fields to work with Charlie.

Margie cooked on a woodstove with a reservoir to heat water and a warming oven on the back. Many of the leftovers from dinner were put in the warming oven so they were ready for consumption at suppertime.

Margie was a wonderful cook, and I don't think she ever owned a cookbook! Once I asked her for her recipe for her molasses cookies. She always had some on hand. They were soft and cake-like, and I have never tasted any more delicious. Charlie laughed at us young wives who used recipe books. Margie's recipe dictated to me went something like this: "Take six or seven good handfuls of flour, mix in a couple handfuls of sugar, a pinch of salt," and so forth.

Several years after Grandpa and Grandma Carmen passed away, Charlie and Margie finally sold the farm and moved to Bath, New York, to retire. The only piece of farm equipment Charlie took with him to Bath was his tractor. Margie often said, "I do hope the Lord will allow Charlie to plow in heaven because I don't know if he will be happy there if he can't!"

As a young pastor and wife, we were there with Charlie and Margie when tragedy struck. There had been a bad electrical storm one night, and the electricity went off in the barn. The next day, Charlie had a friend come to look at it. The friend said it was just a small problem he could fix, so he got the lights on again. He didn't realize the storm caused an electrical short. A couple of hours later, a motorist stopped to tell the Carmens that smoke was pouring from the barn. Thankfully, all the cows were out to pasture, and the horses were not in the barn. But the building and all the hay were total losses. Heath and I felt so helpless, but Margie and Charlie told us they were so thankful we were there to comfort them and pray with them.

I was ignorant about so many things on a farm. One day Margie was telling about a former young pastor they knew. When Grandpa Carmen was complaining that one of their cows had freshened (given birth) way out in the pasture, the preacher said, "Why does he let the cows have calves anyway if it so much trouble?" Margie was laughing because the preacher didn't know that theirs were milk cows, and a cow had to have a calf in order to make milk. I never let on to Margie that I hadn't known that before either!

After spending our first married month with the Carmens, we were able to move into our apartment in Bradford. Bradford was a tiny village that had a general store with a post office inside, Hank Keefer's auto repair garage, a high school, a Catholic church, a Baptist church, some homes, and not much else!

About the same time, we moved into our half of the house, newlyweds George and Bonnie moved into the other side. Bonnie was a music teacher at the high school, and George worked for the railroad in Bath. We became life-long friends.

We had someone plow up a garden area behind the house, and Heath put in a nice garden. As a student pastor, his salary was $30 a week. The church raised it to $35 after we got married, and they also paid our rent of $35 a month. We really needed to earn a little more for our living expenses. I applied and was hired at Westinghouse in Bath. I made the great amount of $35 weekly after taxes were deducted. Making radio tubes at the Westinghouse plant was a real challenge for me. For eight hours each day, I sat at a table with a jig before me and used tweezers to assemble components for radio tubes. Efficiency experts taught us how to make our every move count while exactly assembling the inside parts. After two weeks, I had to assemble a certain number per hour to keep my job! Meeting the hourly quota was nerve-racking! I hardly had time to run to the bathroom once in the morning.

We decided it would be best to live on Heath's salary of $35 a week while we used my salary to make a payment every week on our little black coupe.

That first summer we were married, Heath also took on the brave task of teaching his bride to drive a car! He was very patient with me, teaching me to drive a stick shift. Not only did I have to learn the rules of the road, but the actual driving test at the Bath courthouse was difficult. One of the hardest things was to parallel park at a parking meter on a busy street. Heath was a good teacher because he could do it simply and precisely himself. The examiner allowed Heath to ride in the back seat while I took my test. As I looked back to begin the parallel parking, I saw that Heath's head was bowed, and I knew he was praying for me! With this "outside help," I passed my test the very first time I took it! I was twenty-two years old.

Just a note about Mr. and Mrs. John Roy, another precious couple from the Chapel. Mrs. Roy had severe arthritis and wasn't able to move around a lot. John, our head deacon, was a carpenter and built a beautiful ranch home in Bradford for their retirement years. Mrs. Roy did not know how to drive a car. One day, as they were driving to church, Mrs. Roy asked John what she should do if he ever had a heart attack or passed out while driving. He said, "Here's just what you should do. Reach right over here and turn off the car ignition." John illustrated by turning it off, then there was a loud backfire that blew the muffler off their car! Mrs. Roy told this story, laughing as she said, "I know exactly what to do if John passes out while driving. I'll just blow off the muffler!"

We became lifelong friends with wonderful people we met at the Chapel. They were so loving and forgiving to their inexperienced young pastor and wife. The Lord raised up prayer supporters for us who prayed for us daily then and all the years when we were in Africa.

With Jesus Leading the Way

In February of 1956, an ordination council was called to examine Heath. For the most part, the pastors were kind and serious in questioning Heath on his doctrinal beliefs, and he gave good answers backed by Scripture references. His first question was on the controversial passage of Hebrews 6. Heath handled himself very well, and I was proud of him.

At the dinner that followed, I sat by Gladys Truax. She recounted to me her husband's ordination many years before, including the fact that at the time she had just found out they were expecting their first baby. I smiled quietly and didn't divulge our secret yet – that our first baby was on the way too and would arrive in September!

It was an adventure getting by on Heath's salary of $35 a week. When Charlie Carmen gave him his pay on Sunday evening, we usually bought groceries on Monday and filled our car with gas. By the end of the week, the salary was gone. But at that time, milk came in glass bottles that we paid a deposit on. By the end of the week we usually had enough bottles to return for the deposit to buy another quart of milk!

Yet we lived better on that $35 a week than we have since at higher salaries – our church family was so good to us! In the summertime, they gave us abundant vegetables from their gardens. Every time we were in the farmers' homes, before we left they invariably said, "Just a minute. I want to give you some things from my freezer!" We were given steaks, roasts, and many other cuts of meat that we could never have afforded otherwise.

There were very few restaurants around at that time. Wives put their Sunday dinner into a slow oven early Sunday morning before leaving for church, and it was ready to eat when the family arrived home. A big treat for Heath and me was to go to Bath, fifteen miles away, on an occasional Sunday to eat at a nice little restaurant called The Chat a Wyle. One Sunday during the early months of our marriage, we had our meal and as we were finishing, Heath said, "You do have money to pay for this don't you?" My heart sank! I replied, "No, I thought you had some money with you." Oh, what an embarrassment! As we talked about what to do, a couple sitting at a table close by asked us if we had a problem, so we told them our predicament. The gentleman said, "We live here in Bath, and I publish the little penny saver paper. We will be glad to pay for your lunch, and you can pay us back the next time you come to Bath. We noticed that you bowed your heads and prayed before you ate, and we hardly ever see a young couple do that!" You never know who is watching and how what you do can be a testimony.

We had paid off our little coupe by March 1956, so I quit work at Westinghouse. The gals I worked with collected money and gave me a nice baby gift and card as I left. My friend Norma Haag said she was going to miss me working beside her. She said, "Norma, when you are here at work, the language the women use is so much cleaner. On the few days you have been off sick, it has been unpleasant for me hearing their profanity."

Rebecca's Birth

When the ladies at the church and in our neighborhood realized I was expecting a baby, they had lots of advice for me, including old wives' tales about pregnancy. Almost all of them assured me that I was carrying a boy by the way I walked, by the way I got out of a chair, because I carried low instead of high, and so forth.

On Saturday, September 15th, my labor began, but the contractions were very irregular all day. Finally, since we lived fifteen miles from the Bath hospital, we decided to go to Bath, closer to the hospital. The contractions weren't regular yet, so we found an overnight diner and had some coffee while we timed contractions. It was about midnight when we checked into the hospital.

At that time, there was a labor room with two or three beds and curtains pulled around each so husbands could sit with their wives while they were in labor. Our baby was posterior, which meant the delivery took longer. As I labored in the bed, another woman was taken into the delivery room and I could hear her screams. I thought, "Do I have that to go through next?" (Turned out she was a screamer, and I was not.) When I was fully dilated and about to deliver, Heath was sent out to the waiting room, and I was taken into the delivery room. Dr. Hutchings sat me up for a saddle block injection in the spine. Blessed numbness from the waist down followed!

Dr. Hutchings was young, in his early thirties, and very modern. He gave the spinal and had mirrors adjusted so that I could watch the delivery. Later, husbands could stay for the delivery, which was great. Heath said he was glad to be sent into the waiting room though, thinking he might not be able to take it seeing a delivery!

It was Sunday morning. Heath had been up with me at the hospital all night. When he realized that he probably wouldn't be able to make it to the chapel to preach, he called Rev. Alexander Perry in Corning, New York, to ask if he could preach for him that morning, September 16. Alexander was a retired precision engraver of glass at Corning Glass Works, a lay preacher, and a godly man. He and Mrs. Perry had a cottage on Waneta Lake, so they often blessed us by attending our church when they were at the lake.

Mrs. Perry answered the early phone call from Heath. She said that Alexander wasn't up yet, but she would go ask him about preaching for Heath. Alexander was lying in bed awake. When Mrs. Perry said, "Heath wants to know if you will preach this morning for him at the chapel because he has been keeping vigil with Norma all night, and the baby hasn't yet arrived." Alexander replied, "Yes. The Lord woke me up in the night and told me I would be preaching this morning, so I have been lying here thinking about what message He wants me to bring!"

Rebecca Lynn Bobbett was born about 11:20 a.m. that Sunday. She was so beautiful, not wrinkled or red like some newborns. I marveled at the miracle of seeing her born. Dr. Hutchings said, "As long as babies are being born, God is still performing miracles!" He had a beautiful bass voice, was active in an organization of men's barbershop quartets, and sang in the choir at the Episcopal church in Bath. He looked up at the clock as Rebecca was born and teased me, saying, "Norma, this is just about the exact time our choir is singing, and there was a great bass part in the music this morning that you made me miss!"

Most people didn't have insurance for hospitalizations. We paid for our office calls each time we went to the doctor – $3! For the three days of my hospitalization and Rebecca's three days in the nursery, our hospital bill was $75. Dr. Hutchings' fee for prenatal office visits and the delivery was also $75. We had no insurance, so we had saved to pay the hospital bill. Most doctors at that time did not charge clergy, so Dr. Hutchings never sent us a bill.

There was a constant stream of village and church folks coming to see Rebecca the first few days we were home in Bradford. She received so many nice baby gifts and she had so many dresses and outfits that I didn't need to buy anything for her until she was two or three years old. Of course, that was in the days before disposable diapers, so there were cloth diapers to wash everyday by hand because we had no washing machine, and there were no laundromats around.

My mother came by train from Tennessee to Bath and stayed with me for a whole month. What a blessing she was! She loved holding Rebecca, cooking meals for us, and did the daily dozen diapers handwash too. I wanted her to stay longer, but after one month, my dad's half-brother, Earl Viles, suddenly died in Dayton, Ohio, so Dad wanted her to take the train to Dayton to meet him in time for the funeral.

The church family loved Rebecca and doted on her. I was so happy and content being a pastor's wife and a mother. We went to Highland Falls, New York, to celebrate Rebecca's first Christmas with Jane and Homer Ludington and family. A few weeks later, Heath told me he sensed that it was time for him to resign the church and apply to a mission board for Africa. A new chapter in our lives was about to begin.

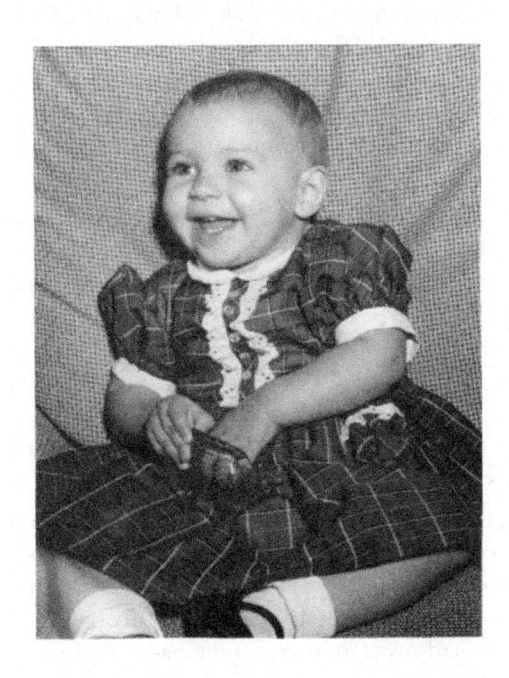

Chapter 6
A Mission Board and Pre-Field Ministry
February 1957 to November 1958

When Heath read his resignation to the Waneta Lake Baptist Chapel early in 1957, the congregation was saddened. Even though he had told them before he ever accepted the call to become their pastor that he was eventually headed for Africa, some thought that others had hurt us and caused us to resign. We told them nothing could be further from the truth, but that God was moving us on now in obedience to His call to Africa. For the rest of our lives, we have been so thankful for the precious friends the Lord gave us at Waneta Lake Baptist Chapel who kept our names lifted in prayer as we obeyed God's call to Africa.

We moved to Horseheads, New York, in February 1957, and Heath took a job selling men's clothing at a Robert Hall store, a well-known chain selling reasonably priced suits. We found a three-room furnished apartment for $90 a month, utilities included. Although the ad said, "No children," they changed their minds after interviewing us and being so pleased with our baby girl, Rebecca.

One day at that apartment, as I was packing away some of our wedding gifts and extra linens to leave in storage in the States when we went overseas, Rebecca, just a toddler, wanted to help me. As I was ready to close a packed box, I saw that she had placed a cucumber in the box with my good table cloths! I was so glad that I saw that and removed it. What a sad day it would have been four or five years later when we came back to the U.S. and opened that box with the lovely wedding gift linens!

We transferred our membership to the Birchwood Baptist Tabernacle in Elmira Heights where Rev. Clyde and Gladys Truax had ministered for many years. While at BBS, Heath had been a member of the Birchwood Church, and Pastor Truax had baptized him. Pastor and Mrs. Truax became our lifelong mentors. Heath's dad had left his mom when Heath was only eighteen, and Pastor Truax became the dad Heath never had. Mrs. Truax was his godly helpmeet, someone I could look up to and emulate.

After working at the clothing store for a while, Heath asked for time off when we were to meet with our mission board, but his boss refused. Heath had to choose to stay with his job or go with mission's work, and so he lost his job at Robert Hall. Our faith was strong that we were following God's leading in our call to Africa, so we knew He would supply another job in His time.

Choice of a Mission Board

During our time at BBS, we had learned about several Baptist mission boards. I was sure the Lord would have sent me to an English-speaking country because I thought I could never learn another language. The Lord must have been smiling and shaking His head at my plans because He then called us to Niger where I had to learn two new languages! Heath felt that God was definitely leading us to French West Africa and that we should contact Mr. Joseph McCaba who had founded Christian Missions Incorporated. Its original goal was to minister in French-speaking Muslim countries. Mr. McCaba started the work in Niamey, Niger. (His story is well chronicled in his autobiography, *The Teacher Who Laughs*.)

When Mr. McCaba spoke at BBS during our senior year, we had made an appointment to talk to him about our call to missions. As a young, soon-to-be-married bride, he really scared me by telling us of the harsh climate in Niger and the many African illnesses. Then he asked, "Are you willing to bury your children in Africa when they die of a disease?" We both realized that if God was calling us there, we would have to lay our all on the altar, even if it meant losing a child.

We filled out our applications to Christian Missions (the name later changed to Evangelical Baptist Mission) and sent them off to their headquarters in Paterson, New Jersey. We also had to have physicals, even Rebecca, for medical clearance and furnish references for the mission to check. We knew that my blood type was O negative, and Heath's was O positive, raising the serious possibility that our future children might have to have their blood changed at birth. The mission acceptance said that it was important that we only have our babies in well-equipped hospitals, so the babies' blood could be changed if needed. We sent our physical reports to the mission in February 1957 and waited for them to check our references.

Finally, we were asked to meet with the board on April 23, 1957. Rebecca was eight months old, and I don't think I had ever been away from her overnight before then. Mother Bobbett came to stay overnight with Rebecca at our Horseheads apartment. She also loaned us her car to make the trip to New Jersey. We weren't sure our old coupe could make the trip.

Now a word about Mother Bobbett's car. She had bought a used Cadillac, which was about six years old. It was running well, and the price was good, but people driving Cadillacs, no matter what the age of the car, were considered well off in life and stared at in gas stations and parking lots. Naïve as we were, we thought maybe the mission wouldn't accept us if we drove there in a Cadillac! So, we parked our car several blocks from the mission office and walked to the mission, so they wouldn't see "our" Caddy! In the years since, we have gotten a lot of laughs out of remembering this.

The house in Patterson, New Jersey, where our mission was lodged, had once belonged to the family of John Stam. John and his wife, Betty, were martyred many years before after a short time as missionaries in China.

Our mission board had always been composed of godly men who have hearts for missions. However, because we were new and didn't know them, being examined by them was scary. We were more than a little nervous, and we reviewed our notes from our oral theology exams at BBS in case they questioned our doctrinal beliefs. To our surprise, they didn't ask about doctrine but mainly wanted to hear about our salvation and call to Africa. One question we were surprised by was, "Would you be averse to or cause division over French Baptist churches that use real wine for communion?"

Later when we had our first shock taking wine from a common cup in a Paris Baptist church – and realizing it was sour wine and not sweet grape juice – we began to understand that we were living in a different culture. Wine was served at meals in France, diluted with some water for French children. Wine drunk in moderation and digested with food does not cause one to become inebriated. French Christians drank wine with their meals just like everyone else and thought nothing of it.

We remembered the story of Charles Spurgeon, the prince of Baptist preachers, who held meetings in Germany. He was shocked and disgusted to see German Christians drinking beer, so he left them and went to a tea shop. What he didn't know was that the tea shop had an unsavory reputation because of those who frequented it, so his testimony was more compromised there in the tea shop than in the beer garden! We met a sweet young German lady in Nigeria who told us another story about Germans drinking beer. She told us that she grew up in a strict legalistic Christian home in Germany. The women did not cut their hair or wear jewelry, but they had beer on their tables with meals every day. She never knew there were Christians in the world who believed it was sinful to drink beer until she went to England to learn English. It was her turn to be shocked when she met Christian women who cut their hair and wore jewelry...but they wouldn't dream of drinking beer!

Later our French landlady, Madame DuQuesne, explained to us that her children often didn't know what to buy for their dad, Monsieur DuQuesne, for Christmas or birthdays because he didn't drink. We knew that he always took undiluted wine with his meals, and it surprised us that she said he didn't drink. She explained that "people who drink" in France are the ones who go into bars at all hours and often get drunk. Monsieur DuQuesne had his own private taxi service for many years, had never had an accident, and was definitely not a drunk!

I know there are many warnings about drinking in the Scriptures, but it isn't expressly forbidden. Heath and I choose not to drink. We were not inclined to adapt to the French culture in drinking alcohol. Although the French people didn't understand why we wouldn't accept wine or other drink, they did respect us when we said we had vowed not to drink. Maybe they thought we were recovering alcoholics!

Soon after our meeting with the mission board, we received word of our acceptance. On May 4, Heath wrote to the mission:

"Your welcome letter arrived last Wednesday with the news of our official acceptance as missionary candidates. It is our prayer that we shall be a credit to our Lord, the mission, and its work as we serve Him. The next days after arriving home, we received letters inviting us to write to two different churches concerning our missionary plans, and we are praying that very soon we will have some deputation meetings scheduled...We feel in definite need of your prayers as I have been laid off work in lieu of our missionary plans, and as yet I have not found another job. If we had the engagements, we could begin to do full-time deputation work but really haven't gotten underway to that extent yet."

In just a few weeks, Heath found a better paying job at National Homes, where prefabricated homes were built. Working hard at that job all summer, he always came home with glue all over his clothes, giving us the impression that those first prefabricated homes were held together with glue!

With Jesus Leading the Way

A missionary nurse to Venezuela, Coralyn Gleason, became our close friend and mentor. When she returned to Venezuela we purchased her used car. It was a 1952 Chevrolet sedan, a little more reliable and roomier than our 1950 coupe. Our payments to Coralyn were $20 a month.

Your Missionaries to French West Africa

Home Address:
EVANGELICAL BAPTIST MISSIONS
146 North 7th Street
Paterson 2, N. J.

"Ye also helping together by prayer for us."
—II Cor. 1:11.

THE BOBBETTS
Heath, Norma, and Rebecca

During the summer, besides his full-time work at National Homes, Heath was busy contacting churches to line up meetings to raise our support.

One night after Sunday evening service at Birchwood Baptist Tabernacle, a couple that we barely knew, Paul and Allegra Whipple, invited us over for a snack. They had three little ones under the age of six. They were living in a cement block home that was still unfinished inside and had a little toy store on the front of their home. Paul also drove a delivery truck for frozen foods.

We were speechless when Paul and Allegra announced to us, "We feel the Lord wants us to provide your passage money to Niger. During this next year, as you work to raise your support, we will save enough to get you to France. And during the year you are in language study there, we will save enough for your tickets to Niger!" This amount would be $1,200. This was a struggling, young couple, working hard to make ends meet and slowly trying to finish their cement block home. What a blessing they were to us, helping confirm that "He who calleth you will also do it." Needless to say, we became very close friends with Paul and Allegra over the years.

God had called us to Niger, and He was showing us that He could supply all our needs as they came up. And yes, all these years later, we can say in praise to Him that He has always supplied our needs, whether they have been physical, mental, financial, or spiritual. What a mighty God we serve, and we are so undeserving of His goodness.

Deputation

We gave up our furnished apartment in Horseheads at the end of August 1957, packed away our meager belongings, and headed out full-time on the deputation trail on September 9, 1957. Our first week of meetings was in Michigan, then on to Indiana, Illinois, and Kansas.

It was hard taking Rebecca away from a settled life in one home. She was just beginning to talk. Our first night on our way toward the Midwest was spent in a motel. She didn't understand the strange room and new port-a-crib, so she kept standing up holding onto the rails and saying, "Where'd you go?" She said it like it was all one word "Weardugo?" We gave her lots of attention on the trip, and she was the darling of the people we met. We celebrated her first birthday in Perry, Iowa.

Seatbelts and baby car seats were unheard of then. There was nothing wrong with holding your child on your lap in the front seat of the car or allowing them to stand behind your shoulder as you drove, so they could see out! We got a port-a-crib for Rebecca, which served as a playpen and bed. The legs could be retracted so it fit perfectly, taking up all the room in the back seat of the car. She could move around, play, or sleep there whenever she wanted to. We also had a folding Cosco high chair and a potty chair with us! The high chair was well made and lasted through all our four children's need of it. We left it in the Niamey guest house, and it was used by various missionary children in Niger for many years after we no longer needed it.

By the end of September 1957, we were thrilled to report to the mission that we had $80 of monthly support promised. The support we had to raise was minuscule compared to that which missionaries must raise today. We needed $400 a month which would cover home office fees, field funds, money put aside monthly for our passage home at the end of our term, and our monthly living allowance. We also needed about $2,500 for equipment, shipping, and customs. There was no thought or mention of retirement and no medical insurance, although the mission did put aside $2.50 a month for any medical needs that might arise.

With Jesus Leading the Way

Along with our acceptance, the mission sent us an equipment list of the things we would need to take to Africa with us. I remember shaking my head in disbelief at the exorbitant fund of $1,000 we would have to raise. I told others I was glad we knew God was calling us to Africa because there was no way we ourselves could raise that much in equipment funds!

Our personal living allowance when we arrived in Africa was $75 per month per adult and $25 per child. Our average monthly support was $25 monthly from churches and $5 or $10 monthly from individuals. Some even promised $2.50 a month. The first church to take on our support was Park Avenue Baptist Church in Binghamton, New York.

We continued traveling to meetings in many states and church folks were very kind to give us lodging along the way. When we came to a stretch of over a week when we had no meetings or places to stay, we drove straight through all night and part of the day to Mom and Dad Christmas' lake home near Rockwood, Tennessee. They were thrilled to have us there and to have grandparent time to play with and spoil Rebecca. Everything she did was "so cute." She liked to get into Grandma Christmas' kitchen drawers and take everything out on the floor. In the mornings, she ate her breakfast sitting up to the table on Grandpa Christmas' lap and sharing his food.

From September to the end of November, we had traveled 5,700 miles in our car. By the end of January 1958, our support level had increased to $154.50. Heath sent our list of supporters to the mission:

Park Avenue Baptist Church	$25
Waneta Lake Baptist Chapel	$12.50
Birchwood Baptist Tabernacle	$25
Birchwood Sunday School Class	$10
North Spencer Baptist	$5
First Baptist, Skaneateles	$10
South Park Baptist – Kansas City	$20
Lake Baptist – Lake, Michigan	$5
Immanuel Baptist – Arcanum, Ohio	$10
Emmanuel Baptist Youth Group	$2
Mrs. Lena Bobbett	$5
Cecil and Jane Roades	$5
Sid and Shirley Blackman	$5
Mr. and Mrs. Ramsey Michaels	$5
Miss Agnes Hot	$10

The business administration courses that Heath had taken at Syracuse University were not wasted. I was amazed at the meticulous accounts he kept for the mission as we traveled from church to church. While at Syracuse, he knew in the back of his mind that God had called him to Africa, but he was not following his Savior at that time. The Lord never wastes any experiences in our lives, and later we realize with thankfulness why He allows us to go down a certain path. Heath has always liked accounting. All offerings were duly noted, down to the last penny, and sent in to the mission. He even accounted for $2 and $5 personal gifts people sometimes pressed into our hands after we spoke at churches.

In December, we stayed with my brother Mickey and his wife, Geneva, in New Carlisle, Ohio. They were always kind and hospitable. Although it was very difficult to find work at that time, the Lord provided for us. Mickey was a mail carrier and was able to get Heath a temporary job in the post office for the delivery of Christmas mail. It was a memorable Christmas. We didn't know that it would be our last Christmas with my mother. Dad and she came up from Tennessee, and Carol and Carl were there also. Rebecca had great fun playing with her cousins, Bobby, Gary, and Ruthie Christmas. I was again experiencing morning sickness (or rather all-day sickness), but we didn't tell anyone yet that we had another baby on the way to arrive at the end of June.

Back in Elmira, New York we looked for a furnished apartment to await the arrival of our baby. We found a three-room apartment upstairs over our landlords. We were praying and setting our sights on a departure for France later in that year. We had always lived in furnished apartments, feeling that if we bought any furniture it should be something durable for us to take to Africa. We were advised not to take wooden furniture because the termites were so bad in the mud houses, and they loved to munch on wood!

In February, we ran across a beautiful $170 dinette set on sale for $80. It was made of chrome-plated steel, and the padded chairs were covered with durable plastic. The colors were red, white, and black! It was beautiful, and we knew the termites couldn't digest it. The chairs and table really brightened up the dining areas of our mud homes. After several terms in Africa, the chairs began to deteriorate, but the table remained our dining table all the years we were in Africa! An African missionary couple from Nigeria took it when we left and even invited us over for dinner at their home, so we could see it still in use!

In a letter written in June 1958 to all the churches we had spoken in, we were rejoicing that we had $227 in monthly support promised. Our prayer requests were:

- For the $168 monthly support still needed and for $1,000 for equipment and shipping.
- For the Lord's leading in selecting the equipment.
- For a place nearby to send, crate, and perhaps store our goods while we completed our French language studies.
- For a safe delivery and good health for me and our new baby, expected any day now.
- And, most of all, for the Lord to prepare us spiritually for the days ahead in France and French West Africa.

Jonathan's Birth

Our second baby was due at the end of June. We wanted Dr. Donald Hutchings in Bath, New York, to deliver this baby but the hospital was at least an hour's drive from where we were living in Elmira. On one visit, Heath asked Dr. Hutchings if he should teach him what to do in case the baby came quickly before we made it to the hospital. With a twinkle in his eyes, Dr. Hutchings said, "You won't need to do anything, but if things progress and it gets to the place where you think you just have to do something, sit on your hands!" He said when he rarely had home deliveries and the father was present, he kept telling the father to go to the kitchen and boil more water. Then after the baby was born, he would tell the new father it was, so they could sit down for coffee!

The baby's due date passed, and nothing happened. On July 8, we were invited to stay at Chuck and Liz Houser's home in Avoca, New York, and the Avoca Baptist Church ladies gave me a lovely baby shower. The next morning when we woke up, I was having irregular contractions, so the Housers thought it would be a good idea if we just stayed with them, much closer to the Bath hospital. They offered to watch Rebecca while I was in the hospital. All day and night on July 9, I continued to have irregular contractions. Heath was to leave on the 11th for deputation meetings, and we were fearful the baby wouldn't arrive until after he was gone. Finally, on Thursday, July 10, I began serious labor. Even though this was to be the biggest baby I would deliver of the four, it was my easiest labor!

Deacon John Roy from Waneta Lake Baptist Chapel came to the hospital and visited with Heath in the waiting room. After his first wife had gone home to heaven a few years before he had sold their home in Bradford, remarried, and lived in Bath in his new wife's home. As I was in the labor room, Mr. Roy informed Heath that he was contributing $1,000 to our passage and equipment funds and hoped we would soon be able to be on our way to Africa! We were stunned! Over and over, the Lord supplied our needs, often through people we never dreamed of!

Jonathan Heath Bobbett arrived at 4:00 p.m. on July 10, weighing nine pounds, ten ounces. He didn't cry but immediately began to suck on his hand. I expressed my concerns to Dr. Hutchings that he didn't cry. Dr. Hutchings, ever the comic, said, "Why should he cry? What does he have to feel depressed about?!"

Then Dr. Hutchings said, "Norma, today is my day off work, and I was up at our home on the lake. Your first baby was born on Sunday and I missed singing in our church choir, and now you have your second baby on my day off!" He was quite a doctor. I really enjoyed having a general practitioner for prenatal care, the delivery, and then caring for the baby afterward. Later, doctors specialized, and I had to go to an obstetrician for prenatal care and birth. Then as soon as the baby was born, a pediatrician took over the baby's care. In all our years of growing up, there was just a family doctor, and he cared for all our family's illnesses.

Hospitals have changed in recent years. Our babies were kept in the hospital nursery and only brought to the mothers at feeding times. Only the mothers and medical personnel could touch the baby as long as he was in the hospital. Children under age sixteen were not allowed to visit in hospitals.

I'll never forget the smile on Heath's face when he walked into my room after being shown his son at the window of the nursery! Sadly, he had to leave the next day for meetings in New England. He asked Dr. Hutchings if he could please just hold Jonathan for a few minutes. Dr. H. said it was perfectly all right with him, but he dared not get into trouble with the hospital by breaking rules. So, Heath kissed me goodbye, leaving Rebecca with Chuck and Liz Houser and Jonathan in the hospital nursery.

With Jesus Leading the Way

Chuck was the one who picked up Jonathan and me at the hospital when I was dismissed, and the children and I stayed a few days with them until Heath came back to take us home to our apartment in Elmira.

I got all choked up when I saw Rebecca again, having missed her so much while I was in the hospital. She was fascinated with her new baby brother and kept expressing her love for him.

Jonathan slept eight hours at night from the day he came home from the hospital, from 11:00 p.m. until 7:00 a.m. What a blessing that was to me to help me regain my strength more quickly. He had arrived two weeks after his due date (as all my children did), so he had a good start in life. He began to smile and coo at only three weeks. A friend told me that it was just gas pains not smiles, until she held him and talked to him to see for herself! She exclaimed, "You're right! He really is responding and smiling at me!"

When Jonathan was just one month old, my brother Carl and his wife, Carol, came to visit us. They never had children and were very much attached to their nieces and nephews. They took Rebecca with them to Watkins Glen and enjoyed her immensely. At twenty-three months, she had a slight lisp and problems with pronunciations. "Oops-ee-daisy" was "up-see-davies." When asked what her name was, she would say "Becca." We kept correcting her to say "Re-becca." After that, whenever anyone asked what her name was, she would say, "Reeeee-Becca Bobbett." Carl and Carol thought that was so cute and remembered her tiny voice saying "Reeeee-Becca Bobbett" all their lives.

At Jonathan's six-week checkup, his size and weight came to that of an average three-month-old baby. However, it was discovered that he had a hydrocele and possible hernia. The doctors said that if we were going to remain in the States, they would just keep a watch on it but because we were going overseas, they thought it should be taken care of by surgery.

When Jonathan was three months old, it was so hard to take our little guy to the hospital, not allowing him to nurse that morning when he had slept all night and was very hungry. The nurse carried him on her shoulder down to the operating room. We waited and prayed in the little hospital chapel, and the Lord answered our prayers, bringing Jonathan through the surgery very well.

We were praying that all our support would be in by November 1958 as we wanted to book passage on the *SS United States*, sailing from New York to Le Havre, France. It seemed that when we set a date for our departure, more of our support began to come in.

In mid-September, Dad and Mom Christmas drove from Rockwood, Tennessee, to Elmira to see us and spend time with us before we left the country. It was the first time my dad had ever come to our home, and it was so special to have them both with us. My mom was having physical problems and was not very strong, but I had no idea that it would be the last time I ever saw her again on this earth. How can I ever thank the Lord enough for her love and prayers for me? She was so proud of Rebecca and Jonathan. Holding two-month-old Jonathan in her arms and playing with two-year-old Rebecca was a great joy to her. I am sorry she was taken to heaven before they could remember being with her. Rebecca is like her in many ways – similar height, makes friends easily and quickly, and loves cherry pie! Our granddaughter Sarah also resembles some of her great-grandma Christmas' younger pictures.

We drove down to Mother Bobbett's home in Johnson City, New York, to celebrate Rebecca's second birthday and Grandma's fifty-eighth. Grandma was thrilled that Rebecca had been born on her birthday.

On October 20, we reported to the mission that in just a matter of days, our monthly support need had been reduced from $113 to $80. We

With Jesus Leading the Way

were booked to sail for France in less than a month! God was working in awesome ways, and it was thrilling to see His hand of provision. How privileged we were to be upheld in prayer by a host of God's people. Most precious of all were the prayer warriors God was raising up for us during our fourteen months of full-time deputation. These prayer warriors served the Lord with us in Niger as they interceded for us every day. We could have accomplished nothing without the prayers of God's people. All glory and praise go to Him.

In early November 1958, we were invited to speak at the Byron Baptist Church in London, Ontario, a church that had been supporting a missionary to Niger named Madeleine Campbell. Madeleine had served for one term but became extremely ill and almost died, so her doctors said she could not return to Niger. Even though could not return, her love for the people of Niger prompted her desire that the support she received from her home church in London, Ontario, might continue to go to other missionaries serving in Niger.

During our four days with the Byron Baptist Church, we were scheduled for overnights and meals in many different homes, so the church family could get to know us. Heath presented our vision and goals to the people, and at the close of the last meeting at the church, Deacon Les Campbell, asked, "Now that your departure date is just a few days away, how much support do you still lack?" Heath informed him that we still needed $30 in monthly support. Les grinned and said, "That is exactly the amount that we have to give!" What a thrill to see again that God was directing and providing for us as He led us along! Yes, He is the God of the last minute, but He is never late!

Sailing to France

Our mission office had written, "You have a four-berth room, B-97, tourist class, Room 141, Deck B on the *SS United States* sailing November 18 from Pier 86 at noon. Embarkation will be between the hours of nine and eleven." The *SS United States* was a modern new ship that could make the crossing from New York to Le Havre, France, in just four days. We were busy getting our inoculations and packing barrels for Africa and some crates and trunks for France. Our barrels were to be shipped to us in Niger after our language study was over in France. Once the ship left them at the coast in Cotonou, Dahomey, they would be loaded on trucks and sent overland to Niger. A Christian man in Binghamton, New York, provided free space in his warehouse to store our things for later shipment to Africa, another kind provision from the Lord for us through some of His children.

Sailing time was fast approaching! Our last meeting, the Sunday before we left, was at a new church plant in the home of our dear friends, home missionaries Rev. Charles and Joy Cuthbertson in Beverly, New Jersey. They were on the ground floor for the city of Willingboro being built. The population was growing daily. There were eighteen people that morning in Chuck and Joy's living room. When we returned four years later, the church had a beautiful building and was running over 100 in attendance! Willingboro is one of the churches that has continued to support us for over 50 years.

On November 18, 1958, some of our family and friends, along with two from the EBM office, gathered with us on the deck of the *SS United States* to say goodbye.

Things were happening so fast, I could hardly realize it wasn't a dream! The mission gave me a beautiful corsage. I cradled four-month-old Jonathan in my arms while Heath held two-year-old Rebecca in his arms on ship board while we were led in a farewell prayer by Tom Clark.

We didn't realize we had climbed the gangplank leading to the first-class deck. Those who came to see us off were quite impressed with the beautiful and luxurious area they saw us missionaries in – we were impressed too! Soon the announcements came over loudspeakers that all who were not sailing had to leave the ship. There were tearful goodbyes, kisses, and hugs. We were standing on the deck in that part of the ship as the tugboats began to pull us away from the dock. We were furnished with streamers to throw out to those still on shore, and a band was playing. Once the ship was out of the harbor and we descended the stairs into the tourist class, the doors were locked, and we never had access to that part of the ship again.

Evelyne Metzler, whom we knew from BBS days, was sailing to France on the same ship, headed to Chad, Africa. She had gone up the right gangplank and was in tourist class when she boarded. When we mentioned how nice it was to have a band playing and to be given streamers to throw out to the people on shore, she said, "What band? What streamers? You must have been in first class for that!" Funny!

This was our first experience on a big ship, and it was like a floating hotel with elevators, corridors, a dining hall, and more. As we went down the flights of stairs to find our cabins, Evelyne heard a little boy say crossly to his mother, "I thought you said we were going on a boat!" His mother replied, "This is a boat!" He demanded, "Then where are the oars?"

We found a bouquet of beautiful bon voyage flowers in our cabin, along with a telegram from BBS's Student Mission Fellowship, saying they were rejoicing with us and praying for us. The president of SMF at that time was our good friend Jess Eaton who later with his wife, Joyce, served the Lord in Bangladesh. The flowers and telegram really touched our hearts. What a thoughtful gesture!

Our cabin had four bunk beds, a small private bathroom and a porthole. The weather was cold, but we were thankful not to have any bad storms on the way over. None of us got seasick, but there were often several other empty places in the dining room. The meals were fabulous. There was a nursery for the toddlers with a lady in a nurse's uniform in charge. We left Rebecca there once, thinking she would enjoy playing with the toys, but she cried and was unhappy. When the nurse sat her on her lap to try to comfort her, Rebecca wet on her lap. The attendant was probably not disappointed that we never took her back to the nursery!

Occasionally, we went up on deck to look at the expanse of water all around us, but it was too cold to remain up there very long. Even though Rebecca was only two, she says she still remembers the loud foghorn suddenly blaring. We all jumped because we were near it. Rebecca wrapped her arms tightly around her daddy's neck and buried her face in his shoulder!

Our cabin must have been over the ship's motors because there was a constant grinding motor sound. When we docked during the night at Le Havre, four days later, the motors went silent, and the silence woke us up! I rushed to the porthole to get my first glimpse of France and saw nothing but a wall of the port where we had docked because our room was down close to the water level.

Jonathan had been such a good baby from the day we brought him home from the hospital, sleeping all night for eight hours. But because we had to turn our clocks ahead one and a half hours every night on the ocean voyage to be on French time when we docked, our baby was thoroughly confused and didn't sleep through the night for months afterward! Once Heath and I plunged into language study, this was hard for us. So, we took turns, one of us getting up every other night with him.

We disembarked from the *SS United States* on November 23, 1958, and for the first time began our lives in a new country, France. All our luggage was loaded onto a train for the journey from Le Havre to Paris. We were young, very green, and so excited about the new adventures God had placed before us.

Chapter 7
In France for French Language Study
November 1958 to January 1960

As our train pulled into the station in Paris, we saw a tall, thin young man standing on the platform to meet us. That was our first introduction to Bob Cowley, an engineer and Moody Aviation Institute-trained pilot who would be serving with us in Niger. He and his wife, Virginia, had arrived in France for language study just a few months ahead of us with their three small children. It was so nice to have someone there to help us get our luggage and a taxi to the apartment awaiting us in Paris.

We had been assured before we left the States that EBM missionaries who had finished their language studies and had gone to Niger had held on to an apartment for us in Paris that was "well heated and very nice." Still in shock and walking with sea legs – bracing as we walked and feeling like the floor beneath us was still going up and down from the ocean trip – we could hardly believe our eyes as we looked over the Rue des Morillons apartment. Bob showed us where we could buy some groceries nearby.

After the thrill of our last days in the States, the luxurious ship, and the exciting train ride from Le Havre to Paris through the beautiful French countryside, we were left in this dismal, dark, depressing three-room furnished apartment. (I left out the word "dump.") Dirty, tattered lace curtains that wouldn't even serve as good rags hung from the only window in each room. By pressing our noses against one of the windows, we could look up at a tiny patch of sky and looking down we could see a tiny cement courtyard four floors below. The sun could never shine into the apartment. The rooms were dark and required that the bare light bulbs on the ceilings be on even in the daytime.

The first night that we slept in the bed, we found it so sunken in the middle that it was like a hammock; thus, we spent the night trying to pull ourselves up on the sides to turn over, only to find ourselves rolling down into the middle again to fitfully sleep against each other in exhaustion.

We had only been in Paris for one day, and in this apartment, we were experiencing dramatic culture shock! We later said that most of our culture shock came in France, so Africa was much easier. I think we expected Africa to be primitive, but we thought France would be much more like the States.

Not many people in France had cars or refrigerators in 1958, and we expected not to have them either. Public transportation and our own two feet would be our modes of getting around. The French shopped daily for their alimentation needs. In wintertime, everyone had a little box sitting outside the kitchen door that served to keep things cold. This apartment's box was attached on the windowsill just outside our kitchen window. Right next to it was a chute to throw garbage down. Not only did our garbage get thrown into the chute, garbage from above apartments was also coming down right next to our food box! It was grubby and smelly.

Heath bravely went out to buy some food for our family at some of the nearby small shops. He spoke no French, but Bob Cowley told him to point at what he wanted and say, "Un kilo." A kilo is two pounds, two ounces, so Heath came back with a kilo of hamburger, a kilo of potatoes, a kilo of carrots, and so forth.

Through the years, our belief that children are wonderful blessings to missionary parents was confirmed over and over. As we tried to assess our new living situation and were wondering how we could stand being in this depressing setting for a year, two-year-old Rebecca found a cardboard box in a corner of the living room with some broken toys. She was excited to have a toy box again and sat on the floor contentedly removing each toy to examine it or to play with it. She lifted our spirits! Had she cried at her new location, we probably would have joined her!

Our wonderful Lord worked on our behalf within the next few days. Bob Cowley came by a day or two later to see how we were doing and to show Heath how to take subways or buses to our language school, The Alliance Française. Heath told him how unhappy we were with the apartment. By God's grace and plan, Bob had heard there was another apartment that was available. He introduced Heath to a missionary and his wife who were nearing the end of their language studies and preparing to go to Ivory Coast. They knew of an apartment in the next block from them that had been vacated by its missionary renters. This was in the village of Crosne, south of Paris. This apartment, connected to the landlord's house, was partially on the ground floor, had a nice big courtyard for the children to play in, and was no more expensive than the distressing city apartment.

Heath went the next day to look at the apartment and meet the landlords. I fully trusted Heath to make a decision without my seeing the apartment. It wouldn't take much to be better than the apartment we were in! He came back with a good report, and we were told we could move in that same week. Our hearts were full of thanksgiving to our Lord.

We decided that the easiest way to move our family and luggage from inner-city Paris to Crosne was by taxi. This was our introduction to French driving rules! We didn't know that their *code de la route* manual's rule is always *priorité à droit* (priority to the right). In other words, a driver is always watching cars coming on his right because they have the right of way on traffic circles and on streets without stop signs. The driver doesn't need to look to the left because he is on the right of the drivers coming from that direction, and he has the right of way over them. We were fresh from the States and accustomed to looking in every direction for the other driver. When our taxi driver got to the Place de l'Etoile (around the Arc de Triomphe), he moved quickly across six lanes of traffic with his eyes always turned to the right. Our eyes were bugging out as we looked to the left and saw six lanes of wild French drivers rapidly bearing down on the taxi!

I remember thinking, "We are going to die here and now!" Then I thought, "No, we will not die here! God has called us to Africa, and we can't die in France!" I was comforted by this thought, and it proved true.

At 3 Avenue Jean-Jaurès in Crosne, we were introduced to landlords Monsieur and Madame Antoine DuQuesne (pronounced "due-cane"). This apartment, on the one side of their beautiful big home, was so big and roomy! The courtyard was large too and looked out on one side into the DuQuesnes' large garden and property that had a small creek flowing behind it. The large dog in their backyard was introduced to us as Darwin. Madame DuQuesne fixed him the same breakfast each morning that she fixed for her family, *café au lait* with French bread. We were so surprised at this but had to smile when Madame said Darwin became grouchy if he missed his morning coffee!

On the ground floor of our apartment was a large kitchen and a large living/dining room. We went up narrow curving stairs to the second floor where there was a bedroom and a tiny American-style bathroom – the toilet, sink, and shower were all in one nicely tiled bathroom. There was one bedroom up more curving stairs to the third floor. The bedrooms were furnished with only a double bed in each and beautiful antique armoires.

Although World War II had been over for about twelve or thirteen years, the French people still carried a lot of animosity in their hearts toward the Germans for the suffering under the occupation. We could only imagine the fear that was upon the occupied at that time. There were three separate locks on our kitchen door and five different locks on the back side of the door leading upstairs.

The living/dining room had a beautiful fireplace and ornate dark wood carvings all around the ceiling borders. The carvings were of gargoyles and other hideous creatures. I don't know how old the house was, but it was classic and interesting to live in. Evening after evening, as we studied French at the dining table, the carvings became familiar to us.

Furniture in the large living/dining room consisted of an ornate dining table and chairs and two wicker chairs. We padded one of our long crates and covered it with an afghan and pillows to substitute for a sofa, and we used some of our trunks for end tables and a toy box. With grateful hearts, we settled into our new apartment.

When we first met the DuQuesnes, a friend translated for us. Not only did we not know one sentence in French, the DuQuesnes didn't know a word of English! Madame was smiling and animated when she spoke, gesturing and acting out what she was saying. She assured us that in three months we would understand everything she said. She was right, but our comprehension was based more on her actions and gestures than they were on our comprehension of her spoken French!

We were thankful for the DuQuesnes. While other missionaries had horror stories to tell about the way their landlords treated them, the DuQuesnes' kindness to us made it easy for us to love the French people. They were wonderful to us and loved our little ones. Jonathan, at four and a half months, was full of smiles every time Madame talked to him, like he understood every word she said. When Jonathan became ill, she told us how to find a nearby doctor. She made delicious creamy vegetable soup for us, wrung her hands at the children's fevers, and was visibly relieved when they recovered.

Before we knew much of the language, we were trying to explain to her that the doctor said to be sure Jon drank lots of liquid. She was totally puzzled by the word "liquid." We had looked it up in our French-English dictionary and saw that the word for liquid in French was spelled *liquide*. Our problem was that we had not yet learned to pronounce the word as the French did. When we finally showed her the word in writing, her face lit up with understanding. *"Ah oui!"* The French pronunciation was "lee-keed!" We learned several times over that just looking up a word in the bilingual dictionary didn't always work! Some words, spelled almost the same, meant the same thing in English or in French, but the French pronunciation was important. Other words, spelled the same as English words, had much different meanings.

Language School

When we arrived in Paris we both enrolled and began classes at the Alliance Française School, an international French language school. We had a one-hour commute each way from our home in Crosne to the school. The route we followed daily was a fifteen-minute walk to the Montgéron train station and a half-hour ride on the train into the Gare de Lyon station in Paris. Then we descended the stairs into the *métro* (subway) to travel on two different underground trains, ascended the stairs back onto a street, and walked about two blocks to school. I was so frightened the first time I made that trip alone. I was sure that if I missed a *métro* stop, I would end up lost forever among people who did not speak English!

Heath rushed off in the morning to attend classes until noon while I cared for the children. When he got home at midday, we had a quick lunch together before I started for the train station and the one-hour commute to attend the afternoon classes. Then it was his turn to care for Rebecca and Jonathan.

The language program lasted about a year, and we progressed by *degrés*. The first degree was one month. Almost all missionaries told us to be prepared to repeat that first month – and we did! From day one, the class was all in French, and I understood next to nothing. My teacher – a beautiful French woman who wore the same suit and blouse day after day, week after week, always looking immaculate – gave our homework assignments orally. Since I understood no French, I never did my homework and wondered how the other students knew what they had to do for the next day's class. Heath's teacher at least wrote the homework assignments on the board, so he could copy them and figure them out at home with the help of dictionaries!

Here are some excerpts from our March 1959 prayer letter: "…It seems as though we just arrived here, and yet more than three months have already passed. We are happy to report that, in answer to your prayers for us, progress is being made in language study. What a joy it is to recall the purpose of our study – that of presenting the Gospel in another language. We long for the day when we will speak fluently so that we might be on our way down to Africa…We have found an older French lady to stay with Rebecca and Jonathan on Tuesdays and Thursdays. Madame Fromand is the grandmotherly type, and Rebecca and Jonathan just love her. Jonathan is eight months old, and we often must 'clear the path' as he goes tearing back and forth through our house with his walker. Two-and-a-half-year-old Rebecca enjoys learning her memory verses. She often prays for Jesus to 'help Mommy and Daddy study French.'"

The classes at the Alliance were good for learning the language. Ever so slowly, we began to make progress in reading, writing, and speaking French (in that order). I remember feeling like there was a fog around my brain for the first six months, then it began to lift as I was able to carry on conversations and hear a lot that was spoken. I regretted my insensitivity back in the States to those who were learning English and my not realizing how important it was for me to speak slowly, clearly, and without using American slang or idioms.

In March 1959, there was a three-month full-time class at Sorbonne University. Heath enrolled in that program and made good progress in his language abilities, but it meant that I had to stop my classes at the Alliance because he was gone all day. I then continued my French studies with a private tutor.

When Heath wondered about how a person could retain their knowledge of French while living in other parts of the world that were non-French speaking, Heath's instructor, Madame Marchand, gave this excellent advice: "Read at least 15 minutes every day in French, and you will not lose your French." We have continued to read our French Bibles daily and have found this most helpful.

For missionaries going to Africa, our mission required progression through the fourth degree and a passing grade on the oral exam at the end of *quatrième*. After I passed the second degree, I had a personal tutor, Monsieur Rusik, for several months to help me with the third degree. I returned to the Alliance Française in the fall and was able to pass the written exams for the third degree. After Heath's classes at the Sorbonne, he returned to the Alliance Française, finished the fourth degree, and passed both the written and oral exams.

Some people feel that the French speak through their noses, with a nasal accent, an example being the way they pronounce *non*. Heath came down with a bad cold just at the time he was to take his oral exam. He said he thought it helped him with his French pronunciations so that he passed!

While the Alliance Française was an excellent place to study and learn French, we were concerned that we also learn a spiritual vocabulary. We inquired about finding a French church to attend and were told that many missionaries attended a Baptist church on Rue de Sevres in Paris. It was a long way to travel with little ones, by train and subway. After attending there a few times, we realized that none of the French people brought their small children or babies to church!

There was a Canadian missionary couple living in the same village we were, so we decided to cooperate. The men went to church every Sunday, but Mary and I only attended every other Sunday. One of us stayed home to babysit our combined five little ones and to prepare supper for all of us.

This worked quite well. Mary and I had sweet fellowship when we could get together.

French really is a beautiful language. A French person speaking English has a pleasant accent to our American ears, whereas an American accent while speaking French is truly harsh to their ears. Heath's professor at the Sorbonne, Madame Marchand, said that from the time we are children, our mouths are shaped by the languages we speak. Americans can almost never get the French R to come from their throats as perfectly as French people do. Americans often can't distinguish between the "u" sound and the "ou" sound in French, and some pronounce the "eux" sound like an "er" sound. An example is when Americans pronounce *deux* (two) as "der." The French, on the other hand, have a terrible time using the English "th" sound at the beginning of a word. Thus some pronounce "this and that" as "dis and dat!"

Children learning another language are a totally different case! Their mouths are young and forming, so they learn young and can speak two or more languages perfectly with no accent! Our children were like that in speaking French and Zarma. In Niger, we sent Nathan, our fourth child, to French school for first grade. At the end of the year, he could speak and write French (cursive) beautifully! When our son, Jonathan, was eighteen years old, the Africans told us that if he was in another room speaking with a bunch of Zarmas, no one could pick out his voice as being a foreigner!

Shopping in France

We really feel like we learned to eat in a healthier way and to eat more fresh things. It was so much fun shopping in their open *marchés*, held once or twice weekly in different locations.

We had never seen artichokes before and were mystified by these little cactuses we saw in the *marchés*. I had no idea how to cook or eat them.

One day in a French restaurant, we saw a lady nearby being served a whole artichoke, so we wanted to watch and see how it was eaten. We couldn't believe our eyes as she plucked off each leaf, put the lower part into her mouth, scraped off that part between her teeth, and then proceeded to make a huge pile of used leaves! We were sure that wasn't the normal way to eat artichokes! However, Madame DuQuesne taught me how to boil them for about forty-five minutes then dip the leaves in a little butter and enjoy. At the bottom was the tender and delicious heart of the artichoke. We loved artichokes from then on. The European ones are large and filling, while those we find (very expensive) in the States are smaller and disappointing.

Buying things in the little shops in Crosne took a lot of time. Shopping was a daily experience for the French ladies because very few had refrigerators in 1958. The beef store sold only beef; the pork store, only pork. There was a store for seafood, another for chickens and rabbits, and a store (marked by a large horse head over the entrance) that sold…horse meat! There were smaller shops called *épiceries* that had some staples too.

All French ladies carried a mesh bag of some kind in their purses or over their arms. I learned why the hard way! Sometimes walking past beautiful displays of fruits, I couldn't resist stopping to buy a half dozen oranges or other fruit. The French shop owners at that time offered no paper or plastic bags to their customers, so I would end up with an arm full of books coming home from school with oranges in my pockets, on top of the books, or in my purse! I soon learned to always carry my own shopping bag.

In the spring of 1959, we were able to buy a small three-foot-high refrigerator from some departing missionaries. How nice it was not to have to shop for milk and perishable things every day. Heath's tutor asked to buy it when we left France. She let us know that she had no intention of plugging it in during the winter months when she could just put things outside to keep them cool.

The Bread Store

They say, "There is nothing better than a fresh baguette and nothing worse than a day-old one!" Yes, the second-day French bread becomes as hard as wood unless you keep it in a plastic bag; then it becomes rubbery! The lady in our little *boulangérie* (bread store) in Crosne didn't seem to like Americans, especially Americans who were trying to learn the French language. Madame had no smile for us when we walked into the shop. She put her hands on the counter and leaned forward with a pained look on her face that said, "I'll never understand what these Americans are trying

With Jesus Leading the Way

to say." But the Lord gave us a wonderful solution. French people love children, so we taught two-and-a-half-year-old Rebecca to say in her tiny little voice, *"Une baguette, s'il vous plaît."* ("One baguette, please.") She melted the cold heart of the bread lady! After that, a broad smile would welcome Rebecca and her parents into the store, while the bread lady looked at Rebecca saying, "Oh! Here comes Mademoiselle Rebecca! What would you like, darling?" (*"Qu'est-ce que tu veux, chérie?"*)

We learned again that using a French-English dictionary could sometimes have you saying words with the wrong meaning. On a special occasion, Heath wanted to ask the French butcher for enough beefsteak for three people. He saw "people" in the French dictionary and ordered "beefsteak for three people." The corners of the butcher's mouth twitched as he tried not to smile. "People" in French refers to a nation or ethnic group! The butcher said, "Monsieur, did you mean you would like enough beefsteak for three persons?" We have laughed about that ever since, and I'm sure the butcher did too.

We got to know the *métro* of Paris quite well from riding it every weekday to and from school, but we didn't have a lot of time for sightseeing. Sometimes tourists came from America to Paris and saw more of the sights in a week than we saw in a year!

We had taken a baby stroller to France with us because we knew we would be living without a car, doing lots of walking or riding trains and the *métro*. The little metal tray footrest could be taken off to convert it into a walker for Jonathan too. His chubby little legs took him all around our apartment before he learned to walk on his own at one year of age. The stroller was made for only one child, but the back could be laid down for when the child was sleeping. We put the back down for Rebecca to sit behind her baby brother, and we literally wore the wheels off that stroller during our time in France. We wished it had an odometer, so we could count the hundreds of miles we probably pushed it!

When I had seen parents in the States put a harness on their toddlers to hold onto them with a leash, I was critical and thought that was awful. My, how our opinions changed in France! Jonathan was an active toddler, and we had to do almost all our getting about in the *métro* system. I was so fearful that he might get away from us in the crowd or fall onto the tracks as we waited for the subway train. So I was very thankful for the harness and leash. Someone said we should put a sign on his back that read, "Too precious to lose!"

A big treat for us was to occasionally visit the American Embassy on Saturdays in Paris. The embassy had a large dining facility, and at that time, all Americans could use it. We were able to buy hamburgers and milkshakes among other things! The prices were reasonable too. Seeing our American flag flying above the embassy and the Marine guard in his full uniform never failed to bring a tear to our eyes and a lump in our throats. It was so safe at that time, and security was lax. The handsome marine who stood guard in his magnificent uniform was only for looks!

Our mail was delivered by a uniformed French postman on a bicycle with his cape swirling behind him. One day while I was alone with the children, he rang the bell and came into our yard because he had a money order for us from the States. He spoke to me in French, but being newly arrived in France, I had no idea what he was saying. After repeating himself several times, he shrugged his shoulders, counted out the money exchange for me, and left. Later I was told that I was supposed to tip him, but this was a forbidden thing to do in the States, so I never thought of it. When Heath came home later, and we calculated the exchange from dollars to francs, we realized that he had taken the tip out for himself!

There were many motorbikes at that time in France, as well as small mopeds. Catholic nuns were still wearing the long black garb with starched white headdress, showing only their faces. Watching one go by on her moped with her long dress and hair covering billowing behind her was an amusing sight for us. We had never seen this in the States.

Getting to know your French neighbors behind their walled-in compounds was almost impossible. We did have good relationships with our landlords, the DuQuesnes. At the *charcuterie* (pork meat store), we found the butcher's wife, Andrée Pillet, to be very friendly too. She really liked Americans and came to visit and help me with my French conversations. I'll never forget the day she talked about the American "Graaas Kell-eee." It took me a while to realize she was saying Grace Kelly, who married Prince Rainier of Monaco.

The Pillets invited us to their home (behind the pork store) for dinner, and we also hosted them for a meal. We tried to share Christ with them and were happy when they allowed their children to come to our Thursday Bible club. Andrée was quite a character with a sad life story. Her husband was a quiet man, and they had three young children. She said she was thinking of becoming a nun when she first met Jacques, but he pursued her relentlessly and finally convinced her to marry him. Although she said she never really loved him and her marriage was empty, she seemed to really love her children, and I hoped she would change her mind about this gentle quiet man she was married to. When we came through France years later we learned that Andrée had abandoned her husband and children and was living with another man. We were never able to contact her or find where she was again.

We also tried to share the Good News with the DuQuesnes. They, as most French people, were Catholic but only went to the church for weddings and funerals. One day as we were talking to Madame DuQuesne, she said to us, "I was born Catholic and I will die Catholic, but if there were two things I could change about our Church they would be: 1) Do away with confessing our sins to the priest and go directly to God for forgiveness. 2) Our Catholic priests would marry and be normal like your Protestant pastors are. The priest in our small town here makes no secret of the fact that he spends his nights at the home of a widow. He parks his car right in front of her house and it stays there all night."

We had good fellowship with other missionaries when we were in France. Everyone was very busy, though, so we didn't have many opportunities to get together. We held a children's Bible class in our home with the help of another missionary friend. When Heath first had the idea, we prayerfully asked our friend Madame Pillet if she would allow her children to come. *"C'est bien,"* she replied. ("Of course, my children can come.")

We were thrilled. Not only was the Bible class an opportunity to improve our spiritual vocabulary in French, but it was an avenue for telling others of Christ's love and power to redeem. Rebecca too learned songs in French that she sang joyfully. We began to understand more and more of the lessons presented each week as our knowledge of French grew. We had five to seven French children who came to the class each week, until we left France for Africa.

Our rides on the *metro* (subway) to language school were very crowded. One morning when our friends Betty and Bud got on the crowded *métro*, they ended up pushed together so tightly, face to face, that they couldn't even lift their arms from their sides. Bud, however, did think that Betty's hand was hanging on to the pole beside them for support when his nose began to itch like crazy. He rubbed the end of his nose up and down on the hand there to make the itch go away. Betty said, "Bud! That isn't my hand!" Horrors! Bud realized the hand belonged to a very feminine looking man! They were so happy when their stop came and they could flee from that crowded train.

One time when Heath and I were on a crowded *métro*, the last man on couldn't get fully in either so the doors would close. In the quietness we were amused to hear his wife call out, *"Pousse, chéri! Pousse!"* ("Push, dear! Push!") This became another of our family joking expressions in other situations!

1959 Vacation in England

When the Alliance courses ended for the summer on June 26, 1959, we were midway through our language studies. We heard of a great and inexpensive trip we could take to London for a short vacation, so we left on June 30. With two suitcases packed for the four of us we met a bus at La Place de la Bastille in Paris. The bus took us to the English Channel, where a small plane picked up the bus passengers and flew us over to the British side. Once again, we were picked up by a bus in England (now driving on the left side of the road) and dropped off in London. This round trip only cost $25 per person!

We made reservations to stay at the Foreign Missions Club on the northside of London. This was only available to Christian workers. It had nice clean rooms in a large building, and the cost was $10 a week for room and meals! Two older ladies ran the Foreign Missions Club. The meals were really different for us Americans, and the servings scant. After a breakfast of spaghetti on toast or baked beans on toast, we caught a bus into the city and spent our days sightseeing.

The Lord gave us a beautiful week of sunshine, which we understood was rare for London in July. We were glad we only took public transportation so that we didn't have to try to drive on the left side of the road. Sometimes we ran to the middle of a block to the bus stop only to find that we were on the wrong side of the street! We had some close calls when we looked the wrong way before stepping off a curb and had a car zoom by too close to us for comfort.

We found the British people to be very friendly and helpful. In later years, we have observed a fast-growing Muslim and Hindu population in Britain, but it wasn't like that in 1959. It was here we learned that we spoke American and not English! We would ask for directions and be told, "Just go down here to the top of the street." British English is beautiful to our ears, though, and we enjoyed our visit. Tourists were sparse at that time. We walked through Westminster Abbey and were able to read the inscriptions on the graves of David Livingstone and others who were buried there. Should I have felt naughty that I was pleased to walk right on top of Darwin's tomb? Later, London was inundated with tourists and the sights were so crowded. (What a disappointment to return to London in 1979 and shuffle through the Abbey shoulder to shoulder with the crowds, not being able to see much of anything.)

Jonathan had his first birthday on July 10, 1959. He loved for us to open the living room shutters so he could stand on the little balcony looking out into the DuQuesnes' backyard. His first words were French words. When he saw the DuQuesnes' huge dog, Darwin, he would point with a smile and say, *"Chien!"* If an airplane flew over, he would point to the sky and say *"Abion!"* He hadn't yet learned to say the V in *avion*, so he pronounced it with a B.

Grandma Lena Bobbett came toward the end of August and stayed with us for three months. She was a help caring for the children while Heath attended classes and I continued learning French with tutors.

Two things that we were unable to buy in France at that time were peanut butter and corn on the cob. The French only grew field corn then, and it was for animals. They couldn't understand how we Americans would eat that! However, after they were exposed to real American sweet corn, they usually changed their minds and thought it was great! Mother Bobbett hand-carried a couple dozen ears of corn to us in France. When the customs agent asked what she had and saw the corn, he wrinkled his nose in disgust and let her pass through. Crazy Americans – eating food grown for pigs!

We have a picture of Rebecca celebrating her third birthday in France on September 16 with Grandma Lena Bobbett. It was Mother Bobbett's fifty-ninth birthday.

That fall we had some vacation time from school. Bud and Betty Shubert; Betty, a single gal from their mission; Grandma Lena Bobbett; and we shared the expense of renting a station wagon to visit Switzerland. We had a wonderful time, seeing that beautiful country and preparing our lunches (tailgate parties) along the way. We will never forget parking our car by the roadside in the beautiful mountainside pastures, watching the cattle graze, and enjoying the sunshine, beauty, and quietness. It was so peaceful, with only the faint tinkling sounds of cowbells the cows wore as they grazed.

We stayed in a Swiss hotel on that long weekend trip. Noticing that people took off their shoes and left them outside their doors in the corridors of the hotel, we decided to do that too. The next morning, we found them all cleaned and polished by the hotel staff!

It was always fun to watch the reaction of first-time Americans in Europe using the "squatty potty" toilet facilities. When we made a rest stop and found this kind of bathroom, we all waited to see what Grandma Lena's reaction would be when she rushed into a public restroom. We all burst into laughter when she came out and said, "I can wait, but I sure wished I had my camera to take a picture of that." In a few short days, we were back at our studies and schooling.

Taking Care of Our Family Laundry

I had to do all the laundry for our family by hand in our shallow kitchen sink, then hang it on the lines in our courtyard to dry. I wonder how I ever did all those things – caring for the children, going to language school, studying the language, cleaning the house, grocery shopping, cooking meals, *and* doing the washing for the four of us by hand! This was in the days before disposable diapers, so diapers were a daily washing chore too. God was so good to me and supplied the stamina and strength I needed. Heath was good about helping feed and bathe the children while also taking turns with me getting up at night with baby Jonathan. At least one of us got a good night's sleep every other night.

My only mishap was when I was (barefooted) washing our sheets in the shallow sink and tried to rush out the kitchen door to hang them on the outside line without too much dripping on the floor. The door was halfway open, and I hit my little toe on it as I rushed by. It hurt so badly. After I got the sheet hung up, I reached down to wiggle my toe, hoping to make it feel better. My little toe went clear out to one side when I tried to wiggle it! Madame DuQuesne helped us locate a clinic nearby, but of course all the doctor could do was tape my broken toe down against the next toe until it healed.

Now that we were in the fourth degree of our language studies, Field Director Bob Richards wrote us that we could begin making our plans for continuing on to Niger. In a letter dated May 27, 1959, he wrote:

"...I would like to take this opportunity to stress the importance of these months you are spending in Paris. Oftentimes you will be tempted to ask, 'Is it necessary?' I can assure you that your studies of the French language are extremely necessary and that all of the French that you can possibly get you will put to good use after you arrive down here. You will use the French language all of your years of ministry in this part of Africa. The entire educational system is in French. All of the government officials and local authorities, whether European or African, use the French language. If you do not have it so that you can use it, you will be very ill at ease and oftentimes times highly embarrassed...I know learning French is extremely difficult, and you are putting in long hours in order to keep up with your homework...so study hard, my dear friends, and keep humble before the Lord in order that He can fill your minds and hearts, not only with the French language but with the ways and customs of the French people. If you have any special requests for prayer, just let us know and we will take you to the Throne of grace...The doors are wide open here, even though there has been a terrific change in government, yet up to the present there has been absolutely no hindrance to our work whatsoever. We praise the Lord for this wide open door, and we want to take advantage of every opportunity which presents itself for the reaching of lost souls for Christ and the establishing of local churches. The Lord is good, and we praise Him daily for His goodness and His faithfulness...May the Lord bless you daily, supply your every need, and prepare you in every way for the day when you can come down here and take up your labors for Him."

Along with our continued language studies, there were so many things we needed to get accomplished. We went to Versailles to apply for our visas, and Bob sent us our repatriation papers that were needed. We began to finalize our shipping lists, ordered mosquito nets and Aladdin lamps, inquired about getting a kerosene refrigerator in Niamey, and made appointments for more inoculations for Africa. We got our inoculations for typhoid, typhus, and yellow fever, and boosters for tetanus and polio at the American hospital in Paris.

Because we left the States when Jonathan was only four months old, he had to have all his inoculations in France. We devised a little game for

Rebecca and Jonathan that worked well for all the injections they had to have. We would play often at home, "It is time for your shot." They would bare their little arms or lay on our laps if it was a hip shot. We would pretend to wipe the arm or hip off with alcohol, then administered the pretend shot quickly, saying "All done!" They thought the game was fun and even played it with it each other. They were perfectly calm when we were at the hospital for shots. When they felt the pain of the real injection and began to pucker up to cry, we would say, "All done!" and they were all smiles again. The doctor at the American hospital said ours were the best-behaved children who ever came to his office for injections!

In November, we received a letter from my sister-in-law, Carol informing us that my mother was diagnosed with breast cancer. Mom had been going to an older doctor in Rockwood, Tennessee. When she told him about the lump in her breast, he told her it was nothing to be concerned about and that he had medication to treat it. Later she told my dad that the lump had opened up and was draining. He immediately took her to another doctor who hospitalized her the next day for a mastectomy. Sadly, the cancer had invaded the rest of her body, and he was not able to remove it all.

I had great hopes that she would survive this cancer, but Carol hinted to us that it wasn't likely. Dad was driving her to Oakridge, Tennessee, every weekday for radiation. Back then, they called it X-ray treatments.

For Christmas in 1959 Carol arranged for us to call Mom and Dad from our landlord's house since we did not have a telephone. It was about noon in France, and only 6:00 in the morning in Tennessee, but Mom and Dad were already up having their breakfast. Even after retirement they couldn't break that early rising habit. Mom sounded good on the phone, and it was a blessing to hear her sweet voice. I couldn't fathom that this would be perhaps the last time I would hear her voice on earth. We caught up on news, and Dad even tried some of his World War I French on Madame DuQuesne. She smiled and thanked him but didn't really understand what he was trying to say. His pronunciation was American! December had been a very busy month as our preparations were in full swing to leave for Africa at the end of January, after our written and oral French exams.

Rest and Renewal before Departing for Niger

Joseph McCaba, the general director of our mission strongly urged us to have a time of rest and vacation before we arrived in Niger and began to learn the Zarma language and culture. We had heard many good things about Villa Emmanuel in the mountains in the southern part of France, not too far from Geneva, Switzerland. The villa was run by a Christian lady named Madame Stocker. Departing from Paris by train, we had ten days at Villa Emmanuel, a nice large home, but at that time snow was everywhere, and the bedrooms were frigid! There were only a few lodgers there at the same time we were, so we all sat around one table for our meals in the dining room.

We became acquainted with an American couple with two small children. He was pastor of the American Church in Brussels. They had a car and very kindly offered to take us on a sightseeing trip with them. We drove around Lake Geneva and also went to Chamonix to ride the cable cars high up to the top of Mont Blanc. The snowy scenes were beautiful.

Another missionary couple who had finished language study in Paris preceded us to Villa Emmanuel for vacation before going to the Central African Republic. While they were at the villa, their only child, a six-year-old girl, began having convulsions. They were able to take her to some of the best doctors in the world in Geneva, Switzerland, but no one could find the cause of her seizures. They were so sad, not only for their daughter's illness but because they would not be able to continue on to Africa. Sitting at the dining room table one day with Madame Stocker, she said, "Your daughter has worms. This is causing her seizures. Treat her for worms." The parents were puzzled but hopeful that this was true. Feeling they had nothing to lose, they obtained the correct medicine and began the treatment. To quote them, "Worms were passed by the millions!" It was true! The little girl had somehow become infested either in the States or in Paris. After the worms were gone, the seizures stopped and the family was able to continue to their field of service in Africa.

When we departed for Niger the end of January 1960, we left a part of our hearts in the spiritually needy country of France. Our time there challenged us because of the paucity of Gospel-preaching churches. We experienced our first culture shock there but came away loving our stay in France and all the dear people we had met and interacted with there. God had been so faithful, and we were confident in His loving care for the next stage of our missionary journey. This photograph of the Niger/Mali team, was taken shortly before our arrival.

Chapter 8
Finally in Niger
February 1960 to March 1960

In the quiet darkness of the early morning hours of February 1, 1960, we at last arrived in the land of God's definite calling for us. Our four-engine plane had crossed the Mediterranean Sea and the Sahara Desert and then circled and landed at the Niamey airport. We then disembarked at the large hangar that served as the Niamey terminal. All the while, Rebecca and Jonathan snuggled down beside us and slept peacefully, not knowing that God was leading them to a unique childhood among a new people. We felt our children were just as called of God as we were to be in Africa at that stage of their lives. What a blessing they were to us as parents and in the work.

In our first prayer letter from Niger, we praised the Lord for the joy of being at last in the land of God's calling, and we rested on His promise, "Faithful is He that calleth you, who also will do it."(I Thessalonians 5:24)

It was a joy (and a relief) to see our field director, Bob Richards, there to meet us. He helped us through customs and checking into the country. After we picked up our luggage, we went out into the unlit parking area. Bob had a small Peugeot truck. I cannot tell you how frightening it was for me to put my feet onto the darkened floorboard when I got in the truck. I felt surely a snake would be there poised to bite me! Our luggage went in the truck bed. Heath and I sat up front by Bob with Rebecca and Jonathan on our laps as we drove from the airport through the sleeping city of Niamey and then out to our mission station at Yantala.

We had received word in France that because of a shortage of senior missionaries, we would not be remaining in Niamey for language study but would be going to the town of Gaya – two hundred miles from the capital – to keep the station open. However, our primary task for the first year would be learning the language.

Early on the morning of our arrival, we were welcomed to the guest house by its hostess, Helen Bechtel and her young son. This was to be our home for six weeks before we moved to the small village of Gaya to replace Paul and Vivian Gustenhoven who were leaving in March for furlough.

With dim storm lanterns, Helen took us to our two adjoining rooms and showed us the closet toilet at the end of the hall. There were no doors inside the guest house, just curtains hanging in each doorway. Each room had a sink and a curtained shower area with a drain on the cement floor that flowed outside on the ground. As long as the barrels on top of the house were filled with river water, we had running water in our sink. The shower had a special bucket with shower-type holes in the bottom. We had to fill the bucket, then when we pulled the chain hanging down, water sprayed over us. The idea was to pull the chain long enough to get wet, then soap up all over and pull the chain again to rinse off.

Helen showed us how to get under our mosquito nets in bed and then neatly tuck them under the mattresses. She also reminded us to always sleep with a flashlight under our pillow. If we had to get up in the night for the bathroom or to attend to the children, we were to shine the flashlight where we walked, always watching for scorpions and poisonous snakes.

The windows and outside doors had screens, but the screen doors had about a two-inch gap between the door bottom and the floor. This was a perfect path for hordes of toads to come into the house at night. We had to be careful not to step on them too. By daylight, they all disappeared outdoors to hide in cool places until nighttime.

We have a picture of our family of four standing in the barren sand that was in front of the guest house – all decked out in our pith helmets! Yes, we were told they were a necessity in the torrid heat and sunshine of Niger. But over the years, the pith helmets began to disappear as missionaries wore lighter and more attractive hats for protection from the sun. In later years, the new missionaries enjoyed mission and rental homes with the many trees former missionaries had planted, so there was lots of shade, and they didn't even wear hats.

After arriving in Niger, we wrote this in our prayer letter: "Sand, sand everywhere! Rebecca (three and a half) and Jonathan (nineteen months) enjoy playing in it, and they think that they live in a big zoo. Camels, donkeys, horses, sheep, goats, and chickens wander outside the house and on the road almost constantly.

Jonathan grins shyly and says, *'Fofo'* (hello) to the locals. This delights them no end. He thinks that 'no stone should be left unturned' and since these are favorite hiding places for snakes and scorpions, Mom and Dad have to keep pretty close tabs on him."

Although the city of Niamey had electricity, the mission had not been able to afford the expensive transformers needed to bring it just four miles out to the property. We learned to live with kerosene storm lanterns and Aladdin lamps. The Aladdin lamps gave a good light, but we had to be so careful not to turn the flame up too high or the fragile white mesh would burn up and we would need to put an expensive new one in before we lit it the next night. There were, of course, no electric fans, so rest hours were pretty miserable without electricity. For more than half the year, all missionaries slept on the cement patios outside their bedrooms. The mud houses protected us from the midday sun, but they really held in the heat, and it was often several degrees cooler outside than in the house after the sun went down.

When we first arrived in Niger, it was the cool season. The days were pleasant, and the nights were cool enough that we could sleep inside under a light blanket. But by the beginning of March, the hot season was coming in. The temperatures were going higher each day, and we had to begin sleeping outside. It was so beautiful to look up at the stars each clear night. There were no electric lights around, so the stars and constellations were fascinating to look at as we lay under our mosquito nets.

Helen's terrace was on the other side of the guest house. Often at night, we heard her and her young son singing before they went to sleep. Hearing them singing, "It will be worth it all when we see Jesus," really touched our hearts. Helen had lost her first son in Niger from rheumatic fever and her husband from snake bite.

There was a special way we were taught to tie up the nets so that when a sandstorm roared up in the middle of the night, we could jump out of bed, untie the mosquito nets at each place with just one quick tug where they were tied, fold up our beds, and wheel them inside. Oh, how upset we became at new house help who hadn't been taught how to tie up the nets properly! While we tried to untie their knots, we were still outside when the sandstorms hit. The flying sand was actually painful as it hit our skin, and our eyes, noses, and mouths were filled with grit!

Those of us who had children had to awaken them from sleep, warn them to use their flashlights as they went into the house, and then set up our beds again inside. If a good rain followed the sandstorm, it cooled off and was comfortable inside the house. But more often than not, no rain came after the sandstorm, and we were sweltering under our nets inside with our gritty sheets. Adventure!

Water was another new experience for us. Former missionaries had put several barrels on top of the houses – one or two over the kitchen and the same over the bathroom. There was a man at the Yantala station whose full-time job was to walk his donkey down to the river, fill the jerrycans that were on each side of his donkey with river water, walk the donkey back up the hill, and empty the two jerrycans of water into a barrel on the ground at the side of the house. The barrel was equipped with a "jappy" pump that he worked by hand, pumping the water up to the barrels on the roof. When the roof barrels began to overflow, he knew they were full, so he moved on to another house to begin the process all over again until their barrels were full. Once our barrels were full, he wouldn't be back until the next day, so it was important to not let the house faucets run for long. We used the river water for bathing but never for drinking or brushing our teeth. That water had to be filtered and boiled daily.

Each room in the guest house had a clay vessel called a *gurgulette*, which held our drinking water. Helen couldn't have guests continually getting into her kerosene refrigerator for a cool drink because, especially in the hot season, the ice cubes would melt and the food would spoil. So after boiling and filtering the river water for drinking, she poured it into the *gurgulettes*. The sweating of the clay pots caused evaporation that cooled the water down somewhat for drinking. She kept clean cloths stuffed into the *gurgulette* opening so that no bugs or lizards could walk (or fall) into our drinking water.

On wash day while we were at the guesthouse, an African man came to collect our basket of dirty clothes. Balancing the basket on his head, he took it and a large bar of yellow soap to the river. He soaped and pounded our clothes on the rocks, washed and rinsed them in the river, then carried them back to hang up on the clothesline for us.

We were amazed that, although the guest house did not have running water or electricity, they did have a telephone. Often the telephone did not work, though, especially after an electrical storm. Once when the phone was not working, Mrs. Bechtel was finally able to get a repairman to come out. Amazingly, when he opened the telephone to check the wires, hundreds and hundreds of "hayni bugs" (earwig insects) fell out of the phone! They were making their home and breeding grounds there. After they were all cleaned out, the phone began to work again.

Orientation

Good flour was hard to find in Niger. And since it was from France and had much more gluten (like pastry flour), it didn't work well to make loaves of American bread. The bread rose beautifully in my bread pan, but when I tried to slice it afterward, the inside was hollow because the heavy dough dropped to the bottom, making it impossible to use. The few times we were able to get one-hundred-pound sacks of flour from Nigeria, we shared it with our coworkers as they did with us when they got some. This wheat was often from Canada or the United States. It was hard wheat with less gluten, so it made wonderful American loaves.

Helen showed me where to buy the right flour sieve in the market. It was shaped like a tambourine with a very fine mesh. American flour sifters weren't fine enough to sift out the weevils and worms. If I was fortunate, the weevils and worms hadn't been in the flour for too many months (or years!) and could be removed. Every month or so, I had to re-sift the flour to remove the worms that had hatched since the last sifting. If the flour had been too long without being sifted, it had a permanent odor and taste that was awful. Even when we were desperate for bread, I learned I had to throw the flour out when it was in that condition. In later years I learned that putting bay leaves in your good flour kept the weevils from proliferating and spoiling the flour.

One of our missionary coworkers never seemed to smell or taste the buggy flour, but when we were offered one of her delicious-looking cinnamon rolls and took a bite, we had to find someplace to discreetly get rid of it without eating it and without offending her!

Helen taught me how to shop in the market and bargain for the little piles of vegetables or fruit lying on the ground. It is a way of life for Africans, so they think we are stupid if we don't know how to bargain. She showed me how to buy large portions of beef and cut them up. I learned to thoroughly wash produce by soaking it in purple permanganate water or soapy Clorox water and then rinse it in filtered water.

We had so many new things to get used to:
- sleeping under mosquito nets
- taking the bitter Nivaquine antimalarial medicine daily
- not brushing our teeth in or drinking faucet water

- sleeping with flashlights under our pillows
- living without electricity or a car
- schools, offices, and businesses closing from noon until 3:00 because of the heat
- siesta time
- buying our vegetables and fly-covered meats in the open market
- trying to hold on to the French language as we started to learn Zarma
- being unable to make phone calls to the States
- getting mail only once or twice a week
- airmail sometimes taking three weeks or more to reach us
- getting used to new sounds (such as a donkey braying outside our bedroom window during the rest hour)
- the Muslim call to prayer five times a day
- sights (too numerous to mention) and smells (open markets and sewers in the capital city)
- camels, goats, sheep, chickens, and cows around our house and on the roads
- naked African children and topless young women (At that time, until a girl was married, she did not cover her breasts.)

It was a new world for us, but we were fascinated and so thankful to finally be in the land and with the people that God had called us to. Our Lord was so good, so faithful, and so loving to us young greenhorns. We had much to learn. As a young mother, I was fearful Rebecca and Jonathan might be stung by a scorpion or bitten by a snake, so I often went out to watch them at play.

Helen Bechtel was our oldest and most experienced missionary in Niger. She first came to Niger in 1934, when I was only one year old! Helen came as a single woman, then later her fiancé, Otto, joined her, and they were married in Niger.

Then in the 1950, Helen and Otto were stationed in Gaya. Otto liked to hunt. While he was walking through the scrub brush to pick up a guinea hen he had shot, he was bitten on the heel by a poisonous viper and only lived a few days after that. Helen told us, "I have experienced living on the mission field as a single woman, a married woman, and a widow."

Helen ran the guest house in Niamey because almost no one wanted that job. She fit in well, and we appreciated arriving there, tired and dusty from travel, to be welcomed with a good meal, a shower, and a clean bed. She gave me the best advice I was ever to receive as a new missionary. She said, "Norma, find your joy here with the local people. Learn their language and customs. You can enjoy other missionaries and expatriates but find your real fellowship and joy with the local people." How right she was! And later we thanked the Lord for sending us off to the village of Gaya where there were few expatriates. It was the best experience for learning the language, and the Lord gave us many wonderful village friends. Helen knew how to live off the land and to do without so many things that weren't available in Niger.

Heath's First Trek into the Bush
by Roger Bacon

Veteran missionary Roger Bacon invited Heath to go on an evangelistic trek with him, evangelist Cecekoy, and Mel Pittman. Roger told about their trip in an article he wrote for our mission paper:

Narrow twisting streets lined with woven millet-stalk fences, beehive-like mud granaries, mahogany chairs brought out into the chief's courtyard, a white-robed man carrying a large Arabic book – such were some of the oddities that made this village seem different from others we had visited. The "we" included Mel Pittman and Heath Bobbett on their first trek, Cecekoy, and myself. We were traveling to a village that was new to us, a few gulleys and many sand dunes beyond the end of the trail leading to Namaro.

The day before, we had churned and pushed the jeep and trailer over the sandy trail to Namaro and there set up our camp: one tent and one small trailer surrounded by a rope fence to keep the children from falling into the rice kettle while we cooked. For Mel and Heath it was a new experience to eat with a crowd of onlookers commenting on every bite, though our food was just rice and peppery African gravy. However, it had been cooked on a little gas burner ("Look! No wood!") and eaten with a fork instead of fingers. Supper was followed by a service with the sand for benches, stars for a roof and two small lanterns for illumination. After two sermons, Mel drew a chalk picture about the way of the cross leading to heaven.

The next day, leaving the trailer behind, we started off to seek out the villages beyond the end of the road. The vastness of this country still amazes me as we stopped on a high sandy hill beside a deserted village and looked over miles of semi-desert, sparsely populated, to be sure, and yet grouped around a well or near the river are numerous villages with people who have only heard of Allah and his prophet Mohammed and who know nothing of the grace of our Lord Jesus Christ and the salvation He offers to them.

Stopping at the village described above, we had the joy of preaching to an attentive audience, gathered around our chairs under the welcome shade of neem trees. We did notice an unusual number of priests (Muslim teachers) in attendance and were amazed afterward to discover that this was "the" Latacabia, the home of a Koranic school to which students came from hundreds of miles around. We were introduced to the imam who proudly displayed his library of Arabic literature. Leaving him some Arabic tracts, we promised to bring an Arabic Bible on our next visit. Very few African Muslim teachers read Arabic with understanding. For most of them it is only for chants and magic phrases to cure illnesses.

We do praise God for open doors such as this in this troubled continent. The entrance of the Word gives light, but we are so few amid so much darkness…Pray with us that the Lord of the harvest will thrust forth laborers into the harvest while it is day, for the night in Africa is fast approaching when no man can work.

During our time at the guest house, our field director, Bob Richards, taught several orientation classes which were very beneficial. He told us, "If you learn the languages well and get a good grasp of the culture, you can consider your first term a success." I remember thinking that we would get these things done quickly so that we could plunge into the work of winning souls for Christ. Over time we realized how right Bob was!

The Lord did give us numerous opportunities to witness, for Heath to preach, and for me to have women and children's classes. But we realized how important it was to learn the heart language of the people so we could communicate with them. They were so appreciative of our learning their language. Interpreters are a poor substitute, for often they are not translating accurately but are saying what the listeners want to hear! Muslim translators are loath to talk about Jesus being the Son of God and the only way to heaven.

Bob also spent many hours taking us to various government offices to get our residence permits in order. We waited and waited, often long after our appointment time, for the various office managers to come in or be free to help us. Bob would smile and say, "In Africa we learn to hurry up and wait!" We were fingerprinted, photographed, and required to give a lot of documentation. The police wanted assurance that we had adequate monthly support, that we had never spent time in jail, and so forth.

Millie Dibble had started Zarma language classes with us during our six weeks at the guest house in Niamey. She had volunteered to accompany us to Gaya for one year to be our language teacher. Her French and Zarma were almost entirely without accent. The Zarmas said, "Some missionaries know more vocabulary, but Millie's tongue stands up," meaning she had no accent. We were blessed to have her as our in-residence teacher. She was patient and encouraging.

EBM had an excellent one-year program for learning the language. It was not easy, and we were required to spend one hundred hours a month learning or listening to Zarma. In French there were many words that were the same as or similar to English; we just had to learn to pronounce them the French way. But Zarma was totally new, so we had to memorize the vocabulary and listen to it spoken to learn it.

I will always be thankful we were required to memorize a number of Bible verses in Zarma. This helped us with sentence structure. We had to write out simple Bible stories for our teacher and then present them to local people to see if they understood. After six months, Heath preached his first sermon in Zarma. There were periodic tests and quizzes during our language program. Toward the end, before our final exam, we had to interview Africans to write a paper in Zarma about one of their customs.

The Yantala mission station was a large piece of property close to the Niger River with much activity. Large adobe (mud) houses had been built to house early missionaries. Closer to the main road the station also had a medical dispensary. Evangelist Cecekoy preached to the crowds at the dispensary, explaining the Good News as the patients waited with their numbers to receive free medications and treatments. Interacting with the Zarma people from morning until noon and again from 3:00 until 6:00 in the evening, our mission nurse, Arlene Spurlock, learned the language so well that she developed a huge vocabulary in Zarma. She was valuable to the translation work of the Zarma Scriptures in the years to follow.

Last, but not least, there was our French government-approved elementary school. When we arrived, it was totally staffed by missionary teachers, but over the years African teachers were found for each of the grades and even as school director.

In 1960, having a sixth-grade education in Niger was sought after and prized. There weren't nearly enough schools for all children to attend. Successfully passing the sixth-grade exam and receiving your certificate meant you were qualified to enter seventh grade or that you qualified to become a teacher or, with one year of training, a nurse.

I must mention here an excellent teacher, Abraham. Although he only had a sixth-grade diploma, he was tremendously successful as a first-grade teacher in spite of the difficulties he faced. Most of the little ones came from homes with illiterate parents who didn't speak French, so the students started school not understanding the language their classes were taught in. The classroom was overcrowded. Muslim parents wanted their children to be in the "mission school" because of the good scholastic reputation it had. Abraham had at least fifty first graders crowded together, two and three to a two-person desk. He was a very strict disciplinarian, but he loved the children, and so as a result the students loved and respected him too. By the end of the year, he had them all speaking French! Until they were able to understand French, Abraham taught the Bible class in Zarma.

The French school was a great testimony to Christ through the years. What a blessing it was to attend their Christmas and Easter programs as the children acted out Bible stories, sang Gospel songs, and quoted Scripture verses for their parents and friends to hear. A large amphitheater was built behind the school where the programs were held. The school and amphitheater were also wonderful locations for our summer teen camps.

Rebecca's first little friend was Mariama. At that time, we had no idea that one day she would become our second daughter.

Our mission's annual conferences, usually held in January, were a time of refreshing as we gathered for several days to pray, share devotionals, hear messages, and conduct business. The children had great fun playing all kinds of games. At meal times, they loved to pick on an "auntie" or "uncle" by saying, "Tell a joke, Uncle (insert name)! Tell a joke!" This was repeated over and over until the aunt or uncle stood up to share a funny story with us all. In mid-morning we had a coffee break and then some fun playing volleyball. Perhaps my least favorite time was the afternoon business meetings. There were all kinds of committees, and with strong personalities, business meetings could sometimes be tense and nerve-racking. The last night of the conference was "Fun Night" when we adults and the MKs did funny skits and activities. To this day we remember some of those hilarious occasions and the great times we had! Probably our children remember them too. It was so good to get together and laugh.

Norma Bobbett

Our First Trip on African Roads

It was March 12, 1960. The end of our six weeks in Niamey had come, and we were looking forward (with some trepidation) to moving to the small town of Gaya with our two small children and our language teacher, Mildred Dibble. We had no car, so we traveled there with Millie in her 1952 Chevrolet truck. It was our first adventure on African dirt roads, and one we will never forget!

Millie thought we should leave at 4:00 in the morning so that we could have the cooler morning hours for travel. The truck was heavily loaded, with just one long seat in the cab. Millie was driving, while Heath and I were holding Rebecca and Jonathan on our laps. Gaya was two hundred miles away over dirt roads.

When Millie came by the guest house to pick us up, we found the two back tires on her truck were quickly going flat. We roused Steve Black, also staying in the guest house, to use his pump, but the tires refused to hold air. Then we woke up Roger Bacon. Mystery solved! Roger and Dave Kepple had put the front tire valves on the back tires thinking they would hold better.

At 6:00, we were at last on our way. We reached Dosso two hours later to enjoy breakfast with Glenn and Ann Nunemaker. While we were having breakfast, another tire went flat. It had a piece of wire in it from the wire sweepers pulled behind trucks to smooth out the washboard bumps of the roads.

By the time that tire was fixed, it was 10:00 a.m. We all piled in the car once more to say our goodbyes to the Nunemakers. Eight miles out of Dosso, as we just rounded a curve, a front tire blew out. It forced us way over to the left side of the road, but we were able to stop before going off the road completely. However, we were then facing oncoming trucks on their side of the road. But the Lord protected us, and no one was coming toward us. If this blowout had occurred when we were rounding that curve!

Some African truckers stopped and insisted on changing the tire for us. Then they followed us back to Dosso. Ann Nunemaker decided to fix lunch for us while the tire and tube were being repaired. After lunch, it was deemed best to not start out again during the hottest part of the day but to rest at the Nunemakers until the sun had passed over a little more.

By 4:00 p.m., we were in route again. All went well for about fifty miles, and then three wild boar ran out on the road in front of us. Millie swerved to miss them. A minute later, smoke began to pour from under the hood. FIRE! Quickly, we stopped. I handed Heath our flask of drinking water, and Millie grabbed a towel. Together they got the hood up and extinguished the fire. While the fire was burning, I kept nervously asking Millie, "Where is your gas tank?"

Heath found the source of the trouble. The air filter had jarred loose, and when we swerved to miss the wild boar, it fell on the hot motor, causing a spark that ignited the grease on the motor. Heath put the air filter back in place, and we were on our way again, praising the Lord that only thirty minutes were lost.

There was no way we could communicate to the Gustenhovens, who were awaiting our arrival in Gaya, about our travel troubles and delays. They had been watching for us all day and just praying that God would bring us there safely.

At seven-thirty in the evening, we arrived in Gaya, tired and covered in red dust from the road but happy to have safely arrived. I was so stressed, tired, hot, and dirty. I thought in my heart, "I will never leave Gaya for the next three years until we go on furlough!" There is no place in the world where a shower is more appreciated and welcomed than after a day on African roads.

We were welcomed by Paul and Vivian Gustenhoven and six-year-old Heidi. They could hardly believe the adventure our thirteen-hour, two hundred-mile trip had been.

This mission house, also made of mud, had no electricity or running water. Again, we had to get used to Aladdin lamps, hurricane lanterns, and pressure lanterns. Water was drawn from a well in the backyard. The floors were made of flat stones with cement in between, and there were no

Norma Bobbett

internal doors, only curtains (even on the bathroom door). The outside doors were just flimsy screen doors, and the windows just had screens too. There were corrugated aluminum pan shutters on the windows, each propped up with a stick. We later learned how quickly we had to take down the sticks to allow the shutters to hang down when dust storms hit!

Before the Gustenhovens left, we drove with them across the border to a village in Dahomey called Bodjékali. They had begun to go there one day a week. Paul held outdoor evangelistic services while Vivian gathered the women and children in another spot for a Bible class. Some of the men had made professions of faith.

As I walked into that small African village for the first time and sat on a log during the Bible class, my heart rejoiced as I thought, "I am finally here in an African village to begin the work the Lord called me to when I was just a young teenager!" What a thrill!

Chapter 9
The First Year in Gaya
March 1960 to March 1961

Gaya is a village on the Niger River in the southernmost tip of the country. Just a few miles east is the border with Nigeria, and even closer across the river is the country of Bénin. It was in this village that we first lived and in which we continued our language studies.

When we first arrived, the Gustenhovens spent some days with us explaining things and taking us around to meet various officials in the village. When Paul explained to one Frenchman that we were new missionary arrivals in Niger, the Frenchman asked, "Why would you ever start new missionaries out in the difficult climate of Gaya?" Paul's reply was, "Can you tell me of any place in Niger where the climate isn't difficult?" With a rueful smile, the Frenchman said, *"Alors, vous avez raison."* ("Well, you are right!")

We were thankful to have Mildred Dibble, our language teacher, there with us. We were very new, green missionaries, so it was good to have an experienced veteran missionary who knew the languages and culture of the people. Niger would be receiving their independence in just a few months (August 3, 1960) after being a French colony for many years. The last French commandant who lived on a high hill overlooking the village had departed, and we were introduced to the new African commandant.

Besides Mildred and us, there were only four other white people in Gaya: Gendarme Molto; his wife; their small son, Serge; and a bachelor agriculture man who wore an awful red toupee! I can't remember his name. He never answered his door without his toupee on and thought no one knew, but the Africans referred to him as "the white man who has a furry hat!"

We were well into March, and the heat was getting more intense every day. Mildred told us that we would know when the hottest days of the hot season had arrived because by then perspiration would drip off of our elbows as we sat at the table to eat! Gaya had a little more vegetation than Niamey since it was closer to the savannah and farther from the Sahara Desert, so the humidity was worse. We immediately began sleeping outdoors at night to get away from the heat the mud house held from the torrid daytime temperatures.

Previous missionaries in Gaya had built a nice little "sleeping house" in the yard. Since it was screened on all sides and had an aluminum pan roof, we didn't need mosquito nets and could even stay out there during gentle rains but not during the dreaded sandstorms. These previous missionaries had no children, so they built the sleeping house large enough for one double bed. We crowded a single bed in there too for Rebecca and Jonathan, so all four of us were practically sleeping in the same bed. Many fast-growing neem trees had been planted in the compound, and their shade was much appreciated.

First on the agenda was to divide the house into two separate apartments, one for Mildred and one for our family. Since Muslim men can have up to four wives, we tried to avoid their thinking that Heath had two wives. Our neighbor Fodi, who was both an *alfaga* (Muslim teacher) and a mud mason, was hired to close off the doorway between our apartments. It was Ramadan, when Muslims don't eat or drink from daylight to nightfall. They aren't even supposed to swallow their own saliva because if they do, they have broken the fast. (This is the reason for all the spitting during Ramadan.) Mud masons put water in their mouths to spray onto their finished mud walls and smooth them out with a trowel. Fodi did this and then carefully took the hem of his robe to wipe the inside of his mouth dry so he wouldn't break the fast.

Heath had many opportunities to share the Gospel with Fodi over the years. Fodi had a gentle spirit, and there was mutual respect between him and Heath. Once after Heath presented the Gospel again, Fodi told Heath, "You are new here, and we only know what we have been taught about God. Be patient and continue to teach. If one day a very important person in the village accepts your teachings, others will follow." Imagine being encouraged to continue our ministry by a Muslim man! Heath was tempted to say, "Fodi, how about you being that first man?" But he didn't think it was the time to say it.

Since Muslims go by a lunar calendar, the beginning and ending of the month of fasting (Ramadan) are different each year. Once they see the new moon, the fast begins and they are not to eat or drink during daylight

With Jesus Leading the Way

hours for the next month. Not eating during the day isn't as difficult as not drinking. If the fast occurs during the hot season when temperatures can soar to above 120 degrees, their suffering is great without water. The "faithful" have dried parched lips, and they want everyone to realize they are fasting. The rules they must follow for fasting are burdensome.

We remember Jesus' specific instructions for fasting found in Matthew 6:16-18.: "When you fast, do not put on a gloomy face…" Every Muslim we saw who was fasting did have a gloomy face during that month. The outcome of their "good works" was not greater joy but only greater darkness without the light of Christ. Their purpose is to gain favor from Allah and also, in their striving, to show their devotion to Islam. Although they are misguided, many are very sincere in their faith and desire to gain favor from Allah.

Although they eat or drink nothing all day, when darkness arrives, they are free to eat and drink all night if they want to. Sumptuous meals are prepared at night, and the rich Muslims in the capital even bought imported fruits (apples and grapes) from France that were unbelievably expensive. In the early morning hours, before the sun comes up the next day, men go around the villages beating on pans or drums telling everyone to hurry and arise, say their prayers, then eat and drink before daylight fasting begins again.

It was to the Muslims that God had called us to take the Gospel. The work would not be easy, and there would not be hundreds of converts as there were in other pagan areas of Africa. In pagan areas, the response to the Gospel is great because most have never heard of Jesus. It is a different story in Muslim lands. How much better it is to have no teachings at all about Jesus than to have false teachings about Him ingrained into you. How grateful we were for the assurance that God had called us to this place and He would always be powerful and faithful. Only He can bring a person to salvation in His Son. We were to learn we must be faithful in giving out the Word, obeying Him daily, and keeping close to Him.

Islam teaches that Jesus is not the Son of God, that He never died on the cross (they only had someone who looked like him) or rose from the dead. For Muslims, Jesus was a teacher, a guide, and a prophet but not a Savior. He was surpassed by Mohammed, the last and greatest of the prophets. Muslims sometimes say, "We believe in your prophet Jesus. Why don't you accept Mohammed?" Islam is Satan's masterpiece. Mohammed taught about the prophets but took the very heart out of the Gospel when He denied Jesus' divinity, death, burial, and resurrection. Without belief in these cardinal truths, no one can ever be saved.

Muslims say that they accept the Pentateuch, the Psalms, and the Gospel of Jesus (the Injil) as being from God but say the present-day translations are corrupted and can't be trusted. They know stories about the Bible prophets, but their stories are perverted and not according to the Scriptures. One of the greatest false teachings from their traditions (Haddith) is that it was not Isaac that God asked Abraham to sacrifice, but it was Ishmael (the father of the Arab nation). Islam says Christians are infidels. They think we believe that God and Mary got married and that they had a son. They repeat *"I mana Irikoy hay, Irikoy mo mana hay."* ("No one gave birth to God, and God gave birth to no one.")They also think we believe in three Gods (God, Mary, and Jesus).

We realized we had to be "wise as serpents and harmless as doves." Winning an argument hardly ever means winning a soul to Christ. We chose not to berate Mohammed, which enrages Muslims, but to tell Muslims of the prophets of old that they revered. Most of their male names were names of the prophets, and they even name some of their boys Jesus (Isa). We wanted to get the message across to them that those prophets of old all looked for the promised Messiah as predicted in Scriptures, and we wanted them to realize that Jesus is this One promised.

Soon after our arrival in Gaya, as we sat at the dinner table one evening, a great cry went up from the village. Mildred told us this meant they had seen the new moon and Ramadan, the month of fasting, was over. In Zarma, to fast is *me haw* or "tie your mouth." The end of the fast was named *Me Feeri* or "open your mouth."

Early the next morning after they saw the new moon, all the men of the village, robed in their finest, filed out of town to a cleared-off area to bow toward Mecca with their faces in the sand. How our hearts ached for these so bound in a false religion.

All the people who could possibly afford it had new clothes to wear on *Me Feeri*. Dressed in their finest, the children went from house to house wishing everyone *Kay Yessi* or "Happy New Year." They were hoping for every household to give them a gift of money too. Sometimes the more well-to-do locals actually left town for the day to go out to the bush to hide from the proliferation of greeters expecting gifts!

During the month of Ramadan, the children had great fun with what they called *Tobway-Tobway*. One of the children was designated to be "the rabbit." White splotches were painted on his body, and he had large fake rabbit ears, a rabbit tail, and so forth. The group went from house to house with drums, awakening people with their chanting, *"Tobway, tobway, to-bai-yeh. Nda fu borey jirbi, ma kar ka tunandi!"* ("Rabbit, rabbit, rabbit. If the people of the house are sleeping, beat the drums and wake them up!") They danced, sang, and did all kinds of performances until they were given food or money gifts. It was amusing to see their creative ideas and dress.

Seventy days after the end of Ramadan was the real New Year's Day. This time when the men went to the special field to pray, the head imam sacrificed the first sheep. Thousands of sheep were sacrificed on that day and roasted over open pits. It was sad for believers to see these who had rejected God's Lamb sacrificing sheep in hopes of forgiveness. The meat was cut up the next day and "sacrificed" by giving it to other families. Once again, everyone wanted new clothes to wear on this holiday, and the children went from compound to compound wishing people *Kay Yeesi* and hoping for money gifts.

Here is an excerpt from our prayer letter to supporting churches on April 10, 1960:

"We have arrived in Gaya after a two hundred-mile trip over roads we will not forget. Someone has said, 'Washboard roads were invented in Africa, and they have the best in the world!' Heath, Rebecca, Jon, and I were happy to see the mud brick (adobe) house and pull in, covered with dust. It is quite an experience living in an African village. The sound effects are greatest at night – donkeys, dogs, drums, and so forth. The mission does not like to send missionaries to an outstation during their first year on the field because it gives them so many responsibilities besides language study. However, we are happy for the privilege of keeping this station open and are trusting the Lord for the added strength and wisdom. We are thankful for the time spent in Paris learning French. All of the local officials and any who have been to school speak French. They don't respect anyone who does not speak the 'educated language.' Our house is made of mud. Can you imagine that? It is really quite comfortable and has a corrugated aluminum roof. One disadvantage of mud houses, though, is that the termites come right through the mud walls, and we must watch that they don't eat the backs of our pictures. The mud walls are about eighteen inches thick. We have simple homemade wooden-framed screen windows and screen doors but no glass windows."

The floors of our home were made of roughly laid out flat stones, cemented in between. They were very difficult to sweep and keep clean. During our second term in Niger, we put a layer of cement down over the stones so the floors were smooth. We bought some rolls of linoleum to put down and were glad the floor could be washed so that the children had a cleaner place to play. There was a long, enclosed veranda, which we used for a dining room; a small kitchen; one bedroom; and a bathroom. Mildred had just about the same thing on the other side of the house except no kitchen. After a year, when Mildred went on furlough, we opened the doorway between our apartments, which then meant we had two bedrooms and two bathrooms. Two bathrooms were handy for when diarrhea, also called "the West African version of the common cold," plagued one or more of us! There were no inside doors, only curtains for privacy. We had to look down under the curtains on the bathroom opening to see if feet were visible before going in, unless the occupant was singing loudly to make his or her presence known!

When our field director had written to us before we left France to say that the Niger field council wanted us to go directly to a bush village for our language study and that we would be living in a mud house, I must admit I was a little nervous about what such a home would be like. Essentially, it is called an adobe and is a natural building material of sand, clay, and water with straw and manure mixed in. Living in a mud house, we really began to understand how distressed the children of Israel were when Pharaoh told them they had to go get their own straw for making bricks – that straw is so essential for binding the bricks together when they are made. The African men actually mixed these ingredients with their feet. The mud pile is covered for a time to ferment, which they said made it more waterproof. Then the material is shaped into bricks using open frames. After the builders mold the brick in the frame, the frame is quickly removed and the large building brick is left to dry in the hot Niger sun. Mud houses have been constructed in various parts of the world for many years. They are advantageous in hot, dry climates since they remain cooler in the daytime.

The same mixture to make bricks, without the straw, is used for mortar and often for plaster on interior and exterior walls. The ceilings of the houses were made of sticks laid evenly on cross beams, then mud was added. Well-made ones usually didn't leak, but it seemed that so many did leak. The leakage that began during a rain continued to drip, drip, drip long after the storm was over. Ceilings and walls in African mud homes sometimes collapsed during rains and could be dangerous. The kitchen of the Gaya house had caved in a few years before we arrived. Sometime after that, all the mission men had gone down to Gaya to remove the mud roof and replace it with a corrugated aluminum pan roof. We were so grateful to have a metal roof. Its biggest disadvantage was the noise during a downpour when you could hardly hear yourself think! Conversation was reduced to a minimum during a hard rain because we had to shout at each other to be heard.

Only the commandant (later called *sous-préfet*) had a generator for electricity in Gaya. Heath had purchased some pressure lanterns that gave a good light but also produced some heat, which we didn't need. We had some more simple Aladdin lamps too. We thought, because we had good light in the house at night, we really didn't miss electricity. We had hand-held fans that we used and even took them to bed with us at night to fan ourselves until we slept. When we awoke again and again drenched in perspiration, we'd once again fan ourselves so we could get back to sleep. We also learned the secret of getting up in the middle of the night to stand under the shower with our pajamas on, then go back to bed soaking wet. The evaporation felt so good, but we soon dried off again.

A humorous true story we were told was about a missionary who sprayed her mosquito net with water before she got in bed. Then for a short time, she enjoyed the evaporative coolness of her net and sheets drying. While home on furlough, a supporting pastor was interviewing her in front of the church. He asked, "How do you ever get cooled down to sleep in that hot country?" Without thinking, she replied, "Oh, that's easy! I just wet my bed!"

In the house during the cool season, we slept under mosquito nets that were securely tucked under our mattresses after we got in bed for the night. Rebecca and Jonathan felt really secure under their mosquito net "tents," and they missed them when we went back to the States for furlough. Heath and I often got up at night to move the children's arms and legs away from the nets if they had gotten up against them as they slept. The mosquitos had a feast then, which often resulted in malaria.

We had an open well in our yard and had to hire a full-time yardman to draw water out, bucket by bucket, transport it to the side of our house to fill the barrel on the ground, then use the "jappy" pump to pump the water to a barrel on top of the house. Unfortunately, sometimes a lizard crawled into the tiny space around the pipe going to the housetop barrel and died! Then our water smelled terrible. It was especially disconcerting when pieces of rotted lizard came through our faucets. We kept big covered clay pots in the house from which we could dip out boiled and filtered drinking water. It was a constant job for me to boil, filter, and cool the drinking water.

Because of the termite problem, we had been advised not to use wooden furniture on the field. We brought a Formica table and chairs from the States, and metal porch furniture for our living room. It consisted of a glider with three seats, two chairs, a chaise lounge, a coffee table, and two end tables. We also had an armoire and two dressers also made of metal. The termites weren't even tempted to chow down on our furniture! For curtain rods, we pounded long nails into the mud walls and then placed a thin metal rod across them. I was very thankful for the treadle sewing machine we had purchased from some missionaries. I made simple curtains from yards of material I bought cheaply in the market. I made dresses for Rebecca and myself and even learned how to make shorts for the boys. I also had to keep taking in Heath's pants because he was down to a skinny 147 pounds at the end of our first term!

Food Preparation Challenges

Our kitchen had a small shallow sink, a little bottle-gas stove, and a woodstove. On the woodstove, we boiled our water and then poured it into a large container that had three stone filters. I had to wash the stone filters often, as they got slimy on the outside from removing the dirt and impurities from our water. The filters got thinner and more fragile after months of use. When they got too thin, they broke and had to be replaced with expensive new ones we purchased in Niamey.

I also cooked and baked on the woodstove, learning how to adjust the oven temperature with how much wood I put into the stove. A donkey-load of wood cost about $2, so it was quite economical to cook with the wood instead of bottled gas. I liked the woodstove in spite of the heat it added in our kitchen. Maybe it reminded me of the first month we were married and living on the farm with Charlie and Margie Carmen.

The kitchen had mud cupboards along one wall. We had a kerosene refrigerator. There was a large reservoir for the kerosene in the bottom with a wick that we lit. The heat caused the gases in the refrigerator tubes to circulate and cool. The heat exited on the top of the refrigerator. Close to the chimney where the heat exited on top was a perfect place for me to place my container when making yogurt because the warm air kept the yogurt warm while the culture grew.

In the cool season, we had ice cubes, but it was another story during the hot season. We tried to open the refrigerator only two or three times a day (at meals), and we kept it covered with a wet blanket hoping the evaporation would cool the exterior. Heath faithfully bought a jerry can of kerosene each Monday to fill the lamps and the refrigerator reservoir. He also had the difficult job of keeping the wicks trimmed just right so the lamps or the refrigerator would not smoke.

For a while, we had a yard man named Hassan who worked for us. He was a cheerful guy but very much from the bush and the primitive way of life. Knowing he had never seen or heard of ice or snow, I brought him into the house once to show him our refrigerator. He looked at the burner flame in the bottom of the fridge, then I showed him the ice in the freezer of the small top compartment. He didn't know what to make of the ice and later told the village people, "You know, these *anasaras* (white people) are so smart, they can cook water until it's hard!"

Preparing meals presented its own challenges as well. Eggs were not readily available in Niger. I used to watch by the edge of the road in front of our house on Tuesdays (Gaya market day) for any Fulani ladies coming from the bush to ask if they had eggs for sale. At that time, the tiny African chicken eggs were two for five CFA francs. It took two of them in an American recipe that called for one egg. I took a bowl of water out to test the eggs before buying. If the egg laid flat on the bottom of the bowl in the water, it was fresh. If only the large end of the egg stayed on the bottom, it wasn't very fresh but might be edible or at least used for baking. And if the egg floated, it was rotten! With no refrigeration and women keeping their eggs for a week or more until the next market day, it was no wonder they didn't stay fresh.

In the rainy season, we bought guinea hen eggs, which have unbelievably hard shells! It was fun to watch new missionaries try to crack them, first gently, then firmly, then really hard! The guinea hens lay lots of eggs in the rainy season. I learned that if I wrapped the eggs individually in newspaper and packed them in a small box, they would keep for several months in my kerosene refrigerator. Their egg whites wouldn't beat up for a meringue though.

In the cool season, we grew a nice garden with lettuce, tomatoes, carrots, and green peppers, but the rest of the year we only found pumpkin squash, onions, garlic, and dried okra in the Gaya market. I often joked that I should write a cookbook titled *One Hundred Ways to Cook Squash and Onions*!

Potatoes were not available in Gaya, only the large yams brought from Dahomey, and they were very starchy. They were a little gummy when I tried to substitute them for mashed potatoes. However, the coastal Africans called mashed yams *fufu*, and the African sauces went well with it. All our family loved buying chunks of yams hot out of the oil with hot sauce, sold by the local ladies. There was also *kudaku*. It was somewhat like our sweet potatoes, but they were whitish-gray not orange or yellow. We ate lots of rice and macaroni to replace the potatoes we couldn't get.

Norma Bobbett

On trips to Niamey, we were able to buy real potatoes. The children loved it when I made French fries with those real potatoes and were careful to count them out so each of them got the same number of fries!

For fruit, we had mangos in the hot season and sometimes guavas. Just across the river, the Malanville market was held on Sundays, and my friend Hadi went over there to buy lots of bananas, oranges, and limes to sell at Gaya market on Tuesdays. She always came to me to sell on Mondays, and we really appreciated these fruits brought up by trucks from where they grew in the south.

A variety of meat was available to us. We could always purchase beef in the market. I bought a large portion and cut it up to use in various ways. With a hand grinder fastened to the table, I made ground meat. The meat was often tough, so I was thankful for a pressure cooker. We also could buy mutton; tiny, scrawny little chickens; and goat (There was no pork in a Muslim village). For local people, the butchers cut up bite-sized pieces of meat, adding some bones for good flavoring to place in little piles for sale. With no refrigeration, the locals bought their meat daily. Meat dishes cooked in tomato sauce would keep for days without spoiling, as long as no one put their hand into the sauce and meat. Although locals mostly ate with their hands, they were careful to only use a clean spoon so they didn't contaminate the meat and sauce when they were traveling and didn't want spoilage.

Several kinds of nuts were also available. African girls boiled peanuts in salt water, put them in little sardine cans to carry on a tray on their heads, then went through the village selling them. They also roasted peanuts in ashes. They were good. These peanuts and the local peanut oil were sold in discarded Johnny Walker whiskey bottles. Sometimes we still got a whiff of whiskey when we opened the bottles for peanuts. We were also able to buy gumsa nuts in some African markets. We were told that the shell of these nuts is unbelievably hard. Cows eat the gumsa fruit, and later we learned that the hard-shelled nuts were found in cow pies! I hoped the Africans washed them well before tackling the difficult job of extracting them from the shells! We didn't eat them raw, only cooked. They worked pretty well for a substitute for walnuts in cookies.

Unless I brought powdered sugar from the States, there was none to be found. I made good pumpkin pies with squash from the market. Other missionary wives shared this recipe for making a chocolate cake without eggs.

Crazy Cake

1 ½ cups all-purpose flour
3 tablespoons cocoa powder
1 teaspoon baking soda
½ teaspoon salt
1 teaspoon white vinegar
1 teaspoon vanilla
5 tablespoons vegetable oil
1 cup water

Preheat oven to 350 degrees. Grease an 8-inch square or 9-inch round cake pan. Combine all dry ingredients in the pan. Make three depressions in the dry ingredients. Pour vinegar in one, vanilla in one, and oil in the third. Pour water over all and mix until smooth. Bake for 30 to 35 minutes until toothpick inserted comes out clean. Allow to cool and top with chocolate frosting.

With no powdered sugar available I used this recipe for a great chocolate frosting (more like pudding) that worked well with Crazy Cake:

Charlene's Chocolate Icing

¼ cup cornstarch
1 cup sugar
½ teaspoon salt
¼ cup cocoa

Mix all ingredients together. Slowly add 1 cup boiling water and cook until thick. Then add two teaspoons vanilla and ¼ cup butter after you remove from cake from the oven. Frost the cake while it's hot.

The way we received our monthly allowance was rather comical. It was sent to us from Niamey by way of the post office. So everyone at the post office (and probably their family and friends) knew exactly how much we got each month. The post office paid us in small denomination old bills that were dirty, fragmented, and torn. Sometimes we had to beg the ladies selling in the market to accept these bills. They really didn't want money in such condition. We saved the very worst bills to buy stamps at the post office, and then I am sure they gave them back to us in our next month's allowance!

In order for me to have time for language learning and to be involved in ministry along with Heath, we employed a houseworker. At that time in

Niger, only men worked as houseworkers, but in other African countries, women were often hired. A houseworker swept out the dust, grit, and dirt (especially after a dust storm) in the house daily; washed the clothes by hand; hung the clothes on the line to dry; ironed the clothes with heavy flat irons heated on the woodstove; heated water to wash dishes; set up our beds and mosquito nets outside in the evening and brought them in the next morning; and so forth. He went home for two or three hours during the hottest part of the day.

Although having a job as a "boy" was something that the locals would be proud of, we learned that the word "boy" did not have a good connotation to African-Americans in the States. We learned to say "house steward" or "house helper" when we were on home assignment. The sad part was that the house steward's relatives all thought he was extremely rich, so they were always asking him for money or descending on him and his family to eat for free. The results were that the house stewards took out loans all over the village without our knowledge, promising to pay for whatever they obtained (street food vendors, grain, and so forth) when they got paid at the end of the month. We thought it was odd that on the last day of the month, several people could be found sitting out in front of our house waiting for the house steward to finish work and get his pay. We were puzzled, wondering why one of our workers always sneaked out our back door to hop over the fence in our backyard to avoid the debt collectors on his payday. One fellow got so he never showed up on payday, claiming to be sick. He sent his wife for his pay!

Since we used the woodstove for cooking, baking, and boiling our drinking water, the first thing our house steward did when he arrived in the morning was to get the wood fire going for me to fix breakfast. I came out one morning to a terrible odor in the kitchen, so I asked our house helper if he had been sick. Sheepishly, he said, "No, I'm cooking some food for myself on the woodstove and that is *bulunga gee* that you smell!" Yuk! What an odor! Then I learned that the English name for this product is shea butter.

Imagine my surprise in later years to discover shea butter wasn't only edible but was used in all kinds of women's cosmetics. I have no idea how they remove the odor to make it have a pleasant fragrance! The karite tree (vitellaria paradoxa) produces its first fruit, which looks like large plums, when it is about twenty years old and can produce nuts for up to two hundred years after that. The trees grow naturally from Senegal in West Africa all the way across to Uganda in East Africa and are found in nineteen countries across the continent.

Europeans had imported neem trees to Africa because they are fast growing and drought resistant. These trees tolerate very high temperatures, thrive in sandy soils, and are evergreen. These trees were great for shade, and missionaries planted many of them on our mission stations. We really appreciated the large trees in our Gaya yard and the shade they gave.

The twigs from neem trees were used for brushing teeth in Niger, so often we saw people walking about chewing on an end of a twig until it shredded to become like a brush. Their teeth were white and beautiful, so it is a most effective form of dental care. They also boiled the bitter leaves from the tree to treat malaria and diarrhea.

Adjusting to Gaya also meant facing different health concerns. Since we arrived in Gaya at the very hottest time of year, Rebecca and Jonathan quickly adjusted to taking showers but soon broke out in prickly heat all over their bodies. Once we got prickly heat in the hot season, it did not go away until cooler weather came. Rebecca, Jonathan, and Heath all got a series of painful boils. We tried bathing them in Phisohex or Dial soap, cleaning the boils with alcohol, but nothing stopped them until they ran their course. Two-year-old Jonathan had over twenty large and small boils on his body, plus an ugly carbuncle on his lower back. I cringe as I write this now. It was very hard for me to see my children suffer so, but they happily played and didn't stress over this as I did.

One day I looked out the window and saw Rebecca pulling Jonathan in their little wagon. For some reason, he fell off the wagon, landing on his back in the dirt where he had the large carbuncle with several heads. Rebecca brought him into the house, crying her heart out in sympathy. I had to wash the dirt and sand off the carbuncle and try to keep it clean. How marvelously the Lord cared for us in the climate, with diseases and germs that were new to us.

As a young mother, I was so very fearful when my children got sick. When we all slept side-by-side in the sleeping house, I could reach over and feel Rebecca and Jonathan's foreheads in the night to see if their fevers were going up. If they had been ill in the daytime, I reached over to them every time I awoke all night. I spent my daytimes watching them carefully, rocking them in our lawn furniture rocking chair and trying to fix food from our limited resources to tempt their appetites.

The nurses at the government dispensary in Gaya were mostly graduates of sixth grade with one year of nurses training. All kinds of sick people crowded into the dispensary each day, sanitation was worse than poor, and needles were used over and over on patients without being sterilized. The dispensary personnel were very kind and didn't seem at all offended when we took our own needles, which I washed and boiled thoroughly before their re-use. This was in the days before disposable needles.

It was quite an experience to see the French-trained African nurses give an injection! Their needles were large. To give an injection they removed the needle from the syringe, then threw it into the hip like a dart. If no blood welled out of the needle, they then attached the syringe and injected the medication. Unfortunately, sometimes the needles hit a nerve that caused the leg to shrivel so that the patient limped badly for the rest of his life.

If our children had an illness that was beyond the nurses at the dispensary, we had to call for the mission plane and take them to the capital, Niamey, to see one of the French doctors. Jonathan was the first of our boys to have febrile convulsions. Eventually, all three of our boys had them. They were so frightening. I can't express how deep my inner panic was each time the convulsions occurred. Although my children are grown and on their own, to this day, I have a sick feeling in the pit of my stomach as I remember how desperate and helpless I felt each time they were convulsing. I prayed aloud as we bathed Jon in cool water, asking God to save our son and bring him out of the convulsions. We did what we could but were forced to realize our resources had to come from our loving Father. We praise the Lord that the boys all outgrew the febrile convulsions.

We wrote in a prayer letter: "We have been having quite a time with our two-year-old, Jonathan. He had a bad attack of malaria, and the high fever brought on a convulsion. We took him to Niamey (two hundred miles), and the French doctor found him to be very anemic. After a series of B-12 shots, he seems better but is thinner and doesn't have much appetite. Please remember him, and us, in prayer. Satan knows one of his best lines of attack with missionaries is in anxiety and discouragement if their children aren't well. It isn't easy when your little ones are sick and the nearest doctor is more than one hundred miles away over African roads."

Our heavenly Father, in His loving care and kindness, sent help our way that first year we were in Gaya. Experienced godly Dr. John Dreisbach passed through Gaya on his way to Bembéréké, Dahomey, where he was going to live and supervise the building of an SIM bush hospital. The hospital was just about three hours south of us, and the one-lane road was paved all the way. It was our joy to host him and get to know him and his wife, Bettie, their first time in Gaya. Dr. Dreisbach told us that whenever our children were sick, we could bring them to him, be it day or night, and he would be happy to care for them. We took advantage of his invitation many times and were so thankful for him. What a comfort it was to us to know that our children could have a competent American Christian doctor's care! The eternal loving Creator God was always there for us! Sometimes it was malaria or fevers or boils that took us to see Dr. Dreisbach. There was no way to let them know we were coming, but Dr. John and Bettie were always so gracious and kind to us. When the hospital was built and staffed, Africans came from all over for treatment and surgeries.

Before Dr. Dreisbach came to Dahomey, Heath got a boil right on his "sitter-downer" and that was no fun either! Either because I found it in *The Merck Manual* or because someone from the States wrote this, I tried heating the neck of a glass pop bottle in boiling water, then placing it over the boil to draw out the core. It worked, although I thought at first there was cotton in the bottle before I realized it was the core!

After only a month in Gaya, again before Dr. Dreisbach came, I became extremely ill with what we thought was malaria and severe diarrhea. At that time we did have Dr. Celestin at the dispensary. He was a *médecin*, not a full-fledged doctor but one who had higher education than the nurses and had taken special training in Dakar, Senegal, for tropical diseases. Dr. Celestin was out of town when I first became ill, and soon I became progressively weaker. When he returned and did some exams, it was determined that I had both amoebic and bacillary dysentery.

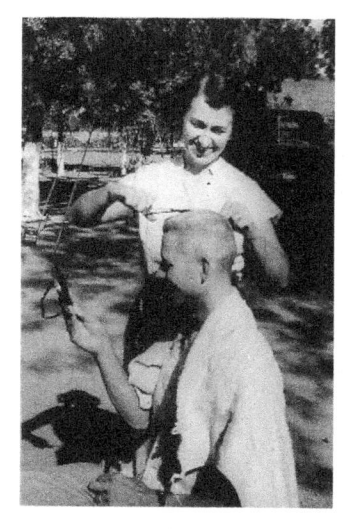

Besides the multitude of pills I had to take daily, there was a very toxic injection that was given for several days to stop the amoebas from causing ulcers in the intestines and even getting into the liver. We didn't understand all the dangers, but Dr. Celestin trusted Mildred to give me the shots with our own boiled needles. He also gave her another medicine to inject after that shot if my heart began to act up! Praise the Lord, I never needed the heart injection. The other ones were painful and left huge lumps at the site where they were given. These solid lumps didn't totally disappear for over a year.

The Lord kept Heath well, although he was getting very thin. He was studying Zarma, caring for the children, doing station work, preaching (through an interpreter while we learned the language), and maintaining our household while I was so weak that I spent most of my time lying down. Mildred helped with meals.

When we arrived in Gaya, God provided a wonderful Dendi Christian man to work with us. Old Soumana had lived a number of years in Nigeria, so he spoke some English. He was such a kind and godly man and loved our children. We have a picture of Soumana pulling little Rebecca and Jonathan around in their red wagon. He was a godly father to us and grandfather to our children. He translated for Heath when he preached in English as we learned the Zarma language.

Soumana was raised a Muslim. When he returned to Gaya after many years in Nigeria, the missionaries who were there were looking for a language teacher. This was before our mission had established the good language program that was in place when we arrived. Soumana, glad to have a job, told the missionaries he would help them learn the language, but he wanted them to know that he was a Muslim and wasn't interested in their trying to convert him. The missionaries agreed but told him the only thing translated into Zarma was the Zarma New Testament, so they had to use the New Testament for their language learning textbook. Soumana accepted this, and the classes began. Day after day, Soumana was being exposed to the Gospel through the Word. Finally, one day the missionaries asked him what he thought of all they had been reading. His amazing answer was, "I believe it is the truth!"

By the time we arrived in 1960, Soumana was quite old, and his health was precarious. He had a small salary, so he mostly just puttered around the mission house, raking leaves when he felt like it, caring for his chickens, and above all, witnessing to anyone who came to see him. Soumana's ankles were quite swollen, indicating he had congestive heart failure. When I was so sick with the dysenteries, he held me up in prayer, asking for restored health. He had no wife at this stage in life, but when I asked him once how many wives he had had in his lifetime, he replied, *"Iboobo"* (many).

Soumana saved everything the missionaries threw away. In his little hut, there was barely a path to his bed because of all he collected. But it was wonderful whenever we needed a small part, some wire, a piece of screening, screws, or whatever. Soumana would say, "I think I have something you can use at my house." He most always had just what we needed.

We were quite cut off from the world in Gaya. The only phone we could use was in the small post office, and it was not possible to call the

States from there. Sometimes we could get a call through to Niamey, and sometimes we couldn't. Even if we could have called the States, the extreme cost was prohibitive. We received mail at the tiny post office twice a week when buses came through. But the heavenly lines were always open! God told folks when we had special prayer needs and even woke them up in the middle of the night to pray for us and other missionaries around the world.

My dad wrote at the beginning of June 1960 to tell us that my mom had been taken to the hospital in Rockwood, Tennessee, in May in the advanced stages of cancer and was in great pain. This letter took about a month to reach us. I realized that it wasn't God's will to heal her, so I began to pray earnestly that He would release her from her suffering and take her home to Himself. Week after week went by, and I received no word of her condition. I began to get desperate, crying out to the Lord for her in her extreme suffering. All of July went by, and I had no word from home. My heart was broken thinking how she must be enduring even greater pain as each week went by.

At that time, missionaries did not go home for deaths, marriages, graduations, or vacations. The only way they went home was if their health was broken and staying in Niger would have hastened their death. God gave grace, and we were able to accept these things, but it seemed so much better in latter days when missionaries could go home for important occasions. Air travel has made it cheaper and possible.

The Lord did a very wonderful thing for me as I prayed for Mom in her suffering. I didn't hear an audible voice, but His peace invaded my heart, and I was sure the Lord was saying, "Don't worry about your mother anymore. She is not suffering. She is in heaven with Me." (Yes, God's telegraph, telephone, and e-mail worked back then too.) I was assured that she was no longer suffering for all of July. In August, another letter came from my sister-in-law, Carol, saying that Mom went to heaven on July 1, 1960. I don't know why my family didn't send a cable gram, but Carol had written immediately after Mom's death, and the airmail letter took a month to reach us.

Dad told us later that Mom's last words to him before she lapsed into a coma were, "Don't worry about me. Remember, 'absent from the body' means 'present with the Lord.'" Dad said her last words were to comfort him and assure him of where she was going.

For the next month, I cried myself to sleep every night because, at twenty-seven years of age, I was motherless. I never realized how much I depended on my mother's love and prayers. At the end of the month, I said to myself, "Norma, you aren't crying for your mother. She is at home with her Savior and forever free of pain. You are crying for yourself!" It was true. My tears at that point were selfish and centered on me. I then was able to thank the Lord for saving my mother, giving her eternal life, and taking her Home. Above all, I thanked Him that I knew I would see her again someday.

The cards and letters from so many friends were a comfort to me.

During the time of waiting for news about my mother, Heath was wrestling with and praying about the huge bill of excessive customs charges for our freight. Our crates and barrels had been shipped to Cotonou to be loaded later onto trucks and brought inland to Gaya. Our account at the mission was depleted with the freight expenses, but we had been told that there would be no customs charges for first-time residents. It was considered to be *changement de résidence* (changing of residence) and customs free. However, there was a new *douanier* (customs official) at Gaya, and when our freight arrived, he was determined to charge us excessive amounts for everything. How would we ever pay it? Some of our personal supporters had not continued, so we were just scraping by each month, and there was not even enough coming in to put aside the customary amount each month so that when furlough time came, we had passage money home. It was a stressful time because we did not have the funds to pay these charges, and it looked like we would have to go into debt to the mission. I want to emphasize that the Lord took good care of us, and we really could live on the $75 a month we received per adult and the $20 per child. It was just that our account at the home office wasn't building up any reserve for customs charges and passage home when it was time for home assignment.

Was the Lord conscious of our stress and frustration? Of course He was! We had been saving and had $200, but now it looked like we would be going into debt to the mission for over $700. This was a lot of money back in 1960. But at the last minute, just in time, the Lord performed a miracle for us. A French customs inspector, Monsieur Poesch, who attended our EBM church in the capital, arrived in Gaya, unexpected by men but sent by God! He graciously helped us fill out the necessary papers and reduced our charges to one third of the former amount asked. Even the customs official had to confess, "God has worked for you." This was the victory of our prayer supporters. To God be the glory! We were learning that though "With men this is impossible, with God all things are possible!"

In July 1960, evangelist Kimba, a recent graduate of our vernacular Bible school in Téra, came to Gaya to work with Heath. The very day that Kimba arrived in Gaya, we received word that the village was in mourning because the *laabukoy* had died in the night. The *laabukoy* was the land chief, a man very well-off by Zarma standards. He had come now and then to the mission station since it opened ten years before, so he had heard the Gospel many times. In earlier years, he had rejected it and argued against God's Son, but in later years he came and listened, saying nothing. Did he believe in his heart but fear man too much to say so? Only the Lord knows. In June, we went to call on him when we heard that he was not well. After explaining again how the Lord Jesus loved him, died for him, and how He would save "whosoever," we adjusted a pillow under his head to make him more comfortable and left. After his death, the *laabukoy's* funeral was done quickly, as all burials in Niger are; without embalming, the bodies deteriorate quickly. We went to the land chief's compound to offer condolences. Heath had Kimba speak to the people gathered at the *laabukoy's* compound and, after hearing him, was confident that Kimba would be a real asset to the work in Gaya.

Kimba grew up in Dosso, Niger, and came to know Christ under the ministry of Glenn and Anne Nunemaker. It is a very serious step when a former Muslim is baptized. Kimba's relatives told him he could turn back and become a Muslim again at any time but not if he was baptized. He was told that baptism would condemn him to hell forever. Kimba was baptized and began to make plans to go to Bible school in Téra. He had gathered all his earthly possessions together in a small box, preparing to take the bus to Téra. His family took the box and hid it from him, so he left for Bible school with only the clothes on his back.

Heath and Kimba trekked into the bush villages where they sometimes stayed overnight, gathering crowds with the village chief's permission and preaching. They also carried literature with them to set up a table in the bush markets. We were advised not to give literature away in the markets because then the people thought the literature was of little value. The people were much happier to pay a few cents for the literature, and then they kept it.

Not all relationships were as encouraging as ours with Kimba. A man named Namata said he also wanted to attend EBM's vernacular Bible school in Téra. The Gustenhovens and then Mildred had literacy classes to teach him to read and write in Zarma. That fall, Namata went off to Bible school and surprised us by taking a young woman he said was his wife with him. A few weeks later, the girl returned to Gaya, saying someone in her family was sick and she had to return to her village. Later, Namata returned to Gaya, and we learned that they had just run off together, wanting to be married, but permission was refused by her family. His attitude was rather belligerent, but eventually he asked us to write a letter to the Washers with his apologies. We had already hired another yard man, so we couldn't take him back in our employment. He stopped coming to church and averted his eyes when he saw us in the village. This was our first big disappointment in what we thought was a young believer who held such promise.

I wrote in my journal: "Namata is giving us lots of heartaches. We have leaned over backwards to try to win him into fellowship again but he seems to delight in running over us with a haughty and very smart aleck attitude. *We need the Lord's strength and grace.* We received a letter from Mother Bobbett, saying that friends from Bible college days woke up one night really burdened to pray for us. They spent nearly one hour in prayer for us! What a thrill to hear such news. How many times we have felt so burdened, down, and alone and have asked the Lord to lay us upon someone's heart at home to pray for us!"

This was one of the many occasions when a missionary's children were a blessing to the work. When Rebecca or Jon saw Namata from a distance, they loudly called out, *"Fofo, Namata!"* Namata couldn't refuse but always broke into a smile and came over to talk to them. While we had been busy studying, memorizing, writing, and reading to learn Zarma, our children were outdoors playing with their friends and assimilating the language so that they were speaking it with no accent.

Gendarme Molto and many other French people serving in the colonies enjoyed the free housing and good salary the French government paid them. At the end of their time in Niger, they liked to take a ship from one of the coastal cities to leisurely make their way up the coast back to France. Once Monsieur Molto asked Mildred what her monthly salary was as a missionary. When she told him, he laughed and said, "I save that much money a month just for drinks on our ocean trip back to France!"

In July 1960, we celebrated Jonathan's second birthday. He was thrilled with the gift of a toy train, which Heath put together for him.

Niger Independence Day

On August 3, 1960, the Niger received independence from France! It was a very significant day, and we were excited about being a part of this historic time. We, Mildred, and Gendarme and Mrs. Molto were invited to the commandant's independence celebration. There were ceremonies, folk dances, speeches, and a delicious *méchoui* (roasted sheep) was served. We never really experienced what it was like to live under French rule since Niger became independent just a few months after we arrived.

Our days were full with callers coming to the house daily. Mildred was faithful about visiting the village women and talking to them about Christ. She took me with her and taught me how to use Bible stories and pictures to help them understand. Mildred spent her mornings in Bible study and prayer, preparing herself to serve in the afternoons. In addition to village visitation and teaching children's Bible classes with Mildred, my work was learning the language and caring for the children. I also shopped in the market for our food, baked our bread, cooked our meals, and later homeschooled our children.

Heath was also learning the language, studying, preaching, trekking, teaching short-term Bible school, overseeing work on our house and yard. He had a time of Bible reading and sharing the Gospel with our house and yard workers, Old Soumana, and any others who happened to be around each day. Heath also did bush trekking with Kimba, preaching in villages. They took literature tables into markets in different towns on market days. He also took Kimba and men from the church to the *faada* in town. This is where many village men gathered in an open space to talk and visit. They were usually willing to listen to preaching too. We also drove to the village of Bodjékali, Dahomey, once a week to preach, have a children's class, and visit in homes. In the evenings, we often had visits from young educated men who had jobs for the government. One man named Prosper worked for the public works on road maintenance and repair. We enjoyed encouraging him in his walk with Christ.

A Muslim Wedding in Gaya

Mildred Dibble and I were invited to a *hiiji hawyan* (wedding) and were told to arrive about 8:00 p.m. The courtyard had been neatly swept, and there were mats for people to sit on. The drummers were busy at their work, and sometimes the noise made conversation difficult. The crowd was just beginning to gather as we arrived. Most conspicuous for westerners at a Muslim wedding is that neither the bride nor the groom is present! We saw the bride, Mariama, briefly as we arrived, but then she went into a hut and hid under a blanket. Most of the men guests sat outside the gate of the compound. Millie and I sat with the women who were gathered inside.

The *alfaga* (Muslim teacher) sat just inside the doorway where he could see all the guests, both inside and out. It was his duty to witness the final negotiating for the bride price. A little before 9:00, a man who was representing the bridegroom entered. The drums stopped beating, and silence reigned as he approached the bride's mother (or aunt) who was sitting on a mat among the women. He asked how much more was required to finish the bridal agreement, and she laid down several specifications of the money needed. The bride needed so much for new clothes, so much to have her hair fixed, so much for pots, pans, blankets, and household needs.

When the bridegroom's representative asked for a total, she said 9,500 CFA ($40). The normal reply is "That's not enough," but then they began to barter about the price. The mother/aunt insisted on the price, so he went outside to talk with his cronies. These are young men helping to pay the bride price, and they will expect him to help them also when their time comes to marry. When he came back and counted out some money in front of the Muslim teacher, he brought it over to the mother/aunt. "Oh no!" she exclaimed. "It's not what I asked for. It is not enough." Once again, they began bartering, and again he went outside for more money, which she also refused as not enough. This time he had brought gifts – six yards of cloth, a pair of shoes, and a can of powder. He promised to bring the rest of the money the next day.

"Nothing doing," she replied. "There will be no wedding until all of the money is brought. You haven't brought the *tugu nooru* (hiding money) yet." This is the money to be used for the bride's food and paying the girl who brings what she needs during the week she is in daytime hiding after the wedding. The bride spends each night with her husband and then hides in the daytime in another hut.

When the final agreement of payment was met, the Muslim teacher, standing outside with the men, shouted many blessings upon the marriage. At the end of each blessing, all the people replied, *"Amin!"* At this point, a woman next to us let out five piercing cries. With that, the wedding ceremony was finished! We all got up, congratulated the mother/aunt, and left. It was 10:05 p.m. Carefully shining our flashlights, Millie and I made our way through the village and back home. Sometime in the night, the young people came to take the bride to her husband under a blanket canopy held over her head. The bride was heard loudly crying and wailing as they took her to her husband. In this way, she honored her parents by letting everyone know they had been very good to her and she didn't want to leave them.

It was a blessing that we had been sent immediately to the bush (small village outstation) to learn the language. We were really immersed in the language and surrounded by the local people. Our first and most important responsibility was to get through the one-year Zarma language program.

Each month, we were responsible for filling out work reports to be sent to our field office in Niamey. We had to keep records of the ministry we had done, including:

- How many visits we made that month
- How many individuals we dealt with about their need of salvation
- How many Bible classes were held
- How many hours were spent in preparing for the Bible classes
- How many children's classes were held and the number in attendance at each one
- How many social contacts were made with government leaders
- How many sermons were preached and how many hours were spent in preparing them
- How many hours were spent in language study (one hundred hours each month required for the first six months, eighty hours each month required for the second six months)
- How much Gospel literature was distributed that month (Bibles, booklets, and tracts)

Although the work reports were bothersome, it was good to be reminded of our main purpose of evangelism and teaching the Word of God and to be accountable for our time each month. I often had thirty or more children's Bible classes a month, besides scores of village visits with the women. Every time a group of children gathered in our yard to play, either they asked me or I asked them if they would like to sing songs and hear stories from God's Word. They were always enthusiastic about the classes. We chose a shade tree and spread out mats for them to sit on. I sat on a low stool, called a *teeta*, in front of them with Bible pictures or my flannelgraph board. They loved the stories and were fascinated by the flannelgraph figures that I allowed them to remove from the board and put up again as they reviewed the story. To this day, I pray I will meet some of these children in heaven. There was much giving out of the Word to children and adults but not much visible fruit, in contrast to missionaries who worked in pagan areas of Africa.

Many Scriptures have come to have a deeper meaning to us, and we need to remind ourselves continually of them. Matthew 5:11-12 says, "Blessed are you, when men revile you, and persecute you, and shall say all manner of evil against you falsely, for my sake. Rejoice, and be exceeding glad: for great is your reward in heaven: for so persecuted they the prophets which were before you."

In November 1960, Heath wrote about an evangelistic trip he made into the bush with Roger Bacon, evangelist Cecekoy, and Bible school graduate Kimba: "Fortunately an administrator had driven out this way earlier in the week, and we could follow his path of bent grass where no road or path was visible. We were going to the village of Yélou, ten miles off of the dirt road into the bush. Our purpose: to proclaim the Gospel where no other missionary had ever been.

"The night before, we had slept under the stars at another village. Yet at the break of day, we were awakened by the shrill cry of the Muslim call to prayer. Islam had preceded us. Approaching Yélou, the centrally located mosque bore mute testimony that neither were we first in this village. What a privilege was ours as we each in turn preached Christ to those gathered around.

"After we had preached some time, we found some who could read and distributed Gospel literature. We are rejoicing that we are now able to witness in Zarma, though our time of official language study isn't over yet.

"Continued prayer requests are: (1) that we might soon have transportation of our own, (2) that Namata might come back to the Lord and yet go to Bible school, (3) for the salvation of the many we contact daily, (4) that Christ might be pre-eminent in our lives in the coming New Year."

From my journal, dated Friday, December 2, 1960: "We took a hurried trip by mission plane to Niamey a week ago because Jonathan (twenty-eight months) was very sick with fever, vomiting, and diarrhea. He seemed better the next day and his last two molars started to come through the gums, so we guessed that cleared up the mystery. Our family of four returned to Gaya yesterday on the crowded African bus."

From my journal, dated Saturday, December 3, 1960: "Old Soumana was so pleased this evening at yard devotions when two of his friends joined the group and listened to the reading of the Scriptures. After we had finished, Soumana witnessed to them using the parable of the sower who went forth to sow and where the seeds fell. He told them again the story of the cross, Jesus' love and death in their place."

In December, Soumana became very ill, having a real crisis with his asthma and his heart. Heath went immediately to the dispensary to pick up the African nurse and take him to Soumana's house; there he gave him two injections. After morning church, where much prayer was offered for our dear Soumana, I went to visit him too. It was so heartbreaking; we loved him so much. Christians of Soumana's caliber were rare there. He continued to suffer all day. I found myself pleading with the Lord to take him. One blessing was seeing the African Christians leaning upon God and pleading for Soumana. Kimba and Sampson's faith was great as they pleaded with the One who healed all manner of sickness when he was here on earth. That evening, we got the nurse to come and see Soumana again. He was breathing easier, which was an answer to prayer; however, he wasn't able to lie down.

When I was crying out to the Lord for Soumana's suffering, the Lord so wonderfully comforted me through Romans 8:18. The sufferings of this present time, seemingly so terrible for our African *baaba*, Soumana, were not worthy to be compared with the glory that will be revealed in him! The suffering seems so great to us. *What must the glory be?* I prayed, "May the Holy Spirit be continually working in the hearts of those to whom Soumana has so faithfully witnessed through the years. Oh, that through this, many precious souls will be saved!"

Two days later, we again went to see Soumana. He was weak but breathing easier. I took bouillon soup and orange juice to him, and he took a little of each. Later in the afternoon, Idé (our first house worker) went to see Soumana, and he asked for ice for a cold drink. We were happy to have some for him in our kerosene refrigerator. When Idé returned with the cold drink, Soumana was sleeping. Later in the evening when Heath went to see him, he was still sleeping.

From my journal, dated Tuesday, December 6, 1960: "'Absent from the body, present with the Lord.' This morning at about 7:00, Soumana went home to be with his Savior. Through our tears, we rejoice in knowing he is with God and has left all suffering and sorrow behind. We feel so lost without him. It is as if we lost our favorite uncle. O Lord, thank You for saving Soumana. Thank You for sending missionaries to this Muslim land to proclaim life eternal in Christ. And, O Father, glorify Yourself through this and bring others to Yourself." The answer to this prayer was abundant and immediate: opportunities abounded for witnessing because of Soumana.

Soumana's Funeral

In the heat of Niger, preparations had to be made quickly for Soumana's burial. We had a nice mahogany casket made. Probably for many, this was the first Christian funeral they had ever seen. Heath read from a number of excellent Scriptures and had prayer at Soumana's compound, then the men loaded the casket into Mildred Dibble's truck and followed on foot to the Christian cemetery. There Scripture was read again and prayer was given. It was so hard for Kimba. Soumana meant so much to him in the Lord, even more than his Muslim parents. Kimba spoke of a dream Soumana had not long ago and how afterward he had exhorted Kimba to continue on in the Lord. Two weeks before, Kimba had returned to Dosso to visit his family, but they refused to receive him because he is a Christian. Soumana too knew what it is to bear scorn, rebuke, and rejection for Christ.

One opportunity came with Soumana's good friend. He had heard the way of salvation from Soumana many times. As Heath spoke to him, it was a blessing to see Soumana's testimony still living. This man knew the Way and could explain it as well as we could! He said, "Soumana wasn't afraid to die. He said he had life eternal because he believed in Jesus!" Heath asked this man if he was afraid to die, as he assured him he could have eternal life too. The man replied, "I am afraid of my friends."

From my journal, dated Thursday, December 8, 1960: "We only had seven in our children's French Bible club today, in contrast to twenty-five last week. When Mildred went to pick up the children, many wouldn't get in her truck because it had transported a dead body yesterday. Mildred and I called on Yacouba's mother this afternoon. She gathered a group together to hear our teaching. One lady looked like she was in an advanced state of tuberculosis and how we prayed she would understand and believe the message of Jesus. About 5:00 p.m., three of Soumana's nephews who are truck drivers came to thank us and asked Heath to show them the grave. When they arrived there, they asked Heath to pray. So Heath read Scripture and prayed then asked Kimba to give a testimony about Soumana and what he meant to him. Kimba told them, 'I'm your brother too because I called him *baaba.*' Afterward we invited Kimba to have supper with us. We were all missing Soumana so much yet thanking the Lord that we knew where he was and that we would see him again someday."

Because the road to Parakou, Dahomey, was paved, we most often went that way to buy supplies rather than over the unpaved Niger road to Niamey. SIM had a number of mission stations down that way, so we stayed in their Parakou guesthouse and got to know many of these dear fellow servants of Christ. Parakou was so different from Gaya, with lots of trees and foliage.

On our December 1960 trip for supplies, Heath bought me a new pair of sandals, and the MacDougals, hosts of the Parakou guesthouse, gave us a large bag of whole wheat flour to make bread. We were also told to take as many grapefruit as we could use from the guesthouse trees. In the evening, the MacDougals took us out to an isolated spot in the bush where we had a picnic on a large rock. They brought their portable battery-operated record player and played Christmas music. It was like a mini vacation for us – how good to meet other missionaries and to speak English!

In Mark 10:29, Jesus said, "No one who has left home or brothers or sisters or mother or father or children or fields for me and the gospel will fail to receive a hundred times as much in this present age." We found these words to be so true after we had left our homes, families, and lands for the sake of the Gospel. God gave us so many wonderful African mothers, fathers, brothers, sisters, and friends over the years – what a blessing they were to us!

Our Christmas celebration that year and years following in Gaya blended our American traditions with new African ones. We tried to bring out a few toys in our barrels for future Christmases and birthdays, but the supply was usually depleted before the term was over, so we had to be creative for gifts. Flashlights bought in the local market always went over big with our boys. Sometimes we could buy a ball too. I made clothes for Rebecca and clothes for her dolls. The children thought it was a big deal to get into our barrels to find gifts to wrap for us. We received toothpaste and soap, often wrapped up in cute childish ways and put under the tree for us.

In later years when we were stationed in the capital, our supporting churches generously sent monetary Christmas gifts for us, which we could use to buy overpriced French toys in the stores of the capital. Our children were thrilled with each toy, and our Christmases were always joyful family times.

In the African Christians, we saw wonderful commercial-free Christmas celebrations. For them, the holiday meant that you bathed, dressed in your finest, and went to the homes of each of the Christians to greet them on the joyous remembrance of Jesus' coming into this world. They did not exchange gifts, but Christmas Day always involved a church service and then gathering together for the celebration meal. The men sat around visiting where they could find shade trees, while the women prepared large pots of rice, sauce, meat, and vegetables.

At Gaya there was an *ancien combattant* (an old soldier under colonialism who served in the French army) nicknamed Quatre-Vingt (Eighty) because of a long recitation he had memorized and quoted whenever asked, much to the enjoyment of the French people. Our French gendarme friend introduced us to him and told us that he was the best cook you could find to prepare the roasted sheep over an open pit for your holiday celebrations. We engaged him for every Christmas sheep roast for the Christians when we were there.

The first Christmas that Quatre-Vingt came to prepare the meal for our Christians, he came to our kitchen door to ask me for a basting brush for the oil, garlic, and spices he applied to the roasting sheep. I told him I was sorry, but I didn't have one. A few minutes later I heard an awful squawking coming from my chicken pen out in the backyard. Quatre-Vingt then came back to the kitchen door to ask me for some string to tie together the rooster's tail feathers he had obtained for making his own pastry brush! We told ourselves that the heat of the roasting coals would destroy any germs put on by the "pastry brush." Quatre-Vingt always brought the fresh sheep liver to us and taught me how to make brochettes of liver chunks and pieces of bread to deep fry. They were delicious! All our family readily ate liver that way. Back in the States, liver never tasted fresh again, so we only ate it in Africa.

That first Christmas in Gaya, the week leading up to Christmas was busy with many activities. Cecelia Dillon and four-year-old Moussa had traveled from Niamey to spend Christmas with us. On December 22, we had a Christmas party with our Thursday Bible club children. There were thirty-two present, and we all had a grand time. Heath reviewed all their French memory verses with them, and Mildred gave the Christmas flannelgraph story. We had races afterward with *bonbon* (candy) prizes. The next day, Millie and I visited the land chief's compound, where she again told the Christmas story with flannelgraph.

Christmas Eve was a most difficult and tiring day. Jon got up with a fever but seemed better enough to go with Mildred to the post office on the other side of the village. She came tearing home, however, as Jon began to have a convulsion. By the time we got him into the house, he was about over it. Heath got the African nurse, and using our boiled needles, he gave Jonathan an injection of quinimax. Each injection was very dangerous – if the injection goes directly into a vein, it will cause death. Needless to say, the process was stressful and draining.

Later that evening, however, we were able to relax and begin our Christmas celebrations. We had invited Gendarme and Madame Molto for the evening, and also our African Christians came for a campfire meeting with a *méchoui* (roasted sheep with rice and sauce). It was a blessing on our first Christmas in Africa to hear Christmas carols sung in Zarma. Heath also read the Scriptures of the Christmas story.

That night, Jonathan's fever returned and kept us busy with cool sponge baths. He had developed a cough and probably had a bad cold. Christmas Day was a bit chaotic – we had a good church service, but we, along with Cecelia, Moussa, and Mildred, had to open our Christmas gifts on the run, and it was very confusing. Our nicest gift was that Jonathan was feeling better! And then, finally, with Cecelia's help, we managed to get Christmas dinner on the table.

From my journal, dated Friday, December 30, 1960: "Soumana's sister and three others came to visit this morning. We spoke to them from John 3. I made my first village visit alone today (without our language teacher, Mildred) to visit the land chief's wives. I spoke to them about the brazen serpent. Advice today from Soumana's sister on how to keep my chickens healthy – feed them onions and red peppers. This was probably a good idea too. Side note: I had told a little girl from a compound I was disappointed because a lady there hadn't come to see me since Soumana had died. This little girl came back to report that the lady hadn't come because every time, I read the Bible to her! I'm sure she got lots of that from Soumana too! Gadjere ("Shorty" who is very tall!) and Yacouba came to visit tonight, and we taped some of them talking to greet Mom Bobbett. They got quite a bang out of hearing their own voices." The next day Rebecca came down with a fever, and Heath was not feeling too well either.

New Year's Day saw Heath preaching in Zarma and doing quite well at it. That day we also had eight little girls come to visit, most of whom were school girls who spoke French. I was able to give them tracts while they were here. In the afternoon, Heath went to Dosso to bring back Mildred and the children who had been at camp since Christmas Day. I was so thankful to hear that Mouskourou, from my sewing class, had received Christ as her Savior while at camp!

From my journal, dated Monday, January 2, 1961: "Rebecca's fever is down today, and she seems better. Today we killed a four-foot-long snake in the worker's washing shelter!" In our first ten months in Gaya, we killed twelve snakes. God protected us and our workers.

The beginning of 1961 saw more opportunities for us to witness and build relationships. Not all were encouraging. During one visit Mildred and I made, a woman in the next compound kept peeking through the grass fence to greet us. We invited her to come over and visit but learned she was in a closed compound and was not allowed out. Then Mildred remembered she had visited in that compound twelve years ago and left some Bible pictures with the women. When she asked to go back to visit again, she learned that the husband found out his wives had allowed an infidel (Christian) to enter, so he beat them and threatened much worse if they ever allowed Mildred in again.

Another day, a lady from Kamba, Nigeria, arrived at my door begging with her twins. According to local custom, the mother of twins has a right to go about asking for money. She is allowing you to do good works and maybe earn your way to heaven. I gave her some money and a little baby shirt, and she started to leave. I was busy, but after a moment's reflection I thought of what a horrible thing I had done. I had given her something for her physical needs but sent her away with no spiritual food! The Lord put wings on my feet, and I caught her just as she was going out the gate. Not only did she come back to sit and listen to God's Word, but another lady friend came in off the road to hear too.

We also had a young man come for devotions one day, informing us that he was going to "come all the time to hear the preaching" so he can have money like Old Soumana did. (Soumana had received $12 a month for going to the market for us, sweeping leaves when he felt like it, and just puttering around the yard.) How sad it is that men come telling us they will follow and even preach for us if we will pay them. So many who work for missionaries profess Christianity as long as they have a job. Thank the Lord for Africans like Soumana who followed Christ and not the white man or their jobs. True followers of Christ suffer ridicule as they are told they are only following the Lord for money. This young man came to the prayer meeting that evening and slept through most of the message. We had to trust that the Lord was able to get ahold of his heart.

One day I could not find my Niger driver's license after Rebecca had been examining my wallet. She couldn't remember what she had done with it. Trying to impress upon her the gravity of losing it, I told her I couldn't drive the car without my license. "Yes, Mommy, you can still drive," she said. "No, I can't drive without my driver's license or the police will put me in jail." After a few minutes of reflection on this, Rebecca began to cry. When I asked her why she was tearful, she said, "Who is going to make desserts for me when you are in jail?" (Not much later, we did find my driver's license, much to the relief of us all.)

We were making good progress in learning Zarma, being able to converse with people in the village and those who visited us in our home. By then Heath was preaching in the church and was making treks to outlying villages. I taught children's classes and witnessed to the women in the village through Bible stories. I, who thought I could never learn another language, was speaking in French and Zarma! Truly God's calling is His enabling!

In February 1961, we took our final Zarma exam. We praised the Lord that we were able to get through EBM's excellent one-year program within a year. Our exam had included two hundred vocabulary words, Scripture to translate (I John 4:4-8), and a five hundred-word paper explaining to Africans a phase of our life. We finished with a dictation given by a Zarma which we translated into English.

Our final exam meant that Millie had completed her year teaching us Zarma. She left Gaya on March 2 and flew out of Niamey about a week later. She left her Chevy truck for us to use. It was old and not very reliable, but we were so very thankful for it. During her time teaching us in Gaya, she often teased us about the fact that she stayed over an extra year to teach us Zarma, thereby missing leap year at home when women are supposed to be able to propose to men! We couldn't understand why she got upset if we went across town to pick up the mail at Gaya's little post office – she let us know that she should do that. Millie was keeping a big secret from all Niger missionaries. What we didn't know was that a widower friend Floyd Adsit, was writing regularly to her! Not too many months after she returned to the States, Millie and Floyd were married.

The day after Mildred left, I seemed to have to force myself to go teach Bible stories to the land chief's wives. The week before, they seemed a little put out to have to stop their work and listen. However, I felt the Lord wanted me to go again. As I started walking to their compound, He brought to my mind, "How shall they hear without a preacher?" I vividly remember looking down at my tired dusty feet and remembering, "How beautiful are the feet of them that preach the Gospel of peace and bring glad tidings of good things." When I arrived, the ladies seemed pleased that I had come. This was an encouraging love gift from the Lord, and I was thankful I had been obedient to His leading. I knew Heath was praying for me as I spoke to them about God's people being delivered from Egypt and how Jesus wanted to deliver us too. As the group quietly listened, one lady was busy looking through another's hair, searching for lice!

With Jesus leading the way for us, we had successfully finished our first year in Gaya and our formal Zarma language program. We learned how to live in a mud house with only old screening tacked on the windows, no electricity, and no running water. And the snakes! We killed about one a month, either inside or outside the house. The Lord so wonderfully cared for us and watched over our children.

Chapter 10
Finishing Our First Term in Gaya
March 1961 to January 1963

When Millie left in March 1961 for her overdue furlough, we were alone on the station for the first time, responsible for all the work. We had spent fourteen months in France learning French and one year in Gaya learning Zarma. In spite of our responsibilities, we were still considered to be rookies because first-term missionaries were not allowed to vote at our field council meetings until the beginning of their second term. I was happy for this, feeling it gave us opportunity to observe the work and learn more before being involved in the important mission decisions.

We received Niger's only newspaper (which at that time was only a few mimeographed pages) by mail. Less than ten days after Millie's departure, we were shocked to read that Ed Zouck, our EBM business manager, had been seriously injured when a truck ran over him while he was on his moped. Through a phone call Heath was able to make to Niamey, he discovered that Ed had been badly injured internally, as the truck had run across all his vital organs. Amazingly, Ed hadn't lost consciousness, but the Africans, trying to be helpful, pulled his legs out of the crumbled motorbike and sat him up in a taxi to be transported to the hospital! French doctors at the hospital had operated three times. We were calling out to the Lord on Ed's behalf.

Two days later, we received a telegram from our field director, Bob Richards: *"Ed Zouck au près du Seigneur."* ("Ed Zouck is with the Lord.") How our hearts went out to Mary, his wife. We had a special prayer meeting at 5:00 p.m. and began to prepare to travel to Niamey. The telegram had arrived too late for us to get to Niamey in time for the funeral. We prepared Millie's Chevrolet truck for the trip.

Once in Niamey, we made our way to see Mary. Mary showed the grace of God and His provision in a wonderful way as she told us about Ed's last days and hours. Many of her and Ed's French friends, whom they had been witnessing to, were at the funeral. Bob Richards gave a simple, clear Gospel message.

Mary and Ed Zouck had been preparing to leave on furlough. Now Mary informed us that we could have the use of their almost-new Peugeot *camionnette* (a small truck with a canvas cover over the truck bed) while she was gone for a year. We were flabbergasted at her kindness and God's provision. How good it would be to have dependable transportation for the next year. Mary said she would use her truck until she left for furlough, at which time we were to return to Niamey to pick it up. We returned to Gaya on Friday and had an excellent opportunity to deal with two of our African friends, Ide and Kata, about Ed's death.

The next days were very busy. We tore out the mud wall dividing Mildred's half of the house from ours, and then did lots of cleaning before moving some of our things over there. After a whole year with all four of us in one bedroom, we then had two bedrooms.

Yacouba's mother and her friend came to visit one morning, and I was able to have a Bible class with them. That afternoon, a Swiss couple arrived with their fifteen-year-old son, Christian. The Coulerouses did colportage work and evangelism throughout West Africa and lived very frugally. We had them take charge of our Thursday children's Bible club that day.

The local children loved to come into our church services to sing and listen. However, sometimes their fathers heard they were there, so they came to call them out to smack them or hit them with a stick as they sent them home, telling them they could not listen to the infidels. One day when Mildred was calling in the village compound and explaining the Word to a young girl, the girl's uncle overheard. He declared, "If you are here to talk about Christ, you can leave. We are good Muslims, not hypocrites." Mildred replied, "Then I take it you don't know what Jesus Christ has done for you?" His retort: "I don't know, and I don't want to know!" It was so sad to realize the hold this false religion had on the people.

From a letter to Heath's mother, dated April 27, 1961: "Dear Mom, Whew! I tried to find a cool place to sit down and write this afternoon, but there just isn't any. It is 108 degrees in the shade. A light rain two days ago has made the humidity worse than ever. We are all popping out with prickly heat. Please pray we will escape the boils this year. I still have some of the yeast pills you sent, and I think we will start taking them…Rebecca (four and a half) has written a letter for me to send you. She is coming along well. I told her what letters to make, and she wrote the letters without other help. She recognizes all capital letters now, and we are starting to learn small letters. She can write the numbers one to twenty and even finds some of the hymn numbers in church…Rebecca and Jonathan sat in a big pan of water and played most of the morning. Lucky kids! They are sleeping now but will probably want to jump in again when they wake up. It helps prickly heat more than anything I know, except for cooler weather…Last Thursday, an Englishman spent the day with us. He came to see the dispensary doctor because he was ill. He is working out in the bush near here, surveying to make new African maps. He has dropped in twice since then but has left now. He was a rather dry stereotyped Englishman, but it was nice to have someone to speak English with anyway."

We had twenty-two supporting churches at that time, with each supporting us with $5 to $10 a month and several with $25 monthly. We realized that though we had only been away from the States less than three years, thirteen of our churches had changed pastors! Although we tried to send communications to our churches every month or at least every two months, only a very small percentage ever wrote back to their missionaries.

Dr. Dreisbach decided that Rebecca's jaw tooth should be pulled since it would be several months before we could get to Jos, Nigeria, to see a dentist. We had quite a time with her, but Dr. Dreisbach was so patient. Afterward she was proud that the tooth was out. We were feeling badly that she lost it so early, but we can trust Him in all things! When Rebecca grew up, her teeth were beautifully even, and some thought she had worn braces.

From my journal, dated April 21, 1961: "Heath couldn't go to Bodjécali to preach this afternoon because we don't have money to buy gas, so I was able to do quite a bit of calling, walking in the village. I called on Tarana's sister again. My! The filth, flies, and suffering in that little hut! We long for her to understand and be born again. I also had a good visit with Mintoon's mother, and she listened well."

Sometimes the difficulties of Muslim work pushed me toward real discouragement. Once when I told an African friend about this, he said, "Oh Madame, please don't feel that way! If you and Pastor weren't here, how would our people ever hear the good news about Jesus Christ?" That really perked me up! "How beautiful are the feet of those who bring Good News."

From my journal, dated May 6, 1961: "This morning, Rebecca was asking about heaven, when we would go there, and so forth. I told her that anyone who believes Jesus died for them and invites Him into their heart has eternal life in heaven. She said, 'I believe, and now I am going to bow my head and ask Him to come into my heart!' I really believe she is serious and has absolute faith in the Lord for as much as she knows. How sweet and precious is the trust and faith of a child!"

We were experiencing our second April and May in Niger, the two absolute worse months of the hot season. If one day seemed bad and the next even worse, although the temperature was the same (115 to 120 degrees in the shade), we had only to look at the humidity indicator to see that the next day had worse humidity. How we looked forward to that first good planting rain. It was an absolute must that the people had a planting rain before the end of June so the crops of millet, guinea corn, and sorghum could grow adequately in Niger's short rainy season. The people told us that the rain had to soak down through the sand at least as deep as from their fingertips to their elbow to qualify for planting. From sometime in September until the next May or June, there was no rain and everything turned brown, dry, and dusty. It was amazing to see the sandy land all around begin to sprout with weeds after that first good rain.

That summer, the chickens that we had purchased from Soumana's family after he died got cholera and began to die one after the other. When I came down with diarrhea at that time, I wondered if I had caught something too, but I was reassured by the good old *Merck Manual* that humans couldn't get cholera from chickens! I tried giving the chickens permanganate water, hot peppers, and onions, but most died anyway. I wanted to keep them alive because eggs were so hard to come by, and it was hard to bake or prepare a lot of dishes without them. Africans usually allowed the hens to sit on their eggs in hope of increasing their number of chickens.

It was interesting to see so many people coming to the market from bush villages, carrying their flip-flops made from old tires on top of their head loads, stopping by our house to put on the shoes before arriving at the market. These poor folks only had one pair of shoes, and they certainly didn't want to wear them out on the long walk into Gaya. The bottoms of their feet were like leather anyway – thick and calloused. Sometimes when they stepped on a thorn, they did not even know it until they sat down and happened to look at the soles of their feet to discover it.

By June, all of our family was suffering with prickly heat. I know why babies with prickly heat were so fussy – it itched! I remarked to Heath that the way we all sat and scratched, anyone who didn't know better might suspect we had body lice! We tried our best to dress lightly and not sleep in the house, even if we were sick, during the hot season because once you got prickly heat, it stayed with you all of the hot season, then gloriously disappeared when the weather cooled down. When we told people in the States how hot it was in Niger, some said, "Oh, but it is a dry heat, so it isn't as bad." A perfect response given by a missionary was, "Yes, the heat coming out of your oven is a dry heat too, but it is hot nevertheless!" We were thankful for a small plastic swimming pool that the children used to cool down.

On June 16, we celebrated our sixth wedding anniversary. We listened to a recording from our wedding. Ironically, a Muslim wedding was being conducted across the street. It was quite a contrast to hear the bride wailing as they took her to her husband, sheep bleating, and people laughing.

It was also Gendarme Buchillot's birthday, so we invited them for a spaghetti supper. We often invited them down to our house to play games, to help keep up practice of using the French language. We had a British version of the board game Clue. It was fun learning the names of the murder weapons in French and then speaking French as we played.

Gendarme Buchillot had an 8mm movie camera. He also had a gun and liked to hunt. One evening, he decided to take his wife for a drive out to the dirt airstrip where our planes landed. He wanted to hunt for guinea hens or wild pigs. When they arrived at the airstrip, there were no pigs but lots of monkeys playing around the area. Quickly they drove back home, left their gun, and hurried back with the movie camera. You guessed it! When they got back out to the airstrip, there were no monkeys but several wild pigs!

From my journal, dated June 26, 1961: "It is sweet to see the way Rebecca and Jon make their way into the hearts of these Africans. Jon (almost three) has begun to speak Zarma and makes us all laugh. The Africans love to tease him just to hear him talk. Our children's love for the Africans is open and unabashed."

Receiving Mail

Our seclusion from the rest of the world made mail a big deal for us, even if the airmail often took a month to reach us. Twice a week we might find mail in our box at the post office the day after a bus went by. Our house was very close to the road, and the only buses that came by were the two carrying mail. If a bus came in not too late at night while Rebecca and Jonathan were still awake in the sleeping house, they stood up on their beds with hands held high to yell, "Hooray!"

Grandma Lena Bobbett and many of our churches' ladies missionary fellowships were really good about sending small one-kilo milk carton boxes with goodies inside that weren't available in Africa. The packages' arrival always was an exciting and happy time for the children...and for all of us! We appreciated so much the many things our friends and family sent that we could not get in Niger – cake mixes, Jell-O, pudding, Dream Whip, Tang, dry spaghetti mixes, and so forth. These packages were sent by boat mail and could take two to six months to reach us.

I had been bothered by a toothache for many weeks. We could not determine what it was but suspected it was dental work that was done in Paris during language study. Finally, we decided I should take the bus to Niamey and see if there might be a dentist at the Niamey government hospital. My trip up to Niamey was uneventful. The one dentist who had been at the Niamey hospital had to return to France for some reason, so there was only a French technician to see me. He x-rayed the suspicious tooth that the French dentist had worked on in France. A large amount of fluid had formed there, and the technician said that was the cause of my pain in the jaw and ear. He was incapable of doing dental work, so he suggested that I just bear with it until it eventually went away. There was nothing else for me to do!

On the trip home, I was the only white person on the bus crowded with Africans, animals, and all kinds of bundles and luggage. The larger pieces of luggage or sacks were tied on top of the bus, and the pile was almost high enough to make the bus look like it was a double decker. The bus was to leave in the early afternoon and to arrive in Gaya shortly after dark. My seatmate was a very nice old African man who had placed some live, scrawny, tied-up chickens by our feet for the trip. We had a nice visit getting to know each other.

The bus stopped at various places to let off and take on more passengers. Then there was always a stop for the Muslim prayer times. Lacking water, the faithful ceremoniously "washed" their hands and feet with sand before bowing toward Mecca to touch their foreheads to the ground the prescribed amount of times. In each small village where we stopped, a great number of food sellers lifted their wares to the windows so the travelers could purchase something to eat – fried yams, fruit, meat sticks, manioc, and water of dubious origin tied in plastic sacks. Another important stop was for everyone to go to the bathroom. Since there were only small scruffy bush-like trees, the driver tried to pick a spot with some hills or dunes on each side. He announced, "Ladies restroom is to the right, gentlemen to the left!" We scurried off to our respective sides and tried to squat hidden from the bus.

The road was not paved, we were very dusty, and night fell by the time we were halfway to our destination. The various stops continued. Finally, we arrived at the village of Malgoro. There was now a single-lane paved road for the last forty-five kilometers to Gaya. Then the tired bus driver announced, "We are stopping here for the night!" Stoically, the Africans accepted this verdict and many got out of the bus to sleep at various places on the ground. My seatmate and I decided to stay in the bus. It was my prayer that there might be less Anopheles mosquitoes (which transmit malaria) inside the bus than outside. Settling in, I laid my head back against the seat and actually slept a little bit. In the darkest part of the night, I was awakened by someone grabbing my ankle and pulling on it! Startled, I sat up straight, realizing that it was my seatmate. He was looking for some of his small packets and chickens down there to rearrange them but accidentally got ahold of my ankle! He apologized.

With the crowing of the village roosters, the bus driver came back to the bus and we resumed our journey. Back in those days, there was no way Heath and I could contact each other. All he knew as he waited for me in Gaya was that the bus didn't make it the night before. It surely was good to see him there waiting as the bus stopped at our house and I descended. I couldn't wait to take off my travel clothes and get under our bucket shower!

From our very first term, we decided it was good to give at least one evening or day for a family time of games, picnics, throwing Frisbees, and so forth. This time was invaluable family time. One evening in June, we went out in the bush and Heath did some target practice with his .22 gun. (At that time, we were allowed to have guns for hunting. After the coup in 1974, all guns had to be turned in to the government.) Jon and Rebecca found a nice gravel hill to slide down on. Such laughter – Jon wore the seat out of his pants! It is surprising what a little change of pace and relaxation can do for you. From my journal: "Sometimes when we see so few results in this Muslim land where missionaries have labored for so long, we are tempted to wonder if it is worth it all to hazard our health and the lives of our children. Then the Lord reminds us of our calling, and His eternal purpose will not be defeated. All our efforts – giving out tracts, trekking, preaching in the villages, children's Bible classes, village visitation, literature distribution – if we were not here, how would they hear? As we returned with the young people from camp, the Lord brought to my mind this fact. If we hadn't been here, these young people would never have known the blessings of camp and seeing that there are other Christians in the world. Perhaps Garba would never have heard the way of salvation. Psalm 62:8: 'Trust in Him at all times, ye people; pour out your heart before Him. God is a refuge for us.'

With Jesus Leading the Way

"I had several callers today and was thankful for opportunities to present the Word. I've been having a hard time with self and Satan. How I long to see results here among these Muslim people, but it seems God could never have called us to a more unresponsive tribe. And yet why should I complain when there are missionaries who have patiently spent most of their lives here with small visible fruit? The Lord is so patient with me! If I can yearn and weep in my earthly state for these people, what must God's love and desire for them be? He loves them far more than we do. The Lord showed me Isaiah 28:13 today: '…precept upon precept…line upon line…here a little and there a little, that they might go, and fall backward…and be taken.' Surely this describes our work among these people. His Word is all-powerful, and one day (perhaps one by one) they will be broken and taken."

Vacation in Nigeria

In July 1961, we took our first vacation since we had arrived in Africa. SIM had a rest home on the cool plateau, twenty-three miles outside of Jos, Nigeria. A coworker took us and a single lady down in his roomy vehicle. It took two or three days, staying at mission stations on the way, and the washboard roads just about shook the car (and us) apart. Much cooler and healthier, the plateau is a boon to the missionaries. At the Miango rest home, we could gain a respite from the extreme heat of the lower elevations.

153

Norma Bobbett

There were many cabins and duplexes for missionary families to stay in. We all ate in a common dining hall. During the hottest months, the rest home was filled up with their own missionaries, but after the rains began, there were vacancies, so they very kindly allowed other missionaries to come. Coming out of the hottest season in Niger into the cool air of the plateau where there was abundant fruit and delicious meals was a fantastic time of rest, fellowship, and sports for us. In the coolness, our itchy prickly heat disappeared overnight! We wives rested from food shopping and cooking. There were local girls available to hand-wash our clothes in buckets, and there were lots of books in the library for reading. There were hikes, tennis, volleyball, and so forth.

One evening at the Miango guest home, we attended a showing of one of Moody Bible Institute's very fine movies from the Sermons in Science series. This one was on the wonders of the human heart. The scientist had a real heart (taken from a man who died at a ripe old age) on the table to demonstrate. Three-year-old Jonathan was sitting quietly on my lap watching the movie. We were amused (and embarrassed) when he said in a loud voice, "What's that big piece of meat?" There was no way a three-year-old could understand that was a real heart on display!

The single-lane dirt road from Jos to Miango that we followed was precarious. Rock formations were everywhere. Someone joked that "God created this area, then sat back and threw rocks at it!"

At the SIM hospital, dedicated missionary doctors gave us physicals, adjusted our malaria medicines, and did the standard lab tests then treated us for anemia, worms, dysentery, malaria, and so forth. They also brought our inoculations up to date for typhoid, typhus, and polio. It was excellent for us to get away from our ministry to look back at it objectively, read great books, hear godly speakers, share our burdens, fellowship with other missionaries, and just have time for sports, hikes, and games. This was all topped with the cool weather on the plateau, abundant rain, and nourishing food. When we returned from our first vacation at Miango, we felt like we had had a mini-furlough.

In August 1961, we set up a volleyball court on the vacant lot on the other side of the church building in Gaya as a means of winning the friendship of young men. It helped us to get to know many. Years later, we often were greeted by men in government offices in Niamey who told us they knew us from playing volleyball in Gaya. Even one of Niger's ambassadors to Washington, D.C., and the UN, Joseph Diatta, told us he remembered attending our Thursday Bible club and playing volleyball as a young man.

Rebecca's fifth birthday was September 16, 1961. I tried to make the children's birthdays as special as possible. We gave her new clothes and a doll with long pigtails. Grandma Lena Bobbett had sent Rebecca a little dollhouse and furniture, but only the furniture had arrived for birthday. I baked a special cake and took a picture of her with the cake and in her new dress and shoes. Nine days later, I began teaching her Calvert Correspondence out of Baltimore, Maryland. I enjoyed teaching her, and she loved being in "school." It only took an hour and a half each day. I was so glad our mission didn't require that we send our small children off to boarding schools but left the decisions about education of our children up to each missionary family.

Before our first furlough, I also taught Rebecca first grade and part of second grade. Calvert was just about the only correspondence course we had ever heard of in the early 1960s. The lessons were well laid out, and we regularly sent Rebecca's papers and tests to Baltimore where a teacher of that grade compared her progress to the children in her Baltimore classroom. We always referred to this woman as "your teacher." When the teacher wrote back suggestions for Rebecca, she seemed to take it better when I said, "Your teacher said you should do thus and so," and it wasn't Mom telling her what to do! I taught her to read from the old Dick and Jane books. In fact, I had the privilege of eventually teaching all our children to read using those books. Calvert School seemed to know what it was like for us living in such a hot climate. They always sent blotters to put under the student's arm so he wouldn't perspire on his papers!

I noted in my September 1961 report that I made 101 visits. Some were my going to call on the village women and others when they came to call on me. I almost always had a Bible lesson with them and told them about Jesus, the world's only Savior. I also had ten children's classes that month and gave out ninety-seven Gospel literature pieces and Bibles.

On October 9, Heath's thirty-first birthday, I wrote this poem in the absence of a Hallmark card store (or any other card store!):

As birthdays go it's true.
I've helped you celebrate a few!
In '55 we were in Bradford town,
New joy in "being one" we'd found.
In '56 your wife was kind of weak
But we had a baby girl at which to peek!
In '57 we were in lovely Kansas City,
The Asiatic flu bug! What a pity!
In '58 we didn't feel so hot
By Doctor Game we had been "shot."
An added blessing of this year
Was our firstborn son, what a dear!
In '59 in gay Par-ee,
We went and had us quite a spree!
In '60, my dear, you wept for 30.
You're handsome as ever and even flirty!
In '61, need I tell you this?
I love each year of wedded bliss.
My darling, each year with you
Is better than I ever knew.
I love you more each passing day.
I thank the Lord for you, and pray…
God will bless you with fruit for Him
And make me worthy of such a gem.
I love you. – Norma

Our ministry through the Thursday children's Bible club continued through the fall. In October, we praised the Lord for thirty-six children who came one week. For the second time in a row, the commandant's children all jumped in the car to come with us. We prayed that some of these children would go with us to camp in December; two of the commandant's daughters wanted so badly to go.

On a village visitation in late October, I called on Tarana, who lived in a compound that Mildred Dibble had taken me to in the past. It was such a busy thoroughfare, with a path going right through the compound where the ladies had all kinds of condiments for sale, such as hot peppers, dosso maray, dried fish, spices, and so forth. It was so busy and noisy I doubted I could ever draw the women together to give them a Bible lesson. However, the Lord gave grace, and I was able to give the whole Gospel story while sitting on a log beside Tarana. Several women gathered around to listen, and even two men paused, listened, and looked at the pictures. After that, I went to a compound where I have always been afraid to return since Mildred and I got the cold treatment from a few Muslim teachers who were there. That day, I paused at the entrance and saw them chanting away, so I gingerly walked on. Next, I got lost in a maze of little pathways, finally coming out near Namata's mother's compound. I went to greet her and asked for little three-year-old Rikiya, who was always wanting to come home with me. They said she was sick, so I went to see her and found out that measles was rampant in the village. So many children in Africa die from measles complications.

During our time in France, we learned that all stores, schools, and offices closed from noon until 3:00 p.m. for *le sieste*, or rest. This gave three hours for the courses of French meals to be served. The French colonialists had carried this custom down to the colonies with them, so Niger practiced this too. After our noon meal, we had family devotions, then retreated to our beds to read and maybe sleep a little. The children knew they had to stay on their beds and not be noisy, whether they slept or not. In Africa, it was really good and beneficial to not be working during the hottest hours of the day. Sometimes the intenseness of the heat was measured by how many quarts of water one drank or how many showers one took. A four-shower day meant you took a shower before breakfast, before and after rest hour, and again before going to bed at night!

In Zarma customs, the left hand is your "bad" hand. It was the hand used for personal hygiene after going to the potty (or "into the bush" as Africans say). It is the hand with which you can make someone else fighting angry by extending it with all fingers pointing toward that person. It means you are silently calling out the private parts of that person's parents, an equivalent of cursing them. Fistfights have broken out in classrooms because a student made that gesture to another student across the room. You are never to receive a gift with your left hand, or you are insulting the giver. When you give someone something, the recipient bends slightly from the waist toward you and extends both hands, palm sides up, to receive it. We taught Rebecca and Jonathan to do this, and it always brought a huge smile to the Africans. They said, *"Ni ize ga waani saabuyan!"* ("Your child knows how to be properly thankful!")

One day in Gaya, Heath and I were rudely awakened by someone tapping their nails on the aluminum of our screen. While I was putting on my robe, we heard the person banging on our front aluminum pan shutter. I arrived at our screen door in time to see a crazy woman, completely naked, leaving. She came back later to stand, ranting and raving, on our little cement patio out front. She spoke Fulani, and we were glad we couldn't understand her, realizing the depths of the filth of unregenerate minds. Believe me, your screen door surely does look thin and flimsy when that is the only thing between you and an insane person (or another time, a rabid dog!). The Lord was our Protector and Helper!

In November 1961, Glen and Anne Nunemaker and their children came down from Dosso. Glen went with Heath, Kimba, and Ibrahim on a trek, reaching seventeen villages in the three days they were out. As far as they knew, many of these villages had never had the Gospel preached there before. They slept in the Hausa village of Yélou where the village chief really had the people under his thumb. When he told them to gather to hear the preaching, they gathered and were silent. After the preaching, they had a question-and-answer period. The first question: "Was Jesus Christ God or God's Son?" This is the vital belief that Muslims reject by saying, *"I mana Irikoy hay, Irikoy mo mana hay."* ("No one gave birth to God, and God never gave birth to anyone.")

Anne Nunemaker and I enjoyed sweet fellowship at home while our husbands were in the bush. One evening, I decided to take Anne and the children to the river to see if we could catch sight of the hippopotami that were there. They gave us a nice surprise by coming clear out of the water. Usually they stayed submerged while we only saw their eyes and noses and heard their grunting! Enjoying our time by the river, we stayed longer than we had expected, so it was already dark when we got home. I had forgotten to bring a flashlight, so consequently I had to feel my way into the dark house to look for the pressure lanterns to light. Quickly getting them lit, Anne and I were busy fixing supper when we heard the children shout excitedly, "SNAKE!" We rushed into the room where they were playing on the floor and saw a poisonous viper just a few feet away! The Lord again showed His goodness to us.

I asked our Muslim house helper to throw the snake into the woodstove fire after we killed it. He refused, believing that if you burn a snake in a fire and later its species bites you, you will die because there is no medicine that can save you. I scooped it up into a dustpan and threw it into the fire, so I guess I was then under a superstitious curse. Later I thought of Paul when the viper fastened itself to his hand, "And he shook off the beast into the fire and felt no harm" (Acts 28:5).

Glen, Anne, Steve, and Sam were with us until after Thanksgiving dinner, then they had to leave to get back for a new converts class in Dosso. It was such a treat to have them with us. It was lonely after they left, and tears came to my eyes as their car disappeared down the road. When Jonathan woke from his nap, he burst into tears, missing Stevie and Sam so much.

For quite some time, Heath had wanted to rent a horse for Kimba to use in going out to preach in the many villages surrounding Gaya. However, he had just about given up the idea because there was no way we could afford to rent a horse from our living allowance. Heath had written a prayer letter about villages where he and Kimba had trekked, saying, "We hope to get back there someday by horse, if not by car." Then he forgot about saying that until we received a letter from our church in Dayton. Mrs. Curtis Cox, had read our letter to the ladies Sunday School class, who were our wonderful and faithful prayer supporters.

We were completely taken by surprise when we received a letter from Mrs. Clyde Lewis, saying, "Our ladies' class has taken as a project *the horse you need*. Please write and tell us the amount needed to buy the horse, saddle, and bridle." We needed $200. The Emmanuel ladies were very enthusiastic about this project. Barney Armstrong made a nice sign with a painted wooden horse on it to post at church with an indicator of how the funds were coming in. Kimba was most often the one who trekked on this horse, taking the Gospel message to many small villages.

During one of Kimba's treks on horseback, he arrived in the first village toward evening and went first to greet the village chief and ask permission to preach. The chief granted permission then called all the people together to hear. After Kimba had preached, he went into the hut provided for visitors and stretched out on the mat. He began to hear the people gathering again outside, and a Hausa Muslim imam began to teach. Not knowing Kimba was there and could hear everything, the Muslim teacher warned, "Beware of those who preach Christ. They will cause you to be lost forever because all they preach is a bunch of white man's lies. They teach that God had a son, and we know God never had a son." After listening to this sort of preaching for a while, Kimba came out of the guest hut and asked if he could say a few words, especially about how we know that Jesus is the Son of God. Kimba explained that we believe this because God Himself said so. It is not the word of man but the Word of God. "Look," Kimba pleaded. "Even the Koran says that God's spirit descended on Mary. If of that Jesus Christ was born, how can we say He was not the Son of God?" A profound silence followed. The imam wanted to argue, but it was late and soon the people left to go to retire for the night. The next morning, Kimba sought out some of the men and told them he wanted to explain more to them. "No," they said. "We understand very well all you have told us, and although we didn't say anything when the imam was arguing, we understand." The village chief extended an invitation for Kimba to come again. "The preaching you did brought rejoicing to our hearts," he affirmed.

One afternoon, I made a visit to a woman in the village who had a sweet new baby girl, but I was appalled by the filth. The mother had a dirty cloth wrapped around the baby that smelled terrible. After holding her, my clothes smelled the same way when I arrived home. There were so many who lived in such dreadful situations. That young mother was sitting on a straw mat with a few dirty rags wrapped around her. A pot of water was boiling on three stones on the sand floor, and the smoke slowly made its way out the small window. In the water were leaves making a solution called *giti*. She would bathe the baby in this solution, and she and the baby also would drink it. There were a few dirty pots scattered through the hut and flies, flies, flies everywhere. Somehow this depressing outward condition only pointed to their spiritual condition, which was far worse. I was very thankful for baby layettes made for me by ladies' missionary class fellowships in our supporting churches. Often there were two little outfits, a bonnet, and a receiving blanket in each set. The new mothers loved those new, clean, good-smelling gifts. Taking soap to a new mother as a baby gift was quite acceptable so I gave soap too.

The Lord gave me many opportunities for children's classes because children were almost constantly in our yard. Their little hearts were so open. I realized that many would never dare to come to us in a few years. We prayed that in those days the seed would remain in their hearts and one day germinate. One day I was working in the kitchen and heard little Settu singing outside, *"Yesu ga ba boro kulu."* ("Jesus loves everyone.") Often as I presented a Bible lesson to the ladies in a compound courtyard, they were shelling beans, nursing their babies, pounding grain, or engaging in some other activity as they listened.

Ibrahim (nicknamed Ariya), from Gao, Mali, came to us in 1961. At a young age, he was given to a Muslim teacher to be trained to become a Muslim teacher. Life is very hard for these young disciples, called *talib-izey*, who ranged in age from around seven to fourteen years old. The Muslim teacher traveled from town to town with them, teaching them to read and memorize long passages from the Koran. Really, all they could do was learn to pronounce the words of the Koran in Arabic. Most often neither the teacher nor the disciples spoke or understood Arabic.

The lives of the *talib-izey* were difficult. When the nights were cold, they shivered with scant clothing and no blankets. The Muslim priest-teacher did not feed them, so they had to go from house to house or into the market to beg for their food. They also begged for money, which they had to turn over to the Muslim teacher.

The *talib-izey* had to go to the bush to collect firewood to be used at night to build a large bonfire so they could read and chant the Koran for hours. The loud chanting (yelling) could be heard long into the night across the street from us where a Muslim teacher lived. He walked among them with a stick or reed to hit them over the head if they hesitated while reciting or weren't progressing as he wanted.

Ariya and the group with the Muslim teacher ended up in Gaya, Niger. One day, as he walked past the mission, he heard the missionary reading the Gospel of John to a converted Muslim, so he stopped to listen. The next day, he came and listened some more. His friends began to ask, "Why are you going to the infidels' compound? Don't go there!" Ariya stopped coming, but the missionary saw him again and asked him why. So he began to visit the missionary and listen again many times. However, when the Muslim prayer call was heard, Ariya would excuse himself to go pray at the Mosque next door.

Finally, one evening as he went back to the compound where the Muslim teacher and *talib-izey* were, they told him he couldn't eat with them because he continued to associate with the followers of Almasihu (Christ). Angry, Ariya picked up his things and went to tell the missionaries. They took him in, and he continued to hear God's Word, eventually opening his heart to receive Christ as his Savior. Eleven months later, he was baptized. The news went quickly to distant Gao, so Ariya's brother and some family came after him, telling him he had to come home. He refused. A large crowd of Hausas gathered in front of the missionaries' home to force him to go home. The missionaries called the commandant who said the boy must choose for himself. Ariya was afraid of his ferocious brother, so he told the missionaries, "I must go with him, but I will come back." The missionaries were very sad because Ariya had shown so much promise.

We did not know any of Ariya's background when he showed up at our door five years later, saying he still believed in Christ but had not been walking with Him. He wanted to repent and study God's Word again. He was intelligent and a good student as Heath taught him. We prayed, and asked others to pray, that he would be grounded in the faith, grow in the Lord, and become a faithful minister of the Truth. He had a marvelous intellect but needed maturity and stability. Satan seemed to be fighting him each step of the way, and we were earnest in prayer for him.

We were glad to have him with us for a number of months, but he left again, returned to the capital, and began working for a French family where he earned more money. They eventually took him back to France with them, and we lost contact. Once he got to France, he wanted to stay there. I sensed a deep hurt in Ariya because his parents gave him to the Muslim teacher, and he was sent off at such a tender age.

In 1961, EBM's first African missionary society was formed and named Union des Eglises Evangélique Baptiste du Niger with four board members, three evangelists, and an appointed missionary counselor, Heath Bobbett. The Niger government officially recognized and gave legal status to this mission as separate and independent from EBM. Offerings from various assemblies and churches contributed to the support of the three evangelists. UEEB President Moses Oyinwola wrote the following letter to EBM missionaries:

"Dear Brothers and Sisters in Christ,

"We always rejoice because of your love to us in bringing this wonderful news of salvation. We thank God because of every one of your lives. We appreciate your great labor for the Lord in your country...Our prayer is that the Lord may richly bless you all and provide for each of your needs. On behalf of the UEEB du Niger, I thank you and praise God for all you have done for the help of this mission...this mission is a fruit of your labor, and our desire is to work hand in hand with your mission. We will be praying for you, and we need your prayers too.

"Yours in His Wonderful love, Moses Oyinwola, president of UEEB"

From my journal, dated December 1, 1961: "Jonathan wouldn't eat any supper last night and had a fever. I didn't get much sleep as I kept watch over him. His fever went down today, and he ate a little supper, but then the fever started to go up again so we took him to the *médecin* (no actual doctor in Gaya) at the government dispensary. The *médecin* was puzzled but gave him a penicillin shot and a quinine shot for malaria. I can't accomplish much else as my little boy is so sick, but I want to be there for him...Two days later, he began to develop sores in his mouth and couldn't eat or chew because it was so painful. It is so distressing to be far from good medical help when you are in a bush village. Two days later, he still had some fever and the very sore mouth, so we drove down to the SIM hospital in Dahomey, to see Dr. John Driesbach. I stayed at Bembéréké with the children while Heath drove on to Parakou for supplies we needed. Dr. D thought there was a possibility Jon was getting measles. He gave him another penicillin shot, treatment for round worms(!), and Gentian Violet granules that I was to make a solution with to swab out Jon's mouth with the sores. Jon had no fever that day!"

Christmas in Gaya

For our second Christmas in Gaya, we celebrated on December 23 because we were leaving for camp at Téra on Christmas Day. Rebecca had made decorations for the house in her kindergarten "class," and we put up all the Christmas cards we had received from the year before, plus our little artificial tree. In Muslim countries, there is no public indication that Christmas is a holiday, so we had to make our own decorations and festive atmosphere.

It was a full day. We had our family Christmas in the morning. Rebecca and Jonathan were thrilled with their toys, many from our supporting church. Elizabeth, a believer living in Gaya, came to make her *farine maasa* (fried donuts) for our celebration in the evening with the Christians. We again had our friend Quatre-Vingt prepare the sheep and roast it for us.

We sat around the fire, singing carols and hymns. I told the Christmas story using my flannelgraph figures. After a season of prayer, Heath presented Kimba with the new robe the church folks had bought for him. Lastly, we had Kool-Aid, Elizabeth's donuts, and delicious pieces of roasted mutton (*méchoui*).

From December 25 to 30, the third Camp de Victoire was held in Téra, Niger. We were excited about going and prayed we would have some campers to take. With fear and trepidation, we had gone to ask if the African commandant of Gaya would allow his two daughters, who attended my sewing class, to go. He said, "Yes, I think it is good for our children to have different experiences in travel!" (Thank You, Lord!) Also, a young Hausa boy named Garba (who grew up to be a republican guard for the government) received permission to go.

After morning service on Sunday (Christmas Eve), we loaded the campers and our family into Mary Zouck's small Peugeot truck for the trip to Niamey. At the last moment, Satan tried his all to keep the kids from going to a Christian camp. One girl dropped out, but the Lord overruled so that the other five could go. We had two girls named Foure and Zelifa and three boys – Yahaya, Hamadou, and Garba.

It was the cold season, and Christmas week brought cold winds with temperatures in the sixties. Somehow, after you have lived a while in torrid heat of one hundred degrees or more, you feel like you are freezing when temperatures fall into the seventies. We got to Niamey in time to take our campers to see the well performed Christmas program at the Niamey church. The church was packed, and the program was excellent, with many Scriptures quoted.

On Christmas Day, we added camp food supplies and a couple of African counselors into the Peugeot, then drove up the dirt road to the village of Gotheye to wait for the ferry that would take us across the Niger River and on our way to Téra. There were some food sellers at the dock, so while we waited for the ferry to return and take us across, we bought African bread and cans of sardines to eat for our Christmas dinner. How happy we were to have these young people going to camp. Rebecca and Jonathan were so good and entered into the adventure of African travel. We realized they didn't know much else, but we were so grateful for these precious children God had blessed us with. The road from the ferry to Téra was terrible – what a rough ride as we bounced through sand, potholes, and ruts! That Christmas Day evening, we arrived at Téra, tired and covered with dust. How refreshing it was to have showers and look forward to a clean bed to sleep in. Dal Washer had shot a wild turkey, and Kay had made a delicious Christmas supper with all the trimmings.

The Washers had transformed the Téra station into a campground. Large grass huts were constructed for sleeping quarters, and many sports areas were cleaned off and ready.

From my journal, dated Tuesday, December 26: "Brrrr! It is very cold in Téra this morning. Heath was out at 6:30 a.m. getting the campers to do gymnastics before breakfast. Kay informed me that I am the camp nurse(!) as well as the girls' handcrafts teacher. Heath is teaching a Bible class, boys' handcrafts, and sports. There were sixty campers. Kay said to not tell anyone that I was camp nurse or campers would be coming to me all day with minor scrapes and ailments because the treatments were free. Many of the adult African Christians enthusiastically took part in camp activities too as teachers, counselors, and preachers."

A real highlight of camp was an early morning hike to the top of what looked like an old volcano. We carried small grills for making pancakes over an open fire. These pancakes, rolled up in sugar and served with hot tea, made a great breakfast. When everyone was full, we split up into two groups, one group going up on a high hill in one direction and one up another, quite a distance apart. Then we took turns singing Gospel songs back and forth to each other. What a joy to hear those who had mostly been raised under Muslim teachings singing about God and His Son, Jesus

Christ. The music echoing from one hill and back to the other was beautiful.

Africans are wonderful actors. One evening Idé Sanda and Cecekoy dressed up as Jesus and Nicodemus, acting out John 3 and quoting the conversations word for word from the Zarma Bible. Other Bible stories were acted out, and we had campfire night also. While the young people sang or gave testimonies, mutton brochettes were being roasted nearby over hot coals.

From my journal, dated Friday, December 29, 1961: "We had a long talk with counselor David Allagbada, who has our Gaya boys in his dormitory. Yahaya and Hamadou told David they had accepted Christ in our Gaya Thursday Bible club. Garba, who has prominent Hausa tribal markings all over his face, said he wasn't a Christian. David explained the way of salvation and asked Garba if he wanted to accept Christ. When Garba said yes, David told him, "Then you can pray and thank God for the Lord Jesus." David told us that Garba's prayer was quite long. He said he believed Jesus is the Son of God and that He died on the cross for his sins. He asked the Lord to help him remain faithful. David said the prayer wasn't perfect, but it was very good for someone's first prayer!"

January 1962 saw us returning from camp and back to work in Gaya. We had been praying for Kimba to be able to find a Christian wife, and in January Kimba asked us to write to a godly Zarma pastor-evangelist, Malam Kano, in Nigeria to ask if Kimba might court his daughter, Esther. Malam Kano wrote back that if it was all right with his daughter, it was fine with him. She was attending school and would not be back home for a few months. At that point Esther and Kimba had never met.

In February, the annual Zarma Christian Conference was held in Gaya. Several carloads of men, over forty, attended. Heath had built picnic tables out of our crates for our meals together. We had great preaching. For the first time, the newly formed African mission society, the UEEB, had charge of the planning instead of the missionaries. The conference was a real blessing to all. Surrounded by Muslims, Christians in Niger are always a minority in their hometowns, so getting

165

together with those of like faith really builds them up in the Lord. Kimba and Ariya were almost tearful when the conference was over and everyone left. It was a little taste of heaven!

Dr. John and Bettie Dreisbach surprised us by coming from the Bembéréké hospital to spend a weekend with us to rest. We had given them an open invitation to do this anytime. They worked so hard at the Bembéréké hospital. Dr. D often didn't have time to make his hospital rounds until 10:00 p.m. The Africans called him "the man who never gets tired!" Bettie was suffering through a bad siege of boils and had eighteen on one leg, so Dr. D asked me to prepare hot cloths to soak her leg.

We asked them what had happened to a little boy named Biyo that we had seen at the hospital the previous fall. Biyo was about six years old when he was brought to the hospital, his body grotesquely swollen because of having untreated hookworms for a long time. Dr. D kept him at the hospital for a long time, and Biyo was so good about taking his medicines. The edema finally went away, but his kidneys were badly damaged. His mother wanted to take him home. Dr. Dreisbach wasn't in favor of this but agreed she could take him home if she would bring him to the Kandi mission station twice a week for medicine. For a while she came, and then the week came when she didn't show up with Biyo for his medicines. The Kandi missionaries went to her home to ask why. They found out that Biyo had died that morning. The last two times, he had refused to go for medicines and had told his family, "I am going to Jesus' house, and Jesus is making a big celebration for me!" Only six years old, but the Gospel had penetrated his heart and he knew Jesus was going to welcome him home!

Jon's Best Friend

Jonathan's best friend was a young boy named Idé (pronounced "e-day"). He was at our house all day almost every day. I noticed his shorts were completely worn out and that his little backside was exposed through the big holes, so I found a pair of Jon's shorts to give him. It was comical to see how thrilled Idé was. He immediately took off the old pair, giving them a final toss and kick after he put on the new ones!

One day I had shared the Good News about Christ with a woman who came to visit as Idé listened by her side. He had been asking me for days to go to his home and meet his mother. So after the lady caller left, we made our way through the village to Idé's mother's compound. His mother, Jo, was very cordial, and as she spread out a grass mat for me to sit on, Idé said, "Now, Madame, I want you to tell my mother the whole story of Jesus just like you told that other woman!" And so it was with real joy that I could again open the Word to these people and tell them of God's love for them in Christ Jesus. I returned to Jo's compound several times after that. Once as I explained that eternal life was a gift and there was no way we could earn it by good works, Jo turned to another lady who was there listening to say, "Now that makes sense! The men in this village saying we'll go to heaven if we say our Muslim prayers can't be telling the truth."

It was great sleeping inside during the cool season, and we dreaded the time when the heat came back with a vengeance. However, it only took one miserable night of sweating and tossing in the house to convince us it was time to move outside into the sleeping house or on a terrace under mosquito nets.

One night, we put Rebecca and Jonathan to bed in the sleeping house then finished up what we had to do in the house before heading out ourselves. We had only a small kerosene storm lantern to light our way out. As Heath was closing the screen door, I saw something coming toward us on the stone path. I thought it might be a mouse or a small rat. Looking closer, we saw a huge black scorpion! It was the largest we had ever seen. We wanted to catch it alive, preserve it in alcohol, and then take it back to the U.S. on furlough. We finally got it into a dustpan, but Mr. Scorpion was rebellious about our putting him into the jar we had. There were some anxious moments with his stinger tail swinging to strike, but at last he was imprisoned in the jar. He struggled for a little while after we covered him with alcohol but finally died and was preserved. We still have him in his jar to this day.

One truth of Scripture was illustrated for us through the way of life in Gaya: the metaphor of God as shepherd. We often saw flocks of sheep passing our home as they came back into the village in the evening. A young Fulani herdsman walked ahead of them with his staff over his shoulders, and another followed from behind the flock. The sheep were protected fore and aft. It was the Lord who led the children of Israel but by the hand of Moses and Aaron (Psalm 77:20). How we need to pray for the pastors of the flocks in our churches and how the people need to remember and respect their pastors! The pastors are the hand God uses to lead the flock, but we must never forget who the real leader is.

The sheep of the flocks know their master's voice. Ariya told us that sometimes out in the bush, just for fun, the Fulani shepherds allowed their flocks to mix together into one big gathering. Then the individual shepherds would go some distance away to call their own flocks one by one. The sheep would all separate in the direction of their shepherd's voice to gather round him! Ariya talked about how the shepherds recognized each of their flock and could identify them. When I expressed my wonder at this, Ariya said, "Madame, the Fulanis know each of their sheep just as your husband knows each book in his library!"

The day before Easter 1962, we spent the morning going all around Gaya to invite French-speaking Africans to our Easter service. We had thirty-eight for the Zarma service and fourteen for the French service. The French gendarme was out of town, but his wife came. Also the Dosso French agriculture man and his wife were in town, so they came. Heath's sermon in French was excellent. We waited until after dark to have our evening service. After the message, Kimba, Ibrahim, Yacouba, and Heath had a skit which everyone really enjoyed. Yacouba and Heath were the disciples behind closed doors in fear of the Jews when Jesus (played by Kimba) appeared to them in his resurrected body. Thomas (played by Ibrahim) wasn't there, came later, and didn't believe. Jesus entered again and said, "Peace be unto you." Then Thomas believed! Africans are such great actors, and this skit made the holiday very real for the believers in this Muslim land where this day was just like any other because Muslims don't believe that Jesus died and arose.

The next day, a couple of our neighbor men came to greet Heath because they had heard we had a holiday on Sunday, and they didn't know what Easter was about. It was an excellent opportunity for Heath to tell them what we were celebrating.

Owning Our First Car in Niger

At the end of April 1962, we took Mary Zouck's small truck back to her in Niamey as she returned from furlough. It was so kind of Mary to allow us to use it for a year, and we were grateful for a dependable vehicle. We learned that missionaries who were to leave soon on furlough would be selling their old (very old!) small Land Rover truck to us for $1,000 when they left. We had tried to start a car fund, but not a lot of money had come in. But by the time the missionaries left in June, we almost had the $1,000 needed to purchase their Land Rover. We were the sixth owners of this well-used vehicle. It had been rolled over by one of its previous owners, so the cab roof was loose. We tried to clamp it down but nothing worked. It bounced up and down as we drove the washboard unpaved roads. In the rainy season, the roof leaked. On the two hundred-mile trip

With Jesus Leading the Way

from Gaya to Niamey, the Land Rover just about shook us apart! We commented that "with a car like this, we really feel like we are missionaries!"

This car broke down multiple times during the years we had it. Our coworker pilot/mechanic tried to keep it running. Once in exasperation when we asked his advice about how to get it running again, he said, "My best advice is for you to park it on a hill that leads down to the river and release the brakes!" The horn did not work either, so when driving through the busy streets of town, someone had to hang out of the window and bang on the side of the car to alert people and animals to get out of the way!

Many tragic accidents occurred on the dirt roads. When we passed a car coming toward us, we entered his huge cloud of dust and weren't able to see what was on the road in front of us. One of our Gaya dispensary *médecins* was killed when his chauffeur couldn't see a broken-down truck on the road in front of him, and he hit the truck at full speed in the dust and darkness. Trucks didn't carry flares, but if they had time, they often placed small branches on the road behind them at ten- to twenty-feet intervals to warn the vehicles coming behind them.

From my journal, dated Monday, May 14, 1962: "Tomorrow is the big Muslim holiday (their New Year), which occurs seventy days after the end of the fasting month of Ramadan. I went to the village to make visits and saw preparations going on everywhere – ladies getting their hair done, preparing food, washing clothes, sweeping and cleaning the houses and courtyards, and so forth. Excitement was in the air. At Tarana's, I taught the story of the rich man and Lazarus. Then she called three Hausa women over and told them the story! Next, I visited a relative of Cecekoy's mother-in-law, Yacouba's mother (not home), blind Zeli (not home), and then Tessie's compound where I had a Bible class with her and six children. A woman started into the compound when I was there but ran back out when she saw me. Sometimes bush people were petrified of white people! Those who know us laugh at the ones who are scared. I couldn't resist telling them that when I was a small child I was terribly frightened of black people!"

From my journal, dated Friday, May 18, 1962: "Our acting field director (AFD), his wife, and their four children arrived for a weekend station visit. Heath and the AFD went to Bodjékali to preach in the afternoon, and I showed his wife around the village. It was so hot that our kerosene refrigerator was unable to make ice. Even though I was trying to keep enough water boiled and filtered for the ten of us, we wound up having no cool filtered water but had to drink it tepid! The children had a lot of fun playing together in spite of the heat."

One night shortly after we had put Jonathan and Rebecca to bed in the house, a huge thunderstorm came up. The lightning flashed and was followed by loud, seemingly close thunderclaps. I hurried to the children's room, thinking maybe Rebecca and Jon would be frightened. But as she heard that loud thunder, Rebecca only asked calmly, "Is Jesus closing His window shutters up in heaven?"

After the rains began and the epidemics of meningitis and measles began to subside, Rebecca, Jonathan, and I went along with Heath and Kimba to a bush market where they were going to preach, distribute literature, and play Gospel records. I took some Bible pictures along but wasn't able to have a children's class because most of the people were Hausa speakers. Wherever the children and I went, we were followed by a huge crowd of children and many adults. It was such a novelty in this bush village for them to see an *anasara* (white person) and her twins (so they thought) that we caused quite a commotion. I was at least able to buy some mangos and some guinea hen eggs while there. We sought refuge back in our old Land Rover, but the crowds all around us cut off any breezes, so we were sweltering.

In June 1962, after spending two hours in the Gaya market with his literature table and giving out tracts, Heath went to see the Gaya commandant to ask permission to conduct jail services, and the permission was granted. Heath and Kimba began the next Sunday. Several soldiers attended, as well as the prisoners.

From my journal, dated Wednesday, June 13, 1962: "Rebecca lost her first baby tooth today! Our little girl is growing up!" In that same month, her Calvert Correspondence school materials arrived. At the end of June, I started homeschooling her, and she was a very enthusiastic student. She loved her books and learning. One day when the winds of an impending dust storm got very strong, we decided we should get under a table in case our metal pan roof blew off (as had happened to some of our fellow missionaries in Tabla and Téra). I told the children they could bring something they considered important with them as we sought refuge. Rebecca brought her school books! She also enjoyed carrying African babies on her back like all of her little friends did.

Since receiving approval, Kimba had been making many trips on horseback (about twenty-five miles one way) over the border into Nigeria to visit his girlfriend, Esther. While she was in school, he depended on us to translate his Zarma love letters to her into English. When she wrote back in English, we translated her letters to him into Zarma. As we took his translated letters to him and hers to him, Kimba always said, "Now you forgot everything that you read or said in the letter, didn't you?" Haha! Yes, we assured him, we had forgotten everything they said to each other. We have to admit that we had a hard time translating "Dearest lover loverest" into Zarma!

Right across the road in front of our house lived a blacksmith named Hassan. He was always cordial when we met him or greeted him, but he never came to our house in the daytime when other Muslims might see him and ridicule him. He came after dark, often bringing a gift to us such as a pan of onions. This is why we called him our Nicodemus. Heath visited with him in the protective darkness. One day as Heath was preparing a Sunday sermon, he asked Hassan the meaning of *fansa* which is to redeem or to set free. Hassan told Heath that this is the word they use when someone purchases the freedom of a slave. After he had explained the word well for Heath and had given an illustration, Heath said, "You know, that is just what Jesus Christ has done for us!" A look of amazement and understanding came over Hassan's face, and a wonderful opportunity opened up to again explain the Gospel message to this Muslim man. Many years later, we learned that Hassan was actually a slave and that he had leprosy, but we didn't know those things at the time.

We were often able to help with the medical needs of those in Gaya. Many Africans could recognize symptoms of malaria, so they came asking us for quinine and aspirin. We kept a good supply on hand, and it was usually effective. If symptoms persisted, we urged them to go (or we took them) to the government dispensary. Mothers also came to me when their babies had sore, infected eyes. They told me they had gone to the dispensary but that medicine didn't help. As I had used a boric acid solution on my own children's eyes when they had problems, swabbing out the babies' eyes was my treatment of choice. It worked very well. The little ones' eyes cleared up, and the mothers were so grateful.

Each year, epidemics swept through and took many lives. Among the worst were measles and meningitis. Before the advent of measles vaccines, a great proportion of young children who got measles died. My friend Mai Dariya told me that the local belief was that you should keep a child with measles in a darkened room and never bathe the child until he recovered.

We learned to watch for meningitis symptoms when our children became ill. We wondered if the dust and sandstorms carried these illnesses from person to person because when the rainy season began, the dust settled, vegetation began to grow, and the epidemics stopped.

One morning, I called across the road to my neighbor to ask how her little boy was. She answered, *"A si no,"* which can mean "He's not here" or "He is dead." When I walked across the road to see what she meant, I learned that after only two days of being sick, he had died. I had treated the little fellow's eye infections many times. The Zarma and Dendi women had to be stoic and accept fatal news without crying. It was Allah's will and not to be questioned.

The Peanut Episode

Rebecca (about four years old) and Jonathan (two years old) were playing doctor when she came to tell me she had administered a peanut "pill" up Jonathan's nose and couldn't get it out. Sure enough, try as we might, our efforts only seemed to push the peanut farther out of sight.

For medical care, all we had in Gaya was the local dispensary. The head of the Gaya dispensary was a man named Chefou. When we took Jonathan to see Chefou he very calmly looked up the nose and said he could barely see the peanut.

He put his hand over Jonathan's mouth, holding it tightly shut, then blew a big puff of air into the opposite nostril. *Et voilà!* The peanut popped right out of his nose. We were so grateful to Chefou – and the Lord. When we got home, I put antiseptic drops up Jon's nose as an added precaution!

Part of African life was the belief in demons and evil spirits. The locals believe there are certain people, called "Carkows", who change into animal-like beings that can fly in the night. If you happen upon one when you are out in the night, it can put you in complete darkness so that you cannot see where to run. They "eat" a person's spirit, which will cause that person to die. And they kill babies. Oftentimes, even in the worst of the heat, the mothers slept inside with their little ones, believing if a Carkow flew over you at night out in the open, your baby would die.

At first, I tended to dismiss the Carkow beliefs as unreal, but then an older missionary said we should not doubt Satan's power to do all kinds of things to keep people living in fear. In the stillness of one night, as we slept outdoors, I awoke and saw a light in the large trees of our yard that shone and faded from tree to tree. It was a very still and dark night. Although it was quite eerie, I felt safe in God's protection and was not afraid.

At times we heard a demon-possessed person screaming or making animal noises in the night. Yacouba says the possessed person will often demand that people bring them a sheep, a goat, or a chicken, which he then kills in a ghoulish manner. A little boy who often came to my children's classes had long braided hair on the top decorated with cowry shells and shaved on the sides. At first, I thought he was a girl because boys usually had their heads shaved. The children called him *Follay Ize* (a demon's child). His mother had been barren for many years, so she went to a demon possession dance to ask what she should do to have children. The demon-possessed person (like a fortune teller) told her that she would bear a son, but she must never allow his head to be shaved. After her son was born, she obeyed this advice. He lived, and she had several children after that too. She came often to visit me, and I was able to present the Gospel to her. She seemed a little slow mentally, so I couldn't tell if she ever really understood or if she actually wanted to stop following demonism.

One day after Millie and I had given a Bible lesson in the home of a widow, some of the ladies asked us to go into the next compound to visit a very sick woman there. It was a typical sight, as we bent low to enter her hut and waited for our eyes to adjust to the darkness. The lady was lying on a mat. Tiny stools (*teetas*) were brought for us to sit on as we talked to her. There was a lull in the conversation, and suddenly we began to sense a presence of extreme evil. I had never experienced something like this before. A demon-possessed woman had come to the small opening in the hut and squatted down to look in. After a few minutes of unintelligible ranting and raving, she stood up and walked away. As she left, the sense of evil receded too. Millie and I were so relieved that we could tell this dying woman about Jesus and His love for her before we left for home.

Demon possession dances (*follay-foori*) were regularly held at certain places in the village. Special drumming on the backs of gourds went on for hours, along with wailing and playing a few notes on homemade violins. Certain people danced around in the middle of the crowd, imploring the demons to possess them. When the demons took over, the person would often fall on the ground, grovel in the dirt, and make animal noises. Later, she or he went into a hut to serve as a fortune teller. People paid them for consultations about whether to travel or not, how to help a school child pass his exams, a charm to wear to ward off "the evil eye" that might kill their babies, what to do for infertility, and so forth.

Sometimes in the still night in the Gaya village, while sleeping outside, we heard our neighbors talking and visiting around the fire until late at night. When the demons came upon someone and the animal noises began, there was total silence and fear.

The Gaya church building was built by preceding missionaries. It was a small, one-room church with definite western architecture. The benches were backless, made of mud, then plastered over with a thin layer of cement. The floor was also cement. There were no window screens, only openings with corrugated metal shutters that could be lowered and latched. Like the shutters on our house, these were in no way thief proof. The ladies held babies out toward the aisle when they were wetting. It didn't take long for the floor to dry in that hot climate! Also, if some of the men wanted to spit or blow their noses, they just hung their heads out a window, held a finger against one nostril, and blew. There was a small folding pump organ (totally foreign to the locals), and the songbooks were Zarma words fitted to English hymns. In later years, local drums replaced the pump organs, although keyboards were beginning to be available, and the Africans really liked these. Also, some indigenous songs began to be written by locals, which was great.

In earlier years, missionaries had translated American hymns into Zarma. However, they didn't know that African music is based on a five-note scale, while Americans have an eight-note scale. The older African Christians really had difficulty singing hymns translated from English, and they were terribly off key, while the younger folks who had been to French school could do well because they had learned music from the eight-note scale.

After the opening songs in the church and just before the message, I would take the children outside to find a good shady spot to lay down some mats and have our children's Bible classes.

Women Friends

The Lord gave me many dear African lady friends. Time after time, I told them about Jesus and why He came into the world so that we could have eternal life. As with the children I had classes with, I pray some of these women will have understood the message and that I will meet them in heaven. They were afraid to openly declare their faith in Christ, for their

Muslim husbands had every right to divorce them, send them back to their families, and keep all their children for himself.

The African Woman
by Brad Hill in Soul Craft

"She carries a large pan of things on her head down a rough path or road with consummate grace. Her hips serve as gyroscope, all forward motion, neatly distributed by the swaying waist, her head gliding along like a snake. Her neck muscles stand out and glisten in the midday sun. She has carried such loads since her short-lived youth and can go for hours without being tired."

Each Sunday, my friend Hadi went across the river to the Malanville Market in Dahomey to buy oranges, bananas, and pineapples. I could count on her appearing on my doorstep on Monday morning so that I could have first choice to buy her fruit. I learned to bargain for everything being sold. This is a way of life for Africans, and they love it. If you pay the first price you are asked, you are considered to be stupid! One Monday, I was very busy. So when Hadi appeared at the door, I hurriedly said, "Today, Hadi, please just tell me what you really want for the fruit and I'll pay it." Her face fell with disappointment, but sadly she gave me the price. I decided I would never do that again, no matter how busy I was. It was important that I play the game of bargaining!

From Zarma language classes, I learned about asking for a *jaara* when we purchased something. Most westerners didn't know they could ask for a "gift" while shopping. After the merchant and I agreed on a price and the purchases were placed in my shopping basket, I asked, *"Man ay jaara?"* ("Where is my gift?") The ladies' faces always lit up with a smile when I said that. If I bought ten oranges, they would smile and put an extra orange in my basket. Other expatriates didn't know this custom, so the ladies said we were like real Zarmas.

A funny story was told to us by Gendarme Buchillot in Gaya. He was in his office when he saw a man come by with a large gourd of tiny African eggs to sell to his wife. Madame Buchillot and the seller agreed on a price, then she went into her house to get the money to pay him. While she was inside, the seller (not realizing Mr. Buchillot could see him) took three eggs out of the gourd and placed them in the pocket of his robe. Madame returned, paid him, and transferred the eggs from his gourd to her own bowl. He thanked her profusely and then reached into his pocket and pulled out the three eggs saying, "Here is your gift, Madame!"

When Soumana's daughter died in childbirth, the baby boy, Hassoumi, was given to Mai Dariya, his great aunt, to raise until Cecelia Dillon returned from her furlough to resume her work at the orphanage in Niamey. Old Soumana wanted his grandson raised by someone who would teach him the Truth. Mai Dariya lived in Malanville across the river. We usually stopped to visit her when we were over there, and she visited us when she came to Gaya. She was a very kind person, and as far as I know, never followed Islam. Sad to say, she often attended the demon dances while carrying Hassoumi on her back. Mai Dariya had a sad life. While young, she was given as a wife to the old land chief who often beat her. She had a number of children that did not survive past infancy. Finally, her family took her back because of the beatings she endured.

Every woman (unless she is insane) is married in Niger, even if she is crippled, blind, or lame. During the time Mai Dariya wasn't married, the village people always accused her of being a prostitute. When a Yoruba man from Nigeria wanted to marry her, she accepted just so the ridicule would stop. Evidently, he only married her because she owned some property in Malanville. She bore him one son, but when she refused to sign her property over to him, he took their son to Nigeria for his family to raise, and she never saw either of them again.

In the Zarma tribe, by custom, a mother is ashamed or timid about her firstborn and won't even say the name of the child. Even if she is carrying him on her back and you inquire about his health, she will not answer. She will pretend not to hear you. She will give him a derogatory nickname, such as It or Black Boy, but she will never say his name. Even if she knows someone else who has that name, she will not call that other person by his name either. When her firstborn is old enough to be weaned, sometime after two years old, he will be given to another relative to raise. Praise God, the believers do not practice this custom and now more educated people don't either.

A Zarma woman will never say her husband's name either. She might call him, "the owner of the compound," or if he has been to Mecca, she will call him by the special title given to all who have made the holy pilgrimage, *Alhaaji*.

One good friend of mine was Tessie. She always listened willingly when I shared the Gospel with her. She was slightly plump and indeed looked as though she was pregnant. She too was involved in demon dances and asking the demon-possessed people for herbs and charms for her needs. I tried and tried to explain to her that one could not follow demons and follow God. She replied, "Madame, you have medicine that works for you, and I have medicine that works for me. Everyone has to follow what works for them." She was such a good friend, and my heart was broken that she resisted the Gospel message.

Tessie told me she was taking special medicine she had gotten from the *zima* (witch doctor) because she had been pregnant for four years. She claimed that her husband's other wife had cast a secret spell on her so that the baby would always stay in her womb and not be born! This *zima* medicine was supposed to break the spell and cause her to go into labor. I carefully explained to her that it was probably a tumor and not a baby. She wouldn't believe me.

Then I learned that it possibly was a baby! We were on holiday in Nigeria, seated at the table with two missionary doctors. When I told them about Tessie, they both said they had operated on women like that and found a calcified baby in their wombs! The baby dies, but instead of being expelled, it stays in the womb and becomes calcified instead of decomposing or aborting. Medical records say there was a woman in her seventies who had carried a calcified baby for forty-six years. A doctor discovered this when she came with terrible stomach pains and in need of surgery.

When we went home on our first furlough, Tessie had a beautiful small local woven blanket made for Rebecca. She said, "I want the people in America to know that Rebecca has a mother here in Africa too." Rebecca still has that blanket. By the time we returned for our second term, Tessie had died, as far as we know, without Christ. I don't know if a missionary woman ever gets over the sorrow and loss of a close friend who dies without the Savior.

Once after a visit from Tessie, Heath remarked, "That woman could write an almanac of local remedies!" That day she had said to take a newborn baby's urine and sprinkle it in the fire. Then the baby will never wet on its mother when he has to "go" because he will feel heat from the fire and start to squirm, so she will know to take him off her back.

Another friend, Kumbu, was such a sweet and kind soul. I always said I was never able to out give her! She was always bringing little gifts to me, and if I gave her something, she always found something more to give back to me. What sharing hearts my women friends had! For many years, Kumbu's husband was a fisherman on the Niger River. They all lived in a small fishing boat and traveled from Gaya in Niger up to Gao, Mali, fishing and selling their catch at the villages. At that time, we were told that fifty percent of children in Niger died before the age of five, but Kumbu's case was even worse. She had eleven children in all, but only two lived to adulthood. Measles and meningitis epidemics that began in the cool season and lasted through the hot season until the rains came were responsible for the deaths of so many children. Kumbu told me that two of her children died on the same day from measles.

I was always welcomed in her compound when I went with Bible stories. She stopped whatever she was doing to gather her neighbor women and children to sit on mats to hear *Irikoy Sanno* (God's Word). At that time, her husband had two wives. The *way chey* (other wife) was not very friendly and didn't stay for the Bible lessons. It was hard for Kumbu. She was kind to the other wife's children, but the other wife did not reciprocate with Kumbu's children. If the *way chey's* children came home hungry from helping chase birds away from their farm field of ripening grain, Kumbu fed them. If it was Kumbu's children who came hungry, the *way chey* would say, "Wait until your mother gets here. She will find food for you."

I explained the Gospel many times to Kumbu. I gave her one of Gospel Recordings' little record players with Gospel records in Zarma and Hausa. She played them and listened to them often. She told me she believed in Jesus, but still she said her Muslim prayers. Was she a secret believer for fear of the Muslims? Did she profess to believe to please me, her good friend? Was she unable to understand that Jesus was the only way to heaven? These are questions for which I have no answers.

One friend of mine was deaf and mute. She was called a *bebe* in Zarma. Malla Bebe came to visit me from the time we first arrived in Gaya. Although I was just learning Zarma and unable to communicate in that language, she and I communicated through pointing and motions, understanding each other unbelievably well. If someone had a baby, I could understand her motions informing me if it was a boy or a girl.

The *bebes* in Gaya had developed their own sign language and could communicate with each other too. Heath and I thought their sign for being married was comical. They pinched and pulled on their nose intimating someone was being led around by the nose! There was one young *bebe* who worked for a truck driver. He regaled us no end by imitating loading the truck and getting the motor started to drive away.

Malla Bebe's beautiful baby girl was named Boulie, which is a nickname for Ramatou. Sometimes Malla's visits were so long I had to give her a stool to sit on in my tiny kitchen so I could get meals prepared. She always said when Boulie was weaned, she was going to give her to me to raise. How sad we were after being away in Niamey for a week for an annual conference to have Malla come to our house with tragedy written on her face. Little Boulie (less than two years old) had contracted measles while we were gone and had died. I hope Malla could understand my Bible pictures and my efforts to explain to her that Boulie was in heaven and that we would see her again one day. She nodded as I showed her pictures of Bible stories and spoke to her about the Savior.

I was amazed that the women, with their tiny one- or two-room huts, could either keep house beautifully or be slovenly housekeepers. They had so many duties to perform during an ordinary morning. They went to the well multiple times to bring back buckets or pans of water for their large clay pots. The water was for drinking, cooking, and bathing. Then the women had to pound millet grain in large mortars with heavy pestles, turning the grain into flour for making millet gruel to have on hand whenever someone was hungry or to make the evening mush for their meat and vegetable sauce. There were grinding machines in the village that ground the flour if the women had the money necessary to have it done. Many men preferred the hand-pounded grain from the mortars, saying it tasted better, rather than the machine-ground grain.

All the women who pounded grain had a huge callus between the thumb and index finger on both hands. At first, I wondered if their hands were deformed! Sometimes the women examined my hand to see if I had this big callus, then commented, "You have soft hands so I can see you do not have to pound grain."

Besides sending someone to the market for meat and spices or going themselves, the women had to bend double to sweep out their yards with tiny handmade brooms only two feet long. The neat housekeepers found clean sand to put inside their huts on the floor, and as they swept the floor inside, they made pretty streaked patterns in the sand. Mintoon was a neat housekeeper. Her pretty enamel dishes were arranged perfectly in her glass-front cupboard along with stacks of hand-loomed blankets that were her wedding presents. White sand was on her floor, swept beautifully. The custom was that one was to leave their shoes at the door when entering. I almost always wore flip flops, as they did, so this was easy.

Not surprisingly, the women's childbirth practices were primitive – sometimes complicated and unsanitary, other times beautifully simple and effective. In the bush villages, there were older untrained women who served as midwives for deliveries. In towns where there were dispensaries with a maternity section, the government worked hard to compel the women to give birth there. The village women delivered from a squatting position, with the baby dropping down on a mat. The older attending woman cut the cord with a sharp shard of broken pottery and tied it with a string. Some babies became very ill with lock jaw from this and died. Every mother nursed her baby. A lactating woman, however, will not nurse the baby of another woman who has died, thinking that the orphan would cause her baby to die as well.

After she gave birth, the Dendi woman stayed in her house for forty days, continuing to boil leaves from a certain tree and using that water to wash herself and the baby. Another kind of leaf was dried, pounded into a powder, and put in the new mother's *komandi* (a fermented gruel the Dendis love). After the forty days, the new mother took the other leaves out to the bush until she found a large ant hill (sometimes taller than a man) where she spilled the leaves and returned home, never looking back. If she looked back, her period would return, and she would not have a long time to nurse her baby because she would become pregnant again. The women nursed their babies for two or three years, so they were very embarrassed if they become pregnant before that time. After she dumped the leaves at an ant hill, she was free to *humpa* (carry her baby on her back) and go about the village.

African babies are happy, loved, and constantly in bodily contact with their mothers, being carried on their backs or nursing around front. The breast is always available until age two, when the babies are weaned quite abruptly.

If their baby was often sick, mothers believed they needed to have the uvula cut out by an African barber because that was what was causing the illnesses. Poor little ones. A visiting U.S. pediatrician was very relieved when I told him this. He had seen so many babies without uvulas that he was beginning to wonder if they were born without them!

Newborns may smell of urine because of the cloth they are wrapped in for the first few weeks when they are too young to be on their mothers' backs. But as soon as the baby is carried on his mother's back, I almost never saw a mother get wet on or messed on. The mothers told me they could tell when the baby began to squirm, it was time to pull him off her back and hold him out over the ground or place him on her ankles, facing toward her while the baby went potty. What a practical potty chair!

Pets

Two of the pets we had at that point were Stumpy, an African dog, and Zacchaeus, a little "green" monkey (a common savannah animal with long limbs and tail). Stumpy was inherited from the Gustenhovens. He accepted us totally and was so affectionate. When we came home from someplace, he always greeted us with joy, violently wagging his stump of a tail and making loud howls. Mildred and I always tried to make sure he was shut in the house when we went out on village visitation because if he was loose, he preceded us into the village, barking, and scaring everyone out of our path. It was embarrassing!

Zacchaeus was given to us by some missionaries when they were ready to leave for their furlough. He was a real source of entertainment. Who needed television when we could watch Stumpy and Zacchaeus wrestle and play? Zacchaeus was attached to a tree in our backyard by strips of inner tube that were cut and tied together to make a long rope. He could go only so far from the tree when the gentle tug around his waist reminded him that was his limit. Stumpy lay quietly relaxed as Zacchaeus searched his hair for fleas to eradicate, but after a while the wrestling and sparring began. They were so entertaining. When Stumpy got tired of the play, he simply walked away, and Zacchaeus could no longer reach him.

Zacchaeus hated water – his species does not bathe – but he did get thirsty. It was necessary that we fill his water pan several times a day because after he drank his fill, he tipped it over and poured it out. One day I gave Zacchaeus a piece of a French baguette. He sat down on his overturned water dish and was enjoying the baguette when, out of the corner of his eye, he saw Stumpy coming over to his tree. Quick as a wink, he lifted the water dish, put his bread underneath in hiding, sat back down on it, and looked very innocent as Stumpy came over. No way was he going to share his bread!

Zacchaeus was one naughty monkey when he got loose! He ran into our house at any opportunity he had, hopping all over and helping himself to any food that might be on a table. If he was outside and loose, he climbed way up into our mango trees. Then he picked a mango, took one bite out of it, and threw it to the ground. Then he picked another, took one bite, and threw it down. There we were down below, trying to lure him down and get him to stop decimating our mangos. No one wanted one that had a monkey bite taken out of it!

From my journal, dated the summer of 1962: "On one of Heath and Kimba's bush treks, they visited three villages quite a distance away. Heath met a young boy at Gueza and had a long talk with him in the hut (*maison de passage*) the villagers had given them to spend the night in. This young boy had never heard of or seen a Bible before. When Heath gave him a Gospel of John and some Gospel literature, the boy's eyes got huge and he thanked Heath profusely. When Heath told him, "God wrote this book," he repeated, "God wrote it!" Heath had a very long talk with him that evening and explained to him the way of salvation over and over. Knowing he might never get to that village or have that chance again, Heath felt led to ask the boy if he wanted to make a decision, and the boy said, "Yes!" So Heath told him he would help him to pray. The boy said, "Just a minute. I want to write it down!" Heath told him what to write down and say that out loud to the Lord as a prayer. This lad seemed most sincere, and we pray he will avail himself of the portion of the Gospel he has."

In August 1962 we were overjoyed that Heath was able to lead a man to a saving knowledge of the Lord Jesus Christ. Germaine was a male nurse, employed at the government dispensary. He had asked Heath to help him learn English, a perfect opportunity for Heath to teach him not only English but the Word. Germaine was raised Catholic and had a lot of questions. He had been stationed up in Filingué before coming to Gaya. What amazed him most was that Heath had good Biblical answers to his questions. Germaine confessed that when he had presented his questions to the priest in Filingué, the priest had no answers for him. After he received Christ, Germaine wanted Heath to be the one to baptize him. Not long after his salvation, Germaine received a scholarship to go to France and study to become a nurse-anesthesiologist. In one of his letters to us from France, he told about how excited he was one morning to see snow for the first time outside his window. He quickly ran outside and promptly fell flat on his back! He said, "No one ever told me it was slippery!"

The window in my kitchen was a favorite place for the village children to watch me at my work table there. If I was rolling out pie dough or making some other dish totally unknown to them, it was fun to hear them trying to guess what I was making. They loved it when I made doughnuts and shared them. The window sometimes was covered with faces, hardly letting any light in for me to see as I worked. If some adults decided to come and watch too, they were tall enough that the window was completely blocked from light, and we had no electric lights in the house either! I loved conversing with these sweet kids as I worked. When I made donuts or cookies and there were just a few children outside, I took some out for them. These children shared! If another child arrived, they were quick to break their donut in two or three to share with others.

Rebecca and Jon learned to like almost all African food, except for the gruel made from millet (pronounced "dough-new").Once when Jonathan had been very sick, I had bought a fresh pineapple, carefully cleaned it, washed it in soapy water, and rinsed it in filtered water to try to get him to eat some. He wouldn't even touch it. A few days later he was better, so I took him with me to visit a customs officer's wife in the military compound. She had some cut-up pineapple lying in a dish on a stool, covered with flies. Shooing the flies away, she offered some to Jonathan. I quickly said, "Oh, thank you, but he won't eat pineapple at all. He doesn't like it." She said, as she held out the plate to Jon, "Of course he likes it." Wouldn't you know, he ate several pieces and didn't get sick from doing so either!

Two-year-old Jonathan had a number of words he used that "stuck." He could not say "Rebecca" but called his big sister "Ga-Ga," so that is what we all ended up calling her when talking to him. He called grasshoppers "hopgrassers." He called washcloths "dra-dra." One day, he insisted he wanted to help me carry some large pineapples into the house. I didn't think he could and kept saying, "They are heavy!" He said, "hebby," and that is what he always called pineapples. ("Mommy, the lady wants you to buy hebby!") Jonathan loved bananas. I couldn't help but smile when he first peeled a banana then came to ask me if he could have one to eat!

In September 1962, there were only six months left in our first term. In our prayer letter, we included praises and prayers for our remaining time.

Our praises were:
- Kimba's leading a Fulani man to Christ on one of his horseback treks.
- The Lord provided a Christian fiancée for Kimba – a miraculous answer to prayer in Muslim lands
- We had $1,000 in our car fund, which enabled us to purchase a used Land Rover

Our prayer requests were for:
- The African missionary society (UEEB), which "represents both the fruit and the future of the Lord's work in this land."
- The proposed French language Bible school (*college biblique*) that Heath was burdened to establish after furlough
- The salvation of those we had contact with daily in Gaya

- A replacement for us so that the Gaya station would not be closed for the year we were on furlough
- For $1,000 yet needed for our passage home

One man that Heath visited with often was named Idi. Idi was a strong Muslim man with multiple wives who worked for the rich Hausa merchant across the street from us. Idi often came over to visit with Heath and the men in our yard. Idi had a superior attitude, and he liked to embarrass people or put them down. There were many opportunities to witness to Idi, but he strongly opposed the Gospel message. One day, he came into our yard while Heath and the men were reading Scriptures and praying. For fear that one of his Muslim friends might see him present where God's Word was being read, he walked over to a corner of our yard to intently regard the garbage hole until Heath had finished. Then he came back to laugh and jeer at the Christians. We were proud of the stand they took for their Lord, but this only served to make Idi furious. He stormed out of the yard, leaving these words ringing in our ears, "One thing I know. There is only one God, and He never had a son!"

In spite of this, Idi continued to come back from time to time, and the Lord gave us a love and burden for his salvation, even though he was so antagonistic. One day, Idi came to Heath to ask about a "friend" who had a lot of pain from a hernia, and he wondered if Heath could take him to the SIM mission hospital in Bembéréké for help. Finally, Idi admitted that he himself was the sick person. He had tried the local dispensary and also African medicines but was not getting better.

We had no car allowance in our support, so we didn't always have money to buy gas. However, Idi had the money and wanted to pay for the trip down to the hospital. We thanked the Lord that Idi was willing to go to a Christian hospital for help, for we knew he would once again hear the Gospel at that institution.

Dr. Dreisbach found that Idi had a hernia, a bad urinary infection, and possibly gonorrhea, among other things, so he was hospitalized for surgery and treatment. Heath left him there with a male friend to help in his care. There were Africans wanting a ride back toward Gaya, so they paid for the gas for the return trip.

Medical Needs and Another Trip to Nigeria

Shortly after Idi's hospitalization, we left for Nigeria for more tests for Rebecca's health. For about a month, Rebecca had been having a series of nine painful boils. We took her to see Dr. Dreisbach in Dahomey where he lanced the big nasty one on her forearm and left a drain in for a few days. He suggested we take her to the SIM hospital in Nigeria for tests that the Bembéréké hospital was not able to do. We were concerned because an infection had been present in her tests in March too. After six days on the strong antibiotic, she developed a fever of 104 degrees, and we found out she also had malaria. Heath wanted to send me and the children to Jos while he remained behind in the work. I also was suffering from a toothache and needed to see a dentist. Our acting field director urged us to go together to Jos.

In mid-September pilot Bob Cowley flew us to Nigeria. Heavy rains delayed our departure in the morning, and the water on the dirt airstrip scared me as we took off. We got to Kano, Nigeria, by mid-afternoon, but customs and immigration told us we had to come back the next morning for visas. Immigration kept us waiting all morning the next day for our visas. Some bribing would have sped up the process greatly, I'm sure. Although missionaries tried not to bribe, we learned that the Africans thought our custom of giving tips was the same thing! They said, "We give incentives (bribes). You give rewards (gratuities). They are the same!" This was one of those cultural differences we needed to think about.

Rebecca's medical tests were done in Jos, and we stayed at the Miango rest home during her treatment. Tests showed Rebecca still had malaria. Our whole family got new shoes at the BATA store in Jos. They were very cheap, and Jon wore right through the soles on his sneakers within a week while playing on the cement volleyball court!

Rebecca had her sixth birthday the next day. She received new patent leather shoes from Grandma Bobbett; a pretty pink dress from the ladies' class at Emmanuel in Dayton, Ohio; a doll dress and matching pants from Jon; a purse from me; and a book from Daddy. It was just a simple celebration with inexpensive gifts, but we all enjoyed Rebecca's happy birthday. She loved being the center of attention. We got to know a lovely Mennonite couple. Rebecca reminded the wife of her own granddaughter. She gave both Rebecca and Jonathan a plastic glass filled with caramels and lots of grandmotherly attention.

We took the opportunity to see the SIM dentist and doctor while we were there. The SIM doctor confirmed happy news for us – we could expect our third child to be born in April 1963!

When we returned to Gaya, we expected that Idi would be back. We were brokenhearted to hear that tests at Bembéréké hospital also revealed that he had liver cancer and that he had passed away into eternity. The man who accompanied him said the hospital staff was wonderful and did everything they could for him. Dr. Dreisbach told us he shared the Gospel many times with Idi in Idi's own Hausa language, but he never gave any indication that he believed. Our hearts still grieve to this day for Idi's passage into a Christless eternity.

The Lord was precious to speak to us when He knew the needs and burdens of our hearts. Early in December, I lay awake in the early morning hours, thinking, "It seems the old devil has been sitting on my shoulder whispering (rather shouting) words of discouragement. True, we have won friends here among the Muslims and have their respect for our lives, but for the most part, they go on living their lives without us. Many avoid us 'infidel followers of Almasihu (Christ)' and would be just as happy if we never came back with our teachings (false to them) about Christ. 'Oh Lord,' our hearts cry out, 'Why have you called us here? It's no use. Satan has completely blinded these people, and they will not heed. They will not hear!'"

As I lay awake thinking of these things, I had to ask the Lord to forgive me. The apostles rejoiced that they were counted worthy to suffer shame for His name. As I confessed my pride and hurt feelings to Him, He spoke to my heart about a verse that has often puzzled me – Philippians 3:10: "That I may know Him...and the fellowship of His sufferings." I've often wondered what Paul meant and also what Christians today mean when they say this is their life verse. What sufferings of Christ do they want to know? Are they asking for physical suffering and sickness? As I thought of our yearning for these Muslim people and their rejection, their unconcern, He brought to my mind how Jesus wept looking down upon Jerusalem, saying, "O Jerusalem, O Jerusalem, thou that killest the prophets and stoned them which are sent unto thee, how oft would I have gathered thy children together, even as a hen gathers her chickens under her wings, but you would not" (Matthew 23:37). Oh, how Jesus suffered in anguish over these lost sheep who would "stone those sent to them."

And then I knew that this which we suffer and which tears our hearts is the fellowship of His suffering. "But rejoice inasmuch as you are partakers of Christ's sufferings that when His glory shall be revealed you may be glad also with exceeding joy." (I Peter 4:13. See also 2 Corinthians 4:17-18.)

Snake Story!

"We are thanking the Lord for His care and protection (and for the Africans' sharp vision)! Baraw was raking by the garage/storeroom when he saw snake tracks in the dirt coming from there. He and Yacouba followed them up to the house and all along the back of the house to an open hole where our cement shower drains out on the ground. They thought it went from the house to the garage, but I asked Yacouba to look in our house, for it may have entered. Sure enough, it was in our cement

With Jesus Leading the Way

shower stall! With a stick, Yacouba got the snake to go back out through the shower hole drain. Baraw was waiting with a stick to kill this very dangerous type of viper that was about two and a half feet long. I would never have observed those tracks and even had trouble seeing them when the guys showed them to me! Time and again we were conscious of the Lord's tender care for us."

In early December, Heath and pilot Bob Cowley laid out two landing strips in these remote villages. The people had never seen a plane on the ground, so they were more than eager to help burn grass, cut down trees, and smash huge ant hills to clear the way. The day that the strips were ready and the plane landed, people came running from all directions to see. Heath and Bob both had a good time telling these people about the Savior.

Later in December, we began preparing for our third Christmas in Gaya. On December 21, we went to the village of Bengou to distribute literature and play Gospel records. We bought two sheep for the church's Christmas celebration. How inexpensive they were at that time! We paid about $6 (1,300 francs CFA) for one and $9 (1,700 francs) for the other.

Rebecca and Jon had fun making Christmas cookies on Christmas Eve. We sent some to the *médecin's* little boy, Leo. That evening, several of our Christians came to practice our Christmas program and stayed until 10:00 p.m., singing hymns.

On Christmas Day, Jon and Rebecca were so excited about opening their Christmas gifts. After three years, our barrels were depleted of almost everything, but we had saved back some new clothing for them to wear back to the States. We carefully wrapped the items in Christmas paper that we had been able to save and re-use for four years and placed the gifts under our little artificial tree. Jon's comment after getting all clothes (except for a car and an airplane from Grandma Bobbett and a coloring book and a game from Aunt Ruby) was, "I only got two presents for Christmas." Clothes just don't count for gifts when you are four and a half!

Our African friend came and prepared the sheep to perfection as he always did. Our meal together with the Christians was great. That afternoon, the African *médecin* came to our house with little Leo to thank us for the cookies. We had been praying for the little daughter of Joseph, a Christian from Nigeria who was living and working in Gaya. Julie was very ill with diphtheria. The *médecin* told us he didn't know if Julie would make it, but five days later, little Julie was walking around and playing! This was a marvelous answer to our prayers for her healing!

As we prepared to leave for furlough, we had two prayer requests: that replacements would be found for us and that we would stay healthy. The first was answered, and we rejoiced that the station wouldn't close while we were gone. Two single ladies, both nurses – Arlene Spurlock and Gladys Gilson – prepared to come to Gaya to stay in our home. Kimba was already in place to do the preaching.

Our second request was due to horror stories about missionaries being detained at health inspection in the States because their children were found to have a rash or sores. One couple told us their children were covered with prickly heat, which they explained to the health authorities at the airport. Their explanation wasn't believed, so all the people on their plane were delayed, with many missing their connections, until a doctor arrived to inspect the missionaries' children. The doctor's diagnosis? Prickly heat!

Mumps were rampant in Gaya, so I was trying to keep Rebecca and Jon apart from the village children during our last few weeks. However, during my Sunday school class under the shade tree, I notice one boy pulling his shirt up over his head and buttoned under his chin. When I questioned him, he told me he was hiding his mumps! Sure enough, he had a full-blown case of mumps. The other children warned me not to laugh at him because "anyone who laughs at a person with mumps will then get them too." So, Rebecca and Jonathan were exposed in spite of my precautions, but they did not catch the mumps Jonathan was especially worried that he might then get them and not be able to leave at the end of January 1963 as we had planned. Since we left the States when he was only four months old, he was anxious to see his homeland for the first time. I comforted him and scolded myself for passing my fears on to this little guy.

Jonathan inherited Rebecca's tricycle when we got to Africa. His sturdy little legs peddled all around our big yard. It was surrounded by a wire fence and the Africans would stand by the fence and watch him in fascination.

I wrote in my journal: "Rebecca and Jonathan are growing rapidly. They will have a lot of discoveries to make when we return to the States. They were too small when we left to remember elevators, snow, tall multi-storied buildings, and so forth. One day I mentioned television. Rebecca looked blank for a moment then asked, 'What's that?' She enjoys kindergarten very much with Mommy as teacher. Jonathan just enjoys life, period! Kimba has been reaching many villages trekking on the horse." We asked for prayer for the children's health because a measles epidemic was causing many children to die in Gaya, and then a meningitis epidemic had begun also.

There were many things in American or European life that Rebecca and Jonathan knew nothing about. One evening, two Frenchmen came to visit. In fascination, Rebecca and Jonathan stood right by their chairs and watched them light up cigarettes then puff away. The next day, I saw Rebecca and Jonathan pretending to "light" their crayons then holding them in their mouths like cigarettes. When I demanded, "What are you doing?" they answered in all innocence, "We are warming our noses!" Why else would someone light a fire under their nose if it wasn't to warm it? Lots of laughs!

I remember reading about a missionary doctor and his wife who served in the Belgian Congo. When furlough time was near, they ordered new clothing from a catalog in the States for each of their six children so that they would look presentable instead of looking like they had spent the last four years in Africa. When the family arrived at the airport in Europe to change planes, the parents noticed that people were laughing and seemed highly amused as they walked through the terminal. Turning around, they found each one of their children were carrying their hand luggage on top of their heads, just like their African friends did!

Our loving Lord had brought us through deputation to, by faith, raise the support we needed, through language study in France, learning Zarma in Gaya, and living on an outstation with two tiny children. He had granted us many blessings during our first term in Gaya. I had many dear African lady friends. God had taken care of us through malaria, boils, dysentery, snakes, and scorpions. Though we lived in a mud house with no electricity, leaky roofs, termites that ate the backs off pictures on the wall, an extremely difficult climate, and Muslim resistance to God's Word, His call sustained us and His presence blessed us.

Heath had kept very busy studying, preaching, teaching, trekking into the bush villages to evangelize, entertaining men visitors, teaching English as an evangelistic tool, putting up literature tables in the markets, calling and preaching in the open *faada* where the African men gathered to visit. In addition to ministry, he kept up all the things that needed to be done in our house and yard, as well as being a great husband and daddy.

Looking back, it is frightening to think that we took two small children into a bush village without a car. We had felt we could not afford one during our first term, but the Lord provided this as well – Millie and her Chevy truck in our first year, Mary Zouck's Peugeot in our second, and then the old Land Rover in our third.

Above all, the Lord provided us with many faithful prayer supporters who lifted our names up to the throne of God daily. Missionaries are so privileged to have people praying for them. We had the assurance that He had called us to Africa and the joy of being in His service. There were many times when we failed Him, but He never once failed us.

I was seven months pregnant when we got on the plane in Niamey. We had been away from the States for four years and three months, and it didn't seem real that we were now headed back to our homeland. How different would we find things from what we had left over four years before? With Jesus leading the way, we were headed for the next chapter in our lives.

Chapter 11
First Furlough
January 1963 to April 1964

It was time for us to leave Africa's heat and head into a very cold Europe. Anyone traveling in the 1960s was always dressed up, so I left Niamey wearing my good dress and nylons. It was the first time in three years that I had put on a girdle and nylons! Heath wore his suit with a white shirt and tie, and we had Rebecca and Jonathan dressed up like they were going to Sunday School. Heath and I still had our old winter coats that had been packed away all term. Some of our coworkers gave Rebecca and Jonathan winter coats that their children had worn on their way back from furlough.

On January 29, 1963, we flew out of Niamey at 4:00 p.m. for our first home assignment. We had been away for over four years. Our third baby was due in just two and a half months. Climbing up the steps from the tarmac to board the Air France plane seemed surreal. Heath always said we knew our furlough had begun when we were seated on the plane in air-conditioning and the stewardess brought us an English copy of the *Herald Tribune* newspaper.

Air France performed a "welcome on board to France" ritual before leaving Africa. Over the loudspeaker, it was announced, "We must now disinfect the plane." A stewardess walked up and down the aisles, holding a spray can over her shoulder with the spray nozzle pointing behind her. Other airlines did not do this. It seemed a little bizarre and of doubtful efficacy. Whatever disinfectant was used, it quickly faded away, and no one seemed to be the worse for it.

It was late evening by the time we arrived at our hotel in Paris. Rebecca and Jon were fascinated by the sights in the big city. They had only known Gaya, where there was no electricity, and the only light at night was when there was a full moon. The small hotel had a cage-type four-person elevator. Rebecca exclaimed, "Look, we get to ride on the alligator!" The four of us with our suitcases barely squeezed into the elevator. We could see out of the cage in all directions as it took us up to our floor. When we walked into our hotel room and saw the beds, Jonathan – bewildered – exclaimed, "There are no mosquito nets!" Rebecca ran to the telephone on the bedside table to examine it, while Jonathan assured her it was "just a toy one." After all, that was the only kind he had ever seen in our Gaya home.

After a good night of rest and a continental breakfast that included fresh and flaky croissants as only the French can make them, we called our friends, Monsieur and Madame DuQuesne, our landlords during our fourteen months in language study. They were thrilled that we were stopping to see them. We followed our old route, a *métro* ride to Gare de Lyon then a train to Montgeron and finally a fifteen- to twenty-minute walk to their home. Heath was quite thin and chilled to the bone. He kept standing on the register vent in the DuQuesnes' home, but any heat coming out was hardly discernible. Suddenly, Madame DuQuesne looked at him and said, "He is so cold, he is turning green!" We had to buy some more warm clothes for him that very day. At the end of our first term, Heath weighed only about 147 pounds, so he didn't have any fat for insulation warmth!

We had learned from other missionaries that we could stop off at many European countries on our ticket from Niger to the States with little or no extra charge. This was a wonderful educational treat for us and our children over the years. After Paris, our next stop was the Netherlands where we stayed in a Dutch bed and breakfast recommended by Menno Travel Agency. Dutch breakfasts were new to us but delicious. There were several selections of lunch meats and cheeses and even chocolate sprinkles to put on your bread! The local people liked pickled herring, which were often sold on the streets with good fries. We did not have a taste for pickled herring, so we skipped that local treat.

Using Arthur Frommer's book *Europe on 5 Dollars a Day*, we got great ideas about where to stay and where to eat economically

We were fascinated seeing people of all ages riding bicycles, picturesque windmills, and canals everywhere. The Dutch people were so friendly, and we always seemed to find someone who spoke English to help direct us on our way. I asked a taxi driver why so many people spoke English in the Netherlands. He replied, "Because it is easy for us to learn English, but Dutch is too difficult for foreigners to learn."

Our time in the Netherlands was shorter than in France. We took a bus tour that included a visit to the Delft porcelain factory, a cheese farm, a diamond factory, and a small village on the Zuiderzee where we met Holland's "Mae West" as we visited a Dutch home. She was a rotund lady, dressed in a local costume, and was quite entertaining to the tourists. We still have the picture we took of Jonathan and Rebecca with her.

Naturally we had to buy some wooden shoes (clogs) for the children to bring home. The young man who took us on a tour at the cheese barn was comical. We bought a delicious ball of sharp aged Gouda that was not available in the States because it was made from milk that hadn't been pasteurized. The guide said, "I urge all of you to take advantage of the free samples of our cheeses here at the cheese barn because when you go to the diamond factory... (long pause)." Then he just closed his eyes and shook his head negatively. We were made to know we could expect no free samples at the diamond factory. He was a comedian!

The small town we visited had ice and snow everywhere. We kept hearing loud booms like explosions. We learned that the Zuiderzee was frozen, but occasionally the shifting waters underneath caused eruptions and explosions of the ice. At the west, Holland is bordered by the North Sea. For years the people struggled with the water as they reclaimed land from the sea for farming. Many floods happened, and lives were lost. Now dikes have been built, so the people live behind the dikes under sea level. All the railroads and many of the roads are built on dikes.

Next it was time to board our KLM Royal Dutch Airlines flight to New York. The flight went well, but as we flew over Idlewild Airport (later renamed JFK Airport) in New York, the pilot announced that the fog was so bad we could not land yet. He said he had enough fuel to circle for an hour. This was rather eerie, flying in circles and only seeing clouds and fog below. After an hour, the pilot said we had to go back to Halifax, Nova Scotia, to land. Several family members were waiting at our mission headquarters in Paterson, New Jersey, to welcome us home. While we were flying back to Halifax, the pilot announced that he had clearance to land at Logan Airport in Boston, Massachusetts. I was sitting by the window as the plane began to descend through the fog. When Heath asked, "What do you see out the window?" I looked and nervously replied, "I see water!" Later we learned that Logan Airport was built on tidal flats and land that was reclaimed from the filling in of Boston Harbor.

As I was seven months pregnant and had traveled for so many hours, my ankles were terribly swollen. We had filled out our customs papers before landing, so I asked the stewardesses if I needed to list my snakeskin African drawstring purse as a piece of luggage, and they assured me there was no need. So when we landed, I sat Rebecca and Jon down on a bench, leaving my purse there for them to watch while we submitted our bags to customs. After our bags were checked and cleared and we prepared to go out with them, what a surprise it was to have plainclothes inspectors stop me and tell me I had to empty my purse out on a table. Evidently sitting a child aside and not putting my purse there for inspection made them suspicious that I was sneaking something into the country! He looked at everything and questioned me about it. I had a small bottle of phenobarbital that a nurse had me keep on hand for Jonathan to prevent convulsions when he got fever. After opening it, smelling it, asking me to explain it, the inspector finally cleared us to repack my drawstring bag and depart.

It was late in the evening by then when a KLM steward announced that they were putting us all on a bus for a six-hour ride back to New York City. Looking back later on our situation, Heath said we were too new and naïve at traveling that we didn't know our rights. If he had known what he learned later, he would have insisted that they put us up in a hotel overnight because of our fatigue and the swollen ankles of his expectant wife. Then they could have flown us down the next day. In spite of everything, after four years out of the country, it was wonderful to be on American soil again. About halfway to New York City, the steward announced, "We are stopping for hamburgers and milkshakes, and KLM will pick up the tab for all of you." Wow! Our taste buds were dancing. What a treat!

One of the mission office staff picked us up at the bus station and drove us to the mission home. As we drove past Times Square Rebecca and Jonathan's eyes grew big, enthralled with all the bright lights.

What a blessing to find that our supporting churches had responded to our need for $1,000 for our passage home. My home church in Dayton, Ohio, had sent the final $500 so we could begin our furlough with no debt to pay back to the mission! We can confidently say that the Lord had never abandoned us; He always supplied our needs in His wonderful ways.

Visit to Florida

In February, after meeting with our mission board, the children and I flew to Miami, Florida, where Dad Christmas and Uncle Dave Christmas picked us up to drive us back to Dad's home in Florida. Dad found the winters in Tennessee still too cold, so he had sold his home there after Mom went to heaven and bought a place in Florida. Heath and his mother drove down to Dad's four days later. Dad had an artisan well which produced sulfur-odored water. Dad got such a big laugh out of Jonathan when I sent him into the bathroom to wash his hands. As soon as he turned the water on, he wrinkled his nose, made a yucky face, and turned his head to the side as far as he could while washing his hands! Dad had devised a system to aerate his drinking water so most of the sulfur smell was taken out of what we drank.

Grandpa Christmas loved children dearly and got along famously with them. The last time he had seen our children, Rebecca was two and

Jonathan was just two months old. Now Rebecca was six and a half and Jonathan was four and a half. Grandpa Christmas doted on them, as he did all his grandchildren. We had never been to Florida before and were amazed at how similar it was to Niger! When the children went outside barefooted, there were the same kinds of "stickers" in the sand, and we also killed a scorpion and a snake in Dad's yard. One big difference was the wonderful beaches Grandpa took us to in Melbourne and Vero Beach. We had lots of sand but no beaches in landlocked Niger. In February, the water was chilly at the Florida beaches, but Rebecca and Jon enjoyed it anyway, never seeming to mind the cold. We have a great picture of the two of them dressed up in their African outfits for Grandpa.

A Home and a Car for Furlough

Our good friends Paul and Allegra Whipple graciously allowed us to live in one of their 10-foot-by-50-foot-mobile homes while we were home on furlough. We also purchased a car, a Plymouth Fury, from some other missionaries who were returning to Africa.

Once we were settled into the mobile home, first on our agenda was to find an obstetrician. When I called for an appointment and the nurse learned that our baby was due in two months, she wanted to know who my doctor had been up to that point. When I answered that I had not yet seen a doctor, she said there was no way he would accept me as a patient at this late date. However, when I explained that we had been in Africa where there was no obstetrician, she understood and gave me an appointment. Dr. Howland was such a kind and gentle man.

Alan's Birth

The hospital in Elmira was going to do extensive remodeling and painting in their delivery rooms, so the doctors were asked to induce all women who were close to their due dates. They took me in at 7:00 a.m. on April 19, broke my water, and gave me some injections, but nothing happened. A few hours later, they began an IV drip, but this only produced weak, irregular contractions. Other women were coming in later than me and delivering quickly. Heath stopped in to see me (and hopefully the baby) several times when he had a few free minutes from being involved in a missions conference, but he couldn't stay with me.

Finally, Heath came to stay about 10:00 p.m., and at 11:00, our new son, Alan Paul Bobbett, was born, weighing nine pounds, five ounces. We were praising the Lord for another gift of a healthy baby! I was placed in an eight-bed ward of all new mothers, and I loved it. After all, we weren't sick or needing to be alone and quiet! We had so much fun visiting and telling each other about our lives.

The summer of 1963 was very busy for our family of five as we traveled to meetings in our churches and visited our families. In July alone, we spoke thirty different times, presenting various phases of the work in Niger. We needed to raise $75 more in monthly support. Our furlough living allowance was $265 per month. After Alan's birth in April, our support was raised to $290 a month.

One supporting church in Michigan, full of wonderful missions-minded people, decided that we should have meals in as many different homes as possible and stay overnight in a different home each night for the four or five days we were there. We had a six-year-old, a four-year-old, and a three-month-old baby! On Saturday night, we were to stay in the home of a new couple. The pastor said, "I need to tell you about these folks. The wife has a lot of problems with her nerves. They have a teenage son born to them later in life. Sometimes when they are driving on a country road, she tells her husband to stop so she can get out and just scream to relieve her nervous tension." I was frightened that our children might upset her.

It turned out that she fixed a lovely meal, and during supper she asked, "How am I doing? I have rarely entertained in my home because I grew up with a mean stepmother who told me I was worthless and couldn't do anything right." We assured her that the meal was delicious and that she was a wonderful hostess. She seemed so pleased.

After the supper dishes were done, the couple announced that they had a small travel trailer back on their property by their pond and that they were going to sleep out there, turning their whole house over to us! My fears were for nothing. What kind lessons the Lord has taught me over the years. Oh, that I would learn to trust Him in every situation, realizing that "the spirit of fear" does not come from Him.

In July, Heath was the missions speaker at the Baptist camp on Lake Lamoka, which was very near the Waneta Lake Baptist Chapel. It was good to renew friendships with some of the staff and meet many new ones too. Rebecca and Jonathan enjoyed all the activities, and baby Alan was easy to care for.

In August, we were with Mickey and Geneva in New Carlisle, Ohio. Dad was there and Carl and Carol. It was the first time my family had been together in over six years. We all were missing my mom but still praising God that we knew we would meet her again in heaven. The whole Christmas family, including Bobby, Gary, and Ruthie were so kind to put up with us and make us feel welcome in their home. By Labor Day weekend, we were back in our trailer home in Wellsburg, New York, for the beginning of the school year.

While living in the trailer park, we became acquainted with several different classes of people who lived there. Jonathan and Rebecca had only learned their English from Heath and me in Africa, but here they began to learn a few unacceptable words in English that we had to educate them about not using! Rebecca fit into her second-grade class well, and her teacher told me that Rebecca was well advanced in her reading and comprehension.

Everyone had been so kind to us that summer as we traveled, but it was hard on the children being in a different church and Sunday school class each week. When fall came, Jonathan did not want to go to kindergarten. He said, "I don't want to be the 'new boy' anymore." We felt badly that the summer of travel had been so hard on him. We had to carry him bodily into his class. I finally stayed in class with him for the first couple of days. He slowly adjusted again and started to enjoy school.

We were young and inexperienced. It did teach me that in future years, I should most often stay home with the children when Heath reported to our churches so the children could enjoy one Sunday school and one church.

Our supporting churches were wonderfully good to us. Anne Nunemaker had told us, "On your first furlough, your churches will spoil you." I do believe she was right! Our Sunday school class at Hillcrest Baptist had a big surprise birthday party for all of us. They put trick candles on the cake that reignited after we blew them out. We had never seen such things before, so we blew and re-blew and re-blew until we realized those watching us were holding their sides to keep from laughing out loud!

In September, when the children were back in school, Heath had to travel alone again. I had the privilege of sitting under the ministry of our dear Pastor Clyde Truax, the godly father to Heath that he always longed for and needed. Mrs. Gladys Truax was a wonderful mentor for me to look up to, besides being a faithful prayer warrior for us year after year.

Early in the afternoon on November 23, 1963, Rebecca and Jonathan were at school, and Heath was traveling home from meetings. While Alan was napping, I turned on the radio for news when the special interruption announcement was made that President John F. Kennedy had been shot in Texas. I began to weep, saying over and over, "This is America. This can't happen here!" A very short time elapsed before the announcement of the President's death came over the air waves. I called the Whipples who were at the trailer park office but then could call no one else because the telephone lines were so swamped with calls that they stopped working. Everyone in America was stunned. Heath arrived home a few hours later. He had stopped at a small restaurant to get something to eat and heard this terrible news announced to all who were in the restaurant.

That evening, I had to go grocery shopping. It was eerie in the supermarket. Everyone seemed to be in shock, and there was total silence as people shopped. We all wanted to do what we had to do, but we could not get away from the horror of the past hours. The story continued in the days that followed. Vice President Lyndon Johnson was sworn in as our new President on the plane that was flying Mrs. Kennedy and the body back to Washington, D.C. Jacqueline Kennedy refused to take off her blood-stained suit but wore it back to Washington, D.C., saying, "I want them to see what they have done to Jack." We can never imagine what this lady went through, seeing her husband murdered right beside her in the motorcade. Lee Harvey Oswald, the man who had fired the shot, was caught and then assassinated a few days later by Jack Ruby. There was much intrigue, and many believe to this day that Lee Harvey Oswald didn't act alone but that it was a conspiracy with others involved.

Packing Barrels

Because of Heath's burden to begin a French language Bible school in Niger, we had been given permission from the mission to go back to France in January 1964 on our way back to Niger. We would have five months of advanced French language studies before beginning our second term in Niger. With a January departure date, we began to pack for our return in the winter.

Our churches had provided so many things for us to take back to the field, so we had been gathering things to pack. It could be four to six months before our goods would actually arrive in Niger.

After much searching, we finally found some barrels to buy that had previously been filled with lard! What a job it was for Heath to wash the lard out of the barrels outside our trailer in the snow! I kept boiling teakettles of hot water to slowly melt the lard and clean the barrels, but the lard congealed again quickly in the snow. We packed the barrels in the small living room of the trailer, and soon we had no living room left. We walked a narrow path between the barrels to get to our bedrooms and the kitchen. Packing barrels is a real art! Every nook and cranny had to be filled. Shoes were packed with socks down to the toes, pots and pans were filled tightly to the brim, and so forth. Heath labored long hours on this big job. Ladies missionary fellowships helped buy or make clothing for the children. We bought things at discount and wholesale stores when we could. I am sure the cashiers wondered at our buying large supplies of toothpaste, toilet paper, and so forth. We heard about one missionary who purchased twelve fly swatters to take back to Africa with him. The perplexed clerk said, "These are reusable, you know."

That winter, we discovered that Alan would follow the same pattern as Jonathan in having frightening febrile convulsions. One cold and snowy Sunday evening, the Whipples took Rebecca and Jonathan to church with them, Heath was away preaching somewhere, and I was alone in the trailer with Alan who was sick. His fever began to go up. My phone was dead, and I felt real panic. I kept bathing Alan in cool water, praying, and giving him baby aspirin. (We didn't know back then that you shouldn't give aspirin to young children because of the danger of Reye's syndrome) His temperature went above 104 degrees. I felt as helpless as if I were back in a bush village in Niger. But the Lord was with me, just as He was in Niger. Finally, the aspirin and cool baths began to work, and Alan pulled through.

Jonathan had suffered with earaches several times. Doctors recommended eardrops and a heating pad. I felt so sorry for this little guy who patiently endured terrible earaches. Sometimes I gave him some aspirin, put in the eardrops, and he would just lie down to sleep. A little while later, the eardrum seemed to rupture on its own, leaving discharge on the pillow. Then he got relief.

In January 1964, serious news reached us from Niger Republic: Nigeriens were not happy about all the government jobs being held by better educated Dahomians after they gained independence. Because of this, Niger forced all of Dahomian origin to leave the country by December 31, 1963. Under colonialism, the French had employed these more educated peoples in schools, dispensaries, offices, stores, and government jobs. Now that Niger was independent, lesser educated nationals were clamoring for these jobs. The most heartbreaking, however, is that our most mature Christians and the most promising students for our proposed French language Bible school were among this number. One missionary wrote, "We are saying goodbye to our best Christians." Some of our mission's French school teachers, our Bible store coworker, plus many deacons and workers in churches had to leave. On outstations where the nucleus of Christians was already small, more were lost to us as well.

Considering those developments and our inability to begin the French language Bible school at that time, our mission board asked us to forgo further language study in France and return to Africa. However, nine-month-old Alan was lacking a number of inoculations necessary before we went to Africa. We had planned to do these while we were studying in France. Our pediatrician told us March was the earliest we could return to Africa. If Alan got sick and shots were delayed, our return could be even later yet.

At that time, doctors didn't like to give measles inoculations until a baby was one year old because they didn't seem to be effective before that age. Our doctor gave Alan the inoculation with no guarantees, only hoping it gave him immunity. It was indeed ineffective; after our return to Niger, all our children were exposed, but Alan was the only one who came down with the measles.

One day that winter, Jonathan was sent home from kindergarten with notice that he had chicken pox. There were only two or three small spots on his chest, and we wondered if he really had chicken pox. However, in just the right time of Jon's exposing our other two, Rebecca came down with a moderately severe case of chicken pox! Last of all, baby Alan got them and was absolutely covered! He even had them on the soles of his feet! When our pediatrician heard about it, he said, "Oh, yes. I forgot to tell you that the more a child is exposed to chicken pox, the harder the case he gets!" Jon was barely exposed, Becca was longer exposed, and poor Alan was exposed to them for weeks!

During our first furlough, I began to have a terrible fear of taking my three little ones back to Africa. I couldn't talk myself out of this terror as it grew within me. I felt something awful was going to happen to us. I didn't share my fears with Heath, and this was a big mistake. I didn't want to alarm him with my irrational fears. One Sunday, Pastor Truax preached about dedication to the Lord and promising to follow Him wherever He led us. I felt like he was talking directly to me, but he didn't know my fears, only the Lord did. As he closed the service, Pastor Truax asked who would stand and say, "Yes, Lord, I'll go wherever you want me to go." A few were standing while I was sobbing and asking the Lord to spare me taking my children back to face this unknown fear. Finally, I slowly rose to my feet and said "Yes." But in my heart of hearts, I was still hoping that He wouldn't take us back to Africa. My fears were terrifyingly real.

Planning to see my dad one more time before we left, we went to Florida, and were all packed up to fly out of Miami to return to Niger. We took Rebecca and Jonathan out of school in April, taking their books with us to complete their studies on the field.

Our time with Dad was again so special. Each time we left for Africa, Dad wrapped his arms around us and told us he loved us. His next words were always, "Well, if I don't see you again on earth, I'll meet you up There!"

On Monday, April 13, 1964, we left for our second term in Niger, packing Dad's car full of our family and luggage and heading to the Miami airport. Our first furlough had been wonderful, lasting one year and six weeks while we raised support to return. We received medical checkups and shots for typhoid, typhus, and yellow fever; raised support; reported to our churches; and Jon had adenoid surgery. We had seen the Lord work in so many ways on our behalf. He gave us a healthy baby boy, a place to live during the furlough, new friends, safety in travel, the support we needed to return, passage funds...the list could go on and on. It was good to reconnect with our supporting churches and individuals and to bring them up to date on how they could pray for us. It was great to be with our families again and see how our nieces and nephews had grown.

Four of us had come back from Africa, and now five of us were returning. Our itinerary was to fly with Pan American Airways from Miami to San Juan, Puerto Rico, then on to Paris, arriving in Niamey on Thursday, April 16. We were hand-carrying Rebecca and Jonathan's school books back with us, and our luggage was very overweight. The Pan Am man who checked us in was friendly and helpful and somehow made adjustments so that we were not charged for the additional weight, which was a real answer to prayer!

We had seven hours in San Juan. With Heath's clergy discount, Hertz gave us a tiny Volkswagen rental cheaply. We enjoyed driving around, seeing this beautiful tropical location – except for accidentally ending up downtown during rush hour! We saw tiny crowded streets lined with shops. The people were extremely friendly. When we got back to the airport, we had a typical local meal of beans and rice before our 10:00 p.m. flight to Lisbon, Portugal. Rebecca was especially excited about this dish and ate with relish! For lack of variety, we had eaten so much rice during our first term in Niger that I never bought any on furlough. One day eight-year-old Rebecca asked us, "Don't they have any rice in America?"

We also had a four-hour layover in Lisbon, Portugal. On the advice of friends, we hired a taxi driver to drive us around to special sights.

Our plane from Lisbon arrived in Paris at 7:00 p.m. The airline transported us from Orly Airport into the city and paid for our meals and lodging for 24 hours. I doubt that airlines do this anymore.

Norma Bobbett

With my secret fears of what our future days in Niger might bring, we were on our way back with our three little ones.

This Is His Place
Anonymous

This is the place of His leading
And I will go
Firm in the thought that He walks before –
He has told me so;
Though the way is steep and the rugged paths
I do not know.

This is the place of His keeping
And I will stand
Strong in the thought of the purposes
That His love has planned;
Though I long to run and to serve Him well
With a ready hand.

This is the place of His blessing –
Here or there –
Though tried by pain and the thousand frets
Of our daily care;
He will give His peace, His will grant
His joy anywhere.

Chapter 12
Second Term in Gaya
April 1964 to August 1965

Our plane trip from Paris to Niamey was stressful. Smoking was allowed on plane flights in 1964, and unfortunately it seemed as though our seats were most often close to the cigar smokers. Alan was only one year old and although he had been good on the long flights, he was getting restless on this last flight. A drunken American (smoking his cigar) was seated behind me, and he didn't like the few times Alan cried. We did have to laugh as he was telling the stewardess with slurred diction he would be visiting Dogondoutchi in Niger, which he pronounced "Dog-on-doo-chee" and that he would be going to Ouagadougou in Upper Volta. He pronounced Ouagadougou "Ew-ga-do-goo!" I'm sure the plane crew was relieved and glad when he was on the ground and off of their plane!

"Stepping out of the airplane to ninety-five degrees at 2:40 a.m. was just a prelude to the heat of sub-Saharan Africa. Daytime temperatures were already 105 degrees or more. We were back in the land where our personal comforts had to give way to being His servants among a needy people." – an EBM colleague

The hot season was in full swing when we arrived in Niamey on April 16. My head was throbbing, and I had a severe stomach ache (due to tiredness and the cigar smoke from our neighbor on the plane, no doubt). We had planned to stay in Niamey one week to get our papers in order and buy supplies before we proceeded to Gaya, but our coworkers informed us that the field council wanted us to take over the orphanage for six weeks because Cecelia Dillon had to leave on emergency furlough, and her replacement wasn't due to arrive until May 25.

Cecelia had such a love for her African babies. By the time we arrived in 1964, Cecelia had taken in five motherless children, and four more were

Norma Bobbett

accepted later. Cecelia had her own two-room apartment in the orphanage, and this is where we were given lodging.

We enjoyed being parents to the little ones. It seemed that there was never a dull moment, so after tucking them in at night, we were happy to crawl under our own mosquito nets for some sleep too. They liked our devotion times with Bible stories and songs. We sang in three languages: English, French, and Zarma. Their favorite song was "Jesus Loves Me."

Cecelia's kerosene refrigerator wasn't working well, so we had trouble with meat and milk spoiling. Heath took the back off to give it a good cleaning, and we started keeping a wet sheet blanket over the whole fridge. We tried not to open it any more than we had to, and it started doing a little better.

This refrigerator had an interesting dent on the bottom grill work underneath the door. When it was new and being removed from its crate, the men saw what looked like a big rubber tire on top of the kerosene reservoir. Closer inspection revealed that it was a large spitting cobra! The dent was inflicted during the missionaries' efforts to kill the cobra and get it out of there. Being near the Niger River, spitting cobras were often seen on the Yantala station. Millie told us she once had one in her dish cupboard on the wall. It was not comforting to know they could somehow get up the wall into a cupboard!

When the cobra "spits" or ejects venom from its fangs, it usually aims for the mouth and nose of its enemy. Some have been known to spit as far as two meters. The venom is harmless to the skin, but unless treated immediately, it can cause permanent blindness if it gets into the eyes. The treatment is to flush the eyes well with milk. Spitting is this cobra's main defense, but they are also capable of delivering their venom through a bite.

Baby Daouda

A few weeks after we started caring for the orphanage children, a Gourma man arrived with a pitiful tiny baby boy who was five weeks old but still weighed his birth weight of four pounds. He was so tiny we could fit him into a shoebox! His mother had died in childbirth, and his father pled with us to take the baby or he would die. We felt we could not turn him away but did not have the authority to admit him to the orphanage. It turned out that Cecelia said she would take him in when she returned from furlough, but the couple replacing her while she was in the States said they did not want that responsibility.

So Daouda (David) became our baby for the next year until Cecelia returned. He remained so tiny and sickly and had constant diarrhea. We finally took him to an American Peace Corps doctor who was working in an African mother-baby clinic. Much to our horror, he pulled a small worm out of Daouda's ear! He said when a baby lies on its side, milk can run from his mouth down to his ear. That is where a fly probably laid her eggs, and the worm was the ensuing larva! Daouda improved on sugar water for three days along with the medicines the doctor prescribed. After his ear infection cleared up, Daouda finally began to gain some weight.

While we were caring for the orphanage children, we celebrated Alan's first birthday on April 19. I had difficulty getting Alan to drink water in the States, but our pediatrician said not to worry about it because mother's milk was supplying the water he needed. My, did things ever change for Alan the minute we got back to Niger into the terrible April and May heat! He gladly drank many bottles of water then.

When the replacement couple arrived to take over the orphanage, we began to prepare for our return to Gaya. We spent a week in the empty house in Niamey behind our Bible bookstore. During our days in that house, my time was fully occupied caring for two babies (Alan and Daouda), Rebecca, and Jonathan; purchasing and preparing food from the market; doing dishes and housework; getting supplies ready for our return to Gaya village; and so forth.

Daouda was still having lots of diarrhea and was even hospitalized for a time. There was no one to stay with him in the government hospital, so I did. That was quite an experience. It was not a clean environment, and the various bad odors were overpowering. The local nurses gave him two injections, one of sterile water under the skin in his back to help rehydrate him and one in his thigh for the diarrhea. About 8:30 that night,

Daouda began to scream and cry in pain from the shot in his thigh, and I couldn't get him comforted or quieted down. A little while later, the European midwife came in for a delivery. She had no idea what the injections were that he had been given earlier, so she just gave him a strong drug to make him sleep. I had to awaken him the next morning when I was able to see the European doctor in his office. I asked the doctor to please let me take Daouda home so that our mission nurse could give him the injections. The doctor thought this was a much better idea than staying in the hospital.

Daouda was a good baby, and all the family enjoyed him. For some reason, he took a great liking to Heath's briefcase. It was so cute to watch him crawl over to it, smile, and pat it. His first words were an elongated pronunciation of what sounded like "I do." We all asked him questions such as, "Who wants to eat now?" or "Who sings a funny song?" His face would light up with a smile as he answered, "Ay doooooooooo!" He knew that would get a laugh from all of us.

While we were staying in the Bible bookstore house, a demon dance was held outside our house on the street. We had passed these dances before, with the large crowds that they attracted and the special drumming on the backs of gourds along with the wailing of their one-stringed violins.

As the large crowd gathered, the drums and violins continued for a long time while a couple of people performed a frenzied dance in the middle of the crowd, imploring the demons to possess them. When the demons came, these dancers fell on the ground, groveled in the dirt, and made animal-like sounds. At that moment, all drumming and violins stopped, and there was an eerie silence. Oh, the horror and power of Satanic activities! After a while, when the demon-possessed person got in control of himself, he went into a hut. A line formed of mothers with sick babies or infertile women or people asking what to do about various activities. One by one, they went into the demon-possessed person's hut because now he or she had fortune-telling powers.

Sometimes people in the States asked us if we ever were involved in casting demons out of someone. Incredibly, these people wanted to be possessed and to have satanic powers! However, we did know people who had demons come upon them before they became Christians who were delivered at their salvation. The demons just didn't return.

One young friend of ours, about fifteen years old, who became an outstanding Christian, came home to find her retarded older sister in the throes of a demon attack and possession. As young as she was in the Lord, she simply prayed over her sister and asked God to deliver her, which He did! The demons left; the convulsive writhing and animal noises her sister was experiencing stopped. Her mother had never seen anything like that in all her years as a Muslim. She was very impressed and later became a believer in Christ.

Return to Gaya

As we prepared to return to Gaya, Heath had the job of getting our old Land Rover up and running again. Then after our semiannual field conference in June he left for Gaya to get the inside walls of our mud house white-washed and some other repairs done. He also got all our stored things out of the *magasin* (storeroom) to get the dust and bat dirt cleaned off them and put them into our house.

One of our EBM pilots took the children and me down by air a few days later. We were amazed at all Heath had accomplished in so few days. When we packed up our things to the ceiling in the *magasin* and left for furloughs, we carefully arranged things so that the things we needed first would be first out when we unpacked. We wanted immediate access to our beds, mosquito nets, water filter, and cooking utensils. We learned early in our married life, as we moved so many times, to make up our beds first so they would be ready for us to fall into when we had worked to the point of exhaustion while resettling in.

The second night after I joined Heath in Gaya, in the middle of the night we were awakened by a large group of young men who were gathered at one side of our compound. Each one had a can or bottle or drum, and they were making a terrific amount of noise as they pounded on them and chanted in Hausa. We couldn't imagine what was going on, and I was imagining all kinds of things that might happen to us.

After a while, they began to march around toward the front of our house, but then they turned into the village and we could hear them marching up and down the streets, banging and chanting. Before long a rainstorm came and all other sounds were obliterated by the wind and the rain pounding on our aluminum pan roof.

The next morning when I asked what the noise was for, the mystery was solved. "Madame, didn't you know something was eating the moon last night, and if we hadn't made all that noise to chase it away, the sun wouldn't have come up this morning?" It was a lunar eclipse!

It took us a while to settle in because we had daily visitors welcoming us back with gifts of live chickens, eggs, onions, manioc, and even a pretty woven blanket. We noticed that the people of Gaya welcomed us back warmly with big smiles. The fact that we returned meant a lot to them. We weren't just expatriates who came for one stay and then disappeared forever. We prayed that they would take more seriously that the message we brought to them was to give them assurance of sins forgiven and eternity with God. It was so important that we returned to continue teaching and preaching the Good News.

Jonathan wanted us to pray that our freight (barrels and crates) would arrive in Gaya for his sixth birthday on July 10 so he could have his small red bicycle to ride. We had gotten it for him during furlough and taught him to ride it while we lived in the trailer court. I tried to explain to him that I didn't think our ocean freight could possibly arrive in Gaya by then. It always took much longer than that for shipment. Jonathan had great faith as he prayed – and Mommy didn't! Our freight arrived three days before his birthday! The truck arrived very early in the morning before I was awake, so Jonathan was the first to tell me, "Mommy! Our freight is here!" His prayers were answered! I made a nice cake for him with six candles, and we had some other gifts, but the red bicycle took the prize.

Our welded-shut steel barrels arrived in good shape but our crates were badly damaged, broken, and water soaked. Our new Maytag gasoline motor washing machine had been stolen on the way. Insurance covered its loss, but we were disappointed that our much-needed washing machine never made it. Once again, we had to hire someone to wash all our laundry by hand in wash tubs.

The French had been gradually pulling out of their former Niger Colony. The last gendarme assigned to Gaya had a Great Dane, named Tarzan, who was their baby. When they prepared to leave Niger, they asked us if we would take Tarzan. On the day they left him with us and departed for Niamey, we could feel Tarzan's sorrow and grief at being left behind. It was uncanny, but on the following Thursday when they flew out of Niamey, Tarzan whined most of the day! He never bonded with us, but he wasn't mean; he only tolerated us. We had to keep him tied up or in the house because he tended to run off and return to the gendarmerie where his presence terrified the African family living in his former house.

Surprise Visitors

We often had surprise visitors requesting overnight lodging. In one month, we had a man on his way to his post at the American embassy in Niamey; two French professors from Upper Volta; a couple who worked for Maison de la Bible in Ivory Coast; and two men working with Gospel Recordings who had just driven down across the Sahara Desert. There were two buses that came through Gaya each week, and sometimes they stopped in town overnight. Since we were often the only white people in Gaya, the Africans believed we were from the same "tribe" as these visitors, so they were sent to our house for overnight.

Through the gift of a Sunday school in the States, we were able to bring back a battery-operated filmstrip projector. It almost looked like a large flashlight. Heath used the Bible story filmstrips in our Sunday evening church, and the believers said they understood Bible stories so much better. Our first experience in a bush village with the filmstrip story of Adam and Eve brought a crowd of over fifty who listened intently. Then at the next village, the crowd swelled to over 200, and Heath had a hard time making himself heard by all. Since there was a school there and some who spoke French, he offered Gospel tracts afterward and was just about mobbed! The filmstrip projector was well received as he continued using it in the surrounding villages.

In October, when Heath went back to the village of Bodjékali to preach, he was warmly welcomed. A man whom he had vaguely known from our last term met him at the edge of the village and took him to the compound where he preached. Heath played Gospel records in Zarma then once again explained the Gospel to the crowd that had gathered. The same man wanted Heath to go to his home too. As they arrived, the man's attractive young wife brought tiny stools for them to sit on and then knelt before them with a basin of water for them to share in drinking. This is an African hospitality custom of welcoming you and one of those times when you must throw your qualms about drinking questionable water to the wind for the sake of not offending. As far as I know, neither of us ever got sick from drinking village water offered in that way. Later as Heath and this man made their way back through the village, Heath asked him about his soul's condition. What a joy it was to hear him say he had accepted Christ five years before when Paul Gustenhoven preached in that village.

During our first term in Gaya, crossing the border at the river bridge was so easy. All we had to do was slow down and wave at the border guards who knew us. However, during our second term, we couldn't go to preach there as often because of the past problems when Niger had expelled all the Dahomey people from their country. Border crossings became more difficult. Just to go to the village of Bodjekcali, we were stopped at four different control points.

I was encouraged with the attendance in the children's classes on Thursdays and Sundays and the village women who came to visit me daily. The women were always willing for me to teach them from the Bible. A Zarma/Dendi custom was to give a gift to anyone who came to visit you to show how much you appreciated their visit. I used to save my five-pound whole powdered milk cans (the brand name was Klim which is milk spelled backwards!) because the ladies loved for me to give these cans as gifts when they visited. They could store food in the large cans to protect from insects, and the shiny lid reflected so well it was like a hand mirror for them. Any tin cans or jars I put in the garbage hole in the back of our yard were quickly seized by the children and taken home for drinking cups or dippers for grain or spices sold in the market.

We had ordered and received a number of Gospel Recordings' little hand-wound record players (they cost $4 to $5, including the customs charges) with Gospel records in Zarma and Hausa. It was our hearts' desire to place the record players in all the villages where Heath and Kimba had preached. There was a little crank that you turned, which made the records go around. The person playing the record couldn't put one on and walk away. He was there listening to every word of the preaching because he was actually the motor to make the records play.

A friend wrote an article for the *Conquest* Sunday school paper with a picture of Heath and the little hand-powered record players he was taking to leave in villages. Here is an excerpt:

"The local person, impressed by such a contraption, will patiently turn the crank causing the record to spin. He listens faithfully to each word uttered from the box with a cover. Over and over again, the Gospel is "preached" in the local language, so the Word continues to echo in this Nigerien village, even after the missionary has moved on to another one. Pray that God's Word sown in the hearts of the Zarma people may bear fruit unto His praise and glory. There are still hundreds of villages to be visited for the first time with the Good News. Remember this unusual 'evangelist' – the record player – as it preaches the Gospel of Christ."

We were thankful for the opportunity to share these gospel recordings with others. One such recipient was Moussa, a young bush man who came to our house seeking treatment for a longtime ulcer on his shin that wouldn't heal. We applied antibiotic ointments and sulfa powder and gave him clean bandages to change every day. Slowly his ulcer healed, and as we shared the Gospel with him, he made a profession of faith in Christ. He was from a distant village called Tondi Hinza (Three Stones). Heath gave him records and a player, which he carried on his head back to his village.

When Moussa visited, we didn't realize how strange our ways were to this bush boy. He had never seen a husband, wife, and children sitting down together at a table to eat a meal. He told us that when he got married, he was going to do that with his wife and be like us. However, when he began to copy Heath calling me "Honey," Heath put a stop to that! He said, "Moussa, I can call my wife that, but you can't!" Moussa laughed when he found out what "Honey" meant in English.

Thus, the seed of God's Word continued to be sown. Rebecca participated in our work. One day she plopped the flannelgraph board on her head in typical African fashion and, in response to Heath's query, said, "I am going to tell my playmate a Bible story." It was our delight and our reason for being His representatives in this place.

Young Alan loved to hand-turn those little record players. We didn't know how his little arm had the strength to continue turning the crank, but he listened to those records over and over, preferring them to toys sometimes. Of course, his all-time favorite toys were little cars and trucks. He and Jon made "roads" in the dirt of our yard, entertaining themselves for hours.

In October, Talibi and his wife, Bouli, arrived, and Heath began teaching Talibi. Because the two vernacular Bible school students were in different grades, Roger Bacon was teaching Cecekoy in Niamey, and Heath was to teach Talibi in Gaya.

Rebecca and Jonathan loved African food, and Bouli was a good cook. I wish I could remember one dish she made with winter squash, clarified butter, onions, and millet. The millet in that dish was much like couscous. It was delicious. Rebecca and Jonathan often decided they should go greet Bouli about the time they knew she was finished cooking the evening meal. Africans are so hospitable, and they always prepare food for extra people. So of course, Bouli always had a bowl of food for Rebecca and Jon too. In Zarma homes, anything that isn't eaten from the evening meal becomes leftovers that they eat for breakfast.

Heath took Jonathan along one day when he, Talibi, and Kimba went out to preach in villages. On their way home, about seven kilometers from Gaya and with night approaching, the clutch went out on our old Land Rover. Six-year-old Jonathan said, "Dad, I sure wish there was a motel out here someplace!" Heath had a hard time finding a scrap of paper to write a note on so that he could send someone back to Gaya for help, but eventually they got the message sent to some newly arrived Peace Corps guys who were able to go out and tow them back to Gaya. After that, Jonathan always wanted to make sure he had paper and pencil on bush trips for sending messages, in case Dad's old car broke down.

There were times when I felt so alone there in Gaya. For a time, I was the only white woman in the village. We missionary ladies often laughed about how much we bush ladies talked when we were in the guesthouse together in the capital. Although the Lord had given me such dear friends among the local women in Gaya, I could not help but long at times for members of my own "tribe" to talk to and fellowship with, in my mother tongue. Compounding the loneliness was the paucity of spiritual fruit among the Muslim people. It is not easy always being the foreigner and missing one's homeland.

The Lord blessed me in a special way as I read words from Samuel Logan Brengle in his twilight years as blindness crept upon him:

"...I have sweet fellowship at times in my own room. The saints of all ages congregate there. Moses is present and gives His testimony, declaring that the eternal God is his refuge and that underneath are the everlasting arms. Joshua arises and declares, 'as for me and my house, we will serve the Lord.' Samuel and David, my dear friends, Isaiah, Jeremiah and Daniel, Paul, John, James, and deeply humbled Peter each testify to the abounding grace of God. Luther, Wesley, Finney, Booth, Spurgeon, Moody, and unnumbered multitudes all testify. Blind old Fanny Crosby cries out, 'Blessed assurance, Jesus is mine!' So you see I am not alone. Indeed, I can gather these saints together for a jubilant prayer and praise meeting almost any hour of the day or night. Hallelujah forever and glory to God!

I was feeling particularly lonely and blue one day, so I asked Heath if we could go someplace to have a picnic in the bush. As the French say, *"Je devais changer les idées."* I needed to "change my ideas" or to be refreshed by doing something out of the ordinary. We had a little kerosene burner and a pancake grill, so I took along my pancake batter to make pancakes. We invited Talibi and Bouli to go down the road with us, across the border into Dahomey. We went past the village of Bodjékali, where we carried on a preaching ministry, and wandered down a narrow dirt cow path to the village of Koubéri to eat on the bank of a small tributary of the Niger River. At that time, Koubéri was quite a bit to the east of the main road. In later years, the Marxist-leaning government made all such villages disband and move out to the main roads. As we were eating our pancakes, two or three men from the village came to see and greet us. We didn't know one of the men was the village chief, but we told them we would like to come into the village later to tell them some good news. The chief then went back and called all the village men to meet in the open market to hear the preaching.

Our hearts were so touched when they told us we were the first ones who had ever come to their village with this Good News. One man received Christ as his Savior that day. We continued to go there regularly to preach and distribute Gospel literature. On other occasions, we took African evangelists, visiting missionaries, and short-term Bible school students to preach also. Later when the village had to move out to the main road, some of our co-laborers built a church there, which still exists today. Beautiful fruit from a simple desire for a pancake picnic.

In 1964, the Peace Corps arrived in Niger for the first time. Two young fellows were sent to Gaya – Bob and Jim. We invited them for a meal from time to time and had interesting conversations. I'm not sure what their projects were to be in Gaya, but I remember that Jim thought he could grow blueberries into a profitable business for the local people! It never happened. The only Americans who had ever lived in Gaya before were missionaries, so the locals were more than shocked to see the Peace Corps fellows in the local bars drinking and flirting with disreputable women. It wasn't long before Bob came down with a full-blown case of amoebic dysentery. The latrine in their compound was a hole in the ground to squat over and was surrounded by a grass mat. We invited Bob to come and stay with us as he recovered. He was ever so grateful for a toilet he could sit on and not have to squat in his weakened condition!

We also became acquainted with another young PCV, George Hatfield, from a town near Columbus, Ohio. Talking to George, we could tell he came from a good home, and it sounded like his mother was a believer. We wondered just where George stood in his spiritual life as we talked to him, and as it turned out God was working in his life. His girlfriend, Dottie, was a PCV too, working in Chad. She was placed at the Baptist hospital there and came to know Christ as her Savior. She wrote to George, witnessing to him of her newfound faith in Christ. He too was saved. They got back together, married, and had four beautiful children. They thought they would be coming to join us in Niger as EBM missionaries, but George's health problems made it impossible. Instead, they moved to Ames, Iowa, to have a fruitful ministry among international students at Iowa State University.

We always wanted to treat the Peace Corps volunteers as we would want our children to be treated if they were in their shoes. We invited them for meals, visits, games, and fun times at our house. Once when we invited two girls to our home, I went through the long process of making hamburgers and French fries for supper. Making something as simple as a meal of hamburgers was a lot of work! First, I had to bake the hamburger rolls (which took 2-3 hours). Next, I had to take the meat chunks I had purchased at the open market and manually grind them into hamburger to form the patties. Since no ketchup was available in Niger at the time, I tried to make a ketchup substitute with tomato paste using a recipe I was given. It definitely wasn't very good! How we enjoyed ketchup when we were on home assignment – as well as potato chips and marshmallows and hamburgers! I had made all from scratch in Gaya and have never bought them ready-made in the States since without appreciating them fully. My hand beater was ruined by all the beating required to make marshmallows.

All my efforts were greatly appreciated. That evening one PCV told us how tired she was of her continual diet of rice and spicy gravy. When she ate with us she said, "Mrs. Bobbett, my taste buds are standing up and cheering!"

During this second term, trouble was brewing in Niger as there were rumors that rebels were training in another land, wanting to overthrow the government. The PCVs told us that in their training they had been told to never ask questions of locals in such situations because "if you ask questions, you are immediately taking sides." They were also told that if they were in trouble, the local prostitutes would shield and help them. I wouldn't be surprised if this was true. Some of these women had kind spirits and wanted to be helpful, in spite of where their lives had led them.

In the nearby country of Ghana, seven communist training camps had developed as a result of president Kwame Nkrumah welcoming Soviet and Chinese communists. Instructors came from China and East Germany to run the camps. In November, Gaya officials informed us that they learned that a number of Niger discontents had trained at those communist guerrilla camps in Ghana and were coming up through Dahomey, through the bush to invade Niger. They expected their arrival in Gaya the next day. These trained guerrillas were told that they had no worries to face because the "repressed" people of Niger would welcome them and join them in their guerrilla efforts.

The gendarmes told us to let down our corrugated aluminum shutters and to stay alert and away from our windows. The fear of bringing my children back to Africa that had begun to possess my heart while on furlough seemed to me to be coming true. We put the children to bed that night, with their beds away from the windows and tucked back in corners of our eighteen-inch thick mud walls. We did not let the children know what was going on but read to them and prayed with them as usual before tucking in their mosquito nets.

There were few cars (less than half a dozen) in the small village of Gaya, but we heard the gendarmes' jeeps going from dirt street to dirt street, patrolling all night. Morning dawned without the rebels having come. A rally began under a big tree across from our house. The village people were gathering with bows and arrows, swords and spears, determined to do all they could to resist these well-armed rebels.

We later learned that the rebels had crossed the river but had gone to smaller bush villages first to raise up people to join them for the big push into Gaya. However, the village people resisted them and chased them out of their villages, so some hid in the bush until they were starving. But still the village people did not feed them. When they came begging for food, the villagers turned them in to the authorities. The invasion was a total failure!

Only then did I tell Heath about the fear I had been experiencing for months. He said, "Honey, I wish you had told me! I could have shared a verse with you that the Lord gave me when we found out the trained rebels were coming!" Ezekiel 20:38 had been on his heart: "And I will purge out from among you the rebels, and them that transgress against me: I will bring them forth out of the country where they sojourn, and they shall not enter into the land...and ye shall know that I am the LORD." At this stage, Heath felt as badly about not sharing this verse as I felt for not telling him of my fears! We learned some things from this experience.

In January of 1965, we had cause for rejoicing: the wedding of Kimba Seidou and Esther Jega. After four years of courting via letters and horseback trips, Esther finished her schooling and was free to marry Kimba. The ceremony was performed in Kamba, Nigeria, where Esther's father, Malam Kano, was an evangelist. Then they moved to Karma where Kimba was stationed at that time. Their marriage truly was a joyous occasion.

All seemed to be working out so well at that time, but later, after Esther had her first baby, she began to have mental problems. We will never know if it was postpartum depression or something else, but all through their married life, she would get better then worse, having babies, going back to live with her parents for periods of time, then returning to live with Kimba again.

From my journal, dated February 1965: "I had nineteen children in Thursday Bible club today. The story was about the boy Jesus in the temple...Alan is amusing us now with his responses and imitations of kitty, dog, donkey, and so forth...Hadi brought me a gift of onions...Kumbu and her friend came to visit. I played Gospel records in Hausa and Zarma for them...Heath had a Gospel filmstrip meeting in the chief's compound tonight...Heath worked almost all day in the hot sun (over 100 degrees) to get our sleeping house repaired and usable...Rebecca and I called on the African gendarme's wives today. One had a split lip from her husband hitting her...Boulie and I called on Kumbu in her new compound. She was making the thick, slightly fermented sour gruel that the Dendis like to have around all day to snack on. This time it was going to be their supper. Mala Bebe came today with a gift of beans and a scrawny chicken. I had washed her baby's eyes every day with a boric acid solution, and he got well. This was her thank you to me."

On February 22, 1965, Bob Cowley flew down in the mission plane. He and Heath worked on our car in the afternoon to get ready for a trek. The next day, Heath and Bob left at 7:00 a.m. for Scia to prepare the bush airstrip and to preach. They expected to be gone two or three days. They got home on February 24 then flew back to Scia, landing on the airstrip where they preached to a very large crowd.

In a February letter to our EBM treasurer, Heath wrote, "We continue to be thankful to the Lord for His daily blessings on us. Last night, Talibi and I went out in the village here to play Gospel records and preach. We had a crowd of over 50 who listened well and even invited us back next Sunday. So in spite of some trying times here in this country, the doors are still open to the preaching of the Gospel. There are also some new young men manifesting an interest in coming to Bible school."

Since there were many of the Hausa tribe in Gaya and most of the people spoke both Zarma and Hausa, we felt we should try to learn some Hausa. In order to learn, we hired a mason, Badje, who had a steady day job with the government. Since the rebels had tried to invade Niger, militias were organized, and Badje was a militia member. He arrived for our lessons two evenings a week with his gun in hand, standing it up against the wall as we studied. Life was too busy and our study time too limited for us to become fluent in Hausa, but we did learn "survival" Hausa to use from time to time. (A "survival" language is when you know enough to ask directions and ask for food, water, and the necessities of life.) We found that even if we only knew greetings in another language, the Africans were so pleased that we had made some effort to learn their language. We had many opportunities to explain the Gospel to Badje, but he stuck to his Muslim ways.

When Badje was a teenager, he had worked for two of our single missionary ladies by washing their clothes. We learned that our ways and customs can seem odd and be wrongly interpreted by the local people. We knew the two ladies he worked for, so we were really puzzled when he told us that they didn't like each other at all. We knew they were fast friends all their years of service in Niger. He said when he washed their clothes, they did not want their clothes to touch, and he was forbidden to mix their clothes in the same wash tub as he washed them. Finally, we figured out what he thought and what actually happened. The local people wash all their clothes in the same water and they do not sort them by colors. Because the ladies instructed him to not put the colored things in with the whites nor the light-colored items with the dark-colored ones, he thought they didn't want their clothes to touch!

Another misunderstanding occurred around Heath's bookends. We fixed up an area at one end of our mud house as Heath's office. His desk and desk chair were there for when he studied. We had a pressure lantern overhead that gave good light for him at night. Our house was in close proximity to the main road through the village, and since there was no electricity in Gaya, we felt like we lived in a fish bowl for people to look in at night. Although we had some curtains at the windows for privacy, when there was a breeze the curtains blew out from the window so people on the street could see in. Imagine our surprise when our house steward told us that some people in the village were saying Heath wasn't a follower of Jesus Christ but he was an idol worshipper! They claimed they had seen him bowing down before idols placed on his desk. We had two nice horse head bookends holding his books on the desk, and to the locals, these were idols that he was worshipping. We had to put the bookends elsewhere so that in the future they would see that Pastor Bobbett was reading and studying books, not worshipping idols!

As I taught Rebecca and Jonathan school each morning, we became quite accustomed to curious little faces peering in the window at us. Many times, I had to ask the children to leave because they were distracting teacher as well as students. One day a young boy named Garba appeared at the window to ask me if I had medicine for "snakes" in his stomach (probably roundworms). He had such large trusting eyes and a beautiful smile in spite of his thinness. After directing him to the government dispensary, I forgot all about him. But when prayer meeting time came that evening, he was there and listened attentively. Afterward, Heath and Talibi had the privilege of talking to him and leading him to the Lord Jesus. The next day, he was one of the forty children in my Bible club, and he was just radiant with the newfound joy in his heart.

Heath asked Garba how old he was, and he replied, "I was crawling when there was famine in the land." When Garba told us the story of his life, it was typical of Muslim homes in the area. His father divorced his mother before Garba's birth. Garba was staying with an aunt. Our hearts ached for children like Garba who never knew the warmth and joy of a Christian home. He was faithfully coming every day for reading classes. The village children taunted him with cries of *"Almasihu,"* which means "Christ or Messiah." This is one of the most insulting things a Muslim in Niger can think of to call another. One who follows the Lord Jesus Christ is considered to be an infidel.

The children weren't the only ones who made it difficult for Garba to follow Jesus. Across the street from our house was the compound of a Muslim teacher. This man had four wives but no children. He seemed to spend most of his time sitting in front of his house on a chaise lounge. In the evenings, through the darkness we could see the bonfire in front of his home and hear all the little *talib-izeys* loudly chanting verses in Arabic from the Koran that they didn't understand. We saw many farmers dropping off grain they had grown and harvested by the sweat of their brows at his house. We learned that he was watching to see anyone who came to our compound so he could report it to their families. He had found Garba's staunch Muslim aunt to inform her that her nephew was frequenting the compound of the infidels, so she forbade Garba to come anymore. We didn't see him for about a month. Then he started coming again, another way through the village and climbing over our backyard fence so the imam wouldn't see him. He said, "When I am grown, I will be able to make my own decisions and I will follow Jesus." He eventually moved across the border back to some of his family in Dahomey. We hoped and prayed that Garba would grow into a strong believer who walked with Jesus.

On March 23, 1965, we heard on our transistor radio that Gemini 3, the first two-man spacecraft, was positioned flying over West Africa. I followed Heath as he ran outside in our yard, and sure enough, we saw it go from horizon to horizon, brightly reflecting the sun! Virgil "Gus" Grissom was the command pilot, and John Young was the other pilot. How proud we felt of our home country!

One afternoon, Jonathan brought his playmate Idé to Heath, saying that Idé wanted to accept Jesus. Heath talked with him and truly felt Idé believed what he understood. When Heath told Idé that the village people would ridicule him when they found out he was a Christian, Idé said, "I won't tell them!" Heath asked, "If your father gave you a wonderful gift, wouldn't you tell everyone about it?" "Oh, yes," Idé replied thoughtfully as he caught on. Heath suggested that perhaps he could go tell Talibi, the Bible school student. He did go tell Talibi and added, "Now Jesus is watching over me day and night!" He came back to tell Heath that had given him courage. Just a few weeks later, both Rebecca and Jonathan sat down and led two of their playmates to the Lord. It was really something to see them sitting out in the shade with Bible pictures, explaining the Gospel to these African children in Zarma!

As I homeschooled, I sometimes used our mud walls for bulletin boards or to display the children's work where we had our class. Thumbtacks held quite well in our walls. Toddler Alan often wanted to be a part of the class too. Without my knowing it, a thumbtack had fallen on the floor. As I looked up, Alan was putting it in his mouth, and he swallowed it! Horrors! I panicked, not knowing what to do in our isolated bush village with no doctor or hospital there. I decided to feed him lots and lots of bread, and I prayed! Every time he had a bowel movement, I examined it carefully, and two days later, the thumbtack came through. More gray hairs for me!

Throughout our time in Niger, we praised the Lord for the wonderful prayer warriors that He raised up on our behalf. We routinely sent off prayer letters to our friends in Dayton, Ohio. They saw that the letters were mimeographed, folded, stuffed into envelopes, and mailed out. Normally, postal air mail took at least two weeks from Gaya to arrive in the States, and by the time the Coxes were done preparing the letters, it might be another two weeks before our prayer supporters received them. By then, the news was old and probably some of the prayer requests no longer valid.

There were times when the children were ill or when there was a crisis that I asked the Lord to please notify our prayer supporters that we really needed immediate intercessory prayer. We are sure He did that. Some wrote us about being awakened in the middle of the night or different times when they sensed the need to pray for us. We would never have dared to take our little ones and live in the African bush if we did not know that God's children were faithfully praying for us every day. What a blessing those warriors on their knees have been to us all through the years.

You Prayed for Me
Anonymous

You prayed for me. You did not know my need
Or that I had a fear I could not quell.
You sensed that with me all was not quite well,
And so – you prayed for me.

You prayed for me. My path had seemed so black,
And yet I knew there was no turning back;
Then, in my loneliness I felt God near,
And down the long, dark road a light showed clear,
Because you prayed for me!

You prayed for me. God did Himself attend
Honored the intercessions of my friend,
And as your prayer, like incense sweet, did soar,
He did, in love, on me a blessing pour
The day you prayed for me!

After the guerrillas from the Ghana Communist training camp had tried unsuccessfully to invade Niger in the fall of 1964, there was still tension in the country. If we were driving the two hundred miles from Gaya to Niamey, we were stopped for questioning many times by the militia, who kept a chain across the road at their checkpoints. Speaking Zarma helped, and they were friendly to us. They also used the checkpoints to help their friends or families who wanted a free ride to the capital. If they saw we had space in our vehicle, they asked us to take them.

On April 13, 1965, an attempt was made to assassinate Niger's president, Hamani Diori. A terrorist hid in the holiday gathering for prayer at the big mosque in Niamey. It was the big Muslim holiday of the sheep sacrifice. The president was in the Mosque courtyard with his entourage of government officials. The estimated crowd was 20,000 people. They were facing east toward their holy city of Mecca and going through the Muslim prayer ritual when a grenade was tossed at President Diori. He was not harmed, but a small boy was so seriously wounded that he died within minutes. Five others were also injured.

Evidence proved that this terrorist who attempted to assassinate President Diori had been trained in Ghana. Niger made this information public in June of that year during a meeting of the foreign ministers of the Organization of African Unity. When Nkrumah denied it, Ivory Coast's President Felix Houphouet-Boigny challenged his denial by releasing evidence of the Ghana training camps with their Chinese Communist instructors.

Heath had been doing some research and praying about the indigenous Bible school program, especially in Muslim countries where churches were few. Sometimes Bible school graduates felt that the mission should employ them full-time after their training. Heath's heart burden was that they would be supported by themselves and local churches, free of dependence on foreign income. Instead of taking them away from their home areas for three years, Heath was interested in men coming for six weeks of short-term Bible school studies and then returning to their usual work in their own towns. This way they could continue serving the Lord wherever they were and supporting themselves. Bob Richards, EBM's General Director, agreed completely with Heath and believed that his recommendations would greatly strengthen the work in Niger. He expressed his hope that the field council would give Heath its complete cooperation.

The Fulani tribe is the largest nomadic group in the world. Fulanis are a proud people, and their cattle are important. They raise large amounts of cattle because their wealth is determined by the amount of cattle they own.

Heath once saw a large gathering of Fulanis in the Gaya market and learned that there was to be a ritual test of manhood between two young men. He watched as a young man waited with his arm raised over his head until another man, dancing around, would finally whack him on his side with a stick. To prove his manhood, he had to survive at least two savage blows without flinching but rather by laughing at his opponent. Heath said the blows were so fierce they broke through his skin, causing large welts. Later this young man came to see Heath, telling him he was now eligible to take a bride! Heath suddenly realized this was a golden opportunity to explain what Jesus suffered for His bride – the church! The young man listened intently to a Gospel presentation that was so vividly related to his culture.

Nyaliya's Story

Nyaliya came from Nigeria in the bush region north of Sokoto. She was an attractive young woman with hair that reached to her waist. The Fulani women had special ways of fixing their hair with silver coins or even buttons intricately woven into their styles. Sometimes their hair styles and facial features made me think of Native Americans.

When the rainy season arrived, her people took their cattle to areas in the bush to find pasture. In the dry season, they had to be near a river for grass and water. Their homes were crude tents made of hides that could be taken down and carried to their next location. During the months they were in the bush, they lived on nothing but milk from their cows. She said that during dry seasons when they moved back into a village where they could eat millet or other grains again, they often had severe diarrhea from the change in diet. She had been married for a few years but was childless. An illness came upon her that totally struck her down. For over three months she was not even able to get up off of her mat in their shelter home. She begged her husband and his family to please take her to Sokoto for white man's medicine, but believing in the fatality of Islam, they said, "If it is Allah's will you will get well; if it isn't his will, you won't get well anyway." This illness plagued her for many years.

She was left with a swollen, painful cheek and sinus passages. Finally she began to get some strength back so that she could go to the distant market to sell milk, butter, and guinea hen eggs on market day. A plan formed in her mind. She had heard that there was medicine for her illness in French country to the north (Niger). She desperately wanted to get well and be pain free again, so each week she began devising a plan, saving and hiding the money she got from her sales at the market until she thought she had enough to walk toward French country (Gaya), across the border from Nigeria.

She asked her husband for permission to go visit her family who were encamped with their cattle elsewhere, and he agreed. Soon after arriving at her parents' tent, she got up in the middle of the night and began walking north. By the time her family realized she was missing, she had traveled a long distance. They had no idea where she had gone.

In village after village, she asked if the local medicine man had medicine for her illness. Their answers were always affirmative, so she paid them some money, stayed under their treatment for weeks, then moved on to another village because their medicines didn't help her at all. She knew no one in these villages, but because she was Fulani from whom all the Hausa butchers bought their meat to sell, she was always allowed to stay in their compounds. And so the weeks and months passed. In six months, she had walked over one hundred miles seeking help.

Finally, one day she arrived at Gaya. The butcher's compound was right behind ours. We only had a fence around our property, not a wall like the rest of the villagers, so she could see us. When she told the butcher's wives that she wanted to ask if we had any medicine to help her, they told her, "No! You don't want to go to their home. They are infidels, followers of Christ." She was trying another herbalist's recommendation of things that were sure to heal, but they were not helping her.

On the morning of Sunday, May 16, I had taken the children out after the song service in our little Gaya church and gotten them settled on mats in the shade so I could have Sunday school with them. I saw her come out of the butcher's compound looking at us, then slowly coming around from the back of our property to the front. She entered the open gate and came to greet me. Instead of having her headscarf tied prettily on her head as the African women do, she had her scarf tied under her chin, and a fold was pulled up to cover her cheek. She asked me if I had any medicine for her illness, then pulled back her scarf so I could see the painful swollen side of her nose and cheek. I asked her if she had been to the government dispensary, to which she replied, "No, the medicine man told me I wasn't supposed to mix his cure (some type of roots) with white man's medicine."

Needing to finish the children's class, I asked if she could come back to visit me later when the class was finished. She said she needed to go back to help the butcher's wives prepare food then too but promised to return. I honestly wondered if I would ever see her again, but at noontime, just as I was getting lunch on the table for Heath and the children, she came back. Leaving Heath to feed the children and get them down for their naps, I seated myself beside Nyaliya in our little mud kitchen.

I asked her if she had ever heard about Jesus. She said she had heard His name but really didn't know anything about Him. I used the Bible pictures we had and began with creation and Adam and Eve, then proceeded to tell her how sin came into the world. She listened intently as I told her about God's promise in Genesis that He would send a Savior into the world. I explained to her that all the prophets believed God's promise that He would send a Savior into the world, and they were all looking forward to His coming. Muslims revere the prophets. They even name their children after them – Moses, Aaron, David, Noah, Abraham, Isaac, Jacob, Jesus, and so forth. But of course they include Mohammed as the last and greatest of the prophets.

Then I came to the time when the Lord Jesus Christ came into the world as a baby. I told her Christians do not believe that God married Mary and had a son (which is what Muslims believe). I related to her about all of Jesus' good works, how He healed the sick, made the blind to see, and told people about God. He even told His disciples that He would die for our sins and that He would arise three days later. As I explained how the religious leaders were jealous of Jesus and plotted to kill him, she shook her head in sadness.

Tears formed in her eyes as I told her about Jesus' cruel death on the cross and why He suffered there – for us. Concluding with the wonderful recounting of Jesus' resurrection from the dead, I sensed the Lord was leading me to ask her if she would like to believe in Jesus as her Savior. I never had done that before with someone to whom I explained the Gospel for the first time, but this time I knew I should do it. Her response was enthusiastic and warm, "O, Madame. I believe!" Even now, my eyes fill with tears as I write this. God was so good to allow me to be there the day He gave Nyaliya the power to become His child!

The next day Nyaliya came to visit and stayed for three hours. The next week, I wrote in my journal, "Nyaliya has been here five times this week for long visits. I pray she will grow in grace." I was teaching her hymns and Bible lessons.

Miraculously, when the Lord brought our paths together, she was able to speak Zarma too. Nyaliya was fluent in the Hausa and Fulani languages. I was able to speak English, French, and Zarma. When I asked her how she was able to speak Zarma, she said that one rainy season her family had lived in a Zarma village for three months! Africans are so much more adept at learning languages than we are. We think we must study, memorize, read books, and then practice using the language. They simply live among the people and absorb the language by using it every day. This is also the way our children learned Zarma. God, in His sovereign plan, took Nyaliya to a Zarma village so that when we met we could speak in a common language.

Two weeks after we met, I persuaded her to stop the local medicine man's treatments and go to the government dispensary to explain her illness. She told them that because of the swelling in her cheek and sinuses, the pain continued on up into her head. She came back with a piece of alcohol-soaked cotton, which the nurse told her to rub on her cheek! I went back with her and asked to see the head nurse. Bonzougou had finished high school and had training in France to become a state-certified nurse. He was a kind man, always friendly with us and so helpful when our children were sick. He examined Nyaliya and then wrote a prescription for her to come to the dispensary twice a week for a series of antibiotic injections.

She said that when her course of medicines was finished, she would have to return to her people who probably thought she had died or had gone into prostitution. I felt frantic! How do you teach a new believer all you want her to learn in just two months' time? All our little Gospel Recordings record players were gone. We had ordered more but had no idea when they would come. Additionally, we were scheduled to leave from June 15 until July 15 for vacation and medical checkups in Jos, Nigeria!

Vacation in Nigeria

When the worst of the hot season was over (April and May) several of our mission families vacationed together on the cool plateau at the SIM rest home. It was July 1965. Afternoons were full of games and sports, and the children had great times playing with their friends. How wonderful it was to be out of the heat and enjoy a steady diet of fresh fruits and vegetables. We had time to rest, relax and recharge our spiritual batteries.

One day, we all decided to take a picnic lunch to the Jos Zoo. What fun it was. There were chimpanzees who thumped their chests, turned summersaults, and then held their hands out through the bars, letting us know they wanted something to eat. This worked well until we ran out of food for them. The next chimpanzee who performed and wasn't rewarded spit at the nearest person he could reach! With the exception of the one who was spat on, we all thought it was extremely funny.

A retired couple who had opened the guest house in Miango stayed on in that location in their retirement. The climate was beautiful and they were in good health, so it was a lovely place for them to retire. This couple came to the dining hall for their meals with the other guests. Mr. C was always the head of the table where he sat with his wife beside him. A teacher at Kent Academy happened to be at their table one morning when Mrs. C was being critical of Mr. C and telling him things he was doing that were not as they should be. When he had heard all he could take, he said to his wife, "Shut up and eat your porridge!" This story brought a lot of laughs when it was retold and became a private joke in our family when one of us was nagging the other. Tension was defused when one of us said, "Shut up and eat your porridge!"

Being out of the heat and stresses of the work refreshed and renewed our spirits. It was always good to look back at your ministry from a distance, share your thoughts and burdens with others, and be edified by godly people. However, I was anxious to get back to Gaya to spend what little time we had left with Nyaliya before she went home.

Just at the end of her medical treatment, with her cheek swelling and pain almost gone, God answered our prayers with the arrival of more Gospel Recordings record players! We may call Him the God of the last minute, but He is never late. How much we learn in those times we are in His waiting room. We had Gospel message records to give Nyaliya in Hausa, Fulani, and Zarma. "His method is sublime, His heart profoundly kind; God never is before His time and never is behind" ("God's Help Sure" by an anonymous hymn writer).

In Galmi, Niger, SIM Mission had a fine hospital. We told Nyaliya that if her illness ever came

With Jesus Leading the Way

back, she should go directly north to Galmi for treatment. We assured her that the followers of Jesus Christ there would treat her with His kindness and wisdom. I gave her a letter of introduction I had written to the Galmi hospital personnel in case she ever went there.

Nyaliya departed on July 25, 1965. As she climbed up onto the back of the truck, my eyes filled with tears as hers did. We did not know if we would ever see each other again here on earth. She was illiterate and was going back into the bush, far from a post office even if she could write.

And so Nyaliya was gone. My heart grieved for this new sister in Christ who had become so dear to me. Heath and I prayed for her as the months went by, wondering what happened to her when she returned to her family or if she was even still alive. We wondered if we would ever see her again. We had no idea of what the Lord had in store for her and for us in the coming months.

Five days after Nyaliya left, I was evacuated from Gaya to the Niamey hospital in a French military plane. Many tensions and stressful decisions had culminated in a panic attack. The mid-thirties seem to be a stressful time for many, and I was no exception. We had taken our sweet little Daouda up to Cecelia in the orphanage, and I was missing him a lot. We were trying to decide if we should send Rebecca up to McCaba Academy's boarding school for fourth grade. She was excited about going and about having American playmates, but it was difficult for me to think of letting her go for that time. Nyaliya had left, and I didn't know if I would ever see her here on earth again. There was the stress of constantly reaching out to Muslims but seeing so little fruit for our labors. There was tension between missionaries and nationals in other areas. I didn't realize how much these tensions were affecting me.

Right across the street from us, a large crowd had gathered to celebrate the upcoming marriage of a Muslim man to a girl who would become his third wife. The drums beat incessantly all day and there was no escape from the noise that almost seemed to be right on our property. As night fell, we began to think they would never stop, and they finally did at 2:00 a.m. – only to begin again four hours later! They were waiting for the bride to be brought from her village.

The next night, I began to have trouble breathing. Even taking deep breaths, I couldn't get enough oxygen into my lungs, and I felt desperate. We didn't understand what was happening to me. The next morning, Heath rushed to the Gaya post office to call Dal Washer in Niamey, requesting the mission plane to come for me. When Dal found out that our mission plane was not available, he called the French military, and they evacuated me on a stretcher in a much larger plane! Dal and Kay were at the Niamey airport to meet me, and I was taken directly to the Niamey hospital in an ambulance.

I wish I could remember the name of the French doctor who worked at the hospital for many years. He had spent many years in Africa and was so kind. We had taken our children to see him when they were sick, and his usual procedure was to sit behind his desk, ask what all the symptoms were, then write three (almost always three, never one) prescriptions. We didn't recall him ever examining any of us. He was also my doctor in the hospital. He felt my big problem had been too much work and stress, so after three days, he released me from the hospital. I learned later that my problem was called hyperventilating and that this is most often caused by anxiety. Some people think they are having a heart attack at the time because the heart rate can be erratic with the heart beating far too fast. The old doctor's book remedy is to breathe into a paper bag.

I recovered and later was taken back to Gaya in the small EBM plane. We thought we might receive a huge bill from the French military, but they never charged us for that special transportation.

We had been back in Africa for seventeen months, again experiencing God's presence and help all along the way. There were new things awaiting us in the next year.

Chapter 13
Continuing Our Second Term
September 1965 to June 1966

When faced with a problem or need, don't complain, panic, or doubt God. Problems are opportunities for us to praise God in advance for the solutions He will give. These are Praise Problems! Thank God for what He is going to do!
– David Jeremiah

On September 8, 1965, we took Rebecca to McCaba Academy in Niamey (200 miles away) to begin fourth grade. The boys also needed some medical attention. Alan had been sick with a fever and had painful sores in his mouth, and Jonathan needed to see a dentist.

Right before we left Gaya, we got a great picture of our children, including Daouda. Though there was no electricity in Gaya, the local photographer was cleverly able to take photographs and then develop them by uncovering a hole in his roof at noon when the sun was directly overhead. He set his son on Rebecca's lap to be included in the photo!

It was very difficult for us to leave Rebecca at the boarding school in Niamey. Jonathan missed his playmate terribly. She had been lonely in the bush, missing other American girlfriends, so it was a new experience for her, and she was happy. The old Lee House at the mission station had been changed into a dormitory for elementary children. It was a stressful time for us, missing Rebecca, but she enjoyed being with girlfriends at school. The dorm parents left in December on emergency furlough. We filled in for a short time until mission pilot Gary and nurse Pat Sheppard could step in as dorm parents – a role they filled well.

In September the replacement for our Maytag gasoline motor wringer washing machine arrived in good shape! We were so happy to have a machine for washing clothes after the years of all our washing being done by hand using scrub boards. The machine was very noisy though. When that loud gasoline motor was started, the whole village knew it was our wash day.

We were happy to have Rebecca home for the Christmas holidays. One day she was standing in our little kitchen, talking to me as I worked. I removed a large teakettle of boiling water from the woodstove to pour into our water filter and when I turned, some sloshed out of the too-full kettle onto her upper leg, giving her a serious burn. I was so upset that this accident happened. During the rest of her vacation, I was very careful to change the bandages and keep antibiotics on it. She seemed nonchalant about the burn and enjoyed the special attention she got. She mostly stayed off of her leg so it began to heal nicely. The healing wasn't complete yet when she returned to Niamey at the end of vacation. I was hopeful it would not leave a scar. Back in the dorm, it did get infected and took longer to heal. When she came home the next vacation, I looked at it and said I thought maybe there wouldn't be much of a scar. Rebecca was disappointed! She wanted to wear the scar as a badge of honor for what she had gone through!

On January 3, 1966, at 5:30 a.m., we all packed into our old Land Rover to take Rebecca back to school and to attend our Niger field's annual conference. Bob Richards was our speaker that year. I wrote, "Our annual conference has been one of the best ever! My own heart has been challenged by this conference. My desire in this new year is to live closer to Him, so the sweet fragrance of 'Christ in me' may be evident to these Zarma people and that they too will desire to know Him."

In addition to the speaker, the conference included devotions, prayer, volleyball, Bible study, business meeting with reports from missionaries, and an evening service. It was always a great time for the missionary kids as they played together and ate together at one table. The last night of each conference was Fun Night when we performed skits, plays, singing groups, and so forth. It was so much fun to just let our hair down and laugh together. I will always remember that our mission nurse had a huge box she called her enlarging machine. Someone was inside the box making grinding and whirring sounds as she put in a small object and then pulled out a large version of it. The last object she put in was a doll baby in a diaper. When our six-foot-tall coworker jumped out of the box wearing a diaper, it seemed that we laughed for fifteen minutes! That was just one example of the hilarious things we did.

It was at this annual conference that Bob Richards asked Heath if he would pray about returning to the States ten months early for our furlough so that he could come back to be the acting field director while the current director was on his year of furlough. This was a total surprise to us.

One night, the McCaba school dorm was invaded by thieves. Pat and Gary, the dorm parents, did not hear the one who came up to their bedside and took Gary's wallet off their bedside table. Rebecca was awakened when a thief untucked her mosquito net and reached under to touch her. Groggily, she asked in Zarma, *"Ifo no ni ga ba?"* ("What do you want?") to which he replied, *"Nooru!"* ("Money!") She thought he was looking to see if she had money tied in a corner of the *zaara* wrapped around her (a two-meter length of cloth that was used as a wrapper by Zarma women.) She called across to Mimi Zimmerman's bed beside hers and said, "There is someone beside my bed." When Mimi came fully awake, she began to scream, so the thief ran away. Everyone was aroused and began to light kerosene lanterns. A missionary had installed some old crank-to-ring telephones in each of the widely spaced mission residences, so everyone got on the line and learned about the thieves who had hit other homes too by cutting screens, going into the houses, and unlocking a screen door to get out.

After that, Rebecca, Mimi and Sharon all began to sleep in one bed under one net, but each awakened in their own beds the next morning. Uncle Gary and Aunt Pat evidently carried them to their own beds and tucked them in while they slept. We thanked the Lord that Rebecca didn't seem to be traumatized by this experience. Maybe it was because she knew the language and had interacted with the local people most of her life.

After the conference, our Land Rover gave us problems on the way home as the gear shift again became very loose, but we made it back to Gaya on January 12 to begin preparations for the short-term Bible school that was to begin five days later. We had four students. We heard that one other fellow decided not to come because he realized that he wouldn't be hired afterward to preach. Thank the Lord, this was just the type we hoped would be weeded out. We went to the village of Coubéri in Dahomey to see if the chief could come for Bible school, but he was sick and also had a terrible toothache. There was so much sickness in the village at that time, along with lots of eye disease.

Heath used our pressure lanterns to light up our little church building at night so the fellows could do their studying there. Some nights they had a songfest before they went to bed. It was great to hear Zarma hymns wafting through the darkness outside. Heath was the main teacher, but others came also.

The Nigeriens are great at making do by repairing broken things. We often saw loaded bush taxies that had split tires repaired with wire, shoes repaired with nails, and many other such things. Although no one in the States would repair Timex watches, we could take ours to the street table repairmen who cleaned the watches for about forty cents, making them continue to run for years.

The most amusing event we experienced was when the expansion watchband on Heath's good watch broke. He took it to the only French jeweler in Niamey and was told, "This is impossible to repair. You must buy a new one." So reluctantly, Heath got a new band and dropped the nice but broken one in our wastebasket. Later that day, our house helper came and asked if Heath was really throwing away the watchband. When Heath assured him it was unfixable, our house helper asked if he could have it. Imagine our surprise when he returned the next day with the band, repaired by a street table repairman for forty cents, on his watch! He wore it for years and always enjoyed showing it to Heath over and over with a big grin on his face.

Heath had not forgotten about Bob's request that he return as acting field director. After much prayer and reflection, he wrote to Bob,

"We have been praying much over the matter you talked with us about. We put it entirely in the Lord's hands, not knowing just how He would speak to us through His Word. Claiming the promise of Philippians 4:6-7, we requested God's will be done. He laid several verses on my heart having to do with the Lord's will and its accomplishment. I was forcibly impressed by Isaiah 14:24: 'Jehovah of hosts hath sworn saying, Surely as I have thought, so shall it come to pass, and as I have purposed, so shall it stand' and also verse 27: 'For Jehovah of hosts hath purposed and who shall annul it, and his hand is stretched out, and who shall turn it back.'...By this and other verses, the Lord has thus assured me that His will would be done in this, as we requested of Him...We are willing and desirous of doing whatever the Lord leads us to do. May He give you and the board wisdom from on high to discern His will in this situation. We trust that as you wait upon Him, there will be a unanimous sensing and peaceful assurance of that which pleases Him...In Calvary's bonds, Heath Bobbett"

Bob wrote back to Heath on March 23:

"At the board meeting last evening, I presented my recommendation for you as the replacement to Dal Washer during the time that he will be home on furlough. With this recommendation went the necessity of you and your family coming home for furlough this year so as to be back on the field by the time the Washers are ready to leave...I want you to know that the decision of the board was unanimous, and several of the men

With Jesus Leading the Way

expressed themselves by stating their belief that you have the necessary qualifications for this big job. Rest assured that the board is here to help you in any way possible and that the men will stand with you as you take up your duties as acting field director. I personally am very happy to have you taking over this responsible position next year. I do believe that you are God's man for the job...I want to express my deep appreciation for your careful and prayerful consideration of this matter after I presented it to you in January. I know that it was a terrible shock to you, but the sweet tone of your letter proved to me that you had prayed much concerning this position and that you were willing to do whatever the Lord had in mind for you. Thank you so very much, Heath, for your open mind and willing spirit. It will be my joy to work with you in this new relationship. We will all be praying for the preparation of your mind and heart for this new work for your Lord. Yours in His love and grace, Robert R. Richards, General Director"

At this time, we were becoming more and more certain that we were expecting our fourth baby. We were very happy about this but more than a little concerned about our Rh issues. Doctors had said I should only have my babies in the States because there was always the possibility they might need to have their blood changed at birth. Later, injections for Rh-negative mothers would prove effective, but they were unheard of when our babies were born.

While none of our family or friends knew we had baby number four on the way and needed to give birth in the States, the Lord knew. He had given us this precious unborn baby, and He had a wonderful plan all prepared. His plan was for us to return to the States for the baby's birth and to be back in time for Dal and Kay Washer to go on furlough. God had, in His usual awesome way, taken care of our need to have our November baby in the States. Truly "our times are in His hands."

We were very happy to have Rebecca home for Easter vacation for 6 days in April, but the time went too quickly, of course. On the last night of Rebecca's vacation, Talibi was bitten by a viper just as he was preparing to go to bed. Heath took him to the dispensary for an antivenom shot, and we applied ice and a tourniquet during the night. The mission plane came the next morning to take Rebecca back to school and Heath to Niamey for an executive committee meeting, so we evacuated Talibi to the Niamey hospital with them, where he was kept for several days. Many Africans urged him to call a traditional medicine man to "remove the snake's teeth" so he could get well. Evidently, when these charlatans were paid to do this, they had something concealed in their hand that they "extracted," claiming they were the snake's teeth and that now the victim would get well.

On April 19, we celebrated Alan's third birthday. I always baked and decorated a special cake for each of the children's birthdays. Our children only received a few gifts each time, but they were so appreciative of their birthday gifts. We tried to keep something hidden in our barrels for them, and we also searched for some things in the open market. It wasn't easy to find birthday gifts there, but our children seemed to appreciate anything they got. Their lives were simple, and birthdays were very special, without depending on elaborate parties or gifts.

We tried to listen to our transistor radio once or twice a day to get world news on the Voice of America or on the British Broadcasting Company. VOA broadcasted some programs in "special English," slowly spoken and clearly enunciated. Since we almost never had anyone to converse with in English outside of our home, it dawned on us one day that we were listening to this special stilted English and not even thinking it was strange!

Living in the African bush, we began to understand Bible stories much more clearly. We understood why straw was needed in making mud bricks, just as the Israelites did in Egypt. We understood what Luke 6:38 was about as it spoke of "good measure, pressed down and shaken over." When buying rice, dried corn, or millet grains in the market, the seller always did this and even slowly poured another measure on top so his measure was heaped up.

Missionary Johnny Grant, that year's annual conference speaker, told a beautiful true story about Africans he knew. There was a wealthy African farmer who was always kind to the local poor people, allowing them to come on his fields after his workers had harvested to pick up grain for themselves. Among the poor who came was a tiny little old woman named Murna. Murna was so thankful for this farmer's kindness and appreciated him.

One day word was sent out that the farmer didn't have enough harvesters to get his grain in, so he was asking for any volunteers who were able to come and help him. The poor who had benefited from the good farmer's largesse came with small baskets to help, but Murna came with the very largest basket she could find! The others criticized her for being so dumb. After all, the farmer was rich, and she was making others who had the small baskets look bad. She replied, "Oh no! He has been so good to me for many years, and this is my chance to pay him back. I want to fill this basket to the brim even if it takes me all day!"

At the end of the day, others came with their small baskets and there came Murna with the huge full basket that she could hardly drag in. She was so happy to do that for her benefactor. Then the announcement was made that actually the farmer had all the grain he needed, so everyone was to take home with them what they had gleaned that day! The others glumly marched off with their little baskets while Murna was singing, shouting, and jumping for joy! Principle: How do we serve the Lord? Do we just get by with the minimum, or do we give Him our all in gratitude for what He has done for us?

Spring 1966

One of our missionary colleagues was a talented artist. In March she came for a visit, and during that time she painted a beautiful picture of the front of our Gaya mud house and yard with all the trees, flower pots, and whitewashed stones. When she set up her easel and paint supplies across the street to begin her work, the local people couldn't understand why this white lady in a big sunhat was standing out on the terrible midday heat, making marks on a piece of canvas! After a while, some stood behind her and were amazed to see the marks were turning into a picture. "Look!" they exclaimed. "She is making a picture of that house!" She even painted in a local boy on his donkey headed out to the bush to collect wood. We have appreciated this beautiful painting all the years that have followed!

In our April 1966 prayer letter, we explained the call Heath had received to become acting field director and the subsequent rescheduling of our furlough. Heath wrote: "We have the assurance in our hearts that this is the Lord's will for us, and thus we accept this responsibility as from Him, trusting Him for His enabling...Being acting field director is not a work we would desire because the burdens and responsibilities are so great. And greatest of all, we have no desire to leave our bush work in Gaya at this time. God has given us fruit in this Muslim vineyard, and we are happy in the work...Pray for funds for a new vehicle when we arrive back in Niger. Our thirteen-year-old Land Rover just cannot handle the difficult roads of Africa anymore...Continue to pray for the work here in Gaya...In the remaining time we have here, we trust to reach as many villages as possible. We are into our third hot season, and we covet your prayers. The thermometer hovers over 100 degrees in our house. We are sleeping outside, but even this offers no relief from the oppressive heat. We are very tired. The hot season lasts through June. Pray for strength. The last of May, we will have the great task of packing our things into barrels to keep them from the hungry termites during our absence."

One of the tasks we thought we would be facing on furlough was to raise funds for a car for the next term. However, God provided for this need even before we left on furlough. Glen and Anna Nunemaker were enjoying the new Land Rover God had provided for them in their ministry. However, they sensed very definitely God was leading them to go home to be with their boys through high school. Very few missionaries had done that sort of thing back then, so they faced a lot of criticism in the homeland and from other missionaries. Anna and Glen felt (rightly so) that their boys needed a mom and dad at home with them at that time and were pioneers in going against criticism to obey God on behalf of their sons.

After they made the decision to return to the States, we received a letter from them saying they felt the Lord wanted them to give us their new Land Rover as they left the field. Certainly this was "exceeding abundantly above all we could ask or think." They only asked that we give them whatever we got from selling our old Land Rover to apply toward their debt at the mission. I wrote, "It hardly seems possible that this burden could be rolled off our shoulders. We thought we would have to struggle along with the old Land Rover until furlough and then would have to try to raise money for the car that we needed. Great is our Lord!"

When we returned from our 1965-66 furlough and were relocated in Niamey, we asked the Nunemakers' permission to sell the Land Rover so we could buy a Peugeot 404 Familial that would accommodate our family of six and was more gas-economical. Anna and Glen answered, "The Lord told us what to do with that car, and we are sure He will tell you what to do too!" We were able to sell the Land Rover to a dear widow friend who needed it in her bush work.

Update on Nyaliya

Our wonderful God knows just when we need encouragement and evidence of His working behind the scenes in our lives. This encouragement came in a letter we received in May 1966 from an SIM nurse, Ruth Hunt, in Galmi, Niger, written on the behalf of Nyaliya. It had been at least eight months since we had said goodbye to her and had seen her off to her people on the back of a heavily loaded truck. Here is Ruth's letter:

"Dear Mrs. Bobbett,

"Just a quick note to tell you that your Fulani girl who made a profession of faith with you last rainy season has finally arrived at Galmi. She came with your letter as well as the picture which had been taken of you and her. She certainly thinks a lot of her 'Madame.' She tells me that I look just like you and that she thought it was you when she came into the dispensary and I was working at the desk that day. After looking at the picture, I think she is insulting you.

"She seems very sure of her salvation. When she arrived, she was staying in town with a former professing Christian that her brother knew. We didn't think this was a very good place for her, so we asked her to come and stay at the hospital. We had a girl from our Bible school there waiting for her baby to arrive, so we put Fadima (Nyaliya) in with her hoping that Abshe would be a help to her.

"You would be thrilled to hear her talk about the records. She knows them forward and backward. Last week we had special meetings for the women with an evangelist's wife teaching. This week two evangelists are preaching in afternoon and evening services. She is staying for all of these, and she really seems to be getting something out of the ladies' meetings. She told my coworker that she would like to stay until she could preach because now all she could do was play the phonograph for the people.

"She is not with her husband now because he had taken another wife when she went back to her town from Gaya. I don't know what problems this may have made for her.

"We are really pleased that the Lord has brought her to Galmi after all these months, and we are praying that she will truly grow in the Lord while she is with us. She wants to learn to read. Do pray with us in regard to her as well as the witness that goes forth from the hospital each day.

"May the Lord richly bless you as you continue to labor for Him there in Gaya.

"Yours in Him, Ruth Hunt (Tuni)"

How good our God was to let us know, just before we left on furlough, that Nyaliya was alive and growing in Christ! While we were on furlough, two more letters came to us from Nyaliya and from Virginia Fridal. The first one was dated December 27, 1966:

"Dear Ramu-Nya, (Dear mother of Ramatou, Rebecca's African name)

"Many greetings to you. I was very happy to receive your letter. I am here at Galmi working. I am pleased to be among the Christians here. I'm glad you sent me here. Now I have been here almost a year. When I fill a year, I am going home for vacation. After vacation I plan to come back here.

"The people here have received me well. They are pleased with me. I have found a friend like you. I am happy with her as I was happy with you, but she is leaving for her country in two months. Her name is Murna (Virginia Fridal).

"My older sister is here visiting me. She came just before Christmas. I was very pleased to see Christmas the way it is. I had never seen the way Christmas was celebrated before. I was the angel Gabriel in the Christmas play.

"I am still remembering how you led me to Christ. Thank you so much for showing me the way of salvation. I am filled with joy whenever I think about it. Even in trouble, I will not leave off following Jesus.

"My nose is healed now. If it bothers me again, I will write you about it.

"On December 5, I went with Murna on a camel trek to a village thirty-eight miles from here. I was able to witness to both Hausas and Fulanis. I also go with Murna to visit around Galmi. There are Zarmas as well as Fulanis and Hausas.

"I am asking how is your father's health, also your brother's? Did your sister-in-law have her baby all right?

"I am greeting you in love in the name of our Lord and Savior Jesus Christ. I am hoping your husband and all your children are well. How is the new baby (Nathan)?

"I am waiting for a letter from you.

"Nyaliya (Fadima)"

Virginia Fridal had written this letter for Nyaliya, translating into English as Nyaliya spoke in Hausa. There was a letter enclosed from Virginia too:

"Dear Mrs. Bobbett,

"I tried to write Nyaliya's letter as she said it. She wanted to write you for some time, but this is the first time we've had time. She is learning to read in Hausa. Her older brother came in August and encouraged her to stay here. Her older sister is here now, having come without anyone at home's knowledge. She wants Nyaliya to go home with her now, but I have tried to encourage Nyaliya to wait until her year is up when she is due three weeks' vacation. We will write her older brother and ask him to come accompany her home and bring her back. I would like to see her read the Bible fluently before she goes back home to live. The Fulani family ties are quite strong. Nyaliya does get homesick, especially for her mother.

"Nyaliya is a real encouragement to us in her sincere desire to follow our Lord. She is a big help in the hospital. Trust you will be able to see her when you come back from furlough.

"In Him, Virginia Fridal"

The months Nyaliya was at Galmi grew into years. She learned how to read in Hausa, and she and missionary nurse Virginia Fridal made numerous treks on camels to evangelize women in many surrounding villages. She returned to her home later to share the Good News about Jesus Christ with her entire family too. Nyaliya never had a child, but down through the years, she raised several of her nieces and nephews, bringing them up with godly nurture. Baa'ra, the first niece she raised, grew into a beautiful girl and married a Christian Hausa man who eventually held a very important position in the Niger government. Muslim superiors trusted him because they knew he was a man of honor who kept his word. As God blessed their home with children, what a joy it was to see them gather as a family each day to read the Bible and pray.

As the years passed, whenever Nyaliya came to Niamey or passed through Dosso when we were there, she came to visit us. She really bore the fragrance of Christ in her conduct and attitudes. She was a lovely graceful lady in all ways.

Many years later we received a letter from another one of Nyaliya's nieces:

"Dear Pastor and Mrs. Bobbett,

"My name is Soutoura, and I am Nyaliya's niece. I grew up in Galmi under her care. I am now twenty-two but was saved at the age of fourteen and baptized in Konni, December 4, 2005.

"I have never met you, but I am very thankful for you. I have heard about you since I was a young child. We thank you more than you could ever know for your part in Christ's work in our lives.

"I would like to take this opportunity to greet your family, including your children and grandchildren. I am so happy to hear that you are doing well. I thank God so much that Nyaliya began her relationship with Christ Jesus through your ministry here in Niger. God truly blessed our family as I grew up in her home.

"I just recently saw the letter and photo that you sent to her. I saw them and was very happy. I greet Alan and his four children, Jon and his four children, Ramatou and her three children and two grandchildren, and Nathan who was just married. God bless him in his marriage.

"I leave you with a verse from my heart. John 15:3: 'There is no greater love than this: that a man lay down his life for his friends.' 2 Corinthians 5:1 also: 'May God richly bless your family. We think about you and pray for you often.'

"Your Sister in Christ, Debora (Soutoura)"

"Translated by Danielle Koepke, missionary among Fulani, IMB (Southern Baptist)

"Debora (Soutoura) and I are sharing the Gospel among the Fulani villages. Your work in God's plan has had a lasting impact. – Danielle"

We first heard the following song at a church in Ohio. It spoke to our hearts mightily about the years spent in Muslim work, causing us to trust that in eternity we will finally know what God was doing behind the scenes. We cannot listen to this song without tears flowing down our cheeks.

Faces
Lyrics by Kurtis Deshaun Williams, Louie St. Louis, Marcus Mybe, and Peter McNulty-Connolly

I dreamed my life was done. I stood before God's Son.
It was time to see what my reward would be.
With love He reviewed my life to count what was done for Christ
For that is what will last eternally.

See I'd done my best to share that Jesus really cares
And He would save if they just believe.
Oh, but seldom did harvest come and so few did I see won
Until the Lord said, "Turn around and see."

Then He showed me the faces of the ones
who'd come because of me.
So many faces that my life had led to Calvary.
All those years I thought nobody saw as I labored in lowly places.
That's when Jesus smiled and showed me all the faces.

He said though you did not see the yield,
You were faithful to plow the field.
At other times you helped me plant the seed.
No matter how small the task, you did just as I asked.
And thanks to you these souls have been set free.

And for those years you thought nobody saw
As you labored in lowly places.
One day He'll smile and show you all the faces.
The faces. You'll see all the faces.

How can I ever thank my wonderful Lord for the part He allowed me to play in seeing Nyaliya come to Him! When we think back of all the people we reached in our time in Africa and seeing so little fruit on this most difficult field, we trust and choose to believe that we will meet some in Heaven that the Lord brought to Himself then or at a later time that we never knew about. God knows just when to part the curtains to let us see a little of what He is doing behind the scenes. "Even when nothing is happening, with God something is happening!"

We got our things out of the house and stored, and then we packed up the old Land Rover for its last trip to the capital. It broke down again on the road, and we had to be towed three-fourths of the way to Niamey.

The Lord had to deal with me, assuring me that the time had come for us to leave our bush ministry and begin a totally new one in Niamey. I took hope in the thought that it would only be for one year and then we could return to an outstation ministry.

There would be amenities in the capital that we didn't have in Gaya: electricity (fans!), city water, McCaba Academy for our children to attend and be able to live at home, fresh vegetables and fruit in the market year-round, and so forth. But it was really hard for me to leave Gaya and face my fears about being a field director's wife in a city ministry after our return from furlough. I knew that when missionaries had to live close to each other, there were often personality clashes and behavior that displeased the Lord. Being alone in the bush for two terms, we had really sweet fellowship with fellow missionaries when we saw them from time to time in the capital city and didn't have to worry about the details of daily life together.

A good friend of ours who served in the Philippines knew just what we would be facing. His advice was, "Heath, when you are field director, station all your missionaries one hundred miles apart, and they will get along just beautifully!"

> *There is joy in serving Jesus, as I journey on my way,*
> *Joy that fills the heart with praises, every hour and every day.*
> *There is joy, joy, joy in serving Jesus,*
> *Joy that throbs within my heart;*
> *Every moment, every hour, as I draw upon His power,*
> *There is joy, joy, joy that never shall depart.*
>
> --Oswald J. Smith

I had already discovered the way my heart filled with joy after visiting the ladies in the villages to explain the way of salvation or after a children's Bible class I had taught. It would be a challenge finding new contacts and opportunities in the busy capital city, but yes, I determined that "If Jesus goes with me, I'll go anywhere!" I was encouraged from John 15:5, without Him I can do nothing, and Philippians 4:13, with Him I can do anything!

Chapter 14
Second Furlough
June 1966 to June 1967

We learned that airline tickets to Europe from Kano, Nigeria, cost the same as ones from Niamey to Europe, so we decided to take that route back to the States. On our way home, we wanted to stop off in Rome, Italy, and Madrid, Spain. We were traveling this time with three children, ages ten, eight, and three, and another on the way. Some of our supporting churches were already lining up DVBS events and meetings for us soon after we got to the States. We hoped to get some refreshment and rest by stopping in Europe as we got out of the African heat.

EBM's small plane was scheduled to take us to Kano, Nigeria, at the end of May 1966. From there we planned to fly to Rome, Italy. However, the unrest in Nigeria had produced instability and a military coup. There were ethnic fighting and uprisings. Some of the Kano market had been burned by different tribes and factions. The Ibo people from the south were well educated and aggressive, mainly professing Christians. The Hausa Muslims of the north were opposed to the Ibos. Later, the violence against the Ibos pushed them to try to secede and have their own country called Biafra. A thirty-month war ensued with much carnage and bloodshed before it finally ended in January 1970.

Because of the unrest in Nigeria, we were on pins and needles, not knowing if we could depart from Kano as planned. At the last minute, word came through that the Kano airport was open once again.

When the EBM plane arrived at the Kano airport, there were armed soldiers everywhere. The situation in Kano was very tense. We were taken to the SIM mission guest house to stay until our scheduled flight out, with warnings that foreigners should not be out on the streets or in the markets. On the day of our departure, there were a number of people at the guest house ready to leave for the airport so we were all picked up by a government bus, well-guarded by soldiers again, and finally able to board and depart without incident.

We arrived at the Rome airport in the afternoon. This airport was actually located thirty kilometers outside of Rome, which meant we had a long bus ride into our hotel in the city. There were not a lot of people on the bus. Our bush family of five was so excited to be out of the heat of

243

primitive living and into a large populated area. Along the route, there were beautiful outdoor markets with fruit we had not seen in years. We looked out the window and exclaimed, "Oh look! Look at those huge strawberries!" "Come over here, Mom! On this side they have apples and peaches!"

There was another American couple on the bus who seemed to be amused at our excitement, so the wife finally asked, "Are you a missionary family?" Oh dear! Was it that obvious? We told them we had come from near the desert and hadn't seen such market-fresh items in a very long time. They were very understanding and said they figured out we had come from a very primitive place by our excitement being in a big city and seeing the fresh fruit.

We had a wonderful time in Rome, seeing the famous sights of the Vatican, the Sistine Chapel, the Coliseum, and the catacombs. At the Basilica of Vatican City, we pointed out the thirteenth century statue of Saint Peter. For centuries, tens of thousands of people have come to the basilica to touch or kiss Peter's foot on the sculpture so that his toe was almost worn off. We told the children this was similar to idol worship that was in Africa and that the Lord never told us to pray to dead saints or to worship at a man-made statue of one. We also got a small booklet with pictures of all that was in the Vatican as a souvenir. I will speak about this booklet again a little later in this chapter.

As we walked through the Sistine Chapel, gazing at this awesome sight, three-year-old Alan whispered, "Mommy! I have to go to the bathroom. NOW!" There was no place in sight, so I urged him to wait. Hopping up and down, he replied, "I can't!" We all tried to ignore the little puddle he left behind on the floor as we moved on! Traveling with small children can be interesting, fun, and sometimes embarrassing!

Again, using Frohmer's book *Europe on 5 Dollars a Day*, we next stopped in Madrid, Spain, for a few days. The very old hotel we stayed in had creaking floors and noisy plumbing. It seemed like a real fire trap, but we were so tired that we were soon in bed and asleep. We trusted our lives into the Lord's hands as we slept soundly that night.

The Royal Palace in Madrid is open to the public when not being used for official state occasions. We enjoyed visiting some of the 2,800 rooms, which were richly decorated by famous artwork, tapestries, porcelain, and furniture. The palace has the world's only complete Stradivarius string quintet!

Spanish people live on a very late schedule. Restaurants didn't even *begin* to serve lunch until 1:00 p.m., and dinner was as late as 10:00 p.m. Of course by then, we all were tired and more interested in sleep than in supper. Then we discovered cafeterias in Spain. They were more like snack bars, and they opened by 5:00 p.m. to serve drinks, sandwiches, and fries. So the Spanish cafeterias well served our dinner needs.

The next combination of circumstances resulted in an embarrassing situation. Serving ketchup with French fries seemed to be unheard of at that time in Europe. Our waiter was harried and not friendly at all. Eight-year-old Jonathan loved ketchup and asked if he could have some with his fries. The waiter, while giving an exasperated look of "whyarethesepeoplebotheringme?" grabbed a bottle and returned. We thought he would just place it on our table, but no, he had to shake the bottle vigorously so he himself could put the ketchup on the French fries. When he removed the lid, it made a loud popping sound and spurted ketchup onto the bouffant blonde hairdo of a lady at the next table! Suddenly, he became very apologetic and humble, trying to blot her hair and blouse. We were glad it was him and not us that shook the bottle and opened it!

We landed in the States at LaGuardia Airport on June 10, 1966. It is always wonderful to be back in your homeland. The customs official who checked our passports and luggage looked up at us and said, "Welcome home!" That warmed our hearts and was very special. We have loved living in and visiting other countries, but there is no place like home.

Jane and Homer Ludington and family met us at the airport and Jane commented that this time we looked like more prosperous missionaries because we didn't have our luggage tied together with ropes as we did the first furlough!

The summer of 1966 was very unsettled for us. Longtime friends Jacqui and Larry Armstrong very kindly told us we could rent their furnished home in Vandalia, Ohio for just the cost of their mortgage payment of $100 per month, but the house would not to be available for us until September.

Gaya was home for Alan. For weeks, we were traveling from church to church and staying in different homes. This was very upsetting for him, and he kept saying, "I want to go home to Gaya!" He was so upset that he began to do all kinds of naughty things, and we had to keep our eyes on him. Examples were pouring salt on Aunt Jane's freshly baked berry pies, turning on the gas burners of a stove in the basement of a pastor's house, and hiding under Paul Whipple's car in the carport while we looked all over for him!

We taught Vacation Bible School in Windsor Locks, Connecticut that summer and were the featured missionaries. Dear longtime friends were away for those weeks, so they offered us the luxury of living in their home. It was strawberry season, and we all enjoyed strawberry shortcake in different homes of Windsor Locks friends.

Another pastor and his wife from West Danby NY went away for several weeks' vacation and also opened the parsonage for us. It was nice to be settled for a while. Finally in September, we moved into the Armstrong home on Buttercup Avenue in Vandalia, Ohio.

For our furlough physicals, we made appointments with the doctor at Baptist Mid-Missions in Cleveland, Ohio. We needed to make a reservation at a nearby hotel for one night, so we looked for a reasonably priced one. That evening when we checked in, we realized that we were not in a good section of Cleveland and that the hotel was a very old building. It smelled old, and the water pipes made all kinds of groaning noises whenever we or someone else turned a faucet on. Not only that, but there was a leaking drip once in a while right over the toilet. It was humorous to find Rebecca sitting on the "throne" with an open umbrella over her head. Last but not least, we were awakened early in the morning by the Muslim call to prayer in the mosque across the street. We were glad to finish up our medical tests the next day and head back to Vandalia.

From our prayer letter, dated September 1966: "We have traveled 7,000 miles in the U.S. during these summer weeks. We are looking forward to unpacking and being settled. Be remembering the children as they begin school and our three-year-old Alan as he adjusts again to a new situation. We will appreciate your prayers too for Norma as we anticipate a "new arrival" the latter part of November."

Rebecca and Jonathan Enroll in Public School

I had grown up near Vandalia, which was just a small crossroads surrounded by farmlands back then. I spent all twelve years of my elementary and secondary education at Butler School. By 1966, the town had really grown, and the small Vandalia airport was enlarged to become the municipal airport for the city of Dayton, Ohio. I was thrilled that Rebecca and Jonathan would be going to the elementary school building where I attended fifth grade. The school was close enough for them to walk. Surprise of surprises, Rebecca's fifth grade teacher was Miss Eleanor Shearer, who had also taught my brothers, Carl and Mickey, when they were at Butler! She was a lovely maiden lady and an excellent teacher. Once when she skipped over the book's teaching on evolution and was asked by her students why, she said, "You can read it if you want to, but I personally believe what is written in this book (the Bible) on my desk." At that time there was no problem with a teacher keeping a Bible on her desk and referring to it!

Heath was gone a lot presenting missions and our work to many churches. The children and I enjoyed the fellowship and kindness of my home church in Dayton and were blessed to sit under the rich biblical preaching of Pastor Nile Fisher.

At Emmanuel, Rebecca was received into the membership upon her baptism. Jonathan also wanted to follow the Lord in that step of obedience and was baptized on Christmas night 1966.

Rebecca and Jon enjoyed bringing different things to school for show and tell. One day, Rebecca asked if she could take the booklet about the Vatican that we had purchased in Rome. When she came home that evening, I asked her what she did with the booklet. She said, "I showed the picture of the statue of Peter with his toe almost rubbed and kissed off, and I told the class there were still idol worshippers in the world today." Wow! This was public school! I asked her what Miss Shearer said, to which Rebecca replied, "She said yes, that is true. There are still idol worshippers in the world today!"

We met some wonderful new friends while living in Vandalia. Walter and Marilyn Baird were new Christians who also attended Emmanuel and they just lived 2 blocks from us. What a precious family! We bonded immediately. Marilyn and I visited often over coffee and peanut butter toast! She was definitely God's special gift to me for fellowship that furlough, and she remains in my heart to this day as a wonderful friend.

My obstetrician, Dr. Magnotta, told me it was good for me to take long walks every day. Alan loved riding his little tricycle, so we traveled many of the Vandalia sidewalks daily when weather permitted. A favorite stopping place was the library. Alan loved to be read to. One day, there was a black gentleman working in the library. I was glad Alan still used his Zarma because he must have thought he was back in Africa as he exclaimed, "Look, Mommy! There's a *boro bi!*" (black man)

Our pastor's wife, Edna Fisher, was Alan's Sunday school teacher. She said she always knew how to spell his name because whenever he was asked what his name was, he replied, "Alan Bobbett, A-L-A-N!" He was the first to teach us a new song he learned in Sunday school, "I will sing of the mercies of the Lord forever." He sang it over and over.

Nathan's Birth

We spent Thanksgiving Day with Mickey and Geneva's family in New Carlisle, along with Carol and Carl. The doctor had said our baby was due November 11, but now it was the 24th and nothing had happened. Back then, no one knew the gender of their babies before they were born. It was a fun family day. Rebecca, Jonathan, and Alan enjoyed cousins Bobby, Gary, Ruthie, and Jeff Christmas. Mickey and Geneva were always so hospitable.

About 10:00 p.m. I began to have irregular contractions. We left Rebecca, Jonathan, and Alan at Mickey and Geneva's, then went to our Vandalia home to see if things were going to progress. My labors were always long, so I had time to do some laundry, shower, and wash and set my hair. We went to bed until about 2:30 a.m. when I awakened Heath for the drive through deserted streets to Miami Valley Hospital. Near the end of my labor the doctor asked me if it was a girl or a boy. Since we already had two boys but only one girl, I said, "It's a girl!"

At 7:36 a.m., Nathan Carl Bobbett made his entrance into the world at eight pounds, thirteen ounces. Dr. Magnotta shrugged and said, "Wrong gender?" It is amazing that no matter what gender a mother says she wants her baby to be, the minute she sees him/her, that is exactly what she wanted! Nathan was a good and happy baby.

We wondered how ten-year-old Rebecca would react when she learned that she had another brother instead of a sister. No problem. She was so happy to have a baby to care for and even made a sign to put up over his bassinet in her room, saying "Welcome, Baby!"

The day after Nathan's birth, hospital photographers had a picture of one-day-old Nathan for us. Heath took it home to show Nathan's older siblings. Alan looked at the picture sitting on our end table for a while but said nothing. He just went into his bedroom and brought out his own picture to set beside the new baby's picture!

Heath wrote in our 1966 Christmas letter, "Little Nathan is eleven days old at this writing, and Jonathan, Alan, and Rebecca join unanimously with us in thanksgiving for this sweet life lent to us by the Lord. Thank you for your prayers for Norma."

An Unforgettable Christmas Day

Christmas fell on Sunday that year, and I had planned to take Nathan to church for the first time but was just too tired and overwhelmed. So I decided it was best that I stay home.

Heath dropped his mother and our children off to enter the church so he could go across Third Street to park in a vacant lot there. As he and

With Jesus Leading the Way

a family with small children were walking back across Third a lady turned into the crosswalk and hit all of them with her car. She claimed that the sun had blinded her so that she did not see them. Heath was thrown to the pavement, as were some of the others. At the hospital, X-rays showed no broken bones, just scrapes and contusions. The first new suit Heath had had in years was ruined! The driver had no insurance, so no compensation was paid to any of those she struck.

Heath didn't get home until much later that afternoon. The children were so thankful their daddy was OK but have always remembered how late they had to wait on that Christmas Day to open their presents!

That spring, we were praising the Lord for things happening back in Niger. Nyaliya was growing in the Lord and learning to read her Bible. The second short-term Bible school was directed by colleague Roger Bacon with increased attendance. Phyllis Bacon had the joy of leading Talibi's mother to Christ out of Islam. One of the first things Talibi's mother did was to take off her Muslim charms and throw them away.

Missions Conference in Kansas

Heath had a busy and full schedule of speaking in our supporting churches and at Bible colleges. One day, he got a call from a church that we had never heard of in Kansas. They were planning their missions conference and begged him to come be one of their speakers. He didn't see any way he could squeeze those meetings into his busy schedule, so he told them that the only way he could come was to fly out between other engagements. He thought they wouldn't want that expense and would look for someone else. "Oh, yes! We want you to come! Please come by plane to the conference."

So he purchased the round-trip ticket and went. It was a great conference, well organized and well attended. Great offerings were taken as the pastor pled for missionary needs. When Heath left, nothing was said about paying for his plane tickets or about remuneration for the expenses of the trip. The next month that church sent $15 to our account for Heath's participation in the conference. Evidently all the offerings went into their church funds to support their own missionaries! Another EBM missionary from Mali was also in that conference, and he received the same amount. There was nothing we could do but shake our heads and laugh!

That was just one unusual situation because usually our churches were so good about giving love offerings or honorariums that did cover Heath's expenses for meetings. We have never been missionaries who received huge offerings, but God has faithfully supplied our every need all through the years.

Grandpa Christmas came by plane from Florida in the spring to spend a week with us. It was always such a joy to have him around and to see how much he loved his grandchildren. I took a picture of him with baby Nathan in front of our dwelling in Vandalia. The family resemblance was uncanny! Nathan definitely looks like the Christmas side of the family. Alan wanted Grandpa Christmas to play a board game with him that involved picking cherries off of a tree. Dad was laughing so hard, saying that he was never allowed to throw the dice more than once, but Alan took that privilege for himself, with no explanation.

On May 28, 1967, Pastor Fisher had Heath speak in the morning service at Emmanuel Baptist Church. On the Wednesday before, the church had voted to complete our needed passage money, which totaled $1,600. Pastor Fisher wrote in the church bulletin:

The Heath Bobbetts Are Returning to the Field

This is the last Sunday that the Bobbetts will be with us before returning to Africa. The church has appreciated their time with us this past year, and we bid them goodbye with mixed emotions.

They will be leaving Dayton on June 2 to sail from New York on June 8. It takes no little dedication and courage to settle in foreign lands in times like these. But the God who so wonderfully calls His servants supplies them with courage fresh from the altar in Heaven.

The Lord Jesus Christ promised those who faithfully carry out the Great Commission, "...and, lo, I am with you always, even unto the end of the age." He said on another occasion, "I will never leave thee, nor forsake thee."

May the Lord who gave these promises richly bless this fine missionary family in their labors in dark Africa. And may we never forget to hold them up in intercessory prayer.

How thankful we were to have a home church like Emmanuel, with a godly pastor and wife and a congregation who had a heart for missions!

Now we were a family of six returning to Niger. Aside from our first boat trip to France for language study, we had always traveled back and forth by planes. Many of our missionaries had enjoyed sailing on the *SS France*, and they urged us to return that way. The ships gave a larger luggage allowance than an airplane, and then a French airline also gave a greater luggage allowance on flights to Africa. We packed accordingly.

We were with friends in Washington, D.C. when we heard the alarming news that war had broken out in the Middle East! We did not know if we would be able to return to Niger or not, how long it would last and what the final effects would be. The conflict was soon named THE SIX DAY WAR and was truly a modern story of David facing Goliath and triumphing! Miracle after miracle had occurred during this amazing war. The commanders of Israel's forces who led it became national heroes.

On the morning of June 7, Israeli paratroopers stormed the Old City of Jerusalem and captured it. What a joyous occasion it was when the Jews returned to their historic capital to blow the shofar at the Western Wall where they hadn't had free access since 1948! By the time the UN demanded a cease-fire on June 11, 1967, Israeli defense forces had seized the entire Sinai Peninsula, reaching to the Suez Canal, the West Bank of Jordan, East Jerusalem, and the Golan Heights of Syria.

It was an interesting experience for us to be with Arab Christians in Washington, D.C., when this conflict broke out. They knew what the Bible says about Israel, but being Arabs, it was very difficult for them to see those nations humiliated. One young Arab said, "Ole daddy-o Abraham sure did mess things up fathering Ishmael and Isaac!"

Cancellation of our Sailing on the *SS France*

Our next shocking news was that the staff of the *SS France* had gone on strike. The ship was still docked in Europe, and we would not be sailing after all but would need to fly back to Niger. At our mission in Paterson, New Jersey, we tried to pare down our luggage. We gave things away and packed a suitcase or two to leave at the mission. Still, our luggage was massively overweight.

Arriving at JFK Airport with our four children, all our luggage was loaded onto two large carts. We felt we had reduced it as much as we could, but we were still beyond our ticket weight allowance. How could we ever pay the charges for it being overweight? I got settled on a bench with the children. Heath had the carts loaded with our luggage, and he said to me, "Okay. I'm going over to check our things in. Please pray!" We did just that! The luggage was so abundant that they had to put the suitcases on two scales to weigh them in. The ticket agent said nothing but calmly filled out the papers. Heath was there quite a while as the ticket agent put the travel tags on the bags. After a while, Heath came back to the children and me with a huge smile on his face. The agent had quietly filled out all the papers, but just as he finished, he looked up to suddenly realize there were *two* loaded scales, and he had only processed one. Then he calmly said, "Oh, that's all right. You could never have paid all those extra charges anyway." Planes flew half empty at that time, so he very kindly took that into consideration, and we were not charged for excess baggage. The Lord surely worked on our behalf once again.

Norma Bobbett

In Paris, we boarded the plane for Niger and the beginning of our third term of service. I knew Heath was very capable of meeting the challenges ahead of him as field director but I wasn't sure about my abilities with the big challenges ahead for me, for now we would be serving in the city and not a bush village.

Chapter 15
Third Term in Niamey
June 1967 to June 1970

Flame of God
By Amy Carmichael

From prayer that asks that I may be
Sheltered from winds that beat on Thee,
From fearing when I should aspire,
From faltering when I should climb higher,
From silken self, O Captain, free
Thy soldier who would follow Thee.

From subtle love of softening things,
From easy choices, weakenings,
Not thus are spirits fortified,
Not this way went the Crucified,
From all that dims Thy Calvary,
O Lamb of God, deliver me.

Give me the love that leads the way,
The faith that nothing can dismay,
The hope no disappointments tire,
The passion that will burn like fire,
Let me not sink to be a clod:
Make me Thy fuel, O Flame of God.

We arrived back in Niger in June 1967 to begin our third term. Dal helped Heath transition to being the acting field director, and Kay filled me in on her ministry with the women and children. Once again, we were asked to begin our term by filling in at a different ministry. Someone was needed to run the guest house, providing hospitality, meals, and lodging for missionaries passing through Niamey until Helen Bechtel returned from furlough. The old mud guest house on the Yantala station was infested with bats. Many nights brought us battles with those ugly creatures. With four children, including a nursing baby, it was a real plunge back into work for me.

Heath's New Job

The ministries of the Niger field for the field director to oversee and assist were the Librairie Chrétienne, or Bible bookstore, and reading room; two medical dispensaries; a small orphanage; a Christian elementary day school in French with a director and six teachers; McCaba Academy with first through eighth grades and a small high school; a guest house; and audiovisual ministry; a radio broadcast; an aviation ministry; church planting efforts on seven stations; committees for translation; literacy evangelism; a Sunday evening English service; plus counseling and encouraging local pastors, evangelists, and missionaries. Besides these things, there were all the government offices he had to contact for various authorizations and signatures, orienting new missionaries, and still having time for his family!

Heath was gone many hours learning the ropes with Dal while I was grocery shopping and cooking for our family as well as for guests in the guest house.

Nathan was not quite seven months old and had just learned to crawl. The rough cement floors in the guest house were chafing and scratching his knees, so he decided very quickly the best thing to do would be to walk on his hands and feet while we were there! He got around very well, but it was humorous to watch him. He reminded us of a spider with only four legs!

Heath wrote to his mother on June 22, 1967: "We have been here just over a week, and the time has just flown. At 3:30 a.m. today, I was at the airport to meet a nurse who is coming to work in our dispensaries for the summer. I haven't been back to bed since, so this will be a long day. The baby [Nathan] has been quite fussy. It has been so hot and muggy. However, we have had some rains, and about four out of five nights we have had to bring our beds and all inside because of either dusty wind or rain or both. Needless to say, that doesn't help with one's sleep either. Nathan just got his second tooth, so that may have been one reason he has been so fussy. I have to go back to the airport in a little while to take some SIM missionaries who are going on furlough.

The kids all seem glad to be back in Africa and have the wide-open spaces to play in, and we all feel like we are at last home again. I haven't gotten to Gaya yet but should soon. Norma keeps very busy with the children and also preparing for and getting meals for the guests coming into our guest house."

Just one month after our return to Niger, new missionaries and their four children arrived on the plane in the middle of the night. It was a tradition for all the missionaries to gather at the guest house to welcome them with coffee cakes, donuts, and other goodies to serve with coffee and tea. After welcoming the new arrivals and having a great visit, they went to bed as the sun was coming up while the rest of us got a very early start on the day!

As we were standing around the table enjoying our food and fellowship in the dim light of storm lanterns, the newly arrived missionary wife said, "Cockroaches!" No one but she had looked at the walls in the dim light and perceived there were hundreds of cockroaches! We were horrified as we all looked. By the time the sun came up, they would all be hiding until night time again.

We constantly battled to keep the cockroach population down all the years we were in Niger. We didn't know what cockroaches looked like when we first arrived in Niger. Huge ones liked to hide under our sinks and in our primitive shower areas. Our language teacher told us those huge things were only water bugs and wouldn't hurt us. We believed her! Later when I repeated that information to another missionary, he said, "Those are cockroaches, not water bugs!"

During my hectic time at the guest house, we asked a young man from Goudel to be our house steward. Amadou worked regularly for some of our other missionaries and seemed well trained. I always washed all our fresh fruits, vegetables, and even leaf lettuce in soapy Clorox water and rinsed them well with filtered water before putting them in the refrigerator. Amadou assured me that he knew how to wash the lettuce.

Not long afterward, we thought Heath must have caught some kind of a tropical bug. He lost twenty pounds in two months. The French doctor prescribed medicines, which he took, and he seemed to get better. But the illness came back as soon as the treatment was over. One day, I watched Amadou wash the lettuce that we bought from piles on the ground in the Niamey market. He was just rinsing the leaves under faucet water! It turned out that Heath had gotten paratyphoid fever, apparently from the lettuce. Next, baby Nathan got sick with diarrhea. When he didn't improve, he was hospitalized for ten days in the French Gamkalley Clinic. The doctor began trying one medicine after another. One night as I bathed Nathan and prepared him for bed, I was upset to see he was breaking out

Norma Bobbett

in a rash all over his body. The nurse told us that he was reacting to the multitude of medications, so the doctor ordered they all be stopped.

Praise the Lord, finally both Heath and Nathan recovered. Heath was glad to lose his "furlough fat" but complained that his clothes no longer fit. From then on, I personally washed the lettuce before we ate it.

From our prayer letter, dated August 1967: "In many ways, we face our hardest term this time. From being bush missionaries, we are trying to adjust to the noisy and busy life in an African city...Please do not fail to hold us up before the Throne of grace. These people have been in Satan's grasp for centuries, and he will not let go without a struggle. How good to know the battle is the Lord's...In the first two weeks we were back, four professions of faith in Jesus Christ were made – one a Peace Corps worker – so we have much cause for rejoicing as we see God at work on this field...Besides all the mission business which Heath must care for as acting field director, there are unlimited opportunities for service – jail ministry, encouraging the local pastors, and visitation. Three Christian men have come to ask Heath about the possibility of beginning an evening French Bible school. This is the work that is close to his heart, so do pray for the Lord's will in this matter...The children are happy to be back in Africa. Somebody's pet monkey found his way to our yard today and adopted Rebecca for a mommy. We insisted he wasn't coming in to sleep tonight, although he climbed up our screen door and screeched terribly at being left out. Nathan (eight months) is enjoying French baguette bread, finding it great for cutting his first four teeth."

When Helen arrived to take over at the guest house, we moved to the Niamey house, even though we had to camp there for the first few days without any furniture.

Emile Ngandi

While we were still taking care of the guest house at Yantala, Heath spent the mornings in his Niamey office then came home at a certain time for lunch. I was concerned one day when he didn't show up for lunch until the middle of the afternoon. He had been occupied about His Father's business. In his own words he wrote to our supporters, "This morning a young school teacher came to my office and said he had some serious questions he wanted to ask me. He was from Togo and was a professing Catholic for a number of years. Then he had married a Muslim woman in Niger and had been practicing that religion. However, it gave no peace, and he realized in his heart he had not found the truth. While visiting in a friend's home, he saw a book titled *Paix et Surete* (Peace and Security). Many things were explained in the book, including the difference between religion and salvation. Emile's heart was prepared, and it was our privilege to see him accept Christ as his own personal Savior there in my office. Please pray much for Emile. He desires to see his wife become a follower of Jesus too and will be bringing her to see us as soon as she returns from the village where she is visiting her parents. What reaction her family takes remains to be seen, so please hold them before the Throne of grace."

In September 1967, Heath received this letter from Emile (translated from French):"My Pastor, would you please invite the brothers to pray for me? I leave Niamey tomorrow for Abidjan to take special exams there. I need the help of Christ. He is the light! He is the shield! With Christ I have nothing to fear. To you, my pastor, and to all my fellow brothers in Christ, I send my thanks. Emile"

Dal and Kay were a wonderful dedicated couple with a deep love for the African people. However, the Lord led the Washers to stay in Greenville, South Carolina, for seven years to get their boys through high school. We really didn't comprehend that Heath's filling in for one year as field director would turn into ten years in that position. In 1974, the Washers came back to Africa under the auspices of a sister mission to open work in Togo. Dal got involved in bush evangelism and church planting while Kay began a school for blind students. They had faithfully labored before in the Muslim country of Niger where they saw very little fruit. In her book *One Candle to Burn*, Kay expressed their thankfulness to the Lord for allowing them to work in Togo where there was much more openness to the Gospel and fruit for their labor.

Introduced to the Gourma People

The Gourmas are a friendly, peace-loving people. Their culture and customs are quite different from those of the Zarma people. The majority of the Gourma tribe is in Upper Volta (later named Burkina Faso), but there were many also in Niger and Bénin. The Gourma people are much more open and receptive to the Gospel. Their background is pagan (idol worship and fetishism), not Muslim. There was a world of difference in working with them compared to working among Muslims. It is better to have no teaching at all about Christ than to have a false teaching about Him. This is true in the States also when one wishes to reach Jehovah Witnesses or the Mormons.

Dal and Kay Washer had been working with a small Gourma church plant located in the little grass hut they had built down by the river as a meeting place. What a joy and blessing it was for us to work with them too. They had looked to Dal for spiritual council, preaching, and leadership, and they accepted Heath in the same way. Kay's comment about the Gourmas will always remain with me. She said, "Working with Gourmas is a bright spot in the midst of working among Muslims." We certainly found that to be true.

Kay took me to meet a Gourma lady who became one of my dearest friends in Niamey. Yenuru was expecting her sixth baby. Kay had met Yenuru in the Niamey market where she sold leafy greens that Africans like to put in their sauces. When Kay invited Yenuru to the Gourma church meeting down by the Niger River, she came, believed in Jesus Christ as her personal Savior, and grew to be an outstanding follower of her Savior.

Yenuru's Story

Yenuru was born near the village of Piéla in Upper Volta and was a very sickly baby. At two years old, she was still unable to walk. Her mother despaired of her life, so one day she took Yenuru outside the village and abandoned her on a trash pile. This sounds terrible to us, but it is only because we don't understand the reasoning of her mother according to their pagan culture. Her mother thought that evil spirits were making her little girl sick and trying to kill her, so if she "threw her away" and paid no more attention to her, the evil spirits might leave her little girl alone. Of course, another relative went out and took Yenuru from the trash pile to raise her.

When she was of marriageable age, Yenuru's family arranged her marriage to a Gourma man named Yabiri who was working in Niamey. They built a grass hut on the Zongo primary school property where Yabiri worked as a guard. As their babies began to arrive, they were being absorbed into the Muslim culture all around them. They sacrificed sheep for each of the babies' eighth-day naming ceremonies, and the Muslim teacher-priest named their babies.

After Yenuru heard the good news about Jesus Christ and believed in Him, Yabiri was not happy. He told her, "We are Muslims now, not Christians! If I had the money, I would send you home to your family!" Yenuru quietly continued to follow Jesus and went to the church. Finally, out of curiosity, Yabiri began to go to the Gourma services too. Pastor Luc and the others talked to him about his soul's need. When Yenuru was going to be baptized, Yabiri decided he would like to be baptized too! It was very hard for him when the Gourma church leaders told him he was not ready yet. But praise God, as he continued to understand the Gospel, Yabiri did become a true believer and was baptized.

Not long after we arrived in Niamey, Pastor Luc asked Heath if he would have a baby dedication for Yenuru and Yabiri's baby (their sixth child). By this time, the Gourma church had moved up from the river to a more central location. They were meeting in a small garage behind our Bible bookstore. Heath and I will never forget that morning. When Pastor Luc asked Yabiri and Yenuru to come forward for the baby dedication, they came forward with all six of their children, saying, "When our other children were born, we did not follow Jesus and so we couldn't dedicate our children to God. This morning, we want to dedicate all six of our children to the Lord."

The Lord gave us the privilege of knowing so many faithful, godly African people. I'm sure that when rewards are given in heaven, God will have them right up in front, close to Him, while we missionaries will be far in the back of the crowd. We did and gave so little in comparison to these African believers.

Yenourou and Yabidi's Difficult Life Situation

Yenourou and Yabidi's grass hut home was located beside the school grounds of École Zongo because Yabidi was the night guard for this elementary school. When the school director discovered that a thief was getting into the unlocked school rooms at night, the principal told Yabidi if it happened again, he would fire him. Yabidi watched carefully, and then one night he caught a thief in a room. The thief began to run, but Yabidi wrestled him to the ground and told him to stay put while someone got a policeman. This was not an easy job in the middle of the night with very few policemen on the streets and no telephone to call police headquarters. When the thief got loose and ran again, Yabidi threw his club at him, hoping to hit his legs and bring him down. However, the club hit the thief in the head and knocked him unconscious. A few days later, the thief died and Yabidi was put in prison because the thief had run off of the school property when he was struck down. We were all concerned. Yenourou and their six children were left without their husband and dad. Yabidi, languishing in prison, had no sentencing for seven months. What a sad day it was when the judge sentenced Yabidi to one year in jail. Thankfully, he had already served seven months of his sentence. The judge said this punishment also would protect Yabidi from the thief's family who could seek revenge on their own. We and others helped Yenourou as much as we could during that year, with sacks of rice and grain to feed her large family. She still sold the spinach-like leaves in the market that women used in their sauces, but because these were so plentiful, they sold cheaply. Only the Lord knew how hard it was for this dear sister to provide for her family. Her faith and trust were in her Savior. Yenourou also stayed awake at night to guard the school in her husband's place, although she was given no pay for it. Heath often visited Yabidi in prison. He suffered greatly but knew the Lord was with him. He said one night it was so hot in their prison cell and with so many men crammed in together, he felt like he could not breathe or last another night. Soon after he prayed, the guard came and unlocked their cell to tell them they could sleep outside on the ground in the walled courtyard.

After one year, Yabidi was released. The school then paid him his whole year's back wages (about $24 a month) because Yenourou had held his job for him. The first thing Yabidi did was go to Pastor Luc to pay his back tithe to the Gourma church! What a testimony!

Busyness and Stress

Our home in Niamey was like Grand Central Station most of the time. We had very little privacy. It seemed that too often there was someone at the front door wanting our help or attention and at the same time someone was at the back door also wanting the same thing...and the phone was ringing! This was typical of our feelings of being pulled in several directions at once.

Heath's office was in a back room of the church next door to our home. There were always arriving or leaving missionaries to be met at the airport, visas to apply for, and freight papers and all other sorts of official papers to be taken care of in French. This work was time consuming but very necessary for the mission and missionaries.

Ours was the only protestant mission in Niamey at that time, so other missions in remote areas called upon Heath to get purchases, airline tickets, visas, and different official documents for them. He was glad to do this for them, and their kindness was reciprocal. We enjoyed fellowship with these brothers and sisters as they passed through Niamey using our guest facilities too. Many became lifelong friends.

We had hired Amadou, a young man who worked for our furloughing coworkers. He was a handsome young fellow with huge dimples that showed when he smiled and he was very meticulous in his dress and grooming. He had heard the Gospel but when presented with his need of Christ, he was so afraid of his family that he couldn't commit to the Savior. He told us once that he would like to become a follower of Jesus Christ but was sure his *baaba* would kill him if he did. *Baaba* means father, but it is also the word Zarmas use for their uncles. Amadou's biological father had died, so he was referring to his uncle.

When the Cowleys returned from furlough, Amadou returned to their employ. A year or two later, his behavior became more and more bizarre, and he could not work. For many years after that, Amadou wandered the streets, dirty, disheveled, with a long unkempt beard and hair, seemingly totally insane. The village people rumored that Amadou's uncle had put a curse on him with witchcraft so that the uncle would get all of Amadou's money. Whenever we saw Amadou, we greeted him and he always recognized us in spite of the faraway look in his eyes.

From our prayer letter, dated December 1967: "One day when an African neighbor lady was visiting, Norma had to leave her alone a few minutes while she gathered the washing. Nathan was loudly wailing for attention, but his mother was busy. Soon, Nathan was quiet and Norma came back to find that Aime-nya had tied him on her back with a cloth just like an African baby, and he was perfectly happy! Pray for our daily contacts with friends here. Winning Muslims is through a day-by-day individual witnessing process, and much wisdom and patience is needed…At present, we are preparing for our annual missionary conference, which will be in January. Pray with us that God will mightily work and give us the best conference ever. Rev. Robert Richards and Rev. Wittig, chairman of the EBM board, will be with us. We are looking forward to their visit."

After the conference, Bob Richards and Rev. Wittig were able to visit several of our outstations to see the fine work being carried on by our bush missionaries. Our hearts were still in the bush work too, but we knew that the Lord wanted us in Niamey at that time. The Lord graciously opened up many new opportunities for us there also.

Rev. Richards and Rev. Wittig planned to fly from Niamey up to Gao, Mali, after the Niger conference so that they could be present for the Mali field's conference. Only one flight a week made that trip. Lo and behold, when Heath took them to the airport, they were the only passengers on the flight. Bob later told us that after the plane got into the air and flew for a while, he had the distinct impression that it had turned back toward Niger. As he looked out the window, he was sure when Niamey came into view. The steward sheepishly told the two passengers that their luggage had been left behind, and they were flying back to get it!

For Christmas 1967, the Frenchman who was head of the Niamey office of UTA airlines, where Heath purchased many tickets for missionaries, surprised us with a real Christmas tree from France and boxes of decorations for it. That was fun, but in the hot climate of Niger, the pine needles soon fell off. We were surprised when the Christmas tree disappeared after we set it outside and even more surprised when it showed up again as we attended the excellent Christmas play put on by the church a few nights later. The various groups from the Niamey church performed several epic dramas during Christmas week, portraying Bible stories. Better acting wasn't to be found in this world! Africans are talented, uninhibited, precise, and comical! That year, they did the whole story of Moses. There on the platform was our balding Christmas tree, portraying the burning bush!

The Gourma Christians invited us to their Christmas Eve celebration featuring rice and peppery meat gravy. The French-speaking church, consisting of many different nationalities, was full on Christmas morning. Our children thought the Christmas vacation went too fast, while Heath said, "What vacation?" He seemed to have enough to do to keep two men busy, but we praised the Lord for His help and strength in this new ministry.

Origin of the Niamey EBM Station
From an article written by pioneer missionary Helen Bechtel

Mr. McCaba and a wonderful Christian named Idrissa decided a church should be built for the Yorouba Christians, a tribe from Nigeria who were the fruit of early missions. They came to Niamey as market traders. Many were Christians and had some schooling. First, they met in a home until it got too small, then they rented a schoolhouse.

They searched for a proper lot. The government gave the mission this elevated lot far outside of the town, but they weren't sure the town would grow in that direction. (Niamey has grown and grown in all directions since then.) Local people told the missionaries to never build there because that location was used for demon worship and sacrifices. It was "the devil's territory."

Mr. McCaba told them that the missionaries were not afraid of the devil. Power was with God. The building was started, the stone and cement walls went up, a pan ceiling was put on, inside benches were made, and a slab stone floor was laid. Finally, the stone steps leading up to the church were finished, and the missionaries were very proud of their stone building.

One morning, Idrissa rushed out to tell the missionaries that lightning had struck the building in the night. The roof had fallen down into the center, twisting the iron structure. The neighbors said to Idrissa, "We told you so!" Tears filled his eyes. He had worked so hard to build the church, and now his health was fast deteriorating from a kidney disease. He knew he could never rebuild it. It was still war time, no cement or materials available. So they cleaned out the shell of the church and put grass mats on the roof. Benches were brought in, and the believers continued to meet in the building until it was repaired.

The missionaries and local believers persisted until the church and property were permanently built to shine as a testimony right in the middle of the city. Our home in Niamey was next door to the church.

Parades

A new experience for us was to attend the fabulous parades for special occasions in Niamey. Hundreds of horses and camels were brought in from many outlying areas, beautifully decorated with gold and bangles. The men in their fancy robes and turbans completed the festive dress. Hamani Diori became president when Niger gained independence in 1960, and the Niger had remained stable while other African countries had many coups and changes of government.

Some countries immediately wanted the French colonists to leave, but Niger, very wisely, had them stay for the transition, to teach the newly independent people how things should be done. In offices, although Nigeriens then held the titles, we saw faithful French men and women in the background helping in the transition from colonialism to independence.

In late January 1968, thirteen heads of African countries met in Niamey. As the camel and horse corteges arrived for the huge parade, we counted more than 100 camels that passed by our Niamey house.

McCaba Academy

EBM had a two-room missionary children's school on the Yantala station, in association with the boarding school, so I did not have to homeschool Rebecca and Jonathan in our new location. Grades one to four met in one room and grades five to eight in the other room. The children had a large play area, and eventually a nice volleyball/tennis court was built. The high school classes met in the back rooms of the Niamey church.

Muslim New Year in March 1968

From our prayer letter, undated: "Life is getting back to normal here in the city after the big Muslim New Year's holiday was celebrated. To us, it is the saddest day of the year, for on that day each household sacrifices one or more sheep for their sins. Coming home through the city on Sunday morning, Heath saw pile after pile of slain sheep lying outside of compounds. These are mute testimonies to the fact that the Muslims reject the Lamb of God who takes away the sin of the world. We prayed much for the African Christians, for although they are ridiculed every day of the year, this holiday is worse because they refuse to make the sheep sacrifice…Heath leaves tomorrow to go on the river with some of our bush missionaries who have a small houseboat that they use as a floating dispensary…Please pray for Emile, the young school teacher who was saved in August. His wife remains unsaved and actually seems to be hardening her heart. Her relatives have threatened to take her away from him now that he has become "a liar and an infidel" (Christian). He needs much grace and wisdom. Pray for Salimou's salvation."

Yacouba Nouhou

We first met Yacouba when he was a night guard at the American ambassador's residence. From the Fulani tribe, he was handsome and brilliant. Although he had never been to school, he spoke seven languages, could write in Arabic, and taught himself to read English and French. A Peace Corps volunteer named Sue had a beautiful horse named Caprice whom Yacouba fed and groomed. She wanted him to ride Caprice too because she didn't often have time to ride. Yacouba came into our yard early in the morning, often while Nathan and Alan were still sleeping under their mosquito nets outside. They were always so happy to see Yacouba and get a ride. Nathan, sitting in his pajamas on the horse, called him Kuba. Rebecca and Jon, being older, learned how to ride by themselves. We had many opportunities to talk to Yacouba about the Gospel, and he readily accepted Gospel literature, but he never seemed to come under the Spirit's convicting power.

From our prayer letter, dated April 1968: "The temperature reads 105 degrees in our house on this warm April afternoon. At night, we are sleeping outside where it is just a little cooler. In spite of all, we are praising the Lord and happy in His work. We have seen Him working in our midst, and we are writing to encourage you in your prayers for us...Nathan is a chubby sixteen months now. He has a vocabulary of half Zarma and half English."

Most bedrooms in missionary homes had an access door outside to a cement patio. Around our Niamey house, Heath and I were on one patio, and our front terrace-porch was big enough for all the children's beds to be set up with mosquito nets over each one. Heath and I had no roof over us, so we had to untie our mosquito nets and grab our linens and mattresses to head inside when it rained. The front terrace was covered, so the children could continue to sleep out there when there was a gentle rain. In the case of big sandstorms, we all had to go inside. By the time we got everything inside, there was dirt and sand on everything, and we were spitting out the grit!

Once inside, we tried to sleep again. But if a cooling rain did not come, we merely sweated and tossed all night, making our sheets somewhat muddy by morning!

One night after we had gotten all the children inside and were settled in our three bedrooms, we were stunned to hear loud knocking on the bedroom door that led from our living room. Who could be inside our house knocking loudly? Switching on our flashlights, we saw that our German shepherd, Hunter, was inside too, right by the door. As he was vigorously scratching behind his ear, his hind leg was hitting the door in a loud staccato! It took us a while to calm down and get to sleep after that adrenaline rush!

Was it noisy sleeping outside in the city? Yes! Many people sat down on the street corner by our house, talking and laughing until very late. The motorbikes and cars were noisy too, but worst of all was the small bars that surrounded us. They played their music at its highest volume until the wee hours of the morning, especially on weekends. It certainly is true that you can get used to anything if you are exposed to it long enough. We slept soundly in spite of the noise and didn't even notice it after a while.

Mariama

Rebecca had always wanted a sister, so the Lord blessed her with one in 1968 when Mariama came to live with us. Mariama was fourteen years old. Her mother had died in childbirth, and her family asked EBM missionaries Steve and Louise to please take this newborn baby, who

With Jesus Leading the Way

would surely die unless someone cared for her who knew how to sterilize baby bottles.

Steve and Louise loved Mariama and cared for her as their very own special little girl. Her biological father – a gentle, kind man – came periodically to see how she was doing. Mariama was her mother's tenth child so she had several brothers and sisters. When Mariama was five, the Blacks had to return permanently to the States. In the years that followed, she lived with many missionary families. She even lived at our girls' school in Dosso for a while. Her resilience was amazing and she grew up very much at home with her African and her American family.

Before she came to live with us, Mariama was living with "Aunt" Gladys Gilson. Gladys also had to leave Niger permanently to care for her aging parents. She asked us about taking Mariama. Our whole family said an enthusiastic "Yes!" She and Rebecca behaved like sisters too, sometimes having great times together and other times going out to their bed at night and sleeping with their backs to each other because of an argument. Overall, they did very well though. Mariama was a blessed addition to our family.

Within one week, we had to break very sad news to Mariama twice. Her "Aunt" Louise Black died in the States of cancer. Then news came that Mariama's father, who had been sent on the pilgrimage to Mecca by his sons, had died there. During the pilgrimage, there is a time when thousands walk around the Kaaba, the building in the center of the mosque in the sacred Muslim city of Mecca. If someone falls, no one can pick them up, so they are trampled. Some believed that Mariama's father had a heart attack and fell as the crowd circled the Kaaba. Muslims also believe that if one dies in Mecca, they are sure of going directly to heaven.

Having grown up with American children, Mariama's English was American with no accent. She also spoke her birth language, Zarma, and completed her schooling in French. So she was perfectly tri-lingual. She loved to play records on our little record player and especially liked a song on one record that said, "Come home. It's supper time." One day I heard her singing, "Bringing in the Sheeps!" When I told her it was sheaves, she asked, "What in the world are sheaves?" When I told her the Zarma word for sheaves, she understood.

Tarzan, the huge dog given to us by the departing gendarme in Gaya, was with us in Niamey too. At that time, we didn't have to have a night guard because there was so little crime and break-ins. With our flimsy screen doors and windows and our sleeping outside, it wouldn't have been difficult for a thief to enter our home. We did have to keep Tarzan tied to a metal chair on our front porch and regularly take him for walks. If he got free, he took off into the city and we didn't see him again for many hours.

One day we were very thankful that Tarzan got out and that no one had attached him to the metal chair. All of a sudden, none of us could find toddler Nathan. We frantically searched the house and yard for him. André ran down on the street to look for Nathan. Our house was located on four busy corners with cars and motorbikes whizzing by. There were open sewers on the street in front and beside our house. Only a narrow cement slab was there to walk across the sewer and onto the street.

As André asked the African people along the street if they had seen a little *anasara* baby, they nodded their heads yes and pointed down the street toward the big market several blocks away. André kept running, and then he saw Tarzan and Nathan. Barefooted, diaper-clad Nathan had descended the five steps out of our front gate, crossed the sewer and the street, and kept going. Right behind him was Tarzan, head down, following close behind Nathan to protect him! As André brought Nathan back, the African people explained, "We wanted to stop him because we knew he shouldn't be out alone on the street, but all of us were too afraid of that huge dog following him!"

Luc Souantieba's Call to Niamey

The Gourma work in Niamey was growing as many responded to the Gospel and became followers of Jesus Christ. When we arrived in Niamey, Pastor Luc had finished Bible school in Burkina Faso then had come to spend time preaching in the church and evangelizing. The first time he witnessed to a group of Muslim men sitting in the shade by the river, they were furious and assured him they did not want to hear the lies about

Christ. They said, "If we weren't afraid of what the government would do to us, we would kill you right here on the spot!" That was a real shock to Luc. When he preached the Gospel to idol worshippers, they were immediately afraid. He decided he would return to his country of Burkina Faso to serve the Lord there. So few in the Niamey Gourma church had work, so they were not able to support a pastor anyway.

Luc's wife, Oukano, (a Bible school graduate) was back in Burkina Faso waiting to give birth to their first baby. When he came to tell Heath that he was going to leave, Heath talked to him a long time about the call of God and how much he was needed in the Niamey Gourma church.

Heath told Luc we would give him employment working for us to supplement the church's pay so that he could support his family. Luc later told us that he really didn't want to hear that! He wanted to get out of Muslim territory and go home! But God dealt with his heart, and he yielded to the Lord's call to be the pastor of the Niamey Gourma church. He was a foreigner as much as we were, called to work on the mission field of Niger.

Luc was a godly man. He came to our house several times a week for me to teach him the Zarma language. We read the Zarma Bible for a textbook. He was diligent and soon had mastered the local language.

A number of Gourma people had come to know Christ through the faithful preaching in the little grass-thatched church by the riverside and were preparing for baptism. They always wanted Heath to participate in baptisms in the Niger River. As we gathered on the bank to sing and rejoice with the new followers of Jesus Christ, scattered groups of Muslims observed this ordinance from a distance. For any Muslim who becomes a Christian, they are told they could always turn back until they were baptized. Then they would be surely sent to hell.

The 1968 school year had begun for Rebecca (seventh grade) and Jonathan (fifth grade). We were thankful our children could live at home with us and yet attend the missionary children's school in town. We asked for prayers for our dedicated teachers. Three teachers in a two-room school for eight grades was a challenge. When Alan had his fifth birthday in April 1968, I began to teach him kindergarten at home.

I wanted to be the one to teach each of our children to read. The Lord allowed me to have that privilege, using the old "Dick, Jane, and Spot" books. When I started teaching Alan to read in kindergarten, he progressed rapidly and went through all the first-grade readers in just a few months. When he picked up a book to read, little brother Nathan would irritate him by saying over and over, "Oh, Jane. Look, Jane. Oh, Dick. See, Dick!" Later when Alan took IQ and Iowa Test of Basic Skills, he scored well above average. We began to realize that God had blessed him with exceptional intelligence.

In the middle of September 1968, tragedy struck Luc and Oukano's household. Oukano brought her very sick six-month-old baby, Malata, to us. Malata had been having diarrhea for several weeks off and on, and now she was vomiting black liquid and looking very poorly.

We rushed Malata to the government hospital. After a two-hour wait, they admitted her, telling us she was seriously ill. The conditions in the children's ward were appalling. There were seventeen cribs in the same room and a mat on the floor beside each crib where the mothers slept by their children to care for them. There was barely space to walk in that room, not to mention the unsanitary conditions, the odors, and the cockroaches everywhere.

Early the next morning, as soon as the sun was up, Luc and one of the other Gourma Christian men came to tell us that little Malata had gone to be with Jesus in the middle of the night. With heavy hearts, this precious little firstborn was wrapped in a white cloth for burial. The small Christian cemetery in Niamey was overcrowded. Twice when the Gourma church men were attempting to dig a grave, it began to cave in, so they knew someone else was buried there. The third try was successful.

I'll never forget Luc carrying this little body in his arms to put her in the grave. We thanked the Lord we could speak comfort to this couple, for Luc and Oukano knew that they would see their daughter again. The Muslims of Niger had no hope beyond the grave; death was an eternal separation for them.

After a while, the Gourma Church was able to launch out in faith to start supporting Luc by their tithes and offerings. We asked prayer for spiritual growth in the lives of the many Gourmas who were coming to faith in Christ.

The members of our Zarma language Bible translation committee could meet only once a month because they were all busy in their ministries. What a job it was to type up Old Testament books on our typewriters, making several copies with carbon paper for the committee to

With Jesus Leading the Way

go over, check, and correct. Then when the manuscript was deemed ready, it was typed page-by-page onto stencils to make mimeographed copies. In March 1968, I typed the stencils for Ruth and Exodus.

I loved teaching in a new ministry we started in Niamey. It was a Sunday school for MKs, African children who spoke English, and children of diplomats, American embassy employees, and Peace Corps volunteers. We requested prayer for our Sunday school classes. So many of these children spoke Zarma fluently and were the best prospective missionaries Niger had.

In January 1969, Malam Kano, a Zarma preacher from Nigeria, came to hold meetings in various places in Niger. We used Gospel filmstrips to draw a large crowd. Malam Kano was a blessing to us all. We looked to him for spiritual and cultural guidance in working with the Zarma people.

Malam Kano had left his home area of Dosso, Niger, as a young boy, to look for work in Nigeria. Because he had no schooling, the work he found was being a house steward for a missionary family. It was there, as he heard the Gospel message over and over, that he opened his heart to become a believer in Christ. As he began to grow in Christ, learning to read in Hausa, he went off to a Hausa Bible school and graduated.

We never knew what the young men who worked for us or who attended our Thursday Bible club or played volleyball with us on the court Heath opened in Gaya would later become. One of the fellows eventually became Niger's ambassador to the United States, and there were many others who worked in government positions who remembered the times we spent with them when they were just children. The missionary for whom Malam Kano worked was later heard to say that Malam Kano was such a problem that he had seriously considered firing him! The transforming power of Christ changed this troubled young man into a godly servant of the Lord.

Some of the stories Malam Kano told us were about demons and evil spirits, which are very real to African people. They know what demon possession and demonic activities are, and they fear their power. After serving many years as an evangelist, Malam Kano and his family settled in a small village, Fingilla, in northern Nigeria, not far across the border from where we had served in Gaya, Niger. As we were visiting one day, he told us the following story.

Demon worshipers had set up fetishes and a place to offer sacrifices on a large stone in the field of a rich Muslim man. Malam Kano was irritated in seeing it every time he passed by, so one day he asked the rich man why he allowed the demon worship and sacrifices in his field. The Muslim man said he didn't like it either, but he was afraid of the demons' power, so he never touched the things or tried to remove them. He told

Malam Kano, "I am afraid to do anything, but if you want to destroy that place, I don't care if you do it."

Malam Kano went right out to the big stone, destroyed the fetishes, and scattered everything to clear it away. There was a lot of screaming and wailing when the demon worshipers arrived to see what had happened. They were told that the Christ follower, Malam Kano, had done it and the field owner had allowed it.

They pronounced a curse on the Muslim field owner and on Malam Kano, saying they both would die in a short time. True believers in Christ are not afraid of the devil's curses placed on them. The next week, the Muslim man got a ride on a transport truck to go to a larger town to conduct some business. On his way back home, the truck rolled over and he was killed. He was not under the protecting power of our Father in heaven. Malam Kano told us, "That was many years ago, and I am still alive. God controls my destiny, not Satan!"

Alan's Injury

When Alan was about six years old, he began to limp badly, and we couldn't find out why. He said he hadn't hurt his leg. At the Gamkalley Clinique, there were young French doctors doing their residency for two years. If they spent two years in Niger, it counted as their two years of French military service. The two who were there examined Alan, took X-rays, and seemed really puzzled about what his problem was. Finally, they wrote a prescription for a strong antibiotic for us to give him. We were not happy about doing that.

What we needed was an orthopedic doctor to examine Alan. *God dropped one out of the sky for us the next day!* In a casual conversation with one of our coworkers, she mentioned that a doctor from her home church would be passing through the next day to visit them on his way to visit his missionary daughter in Nigeria. He was an orthopedic specialist! When we asked if she thought he would be willing to examine Alan, she was sure he would say yes.

With Jesus Leading the Way

He examined Alan carefully, working his leg and asking questions. Finally he said, "I wouldn't give him the needless antibiotic. He either has a sprained hip or Paget's disease, which is very serious. In that case, you will need to return to the States for treatment. I don't think it is Paget's disease. I am more inclined to think Alan has a sprained hip. For the next week, he must be off of his leg completely and in bed. He is not to even walk to the bathroom. You'll have to carry him there. After one week of this care, if it is a sprain, he will be fine."

We carefully kept him immobile for a week, and then Alan was fine, praise God! After that, he remembered that one of the other children was pushing him on his little go-cart, and his leg got twisted back! *Voilà*, the sprain! We will never forget the miracle of the Lord dropping the precise doctor we needed out of the sky for us!

Since EBM had been the only Protestant mission in Niamey over the years, invitations were occasionally issued to us to attend government receptions at the palace. Dal and Kay Washer had told us to bring some formal attire back from furlough. Heath had a nice tuxedo-type white coat. I often bought pretty material in the market to be made into long dresses. No matter how I dressed, I always felt very plain compared to the African ladies in their elegant dresses with their gold jewelry and fancy head coverings.

Dec. 18, 1968
President and Madame Hamani Diori
Reception given at Presidential Palace
Niamey, Niger Republic

We knew it was a great privilege to be invited to these occasions. At the palace, we always had to walk up the steps and stand in line to personally greet President and Madame Diori then walk through the palace and out onto the huge back terraces where tables were waiting. At the appointed time, we all stood as President Diori came out with the visiting dignitaries. They paused regally at the top step while the Niger military band played the Niger national anthem and the national anthem of the visiting head of state. Sometimes there were traditional dancers who entertained the invitees, and there was always excellent food.

As embassies from different countries opened one after another in Niamey, we were also included on their guest lists for their Independence Day celebrations. We met many different nationalities and had opportunities to speak and minister to them also.

From our prayer letter, dated March 1969: "The bleating of many sheep is in the background as we sit down to write. Within the next hour or two, thousands upon thousands of these will be sacrificed on this Muslim holiday Eid Al-Adha. With this, they hope that their sins of the past year will be forgiven. How we thank God for a living Savior to present to these people and that we can show them from God's Word the Lamb of God who takes away the sin of this world. Only the Holy Spirit can persuade them of these truths though, and for this reason we are so very dependent upon your *prayers* as we labor here for Him."

Looking for Giraffe

From time to time, especially during the children's school vacations, we would hustle them out of bed at 5:30 a.m., along with some of their African friends, to head for the bush. About twenty-five miles up the Tillabéry Road, we almost always began to see the wild giraffe that we were looking for. We had the feeling that the pleasure was mutual as far as the sightseeing went because they seemed as curious to look us over as we were to see them. Niger has some of the tallest giraffe in the world, known to have knocked down telephone wires when they were running. On one occasion, Rebecca and Jon ran beside some giraffe as they were leaving. Later we learned that a giraffe kick can be lethal, so we were glad for the Lord's protection as the kids innocently did that.

This was the era of the hippies who often traveled in Africa seeking adventure. Africans were puzzled by the hippies' long unkempt hair and different clothing. One morning the local villagers told us, "Giraffe don't like hippies, but they like your children and they won't harm them."

On one outing along a dirt road, we looked and looked for our tall friends, finally stopping when we saw giraffe quite a long distance from our car. As we looked out the right side of the car, exclaiming excitedly about how many there were in the distance, someone looked to the left. There were three large giraffes right beside the road, looking down at us with all curiosity before they leisurely went on their way!

I usually prepared some homemade donuts or cinnamon rolls for our breakfast on these outings, along with hot chocolate and coffee. I hope our children remember those good times as fondly as we do. We enjoyed going to zoos but seeing animals in their natural habitat in the wild was much more thrilling.

Our first year in Niamey brought many trials and heartaches that we had not faced in all our preceding years when we were bush missionaries. Besides the difficulties with the African mission group, led mostly by a disgruntled Hausa Christian who had a high position in the government, there were some of our men missionary colleagues who felt they were passed over by our home board in not being chosen as acting field director. My admiration for Heath's Christ-like reactions to those men in spite of their attitudes and actions grew daily. I knew where the grace and strength he manifested came from. He began his days on his knees, committing all into the hands of His Lord. I never heard him say anything against any of those men, but I only saw him serve them with kindness and humility. What a testimony he was to me and our children.

I was very thankful for other colleagues who did accept Heath's work as God-appointed. We didn't always agree on everything, but there was grace and love that gave latitude to each servant of Christ and their service in Niger.

In the spring of 1969, we went on a station visit to Filingué where Roger and Phyllis Bacon were serving. It was a great joy to visit with a dear old woman who came to Christ in the sunset years of her life. What a thrill to sit on the floor of her little grass hut and have her tell us of her new life in Jesus Christ. She wanted to learn to read the Word of God, but her eyesight was almost gone. We praised God for His saving power and prayed for her witness to those all around her. She may not have been able to see much, but it was those around her who were in darkness – the spiritual darkness of not knowing Christ. The colorful cliffs, canyons, and rock formations around Filingue reminded us a lot of the American West.

Children's Bible Class at Yabiri and Yenuru's Home

In 1969, I began holding open-air children's classes in the school yard of Zongo primary school where Yabiri and Yenuru lived with their large family. I never knew how many children would come, and their ages were approximately from toddlers to junior high. It wasn't easy to keep control of a large group outside with people passing through the schoolyard. Some of the children were there every week, and there were even some adults who sat to the side and listened too. This was the only time I prayed that a class wouldn't be too big! When there were more than forty or fifty, pandemonium could reign!

Yenuru and Yabiri were a wonderful help in settling the children on benches and mats then telling them to be quiet and listen. For the most part, the children behaved quite well. They loved singing the Gospel songs I taught them in Zarma or in French. One of the first songs they learned was *"Joie, Joie, Mon Coeur est Dans la Joie"* ("Joy, Joy, My Heart is Full of

Joy"). From this they nicknamed me Joie-Joie. No matter where I was in the city, when a smiling young person greeted me as Joie-Joie, I knew he or she had attended my children's classes. I continued having classes for the next seven years using visual aids of Bible stories and went through many series of lessons.

Our prayer letter described our open-air children's classes: "Picture in your mind a sandy hill with two grass huts perched on its knoll. One hut is so old it looks like any good puff of wind will level it. This is home for a family of seven, and it is freely open to us for Bible classes each week. We drive the car as close as possible, avoiding getting stuck in the sand (we hope) to park under a shade tree. The children have spotted the car and come running toward us from every direction.

"'Joy-Joy! Here comes Joy-Joy's car! It's time for our class!' A dozen or more hands reach to carry my Bible pictures and whatever else I have with me. We receive such a glad welcome each week. Within ten minutes, there are more than forty children eager to begin, so we place a few benches and spread out mats in the shade to begin to sing. More children of all ages are arriving. A few men and two women settle themselves near enough to hear too. How we pray for wisdom to make the Gospel message as clear and simple as possible to these for whom Christ died. Songs, a Bible story and application, memorization of Scripture verses, and the class is over. We wish you could be here in person for we know you couldn't help but love these young people as we do."

To maintain quietness and attention during the lessons, I brought along a bag of hard candies from the market. If the children were well behaved, everyone got a piece of candy at the close of class. If they were noisy and troublesome, no one got candy! It worked quite well. There were very few times that I didn't give out candy at the end of the class.

One week when I sent our house helper to the market to buy a bag of candy, he came back with a bag of cough drops. I reasoned that the children wouldn't know the difference and would think they were candy. Wrong! After we had given everyone a cough drop, several came back pretending to cough, asking for more because they had a cold!

Years later, another missionary friend brought a university student to see me. He blessed me with this testimony: "My name is Sidi, and when I was a young boy, I attended your open-air children's Bible classes at the Zongo school. I remember all the songs and Bible stories that you taught us. Now I am a Christian. Next Sunday I will be baptized at the Bible center on the other side of the river." The smile on the face of this young man made going to those classes in the heat of the day all those years more than worthwhile. My prayer is that someday in heaven I will meet many others who heard and believed too.

One Thursday during the hot season, Yenuru was not home when I came for the class, and I was disappointed. However, before I even got started, I saw her hurrying across the sand to join me. She had taken one of the Gospel Recordings' record players and Gospel records to homes of her lady friends to do some evangelizing. The heat was beastly as she rushed back for our class. She carried the phonette balanced on her head, her baby tied on her back, and she was perspiring profusely. Still she arrived with her happy smile to greet me.

The thermometer in our living room reached 109 degrees in April, the highest it had ever registered in the house. Any breeze that blew felt like it was coming out of an oven door. During such debilitating heat, patience and tempers became short. No missionary could afford an air conditioner, much less pay the electric bill to run one. Once a French doctor came to our house when Jonathan was sick with a fever. He asked why we didn't have Jon in an air-conditioned room, so we had to tell him we had none. He replied, "Having an air conditioner in Niger is not a luxury. It is a necessity! I must have you check your son into the Gamkalley Clinic to help bring down his fever."

The French in Niger always had air conditioners, at least in their bedrooms. The American embassy and A.I.D. employees had an air conditioner hanging out of a window in every room in their houses and even out of the storerooms for their canned goods. It was always amazing to us that the Americans left many of their air conditioners running day and night for the month or two when they were in the States for vacations. Since the U.S. government paid all their utility bills, they weren't concerned.

How could we complain though? The Lord was so good to us, and our lives were much easier than our African friends'. At least we had fans to help cool us.

A blind man named Seidou came often to our house. Kay Washer had taught him to read Braille. She had prayed for him and witnessed to him, but he remained a staunch Muslim. When Seidou requested something to read in French from one of our other blind students who was attending school in Nigeria, he loaned Seidou his Braille copy of the Gospel of John. Seidou began to see the light through his fingers! As he read the book of John, he began to realize that Jesus was truly the Son of God. He visited us often, and we read Scriptures to him. Later I read French Bible correspondence courses to him and wrote down his answers to the questions. He eventually got a certificate for finishing all of the courses.

In May 1969, we wrote to our supporters rejoicing that Heath had just baptized six new Gourma believers, my children's classes were going well, and blind Seidou had become a believer. We also wrote, "The devil hasn't taken a holiday though. He never lets us forget that we are in his territory, and he fights us each step of the way. Pray that we will use our *shield of faith* when he sends his fiery darts of discouragement our way. This has been one of the worst hot seasons we can ever remember in Africa, and we are all so very exhausted from the heat."

McCaba Academy Faces Trying Times

The Glessners had finished their term as teachers for McCaba Academy and left for the States. Attempting to have a high school on our field was an experiment that wasn't working very well. We found that a high school is a whole different ball game from having an elementary MK school. However, we were quite thrilled that a couple with a young son was raising their support to come to Niger. She would teach in the elementary school and he in the high school.

She was a sweet Christian woman who testified she had wanted to serve on the mission field since she was just a young girl. As the months went by, we were puzzled by the behavior of her husband. He made some statements in his classes that made the students wonder where he stood on Christianity. On Sunday evenings, everyone attended our English service. We were all grateful to worship in our mother tongue and to reach out to other English-speaking people in Niamey – Africans, Peace Corps volunteers, diplomats, embassy employees, Europeans, and others attended these services. This young teacher always made sure he needed to take his small son out of the service just before the message. Then he sat outside during the remainder of the service. He was not a happy man.

In addition to this strange situation, we had elementary dorm parents who also had serious problems. They were overly strict with the children entrusted to them and were unhappy with some of the parents of the children in their dorm. A couple of children from Mali actually ran away from the dorm and showed up at our house! We talked with them and prayed with them, encouraging them to return to the dorm. They did return, even though it wasn't easy for them.

These two couples became friends and each fed the others' dissatisfactions. They both decided to quit missions, return to the States, and seek secular work at the end of that school year. This was a very trying time for all of us. Who would be our dorm parents for the following year? This meant we also would need an elementary teacher as well as a high school teacher.

I'll never forget the way Heath laid the whole situation out to us remaining missionaries after these couples left. There was a sadness that pervaded our group as we met for prayer. The Lord gave Heath faith and courage to calmly communicate to us that God was going to supply our needs. He assured us that God was faithful and would not let us down. I'm sure I was silently listening to him and thinking, "But how?"

God's Provision for McCaba Academy

In July, we welcomed Bob and Liz Schultz to teach for the next two school years. They were raising support to go to Algeria where Liz had grown up but graciously were willing to come to Niger first. Word came also that Ron and Sherry Yeater were coming to teach in the elementary school. We were praying for the Yeaters' needed support. The Lord worked mightily so that they arrived one week before school opened. Veteran missionaries Frank and Eleanor Marshall left their work in Timbuktu to become the new (dearly loved) dorm parents for the next year. Yes, we found God faithful, as always, and the Supplier of our needs.

That year saw our largest student body at McCaba Academy. Ron Yeater taught eighth grade, and I was sure some of the eighth-grade girls had a crush on him! Ron was an amateur taxidermist and made great preserved exotic African birds. He also knew how to take remarkable pictures with his cheap Instamatic camera. He always had his camera handy in class. The students knew exactly when to "freeze" and be very silent went he saw a picture he wanted to take of something he saw outside the classroom.

Vacation in Nigeria

We were hoping we could go down to the SIM rest home on the cool plateau in Jos, Nigeria, for the month of June 1969, so we made plans to go with colleagues Jim and Sandy Brock and their children who were on our old station of Gaya. Nigeria was preoccupied with the Biafra war (from

July 6, 1967, to January 13, 1970), and no visas were being granted to Nigeria. Rumor had it that we could obtain visas at one of the borders entering Nigeria, so we packed up our travel supplies of food and water and headed across the border in Gaya for Kamba, Nigeria.

When we came to the police barrier entering Nigeria, the border authorities told us to go back, that they wouldn't give us a visa. We always knew that other Europeans got across borders by giving a good bribe to the right people, but we didn't feel right about doing that. We often gave out tracts, Gospel calendars, agenda books, and Bibles. Many were happy to receive them and accepted them, then waved us on across the borders.

Nigerian journalist Dr. Peter Enahoro, had written a book titled *How to Be a Nigerian* which described Nigerian idiosyncrasies and customs. Evidently it was really amusing to read his comments about Nigerian culture, and Europeans were buying the book in large numbers. We hoped to buy a copy, but alas, the Nigeria authorities decided the book made fun of Nigerians so they banned any future sales in Nigeria.

In that book, Dr. Enahoro talked about bribes (which Africans give) and tips (which Europeans give). He said to the African mind, one is the same as the other. Dr. Enahoro said, "Africans give incentives before, while Europeans give rewards afterward." That statement is worthy of consideration.

He also mentioned how important long greetings are to Africans. "How are you? How is your family? Your father? Your children? All in good health? and so forth. He told about two Africans who were living in London, driving opposite directions down a narrow street when they saw and recognized each other. They stopped, smiled, and went through all the greetings, oblivious to the long lines of traffic behind them blowing their horns!

Meanwhile at the border, our pleas of dental and medical needs and the fact that we were exhausted from the Niger hot season finally got through to the border authority. He announced that as an act of grace, he would give us visas to go on! (Thank you, heavenly Father.)

Our children always entered into our adventuresome travels in good spirits. There were lots of laughing and sharing of stories with the Brock family too. When we made potty stops in areas that afforded a gulley or a few bushes for privacy, someone jovially announced that the men's restroom was to the left of the road and the women's restroom was to the right. There were always lots of deserted places along the Niger roads, but in Nigeria, Africa's most populous nation, it was more difficult to find a good isolated "restroom."

There was a small bridge that was washed out by the rains on the road near Kaduna, Nigeria, so our group of nine spent the night with a hospitable Canadian bachelor. He gave us instructions on how to make proper British tea. Use loose tea leaves, never tea bags. Be sure to "hot the pot" by filling it with boiling water for a few minutes. Pour that water out, then "never bring the boiling kettle to your tea pot, for it might cool some. Take your tea pot to the boiling kettle. Allow the tea leaves to steep for three to five minutes then pour the tea into fine teacups to serve. Since many British prefer milk in their tea, the milk should be heated and poured into the cup before you add the steeped tea." The tea was really good too!

No one had any idea when the bridge would be repaired, but there was a place a little way up the creek that was being used to cross over. Enterprising Africans were there to push our cars (for a sum) through the water toward the small embankment on the other side. Our Canadian friend told us they were disappointed when the waters began to dry up, bringing their source of income to a halt. They were known to bring water to the dry spots to stir up and renew the mud so cars still needed their pushes to get through.

Once our holidays were over, we again bounced over the difficult dirt roads on the two- or three-day trip back to Niger. We had two flat tires before we got home, the last happening just fifteen miles from home. Niger just had its first good rain, which brought out the big flying ants at dusk. They fly toward light of any kind. Our children laughed at my squeals when the ants constantly came at me while I held the flashlight for Heath to change our flat tire.

In July 1969, Jonathan had his eleventh birthday, requesting *tigidugey foy* for his special meal. The whole family enjoyed the peanut butter meat sauce over rice. It was, and still is, one of our family's favorite dishes.

Kano's Peanut Butter Sauce (Tigidugey Foy)

3 to 4 tablespoons oil
1 to 2 pounds bite-sized beef chunks or chicken breast or thighs
1 small onion, diced
2 to 3 cloves garlic, diced
1 8-ounce can tomato sauce
4 cups water
Beef or chicken bouillon
½ cup peanut butter
Salt and Cayenne pepper to taste

Heat the oil in a 4- or 5-quart Dutch oven or soup pot over medium heat. Brown the beef or chicken in the oil along with the onion. Add the garlic and cook for a minute or two until fragrant. Stir in the tomato paste and when the meat is almost browned. Add the tomato sauce over the meat mixture and stir until the meat is coated. Add enough water to cover the meat by about ½ to 1 inch and stir. Then add the beef or chicken bouillon. Simmer until the meat is tender. Put ½ cup of peanut butter in a bowl then spoon some of the hot sauce into the bowl. Mix it well so it thins out. Then add the peanut butter mixture into the sauce and meat mixture. Add salt and cayenne pepper to taste. Nigeriens like it hot! Serve over hot rice.

We missionaries gathered each month for a day of prayer. It was good to spend that time together before the throne of grace, asking that we would number our hours and days to be used just as He would have us use them. We mimeographed a copy of the prayer and praise items that we all submitted with our monthly work reports. In the evening of the day of prayer, everyone usually gathered at our house to listen to a taped message from home. While Heath met with the adults, I had the missionary children for their Bible study and prayer time. They were a grand group, and I really enjoyed working with them.

It was sad for all of us when a local evangelist took a second wife. He made all the arrangements with the father of his cousin, and the ceremony was performed in a bush village. Zarmas do marry first cousins. However, when this Christian girl found out about it, she absolutely refused to become his wife, so the marriage was annulled. His defense of taking a second wife was that so many of the Old Testament prophets took several wives, so it must be all right for him to do so too. Heath and other missionaries filled in preaching at the church as we prayed for the Lord to provide a national pastor to fill that position.

We thought maybe Alan had picked up malaria while we were in Nigeria. He was seven years old and gave us a terrible scare when he had febrile convulsions. We rushed him to Gamkalley Clinic, and they kept him hospitalized for three days.

On August 10, 1969, our nephew David Ludington, an Air Force Academy student, was killed in an automobile accident. We could hardly believe this shocking news that came to us in a telegram. Twenty-year-old David was home in Cazenovia, New York, on a short leave from Colorado Springs, Colorado. He and his parents, Jane (Heath's sister) and Homer Ludington, had a great vacation time together, never realizing it would be their last with David. On the fateful day, David had a date with Karen Woodward, a girl he had known since childhood. Their parents attended the same church and were good friends. David and Karen took a picnic lunch and were driving to Ithaca, New York, to spend time at one of the beautiful parks there. It was a warm summer day; the windows were open.

With Jesus Leading the Way

No one will ever know why David veered into the oncoming lane and hit a truck head-on. David was killed instantly. Karen lingered for a week in a coma before she passed away.

David was a fine young man who loved the Lord. How our hearts went out to Jane and Homer as we lifted up them and all the family in prayer. They saved a tape recording of the funeral for us to listen to when we got home the next year. The funeral closed victoriously with the "Hallelujah Chorus." We immediately decided that we wanted that music played at the end of our funerals too.

About one week later, Karen Woodward's funeral was held. The grace of God was gloriously put on display through her parents, George and Shirley Woodward. They could have been bitter and could have blamed David, but they did not. George stood at the funeral to say, "We want everyone to know that we do not believe there are any accidents in the lives of God's children. He is always in sovereign control, and we accept what has happened as from His hand."

Luc and Oukano were expecting another baby. Oukano was really getting big. I began to tease them saying, "If you have twins, one of them will be mine!" Her legs were quite swollen, so we decided to take her to the midwife at the maternity section of the government hospital. The midwife was concerned with the signs of toxemia and decided that Oukano should stay at the hospital. This time there were no beds available, so Oukano was settled in on a mat in the hallway. We hated to leave her there, but at the same time we were glad that at least the midwife was close by to monitor her.

Luc appeared at our door early the next morning with a big smile on his face. "You were right, Madame! Oukano gave birth to twin boys in the night!" I rushed to the hospital to see her and these two little gifts from God, but my joy turned to great sorrow when we found Oukano unconscious in her bed, having seizures, and with her eyes rolled back. It was postpartum eclampsia. I knew these symptoms were often fatal, and my heart was broken for Luc and these baby boys. After praying there with her, I went home and fell on my knees at our bedside in tears, praying for the Great Physician to heal Oukano. God, in His gracious love and provision, did heal her. She even went on in later years to have four more children with no complications.

The Gourma people have a beautiful custom. If you give them something or do something really nice for them, they do not come to thank you. Instead, they tell their friend what you have done and ask that other person to thank you for what you did. In some other African tribes, there is a great tendency to be jealous of another receiving good things. Certainly there was no room for jealousy when a person came to thank you for what you had done for another. The Gourmas even do this with the Lord. How many times Luc came to tell us of some gift or blessing they had received from the Lord, then asked us to thank the Lord for him. Also, when he prayed, he thanked the Lord for what He had done for others.

Our Bible bookstore in Niamey proved to be a great door of ministry in a Muslim land. Many would come into a bookstore who would not come into a Christian's home, much less a church. Each customer was given a Gospel tract, which most of them accepted.

About that time, we met Dominique, a brilliant young French teacher who was in Niger for a month to teach new math to African teachers. She asked, "Why are you missionaries here in Africa?"(Yes, we had heard it said that anyone who lived in the tropics was either after money or after souls or was crazy!) Although friendly, Dominique was very cynical about our work, stating that Africans have a religion suitable to their environment so why didn't missionaries leave them alone. We had opportunity to give testimony of faith in Christ and everyone's need for Him. We wished Dominique could have heard the testimony of born-again Africans who thanked us for bringing them the words of eternal life.

We often sent Mom Bobbett money to ask her to purchase and mail things we needed. In a letter Heath wrote, he asked her to purchase a pair of the Hush Puppies shoes that he liked so well. His instructions were for her to mail them in two different packages several days apart because if someone in the post office or customs office was tempted to steal, they wouldn't be interested in just one shoe! Heath also wrote to his mom, "I think it best that you don't send me any more underwear as you seem to have forgotten that I am a slim 36 and don't wear 44 shorts! Ha! I may return these to you unless we can find someone here who wants them…Sorry I have been so busy lately. These have been very hectic weeks. In fact, our whole term has been, and it has all gone by so swiftly. If Norma hadn't become our letter writer this term, no one would have heard much from us, that's for sure, and this includes our churches as well as our family and friends. We are praying for you and appreciate all you do for us. The Lord bless you. We love you very much. Heath"

When the Gourma church was able to support Luc, he stopped working for us as gardener and groundskeeper. He brought a young man named Dieyabidi to work in his place. Dieyabidi was fresh from a small village near Mahadaga in Upper Volta (later called Burkina Faso). He watered flowers, raked leaves, and swept the dirt yard. Nathan was just a toddler, so Dieyabidi kept an eye on him when he was playing in the yard.

Alan loved animals and always had pets of one kind or another. At that time, he had a duck. One day Nathan was chasing the poor duck all over the compound, and Dieyabidi did not know how to get him to stop. He came to our screen door all excited, saying in fractured French, "The duck, the duck, he is dead!" When I ran outside to see what was happening, the duck was very much alive. Dieyabidi was trying to tell me he was afraid Nathan would kill the duck by chasing it all over the yard!

That fall, Dieyabidi came down with measles that almost took his life. We fixed a bed for him in one of the Sunday school rooms in the back of the church. I took food to him, but he could not eat much. Sometimes he knew I had come with food and prayed over him, and other times he didn't even realize I had been there.

We took him to the government dispensary nurse who finally decided that he should be hospitalized in the big government hospital. Whenever a patient is hospitalized, a family member or friend accompanies him to care for him, bring food to him, and help in all ways. Dieyabidi was admitted to the hospital with no companion or relative to help him. Pastor Luc and some Gourma church members called on him when they could. We visited him also with food and gifts. We will always remember how the Lord lovingly cared for this child of His.

The following is what Dieyabidi recounted to us afterward. Far from home, desperately ill, hospitalized for the first time in his life, knowing very few people in Niamey, and not speaking the Zarma language, Dieyabidi was surrounded by Muslim patients in his ward. One cruel man would stand at the foot of his bed and taunt, "Gourma, you're going to die. You are an infidel because you don't pray (toward Mecca in Muslim ritual prayer). Just die! No one will bury you. We'll just throw you on the garbage heap outside."

But miraculously, there was another man who went outside and bought food from the ladies cooking and selling along the street outside the hospital. Time and again, he would buy special nourishing food and then bring it to Dieyabidi saying, "You won't die! You are going to get well. Here, eat this food. It will make you strong again."

After a month, a thin and weak Dieyabidi appeared on our doorstep to tell us he had been released from the hospital. He never knew who the man was in the hospital who encouraged him and brought him food. Although he went back to the hospital to look for him and ask for him, he never saw him again. He and I believe it was one of God's angels, ministering at his time of need.

After one month of being surrounded by Zarma-speaking people in the hospital, Dieyabidi spoke Zarma! The African people are so good with languages. They don't learn it by reading, memorizing, and studying as we think we have to do. They just live with the people and absorb the language the way our children did playing with other Zarma children.

It wasn't long before we decided to bring Dieyabidi into the house and teach him to be our house steward. It was one of the best decisions we ever made in our lives! We were so happy with him, and he soon became a beloved part of our family. When we had to be away on trips, we always knew he would take good care of our pets and our house while we were gone. What a blessing to have a trustworthy steward to help our busy household run more smoothly. He often sang hymns and praise songs as he worked around the house, which made for a great atmosphere in our home.

Once he confessed that he played tricks on me when I didn't realize it. He said he would sing a song two or three times, then go silent. After a while he became amused because he heard me singing the same song over and over as I worked around the house, too.

From our prayer letter, dated November 1969: "'It's coming! It's coming!' Missionary children and adults alike were gathered at the river's edge as the Trans-African Hovercraft Expedition stopped in Niamey. A hovercraft travels on a cushion of air over either land or water. This British team had traveled along the Senegal and Niger Rivers, starting in Dakar...

"A special delight for us was to meet F. Nigel Hepper, the head botanist among the twenty-six people on board, and to find that he was a genuine born-again Christian. He took time from his busy schedule to take a nature walk with the children of McCaba Academy, telling them many interesting things about African vegetation...We were all greatly impacted by his comments about the acacia trees.

"As they were walking across the mission compound, Dr. Hepper stopped, pointed out one of our trees, and said, 'This is an acacia tree. It was of this species that God told Moses to use in building of the Tabernacle. It is a very hard wood, yet very light and could easily be covered in gold and still be carried without too much difficulty. Acacia wood would have been plentiful and quite accessible where the Israelites were camping in the desert.' One of the MK teachers got a funny look on her face and said, 'You know, just the other day I asked an African man what that type of tree was good for and he replied, 'Oh, that one is good for *nothing!*" Isn't that just like God to take something that in the eyes of man is worthless and use it to raise up unto Himself a Tabernacle in the wilderness – to take that wood, shape it, cover it with gold, and make it a pillar in the Holy of Holies where he housed His Glory! What a perfect illustration of what God does in our lives. We are nothing. But God can take a worthless sinner and strip off the bark of our own self-righteousness, save us, clothe us with the righteousness of Christ Himself, and make our bodies a temple for the Holy Spirit of God Himself to dwell in and reflect His glory. Like pillars in His temple, we will be strong in His presence. His own name will identify us. What a promise that *He* is the only one that can make something out of nothing and use it for his glory."

In his published report, Mr. Hepper wrote about the missionaries he met all along the way during this trip: "As I flew back over the wide Sahara in a luxury DC-8 jet, I thought of those I had met, those serving the Lord in full-time service in Africa. My visit was over; I was soon home with my wife and family. But they stayed on in an environment very different from home. Many are in isolated spots, in dust and heat, without what we consider normal facilities.

"Yet how often have I heard people, even Christians, begrudge the missionaries some items that help to make their lives tolerable. Sheer ostentation may well be condemned, but that is not in question. From my own experience, the majorities of evangelical missionaries are making the best of humble circumstances and continually eat simple meals that put to shame their critics who invariably fare very much better. 'The laborer is worthy of his hire,' said the Lord Jesus. He also said, 'Blessed are the peacemakers, for they shall be called the sons of God...'Those who lead others to God are indeed the peacemakers, and their reward is eternal too."

Trip to Mali

Toward the end of 1969, our family of six embarked on a four hundred-fifty-kilometer road trip in our little Peugeot station wagon from Niamey to Gao, Mali. We had a long-standing invitation from friends Ann and Dan Zimmerman to visit them in Gao whenever we could. I had prepared food for the journey, including lots of filtered water (and a couple rolls of toilet paper) to carry with us. The unpaved roads were worse than we even imagined. At times, the road ran close to the Niger River, which was at peak level. Where the water overflowed the road, Heath took off the fan belt, hoping the car wouldn't stall in the deep water, while the children and I walked barefoot through the water trying to keep on the road to guide him. Arriving across the border in Mali, we then encountered deep sand with ruts so bad our car got hung up on them. Sometimes it was better to leave the road altogether and travel along the side of it. Then we encountered thorns so big they could cause flat tires.

Our children were great pilgrim travelers. Rebecca was thirteen; Jon, eleven; Alan, six; and Nathan, three. We had lots of fun joking, singing, and enjoying our travel adventure. The older kids liked to teach Nathan funny things to say, so when someone needed to make a bathroom stop, he would announce, "We gotta go booooosh!" The Africans often said when someone went outside of the village to relieve himself, "He went to the bush" because that is literally what they did. A very special bonus during the Gao trip was counting all the wild giraffe we saw along the way. We counted fifty-nine that first day.

We arrived tired and dust-covered at the Zimmermans' and were warmly welcomed with cold drinks from their refrigerator. During our three-day visit, they showed us around Gao. One of the highlights was a visit to the Rose Dune. This huge sand dune gets its name from its beautiful pinkish color at sunrise and sunset. To arrive at the dune, we had a fifteen-minute ride in a dugout canoe through small fishing villages found on islands in the Niger River. Climbing to the top of the dune was challenging, but we were rewarded with a fantastic view for miles around. It was beautiful, so peaceful and quiet. There is perhaps nothing like the tranquility and stillness of desert scenes.

The Gao Songhai language is similar to Zarma of Niger, but there were enough differences that we could only greet the local people, not have a conversation with them.

Rebecca was maturing into a lovely young woman, although she was only thirteen. When we were in Gao, Muslim men were taking note of her looks. A missionary daughter at this age often has to stay home unless she is accompanied by family or friends on the streets to avoid men who make suggestive remarks to her. I lost my cool in Gao when a turbaned and robed man leered at her said, "Girl, I want to go to bed with you." His mouth dropped open when I scolded and shamed him saying, "You should be ashamed of yourself, talking to a young girl like that! Here you are in Muslim dress with your prayer beads in your hands, talking dirty to a young girl!" I was furious. He backed off and said no more, while we continued down the street. Who knew how many wives and children he had at home; maybe even some of his daughters were Rebecca's age. He definitely ruffled my feathers, and I wasn't about to let him get by with it.

We were glad we got to spend Sunday at the Gao church to meet and fellowship with the believers. One outstanding man, Attino, had been saved years before and was a blessing to locals and missionaries alike.

With Jesus Leading the Way

Youth Camp

Our youth camp, still held during the Christmas break from school, was no longer in Téra after the Washers left but instead was held at our French elementary school. Classroom desks were removed or stacked to one side of the room. The campers brought their own sleeping mats and blankets, and the classrooms were designated either girls or boys dormitories. Coworker Florence Houck's wisdom and planning with the African staff made each year outstanding.

The time away from their villages and surrounded by a Christian atmosphere opened doors to reach young hearts for Christ. The outdoor amphitheater behind the French school was perfect for chapel each day and also for the plays and skits the youth did during camp. Abraham's wife, Agathe, was the head cook. She made delicious meals in huge pots posed on three stones over wood fires. I was often designated to take Agathe or some of the other lady cooks to the market to purchase meat, vegetables, yams, rice, couscous, and other supplies for the meals. It was a happy time and thrilling to see how God worked in the children's lives. Many young people were saved at camp, and those who already knew Christ were strengthened in their daily walk with Him. As an aftermath of this camp, seventy young people enrolled in our New Life for Christ class.

During one camp, there had been an unwelcomed guest on the property the first night. Heath and Roger Bacon were walking on a path with only a storm lantern for light when they saw what looked like a car tire beside the path. In seconds, they realized it was not a tire but a large coiled spitting cobra. Needless to say, there were two missionary men making a hasty exit from the scene! By the time they came back with proper lights and a gun, the cobra was nowhere to be found. We hoped he realized he was neither qualified nor welcomed for camp! We thanked the Lord for His protection.

Although the cost of camp was very minimal, many of the campers could not afford even that amount. But those who couldn't pay were not left out; they could earn their way to camp by memorizing a significant number of Scripture verses. Many of the campers paid their way to camp in this manner.

Death of Heath's Father

As with all children of divorced parents, Heath's parents' divorce had a profound effect on him. Jane and Shirley already were married and had their own homes when their parents divorced, but they were broken up about it too. I don't know why George never held onto his son or contacted him after that. Neither Lena nor Heath ever saw "the other woman." Later, Jane and Shirley invited them to their homes. But they did not see their dad and her often. The girls tried to keep their mother from knowing when they invited their father and his wife to their home because she highly disapproved.

After Heath became a student at Baptist Bible Seminary, he called his dad when he was in the Syracuse area to ask to meet him for a visit. George never came to where Heath was or tried to look him up.

During the first year of our marriage, word came that Heath's uncle, Irvin Bobbett, was hit by a car and killed. We drove to Skaneateles for the viewing. Heath introduced me to his dad at the funeral home. That was the first time I had met him.

There was only one other time that I saw Heath's father. On our first furlough from Niger, we were traveling through Syracuse, New York, with Rebecca, Jonathan, and baby Alan. Heath called his dad at his work, and they arranged to meet in the parking lot. He brought some ice cream bars for the children. I never saw him again.

In the fall of 1969, Heath heard from his sister Jane that his dad was very ill with Hodgkin's lymphoma and in a nursing home. Jane, living the closest to Syracuse, was able to visit him just about every Sunday. On December 31, 1969, from Niamey, Heath wrote a letter to his father:

"Dear Dad, we just recently heard that you were ill and today received a letter from Mom saying that you were being cared for in a nursing home. We were all sorry to hear that you were sick and want you to know that we are praying for you.

"Though we have not seen each other very often in the last twenty years, I have prayed for you, especially for your salvation. I was thrilled when I heard that you had told Jane's pastor that you were trusting Christ as your Savior and thank the Lord for His answer to our prayers, even though late in your life. May you be conscious of the Lord's presence with you in this time of physical suffering. He never leaves nor forsakes His own and has said, 'Lo, I am with you always.' May your realization of His presence strengthen you each day.

"We are all well and 'thanking God' as the Zarmas have a habit of saying.

"My constant prayer for you is: 'The LORD bless thee and keep thee: The LORD make his face shine upon thee and be gracious unto thee: The LORD lift up his countenance upon thee and give thee peace." (Numbers 6:24-26) Love from your son, Heath"

On January 1, 1970, before the letter arrived, he passed away. It fell to Shirley and Jane to clean out their father's house and put it up for sale. Jane was going through difficult struggles after her son David's death and now her father's death. She wrote in the same letter about her dad's death: "We love you all so much and feel so close to you even though thousands of miles separate us. We just know you pray a lot for us, and we can feel the power of your prayers. We are so grateful for them and are counting the days until we see you in June."

Heath and I have always been so thankful for the loving relationships we have had with his sisters Shirley and Jane and their families, as well as my brothers Melvin and Carl and their families. Our homes have always been lovingly open and welcoming to each other. Through the years, we met many families who did not have good relationships between parents, children, siblings, children, or in-laws. When families are divided by lack of forgiveness or holding grudges, everyone in all the generations is affected adversely. It is a sobering fact to read that God will not hear the prayers of the unforgiving person.

Blind Kommi

Amadou Issaka (Kommi) was an intelligent and handsome little boy who attended our mission's French primary school. His best friend and classmate was an MK named Daniel Cowley. During recess time one day, Kommi saw that Daniel had candy, so Kommi asked for some. Daniel said, "Kommi, I have something that is sweeter than candy." Intrigued, Kommi asked what that could be, so Daniel told him about Jesus who could forgive his sin and give him everlasting life. God began to work in Kommi's heart through this testimony from Daniel.

Not long after this, Kommi got measles and a bad eye infection. The infection became so bad that he lost his eyesight. That meant he could no longer go to school but was relegated to begging to make a living.

When Kommi was a young adult, one of our missionaries took an interest in him by teaching him to read in Braille so that he could apply to go to a Christian school for the blind in Nigeria. His belief in Christ was affirmed there, but it took a long time for him to be able to tell his family.

He knew he would be ostracized and scorned for his faith in Christ, but eventually he did tell them.

In January 1970, Kommi preached for the first time in our Sunday evening English service. At that time, he was home on vacation from Nigeria schools. We wrote, "How our hearts were warmed and challenged to see a blind Zarma with a 'seeing heart.' It has taken much courage for him to witness to his family and friends, but his testimony to us was this, 'I thank God for my blindness, for it was through this that I came to hear the Gospel and accept Jesus as my Savior.' As Heath closed the service, he asked us all to stand and sing 'I Surrender All.' We did so in rededication of our hearts, earnestly thanking God for the great work that He has done in the life of another blind person here."

Amadou, Our Egg Seller

The little old Fulani man Amadou showed up periodically on our doorstep with eggs he had brought from his bush village to sell to us. Sometimes his wife was with him. She must have been at least thirty years his junior and had a small baby on her back. He was a lot of fun to visit with and never ceased to tell us how unusual it was to have two white families in a row who were so nice (the Washers and us). From time to time, he asked me for malaria medicine or aspirin, but there was something else he begged me for each week – medicine to make his wife fat!

In Niger, it is a great compliment to a husband if he has a fat wife. It shows that she doesn't have to work hard and that he makes sure she has enough to eat. When Amadou's little wife took her milk and butter to market to sell, the other ladies would make fun of her because she was too thin. Once they even threw her milk and butter on the ground, ruining it so that she came home in tears.

Pastor Kommi used to say, "I don't understand it. If American women lose weight, they are proud. If African women gain weight, they are proud!"

Knowing that he would never believe I didn't have medicine that could make a person fat, I gave him vitamins for his wife and told him (truthfully) that I took one of these pills every day. He was so happy to take them home for his wife with great hopes of her becoming fat!

In March 1970, we wrote about our egg man, Amadou, in our prayer letter: "'Really? A book with no words, and yet it has a story to tell me?' Amadou, the Fulani herdsman, was all eyes and ears as we presented the Gospel to him by means of a 'wordless book.' Our hearts are burdened for this dear old illiterate man who has been open to our Gospel witness. Only God, by His Holy Spirit, can redeem his soul, and for this we are so dependent on your prayers. Our friend Fadima, who received Christ when we were at the Gaya station, is coming for a visit, and we have told Amadou that he will hear about Jesus in his own Fulani language. We use the Zarma language with him, and he speaks it fluently, but we feel there will be great value in his hearing the Word from one of his own people in his own language too."

In the spring of 1970, we held special evangelistic meetings, with Malam Kano and Pastor Kommi doing the preaching. A number of young people from the village of Goudel had received Christ as their Savior during our December camp, and we were burdened to reach their Muslim parents. Muslim men did not want to walk into a church, nor be seen visiting the home of a follower of Jesus, so we elected to go to them. After permission was obtained from the village chief, our men set up lights and our portable loudspeaker system in the Goudel marketplace. A sheet was tacked to a mud wall for our filmstrip projections. Pastor Kommi and Malam Kano did the preaching and explained the Bible stories excellently. Hundreds of men who came to the marketplace in the cool of the evening heard the Gospel. Later, the same type of meetings were held in Yantala.

Heath was also meeting on Sunday afternoons with the nucleus of Gourma believers, teaching them Bible doctrine and about the organization and work of the local church. Working with the Gourmas continued to be a joy for us. We asked our prayer helpers to hold them up at the throne of grace "that they will grow and that the sweet spirit of love and cooperation will continue in their midst."

Hepatitis Strikes Our Family

We were concerned when three-and-a-half-year-old Nathan lost his appetite and was listless. One night, we had him sleep with us so I could keep checking on his fever for fear it might spike a febrile convulsion. Very early in the morning, he awakened me saying he needed to go "tinkle." When I saw that his urine was coffee colored, I felt pretty sure that it was hepatitis. Then I took a good look at the whites of his eyes in the light and realized they were jaundiced.

The French doctor immediately put Nathan in the Gamkalley Clinic down on the river road. It was necessary that one of us stay with him at all times. During his twelve days of hospitalization, when someone else could stay with Nathan, I rushed home to fix meals and be with our family for a while. The French doctor gave Nathan vitamin B intravenously to improve his appetite. He began to eat well and have an abundance of energy. The doctor said to keep him quiet, but he began to hop all over the bed once he had a good appetite, and it was hard to keep him still.

The strain of the full days from the clinic to the house left me exhausted. One night when I had made a special treat of hamburgers for supper, eleven-year-old Jonathan just picked at his food and wasn't hungry. He hadn't been feeling well for quite some time, but he wasn't jaundiced nor did his urine turn dark.

On the afternoon of the day Nathan was released from the clinic, Jonathan's tests came back positive for hepatitis, so he then was admitted for ten days. I wrote, "The boys did not like the daily intravenous feedings, but they were necessary as one dehydrates so quickly here in the intense heat."

Even though Jonathan did not show the outward signs of hepatitis, we found out during his physical at our next furlough that permanent damage had been done to his liver.

Several of our missionary kids came down with hepatitis at that time, but we could not pinpoint the exact source of the infection. I believe the Lord protected me as I took care of Nathan at the clinic. When the nurse was trying to take blood from him for exams, he squirmed and the contaminated needle scratched me. Then when Jeanne Brock was admitted a few days later, she threw up on me as I was trying to help her with an emesis basin!

From our prayer letter, dated May 1970: "This Sunday we will have the joy of seeing four more Gourma people follow the Lord in believer's baptism. Yabiri, who was refused baptism by the Gourma church leaders last year because of certain habits in his life, will be baptized this time. We are glad for the work of the Lord in his heart and life and for his godly wife, Yenuru, who is a blessing to all.

"Furlough time is rolling around too quickly. We keep wondering when we will ever find time to pack our things away. The Lord has wonderfully provided a home for us this furlough at the Cedar Lanes Missionary Homes near Philadelphia. We will have a four-bedroom house completely furnished down to the last teaspoon for just $50 per month, plus utilities. Even better yet, there is a Christian school in the area for our children...

"We hope to begin visiting our churches after September, the Lord willing. We will be contacting you for dates in the future. Once again, we say a heartfelt 'thank you' for each and every church and individual who made it possible for us to be here. It will be a joy to share with you how God has worked this term in Niger."

Three blessed events occurred before we left for furlough in June 1970. The Bible classes Heath had been having with the Gourma believers were completed, and the Gourma Evangelical Baptist Church of Niamey was officially organized. On one of our last Sundays in Niger, Heath and evangelist Luc had the joy of baptizing four more Gourmas. The greatest news of all was that Salimou, Emile's wife, professed Christ as her Savior in our living room the night before we left Niger.

As we were traveling back to the States in 1970, we visited Holland. This is where my very favorite picture of our four young children was taken. A Dutch photographer had our children dress in national clothing for the picture. After he took his picture and we paid him to mail it to us later, we asked if he minded if we took our children outdoors to take a picture on our camera. He was totally agreeable to this. There were many international tourists outside who then began excitedly taking pictures of "the darling little Dutch children" too! I wonder where in the world their pictures went!

Chapter 16
Third Furlough
June 1970 to August 1971

The McGuffey Reader's Version of The Ten Commandments

Above all else love God alone;
Bow down to neither wood or stone.
God's name refuse to take in vain;
The Sabbath rest with care maintain.
Respect your parents all your days;
Hold sacred human life always.
Be loyal to your chosen mate;
Steal nothing, neither small nor great.
Report, with truth, your neighbor's deed;
And rid your mind of selfish greed.

When we arrived back in the States, we settled into Cedar Lanes Missionary Homes in Laurel Springs, New Jersey. We could hardly believe the blessings that were ours, to just move into a four-bedroom, fully-furnished ranch home.

Cedar Lanes Missionary Homes were born out of the vision of Dr. Robert and Estelle Dawson who were concerned about missionaries returning for furlough with no place to call home. The Dawsons had served with Mexican Indian Missions.

We were especially thrilled that Rebecca (ninth grade), Jonathan (seventh grade), and Alan (second grade) could attend nearby Christian schools. Because we were missionaries on furlough, the high school reduced Rebecca's tuition by 75 percent. What a blessing and a help! When second-grader Alan was being tucked into bed a few weeks after school started, he asked his dad, "Do you want to know what I learned in school?" He then amazed his dad by giving excellent definitions for justification and sanctification!

These three Bobbetts weren't the only ones poring over the books during that furlough. Heath decided to begin working on his master's degree by taking classes at Faith Theological Seminary in Elkins Park, Pennsylvania. After fifteen years out of school, working mostly in the French and Zarma languages, his Greek and Hebrew were more than a little rusty. We asked for prayer during his busy year of study and the weekends of deputation ministry.

Four-year-old Nathan was the one who amused us as he discovered civilization this time. His eyes were as big as saucers the first time he saw me use a vacuum sweeper. Afterward he liked to be the official one to "brush the floor." When I ran the vacuum sweeper for longer periods of time, he warned, "Watch out, or you'll run the batteries down!"

There was a basement room in one of the Cedar Lanes residences where used clothing donations for the needs of furloughing missionaries were received. We looked there for winter clothes and pretty much found things each of our family members needed.

Nathan had never worn winter clothes. The day I dressed him up in boots, hat, winter coat, gloves, and scarf, he stood in front of the mirror looking at his strange reflection then burst into laughter at the sight!

Our plans were to attend a large Baptist church in the area so Rebecca and Jonathan could be part of the youth groups. However, shortly after we moved into our home, there was a young home missions pastor on our doorstep. Jim and Carol Smith were working to establish a self-supporting church in nearby Clementon, New Jersey. Pastor Smith pled with us to come to his church (meeting in a one-room schoolhouse) to be a part of the ministry. He said Rebecca and Jonathan would be a blessing and example to the youth group there.

We promised to at least visit, but after our first time there, we knew that was where the Lord wanted us that furlough. It was great to get to know that church family and to sit under Jim's fine ministry. He was strict with the youth, and it must have been just what they needed because they loved him and respected him.

I was asked to start a children's JOY Club in an especially needy area nearby. In December I wrote, "Praise the Lord, the attendance in Pine Hill Club is now four times what it was when we began. Mrs. Balcer's living room is getting very crowded." I loved teaching children's Bible clubs and classes. It was a special blessing to me to have that opportunity while on home assignment.

I met with resistance to the Gospel in the States too. The very first time little Cathy Devlin came to JOY Club, she was so thrilled about the things of Christ that she stayed after class to tell us she wanted to receive Christ as her Savior. In the weeks that followed, her enthusiasm never wavered as she came weekly with her memory verse well memorized. Evidently these verses were shown at home, and her mother became enraged. She forbade Cathy to ever return to JOY Club. When two ladies from our church called on Mrs. Devlin, she informed them that she believed in God but not in the Bible. As the ladies dealt with her about her need of a Savior, she slammed the door in their faces. Our hearts were so sad for little Cathy who was cut off from spiritual help.

After a Sunday school class one Sunday at Faith Baptist Church, Nathan's teacher said to me with a smile, "You certainly have Nathan well grounded." She had been telling the story of twelve-year-old Jesus in the temple and how his parents couldn't find him on the way home. When she asked, "After Jesus' mother and father searched and searched for Him, where did they find Him?" Four-year-old Nathan raised his hand to answer, "In the Baptist church."

In December 1970, we asked our supporters to pray because we were wondering if the Lord wanted us to stay in the States during Rebecca's high school years. We knew He would open up a different ministry for us if that was His will. Ivory Coast Academy, was a well-established missionary children's school, but I didn't see how I could ever send my children a thousand miles away for high school. However, this was the path the Lord was leading us down, and once again, we found His sufficient and enabling grace for this.

Children's Activities

Rebecca and Jon had a great time on a retreat with their youth group. Nathan's little friend across the street from us, Debbie, gave him chicken pox, and Alan was collecting quarters for his teeth that fell out.

There were extremely tall trees around the Dawsons' home at Cedar Lanes. One Saturday, Alan decided to climb to the very top of one of the trees before I discovered him. I, who have a great fear of heights, almost fainted with fear when I called him to "Get down here!" The other ladies said, "Norma, don't watch! He'll get down all right, but it is better if you aren't watching!"

By May 1971, we were confident that God was leading us to return to Africa. We planned to return in August, and the mission board asked Heath to again assume the duties of field director.

Prayer requests from our prayer letter, dated May 1971: "Pray that the construction of the boys' dorm will be completed by August and the needs supplied for it. Pray for medical clearance for Jonathan who is experiencing liver tenderness after having hepatitis last term; pray this will clear up. Because of the increased expenses for our children's education and transportation, we still need another $100 per month."

I was thrilled when four children from my JOY Club came to Sunday school on their own. We had a closing rally of all the JOY Clubs at Faith Baptist Church in Clementon. There had been sixty-three enrolled in my Pine Hill Club. Twenty-three received Christ as their Savior! This was the highlight of my furlough!

In the summer of 1971, we were invited to go as a family to a camp in northern New Jersey. Heath was the missionary speaker. We had a great week of ministering together with Heath teaching and both of us giving our testimonies and performing a skit about Niger.

Our children had the fun of being campers too. Pastor Richard Pettit was with us at that camp when there was a really humorous incident. The campers had adopted a really odd looking stuffed doll as the camp mascot that they named Gunk. Gunk showed up everywhere – in the dining hall, at chapel, for sports, and so forth. The camp sports director was a retired military man who seemed to want to run the camp with strict military rules. One evening as everyone was standing at attention for the lowering of the flag, the campers began to snicker, then chuckle, then laugh out loud! Gunk was coming down the flagpole with the flag! The ex-military man was horrified! He demanded that the youth who were responsible for not honoring the flag step forth. Then he directed Pastor Pettit to "take these youths aside and lecture them about the terrible thing they had done."

We wondered how Pastor Pettit handled this situation, so we asked him later. He said he took the youth around out of sight of the strict director, and then they all had a good laugh at the whole situation! Their intentions weren't disrespectful. They were just kids having fun.

It was a busy summer for us with passports, visas, and inoculations to be obtained and barrels to pack. Cedar Lanes had a large shed-type building that was perfect for packing and storing barrels for shipment.

One day while Bob Dawson was working in that shed, a compressor blew up, and something hit his leg hard enough to break it. He was taken to the hospital and returned with his leg in a cast. Bob and little Nathan were buddies, so that evening Nathan went over to see his special friend. By then, people were bringing food, candy, and other goodies to Bob. Nathan looked at the things being brought, then said, "Mr. Dawson, I wish I had a broken leg!" The next evening, when the pain was pretty intense, Bob called us to say, "Tell Nathan he can have my broken leg!"

Rebecca and Jonathan Leave for School in Ivory Coast

August 1, 1971, arrived all too quickly. The plans were for us to meet the Frank Marshalls and the Kepple children at JFK Airport. Frank and Eleanor were assigned to be house parents at the boys' dorm and were accompanying eight young people to Bouaké for the opening of school on August 3. We encountered torrential rain on our way to the airport from Cedar Lanes so that the trip took four hours instead of two.

Thankfully the plane was late leaving, so we made it. This was the first time any of our family had ever been on a 747. At that time, you could go out close to view the planes from behind the fence. When I looked at that huge aircraft and realized Rebecca and Jon were flying away on it, I prayed, "Dear Lord, please get that huge thing off the ground and take my children safely on their way!" Although I had said I could never send my children away for high school, God's grace was sufficient when the time came, and He gave me perfect peace that we were in His will.

I am so thankful all four of our children enjoyed their high school years at Ivory Coast Academy. They had positive experiences and made lifelong friendships. When I talked to Rebecca about it recently, she said, "Mom, at the time I didn't realize our going away to boarding school was much harder on you than it was on us."

Years later, Nate wrote us this letter, which meant so much to us:

"Hi, Mom and Dad.

"For some reason today I had a memory of something. I remember when I was 16 you took me to the airport in Niamey, and I climbed onto that small mission plane that would take me to Bouaké and to boarding school. I was excited! All my siblings had gone there. I was excited about having kids my age to go to school with and play with. I was excited about living in a dorm and playing sports. So I remember my excitement as I climbed up the wing and squeezed into the cabin. I found my seat and buckled up.

"Then I turned and looked out the window to give you guys a fast wave before leaving. I remember you both standing there next to each other, and you were crying. We waved at each other, and then the plane started taxiing away from you. I think back on that moment every now and then. It is a picture to me of one of the thousands of sacrifices you made so that you could share Jesus with those who have never heard. It was a sacrifice to you that we had to go to boarding school and only come home three times a year. I can't imagine doing that now that I have kids. But you did it with four of us because you were living for a kingdom that is not of this world, and you were looking for a city whose builder and maker was God. You chose to forgo many of the comforts of this life so that others could hear about Jesus. You chose to allow your kids to go to a school a thousand miles away so that you could stay and do what God had called you to, and you never quit. Thank you for making that choice daily for 35 years. I love you. Nate"

It was difficult returning to Cedar Lanes without Jon and Rebecca. A few days later, Alan expressed all of our feelings when he commented, "Everything around here is gloomy!" However, we were very busy during our final days in New Jersey, finishing up Nathan and Alan's dental work, packing, and then cleaning to leave our home spotless for the next residents.

Mrs. Dawson asked if we had left our application to live at Cedar Lanes for our next furlough and said they would be very happy to have us back again! That was sweet, and we were glad they felt that way about us.

Jonathan's first letter from Bouaké told about their trip and his dorm parents. This was his first time away from home, and we could sense his homesickness. He mentioned really missing Alan and Nathan. In a postscript, he asked his dad if it was okay if he bought a pellet gun. Then we could see he reconstructed the sentence to tell his dad he *was getting* a pellet gun!

During her years in boarding school, Rebecca was great at writing long descriptive letters, letting us know what was going on. Her brother's letters were a lot shorter!

We finished cleaning the house and then drove to Mickey and Geneva's home in Ohio, arriving on August 11. That evening, Alan met with the deacons for baptism and church membership at Emmanuel Baptist Church. Heath dressed in his African outfit and spoke at Emmanuel's closing DVBS program, then on Sunday he preached at the morning service and Alan was baptized. We said our final goodbyes to our Emmanuel friends and prayer warriors.

Unexpected News

That evening, we received a call from Dr. Wittig, saying he could not clear us to return to Niger because our account was in the red and we had no money to ship our barrels. We had no way to go but forward – no home in the States, Rebecca and Jonathan were already in Ivory Coast, goodbyes were said, and our bags were packed! Our barrels had to be left in storage until our account at the mission had enough money to ship them. On August 24 at 10:00 p.m., we were aboard a Belgium World Airlines Sabena 747 with Alan and Nathan, heading for our fourth term of service in Niger, with Jesus leading the way.

Chapter 17
Fourth Term in Niger
September 1971 to July 1974

Return from furlough is in three stages:
First, the exaltation and pleasure of seeing old friends,
then the awful depression as one feels the weight of the many problems,
then the return to the normal level. – Dr. Nelson Bell,
missionary to China

On August 24, 1971, we flew out of New York at 10:00 p.m. The 747 aircraft was not crowded, so we each could stretch out across several seats to sleep. That was a nice luxury. When crossing the Atlantic from west to east, it is always fascinating to see a beautiful sunrise from the plane window at about 2:00 or 3:00 a.m. We arrived at 5:00 a.m. New York time, but it was already 10:00 a.m. in Brussels.

We had two days and one night in Brussels before our plane left for Niger, so Sabena Airways put us in the elegant and historic five-star Metropole Hôtel, providing all our meals also. The Metropole, the largest hotel in Belgium, was built in 1895 and it is the only nineteenth century hotel still in use today. Sabena Airways was always so kind to us in this way. However, Air France soon pushed them out of Niger, so we didn't have those privileges after that.

We were greeted by many friends when our flight landed in Niamey at 7:20 a.m. on August 27. I got choked up when I saw Mariama again.

I wrote in my journal on August 29, "We are trying to sort and get a few things into the house…and clean, clean, clean. Everything is so dirty! We are encouraged that when Yacouba Nouhou came to see us, he asked for another tract on the way of salvation in English. Oh, what a joy it would be to see this man saved!"

Alan was already an avid reader when he started school at McCaba Academy. His teacher, Virginia Cowley, was able to keep him challenged with books from higher grades. Having the first through fourth grades in one room had many advantages. The slower learners could listen in as the teacher helped the younger grades, and the fast learners listened in on higher levels. Virginia Cowley told us that in first grade Alan was reading well on the fourth-grade level and beyond.

Although Jonathan's liver tests had finally gotten within normal range so we were able to leave the States, word came to us that he was having some health problems at boarding school. Because he was experiencing stomach pain, he had been put on a special diet and complete bedrest. It was extremely difficult for Heath and me to be so far from Jonathan when he wasn't well.

From my journal, dated Friday, September 3, 1971: "We have been trying to call Bouaké but without success. The school is outside of town, and we aren't even sure if they have a telephone. We have written and asked the school nurse to call us about Jonathan's health, if not from the school then from the post office in town."

Ten days later, we got a call from Jonathan, saying he was a little better and had been allowed to go to classes. He had lost quite a bit of weight.

The Arrival of our German Shepherd Puppy from Timbuktu, Mali

Frank and Eleanor Marshall wrote, saying they had a new litter of German shepherd puppies and asking if we would like to have one. We said "Yes!" So they telegrammed us to say that the puppy would be arriving on September 16 by Air Mali. Security was so lax between the countries in 1971 that the Marshalls just went to the airport, found a French couple who were flying to Niamey, and asked if they would deliver a puppy for them. At the Niamey airport hangar, we inquired and soon found this couple who pointed us to a cardboard box. Inside was this darling puppy, looking quite forlorn, with a red gift ribbon tied around his neck!

When we got him home, he soon perked up and was happy to be with us. Alan claimed him for his own and named him Hunter. Five-year-old Nathan received a kitten soon afterward and named it Cuppa-T. Cuppa-T looked like a thoroughbred Siamese cat. The mother kitten was a Siamese cat but unfortunately had bred with a black cat. She had four kittens: two were black like the father, and two looked totally Siamese!

From our prayer letter, dated September 1971: "We are rejoicing in a special way to see progress in the Zarma church four miles outside of town. The African brethren have completely taken over and are doing an admirable job in the preaching, song leading, and affairs of the church. There have been many hard years of labor to see this fruition in a Muslim village. Please pray much for this nucleus of believers. Just to be seen walking into the little mud church building brings much ridicule and scorn from the villagers.

On September 21, 1971, Jon's dorm parent, Herb Nehlsen, called to say Jon was not improving much and asked me to come down to school. The big problem was that the French consulate in Niamey wasn't allowed to grant visas to Ivory Coast at that time.

On Wednesday, September 22, we received this telegram from Herb: *"Venez urgent fils malade Bouaké. Nehlsen"* ("Come urgently. Your son is sick in Bouaké.") This really shook us. Then the Lord reminded us that this was probably no new development but that Mr. Nehlsen sent it to help me get a visa. Heath took the telegram to the French consulate, and they telegraphed Abidjan, Ivory Coast. I had a visa by 5:30 p.m. The consulate secretary said they had never had a visa granted so quickly.

At 3:30 a.m. on September 23, I flew out of Niamey for Abidjan. It was a surprise to find U.S. embassy personnel meeting me at the Abidjan airport to help me get into the country in case I hadn't been able to get a visa. They were so kind, and I really appreciated their doing that.

The crowd was getting impatient as we waited for our next flight up to Bouaké. Finally, at the desk, I was told that the plane was full and the rest of us could not get on the flight until the next day. A French man ranted and raved to the clerk and to the airlines about the fact that we had tickets and we should have a flight also! Shortly thereafter, the announcement came that they were putting the rest of us on a second plane that was being put into service! I, the meek American, could only accept this injustice, but the French are great at "throwing a fit" to insist that things be corrected. I had to say I was thankful it worked!

Dr. Slater came down from the CB mission hospital to Bouaké just at the time when we needed him. He thought Jon had chronic liver damage from the hepatitis that would affect him the rest of his life, requiring that he watch his diet and exercise. Being a surgeon, though, and not an internist, Dr. Slater sent Jon and me to Abidjan to see a French internist for a diagnosis.

I was having a spiritual crisis alone there in the Bouaké missionary guest house. I realized my heart was not right and that I only returned to Africa that term because God sent us back. I was fighting bitterness about being separated from my children for their high school years. Alone, on my own for a day in the guest house, I read God's Word, letting Him speak to me as I repented and surrendered myself anew to my wonderful Lord.

His plan for our lives is perfect and good, but I had not been accepting of it.

I wrote in my journal: "Lord, I have nothing to offer You. Perhaps it is proud to even consider myself a lump of clay to lay at Your feet. Mud would be a better description of me. But, dear Father, You are the Master, the Potter...whatever you can make of me, in whatever way You can use me, please do! Dear God, I yield myself, I lay myself upon Your altar. Everything I have, I give to You – my husband, my children, my time, my talents, my abilities are Yours. Please use me! Glorify Yourself through me."

Refreshed and with a revived heart, I experienced His peace once again as I looked forward to serving Him back in Niger.

Jon and I took a crowded thirty-passenger mail bus to Abidjan where we saw the cold and uncommunicative Dr. Baudin. He said Jon was okay but sent us for blood tests the next morning. Jonathan was very patient with all the blood vials they took.

Abidjan was a beautiful modern city. Many called it Petit Paris. We were amazed to find an ice skating rink at the Hotel Ivoire. I took Jon there for the treat of a hamburger and let him shoot in the galleries and play pinball and other arcade games. I gave myself a home permanent at the guest house, and Jon even helped me neutralize it. Looking for a restaurant that day for lunch, we finally found one. Only afterward did we see the large horse head over the door and realize their meat was horse meat. There probably is nothing wrong with eating horse meat, but we just didn't like the idea.

On October 1, the French doctor told us Jon's tests were in the normal range so he was okay "for now." We were very thankful that we could ride back to ICA with a friend that evening, and not public transportation. Jon was anxious to return to his friends at school. I stayed on for several days at ICA to fill in at the high school boys' dorm and the high school girls dorm so the dorm parents could get away for some R&R. MKs are special kids and so much fun to be with.

One sad story, however, was when I spent time with one of the high school girls who was struggling with the fact that her parents sent her away to boarding school from first grade on. My heart was broken when she told me that going for so many months without seeing her parents bothered her so much because sometimes she could not remember what they looked like! At that time, her parents' mission required the parents to send their little ones away to boarding school, but they no longer require that now. We are thankful that EBM always left the children's schooling up to the parents' prayerful decisions.

Another missionary mother traveled back to Niger with me, by train from Bouaké to Ouagadougou, then by plane to Niamey. It was great having someone to travel with, although in Africa you never travel alone. I always found Africans to be friendly, helpful, and wanting to share conversation and their food with me. I never lacked for companionship and someone to talk to when traveling alone.

Other Expat Friendships

An American friend who had married a Hausa man asked me to take her to the maternity when she began labor. After the birth, I finally got home and to bed at 3:00 a.m. then was up the next morning to get the children off to school. I was never afraid being out on the streets in the wee hours of the night. Niamey was so safe at that time, with city crime being almost unheard of. When a single gal colleague had trouble with painful kidney stones and needed to be taken to the clinic in the middle of the night, Heath would stay in bed sleeping while I went to get her. Men who were sitting around visiting on the streets would say, "Madame, all you all right? Is there anything I can do to help you?" We also never locked our car when we went shopping. Unfortunately this all changed in later years.

Thanksgiving 1971

November 25, 1971, was Thanksgiving and Nathan's fifth birthday. I planned for his party to be from 9:00 to 10:30 a.m., but the boys had so much fun that they stayed all morning. Nathan's favorite gift from us was a jet airplane that ran by battery and lit up.

That afternoon I had fifty children in Bible club. After Bible club, Kumbu, a lady Yenuru had introduced me to, came home with me because she wanted to see my house. She was a loveable old lady. How wonderful it would be if she really understood and believed the Gospel as she sat nearby on Thursdays listening as I taught the children's open-air classes. There were some other adults who seemed to make it a point to be there listening in on my children's Bible classes too.

That evening we were invited to Thanksgiving dinner with other missionary families. I furnished the pumpkin pies (made from local squash that tasted like pumpkin).

Right after Thanksgiving, Heath started weekly classes with the Goudel believers on the New Testament Church. The first Sunday, drummers were outside the building located in the market, advertising meat that was for sale at the meat table. Heath came home hoarse from talking over the noise.

A Surprise Invitation to the President's Palace

One Sunday afternoon, we received official notice that all EBM and SIM missionaries were invited to the palace that evening. Wondering why, we all scrubbed, curled, and donned our best clothes. It turned out that President Diori had decided to invite some friendly nations for dinner on his terrace – what an honor! That night, he had invited Americans, Israelis, and Nationalist Chinese. It was really a lovely evening and quite a change of pace from our everyday routine. How we thanked the Lord for President Hamani Diori's friendly attitude and for the open door set before us in Niger. That evening, we renewed contact with a Jewish couple to whom we had given a New Testament during our last term.

Rebecca and Jonathan and the other MK's returned for Christmas vacation on December 8. Rebecca and Sharon Abuhl took over my English Sunday school classes while they were home. McCaba Academy's Christmas program on December 14 was excellent. Alan got a lot of compliments on his acting as he was a little hunchbacked boy named Joshua, son of Asher. He gave his lamb to baby Jesus, then later when he was grown up, Jesus healed him. Yacouba Nouhou went with us to the program.

Our youth camp at the French school had *Astronauts de Dieu* (Astronauts of God) for our theme with fifty campers. I was a girls counselor with thirteen in my room. We slept on the classroom's cement floor. On closing night, I had the privilege of leading four girls to Christ. Several others said they had been saved during that week of camp too. We wrote to our supporters asking prayer for those who indicated they wanted to become followers of the Lord Jesus Christ because almost all were from Muslim homes and would not be receiving any encouragement there.

Carol Anderson came to Niger to teach MKs for two years. She was a delight to have around and was so sure of her calling. Even though she had to miss her fiancé's graduation from Bob Jones University and his ordination, her only brother's wedding, and her parents' twenty-fifth anniversary, she did not brood over those things. She knew she was where God wanted her to be, and she rested in that. Her fiancé, Spencer Brown, came to Niger for Christmas and stayed with us.

On Christmas Day, I made my traditional Swedish tea ring (fancy cinnamon rolls) and scrambled eggs for breakfast. Nathan got a bike; Alan, a watch. Rebecca, Mariama, and Jonathan mostly got clothing. For our Christmas dinner, we had two small African chickens, homemade stuffing, and all the trimmings.

About 4:00 p.m., we went to see the Gourma believers gathered in the Bible bookstore compound. They were ready to enjoy their feast and were so pleased we had come to join them. We had already eaten dinner at home, so I urged the servers to give us small helpings. Jonathan objected, saying "Speak for yourself, Mom!" He always loved African food, so he had a big plate of rice and sauce. We had a sweet time of fellowship. They sang several songs for us, then asked us to sing a song in English for them. We sang "Nothing but the Blood of Jesus," and they applauded us. Luc said, "We rejoice together because even though we are different nationalities and races, we all have the same Father." Amen.

One day we loaded Spencer, Carol, and our family into our Peugeot at 5:00 a.m. to visit Gaya. It was wonderful to see all our old friends. The Brocks were still home on medical leave, so we planned to camp in their empty house.

In the afternoon, we went over the border to Dahomey (later renamed Bénin) to the village of Coubéri where we had started a work during our second term in Gaya. The Brocks had continued that work faithfully, and it was a joy to see that a meeting house had been built for the believers.

During our visit, Spencer had an embarrassing moment as a first-time visitor to Africa. In bush villages, women who were working in their compounds often did not wear a blouse or a top. We had become accustomed to this, as well as seeing women openly nurse their babies, but poor Spence turned red when a bare-chested older woman came over to shake hands with us to welcome us as we entered her compound!

Heath and Spence met with the older Christians while Carol and I had a children's class. Jon sat by Spence to translate when some of the Christians gave their testimonies. The village people really appreciated some simple medicines for sores, fevers, and malaria that I had brought along to treat them with.

Back at Gaya, we bought some roast chickens from street vendors to have for supper along with pumpkin bread I had made. The children slept in the car, and we brought cots for the rest of us. With so many Gaya friends coming to greet us the next morning, we did not get off for Niamey as early as we had planned. We realized the Lord had delayed us for a purpose when SIM missionaries arrived from Kamba, Nigeria. Mr. Crane had had a heart attack the day before, and a plane was coming from Jos to Gaya for him. Heath took Mrs. Crane (who didn't speak French) to inform the commandant that an unauthorized plane would be landing at the Gaya airstrip and why.

We arrived back in Niamey that evening to the house Dieyabidi had cleaned meticulously. What a blessing he was to us.

Anne and Glen Nunemaker had opened a dispensary in Tabla. One day, Anne brought in Kadi, a woman who had a prolapsed uterus. I had never seen anything like it — I think her bladder was outside too. She constantly dripped urine, so many flies followed her, clinging to her wrapper-skirt. She told us this happened after her (20-year-old?) son, Zakou, was born in the bush, and her husband would have nothing to do with her after that. I took her into the hospital to see a doctor. When the Chinese doctor examined her, he turned his head away in disgust but did admit her for surgery.

Anne and I went to see Kadi after the surgery, but there was no one watching over surgical patients in the recovery room. There were flies all over her, and her IV wasn't dripping fluids into her veins. We tried to get help, but there was only a student nurse and an aide and they didn't do anything.

Somehow Kadi survived and showed up on our doorstep one day, very weak, asking to stay with us because the doctor wanted to see her again in six days. We fixed a place for her to stay in a back room of the church and hurried to prepare some food for her. I prepared spaghetti. Big mistake! She had never seen spaghetti before and was horrified because she thought I was serving her worms! I tried to explain to her that this was not worms but food made from flour just like macaroni, but she didn't know what macaroni was either! Her bush diet had only been millet, sorghum, and corn meal. Finally, I went down on the street in front of our house to find a street vendor to buy real African food for her.

Prayerfully, I used Bible pictures to explain the way of salvation to Kadi. Another time I explained The Wordless Book to her. (Like most bush women, she had never been to school.) She said she wanted to follow Jesus. I prayed she would completely understand and be saved, but I knew only the Holy Spirit could accomplish that work in her heart. When the time came for her to return to Tabla, I gave her The Wordless Book. She told me she would look at it often, and she would explain it to others.

One day when Kadi's son, Zakou, came to our house I noticed that he had some reddish dirt smeared on his forehead. He told me that he had a terrible headache and that people told him if he found some bloody sand from where the holiday sheep was slain, its magic would cure his headache. I asked if his headache went away, and he said no. So I urged him to wash the dirt off while I went to get some aspirin. He was very happy to do so, and the aspirin worked.

A Month of Many Challenges for Us

On January 9, 1972, some coworkers left at 9:30 p.m. to drive their children and Rebecca and Jon to Ouagadougou, in Burkina Faso, where they boarded a train for a twenty-two-hour ride back to boarding school. Nathan had a good hard cry when it was his bedtime that night because Jon wasn't there.

On January 10, Luc and Oukano had a baby girl and named her "Rebecca" after our Rebecca. Our annual conference began that day with special speaker Iver Ruten, a precious man of God.

God's providential alignment of our life circumstances was shown to us again in a marvelous way. The first evening that Iver spoke, he told about when the invitation had come from Heath for him to be speaker at our conference. As he was praying about this, seeking the Lord's will about whether or not to accept the speaking invitation, the Lord spoke to his heart through a passage in Luke 5. He was especially drawn to verse 5 where Peter said, "Master, we have toiled all night and caught nothing, *nevertheless, at thy word...*" While Iver was pondering the teachings of those Scriptures, he received another letter from Heath informing him that the theme of our conference was to be "Nevertheless, at Thy Word!" This confirmed the peace Iver had in his heart about coming to speak at our annual conference.

On January 22, one of our newest missionaries, Harold Curtis, was admitted to the Gamkalley Clinique with hepatitis. In just a few days Harold's skin and eyes turned yellow. The Curtises had visited some friends a few weeks before who didn't feel it was necessary to boil river water as well as filter it for drinking. .It made us shudder to think of all that went on at the river in that village – people bathing themselves, washing their dishes and clothes, and animals drinking, wading, and defecating in the water. It was pretty obvious where Harold contracted hepatitis.

January 24 was the official visit of France's President Georges Pompidou to Niger. He was elected president in 1969 after Charles deGaulle resigned. The Niger officials were excited about President Pompidou's visit and worked hard painting, paving, and cleaning up Niamey. Everything looked nice, but three days before his arrival vandals had painted graffiti saying *"Abat P"* ("Down with Pompidou"). They even got the wall beside our church and the side of our Bible bookstore. The government sent teams of men out immediately to erase it all.

Heath and I were invited to an evening reception at the palace for Monsieur le President Georges Pompidou et Madame. Many people were already seated and eating on the upper terrace, so we chose the lower one. After we took our seats and looked around, we realized we were sitting straight in front of the Niger and France presidents as they finished their evening meal! Ringside seats! After each president made a speech, we were entertained by folkloric dance groups.

There were also parades for the visit. The Niger parades at that time were regal, colorful, and outstanding. Hundreds of decorated camels and horses with their turbaned and robed riders were brought into Niamey for these occasions. School children dressed in the same patterned material, military men in full uniform dress, different groups and associations each dressed in the same patterned material, and others were included. This parade lasted for two hours. Niger protocol gave us ticket invitations to sit in the platform stand behind the visiting dignitaries, so we once again had ringside seats for the parade.

Emile Ngandi left in February for pilot training school in Fort Worth, Texas. He later told us how scared he was of the States because of the movies he had seen. He thought there must be gangsters everywhere and that it was terribly dangerous to go out at night. He said early on during his time in Texas, after eating his evening meal, he secluded himself in his dorm room to study when other friends were going out. Their urging didn't budge him to go out where all the gangsters were.

The day he first saw one of the Tarzan films was the day light began to dawn on his ideas about America. *Tarzan of the Apes* was written by Edgar Rice Burroughs, who had never been to Africa. Emile found Burroughs' conception of what Africa was like to be incredibly off base and then began to see that his beliefs about the States, derived from movies, were just as silly. After that, he relaxed enough to be able to have a good time out with friends in the evenings.

On January 30, our fears were realized about Charlene Curtis, who was carrying their fourth baby. We had prayed so strongly that she would not come down with hepatitis as Harold had. She had not been feeling well, and on this date, we realized her eyes were becoming jaundiced. Because she was expecting a baby and the French and the American methods of treating hepatitis were different, we all felt it would be better for Charlene to go to Jos, Nigeria, for treatment at the SIM hospital. The three Curtis children remained in Niamey, being cared for by several of us missionary families. That was a difficult first-term experience for Harold and Charlene.

We praised God that they both recovered and their baby was fine when he was born the following July.

In December, we finally had enough funds in our account so that the barrels we had left in storage in the U.S. could be shipped. It seemed like Christmas when they arrived eight months after we had packed them!

On March 16, Betty Abuhl and I made the long trip to Bouaké to visit our children at boarding school. We flew from Niamey to Ouagadougou in the middle of the night, then got the 6:30 a.m. train for Bouaké. That was always a long tiring trip of twenty to twenty-two hours. We had packed some ham sandwiches. My cup of strong French coffee in Ouaga had me wide awake, but Betty was sleepy. She ate only half of her sandwich then finished the rest several hours later, not realizing the heat had begun to spoil the sandwich. By the time we got to Bouaké, she was coming down with food poisoning – nausea, vomiting, and diarrhea. Thankfully she began to revive the next day and was able to enjoy her visit with her children. We attended activities at the school, met their friends, and even took them into the city one day for shopping and the treat of dinner at a Lebanese restaurant.

Our trip home was another adventure. It was often difficult to find a seat when boarding the train in Bouaké, so we started out sitting on our suitcases in the aisle. When some people vacated their seats, we quickly took possession of them. We sat on that train all night, but it never moved! The next morning, we were finally told there had been a derailment on the tracks (not unusual). A Conservative Baptist missionary gave us a ride in his car up to Férékésédougou where their hospital was located. The next day, we got on a beautiful air-conditioned train car. That was wonderful – for two hours. Then the air-conditioning stopped working. We couldn't get the windows open, so the interior of the train was like a pressure cooker in the heat. That train dumped us at Bobo Dioulaso at 1:30 p.m., and we waited until 6:30 p.m. for another one. After leaving Bouaké on March 22, we finally arrived home on March 25.

From our prayer letter, dated May 1972: "We have become close friends with an Orthodox Jewish family, Simon and Rivka Shahel, from Israel who are to be in Niamey for two or more years…The other evening, they invited us for dinner, and we had a long talk about God's Word. It is amazing that they are so open and willing for us to talk to them about Christ, and yet they are so blinded. They love Jehovah and are zealous in their worship of Him but cannot believe Jesus is the Messiah."

Our friendship developed quickly, and we came to love these Jewish friends. They told us that because their parents were Orthodox Jews, they would never have been allowed to be our friends in Israel. Simon and Rivka had a young son and a younger daughter.

The Shahels never ate beef in Niger, but Simon had taken special training in the proper (kosher) way to kill chickens. They only ate chicken and fish in Niger. They strictly observed the Sabbath, preparing their Sabbath day food on Friday and never driving their car on Saturday. If their house steward did not turn off the lights in the house when he left on Friday evenings, the lights burned all night because turning lights on or off was work equivalent to building a fire or putting it out on the Sabbath.

One Saturday, their small son got food poisoning from Sabbath food that had spoiled in the heat. He was seriously ill all day Saturday, but they could not drive him to the doctor's until after sunset. The French doctor told them he was so dehydrated he was close to dying before they got him to the clinic. Simon's only comment was, "It is very dangerous to drive on the Sabbath."

Whenever we were with the Shahels, our conversations almost always turned naturally toward spiritual things. We had opportunity after opportunity to tell them about our Savior. Once Simon smiled and wagged his finger at Heath saying, "You always are doing your missionary work!"

Once our conversation was about Jesus being the Messiah. Rivka said, "Jesus wasn't a good Jew because he broke the Sabbath!" This led to discussing prophecies about the Messiah in the Old Testament. Rivka was amazed that Heath could remember so many references, saying that although she had gone to Hebrew school since she was a young child, she couldn't remember references like he did.

Heath mentioned that the Old Testament predicted that the Messiah would be born of a virgin (Isaiah 7:14). Rivka disputed that, so she got out her Hebrew Bible to look at this reference. In a quiet and amazed voice, she acknowledged that "was what the verse says." Written all around the edges of her Hebrew Bible verses were explanations by the rabbis. She read the rabbis' words, then said, "Oh, it isn't talking about the Messiah." We continued to pray for these dear friends who loved Jehovah and were trying their utmost to keep the Law.

Niger had good relations with Israel at that time and was happy to receive Israel's technical aid. The Israelis opened a large farming project near the Niger River where they planted all kinds of fruit trees and vegetables. We thought they would surely eventually have this desert area blossoming like a rose.

One night we were invited to the Shahels' for dinner to celebrate Rivka's being awarded her master's degree from a university in South Africa. We were honored in being the only Gentiles (and the only ones who didn't speak Hebrew!) invited that evening.

Another time, during the Feast of Tabernacles (Booths), the Shahels invited us to their house for tea – inside the rustic booth they had built in their yard. Simon was born in an Arabic country, but he never wanted to tell us what country. He said, "It isn't important!" When Simon told Heath he knew one day he would meet the Messiah, Heath gently told him, "And when you do, He will have nail prints in his hands."

Sometimes Simon and Rivka argued in Hebrew. I quickly learned the words for "yes" and "no" in Hebrew when Heath asked them if they believed the Temple would ever be rebuilt in Jerusalem. They disagreed on this answer and argued, "Ken, ken, ken!" and "Lo, lo, lo!"

One day after I returned from visiting Rebecca and Jonathan at Ivory Coast Academy, Nathan became desperately ill. In our April 1972 prayer letter, Heath wrote to family, friends, and supporters: "Were you praying for us in a special way on Sunday, March 26? We asked the Lord to lay us on your hearts that day as we fought to get control of the disease and fever that was wracking the body of our youngest child, Nathan.

"Nathan had had a cough for a few days, and then he began Sunday with a fever that quickly went higher and higher. We were thankful for the willingness of the Peace Corps doctor to come and see him. The doctor's initial diagnosis was pneumonia, so he gave him some penicillin and promised to return later. All day we continued to sponge Nathan with cool water, gave aspirin and antimalarials, but nothing brought down the high fever. In his delirium, Nathan asked if he could go out and lay on the wall surrounding our house, then later spoke about the Indians he was seeing! Next, he developed severe diarrhea, so the doctor gave him another type of broad-spectrum antibiotic at his evening visit.

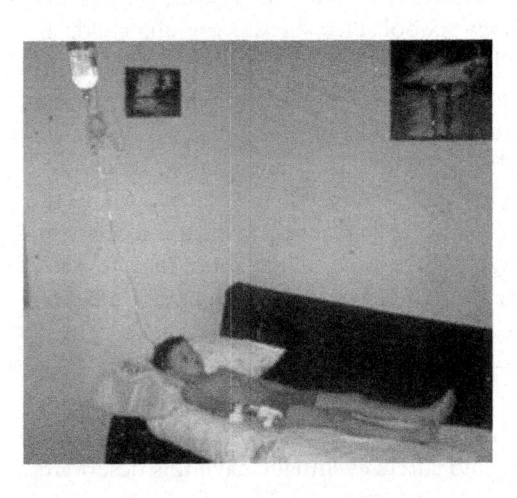

"A short time later, Nathan went into convulsions while Norma was alone with him and I was next door at church. Again, the doctor was summoned. Altogether, he was at our house four times that day. (Normally Peace Corps doctors only care for PC volunteers, but this doctor was so kind. We thanked the Lord for him.) Because one dehydrates so quickly here in the heat, the doctor started an IV dripping into Nathan that night. Nathan was lying on our couch, and the IV was hung above him on a curtain rod. Norma and I took turns being awake all night with him. About 4:00 a.m., the fever began to go down and we began to see some improvement the next day."

Heath only got one and a half hours of sleep that night, and I got about three. That morning, the PC doctor called to say Nathan had Shigella (bacillary dysentery).

Usually we looked up the illnesses of our family in *The Merck Manual*, but we were so occupied with Nathan's care that we didn't have time to get the book out and look. Later we knew the Lord kept us from looking up his symptoms during his illness. It was frightening when we read the manual's description of a type of dysentery that can progress so quickly that it takes the life of a child in twelve to twenty-four hours. How we thanked the Lord for healing Nathan and allowing him to recover.

The Effectiveness of a Grandmother's Prayers

When we asked the Peace Corps doctor where Nathan could have contracted this disease, he said, "The city has left open sewers in many places, and you have two around your property. A fly from one of those sewers could have carried the germs to the food in your house." We had asked city workers many times when they were going to cover those sewers, but they always said there was no money to do it. When Grandma Lena Bobbett heard this, she wrote, "I'm going to pray every day until those sewers are covered!" Not long after that, Heath saw trucks with cement and gravel parked on our street corner. They had come to cover the sewers!

In the afternoon of April 12, we received a long letter from Rebecca at Bouaké. While I was reading it, Nathan started asking me questions about an illustrated songbook we had of "To God Be the Glory." As I talked with him, he said he wanted to be saved! We knelt together by the bed. I wrote, "Thank God! O Father, make it real to him! Help him to understand and truly believe." Nathan was five and a half years old.

That spring we also received a letter from Jonathan at boarding school, saying his right arm was in a cast because he had fractured his wrist. He wrote, "The cast makes it hard doing my school work, but it doesn't bother my basketball game much!" Talk about concerned and puzzled parents! We were longing for more details!

On April 19, 1972, we invited eight boys to celebrate Alan's ninth birthday with us. He was very happy with the Zorro outfit we gave him and a toy car from Nathan. Eggs were almost impossible to buy in hot season, so it was a struggle to find some for making Alan's birthday cake. Once we brought powdered eggs from the States, but they didn't work well for baking and had a funny, yucky taste. Alan's birthday came during the hottest month of the year. He had to blow out the candles quickly after they were lit because in the heat, each soon melted into little puddles on the cake.

Mariama Moussa became our very good friend. She had a black belt in Judo, which was very unusual for a woman in Niger. Mariama had grown up in a bush village and was married off by her family when she was just fourteen years old. Her son's nickname was Tondi, which means "stone," indicated that the husband had taken another wife while his wife was pregnant. Even though the mother's heart was broken by sadness, the baby was strong like a stone and survived.

Mariama Moussa had hard times in life, so she became an independent woman. She was a lot of fun to be with, and our kids really liked her. Nathan always wanted her to show off her Judo strength to him. We took many opportunities to talk to her about the Lord Jesus Christ. She seemed interested and polite, but that was as far as it went.

One day after my children's class, I stopped to see Mariama because she had just gotten out of the hospital after a surgery. She wanted to keep my Bible storybook to read. That lesson book starts with creation and goes through Jesus' resurrection. When I went back the next day, she said she had read the book all the way through, as did her husband. I was very happy to hear this.

One evening, we were invited to a friend's house for supper. There were a number of French-speaking Africans there, including Mariama, and it was a fun evening. They began to tell African stories that had two choices for the conclusions. Then they would ask us which ending we would choose. Here are two examples:

An African woman is walking to the river one day to fill her clay pot with water for household needs. She sees a huge lizard lying across her path who then speaks to her saying, "If you walk around me, your husband will become very rich. If you jump over me, your parents will become very rich." Which should she do? We thought she should walk around the lizard so that her husband would become rich. "No, no, no!" Mariama declared. "If her husband gets rich, he will take another wife!"

Here's the second story. A married man had problems with wetting his bed at night. Who would he want to wash his bedclothes the next morning – his wife or his mother? We thought he would want his mother to wash the bedclothes. Again, Mariama declared, "No! If his mother had to wash the bedclothes of her grown son, she would be muttering under her breath about what a disgusting person her son was, and everyone would learn of his bed-wetting. But his wife would be very embarrassed, so she would silently do his wash, hoping that no one found out about her husband's embarrassing problem!"

Asking for a Miracle

It almost seemed as though we went from one crisis to another in 1972. On April 27, Heath drove a coworker to the airport for his departure on our small mission plane. As he unloaded the other man's things from the back of our small Peugeot station wagon, Heath placed his briefcase on top of the car to get it out of the way. Then he forgot it was there as he shut the back hatch and drove off. About halfway back to the city, he remembered, but the briefcase was gone! Even though he followed his route all the way back to the hangar, there was no trace of the briefcase.

We prayed earnestly, knowing that God was able to help us find the briefcase. A song that Doug Oldham often sang kept going through my mind, "A God of Miracles is He." The briefcase contained many important papers, the mission checkbook, Heath's health card, and less than $50 (5,000 francs of petty cash and 5,000 francs to pay for a visa for a missionary coming from Ghana).

Our African friends told us we would never get the briefcase back because there was money in it. The next day was our monthly day of prayer. Many prayed for the lost briefcase. That noon, a man who worked at the airport appeared on our doorstep with the briefcase in his hand. He said someone else had brought it to him to turn in. The money was missing (not important), but everything else was there! Yes, God answered our prayers and showed us yet again another instance of His goodness! I wrote in my journal, "I should write a book – *How I Know God Answers Prayer!* We have seen so many instances of His goodness to us."

Also in April, Heath performed the wedding ceremony for a young Gourma Christian couple. This was a special blessing to many of the new believers who had never seen a Christian wedding before.

We were asking prayer for health and strength in another hot season. "The devaluation is hitting us hard, having reached 13 percent now and giving us 26 francs less per dollar. In the face of rising living expenses here in Niger (about 30 percent in the last five years)…it makes it even more difficult to make ends meet." The Lord certainly proved Himself faithful to us though, and we never lacked food on the table.

Crooks, Swindlers, Dishonest Persons, Scoundrels, and Those Who Act in Disreputable, Unethical, and Unscrupulous Ways

Yes, we met so many of them over the years we were in Niger! They appeared on our doorstep, their most frequently repeated statements being, "I was traveling, and I was robbed. They stole my money and my passport, and I haven't eaten in days. Please help me." Over time, we learned our lesson that about 99 percent of these people belonged to the categories mentioned above. We heard their stories about being robbed so often that once when one appeared at our door, before he could speak, Heath said, "You are traveling and have been robbed. They stole your money and passport. Besides that, you haven't eaten in days, and you desperately need money from us!" The stranger's eyebrows went up as he said, "How did you know?"

At first, we tried to help people like this as much as we could, only to discover later that they made their living with these lies and were sometimes found in a bar not far away, enjoying alcohol at our expense!

We prayed for wisdom from the Lord when these people came to our doorway. We never wanted to refuse help to a person truly in need, and there was that 1 percent who were not scoundrels.

Once a man from Cameroon came for help. He had been kicked out of Algeria with his wife and three children. We felt he was truthful, so Heath helped exchange his Algerian money so he could get to Ivory Coast where there was a Cameroon embassy to help him.

A man from Yugoslavia came and told us of his being imprisoned there because he was anti-communist. We invited him for dinner and talked to him about the Lord. He showed us the prison number tattooed on his forearm and explained that he was looking for work in Africa. We felt he was sincere, so we helped him. A few days later, he came back to thank us, telling us he had found a job and wanted to give us an American $5 bill that he had carried in his wallet so long he had forgotten it was there.

On the negative side, there were people who came saying they were taking a collection for a great cause. When we insisted we needed to see official papers, they became indignant and tried to make us feel guilty for not just handing over money to them. Sometimes they professed to be plain clothes policemen or soldiers or representatives of a charity.

We often recommended that these strangers who came to our door go to their own embassy in town or seek out some of their own countrymen for help. We explained to them that we were just a small mission and did not have great funds to give out to everyone who came. Of course, they didn't believe us because we were Americans or Europeans whom they were convinced had unlimited money resources!

One day, an American tourist world traveler-type came up our walk with a beautiful expensive camera hanging on a strap around his neck. I was the only one home that day. Before he even got to the steps of our porch, he started in, "I have been robbed. They took everything. I have been everywhere trying to get help so you are my last resort, the only one who can help me at this point!" As he continued to tell me how we had to help him, I said, "We are a small mission and do not have funds to help you at this time. I guess the only thing you can do to get some money is to sell that expensive camera around your neck." (We had had so many of these people wanting money!) His face fell and the "come on" smile faded as he turned around and left.

Another fellow came one day, puffing on a cigarette, telling us that he was a Christian and that he was very active with another mission agency in Nigeria. Everything he owned had been stolen. He had no money and no food in days. Heath asked how he had money for cigarettes. He quickly jerked the cigarette out of his mouth and stamped it out on the ground, flustered as he said, "Oh, somebody gave me the cigarette. I didn't buy it!" We questioned why someone would give him cigarettes but no food!

Some of the most heart rending situations were when a child was sick and the father carried a written prescription for treatment from place to place, with the sick child in his arms, asking for money to pay for the prescription. It was a way to make a pretty good living from folks whose hearts were touched by the needs of this sick child. Sad to say, the money given was never used for the prescription. Wisdom in this situation was to take the prescription yourself to have it filled for the child, but the swindling parent didn't want to give it up. Our hearts broke for their little ones who would undoubtedly die.

Not only did we have to pray for wisdom to know the truly poor folks who were in distress, but we had to pray for ourselves because it was easy to become cynical over the abundance of these charlatans and not to trust any stranger's request.

Rebecca's Surgery and a Trip to Nigeria

It was with great joy that we anticipated Rebecca and Jonathan's return for the summer of 1972 after their first year at boarding school. Having them home felt like our family was whole again. Jonathan was a faithful and hard worker. He always asked us to tell him any jobs he could do at home. He painted, repaired, brushed old whitewash off of the big stones lining our yard paths, then re-whitewashed them after rainy season. What a help he was to his dad and me in all he offered to do every time he was home!

Rebecca began to complain of stomach pain soon after arriving home from boarding school. On May 27, she awoke with the pain localized in her lower right side. We were not able to get her to the SIM hospital in Nigeria on such short notice. At 5:45 p.m., she had an emergency appendectomy performed by a French military surgeon at the Gamkalley Clinic.

Upon reading this memory recently, Rebecca commented, "I remember that the French military surgeon was very good looking, and I was embarrassed that he had to see me undressed and with my hair unwashed! I remember that in the surgery he did not even wear scrubs or cover his hair, and right before the anesthesia kicked in, he looked down at me and promised that he would leave such a tiny scar that I could still wear a bikini. Ha! And he did! My scar is hardly visible. I remember the Dowdell boys coming to the clinic to visit me and making me laugh so hard I nearly tore my stitches, and I was begging them to stop being so funny."

It was just two weeks before our planned vacation time in Jos. We were so thankful the Lord didn't allow Rebecca's appendicitis to happen the week before when she was on the long train ride from boarding school or while we were on the road traveling to Nigeria.

She was released from the clinic on June 2, and we left on June 9 for Nigeria. We had our first flat tire at Dogondoutchi after we picked up three pieces of broken wire and our second just after crossing the border into Nigeria. We arrived at Miango in time to unpack in our cabin and go to the ritual tea time held each afternoon in the dining hall.

There were large woodstoves in the guest house kitchen. Any wood smoke I encounter to this day always reminds me of our good times at Miango. I arrived this time, however, with a bad toothache and couldn't see the dentist until the following Monday. He found I had a partially impacted wisdom tooth that had decayed, so he extracted it. The next day, I was in a lot of pain that lasted for seven days. I had never heard of a dry socket before, and I hope I never have one again!

Harold and I were with Charlene at the French Clinic when Jonathan Edward Curtis was born on July 31.The clinic called the *médicin accoucheur* (delivery doctor) to come for the baby's delivery, but he hadn't arrived when the baby was ready to make his appearance! The young French intern admitted he had never delivered a baby, but he was now forced to. Just as the baby's head crowned, the delivery doctor arrived. We couldn't believe what he did next! As the intern peeled off his rubber gloves, the doctor held that inside-out glove in his hand to catch the baby. He did not even bother to wash his hands and was rather cocky, besides not having good bedside manner. The biggest shock for Charlene and me was next. To sterilize some of the medical instruments in a basin on the table next to Charlene, the nurse poured alcohol on them and set them afire. Poor Charlene! After all she had been through, I'll never forget the look on her face as she saw this two-foot blaze of fire next to her while the alcohol burned away. I have read since then that this is not an effective way to sterilize instruments.

Fun activities we had as a family were playing table games and volleyball, having picnics on a plateau overlooking the Niger river, throwing Frisbees, watching beautiful sunsets, letting the kids drive the car on the dirt camel racing track or bush airplane dirt runways, getting up early to go giraffe hunting, swimming in one of the hotel pools, and hosting birthday parties. For a time, for 250 francs ($1) each we could eat at the air-conditioned Sahel hotel restaurant. They served a steak and French fries plus good French bread! The seven of us ate out for $7! Because we spoke Zarma to the waiters, they took good care of us. Normally the French did not serve butter with bread, but when our children asked for it, the waiters brought the butter and there was no extra charge. Of course, some of the staff asked how much it would take for them to become engaged to our beautiful Mariama too!

That fall, an evangelists conference was held in Niamey. Malam Kano talked about soul-winning, telling us missionaries that we shouldn't just sit back and say, "Now let the Africans do the evangelizing." *"Nda baabo si koy fari, zankey ga koy, wala?"* ("If the father doesn't go out to work in the fields, will his children go?") Evangelist Cecekoy preached on "We are the salt of the world," then asked, "Are we good salt for food or Epsom salts?" (!)

321

Luc gave his testimony of how he came to Niamey for two months in 1966 to work with the small Gourma church plant. There were only five or six faithfully attending then. He was glad to return to his home village of Mahadaga in Burkina Faso, but then the Lord impressed upon his heart that He wanted him to return to Niamey to work. He resisted but did ask his wife, Oukano, "If God says we should go to Niamey, will you go?" Oukano answered, "Yes. If God says to go, let's obey!"

He needed a way to support his wife and daughter. Luc said he was secretly hoping so very much that Heath would say nothing could be offered, but Heath wrote back and told him we would give him work. With great misgivings, Luc was assured that God wanted him in Niamey! Life was much more expensive in Niamey. He told about a day when he and the family where he was staying had nothing to eat. Just then, a former missionary he knew in Burkina Faso stopped by to give them a big sack of beans! In no time at all, the Gourma church began to grow and was able to help with some support for him too. Luc was one of the greatest soul winners and evangelists we ever met in Africa.

In my journal, I wrote highlights of other evangelists' testimonies at the conference. They all were so encouraged to be together with other believers because they were so alone in their villages. It reminded me of a woman who was the only woman in her village to become a Christian. When she was taken down to a Christian women's conference, she spent the first day just weeping. When asked why, she replied, "I thought I was the only one! Now I am seeing and meeting all my sisters in Christ that I never knew existed!"

Pastor Luc was making many trips out into bush villages on the road to Burkina Faso, preaching, winning souls to Christ, and starting churches. The Niamey Gourma Church continued to grow under his ministry.

On September 11, Rebecca and Jonathan left to return to boarding school. I wrote, "It has been a long and lonely day. We miss them so much." Sending my children away to boarding school was probably the most difficult thing I have ever done.

We were thankful that Ivory Coast Academy was on a trimester system so that about every three months, the children came home. They had a long Christmas vacation (Thanksgiving until after New Year's) and also several weeks at Easter, then they were home with us for about two months in the summer. How we looked forward to their times at home with us! It was so difficult and sad for Heath and me to say goodbye when they returned to school. The first loads of wash after they left brought tears to my eyes until their things were washed and put away again. September 16, 1972, was Rebecca's sixteenth birthday. I wrote, "How we miss her. She has been so sweet, thoughtful, and helpful this summer. Such a joy to us. Thank You, Lord."

October 2 was Nathan's first day in French school, Cours la Fontaine. He looked so cute going to school with his little book bag! McCaba Academy didn't have kindergarten, and his birthday was too late for him to enter first grade. The French school decided to put him into first grade there. They said if it was too difficult, they could always put him back in kindergarten, but if kindergarten was too easy, they couldn't advance him.

Shortly before the first day of French school, Nathan got cold feet, telling me that he didn't want to go to school. "Honey, it is really important that you go to school. See those men in town who are shoveling out muck from the open sewers? They have to take jobs like that because they have never been to school." He pondered that for a while, then later in the evening he told his older brother, nine-year-old Alan, that when he grew up, he would have to shovel out open sewers because he didn't go to French school!

Amazingly, Nathan did very well in French school. By the end of first grade he could speak French without an accent and write in cursive! Nathan received this note from his teacher: *"Bon travail. Nathan s'est bien adapté à la classe et a surmonté son problème de langue."* ("Good work. Nathan has adapted well to the class and has overcome the problem of not knowing French.")

Another amusing story about Nathan's French school experience was when our Israeli friends, the Shahels, with whom we carpooled, forgot to pick Nathan up when school was out at noon. They were often late in delivering him home, so I thought they had been delayed on the way. Then I saw Nathan's French teacher coming through our front gate with him. She had observed him waiting in the schoolyard until all the other children had been picked up, so she realized no one came for him. She very kindly brought him home!

I was frustrated, trying to talk to her in French, while Nathan kept pulling at my arm and saying, "Mom! My teacher has a fast Deux Chevaux (a small French car named Two Horses, which is now obsolete)!" While trying to listen and understand the teacher in her rapid French, I thought Nathan was saying "My teacher has a horse face!" What he was really saying was that her car went really fast. Mortified, I kept trying to get him to go on into the house and hoping the teacher didn't understand what he was saying! At least this was good for many laughs in the years afterward! Nathan was always thrilled to ride in any different car, and he thought his teacher drove fast – which she probably did.

On October 5, 1972, I celebrated my thirty-ninth birthday by having my first JOY Club meeting of the year, with forty-five children attending.

Some new Arab children came. They all listened so well. I was thrilled that Dieyabidi started going to JOY Club with me because he wanted to learn how to teach children too. We learned the value of praying before class for the Lord's help and that Satan wouldn't be victorious when we taught a series of four Bible lessons about Satan, God's enemy. The first week we had fifty-three children with lots of problems and interruptions. We felt that Satan was agitating them, not wanting them to know what the Bible had to say about him. After that, we fortified our teaching with much prayer. The classes went better as the children learned about Satan's origins and his work in the world today.

A couple of months later, I asked Dieyabidi to teach the class. He was very nervous about this great responsibility. We went over and over the lesson beforehand. His hands were trembling, but I could really sense the Holy Spirit was helping him. Our lesson was about demons and Jesus' power over them. As a child, I had not really understood this lesson and thought there were no more demons today. Not so for these African children! They knew what demon possession was all about. Dieyabidi talked to them about reality, and he did an excellent job, telling them God is more powerful than demons.

Each Sunday after services at the Goudel church, Heath was having classes about how to organize a New Testament church. Since the little church meeting place was in the middle of the Goudel market, there were disturbances to try to hinder the meetings. Even Pastor Kommi told how as a boy, and before his salvation, he liked to throw stones up on the metal roof to make noise to trouble the preacher. One Sunday, we arrived to find that someone had thrown a dead chicken into the meeting place. The stench was terrible. After it was all cleaned up, one of the Christians went out into the market, bought a bottle of cheap perfume, and poured it all around. Services continued as normal!

Answers to Prayer for Kommi

After Kommi (Amadou Issaka) finished all his Braille schooling in Nigeria, he requested prayer because he felt the Lord was leading him to go to Bible school. By then he spoke impeccable English, and he was accepted into a Baptist Mid-Missions school in Wa, Ghana. The school officials were very gracious in his case because they had never had a blind student before. His second request was to find a Christian wife. Muslim relatives always tell (threaten) young men who become Christians that they will never get a wife because no one would want their daughter to marry an infidel.

Kommi went off to Bible school and the other students helped him with his studies. With his Braille typewriter he wrote something and stuck the paper up on the headboard of his bed. The sighted students often asked him what was written there, but he wouldn't tell them what it was. One day, another blind man came to visit with him during rest hour. As the other blind man lay on Kommi's bed, he reached up and felt the Braille writing. He read it out loud: "God, please give me Mariama." Mariama was the daughter of a professing Christian in Niger. Kommi's secret was out because all the other students learned about it too! When he came home on school vacation, Kommi visited Mariama's father to ask permission to court her. Mariama was impressed by Kommi and accepted his proposal of marriage! They were married in 1974 while we were home on furlough. Mariama was a great asset as a pastor's wife. She had a photographic memory and could easily memorize whole chapters of the Zarma Bible. Then she set the words to music for her Sunday school children, having them sing whole chapters of Scripture too.

During our last furlough, we had bought a vinyl La-Z-Boy chair for Heath on Father's Day and packed it into a crate for shipment to Niger. When it arrived, the crate had been broken open, the chair was broken, and the nice seat pillow had been stolen! An African carpenter was able to repair the chair. We wrote to the company in the States, telling them the color of the chair and what happened. We explained to them that Heath's mother was coming to visit us for Christmas and could carry the seat pillow under her arm if they could replace it. Those dear people only charged us $8 for the cushion, mailed it to Mother Bobbett, and she carried it out to us! All the family enjoyed that chair for the rest of our years in Niger, except in the hot season when the vinyl was too hot and sticky to sit on!

Christmas 1972

I wrote, "Our children home from boarding school, a Christmas tree fresh from France (gift from UTA French airlines), a nineteen-pound turkey (gift from the director of the American Cultural Center), the arrival of Grandmother Bobbett and Rebecca's friend Paula from the States, the fellowship and special services and get-togethers with local Christians – these give you some idea of our joy and thankfulness to the Lord for His special blessings upon us as we once again celebrated the Savior's birth here in Niger." The Africans greatly respect those who are aged, so they honored Grandmother Bobbett like she was a queen!

In January 1973, Dr. Joseph McCaba, founder of our mission in 1928, went home to be with the Lord. There were some Africans around who still knew him and the great work he did for the Lord beginning in 1930. They were very touched by his death and came to express their sympathy. One dear old lady named Grace could just barely make it up the two steps onto our porch to come, but with beaming face she said, "I was the first one Malam McCaba baptized here in Niamey!"

Being of Syrian background, Mr. McCaba had a gift for languages and spoke English, Arabic, French, Hausa, and Zarma fluently. He worked with a Hausa man to produce the first Zarma New Testament, published in 1954. We were so thankful to have it when we arrived in Niger. Some Hausa words had been used in the text though, and the spelling was greatly changed by the independent government in later years, so it was revised and re-published in 1977. It was again extensively revised with Zarma translators from 1984 to 1990 as the whole language committee completed the translation of the Old Testament, and the complete Zarma Bible was published in 1990.

We were saddened in January 1973 when the Niger government asked all the Israeli aid workers in Niger to leave. A few weeks before, King Faisal of Saudi Arabia had made a trip to several African countries, promising them monetary aid with the condition that they removed all the Israelis and their embassies from their countries. The Israelis were given short notice. Fearing Muslim terrorists, they began to travel in convoys when they took their children to school or went out for needed things.

We went to the airport to bid the Shahels goodbye when they left. From my journal, "Our Israeli friends, Simon and Rivka, got off with no incident. They had to leave in such a short time and were concerned about six families going out on the same plane, but they had no choice. We lost some very dear friends. Simon kissed Heath on both cheeks when we said goodbye, and they both had tears in their eyes. It is our prayer that they will be convinced by the Holy Spirit that Jesus is their Messiah. More than anything, we want them in heaven with us." Heath had obtained a New Testament in Hebrew that he presented to Simon as a farewell gift.

The Shahels told us that they always went to Jerusalem first when they returned to Israel, although their home was in Tel Aviv. Simon said, "There is something very spiritual about Jerusalem. I don't know what it is, but we must go there first."

In a letter we received from Simon a few months later, he said, "Thanks for your two letters and the photo. It was very thoughtful of you to send it over to us. We were too busy trying to settle down in Israel. Thank G_ _ the children are very happy here and doing well in school. Elihay climbed to the top of his class in a very short time. Oriel has forgotten all her French and does well in kindergarten...How do you keep in these hot days? We have read about the starvation in all the countries of West Africa...Love from all of us. Hope to hear from you soon. Heath, we appreciate your Hebrew progress." We tried to keep up a correspondence with them, but after several months we did not hear from them anymore.

All the lush vegetation at the project the Israelis created was supposed to be taken over by Arabic countries, but the vegetation quickly deteriorated and returned to its desert-like state.

What an encouragement it was when God led us to hearts He had prepared for the Gospel! In February 1973, we met Youssouf, a young man from a village in Mali, not far from the Niger border. He had completed elementary school but his father would not allow him to continue beyond that. Youssouf was drafted into the army for two years, serving in Bamako and Timbuktu. Afterward, he returned to his small village, helping at home and caring for their herds. In the market one day, he saw an American missionary with a literature table and was intrigued seeing Billy Graham's book, *Paix Avec Dieu (Peace with God)* so he bought it for 500 francs (about $2 at that time). One day quite sometime later, he had nothing to do so he began to read it. Struck by the message of salvation, he couldn't put the book down, even when he was called at meal time. The more he read, the more he wanted to know. He decided he couldn't say his Muslim prayers anymore. His mother and father couldn't understand why.

"Will you make us live in shame when the neighbors reproach us because you don't say your Muslim prayers?" his parents asked. Youssouf replied, "I do pray, but not like before." Still searching and wanting to find out more, he came to Niamey, and the Lord brought him to Heath's office in the back of the Niamey church. What a joy and privilege it was for Heath to lead him into the assurance of salvation and what it means to be born again.

Afterward, Heath brought Youssouf from his office up to our house to meet me. His face was absolutely radiant! He was so thrilled over the Gospel. Heath took him to our Bible bookstore for a New Testament and started him on a correspondence course in the book of John. The next day, he came back with the first twelve lessons and answers already completed! Only four days after he was born again, Youssouf had read all the Gospels and was starting on Acts.

When Youssouf's uncle, with whom he was lodging, found out, he told Youssouf he could not eat at his house again. "No dog is eating at my house," he said. Mariama gave him some of her tithe money for food, and we tried to help also as he looked for work. We had to guard against just handing out money indiscriminately to new believers, not wanting them to become dependent on handouts from foreigners. Youssouf found work as a night guard soon after, which was a real answer to prayer.

At this time, I was having classes with blind Seydou. He had enrolled in a Bible correspondence course. I read each Scripture passage and lesson to him, then asked him the questions at the end. He retained what he heard very well and passed course after course until he had finished them all. With the advanced courses, he had to memorize a verse with each lesson, and he memorized quickly. He was a big help to me too as I translated English Bible lessons into Zarma for my JOY Club. Seydou spoke Fulani, Hausa, Zarma, and French fluently.

April 19, 1973, was Alan's tenth birthday. I made a special cake for him, and he was happy with his gifts: books, materials to build a chicken pen, an army suit, pajamas, a dart gun, and a dollar.

I noted that there were sixty in my children's open-air Bible class that day, and many earned prizes for knowing their memory verse from the week before. Alan had developed a boil on his chin and one on his leg. The one on his chin came to a head quickly with hot packs, but the one on his leg wouldn't come to a head. Nurse Arlene Spurlock treated him with Gantanol and then penicillin shots. When the boil finally opened, we realized it was a carbuncle with at least three heads! I felt so badly to see Alan suffer like that, but he, like our other children, never complained about such things. They just accepted them as a part of growing up in Africa.

Just before Easter, we received a surprise conference call. We heard Dad's voice in Florida, my brother Mickey's from Ohio, and my brother Carl's from Arizona! Carl's wife Carol had arranged for the call and we appreciated it so much. We never made phone calls to the States except in dire cases. It was unbelievably expensive.

Pastor Truax Promoted to Heaven

During this time, we received word that our beloved Pastor Clyde Truax was promoted to heaven. When he retired from Hillcrest Baptist Church a few years before, he had asked the Lord to allow him to preach until he died. The Lord granted his request, and he was invited to fill pulpits and hold conferences up until the last month before the Lord took him home. His counsel and encouragements to pastors in churches earned him the title of The Pastors' Pastor. The news of his homegoing was very difficult for us, and we wept.

From my journal, dated Easter Sunday, April 22, 1973: "The Lord gave us such joy and blessings today as we saw Youssouf, Emile, and Seydou follow Him in the obedience of baptism. Cecekoy had a hard time finding a good place for the baptism in the Niger River because the water level was so low. Each of the fellows gave a testimony before they were immersed, and it was thrilling to see how God had worked in each life. Heath and Cecekoy did the baptizing. The heat was a real scorcher today, 107 degrees in our house." A few days later, our living room thermometer read 110 degrees, but that was at the top limit of the indoor thermometer, so we could only guess how much higher the temperature really was. I noted in my journal that we had not had a good night's sleep in three nights because of the heat and humidity.

Papa Ibrahim Keita, a retired postal chief, was a stalwart in the Niamey church. As he grew older, his doctor often hospitalized him in the hot season to get him into the air-conditioning because of his high blood pressure. We went to call on him that month. As Heath was preparing to have prayer with him, Ibrahim's eyes welled with tears and he said, "We are so grateful for you missionaries who came to Africa to tell us the Good News of the Gospel so we could be saved." Needless to say, that touched our hearts and encouraged us to keep on keeping on for the Savior.

The drought in West Africa was getting very serious, and cattle were dying by the hundreds, I wrote, "If we don't have a better rainy season this year, I don't know what these people will do." A measles epidemic was killing many children also.

April 1973 was a happy month for us, having Rebecca and Jon home between trimesters. After they left, I wrote in my journal, "The goodbyes get harder each time." A few times, Rebecca and Jon made tape recordings for us at school and talked a long time. How happy they made us when we received those recordings. From my journal: "They are growing in grace and knowledge, as well as maturity. Thank you, dear Lord, for answered prayer."

We had so much work to finish before we left on July 5th for the cool plateau in Nigeria that we were in the mission office until midnight.

We praised the Lord that we made it to our first overnight stop with no flat tires. The next day, less than five miles out of Gusau, we came to a bridge that was washed out by a big rainstorm. We went back to the SIM station and were kindly received for another night. Heath spent all day typing and finishing work he had to do before his vacation began anyway.

We arrived at Miango on July 7, and on July 20, Bob Cowley flew Rebecca and Jon in from Bouaké. We were always surprised at how Jonathan grew each three months we were apart. When we left the States in 1971, he was shorter than Rebecca, but in just two years he was towering over her. We enjoyed the rest of the month together in the cool plateau climate.

Famine

All of our missionaries, by faith, gave so that we were able to purchase one hundred sacks of grain. We asked the African church to distribute the grain because they knew who the truly needy were. We learned the difficult way that when word got out that we had grain to distribute, everyone tried to get into the line for a free handout, even those who had sufficient income and granaries full of millet. Our prayers were that this help with grain during the famine would result in a testimony for Christ.

Niger had come to the attention of the world because of these famine years. Many of the light-skinned Touareg tribe (Tamachek) and their slaves, the darker-skinned Bellas, were coming down from Mali and the desert into Niamey. Their cattle had died, and they were starving. America and other countries were sending grain, but it wasn't reaching the people as it should have. Our supporting churches were also sending gifts for grain to EBM's Niger famine relief funds. I determined at that time that if I ever wanted to send money for food to a country, I would prefer sending it to missionaries because 100 percent of what was sent was used for grain. Some other organizations had high overhead costs, sending out their representatives to stay in Niger's best hotels while they "observed" the conditions and so forth.

A prayer request from our prayer letter, dated July 1973: "Insane people are allowed to roam the streets, and at present we have three very deranged men who come to harass us from time to time. Because of the heat, we must sleep outdoors, and it doesn't always make for a restful night when you know these men may walk into your yard at any time. Pray for protection and that the Lord will cause these men to go elsewhere."

The church building next to us was never locked. One mentally deranged man went in many times to ring the church bell at any time of day or night. One day, the Catholic priest came to our house with a stack of the church's hymn books. The demented man had carried them across town to the Catholic church to distribute them to people at early mass! At last, this insane man ceased coming to our church after he yanked the church bell one night and it came crashing down to the floor! The timbers and mud construction holding it in place for years had been ravaged by termites!

On September 3, 1973, school started for Alan and Nathan at McCaba Academy. Nathan was happy to be in an English school where he was taught a new Bible verse each week and "had neat Bible stories." Rebecca and Jon returned to boarding school the next day. It was Rebecca's senior year and Jonathan's sophomore year. The fourteen seniors would be ICA's second graduating class. Jonathan loved being on the basketball team and proudly proclaimed his one distinction on the team – no one had bigger feet than he did!

Tragic news came to us on September 18 that a senior, 17-year-old Mark Olsen, was accidentally killed when he touched a live electrical wire while working on campus. Mark was a godly young man, and he left a tremendous testimony. When his coach had asked him if he was ready to play ball that year, Mark answered, "Yes, but you know, this is not exactly what I really want to do. There is something deeper than this, and I can't explain it. What I really want is to have an impact on the kids in my school."

The dorm boys remembered him as the fellow who knelt to pray. A former roommate wrote to Mark's parents: "Last year, I was coming to the point of throwing Christianity out the window because of all the doubts I had about God. But watching Mark having his devotions every morning and night and seeing him kneeling to pray made my conscience bother me. He was close to the Lord and I kept drifting away, not having my devotions and not even going to Sunday school. When I got the news, I was really struck as I realized that if it had been me killed, I'd not have gone to be with the Lord. I've been doing some hard thinking today, and I realize now that I really do need God." Mark's missionary parents amazed us all as they were sustained by the Lord, bearing remarkable testimonies for Christ through it all.

At my Thursday open-air children's classes, one lady, Djingiri, listened faithfully each week and then started going to the Gourma church with Yenourou. We were all praying for her. She had a difficult life with several children and a husband who was far away working in another town. What a joy it was for us when Djingiri stepped out for Christ one Sunday and also her two oldest sons accepted Jesus as their Savior. They were faithful week after week and began to grow in the Lord. Two months later, her Muslim husband returned with two more wives he had married where he was working. He forbade Djingiri and his sons to attend church again.

For Christmas that year, we invited some university students (Desiré and Blaise) and another young man (Elisha) for Christmas dinner. Two Peace Corps girls came for morning coffee. After dinner we played table games. The Gourmas met at 5:00 p.m., and Heath preached. In the evening Jonathan showed us a film borrowed from the American Cultural Center. The film was *Rio Bravo* with John Wayne "speaking" French. Many laughs!

Our dear Zarma friend Kano had her second baby, Elizabeth, on January 4, 1974. Liz's birth was a real answer to prayer and had quite a history behind it. Kano's firstborn, Amina, was five years old, and Kano had not been able to conceive again. Although her husband was a professing Christian at that time, she was very concerned because every African man wants many children and especially, to have a son. She was devastated when a Niamey doctor told her she had fibroids, could never have more children, and needed a hysterectomy. We sent her to a hospital in Bénin, where the mission doctor told her the same thing. Kano was sure that her husband would take another wife who could bear more children for him.

In desperation, we wrote to Dr. Long at the Galmi hospital in Niger to ask if there was any surgery he could do to remove the fibroids without doing a hysterectomy. He said he would at least try to do that for her. Kano went off to Galmi with a little hope in her heart. Surprise! When Dr. Long opened her up to do the surgery, he saw that she was already about three months pregnant! He carefully sewed her up and said, "We doctors goofed!" Kano told us that when she was conscious again after the surgery and heard that she was pregnant, she was so happy she never felt any pain! Elizabeth was a beautiful little girl, and in the following years, Kano also had two sons.

Dieyabidi's Parents

Out of all of Dieyabidi's siblings, only he and his brother, John, lived to adulthood. His parents were idol worshippers. When a parent dies in the Gourma culture, the children hold a big homemade beer party for the dead one. When both Dieyabidi and John became Christians at the same time, their father's sad comment was, "Now no one will have a big beer party for me when I die." Nevertheless, Dieyabidi always spoke highly of his dad and the wisdom he had passed on to his sons. He was the one who urged Dieyabidi to travel, resulting in his coming to Niamey for work. His father counseled that if you never traveled, you would never be *cerrem* (clever) because you learn so much from being in other places and with other tribes.

Dieyabidi often remembered when he was a little boy hearing his dad say, "I didn't sleep all night. I was walking." He later realized that his dad was awake thinking of ways to feed his family and provide for them. His father had two wives, and their family situation was unique. Dieyabidi's mother and the co-wife got along very well together. He said his "other mother" was always kind to him, so when he bought a gift for his mother, he bought one for her too.

In January 1974, Dieyabidi received word that his mother was seriously ill. His heart was broken that neither of his parents had believed on the Lord Jesus Christ for eternal life. We gave him vacation time so he could go home to see her. He asked us to please pray for his parents to be saved. We prayed much for his mother especially at that time because of her precarious health. Dieyabidi rode as far as he could on a bush taxi then had to rent a bicycle for the rest of his journey home. He said that over and over, he would ride a while then get off and walk, pushing the bike and praying for his mother. What joy was his when he walked into her hut and heard her say, "Don't worry about me. Jesus is now my Savior!"

Dieyabidi wrote to us, "I have arrived home safely. My mother is still quite ill, but she has accepted Christ as her Savior! My heart is at peace because I know that whether the Lord heals her or takes her home, she is ready." When we received his letter telling about this, I was so happy I literally danced for joy as I thanked God for answered prayer. Then we began praying more earnestly for his father.

C.H. Spurgeon said, "Prayer pulls the rope down below, and the great bell rings above in the ears of God. Some scarcely stir the bell, for they pray so languidly; others give only an occasional jerk at the rope. But he who communicates with heaven is the man who grasps the rope boldly and pulls continuously with all his might."

What a marvelous example Daniel is to all of us in Daniel 9:3. Day in and day out, often multiple times a day, Daniel "set his face toward the Lord God" to discover His will and obey Him in everything. Dieyabidi returned on February 26. His mother had gone to be with the Lord on February 15. I was so glad to have him back to help me

Art Linkletter's Visit to Niger

Art Linkletter, the famous television host and author of *Kids Say the Darnedest Things*, toured Niger in 1974. He came with the president of World Vision and a camera crew to make a film about the famine in Niger. Art, America's goodwill ambassador to Australia (where he had a huge sheep ranch), was really friendly and very entertaining. We were told he had become a Christian not too long before visiting Niger. Heath asked him to speak in our Sunday evening English service. Pastor Tambaya from Nigeria was sitting on the front row. Mr. Linkletter told a story about asking a little boy what his favorite Bible story was. When the little boy said it was about Noah's ark, Mr. Linkletter asked him to tell him about it. The boy described the building of the ark and how all animals went aboard two-by-two. Mr. Linkletter then asked, "What did you learn from this story?" The boy replied, "If you want to go to heaven, you'd better get married!" Pastor Tambaya laughed so hard he almost fell off of the church bench!

Heath also asked Mr. Linkletter if he would come to speak to the children at McCaba Academy. He replied, "Yes, I'll come and I won't even ask for a fee because you wouldn't be able to afford it anyway!" He told the children about baby kangaroos. He said when they are born, they are only about the size of a bumblebee. They crawl from where they are born up into their mother's pouch where they can get nourishment, and they don't come out until they are big enough to hop around. He said, "In a way, you can say that kangaroos are born two times." Seven-year-old Nathan raised his hand to ask, "Do you mean that kangaroos are Christians?" Mr. Linkletter smiled and said, "You have been listening well to your Bible lessons, I see!"

The film crew took Art out to the Lazare refugee camp and had him seated on a mat under of one of their grain sack tents to film him having Touareg tea with the men. Art said there was a dead fly floating in his little glass of tea, so he brought it to his lips as if he was to drink with the others, but when the camera man panned around to photograph the others, he quickly dumped his into the sand then raised the empty glass again to his mouth as if he had drunk it!

One Thursday I took Blind Seydou with me to the children's open-air class. I asked the children, "Do you believe a blind man can read?" Many were sure this wasn't possible, so when Seydou began to read from his Braille Scriptures, the children were fascinated. I loved watching the expressions on their faces when he spoke. It was amazing how well they usually listened as we taught.

Seydou's mother and cousin were beginning to give him a very hard time, saying harsh things to him because he had become a Christian.

"There is no one in this world worse than you. You are an infidel, a Christian! I will never trust you again."

After class, one young boy came up to me and said, *"Joie-joie, Cawyan wo ga kaan gumo!"* Loosely translated, it meant "Joy-Joy, the teachings you are giving are very pleasing to me." Then he smiled, clutching the tract I had given him, and went home.

The Cost for a Muslim Who Turns from Islam to Follow Christ

This testimony was passed on to us through a prayer letter from fellow EBM missionaries:

"To all my new Christian friends, I send greetings. You don't know but my experience is typical of every Muslim who hears the Good News of the Gospel of Jesus Christ and receives Him as personal Savior and Lord. Let me tell you about it.

"In this area, we have what we call *un telephone sans fil*, a telephone without a wire. All news travels very quickly by word of mouth. Yesterday I received a letter from my mother and my uncle which I would like to share with you:

"'Dear Son, I am not sending you greetings. This is what I would like to say to you. Your mother is here with me. She and I, we both say to you, if it is true that you have decided to leave Islam and become a Christian, all we say is don't come home. I believe that will be best for you. Being a son of a Muslim, we cannot now permit an infidel here. No one here greets you, for you are no longer our son. You must stay there where you made your decision.' (Sent by your Uncle)

"It only took thirty days for the news that I had accepted Christ as Savior to go ninety miles and for the above letter to be sent to me. Pray for me. I have no family here. I am going to school here. Praise God for some Christian friends who are assisting me. Thank you for sending missionaries with the real way of salvation from sin. But the wedge of Christianity has been driven between me and my family. Pray for me and for them. Thank you, A New Christian"

We were praying much for a friend's husband who had a serious alcohol problem. One day, she brought him to our house, saying he wanted to talk to me. He had been drinking but was coherent. He wanted me to explain the way of salvation to him and asked what he should do to become a Christian. I explained the way to him, but I told him that an oral profession wouldn't mean anything; it had to come from his heart. I asked him if he was ready to confess in his heart that Jesus was the Son of God. He said he wasn't. We gave him the book *Paix avec Dieu* (*Peace with God*) by Billy Graham. Later he did truly become a child of God. I was amazed when later she told me that he believed that day after our conversation.

Coup d'Etat in Niger

Although many African countries had several government overthrows since their independence, Niger stood out with a stable government and the same president for fourteen years. President Hamani Diori was the first president after Niger's independence in 1960 and was reelected in 1965 and 1970. Typically, when someone got into power, his party outlawed all other political parties so he was the only one running for reelection. President Diori was a good man, but more and more, he was becoming surrounded by corruption in his administration. He was criticized for not being able to deal with the famine that was ravaging the land. Much of the grain sent by other countries during the famine was not reaching the starving people out in the bush villages. Some of the government ministers were actually getting the grain themselves and storing it in their garages to feed to their horses or other livestock! Not least of the corruption around President Diori was his clever Fulani wife, Haissa. She was an attractive woman and astute in business, although she had never been to school. She amassed personal wealth over the years wherever she could. Many of the local people resented her.

In the night hours of April 15, 1974, Heath awakened at about 4:00 a.m. and was unable to get back to sleep. So he was sitting in our living room when he heard a large truck pull up in front of the church, which was next door to us. Soldiers began to pour out of the truck and take positions in front of the church and at our front gate, as well as at our car gate behind the church. Our German shepherd, Hunter, began to bark furiously, so Heath went out to get him. He greeted the soldier by our front gate and the soldier replied *"Tranquillisez vous."* (Be calm.) Soon there were gunshots, so Heath got Mariama and Rebecca, who were sleeping out on our front porch, to come inside. Then he went to the side terrace to call Jon, Alan, and Nathan into the house. I was sleeping inside when he awoke me. We did not turn any lights on because our house would be like a lighted fishbowl for those outside to see in. We also spoke in whispers and wondered if this was an attempted government overthrow, but we were not afraid.

A radio station normally came on the air at 6:30 a.m., but when we turned it on there was only silence. The station finally came on at 8:00 a.m., playing military music. This was as good as a statement that there had been a military overthrow of the government. At 9:45 a.m., the official announcement was given on the radio that the rule of Hamani Diori and his party was ended by a military coup led by Lieutenant Colonel Seyni Kountché.

The French had a large military camp right in the center of Niamey, and they were there to protect the president and ministers in such an attempt. But before they knew what was happening, the Niger military had completely surrounded their base in those night hours telling the French military that as long as they stayed in their own camp, they would not be harmed. So they sat tight and didn't leave their military camp. (After the coup, the French military were asked to leave the country.)

Niger soldiers had surrounded the palace, there was an exchange of gunfire, and some were killed. When they entered President Hamani and Madame Haissa Diori's private quarters, she pulled out a small gun and began to shoot. Immediately she was shot and killed. The president was arrested and secretly transported to a military camp in the desert town of Zinder. He was not put in prison but was under house arrest and guard. We were so glad the military were kind to him. We were told that a neighboring African country had their former president rolling barrels of water in the desert in hard construction work. After 11 years Former President Diori was allowed to move to Morocco and eventually died there at age 72.

After the coup, curfew was immediately imposed on the city from dusk to dawn. We had to cancel our Zarma Christian conference, which was to begin the next day. The eerie silence that descended on the busy city as soon as the sun went down seemed strange. We were used to loud conversation on our street corner, motorbikes, cars and vendors passing by, and the music from nearby bars that went on until the wee hours of the morning. Under curfew, there was only silence.

The next day, we saw the death trucks from the hospital morgue pass our house on their way to the Muslim cemetery to bury those killed in the coup.

There was much to do during the next couple of months as we prepared to leave for furlough. A coworker reluctantly agreed to be acting field director while Heath was gone. Heath was busy teaching him those responsibilities and introducing him at government offices.

Easter break was a nostalgic time for Rebecca as she said goodbye to many of her friends in Niger. After her graduation from Ivory Coast Academy in July, we would be leaving from there to go on furlough. She had been accepted as a freshman at Baptist Bible College that fall, and she didn't know when she would be in Niger again.

On May 29, I had my last JOY Club at École Zongo for the year. I was thrilled that Dieyabidi and Alzouma wanted to continue it the next year while we were in the States.

On June 30 we traveled to Ivory Coast Academy for Rebecca's graduation on July 3. There were thirteen seniors in the class of 1974. Mark Olsen's parents came too, and it was very touching. Even though their son had gone to heaven months before, this dear couple wanted to be there to see his classmates graduate.

It was hard saying goodbye to Mariama as she returned to Niger and we prepared to leave for the States. On July 5, with a large group of missionaries leaving for the States, two African *rapides* (small buses) were hired to take all of us to the Abidjan airport. There was a torrential downpour of rain as we got to Abidjan, but when the rain stopped, a patch of sunshine showed briefly through the clouds and we saw the end of a beautiful rainbow in a field. There wasn't any pot of gold, though! We had five hours to wait at the airport before our plane left at 11:00 p.m. In the ladies room, many of us were changing into travel clothes; some of the women were putting on panty hose for the first time in three or four years. One gal stood with hers poised in her hands declaring that she had forgotten how to put them on! We all laughed and understood her frustration.

Our fourth furlough was about to begin. It didn't seem possible, but our firstborn, Rebecca, had finished high school and would be a college freshman in just a few weeks.

Chapter 18
Fourth Furlough
July 1974 to August 1975

We wanted to rent a home near Baptist Bible College so Rebecca could live at home her first year but were shocked at the rental prices for a furnished house for a family of six. Then we heard about an old house for sale just one mile from BBC. A friend of ours at the college looked at it for us and said if we didn't buy it he would buy it himself for an investment!

The price was $8,500. Sight unseen, we borrowed some of our insurance money for a down payment and accepted the offer of purchase! The two-story, four-bedroom house was over 100 years old and had been built on a foundation of stones. Someone had put extra support poles in the small basement to jack up the house, but the floors were still sagging and very uneven. We had to put wood blocks under some of the legs of the beds so they would be level for sleeping. It looked pretty bad on the outside, but we fixed it up nicely on the inside and found it to be a comfortable place for our family.

Answers to Eleven-Year-Old Alan's Prayers

When we were still in Niger and wondering and praying about where we would live during this furlough, Alan had told us, "When we go to the States, I want to live in a big house in the country that has an upstairs. (Quite novel for Alan since we had only lived in one-level homes.) I want to have a yard to play in and a place to go fishing nearby." Oh, the faith of a child! We didn't have that kind of faith, so not wanting Alan to be too disappointed, we told him to just pray about it and we would be content with what the Lord provided. Our furlough home on Griffin Pond Road in Clarks Summit, Pennsylvania, was a two-story house (had an "upstairs") in the country with a large yard with trees and two fishing ponds nearby! All we could say was, "Thank You, Lord!"

After years of boarding school, Rebecca was thrilled to be living at home her freshman year, instead of in a dorm. The ladies at my home church gave Rebecca a lovely personal shower which helped greatly with her clothing needs for college. Many other friends sent gifts to help pay her tuition for the first semester. If I am remembering correctly, a year's tuition at BBC in 1974 was $3,400. My how things have changed!

Rebecca got her first job working evenings as a waitress in a restaurant called Elby's Big Boy. One thing on her job caused her to cry. She was told that a basket of rolls put on the table had to be thrown away afterward even if nobody touched the basket. With her vivid memories of coming from the terrible famine in Niger and seeing so many starving refugees, it broke her heart to have to throw away good food.

We had an unusual experience with some of our support. For many months, we had not received any support from a faithful church that had partnered with us since the beginning of our overseas ministry. Sadly, we thought they had just dropped our support without saying anything. Then, Heath saw the pastor of that church at meetings, and he was very enthusiastic about "the Bobbetts being our missionaries." Heath then told him that we had not received any support in quite some time, so we assumed they were no longer with us. "Oh, yes!" said the pastor. "Our treasurer is a dentist, and he probably just wants to send your support quarterly or yearly. We definitely are still supporting you."

The months continued to pass with no support being sent. Then one day, we received a letter with profound apologies from the new treasurer who had been elected. Going over the books, she found that the dentist had been pocketing the missionaries' support! The church confronted him and told him they would not press charges if he paid it all back. The Lord worked it together for our good because the nice sum of back support we were given helped us buy a used car for this furlough. The new treasurer wrote, "The dentist no longer attends our church."

Jon, Alan, and Nathan were enrolled in public school. It was very hard for Jonathan to experience the interruption of a new school (Abington High School) for his junior year. His heart was still back in Africa. He was a great son, though, and never gave us one day of grief because of his attitudes or running out late at night. He liked playing basketball, but other than that, he was home, playing games with his siblings, doing homework, watching TV, or wrestling with his little brothers.

Larry and Joan Nielson gave us the use of their second car during that furlough. That was a wonderful gesture. I don't know what I would have done when Heath was away in meetings because living way out on a dirt country road, I could not walk to a store or to church. For almost all of our married life, we have gotten along with just one car.

Jon, Alan, and Nathan sometimes went to the gym at BBC to play basketball with the college guys. One student who was a basketball star, had fun with the boys, and Nathan thought he was wonderful. When this student asked Rebecca out on a date, Nathan just couldn't understand why he would want to hang out with a girl! We were all amused when Nathan waited at the end of our driveway for the fellow to arrive that night, trying to waylay him before he took Rebecca out!

Thanksgiving 1974 was wonderful for us. Carol, Carl, Mickey, Geneva, and young Jeff came to our house from Ohio. Jane and Homer and some of their children came to Mother Bobbett's, as well as Shirley with some children from New Jersey. After our Thanksgiving dinners, we all got together for fellowship and dessert. Having all our family for that holiday gathering was very special to us. My family will never forget their trip home! Snow began to fall heavily, and troopers urged folks not to travel. But the men had to get back to work, so they started out in terrible conditions. After a while, they had to head south to a longer route home in order to get south of where the snow was falling and cross back to Ohio. Thank the Lord, they made it safely!

Up until this furlough, the Lord had always given me a special woman friend to fellowship with. These special sisters meant much to me as we encouraged each other to go on growing in Christ. This fourth furlough was different though because two different women with severe emotional problems began to demand my time. The children would often intercept their phone calls because when they called, they wanted to talk on and on, taking my time from my family. I wanted to be of help to them, but I came to realize their needs were far beyond my abilities to aid them.

We were very thankful for news that for the first time in seven years, Niger had a good rainy season. The crops were much better, but of course the many tragic results of the famine would continue for years to come.

We received the sad news in January 1975 that our friend Emile was killed in a plane crash near Lomé, Togo.

Heath concentrated on reporting to our supporting churches and speaking in mission conferences. On March 11, 1975, we wrote, "Deputation travels this month will take us as far south as St. Petersburg, Florida, and as far north as Windsor Locks, Connecticut. How wonderfully the Lord has watched over us as we travel. We haven't had to miss one meeting so far because of bad weather. We thank the Lord for the joys of renewed fellowship with old friends and also for the privilege of getting to know many of God's children for the first time in various churches."

Ladies missionary fellowships wrote asking for lists of things they could help supply to pack into our barrels. What a tremendous help they were to us, enabling us to check off needed items on our lists.

Looming over us was a sadness that we would be leaving one of our family behind in the States this time because Rebecca was in college. We were asking prayer for her and all of us as we faced this difficult separation.

August 11 found us back at Mickey and Geneva's. Dad was there and bought a twenty-one-pound turkey so we could all have one last family meal and celebration together. My Aunt Stella and Uncle Ermel Burns came to see us and gave me money to buy my first instamatic camera.

We drove all night on August 21 back to Clarks Summit. From my journal: "missionary Carson Fremont called today to say he will buy our car! How great is our God! He knew we needed it until the last minute, then He sold it for us!" Friday, August 21, 1975, was our departure date for our fifth term in Niger. Jane and Homer picked us up in a large van shortly before noon to take us to JFK Airport. During the three-and-a-half-hour trip, I was frantically working to finish an afghan I'd made for Rebecca's room in the BBC dorm. It was heart-wrenching to say goodbye to her. We knew that when we landed in Niger, we would also be saying goodbye to Jonathan because he would continue on to Abidjan for his senior year at Ivory Coast Academy. Jon was really looking forward to being back on African soil. He once told us, "If you don't go back to Africa, I'm going back without you!" Only God's grace sustained us for these separations. Yes, as the Scriptures say, "His grace is sufficient."

When we were having our hand luggage searched in Paris before boarding the next plane for Africa, the French inspector made us all laugh when he pulled one of Jonathan's size twelve sneakers out of his handbag and exclaimed, "*Oh là!* Can anyone have feet that big?"

Our September 1975 prayer letter from Niger: "We are so happy to be back in Niger. We do thank the Lord for the wonderful furlough, now past, and for all of you who prayed and helped in so many ways to bring us back here. When we were at EBM headquarters in Kokomo last month, we still lacked passage funds. The accountant said, 'God will supply!' We really had to chuckle this morning when our statement arrived from the mission, indicating that, sure enough, He had supplied and our passage account even had a balance of $2.50. This is only one example of the many needs God has supplied in these last months in answer to your prayers."

Chapter 19
Fifth Term in Niger
September 1975 to August 1977

We arrived in Niamey during a hard downpour and before getting off the plane, we had another goodbye to say. Jonathan was continuing on to boarding school. I hugged him hard as we said goodbye looking forward to seeing him for Christmas break. The separations never got easier.

Niamey had had a good rain, so our feet were really wet by the time we walked from the plane into the terminal. It was so good to see everyone again. Our beds were in the house, so we slept there, but we were awakened by a rat chewing on something in the house. The next day we left him a snack laced with rat poison and never heard from him again! The house needed painting, and there was so much to do we didn't know where to begin.

Dieyabidi married a young woman from his hometown. He was ten years older than Kwampwa and could even remember when she was born. Kwampwa's mother died when she was just a baby, so she was brought up by an aunt. From the time Kwampwa was just a young girl, she declared that she was going to marry Dieyabidi, and if she couldn't marry him, she wouldn't get married at all! Since her parents were not living, an uncle had the say over whom she would marry, and he had chosen someone else for her. After Kwampwa's declaration along with many negotiations on Dieyabidi's part, the uncle finally relented.

By the time we arrived back in Niger, they were all expecting the arrival of their first baby, but the situation took a bad turn. The local midwives allowed her to labor for two days and even tried to induce her for the birth. Dr. Bianci arrived in the late afternoon of the second day and was furious that he hadn't been called earlier. The baby was transverse. Dr. Bianci performed a cesarean section, but it was too late. The beautiful healthy baby boy had died in her womb. Dieyabidi was very upset because they would not allow him to see Kwampwa until the next evening. About 9:00 p.m., he came to our house saying that the maternity had given him the baby to bury. Heath and the Gourma men went with flashlights to bury the baby while Dieyabidi and I stayed with Kwampwa.

Dr. Bianci had done the cesarean in such a way that she should be able to have her next baby normally if it was in the right position. In the years afterward, Kwampwa carried six more children (including twin girls) and had them all by natural birth.

On Friday, September 19, 1975, Heath was asked to have a funeral for a Swiss couple's sixteen-month-old son who accidentally swallowed antimalarial medicine and died. It was so sad. Madame Mermod was a Christian, but her husband wasn't. She gave a marvelous testimony in our evening English service a few weeks later, but Mr. Mermod seemed to have no comfort, only bitterness and anger.

A few days later, we had a long-distance call from Rebecca saying she had contacted mononucleosis and was staying with Grandmother Bobbett. (She later wrote about the details of that phone call: "I was in my second year of college, working way too many hours at Big Boy to pay my way and trying to keep up with my studies when I was diagnosed with mono. My parents were in Africa, but my grandmother lived near the college so I crashed on her sofa for several weeks. I was so sick and lonely. One night, three other lonely missionary kids came over to visit and cheer me up. They presented me with a check for $13.25 so I could call my parents in Africa, for three minutes, on a land line. There was no free long distance on your cell phone in 1975. Those MKs were just as poor and lonely as I was, and it touched my heart so much that they scraped this money together to give me such a gift. I have never forgotten their kindness.")

A severely raw sore throat and lack of appetite (side effects of mono) caused Rebecca to become very thin, so there was one thing that she was happy about in her illness! She was missing classes and of course had to give up her job at the restaurant for a while. We wrote our churches, "Pray for the Lord's healing hand upon her and that she might have wisdom not to overdo. It is good to know that we each belong to the Lord and that we are in His care." Jonathan had been elected president of his senior class, already showing qualities of leadership.

Heath was working with the translation committee on the Zarma Bible, but progress was painfully slow. Everyone had full schedules of ministry, and they could only meet a couple of days a month. Slowly, the Old Testament books were being worked on. We wrote, "We joyfully anticipate the day when we can preach from a complete Zarma Bible."

On December 18, 1975, Heath and I were invited to the palace for the celebration of the day Niger was declared a republic. This was the first time we saw the new president, Lieutenant Colonel Seyni Kountché, up close. He always had a stern, unsmiling demeanor in his pictures, but when we smiled he returned a warm smile to us. The sumptuous, expensive receptions and parades of the past were no more. The receptions became smaller and eventually ended. The country was trying to recover from the many years of famine when the government officials celebrated and spent in spite of their country being in crisis.

Christmas 1975 was our first Christmas without Rebecca. She spent the holiday with her Uncle Mickey and Aunt Geneva in Ohio. They were so kind and loving to our children all through the years. Rebecca was able to call us briefly the day after Christmas.

The Gourma Christians came to our yard for Christmas dinner, about fifty-five in all. Our meal was prepared by the Gourma ladies in big pots set on three stones with burning wood underneath. I made Kool-Aid and cupcakes for dessert. We had roasted sheep, and the ladies made macaroni cooked with all the sheep's meticulously cleaned intestines in a tomato sauce. It tasted better than it sounds, and we had a very nice day. Two of our favorite beggars from the entrance to the post office gladly accepted our invitation to come for the Christmas meal too.

Beggars in Niamey

There are many beggars in Muslim countries. One of the tenets of Islam is giving alms, so these beggars were helping you earn your way to heaven by allowing you to do a good work. The blind, the lame, and any with a physical disability were in front of the stores, at the entrances to the open market, on street corners (especially at traffic lights), at the entrances to mosques, and so forth. It is actually a good way for these people to make a living. You can even honorably beg if you are the mother of twins.

Probably most of us developed a liking for certain beggars, especially for those crawling on the ground with withered legs. Some actually had wheeled carts they could sit in with a means of pedaling by hand so they could get around. We missed one for several weeks in front of the post office, so when we saw him again we asked what had happened. He replied, "I was on vacation and went home to Nigeria to see my family!" Sometimes store owners gave them sugar cubes or little food gifts. One made us chuckle when he complained, saying, "I don't need food gifts. What I need is cash flow!" We could not give to all or we wouldn't have anything to live on for the rest of the month, but the beggars I could not fail giving to were the lepers without fingers or toes, with deformed faces, and sometimes blind. How they touched our hearts.

The day after Christmas I gave Mariama her first driving lesson and she drove most of the 25 miles to Karma. She was a little nervous and once remarked to me, "Aunt Norma, this car keeps going faster and faster!" I had to remind her to let up on the gas pedal!

Johnny Grant was our conference speaker in January 1976. He had awesome, challenging messages on prayer. Here are some quotes from his messages:

"Our endowment with power will be in proportion to our praying. If the Son of God's ministry depended on prayer, how can we think we can do ours with only brief devotional periods?"

"We missionaries give up home, comforts, even our children, but we aren't willing to give up the one thing that will make our ministry really effectual – time for prayer." "The church is looking for better methods. God is looking for better men." "We put the Word in their ears; the Holy Spirit puts it into their hearts. How? By prayer!"

Cheryl (Sherry) Adams arrived in Niger after a call from Dave Marshall, telling her how desperately we needed a teacher for McCaba Academy. She stayed with us for several days before we moved her into her apartment at Yantala. She became one of our dearest friends and like a daughter to us. Nathan and Alan were on their best behavior during her initial days with us, so Sherry wrote to her parents, "The Bobbetts are a wonderful family. Their sons are so well behaved and never argue." Toward the end of her days with us, she wrote: "The Bobbetts are still a wonderful family but scratch the comment I made about their boys never arguing!"

In February we made a short trip to a game reserve in Burkina Faso with the three Nunemaker families and Sherry. There were fifteen of us. We lost two hours at the Diapaga dam where traffic was blocked both ways. A gas truck was leaning precariously on a rock path we had to take through the swamp. I was very relieved when we got past that truck (on the leaning side)! We arrived at a rustic little motel on the edge of the park at 2:00 p.m. Alan and Nathan enjoyed the pool. Sherry made us all laugh when she accidently locked herself in her bathroom, and it took some time for the rest of us to find out her plight! Thankfully, she hadn't undressed, so it was okay when an employee was finally able to get her door open. We went out into the park at dusk and saw some animals, then enjoyed supper at the motel restaurant – antelope meat, fries, green beans, salad, and fruit cups. After our trip, when we threatened to tell about Sherry's locking herself in the bathroom, she threatened to show a picture she had of me coming out of the bushes with a roll of TP in my hand!

On Valentine's Day, we went into the park as the sun was getting ready to come up and saw elephants, antelope, baboons, hippos, wild pigs, and all kinds of birds. We had brought breakfast supplies along with us, so we ate near the hippo pond. By noon, we had arrived at a stream, so we had our lunch in this lovely place. Most of us adults waded in the stream, and the children swam.

When we were riding along, Dave Nunemaker read us a hilarious account of some man who had paid $3,000 for a 3,000-mile trip by Land Rover from Mali to Niger! His description of when several people got "the West African version of the common cold – acute diarrhea" was hilarious. That night all the tourists were sleeping in one long room with the water closet, or toilet, at one end. The WC had only a curtain – no door! As everyone suffered with diarrhea and not wanting to use the toilet, he said it was "the night of the living dead!" The writer found that the diarrhea medicine Imodium was effective because "it closed you up like a Japanese camera lens!"

We started having all kinds of trouble with our car on the way home: two flat tires, our battery discharging, and after dark we had no lights but had to follow the tail lights of the Nunemaker car in front of us. The Lord helped us at least get back to Niamey, but the car died completely just as we crossed the bridge over the Niger River.

Another Coup d'Etat?

On March 15, 1976, we awakened at 6:00 a.m., realizing the electricity was off. Then we began to hear machine gun fire. At 6:30 a.m., the radio station did not sign on. We brought Alan and Nathan inside the house from under their mosquito nets on the front porch. Since our route to McCaba Academy was past the president's palace and the military camp, we decided not to try to take them to school. The gunfire continued until 10:00 a.m. Mariama went to her school but was sent home. Eventually the *ministre de défense* announced that there had been a rebellion led by three men, but they had been captured and the government had things in control. This announcement was repeated every few minutes all morning. He asked everyone to remain calm.

At 5:00 p.m. the death trucks from the morgue began passing our corner on their way to the Muslim cemetery once again. It was a huge funeral procession of ninety-three cars and trucks to bury the eight soldiers who had been killed. A curfew was announced from 7:30 p.m. to 6:30 a.m., and again the empty streets and silence were eerie. On the 8:00 p.m. radio news, they played a recording of the eulogies for the soldiers who were killed. The French version of "Taps" could be heard as it echoed over all the radios in the compounds around us.

The radio said the arms the army had captured were from outside of Niger. Two days later, they were put on display at the youth center. They had also captured three kilos of witchcraft charms. The announcement was made urging all to report anyone they saw who looked suspicious.

Cars and taxis were not allowed to go out of town. Eight days later, when travel was allowed again, every car and truck was meticulously searched.

One day Dieyabidi and I loaded Yenourou and her seven children into our car to see a DC-8 take off at the airport. Though she had lived in Niamey for sixteen years, Yenourou had never been to the airport, which was several kilometers out the Dosso road. It was so much fun to see this experience through the wonderment in their eyes! On the way back into town, Yenourou said that would be all her children would talk about for days.

March 20, 1976, was my dad's eightieth birthday. I wrote in my journal, "How I thank the Lord for my wonderful dad!" Also on that day, our friend Daniel Osée came to our gate at 7:10 a.m. to say that his six-year-old niece had died suddenly the evening before and they wanted Heath to perform the funeral. At this sudden and sad event, the Lord enabled Heath to speak with comfort and assurance from the Scriptures, while also making the Gospel very clear.

It was wonderful to have Jon home for spring break at the end of March. From Heath's journal: "While Jon and I were peeling potatoes for Sunday dinner to make French fries, I casually asked Jon if he had given more thought to his plans after high school. He said, 'You know what? I think God is calling me to preach. I have been fighting it long enough.' That broke up the potato peeling for a little bit as Norma and I wept and laughed for joy and hugged our son."

Mangos were in season and children were walking the streets with huge pans of these yellow and orange treats for sale. The mango trees amazed us that their leaves were green and their fruit ripe right during the hottest, driest season of the year. They made us think of what working with Muslims was like. Through the prayers of God's people, in spite of the withering heat of Islam's attack upon Christianity, we trusted we would see His church built. When I brought the first mangos of the season home from the market, nine-year-old Nathan exclaimed, "Mmmmmm! My first mango in two years!"

On Thursday, April 22, 1976, Heath and two missionary colleagues started a Zarma Thursday evening Bible school. Heath taught Old Testament chronology, which took a lot of hours of preparation because he either had to write or translate all of his material into Zarma. Dieyabidi was so thrilled to attend these Bible classes. The next month he said, "This is serious study! We are learning so much!" He also said he wished Heath wouldn't look at his watch and stop when his hour-long class was over. "We don't care if he goes on and on because it is so interesting!"

With Jesus Leading the Way

In June Rebecca and her friend, Cindi Nielson, arrived from the States to spend the summer with us! It was wonderful to have them with us for several weeks.

Jonathan's Graduation from Ivory Coast Academy

On June 26, 1976, Heath, Rebecca, and Cindi flew to Bouaké where Heath had been invited to preach the next morning. Alan, Nathan, and I followed by plane a couple days later. We had bought our tickets back to Africa the summer before from New York to Abidjan, so we still had this unused portion of our tickets to use. At the Abidjan airport, we got a taxi to drive us to the train station. The taxi driver was absolutely nuts and drove like a banshee to the train station because he wanted to get back to the airport to pick up more passengers from our flight who needed a taxi too! We just thanked the Lord that we weren't killed or seriously injured by his erratic driving! Thank the Lord we had an enjoyable seven-hour train trip to Bouaké.

June 30 was the senior, parent, and alumni reception. There were twenty-six alumni who came back for this graduation. We all were amused when Miss Jan, who had taught all these alumni, still got their attention and respect! They were moving around and goofing off while she was trying to set up a group picture until she called their names and said, "Mike,

Norma Bobbett

get up there in the back row and be quiet!" and so forth. "Yes, Miss Jan," was their meek and obedient response! It was humorous. Miss Jan loved these kids and had dedicated her life to teaching them.

Jonathan was planning to stay in Niger with us for the next year and was hoping to find work (which he did) at the American embassy so he could save money for college. He had decided that he too wanted to attend college at BBC.

On July 1, 1976, our "number one" son, Jonathan, graduated from high school. This was an outstanding class of 26 great MK's. The reception line was long afterward, with lots of hugs and tears. It was very touching.

The rest of that summer flew by. Both Rebecca and Cindi got secretarial jobs at the Peace Corps office during the rest of the summer. The Peace Corps even let the girls set their own hours. At the end of the summer, the Peace Corps office asked if they knew anyone else who could work in the office after their departure, so they suggested Mariama. The Peace Corps personnel tested her typing and reported, "Eight words a minute, but she was very accurate!" Her abilities in French, Zarma, and English helped her to be hired, and she worked there several summers afterward too.

A French girl at the Peace Corps office gave us a beautiful white long-haired kitten who had one blue eye and one green eye. Nathan named her Frosty. She was very haughty, and it seemed as though she must have known how pretty she was. She became very attached to Nathan only, playing with him as long as he gave her time.

Frosty (and all our cats) liked to catch lizards outdoors and then play with them for hours. When I wasn't watching, the cat sometimes carried dead lizards into the house, finally abandoning them when they were no longer active. One day as I was sitting at the desk doing some typing for the field office, I felt something fall into my lap then hastily run down my leg. It was one of the cat's lizards that had eventually revived then hid under the desk! Even worse was when one was on top of a doorsill and fell onto my head when I opened the door. My family found it so amusing that I could scream so loudly while doing a very lively dance until that lizard got off of me!

We had Frosty for thirteen years. It is

uncanny the way some animals act. Once, when we left for furlough, we were told that she went into Nathan's bedroom and curled up on his shirt that he had left on the floor after getting dressed for the airport. Another time, when he had been away for quite some time, we were amazed at her actions. Although she usually slept on a chair in the front room, that day she went into his bedroom to curl up on his bed, as if she somehow knew he would soon be there for her.

Just before Rebecca returned to College that fall, she wrote a postscript in our prayer letter: "Hi everyone! Thanks so much for praying me through school and out here to Niger for the summer. It is a great feeling to know you all care so much. I've loved my first two years at BBC and am looking forward to the next two. I am majoring in missions, and I've really enjoyed the chance to come home again to Niger to be a part of Mom and Dad's work. God bless you all!"

It was amazing to see the variety of people from many countries who came to our door, giving us opportunities to talk to them about where they would spend eternity. One day it was a blind Hausa man named Amadou. We explained the Gospel to him in Zarma, but that wasn't his heart language. At that moment, blind Seydou "just happened" to stop by for a visit! What better testimony than from another blind man in Hausa who had seen the Light of Life, Jesus Christ!

Another day, an American university student came and spent several days with us. We felt he was very open and close to believing in Christ, but he didn't make a decision at that time. His parting words were, "Wouldn't it be something if I had to come to a Muslim country to learn how to become a Christian?"

From our prayer letter, "'Don't try to talk to me! I don't believe.' These words were from a French hotel manager who was bitter over his wife's sudden death of a cerebral hemorrhage. We could only listen and pray for this one in his grief and anger.

"'We accept Jesus as a prophet. Why don't you accept Mohammed as a prophet?' asked two young men who often came to visit us. They had gone through our mission's elementary school program but were then going up the ladder of success in life, not wanting to be condemned as Christians.

"'These words about Jesus are wonderful! I will bring my friend Zelica next week so that you can tell her everything you have told me.' Raabi is a Zarma woman who has been attending church with us for a few months and is interested. Her husband is from a pagan background but is willing for her to attend church."

The years were flying by so quickly, and now another one of our children, thirteen-year-old Alan, left us in August 1976 for eighth grade at

Ivory Coast Academy in Bouaké. This was his first time to be away from home, and we missed him terribly. His dorm parents, Howdy and Jody Filkins, sent us a picture of him sitting in a wagon outside the dorm shortly after his arrival at ICA; he looked so forlorn. That really tugged at our heartstrings. He wrote that he really missed feeding and caring for his chicken project at home. I think he missed his family too!

McCaba School, where Nathan attended, started up again in September with a good number of diplomats' children attending. There were American, Vietnamese, and Nigerian children in the school. It was a great outreach for our MK teachers. We were able to get a number of these children to attend our English Sunday school classes for more Bible teaching.

Humorous Words from One Language to Another

When Sherry Adams first started teaching at McCaba School, she did not know any of the Zarma language. We missionaries were always unconsciously mixing French or Zarma into our English conversations. One day, Virginia Cowley saw an African lady walking by the school window lose the balance of the large pan of millet on her head. (Millet is pronounced "high-knee" in Zarma.) Virginia exclaimed, "Oh, that poor woman! She dropped her high-knee!" Sherry didn't know what she would see when she ran to the window to look!

Jonathan worked for the American embassy from the summer of 1976 through the summer of 1977. The team of African men working under him loved him dearly. Some of their reasons were because he spoke fluent Zarma and French. They also felt like Jon was one with them. He had an interested and sympathetic heart for some of their frustrations working for embassy personnel who were only there for two years and didn't know the language or local customs. We didn't know at the time that some embassy officials were pressuring Jon into other work burdens that they shouldn't have. They appealed to his youth, inexperience, and patriotic spirit for America to use him for their own advancement. We did not learn about this and the heartache it had caused Jon until many years later.

"I had a chance to witness to two fellows at work today!" These were the words with which Jon greeted us when he came home for lunch one day. We were so thankful Jon could be with us for that year and for his burden to be a witness and testimony among his coworkers. He is helping in a Wednesday evening French Bible study and seems to bring someone to church with him most Sundays. Please pray for Jon as he is here this year.

For quite some time, our car horn only gave a weak moan. So, as a birthday gift, I bought Heath a new horn for our Peugeot, and Jim Brock secretly installed it. We had lots of fun waiting for Heath to notice it was on his car! Surprised to hear it, he only thought his old broken horn was working again!

In November 1976, we had the joy of seeing Pastor Luc Souantieba ordained to the Gospel ministry. God used Luc in so many ways, and he was an ardent soul winner.

Alan came home from Ivory Coast Academy and was with us from November 25 until after Christmas. It was so good to have our boys all with us again. Alan loved to do magic tricks when he was younger and entertained all of us around the table with jokes and riddles.

We talked much about the difficult hot season in Niger, but we also had a cool season which could last from December through mid-March. We could sleep inside the house then and even under a blanket! The morning temperatures could be down in the sixties or fifties, causing us to need sweaters, jackets, and socks, but by afternoon it was pleasantly warm again, not hot. Even with temperatures in the seventies, we felt so very cold! It was the lack of humidity at that time. The cool season was also the dry season! Then we suffered cracked lips, split heels, dry skin, and (as one lady said) "hair so full of static that I can turn the lights on during a power cut!"

I had been burdened to start a ladies Bible class and to use knitting or crocheting as an evangelistic tool. Each week I brought a carload from Niamey, and coworker Nadine Anagnost transported ladies from Goudel, while some walked to our class which began at 3:00 p.m. I started each time with a Bible lesson. It was a unique opportunity to give a Bible story and the plan of salvation. We had some Christian women who came as well as a number of Muslim women. Usually there were about a dozen ladies who came with five or more babies. Working with these ladies was a great joy to me.

Volleyball!

A highlight of our week was the organized volleyball games on Friday nights. We had a cement basketball court beside McCaba School and lights for nighttime playing. There were missionaries, young African students, those working with various non-governmental organizations, and others who came together for those times. It was a relaxing, fun time and great to have a little time with others because we all were so busy all the other days of the week. This was an outlet for Jon whose social life was almost non-existent during the year he stayed in Niger to work.

Heath always took off his glasses when we played volleyball and left them in the glove compartment of our unlocked car. One night, we found that thieves had gotten into our car in the darkness, and Heath's prescription glasses were gone. He could see very little without his glasses, so this was a tragedy for him. It would take weeks for him to send his prescription home and have new glasses sent.

He was really handicapped without his glasses. We prayed much for a miracle and that they would be returned. Certainly no one else could wear them or see through them, but there was a lurking fear a thief might just break out the lenses and wear the frames!

The next morning, Dieyabidi, Mariama, Alan, Nathan, and I decided to go back to McCaba School to comb the area, searching to see if the glasses had been thrown away or if anyone down at the riverside gardens might have found them. We looked all along the dirt road leading down to the river and around the edges of the yard but to no avail. We even went outside the mission property to ask the gardeners down by the river if they had seen the glasses. Having no success, we got back in the car to go home. As I was driving up the hill to leave, Dieyabidi suddenly said, "Stop!" Someone had placed Heath's glasses, still in their case, right in the middle of the road so we would find them as we left! We will never know who looked over a wall or who informed someone down by the river, but in answer to prayer, Heath had his glasses once again! Surely the Lord laid it on the heart of that thief to return them. Thank You, Lord!

When we got back to the house, Dieyabidi wanted to be the one to tell Heath we had found his glasses, so he put them on and staggered (with exaggeration) into the house, looking through those strong prescription lenses until Heath realized in amazement his glasses were found! Our laughter was mixed with thanksgiving to the Lord.

Heath's work kept him so very busy and constantly on the go. In early March, he came down with a high fever and extreme lower back and leg pain. We thought it might be malaria or the flu, so we treated him accordingly, but the fever persisted. On the fourth day, he thought he felt well enough to go to Sunday morning Zarma church, but by afternoon the fever started up again. When the telltale rash began to break out all over his body, we realized he had dengue fever (also called breakbone fever because of the intense headaches and joint pain).

With Jesus Leading the Way

Jim Brock and Heath had planned to take their boys – Danny, Jimmy, Jon, Alan, and Nathan – for a couple of fun days in the Park W game reserve. Heath was too sick to go, but Jim and the boys went. They came back covered with dirt and dust (I have a picture of them to prove it) but laughing about all the good times they had seeing the animals. Heath was so sorry to have missed that last trip to the park before Jon left for college.

Heath went back to work too soon because there was so much to be done and no one else to do it, but the Lord enabled him. He had very low blood pressure as an aftermath and had to be careful not to stand up too quickly, which caused light-headedness and almost caused him to pass out. A more difficult aftermath of the dengue fever was Ménière's disease that developed in Heath's left ear. A doctor thought it may have been caused by the high fever that upset the balance of fluid in his ears. Heath suffered greatly many times in the ensuing years with severe vertigo episodes. With the room spinning, he became very nauseated. The Ménière's disease destroyed much of the hearing in his left ear.

Tembengou was a young man who was faithful to the Lord. When he found the girl of God's choice, he asked Heath to marry them. The following account happened before he was married. Tembengou bought a new motorbike and loaded it onto a truck to return with it to his home village. In the bush, the truck broke down. He needed to get back because his time off from work was up, so he decided he wouldn't wait. Who knew how long it would take for the truck to be repaired? He only had 600 francs in his pocket (about $2). Another person with him had no money at all. Tembengou told his friend he would go on alone with the bike, but first he gave his friend 300 francs. It was still a long way to his home village. He bought one liter of gas for the bike for 150 francs

Tembengou reasoned, "God will help me, so I will go!" He bought some bread (50 francs) to take along, which left him 100 francs with which to begin the long trip. Knowing he would need four or five liters of gas, he prayed: "Lord, I am Your child. I will go, trusting You!" As he was going, he saw a man with leprosy begging beside the road, so he broke the baguette in half to share with the leper.

As he continued along the dirt road, suddenly Tembengou saw a 1,000-franc bill lying on the road, far out from any village! "Lord, is this mine?" he asked then decided it was, so he picked it up and continued on the road. Before he reached another village, he saw another 1,000-franc bill again on the road. He said he was so shocked, he just sat there for fifteen minutes, talking to the Lord. "Lord, now I see that You are with me!" Tembengou made his way safely all the way to his village with money left over! African friends often told us stories of how God met their needs in powerful, unusual ways.

In April 1977, Heath surprised me after the executive committee meeting by asking if I would like to return to work outside of Niamey again! We had originally come to Niamey in 1967 to replace missionaries going on furlough for one year. They did not return, so ten years later, we were still serving in Niamey.

The Curtises were leaving Dosso for a year's furlough and were very desirous of missionary replacements to continue in this growing work. We were thrilled at this opportunity to return to an outstation again. The field council asked Heath to continue as field director but promised that a coworker would be business manager for the next year to keep track of day-to-day business. This meant that we would be coming back to Niamey at least once a month for the field director work in addition to continuing the Dosso work.

I had been so reluctant to leave Gaya ten years before because I loved the bush work, but I know God worked our living in the capital for our good. It seemed like a dream that now we were going back to village work again. We ordered correspondence courses for me to teach Nathan sixth grade and Nebraska courses for Alan's ninth grade. We were happy Alan had decided to go with us to Dosso and continue his schooling at home.

But first, we had a busy summer ahead of us. Rebecca was coming for June and July as part of the Missionary Apprentice Program, a requirement for her degree in missions at BBC. We had her lined up to teach children's classes, go on village visitation, and participate in other ministries in Niger. Rebecca's plane arrived on May 31 but it was an hour late! After such a long separation I couldn't wait another minute! An African friend who was at the airport said that as we watched Rebecca descending the steps from the plane we "ate our daughter up with our eyes."

I noted in my journal that "Jonathan preached his first sermon in French on June 12, 1977." Also, on that Sunday, Heath and Pastor Luc baptized four new believers in the Niger River.

Mariama was finishing up her first year at the University of Niamey and was also working at the Peace Corps office again, hoping to save enough money for a plane ticket to visit us in the States the following year.

Trial by Stolen Check

In July 1977, Heath realized there was a check missing from the mission's checkbook and reported it to the bank. They said the check hadn't come through, so they accepted a letter from him saying not to honor it. Shortly thereafter, we found out the check had been forged and cashed on May 5 for $5,000! We thought the thief may have been someone at the American Recreational Center where Heath had forgotten his briefcase once, then went back to retrieve it. We also felt sure that the thief was in cahoots with a bank employee who accepted and cashed the check. When we wanted the bank clerk questioned, the bank said he was no longer at that bank. The bank took responsibility for $2,500, and it was up to our mission to pay back the rest. One of our coworkers had an account that was in good shape, so they helped too. We were very grateful. Of course, all these negotiations involved much time with phone calls, letters, meetings with bank personnel, and much stress added to our daily activities.

Before Jonathan left for college he made a short trip to Bénin and brought back a surprise for little brother Nathan – a pygmy goat! Pygmy goats were rare in Niger. Nathan named her Pepper.

Rebecca and Jonathan paid for Heath and me to spend two days resting at the Les Roniers hotel outside of town. The peace and quiet was blessed. A number of events that summer were heart-rending, we were so tired, and I was personally discouraged. How good the Lord was to allow us to look forward to living in Dosso the next year, away from the hustle and bustle of the big city. Life would be slower there; we would have more time for the Africans, and they would have more time for us.

That August we saw Jon off at the airport as he headed for Baptist Bible College. This had been a good year for him, although I know he was often lonely for other young people. His work at GSO seemed tailor-made for him, and he saved $4,000 for college fees. Our biggest joy was his Christian witness to his co-workers and how well he got along with the Africans and how much they liked him.

357

Jonathan wrote a beautiful letter to us once he was in the States. One statement he made was to the effect, "I will never apologize for growing up as an MK in Africa. I am so blessed to have had that privilege!"

We are so thankful that all of our children have grown up loving their African friends and are thankful that they grew up in Africa. Life as an MK is a great privilege. Even though there are hardships, the blessings and life experiences far outweigh them. MKs often have a maturity and outlook on life that is a great advantage to them. All EBM MKs are very special people, and we love them dearly. What a privilege to be Uncle Heath and Aunt Norma to them all!

As we passed the presidential palace each day, taking our children to McCaba Academy, we were saddened to see a large sign proclaiming, "Our Prophet is Mohammed. Our Book is the Koran. Our religion is Islam." Yet with all the opposition and persecution of new believers, we were thankful the door remained open in a country that called itself more than 95 percent Muslim. Much of Islam in Niger is mixed with animism though.

A week after Jonathan left, we were packing our furniture away and loading the car for our move to Dosso. Our hearts were filled with joy to be leaving the city and returning to a church planting ministry again.

Chapter 20
Sixth Term in Dosso
August 1977 to April 1978

We certainly resembled The Beverly Hillbillies as we loaded our Peugeot 404 for our move to Dosso. Pots, pans, and clothing for ourselves and our passengers were put in the back, while suitcases went on the top car rack. On top of the suitcases was an African straw mattress that a friend had asked us to purchase and bring for her. Dieyabidi and his two little nieces were already in Dosso, so Heath and I were packing in Kwampwa and baby Manguiama, Alan, Nathan, our German shepherd, Hunter, the pygmy goat, Mindy, and our cat, Frosty.

Early in Hunter's life, we found out he got carsick, so we never took him for trips in the car with us again. But this day, we were moving. He stood nearby looking so sad and forlorn because our house was emptied and we were all getting into the car. If we ever saw a happy dog, it was Hunter when we invited him to hop into the car. He sat on the floor between Alan's knees, and he never budged or gave us any problems on the one hundred-mile trip. The pygmy goat lay quietly at my feet up front. The animal that gave us the most grief was Nathan's cat, Frosty. We had no air-conditioning, so all the windows were down. Frosty wouldn't stay still. She moved from lap to lap, from back to front, from seat back to seat back, and her long white hair was blowing in the breezes, causing all of us to sneeze or spit out her hairs!

We were so glad Dieyabidi and Kwampwa were willing to move with us and to become a part of the work of the church in this needy area.

Heath was obligated to drive the one hundred-mile trip to Niamey once or twice a month to continue his duties as field director. The road was thinly paved with an abundance of small loose pebbles placed over the tar. Unfortunately, these small pebbles flipped into the air as cars traveled at high speeds, so the road was littered with broken windshields! We counted at least twenty-five on one trip. We had that frightening experience once in Niamey. It sounded like a gunshot, and then the windshield fell inward in a thousand pieces! There was no safety glass for sale in Niger, and the insurance companies stopped covering broken windshields, which were expensive. We asked for prayer for Heath as he traveled, for wisdom from God in all his work as field director, and that our car windshield would not be shattered on these trips.

Prayer Warriors

What a blessing it was on our next furlough to have friends in a supporting church tell us they prayed much that our windshield would not shatter. We were so thankful to them and told them their prayers were answered! But more important was hearing they prayed for our African coworkers because they were asking about them by name. How these dear ones needed our prayer warriors to be lifting them up. We will never know how difficult it was for them to often be lone Christians surrounded by Muslim families and neighbors.

The church in Dosso was meeting in the former main missionary residence with about twenty to twenty-five in attendance. We thanked the Lord that we had a wonderful core of believers, comprising at least five different tribes so it was a cosmopolitan church. We praised God that so many of the men had godly wives to labor alongside them.

Heath preached in French, and this was translated into Zarma or Hausa. Sometimes translations were done into Gourma or Yoruba too. Most of the people understood French (the official language of Niger) or Zarma (the predominant local language) but not all. What a joy it was to see the church begin to grow.

When the church folks decided they needed to build a baptismal, they wanted it to be outside in front of the church for all outsiders to see the baptisms. They wanted to openly show they were sincere believers in Jesus Christ and willing to be obedient in baptism.

Baby Dedication of Paul Ora

One of the first things Heath was asked to do was to have a Christian baby dedication at the home of Ladi and Felix. The Muslim baby ceremony was always on the eighth day. A sheep was provided by the father for sacrifice and acknowledgement that the baby was legitimate. The baby's head was shaved, and the Muslim teacher was there to give the baby a Muslim name. From birth, those babies are considered Muslims. Ladi and Felix wanted to be a testimony to their neighbors with a Christian ceremony. They proudly stood by Heath as he made it plain to the people that this little boy would one day need to decide to become a follower of Jesus Christ himself. Muslim neighbors looked on in silence as Felix and Ladi promised to faithfully bring the baby up in the nurture and admonition of the Lord.

Encounters with Snakes in Dosso

One evening, we came back from our evening walk tired and hot. I had prepared supper earlier, so I suggested that we just fill our plates and take them out to eat on our front cement patio where it was a little cooler than in the house. After supper, we came into the house and were reading in the living room when we heard Frosty making hissing sounds from outside the screen door. When we let her in, she went directly to my chair at the dining room table, showing us a poisonous viper hanging from the chair rung! I usually was barefoot in the house and put my foot on that rung often while eating. Alan and Heath killed the viper. The Africans who saw it the next day said it was a really bad one. We weren't sure if it was a minute snake or not. A minute snake in Niger is called "it bit" because they say you are already dying before you can finish the sentence, "It bit me!" So many, many times over the years, God protected us from snake bites and scorpion stings.

One day, Nathan and Alan's young friend Soumana pointed out a thin snake that was about two to three feet long. As they followed it, wanting to kill it, it slithered up and through a space where the wooden shutter didn't meet the window of the storage shed and went inside. They called Heath to tell him about it, but when we opened the door, we had no idea where Mr. Snake was hiding among the barrels and boxes. Heath got an aerosol can of poison for flies and mosquitoes called Fly-Tox. He kept the door as shut as possible and put his arm in to spray, hoping it would drive the snake out of hiding. But when he opened the door, he couldn't see the snake anywhere. Circling behind the storage shed, we saw Mr. Snake with just his head out of the window, apparently gasping for fresh air! Next, he made the mistake of trying to escape through that window, but the guys pinned him down and disposed of him. We wished we had taken a picture of Mr. Snake with his head out the window, looking for clear air!

We were happy Alan had decided not to go back to Ivory Coast Academy for ninth grade but to stay home and work through the Nebraska correspondence courses. He was self-motivated, working diligently at his courses, mostly on his own.

Alan got busy building a nice grass mat roof over the cement patio out front. It was quite a job, but he tied it down securely, and we really enjoyed the cooler place to sit in the evening when we had company. Koché was a very active little boy who lived nearby, and he could wreak havoc on areas around him, so he had quite a reputation of being a demolisher! We were so amused when Alan assured us of how securely he had built that grass mat roof on our patio by saying, "Even Koché couldn't tear it down!" Yes, that was the ultimate test!

A large wooden spool for cable, found abandoned along the road, served well as our patio coffee table. Alan and Nathan slept on this patio during the hot season. Heath and I had another small cement patio just outside our bedroom for sleeping outside also.

The local people soon caught on to the fact that we were making trips up to Niamey every month, so they began asking if they could get a free ride with us instead of paying a bush taxi. We were glad to help them out if we had room. We told them the precise hour we would be leaving so they could be at our gate when it was time to go, but we warned them that if they weren't there, we couldn't wait and had to leave without them.

Two village ladies came one day to ask for a ride and were thrilled when we told them we would have room for them. About 2:00 a.m., as we were all sleeping outside under our mosquito nets, we heard voices and looked over to see the two women sitting on porch chairs beside Alan and Nathan's beds, talking to each other! "Ladies! What are you doing here at 2:00 a.m.? We won't be leaving for Niamey for another four hours!"

They said that they heard their rooster crow, so they thought it must be time to come to our house for their ride! We explained to them that it was still the middle of the night and not morning, so they should go back home. We couldn't help but laugh when they said, *"Wūza! Gorongari ga taari!"* ("My goodness! That rooster lied to us!") It was true that we often heard roosters crowing at midnight and other strange hours.

One rooster Alan had in Niamey took it upon himself to circle our house, going to the patio where Mariama and Rebecca slept to crow loudly. Then he came around to the terrace where Heath and I slept and finally around to the front of the house where Alan, Jon, and Nathan were sleeping. Crowing loudly just before dawn, he evidently had appointed himself to be our alarm clock.

Alan and Nathan made a little pond and fenced enclosure for Alan's ducks. The ducks really enjoyed the water. Once after we had a good rain, Alan allowed his ducks to go outside our yard to enjoy the puddles. He followed them so he could guide them back home after a while. Two enterprising local teenagers came by. When they saw Alan's interest in the ducks, the teens claimed the ducks were theirs and offered to sell them to Alan!

Heath bought a small used dirt bike for Alan and Nathan. They had a lot of fun with that! They also rode bicycles and a Belgian doctor's horse. We have a picture of Nathan with a cart they built from old wheels and pieces of plywood. They also spent hours playing soccer with their local friends.

Nathan and his pygmy goat, Pepper, entertained all of us when they played. When Nathan knelt on all fours, she jumped up and stood on his back. He took her to the far corner of our yard, then raced to see who could get to our front door first. Pepper cheated! As they both were running full speed, she would veer into Nathan's path to cause him to stumble or slow down so he wouldn't fall over her. That way, she won the races. I had to be careful if I was sitting on the patio reading because she would come up quickly to rip a page out of my book before I knew what was happening. Then if I didn't get it away from her, she chewed it up and swallowed it!

Christmas 1977

In December, Rebecca and Jon attended EBM's MK retreat in Kokomo, Indiana, reporting that it was a great reunion and a wonderful time for all the missionary kids. MKs are identified as "third-culture kids," and there is a strong bond among them.

For Christmas Eve, we invited everyone to our house for the evening, and more than forty people came. I don't know where we put them all in our small house! Alan and Nathan were particularly happy that many of their neighbor friends came. Ladi cooked a delicious mutton sauce that we served over rice and Nathan commented, "Ladi is the best cook in the world!" We played games, sang hymns together, and then Heath gave a filmstrip presentation of the Christmas message.

However, before the evening was over, Dosso policemen came to our house. Heath went out to greet them and learned they had been notified by a telephone call from Niamey police that our dear colleague Cecilia Dillon had been killed in an automobile accident a few hours before. Though we were numb with shock, we felt it was best to wait until the next day to inform the church family, knowing that the news would have dampened the celebration of our Savior's birth they were enjoying together.

At the morning service, we informed the church folks about Cecelia's death, then left shortly after noon for Niamey. It is the duty of family members to go to the hospital morgue to bathe the body and prepare it for burial. Dear Christian sisters from the Niamey church – Mama Keita and Abigail, the pastor's wife – went with two of our mission sisters to prepare Cecelia's body in the morgue.

In the shock of Cecelia's family receiving the news about her, they said they wanted her body shipped home. This opened up huge problems for Heath as he inquired about the cost ($4,000), special treatment of the body, encasing it in more than one casket for shipment, and so forth. We prayed much about the expense and all the complicated procedures. Then on one of Heath's calls to Cecelia's family, they said they had found a letter she had written years before, saying if she died in Niger she wanted to be buried there! This was a great answer to our prayers. After that, missionaries on the field put a similar notation in their files.

The church was full for Cecelia's funeral. Heath preached in French, and Abraham translated into Zarma. The orphaned children were devastated. Cecelia was sixty-three years old. We all loved her and appreciated her godly life and the way she cared for and loved her orphaned children.

I enjoyed teaching the Dosso ladies Bible study each week. Sometimes we met at different homes or out under a shade tree at the church or at someone's home. Ladi, helped me teach and was very enthusiastic about the things of the Lord.

One of the ladies had a problem with drowsiness during one of the meetings at our house. Ladi quickly called out her name, "Atou, wake up! The devil is making you sleepy! He doesn't want you to hear this Bible lesson Madame Bobbett is teaching."

A few minutes later, Atou was nodding again, so Ladi said, "Atou! You go right out in the kitchen and wash your face with cold water so you will wake up!" Atou wasn't a bit offended as she obediently went to wash her face!

On Wednesdays, we had JOY Club in our home too. I loved teaching children. It helped to have several children from our church group attending as well as our neighbor children. Felix and Ladi's children kept a perfect record in knowing their Bible memory verse each week.

"If someone new in town asked your neighbors to introduce them to a Christian, would your name be given to them?" Heath asked this question on our next furlough as he told about two Hausa men, Hassan and Marafa. They had recently moved to Dosso from a small village where they had witnessed a man who had been honest about paying his income taxes, although he could have gotten by with lying. They were impressed that this man was a Christian, so when they got to Dosso, they asked if anyone knew a Christian there because they wanted to learn more about Christianity. God, in His providence, saw to it that they were sent to Felix. Felix explained the way of salvation, and they opened their hearts to Christ! They started coming to church regularly, in spite of the taunts and ridicule from their Muslim neighbors.

I was especially happy when their wives came to one of my ladies Bible study meetings. That week we had twenty-four present, twelve ladies and twelve babies! Seven of the ladies spoke Zarma and five only spoke Hausa, so Ladi translated into Hausa as I taught in Zarma.

Mokko was a small village about fifteen kilometers from Dosso out a dirt road. One day while Heath was busy, Alan, Nathan, some of their friends, and I drove out the dirt road to the Mokko market to see if I could find some fresh things to buy. As I parked the car, there was a huge crowd nearby, and in the center of the crowd was a man handling snakes. He told the people the snakes would not bite him because he had special charms for sale that would protect them from snakes while they were farming. "Just buy my snake charm, wear it on your arm or around your neck, and snakes will never bite you!" I went off through the small market to shop, not realizing Alan, Nathan, and their friends had climbed on top of our car so they could see the middle of the crowd and watch the medicine man show.

He pulled a young boy out of the crowd and asked the boy to bite him. The boy's mouth froze open! He began to cry because he could not close his mouth. Alan's comment was, "That's pure demonism!"

That afternoon, Alan and Nathan were visiting with several of their friends on our patio. They got out the pictures from our JOY Club lesson the day before (David and Goliath). It was interesting to hear Alan, Nathan, and Souley retelling the story to a neighbor boy named Daouda. They had listened well and knew the story. Of course, Souley's dramatic expressions and reenactments were a riot!

From my journal, dated March 3, 1978: "We invited Dieyabidi, Kwampwa, Manguiama, Phillipe, Poinyago, two children, Jonathan Dasa, Florence, Nadine, and Charles (English teacher from Ghana) to have supper with us. We had such a happy time with so many different languages involved. We decided everyone should give a five-minute lesson and talk in his own language. There was Tri (Ghana), Gourma, Zarma,

English, and Yoruba. With lots of laughter, we began singing and clapping in our languages. Jonathan Dasa said, "Oh, this is like a taste of heaven!"

As furlough time approached, our hearts were pulled in two directions. We longed to see Rebecca and Jon, our parents, and friends in the States, but it was difficult to say goodbye to our African brothers and sisters. We were so grateful to the Lord for allowing us to spend the last months of that term back on an outstation. Deacons Phillipe, Felix, and Dieyabidi would take over Heath's preaching duties when we left.

On our next to last Sunday in Dosso, the church folks surprised us with a colorful hand-loomed Zarma blanket. They also had a local photographer come to take a souvenir picture of our church group. By God's grace, our church attendance had doubled to over fifty attendees.

Chapter 21
Fifth Furlough
May 1978 to August 1979

It was the middle of the hot season when we left Niger. There had been no rain for eight months, so it was extremely hot, dry, and brown. We were almost blown away by the contrast when we reached Holland! There was water everywhere, everything was green, and the tulip colors were gorgeous. We visited some of the flower markets where flowers are exported all over the world.

Next, we stopped off for a few days in London where we stayed at a bed and breakfast for Christian workers. In the daytime, we visited the London Tower, Houses of Parliament, and Westminster Abbey. We thought that we would miss the summer tourist crowds by traveling there in May, but it was already too late. When we went through Westminster Abbey years before, we could do so at a leisurely pace and read the inscriptions on the floor where famous people, such as David Livingston, were buried. This time it was shoulder to shoulder crowds, and we couldn't even see the floor!

We flew into Philadelphia where Jonathan, who had just finished his first year at BBC, met us in his big (ugly) mustard colored car. We had lots of laughs about that cheap car, but Jon kept it running and even sold it for a little profit when he got his next car. We arrived at our home in Clarks Summit in time for Rebecca's graduation from Baptist Bible College.

Jon had spent his first year in the dorm, but we were so glad he moved home with us for that furlough. As always, Jon was working hard to help pay for his schooling. He has lots of stories to tell about working in a slaughterhouse but even more about his work at Strick Tires. When he left Africa, he was a skinny beanpole, but he had put on weight during his year in the States and was muscled from all the hard work he did at the slaughterhouse and Strick.

We took advantage of the summer months to visit my family in Ohio and report to our supporting churches and then were able to enroll Nathan and Alan in Christian schools.

Nathan's male teacher in Clarks Summit was inexperienced and very consumed with legalism, which he considered to be a sign of true spirituality. Nathan, like all boys his age, was thrilled by the TV program "The Hulk." His teacher scolded him for having a small picture of The Hulk in his desk cubicle and told him to take it down. He put a guilt trip on us parents too for allowing Nathan to have such a picture. (Give me a break!) As expected, the school let that teacher go before the next school year.

Alan became very quiet that year of furlough and undoubtedly was suffering the transitions of becoming a teenager and adjusting to life in the States. I'm sure that Satan was throwing a whole host of temptations at him. One day when we were arguing, I asked him to go up in his room to pray and talk to the Lord about which path he wanted to follow. He came down a while later and with tears in his eyes said, "Mom, I choose Christ." His heart's desire was good, but Satan wasn't giving up yet. We put our children in Christian schools, hoping their friends would want to walk with the Lord too. However, Alan later told us, "Those guys at that Clarks Summit Academy were a bunch of hoods, and I was one of them too!"

In late summer of 1978, I was broken-hearted over a situation and hurt that came into our lives. I don't think I had ever been to such a low point of discouragement and sadness before. I was going to bed at night and even wishing that I wouldn't wake up in the morning. How blessed to know that the Lord "is nigh unto him whose heart is broken." The Lord came to me through His Word and also through one special friend who came to sit with me in my grief. Perhaps she will never know what love and sympathy she communicated to me that day. The Lord used her to comfort me, just by her presence and silence! My journal is taken up with many pages I wrote, crying out to the Lord. "Lord, I want my prayers to be fervent and effectual. I know there is so much You want to teach me about faith and forgiveness. Help me to learn – to appreciate, to apply, and to appropriate what You want to teach me."

In October, Heath spoke at the beautiful old church he grew up in, First Baptist of Skaneateles, New York, which was established in the early 1800s. The church bulletin gave a brief history of Heath's background and concluded with this statement: "The Bobbetts' greatest joy has been in seeing Africans come to Christ and become established in a church so that they can grow. It is a difficult area in which to work though, for about 98 percent of the people in the Niger Republic are Muslim and very much opposed to Christianity. The believers in Niger need much prayer, for they are subjected to ridicule and persecution for their stand for Christ."

On November 20, 1978, I wrote, "Psalm 55:22: 'Cast thy burden upon the Lord and He shall sustain thee.' And I read that Hebrew word 'burden' used in this verse means 'what He has given you.' If I view my burdens like that, it truly sheds a new light on them! Father, help us to accept Your invitation to cast it upon You. We must! You are so faithful. You are our Rock, our Strong Tower, our Burden Bearer, our Savior, our Shepherd, our Guide, our Leader, our Enlightener, our Source, our Father, our God!"

One of the things I trust I have learned over the years, and in looking back at my prayer requests, is that God knows what is best, and He answers our prayers, not according to our agenda or our timetable but in His timing, which is perfect. Actually, he is not bound by time as we are. One day is as a thousand years with Him. How awesome that He works all things together for His glory and for our good!

The Lord has always brought such comfort to me from 1 John 5:14-15: "And this is the confidence that we have in Him, that, if we ask anything according to his will, he hears us: And if we know that He hears us, whatever we ask, we know that we have the petitions that we have asked of Him."

In Jesus Christ our Lord and through faith in Him, we may approach God with freedom and confidence. "For this cause I bow my knees unto the Father of our Lord Jesus Christ, of whom the whole family in heaven and earth is named, that he would grant you, according to the riches of his glory, to be strengthened with might by his Spirit in the inner man; that Christ may dwell in your hearts by faith; that ye, being rooted and grounded in love, may be able to comprehend with all saints what is the breadth, and length, and depth, and height; and to know the love of Christ, which passes knowledge, that ye might be filled with all the fulness of God. Now unto him that is able to do exceeding abundantly above all that we ask or think, according to the power that worketh in us, unto him be glory in the church by Christ Jesus throughout all ages, world without end. Amen (Ephesians 3:14-21)." Neither God's love nor His power is limited by human imagination!

I know not by what method rare,
But this I know – God answers prayer.
I know that He has given His word
Which tells me prayer is always heard
And will be answered soon or late,
And so I pray and calmly wait.
I know not if the blessing sought
Will come in just the way I thought.
But leave my prayers with Him alone
Whose will is wiser than my own.
Assured that He will grant my quest
Or send some answer far more blessed.
– *Eliza M. Hickok*

Mariama's First Visit to the States

Mariama promised us that if she passed her university exams and if she had good summer employment in the Peace Corps office, she would buy a ticket to visit us. All this came to pass, and it was a joy to have her with us for the whole month of October 1978. Lifelong habits were hard to break! She still slept with a flashlight under her pillow every night, although we assured her she would not encounter a snake or a scorpion if she got up in the dark. She loved the shopping mall, was petrified of escalators, and decided that Americans have an awful lot of push buttons to do their work for them. She told us that the thing which impressed her most was all the Christian fellowship we have here. She longed for that in her home country. When she returned to Niger, she entered her final year at the University.

Jonathan was very busy with school and work. He continued to be active with the MK team on weekends. I wrote on November 18, 1978, "Lord, Jon has a lot of traveling to do this weekend, and he will speak tonight (Saturday) at a youth rally and tomorrow in a church in Sellersville, Pennsylvania. Please watch over him, help him to be humble and to seek Your face, to realize in himself he can do nothing. May he rely on Your Holy Spirit."

Once again, we were praying about whether the Lord wanted us back in Niger and where He would have us serve next. Dr. and Mrs. Dreisbach were serving the Lord up in Filingué, Niger, at that time. Without knowing we weren't sure of our return, Bettie wrote, "Our team voted 100 percent that you are the people we want most to see back in Niger." That meant a lot to me. If the Lord led us back, we wanted to go to an outstation again.

I wrote in my journal, "Lord, we want to be sure of Your will. Help me, Father, to say, 'Anywhere You lead me, I will go – even back to the city!' You have always undertaken for us and led us. We put our hand in Yours in faith."

Heath had extensive testing for his inner ear problem that he had suffered since he had dengue fever in 1977. The specialist concluded that the trauma of the high fever caused an imbalance of the fluids in his ear and said he might get over it. It was later diagnosed as Ménière's disease. When he started to feel fullness in his ear, extreme vertigo would come, followed by nausea and vomiting. This continued for years, especially when he was stressed, and eventually destroyed much of the hearing in his left ear.

Rebecca and Richard Ahlgrim were married in October of 1978. Rebecca wore a wedding gown borrowed from her best friend, Nansie Burns Ike. It was lovely to have Mariama with us as well, and she was a bridesmaid. Rebecca had graduated from BBC, and Rick was no longer a student there, so they moved to Crown Point, Indiana, to begin their life together.

I was hospitalized in early December 1978 to have the varicose veins stripped out of my left leg. My doctor at the Scranton hospital was from Iran. As they were testing me before the surgery, we learned that I was allergic to injected dyes! I broke out in an itchy rash all over my body, and my face swelled badly. The doctor in radiology watched me closely as they gave me injections to counteract my swelling and rash. He kept asking if I was having any problem swallowing or breathing. Thankfully I wasn't. I wished someone would get sandpaper to rub on my itches! I ended up being in the hospital for seven days instead of three or four.

From my journal, dated February 22, 1979: "Lord, forgive me for my 'love of the world,' for being more concerned about my reputation than my relationship with You. Thank You for the trials you have brought to us. How much more precious the Psalms seem as I read them through tear-cleansed eyes. Thank You for my dear husband and children, for precious African brothers and sisters. Thank You for all the ways You help us. I can't even name them all! You do so many things that I am not even conscious of. Thank You that I can trust each of my children into Your care for each of their needs. I just ask, Lord, that You will open their eyes, each one, to how wonderful You are and how they need to love You and thank You."

On March 15, 1979, Nathan followed the Lord in baptism was at Heritage Baptist Church in Clarks Summit. "Father, guide in his young life for Your glory. Help him to know Your will and follow it. May he be loving and tender towards You. Call him into Your service if it is Your will. Keep him from sin. Lord, may he know the thrill of answered prayer." We were so thankful to see how faithful thirteen-year-old Nathan was in having his daily quiet time. Even Jon mentioned, "I wish I was as faithful as Nathan is in having devotions!"

We had put our old house on Griffin Pond Road in Clarks Summit up for sale. It was over one hundred years old! The newspaper ad read, "A genuine antique!"

In late spring, our first grandchild, Nansie Lynn Ahlgrim, was born in Crown Point, Indiana. I was able to fly out to spend a week with them. What a thrill it was to hold this beautiful little girl in my arms.

From my journal, dated June 13, 1979: "When praying, do you give instructions, or do you report for duty? Lord, I want to report for duty today. Help me to be 'Your person' and not to worry. Oh my! Satan has a whole new list for me today, and I gullibly took them! I'm praying for each of my children. You love them even more than I do. O for a quiet faith that peacefully smiles and trusts You in all circumstances.

"'My grace is sufficient for thee.' How wonderful, Father! George Mueller said he prayed many hours as he went about his daily duties, and 'The answers are always coming.' What a privilege is mine to trust You for my salvation, daily needs, and tomorrow too!"

In June of 1979, we drove to Springfield, Missouri for Jon's wedding to Judy Weidman. About twenty-five MKs showed up to attend the wedding as well, and a picture was taken of all with the bride and groom. A real ICA reunion. The wedding was very sweet and God-honoring with both of their fathers having a part in the ceremony.

We had been praying about our next term of service and finally wrote to the Niger field council and asked to go back to Dosso to serve, but before our letter reached them, the council had already met and voted that we go to Dosso! "When the Great Pilot is at the helm, why should the passengers pace the deck?"

We looked for a home to buy in Ohio near New Carlisle and found one, but the deal fell through because our home in Clarks Summit hadn't sold. The Lord was stretching our faith, saying, "Trust Me. I have all under control. Your Clarks Summit house will sell in My timing." We didn't realize that the day would come, years later, that we thanked the Lord for not allowing us to have that house in New Carlisle!

Dad had sold his home in Florida and was giving $10,000 each to Carl, Mickey, and me, which would have been a big help. But he didn't give me mine since we didn't find a house to buy before we left the States. I thought that was a disappointment, but it was actually God's appointment. Dad put my inheritance into a CD when interest rates were incredibly high. When we returned to the States three years later, it had increased from $10,000 to $13,000.

The summer was a very busy time as we had meetings; sorted, purchased, and packed barrels; and cleaned out our house. Heath had another bad attack of Meniere's syndrome and was too sick to take some of our furniture to New York where we planned to store it. His sister Jane had graciously offered storage space in the old hayloft over their garage. Jonathan, took a day off work and drove the U-Haul truck and unloaded the loads for us. He has been a loving and helpful son all his life.

Chapter 22
Seventh Term in Dosso
August 1979 to March 1982

After twenty-one years of missionary service, we realized our greatest needs were in this list:

The Missionary's Equipment
Author Unknown

A life yielded to God and controlled by His Spirit.
A restful trust in God for the supply of all needs.
A sympathetic spirit and willingness to take a lowly place.
Tact in dealing with men and adaptability toward circumstances.
Zeal in service and steadfastness in discouragement.
Love for communion with God and for the study of the Word.
Some experience and blessing in the Lord's work at home.
A healthy body and vigorous mind.

Our departure date was set for August 12, 1979. This time, we returned to Niger with just Alan and Nathan. Rebecca and Rick were living in Indiana, and Jon and Judy were in Clarks Summit where Jon was a junior at BBC.

How beautiful it was to look out of the plane when it is circling to land during the rainy season in Niger. The fields were green, and the Niger River was flowing swiftly. Once again, it was another goodbye as we saw Alan off three days later for his junior year at Ivory Coast Academy. I sensed Alan was struggling in spiritual battles and with the pull of the world. He had switched from his bright and happy spirit into some sullenness and was not very communicative, which isn't uncommon for young teenaged boys.

My journals record many prayers for this precious son, asking for God to help him and hedge him about.

We also saw Mariama off to the States where she planned to study on full scholarship for her master's degree at Southern Illinois University.

Our first job was to get our things out of the storeroom and cleaned up from the dust and dirt that had accumulated during our year's absence, then pack them for the one hundred-mile move to Dosso. As we stopped at the police checkpoints, it was fun to see a big smile and a look of remembrance when we greeted the officers in Zarma, French, or Hausa.

The Christians in Dosso gave us a warm welcome. What a precious group they were! They really loved the Lord and each other. We thanked God for this little group and their testimony for Christ in their Muslim surroundings. We were so thankful the doors were still open to us to be there and to preach the Gospel. We weren't as free anymore to hold public, open-air meetings, but we had permission to worship and preach openly on mission properties. We were praying God would use us in teaching the believers and organizing the church as well as in having an effective outreach in the community.

In the first twenty-four hours that we were back in Dosso, our electricity went off four times, so we were quickly introduced to some of life's daily frustrations.

We requested prayer for two young men, apprentice tailors who were desirous of attending church. But their pagan uncle, for whom they worked, did everything he could to keep them from coming. When one finished his training, he moved to Bénin, but the other one, Joseph, stayed with us and became a fine strong Christian. Heath had the joy of baptizing him in the large water cistern in our backyard the next year. (God's marvelous plan was that one day Joseph would be the pastor of the Dosso church!)

Another prayer request was for a man in Dosso who had been a real witness for Christ but had fallen into sinful habits and damaged his testimony in the town. Every month, he told his wife his salary was stolen or that it never came through. However, in reality it was going for drink and not to his family. Praise God, years later when he was dying of cancer, he did turn back to the Lord and abstained from drinking. It was sad when he grieved over the years he had wasted. We have a patient and forgiving Savior!

Homeschooling

I always enjoyed homeschooling our children and reviewing geography, history, mythology, and archeology that I had forgotten over the years. However, in Dosso, I discovered that seventh-grade math was too difficult for me to teach! That day, Nathan was to learn a complicated formula and then use it to solve his math problems. We worked and worked and worked on this, but the answer didn't come. Heath came from his office to try also. After a long struggle, he finally was able to solve it. We decided that from then on, Nathan's dad would have to teach his math while I cared for the other subjects.

Now for the amazing and humorous side of this story. In the kitchen as I was preparing the next meal, I told Dieyabidi the math problem. Dieyabidi had never been to school a day in his life, but after he became a Christian he learned to read his Gourma New Testament and how to write. He was a brilliant man, having learned Zarma and was working on English and French. He also had a market stand where his wife sold various food items. The market vendors, who were mostly illiterate, kept their accounting books accurately in their heads. They always knew exactly how much they owed and how much they were owed. So Dieyabidi's mind was accustomed to doing all kinds of bookkeeping.

When I told him the mathematical equation we had struggled with, he thought for a minute or two then said, "The answer is this," and he was right! I asked how did he ever reach that answer so quickly? He gave me the simple formula he worked out in his mind (not the complicated one taught by the math correspondence course). I gave him several other math problems, and he figured the answers quickly again with his formula!

That evening, we had invited Peace Corps volunteer Ray for supper. In conversation, we mentioned how we had struggled with the math problem that day. Ray confidently said, "Well, I am a math major. Give me the math problem, and I can probably figure it out right away." Forty-five minutes later, he finally had the answer! Then we couldn't resist telling him that Dieyabidi had figured the answer in just a few minutes!

Baptisms

In November 1979, Heath was leading a baptismal class with six candidates. Three in the class had been recently saved through the outreach in Dosso. This time we used a water reservoir in our yard, but the believers later built a cement baptismal in front of the church. What a challenge the African believers were to us. One Wednesday night, Heath suggested that we split into a men's group and a women's group for prayer. The believers said they wanted to pray in a mixed group because the people of the village could see us in our lit-up room at night, and they might think we were saying men were better than women, so they couldn't pray together. Muslim men pray up front in the mosques while the women are sequestered in a smaller room behind. They never do their prayer rituals together.

From my journal, October 1979: "Lord, I do believe in the power of praise and that 'Satan does tremble when he sees the weakest saint upon his knees.' Help me, remind me to praise You. Oh, that I would 'praise the Lord for His wonderful works to the children of men.' Father, have my heartaches made me more empathetic to others who have children who are grieving them? More loving? More understanding?"

May Jesus Christ Be Praised
German Hymn, Translated by Edward Caswall

In heaven's eternal bliss the loveliest strain is this:
May Jesus Christ be praised!
The powers of darkness fear when this sweet chant they hear:
May Jesus Christ be praised!

Our barrels arrived safely, and we opened them exactly four months from the day Heath and Jonathan took them in a U-Haul to New York.

Heath brought a series of messages on the doctrine of the church and asked for prayer that within the next year we might see the Dosso work organized into a strong and growing church. For neighborhood evangelism, he was also showing Gospel filmstrips weekly in the various compounds of believers who invited their neighbors in.

In December, we were happy again to have Alan home from his junior year at Ivory Coast Academy. He had been elected class president and was on the basketball team. The Lord had been working in his heart.

Alan and Nathan were singing in the youth choir as they prepared special numbers to sing at the Christmas get-together at our house. The choir members didn't want us to hear them rehearsing because they wanted to surprise us on Christmas Day. They sang "Joy to the World" in Zarma (*"Farha ma te ndunnya ra"*) accompanied by African drums. We decided it was the best version we had ever heard of that song!

With Jesus Leading the Way

The December 1979 issue of Baptist Bible College's *The Anchor* had a wonderful article written by Jonathan:

The Christmas Story in Niger
by Jonathan Bobbett

Editor's note: As Christmas approaches again this year, we see the familiar decorations, the snow, the Christmas tree. But in many parts of the world, the season of Christmas is not celebrated in this way. Jon Bobbett, a junior here at BBC, spent the first part of his life in the country of Niger, West Africa, where he learned of a different sort of Christmas. We asked him to relate some of that to you.

"The sky is just beginning to show touches of orange as dawn approaches. Suddenly from a high tower overlooking the city, a Muslim priest shatters the morning calm with a call for the people to rise for their morning prayers. Roosters crow in the background as the people of Niger are awakened for just another day.

In another household, the kids have already been up for an hour. Christmas morning has arrived and, for once, the missionary kids are out of bed early. They are all gathered outside the door of their parents' bedroom waiting to throw it open at 6:30 a.m. and awaken them.

In many ways, this is like no Christmas in the States. No snow will fall during the Christmas season. Rather, the air is so dry that dust will hang in the air for the entire day. No one will bundle up to go outside on their sled because at noon the temperature will climb to over 100 degrees.

But Christmas has very special meaning for many missionary families. After attending boarding schools from September to December, kids enjoy being back home with the rest of the family. As in Christmas celebrations everywhere, the presents are opened and soon the new toys are spread out all over the room. However, all these are second to the joy of being together as a family. For many families, the Christmas season holds a measure of loneliness as the day is spent apart from sons and daughters who remain in the States for schooling and from other family members.

The Christmas dinner will consist of two chickens, as turkeys are not readily available. But the missionary mothers can make the meals taste just as delicious. After the food has been devoured, the family gathers in the living room for family devotions. The Bible is opened to Luke chapter two, and the Christmas story is read. The realization that the birth of Jesus Christ was for every nation becomes very vivid. Missionaries are the outworking of the very purpose for which Christ came.

The missionary and national Christians gather in the Christmas afternoon for a feast and for fellowship. They roast a sheep over hot coals in a shallow pit outside. They have all come together for one purpose – to celebrate the coming of Christ so many years ago.

Although the missionary does not get to see the snow, participate in the winter fun, enjoy a large Christmas tree, he will participate in the very meaning of Christmas: Christ came to earth for sinners. This is His message."

Each of the seasons in Niger had its good aspects and its bad ones. During the cool season, we could sleep in the house under a blanket, and we wore sweaters during morning hours when sometimes the temperatures got down into the fifties or sixties, but even when they were in the seventies, we felt quite cold. There was no heat in our houses, and often no glass windows either, so the cold winds came right through the screens. By afternoon, the temperature was back into the eighties or nineties and quite comfortable. We often suffered from cracked lips and heels and fingers because of the dry air.

From the end of November to the middle of March is when the dry, dusty Harmattan winds blow south from the Sahara toward the Gulf of Guinea. On its passage over the desert, the wind picks up fine dust particles. A few hours after our furniture was dusted, we could again write our names in the dust and fine sand on the furnishings! We have pictures of "Dust me!" or "Major big-time dust storm!" written on the dusty furniture by our kids.

The heavy amount of dust in the air limited visibility like fog does in other countries. Often air flights were canceled or diverted to other countries for landings. The Harmattan dust storms on our bodies made Caucasian skin and hair look brown and reddish, while our African friends' hair and skin looked white!

The Harmattan winds and dust can severely limit visibility and block the sun for days. When we could see a little bit of the sun through the haze, an author described the sun as resembling "an Alka-Seltzer tablet floating in a vanilla milkshake."

When we saw the huge red rolling dust storms approaching on the horizon, we immediately dropped whatever we were doing to fly into action. We had to close windows (if we had had them), let down shutters, put food away, get laundry off the lines, and so forth. The dust and sand blasting on the damp clothes we hung out turned them muddy, and they had to be rewashed.

Sometimes as we were sleeping during the hot season, we would feel a cooling breeze begin. Half-awake and half-asleep, we enjoyed the coolness but realized if the rain came we would have to get up in a hurry. If the rain never came, we continued sleeping but laughed at the spectacles we saw when the sun arose. Our hair and skin were reddish, and we could see the outlines of our bodies on the sheets where the reddish dust had settled all around us as we slept. We had to head for the shower, take off the sheets to be washed, and then start all the sweeping and dusting that the inside of our house required.

At other times, the sandstorms so completely blackened the sky that it became like midnight (with no moon) at noon! Sheep and goats that wandered freely about could be heard pitifully crying out, lost along the roadside and not knowing what was happening. Also, small children were heard crying for their mothers. We literally could not see our hands held out in front of us until the storm passed.

The epidemics of measles and spinal meningitis are believed to be carried on this dust. When the first good hard rains come, they seem to settle the dust and stop the epidemics.

The Hot Season in Niger

From March until June, we tied up mosquito nets and slept outside because of the heat. Often it was 110 to 115 degrees or more in our house. We found ourselves often tired and unable to accomplish nearly as much as we had hoped each day. Productivity declined, and conversations often centered around the heat. Patience was stretched and tempers often flared between people as the heat wore us down. Even Africans greeted us with "How is the heat?" The traditional answer was *"Fufule go no!"* ("It's hot!")

The World Reference Atlas (2007 edition) lists Niamey, Niger, as one of the hottest inhabited places on earth. There were times when I felt like I could not bear the heat for one more day (or night). I sometimes had nightmares about being in Niger in the relentless and repressive heat. I remember thinking, "How can I ever endure another hot season in Niger?"

Niamey electricity was very expensive, so we could not afford the high electric bills that air-conditioners produced. Once a friend gave and installed a used air-conditioner in our bedroom. We only ran it two hours a day during the rest hour. All six of us (plus our German shepherd, Hunter) spent rest hours in that crowded room! Toward the end of our time in Niger, many missionaries had evaporative coolers, which used less electricity because they didn't have compressors. They were a great help.

In Lilias Trotter's biography, *A Passion for the Impossible*, she wrote about the debilitating heat in Africa. "Nerves get overstrung in these climates in a way they never did before, and little things bring a ruffle and jar and cannot be shaken off again; and a sense of exhaustion comes through the body to the spirit, even apart from the consciousness, so vivid at times, that the very air is full of the powers of darkness; and the enemy launches his fiery darts in showers on those who come to attack his strongholds. How many of us have gone through the testing of every fiber of our inner life."

My heart went out to the local people who never got relief year after year. We missionaries at least got to go back to our home countries every three or four years to get out of the heat.

Water Challenges in Dosso

Wells supplied the large water tower that was closest to our home. The whole landscape looked very flat, but actually we were at the highest part of the town, so during the hot season we were the first to lack water. The water supply in the hot season was just not adequate for the town or the schools.

The water began to go off for two or three hours a day during the hot season, then the hours increased until we only got water for an hour or two in the middle of the night. Since we were sleeping outside under our mosquito nets then, we were never sure when the water came on. Clever people that we are, we devised a method!

We turned on our outdoor hose, draped it over the end of our beds outdoors, then went calmly to sleep. About 2:00 or 3:00 a.m., we heard the "splat" of water as it hit our cement terrace, and we were mobilized into action. We filled the water barrels supplying the house, watered the garden, filled washtubs, flushed the toilets, filtered drinking water, wet down new cement on a wall being built, and even filled a neighbor's barrel for him. Then we finally climbed back into bed for a few more hours of sleep before the sun came up.

Ladies Retreats

Once a year, the ladies from churches in Goudel, Niamey, and the Dosso got together for two days of fellowship and learning from the Word of God. These times were such a blessing. In March 1980, our Dosso Ladies Fellowship hosted the retreat. We all slept on mats on the cement floor or wooden benches at the church. Some of us were full of groans and aches the next morning. However, I had a bottle of ibuprofen sent to me in a small package from the States which I shared with the ladies. The pills helped all of us, and the ladies declared them to be a miracle medicine! Just to be together with other believers meant much to these women who were surrounded by the hostility of Muslim neighbors. Their testimonies were precious as they stood for Christ.

Kano – "I want all my family to know the hope and joy I have in Christ."

Gambi – "I thank God for missionary friends. When I was sick the village women offered no help, but the missionaries ministered to me and cared for me. I would dearly love to start a children's class in my compound but I believe the village people will tell their children to stay away from us and call us infidels."

Ladi – "When I go to the market, they call me 'Christ' (Almasihou), thinking I will be ashamed and hurt. I tell them to say that beautiful name over and over again, because I love to hear it. The hardest part for me is all the terrible things said to my children. They insult them and call them infidels and say that their father is a cannibal. When my children come to me with their hurts, it is more difficult for me than when village people curse me."

I prayed, "Lord, please comfort these dear sisters. Strengthen them through Your Word. Thank You for Hebrews 12:3." The Phillips translation reads, "Think constantly of Him enduring all that sinful men could say against Him and you will not lose your purpose or your courage."

Right after the retreat, twelve-year-old Nathan came down with a 104-degree fever and diarrhea. We were thankful for husband and wife doctors from Belgium who lived not far from us. Heath went to summon them for help one evening at 9:00 pm. Dr. Inga came immediately. We were giving Nathan antimalarial medication and aspirin for the fever. Dr. Inga said if he wasn't better by midnight to come again for her. The next day, tests revealed that Nathan had bacillary dysentery, so she started him on Bactrim and he began to recover.

We were so happy to have Nathan with us, but sometimes he felt very lonely in Dosso. Although he played with his African friends, he couldn't help but miss playmates from his own "tribe." While Alan was there with us, they had fun doing things together. We played a lot of table games, and they rode their dirt bike, camped overnight in the bush, and spoke the Zarma language fluently.

Easter 1980

On Easter Sunday morning we met in our church yard at 7:00 a.m., shortly after it got light. One of the highlights of our service was special music in a number of languages. Would you believe – Yoruba, Ibo, Gourma, English, and Arabic, as well as our regular songs in French, Zarma, and Hausa? What a blessing to share the resurrection joy together in song and through the preaching of the Word. We had sixty to sixty-five in attendance, including some we have been seeking to reach for the Lord. In the afternoon, Heath baptized one man and two women.

We recognized the open attacks of Satan on God's church family in Dosso. I like what one missionary in said about his work: "Everything is going great. God is blessing, souls are being saved, and the devil is really mad!"

Wherever God puts us to serve Him, there will be difficulties, heartaches, and satanic oppression. However, in spite of all these things, we loved the work and the Dosso believers. What profound blessings are ours in Christ! He tells us to cast all our cares upon Him; to not worry about anything; to come boldly into His throne room, robed in Christ's righteousness; to present our requests to Him with thanksgiving; and then to know His peace, which is too wonderful to fully understand. Our riches are incredible!

"Oh, the depth of the riches both of the wisdom and knowledge of God! How unsearchable are His judgments and His ways past finding out! 'For who has known the mind of the Lord? Or who has become His counselor? Or who has first given to Him and it shall be repaid to him?' For of Him and through Him and to Him are all things, to whom be glory forever. Amen." (Romans 11:33-36)

"Satan dreads nothing more than prayer. His one concern is to keep the saints from praying. He fears nothing from prayerless studies, prayerless work, prayerless religion. He laughs at our toil, mocks our wisdom, but trembles when we pray." – *Samuel Chadwick*

"Satan desires to limit our prayers because He knows how our prayers limit Him." – *Anonymous*

In July 1980, I wrote in my journal, "Father, I've looked over prayers of past weeks and see how You have marvelously answered. What a privilege You give us! Please give me wisdom to pray in Your will. Thank You for answers that we don't see yet. Thank You for the Holy Spirit who prays for me with groanings that cannot be uttered and for Jesus who is making intercession for me."

We were very happy to hear that Harold and Charlene Curtis were coming back to Dosso to work with us! Sherry Adams was coming also and would be teaching the Curtis children.

Preparing for Sherry Adams to Come to Dosso

We found a house for Sherry just across a large open space outside our front gate. The house needed a lot of repairs. The old gentleman who co-owned this house with his daughter had served in the French army in World War II. His daughter worked for the government. They both were really nice, and the father was at times comical. When he found out it was *anasaras* (white people) who wanted to rent the house, he said, "Yes, rent it to these people because they do what they say." This is a loose translation of his Zarma-French, which actually said, "These people walk a straight line!"

The house had been rented previously by a Peace Corps volunteer, and the large, weird, almost satanic-like drawings on the living room wall were the first to go, thanks to a good amount of white paint. We prayed for cleansing from any satanic rituals that may have been conducted in the house.

Alan was home from boarding school for the summer and had grown as tall as his dad. He was already showing great manual work capabilities and he was able to get the electricity working again in Sherry's house. Then he painted and repaired the interior.

It was hard to find someone to work on another huge problem – a leaky aluminum pan roof. We had someone who was recommended locally, but he never could get all the leaks stopped, which meant Sherry had to place her furniture strategically between the leaks or sometimes move them again during a rainstorm. When the rains came the next year, Sherry wrote in her prayer letter, "May's weather has been a definite change. We've had several orange dust storms and some very beautiful rains as well. I hadn't realized that my home came complete with sprinkling system and moat…but the break in the heat more than makes up for these little extras!" The "moat" was the large puddles that had to be carefully circumnavigated going from her house to ours. In the dry season she referred to that open area as the "poop deck." In the dark of night, many squatted in that area unfortunately. It always paid to laugh at trying situations!

Not only did the Lord bring the Curtis family and Sherry Adams to Dosso that summer but also a sweet Peace Corps girl named Barbara Wilson. It wasn't long before we bonded with Barbara, and she became like a daughter to us too. She had worked in the Dosso hospital laboratory. Her parents were so happy to hear there were missionaries where she was stationed. Barbara married a fine Christian man when she returned to the States. We felt honored that they named their first son Heath!

We met many Peace Corps volunteers over the years as we served in Niger. We wanted to be lights for the Lord Jesus Christ among them and to treat them just as we would like to have our children treated if they were PCVs.

There was a good crowd that came out to see a Moody Bible Institute film we projected in the church yard. Although some rudeness and insults were to be expected, there were those who also had sincere questions. One young man asked, "Why is it if you light a match to the Bible and to the Koran, the Bible will burn but the Koran won't?" (This is a common belief among Muslims.) When asked if anyone had ever tried the experiment, he admitted they hadn't. Of course, a Muslim would be very fearful of desecrating the Koran in any way.

Upkeep on mud buildings was always a big chore because of termite infestation and the rainy seasons. The men of the church donated many hours working on our meeting place, knocking out walls of the former missionary residence to enlarge our sanctuary. They chopped off the outer layer of dried mud, nailed chicken wire over it, and then applied a thin layer of cement on the outside. The building began to look much better, and we knew it would be good for many years to come.

When Heath and Harold challenged the church folks about tithing, they began giving as never before. One believer testified in church, "I can't tell you how greatly God has blessed me since I started to tithe and stopped stealing from Him!"

In our October 1980 prayer letter, we wrote, "Thank you for your continued prayers for the future establishment of a church here in Dosso. Since our last general letter, Satan has tried and sifted the believers, but their faith has not failed. God continues to bring out new people to the services – three this last Sunday. The presence of the Curtis family and Sherry Adams has also been a real boost to the work."

The Bible Bookstore in Dosso

In 1972, Phillipe Dahani, a godly man, felt led of God to accept the invitation to open a Christian bookstore in Dosso. He began with about

$100 worth of stock in a little 8-by-10 movable tin kiosk. Some of us missionaries helped in his support until he could make enough for his family to live on. In the hot season, Philippe had to sit outside because the little kiosk was like an oven. Many Muslims laughed at the store's beginning and predicted its failure, but Phillipe and his wife prayed that God would enable him to stay as a testimony in Dosso.

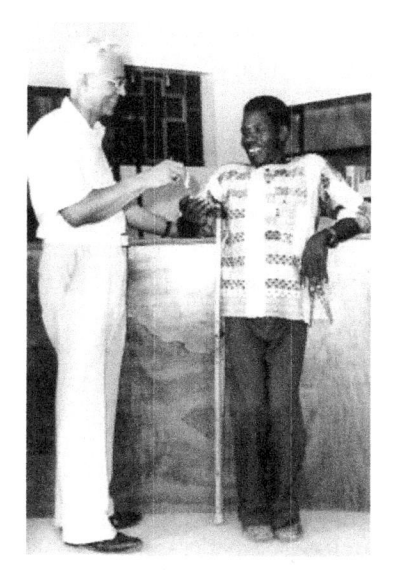

Phillipe, who always had a radiant smile, was a good witness for Christ during those eight years. Despite hard times, he stuck faithfully to the task. By God's grace, in the fall of 1980 Phillipe was able to support himself and had a good stock of materials. Besides Bibles, Christian books and literature, and Gospel tracts, he carried school and office supplies as an attraction. Many Muslims who would never enter a church came to the store to shop for supplies. Phillipe used these opportunities to talk about his Savior. In the previous nine months, Philippe had given out 2,146 Gospel tracts. He also invited any new arrivals in town to our church.

A big surprise came to us that fall when the space allotted for the kiosk was taken over by the town for other purposes. Philippe was informed that he would need to move to a permanent store building. God gave us a kindly mayor who offered Philippe a choice location in town on which to build. We needed $10,000 to purchase the lot and build a thirty-square-foot building that would give Philippe store area and storage space, with room for future expansion.

We, along with the Curtises and Sherry Adams, prayed about this huge need. None of us felt we had ever been big fundraisers, but with God's help we would let our churches know about this need. We also let our general director, David Marshall, know. Then we waited to see what God would do.

EBM Director, Dave Marshall, came to Niger to be the speaker at our next annual conference. When he asked Harold and Heath to come up front in one meeting because he had a presentation to make, we had no idea what it was all about. Mr. Marshall presented them with a $10,000 check given by one donor for the building of the Dosso bookstore! There were many tears of grateful rejoicing at God's miraculous supply. When we returned to Dosso with this news for Philippe, his familiar smile spread across his face as he said, "I have always prayed that the Lord would cause the bookstore to go ahead for His glory, even if He had someone else to take my place and further it."

Harold Curtis supervised the plans and construction of the new Bible store. He bought many building supplies in Niamey besides what he could find to buy in Dosso. The walls were up by April 1981, and the roof was soon put on. We asked prayer for protection and strength for the men working on the building. It was the hot season, and the temperature was soaring.

Robbery in the Curtis Home

Since Harold and Charlene were to be in Dosso for only one year before their next furlough, they rented a house in town about a kilometer from ours. Evidently, some criminals saw that Harold was spending a lot of money on cement and building supplies, so they thought robbing him would be very profitable. What they didn't know was that Harold had used all the funds he had on hand to buy Bible store building supplies. In the middle of the night, these men broke into the house and appeared in Harold and Charlene's bedroom demanding money. Harold told them he had spent it all. They thought he was lying so they hit him with a rubber hose to make him talk. Finally, he showed them his empty briefcase. The men rifled through the Curtises' things and took Charlene's purse and some jewelry. It was mostly costume jewelry, except for her nursing pin and she did regret seeing them take something that was irreplaceable.

By then, the Curtis children were awake and crying. Although Harold and Charlene begged the robbers not to, the men locked Harold and Charlene in their bedroom with the children crying loudly down the hall. After the thieves left, the children were crying outside their parents' room until Charlene could get them to quiet down enough to look for the key to open the door!

Although they reported what had happened at the police station, and that there were robbers circulating in town, the police only filled out a report!

What a traumatic experience for Harold and Charlene. Yet they very calmly told us what had happened and didn't even want to tell Sherry or Peace Corps volunteer Barbara, not wanting to make them nervous and fearful. Harold and Charlene were truly selfless servants of Christ.

The Bible bookstore exterior and roof were up by June 1981, but due to the increased cost of cement while the building was being constructed and some underestimates, we were $1,000 short of the funds needed to complete the interior. The Lord met those needs through donations from supporters in the States. One contribution came from the ladies missionary fellowship in a New Jersey church. "Instead of sending Christmas cards to each other this year, we put one card to everyone on the Christmas tree at church. The money we would have used for cards and stamps has been sent to your account to help pay on your $1,000 indebtedness for the bookstore. We collected $191.70." Another blessing was that the students of Ivory Coast Academy gave over $800 from their chapel offerings for Philippe to buy Bibles and Christian literature to stock the store.

We had thoroughly enjoyed the year of working together with Harold, Charlene, and Sherry. In the summer of 1981, the Curtis family left for home assignment. Sherry transferred to Ivory Coast Academy to teach. The Bible store building was up, the doors and windows put in. Heath was painting the interior and working on getting shelving and counters made for the grand opening.

Alan's Graduation from Ivory Coast Academy

Alan had expressed the desire for many years to become a veterinarian, but during his senior year, he was under conviction to yield his life and ambitions to the Lord. He wrote, "I haven't even sent in my application to veterinary college. It's become obvious that God wants me in Bible school, most likely to preach…" Our hearts were praising the Lord for that. At graduation, he received the Mark Olsen Award for Christian walk and character. We were so proud of him.

We sent Alan to the States where he stayed with Rebecca and Rick in Indiana for the rest of the summer and found a job detasseling corn. Sadly, he also renewed acquaintance with a friend who was walking far from the Lord. They both headed off to Piedmont Bible College in Winston-Salem, North Carolina, where the tuition was affordable for children of missionaries.

Alan began to rebel against the things of the Lord. The school president later told us he was very concerned when he saw Alan in chapel because he looked extremely unhappy in Christian surroundings. Although his MK friend was dismissed from the college for his conduct, Alan finished his semester before he dropped out. It was the beginning of his descent into "the far country." We cried out to the Lord for Alan day by day. It was more than difficult to be so far away and not know what was going on.

Nathan left for Ivory Coast Academy in August 1981, and for the first time we had an empty nest.

A Goal Reached!

As Heath taught the people week by week, it was his desire and goal to see the believers in Dosso organized into a New Testament church. In January 1982 we wrote, "Rejoice with us! Last night the Evangelical Baptist Church of Dosso was officially organized. We praise the Lord for His faithfulness in saving souls, blessing His Word, producing spiritual growth, and bringing this local church to birth. We praise Him too for those who have sowed before and with us to bring this to a reality. *To God be the glory!*

"Eighteen of the members (two were away studying) were present at the meeting, and the Lord gave us unity and understanding as the church constitution was unanimously adopted and the church officers elected. Pray much for all our church family who are surrounded by the hostile atmosphere of Islam. May their lives continue to be a testimony and bear fruit." Sunday morning attendance had grown to about sixty people.

Dad Christmas Promoted to Glory

On January 20, 1982, we received word that my father, Eppy Carl Christmas had passed away. Dad had been hospitalized with stomach pains, then had a massive heart attack and was gone – into the arms of His loving heavenly Father. I thanked the Lord for the wonderful dad He had given me for forty-eight years and for bringing him to repentance and faith in Christ all those years ago. Rebecca, Jonathan, and Alan traveled to Ohio for the funeral.

My tears flowed, but I knew where Dad was and that I would see him again. He wasn't dead! "He that believeth in me shall never die!" I thought of the wonderful experience for Dad – totally healed in mind and body and ushered into the presence of his Savior.

We received an invitation to be the speakers at Glory Week (February 1 to 7, 1982) at Ivory Coast Academy and wrote, "We are not sufficient for this ministry but are asking the Lord to use us as His channels of blessing." This was a big assignment, but we received help, comfort, and strength from the Lord as our prayer warriors held us up in prayer.

I had two sessions a day with grades one through six, and Heath had grades seven through twelve. In addition, Heath was the evening speaker. Thanks to the Lord's working, many students made important decisions, and one MK announced that he had received Christ as his Savior that week. We prayed much for the Word sewn in young hearts and for future results too. Heath said that being the speaker for Glory Week that year was one of the highlights of his missionary career.

Alan was living in Winston-Salem but was walking farther away from the Lord. In March, Jonathan called and told us we needed to come home to see if we could get hold of Alan.

There were things that needed to be finished up before we left the work in Dosso, so we decided that I would pack away as much of our things as I could in just a few days' time and go back to the States while Heath finished up and followed me a few weeks later. We couldn't let the Dosso church family know I was leaving until I got a lot of packing done because, in their love for us, once they heard, there would be a constant stream of folks coming to say goodbye.

I'll always remember Ladi coming to visit me before I left and trying to comfort me about a wayward son. She said, "We women cry because we don't have children, then later we cry because we _do_ have children." How true.

Words of Wisdom for Mothers
Taken from Ruth Bell Graham's writings

- We mothers must take care of the possible and trust God with the impossible. We are to love, affirm, encourage, teach, listen, and care for the physical needs of the family. We cannot convict of sin, create hunger and thirst after God, or convert. These are miracles, and miracles are not in our department.
- I have, as wife and mother, a good cause, the best cause in the world. But I lack the shoulders to support it. The job isn't too big for me. I'm not big enough for the job.

- As a mother, I must faithfully, patiently, lovingly, and happily do my part then quietly wait for God to do His.

It was with a heavy heart that I said goodbye to Heath at the Niamey airport. Earlier, we had clung to each other and wept as we made arrangements for our time apart. There are few experiences as painful as when a family member or friend turns away from God. I seldom traveled alone, so I wasn't looking forward to that journey. Alan was heavy on our hearts, and we were praying constantly that we could get him back to live with us and straighten out his life. (We still thought we as parents could fix things. We had so much to learn.)

> ### Don't Let Go
> *by John Piper*
> *"Those who sow in tears shall reap with shouts of joy!" (Psalm 126:5)*
>
> My main memory of my son, Abraham's, prodigal years is tears. As I knelt in prayer, I would remember nine-year-old Abraham walking with me to 6:30 a.m. winter prayer meetings – willingly. I would take hold of Jesus' cloak and cry: "O Jesus, please, don't let go of him."
>
> He was never more than a breath away. One moment I would be rejoicing over some simple blessing, and then suddenly he was there, a heaviness, an ache. I would wonder what he was doing. And I would pour another prayer into the great censer before the throne.
>
> Then there was fear. Will he destroy himself? Will he ruin a girl's life? Will he get a disease? Will he turn out to be an Esau? To survive I had to make the daily transfer: "Cast your burden on the Lord, and he will sustain you (Psalm 55:22)." Every day the sorrow was new. Every day sustaining mercies were new (Lamentations 3:23).
>
> All the while God was making me a broken-hearted pastor. God loves His people through the pain of His shepherds. None of our suffering is wasted. We do not graduate from the seminary of sorrows in this life. But oh, how glad I am that this class is over, and Abraham is home. Thank you, Jesus, for not letting go.

"With whom do you identify when you hear Jesus' story of the prodigal son? Is it the rebellious boy? The worried father? Or the older brother? I'll tell you which one speaks to me – the waiting dad. I'm not sure parents can ever know the maximum test of their love until one of their grown children walks in another direction, away from the Lord. If you have been there, then you know what I mean. Your heart may be broken, but you can never wave a magic wand to make it go away. You can't preach loud enough for them to listen. Your notes and phone calls are ignored. So, you wait, you hope, you endure. Take it from this old veteran of that experience, it's a tough journey to endure. When they finally turn around and come back toward the Lord, you understand the father of the prodigal." *Chuck Swindoll*

The Lord had much to teach us in the days ahead. We really didn't want to be enrolled in this school of learning, but our loving heavenly Father proved Himself faithful each step of the way. We had to remind ourselves over and over that He was sovereignly in control, and He loved our son even more than we did. It is said that one of the greatest blessings of growing older is that we can "look in the rear view mirror" to see how God was with us, working in unseen ways in every circumstance of our past.

He Was There All the Time
Lyrics by Gary S. Paxton

Time after time I went searching for peace in some void –
I was trying to blame all my ills on this world I was in;
Surface relationships used me till I was done in –
And all the while Someone was begging to free me from sin!

He was there all the time, He was there all the time;
Waiting patiently in line, He was there all the time!

Never again will I look for a fake rainbow's end –
Now that I have the answer my life is just starting to rhyme;
Sharing each new day with Him is a cup of fresh life –
But O what I missed! He'd been waiting right there all the time!

Don't Quit
Anonymous

Keep me from turning back;
Ne'er let the reins be slack;
The handles of my plow with tears are wet,
The cutting shears with rust are spoiled, and yet –
My God! My God! Keep me from turning back!

Chapter 23
Extended Furlough
March 1982 to September 1984

"He [Caleb] followed the Lord, the God of Israel, wholeheartedly."
Joshua 14:14

Jonathan and Judy met my plane in New York and took me to their Clarks Summit home. They were expecting their first baby in August, and Rebecca was expecting her second in September. Judy was working in the bookstore at BBC and Jonathan was managing three Athlete's Foot stores while finishing his senior year.

Nathan had adjusted to school in Bouaké, but he needed to make a decision. Would he come to Niger for spring break then go back to the States with Heath to finish ninth grade, or would he return to Bouaké, finish ninth grade, and return to the States in the summer? He decided he would stay on at Ivory Coast Academy to finish ninth grade. That meant I would not see him from New Year's until July 1982. Only a mother knows how difficult it is to be apart from her child for so long.

Once I was in the States, I arranged to go to Winston-Salem to see Alan as soon as possible. During the flight down, when feelings of hopelessness and helplessness overwhelmed me, many Scriptures verses recalled from memory helped and strengthened me. We wanted to do everything within our power to get our son back.

Dear friends in Winston-Salem kindly took me in during that time. I spent the days in Alan's apartment while he was at work, then we talked when he got home. After a while, he promised to come back to Clarks Summit after his dad returned from Niger.

We had left Niger three months before our scheduled furlough. God had given us one of the best terms we had ever experienced and we knew our prayer warriors and supporters had a big part in that. The Dosso Bible bookstore was completed and functioning well, the church was organized, and the deacons were prepared to carry on the preaching as they anticipated the Curtis family returning to Dosso in July. It wasn't easy saying goodbye to the believers in Dosso, but we knew God wanted us on the other side of the ocean at that time. They were backing us in prayer for Alan, whom they knew and loved.

From my journal, dated May 10, 1982: "Isaiah 41:13, 'For I am the Lord, your God, who takes hold of your right hand and says to you – Do not fear; I will help you.' Thank You, Father, for holding my hand, for telling me not to fear. Lord, You will work it out for a place for us to live, for Alan's life – to move to Ohio with us or not, for Alan's future schooling. Lord, I believe You will bring him back to Yourself. I pray for the convicting power of Your Spirit in his life. May he not be able to forget You. Give him no peace, I pray, until he says 'yes' to You."

We stayed with Jon and Judy for a month or more and will never forget their kind and loving hospitality. It had to have been hard for Judy to have her mother-in-law there all that time, but she never made me feel that I was a burden. In fact, the day before we left, she reached across the table, grasped my hand and said, "I'm going to miss you, Mom."

House Hunting

We had some funds from Heath's inheritance when his dad died, funds from my inheritance from my dad, some savings, and some profit we had made from the sale of our one-hundred-year-old house in Clarks Summit. Now we wanted to invest in a home for when we retired from Niger. Finding nothing in Clarks Summit, we decided to look again in Ohio, this time in Springfield. Jon wanted Alan to stay in Clarks Summit with him and not move to Ohio with us.

With my brothers, Carl and Mickey, and my sisters-in-law Carol and Geneva.

The realtor showed us a number of houses in Springfield, not far from my brother, Mickey, but we didn't sense any peace about purchasing one until the day he drove us up north, just outside the city limits, to see which houses were for sale in Northridge. He stopped in front of a house with trees all around and a well-kept lawn, but there was no "for sale" sign out front, saying

"I go to the same church as this couple and I think they are planning to sell." After about ten minutes, he came back out, saying, "It's for sale! She is scurrying around straightening up so you can come in and see it."

The three-bedroom brick home with one and a half bathrooms and a partially finished basement was lovely and we knew almost immediately that this was the house God meant for us. The owners were moving to Georgia. We were able to take over the mortgage at their rate of just 6 percent. With the funds we had, we felt we could pay off the mortgage in a few years. The Realtor told us later the possibility of a 6 percent mortgage was taken away just a short time later, but the Lord had gotten us into that little time slot!

Jonathan's Graduation from Baptist Bible College

Jonathan graduated from BBC on May 14, 1982. We were so proud of him. He had to work hard to pay his way through school, and thus it took five years instead of four. At graduation he was extremely busy, managing the three shoe stores.

Mariama was still in the States and came to celebrate with us along with Rebecca and Nansie.

A prayer for Alan from Psalm 80: "Return to us, O God Almighty! Look down from heaven and see. Watch over this vine, the root Your right hand has planted, the son You have raised up for Yourself. Restore him, O Lord God Almighty. Make Your face shine upon Him."

"'The children of your servants will live in your presence; their descendants will be established before you.' Our earnest prayer is that our children and their mates will love You, look to You for their needs, live in Your presence and be established before You, dear Father." And from Psalm 119:125: "I am your servant. Give me discernment that I may understand your statutes. I have put my hope in your Word. I rejoice in your promise, like one who finds great spoil!"

We were eagerly waiting Nathan's return to us in early July. I had not seen him in five months! Then, what a disappointment when we met the plane in Vandalia and he was not on it! The airline would give us no other information except that he wasn't on the flight. I was close to panic, but finally we got information that his flight from Europe was late, and thus Nathan missed his flight out of New York hours later. What joy filled our hearts when he got off the next plane! It was the Fourth of July, and beautiful fireworks were illuminating the sky as we returned to Springfield. The next Sunday, Pastor John Greening told Nathan at church, "All those fireworks were in celebration of your arrival and don't let anyone tell you differently!"

Heath flew to Scranton on July 12, 1982. Alan was nineteen years old. I was at home, crying out to God for our prodigal son. Nathan was sad to see me in tears so often. Oh how tenderly God cares for distraught mothers as He teaches us to trust Him as we pray for our children. How often I have been touched and blessed by Ruth Bell Graham's writings.

A MOTHER IS PRAYING

"Listen, Lord, a mother is praying low and quiet: Listen, please. Listen what her tears are saying, see her heart upon its knees; lift the load from her bowed shoulders till she sees and understands, You, who hold the worlds together, hold her problems in Your hands."

–Ruth Bell Graham

In my journal, I wrote out many Scripture verses and made them into prayers. "Lord, help us to see our problems as fitting into Your plan for our growth. We love You, Lord. I trust You. I believe You will help Heath, give wisdom for him to talk to Alan. I believe you will bring back our prodigal son...Lord, may Alan not lose sensitivity to sin. May the teachings of his life continually convict and rebuke him." From Lamentations 3:25, "The Lord is good to those whose hope is in Him, to the one who seeks Him. It is good to wait quietly for the salvation of the Lord." I was reminded to trust His love, His timing and His promises.

In tears I called our special prayer warrior and my most wonderful mentor Gladys Truax Carpenter, just needing to hear her voice and to share my prayer request with her. It happened to be her birthday! What a blessing this precious mother in Christ was to me.

Though Heath pleaded with Alan to come to Ohio to live with us, Alan was not willing. Heath talked to him about the Bible story of the prodigal son and told Alan that he too was looking down the road wanting Alan to return home. God was working, even though we could see nothing encouraging at that time. As Heath was saying goodbye to Alan to return to Ohio, Alan said, "Dad, keep looking down the road!"

Parents who have prodigals feel guilty and as if they have been a failure. I knew that we wanted each of our children and loved them with all our hearts. Still, being human, we weren't perfect and had made mistakes. Satan knows our vulnerable spots, and he aims his fiery darts at them. I needed to be reminded of this, "Remember that as parents we are only accountable for how we train our children. They must account for what they do with that training. Keep on praying. God knows the value of correct timing. We are to keep on praying – ask, seek, knock, and be persistent!"

On August 22, 1982, our first grandson, Stephen Heath Bobbett, was born. We were all so excited! Heath and I felt so blessed to have Nansie and now Stephen as grandchildren!

Nathan always hated change, so when he came home to a new town, a new home, and a new school for tenth grade, it was very difficult for him. We enrolled him in Springfield Christian High School which met in a downtown church. I sensed a coolness and indifference in Nathan to spiritual things that fall, and I prayed the Lord would reawaken in him an interest in God, His Word, and His will. I prayed, "Lord, please help Nathan as he adjusts to a new school, new students, and teachers. Awaken his spiritual life. Protect him from wrong companions and help him to love Your Word and obey You." Praise the Lord that all through Nathan's life, he always chose good friends.

We were amazed at the great loneliness Nathan, Heath, and I experienced that fall – in a new home, a new location, and slowly making new friends. When Heath was home, we drove forty-five minutes to Dayton to attend Emmanuel Baptist Church where we were members. Pastor Nile Fisher was such a great preacher and teacher, so we never came home after a service without knowing we had been taught the Word and challenged. The whole church family was warm and cordial to us, and we felt very much loved there. We were just sorry it was so far from Springfield.

In Dosso the deacons were doing the preaching each week. A friend wrote this about deacon Dieyabidi, "His preaching for the last two months has been great. Not that he wasn't good before; it's just that suddenly there seems to be more power in his messages and all the other deacons too."

Before leaving Niger, we realized our 11 year old German shepherd, Hunter, was getting deaf and beginning to have a weakness in his back legs. He was such a part of our family, and it was sad to see him deteriorating. We left him in the kind care of Dieyabidi knowing he would be well cared for and not mistreated. One morning Dieyabidi observed Hunter curled up and sleeping under a shade tree. As the day wore on and Hunter didn't get up to come to the house, Dieyabidi went over to check on him finding he had quietly died in his sleep.

Sadness overwhelmed me at times for Alan who was far from us and not communicating. In my journal I wrote, "I ask, Lord, for Your ministry to Alan's needs. We can't be there with him, but You can. He cannot flee from Your presence. Lord, keep and protect Alan in spite of himself. Help us to trust Your timing, power, and working..."

On September 20, 1982, our third grandchild, Sarah Beth Ahlgrim, was born. I was on my way to Indiana, (130 miles) the next day to spend five days helping Rebecca and cuddling Sarah.

Thanksgiving and Nathan's sixteenth birthday fell on the same day in 1982. My journal prayer for Nathan was "Dear God, I thank You for this fine son; for Your hand upon his life; for giving him health, growth, and intelligence. Thank You for allowing us to have him in our home for sixteen years. Help him, Lord, to be sure of his salvation. I ask for the working of Your Spirit in his life, that he will know the joy of Your sweet and warm fellowship. Burden him for the lost about him and give him a hunger for Your Word. Oh Father, help him not to be indifferent to You and Your will. Help him to have a desire for fellowship with You, to live a lifestyle that glorifies You."

Christmas 1982

We were so excited because this would be the first Christmas in eight years that we would have all four children and the grandchildren with us. It was a wonderful time together! We will never forget that Christmas. Heath always called it "the best ever!"

By spring of 1983, Heath had reported to all our supporting churches. As he met with the pastors and deacons, he asked for prayer for Alan and told them we might have to remain in the States for longer than our one-year furlough. We were amazed that as we opened up to folks about our prodigal son, pastors, deacons, and friends also opened up to tell us that they were crying out to the Lord for their prodigal sons and daughters too. They all emphasized the importance of our family and encouraged us to extend our time at home if we felt we should, assuring us of their understanding and continued support if we did so. We thanked our Savior for these wonderful prayer and financial supporters He had raised up for us. EBM granted us permission to extend our furlough through the summer of 1984.

The Niger field, though disappointed by the news of our delay in returning, was also completely supportive. They asked Heath to plan to head up the translation ministry for the completion of the Zarma Bible when we returned and while he was home to research the word processor that would be the best adapted for the needs of the translation work. We were all realizing that a word processor would greatly increase our speed and efficiency in translation work. Heath was also planning to take special training in the use of the word processor.

The verse I chose for 1983 was Romans 12:12, "Be joyful in hope, patient in affliction, and faithful in prayer."

A quote from Edith Schaeffer: "No one is shut up from expressing trust in the most adverse of situations. In the depths of despair, in deep sorrow, pain, or in terrible disappointment...it is sufficient to whisper, 'Lord, I can't understand this, but I still love you and I trust you.' What takes place here? It is a victory in the battle between Satan and God as Satan tries to rob God of our love, to steal our attention and fix it on our troubles rather than on God's faithfulness and His promises."

The months trailed on as we fervently prayed for our beloved son who had gone "to the far country." God is so good to not let us know the time when He has chosen to answer our prayers in miraculous ways. Oh, how I was being stretched and challenged as I prayed but saw little or no encouragement in response. My heavenly Father was teaching me to trust Him, to cast all my cares on Him, to leave my burdens with Him.

"When all kinds of trials and temptations crowd into your lives, my brothers, don't resent them as intruders, but welcome them as friends. Realize that they come to test your faith and to produce in you the quality of endurance (James 1:2-4)."What peace and joy comes into our hearts when we trust our loved ones into His care!

I was asked to speak at ladies missionary fellowships, Sunday school classes, and Mother's Day banquets and workshops. These drove me to my knees as I realized what a great privilege and responsibility the opportunities gave me to magnify my Lord. Pastor Greening also asked me to lead a women's home Bible study in Springfield that furlough.

Florida Deputation Trip

We invited Nathan's good friend, Todd, to accompany us to Florida so Nathan would not be lonely. Todd's family was a delight to fellowship with. His dad, a fire chief, told us that he was saved one night as he read Scriptures during his duty at the firehouse. He read into the wee hours of the morning before the Light broke through. He was so happy that he wanted to tell someone, but all the other firemen were sleeping. He said he just walked around hugging his Bible to his chest, with tears running down his cheeks as he sang "Jesus Loves Me."

Heath spoke at our supporting churches in Florida. We were warmly received in each church, and it was a blessing to fellowship with old friends as well as to meet new ones. Heath took Todd and Nathan to Cypress Gardens on the day I spoke at the West Coast Florida Ladies Fellowship in Lakeland. The ladies surprised me with a shower of cards with money and gift cards! I was able to buy some new lingerie and even a new dress. How kind and thoughtful those ladies were! It was a good trip, filled with many blessings, and God gave us safety as we traveled.

Nathan returned to classes at Springfield Christian after we arrived back in Ohio. I found this entry in my journal that, although it was my serious prayer, it is humorous in retrospect! "Nathan just left for school this morning. Father, I ask for Your working in his life by Your holy and pure Spirit. Help him, guide and protect him through these difficult teenage years. Awaken him to his spiritual needs. He's like a light bulb not screwed in. Lord, turn Your power on in his life, please. Help me to live my faith and to especially be a testimony to Nathan in trust so that he will see how real You are to me."

On Alan's twentieth birthday I prayed, "Father, thank you that I can come in the name of Jesus. Thank you for Your power, for Your grace, mercy, love, and timing. I thank you for your love for Alan. I place him in Your hands, trusting the power of your Holy Spirit to work mightily in his life. Lord, Your hand was on my life as a teen-ager when I was far from You. Your hand was on Heath's life then too. I ask You to break the power of sin in Alan's life – to bring him to his knees before the cross, that he may see the horror and ugliness of sin. We trust You to build a hedge of thorns about him and cause him to see the only way to look is up. I thank You."

From my journal in May 1983: "My Father, you are omnipresent, omniscient and omnipotent. (You are everywhere, You know everything, and You have all power!) Thank you for this assurance that your attention is upon every circumstance in my life and that nothing is beyond your control! How blessed I am to know that You are with me, no matter where I go, and You know everything that will happen to me. No circumstance, no obstacle, no problem is beyond your capabilities to solve! Nothing is too hard for You! I am never alone, never forgotten, never beyond hope."

Our Trip from Ohio to California

We had always wished we could drive West to see America beyond the Mississippi River while our family of six was still with us, but we were never able to do that. In June 1983, we decided to take the trip with just Nathan with us. He wasn't enthused about spending all that time with Mom and Dad, but good kid that he was, he did agree to go with us. One thing that made him happy was that he was then sixteen and a half and had his driver's license, so he drove most of the way! Heath lined up many meetings, we visited family and friends, and we saw many of the national parks. Day by day we marveled at the diverse and magnificent beauty of America that we had never seen before.

It was our first time to visit my brother Carl and his wife, Carol, in their Lake Havasu City, Arizona, home. While we were there, the temperature was 110 degrees! It was as bad as Niger! I asked Carl why they moved there from Ohio in retirement. His answer, "You come back in December, and you'll see why we moved here!" Carl had a very nice inboard boat, so they took us out on beautiful Lake Havasu where they gave Nathan a lesson in water skiing. He did a beautiful job and hardly ever fell, even though it was his first time doing this.

On our twenty-eighth wedding anniversary, we visited the Grand Canyon. Words are totally inadequate to describe its immenseness and beauty! How can anyone ever see this fantastic place and not believe in our Creator God?

After leaving Carl and Carol's, we crossed the Mojave Desert and headed to El Monte, California, where we stayed with a lovely saintly widow from Gene Barnes' church.

Thursday, June 23, found us in Yosemite National Park marveling at the Sequoia trees. These trees are hundreds and hundreds of years old, yet they begin from a tiny seed. It takes 91,000 seeds to make a pound! The ratio of one seed to a full-grown tree is the same as one tree to the earth!

Heath preached in several churches in California, and in between those times we visited Fisherman's Wharf in San Francisco, saw the Golden Gate Bridge, drove down Lombard Street (the crookedest street in the world), and toured San Quentin Prison.

We drove across the Great Salt Lake Desert to Tooele, Utah. We knew some missionaries to the Mormons in that area and they invited us to stay in their small travel trailer.

Some folks from their church invited us to their home for dinner. After dinner they asked if we'd like to see their backyard where they had a horse and a dog. The big dog was so friendly, laid on the ground so I could scratch her tummy and play with her. When I finished, the lady of the house asked, "Did you realize she is a full-blooded wolf?" I could hardly believe it! They had her since she was a puppy. The lady said the veterinarian told them they would have to be careful if she ever had puppies. At that time she considered the family to be her "pack," but it might change when she had her own litter of pups!

We were urged to visit Temple Square in Salt Lake City to learn more, since it was free, and we could see first-hand what was there. A very suave retired business man conducted our tour. At one point, he had us sit down in the chapel while he held up a Bible and said they believe the Bible, but soon the Bible was put aside as he expounded the "wonderful teachings" of the Book of Mormon!

We drove through Jackson Hole, Wyoming and The Grand Tetons which were snow covered and beautiful. We then traveled on to America's first national park, Yellowstone (established in 1872).

The Yellowstone "super volcano" is a marvel to visit! Even in June there were still patches of snow in shady spots. Buffalo were abundant, and there were grizzly bears, wolves, fox, elk, and eagles, among other animals. After Nathan observed the bubbling mud, caves belching hot water, thermal springs and geysers, he commented, "This place is going to blow one of these days!" This certainly is a possibility!

Heath preached at a church in Rapid City, North Dakota, and on the Fourth of July, very appropriately, we were at Mt. Rushmore for the Fife and Drum Corps music and to see the presidents. The Badlands were the last stop on our journey home.

Arriving in Springfield, our house was as clean and spotless as we had left it. Remembering how dirty our home in Niger became from dust storms while we traveled, we asked our neighbor if she had cleaned our house when she came in to water our plants. Her reply was, "No, I didn't clean your house…or mine either that month!"

In our August 1983 prayer letter, Heath wrote, "We have wandered through woods and forest glades, looked down from lofty mountain grandeur, heard many brooks, and our souls many times have spontaneously sung, 'How Great Thou Art,' as in recent weeks Norma, Nathan, and I fulfilled a longtime family dream of a trip to the west coast.

"Besides the magnificent scenery, we had the joy of renewing fellowship with many dear friends who, because of their love of our great God, opened their hearts and homes to us. How great a blessing it was to have the opportunity to share the ministry and needs of Niger Republic in many churches from Kansas to California."

Very soon after our arrival back home, Heath was off to Indiana, to teach some classes in EBM's summer candidate school.

In the fall, he left for a month of meetings in churches and colleges. This trip included being at Baptist Bible College in October where he was honored as Alumnus of the Year. I was happy that my life-mate received this honor that he earned and deserved. The only one of our family who was able to be there to see him receive that award was Alan. Heath was really pleased to see him again and that he was there.

That fall Nathan had to adjust to another new high school, Kenton Ridge. That was his third high school in three years. Springfield Christian had closed after only one year. This is often "the story" for MKs; however, once again, he chose good friends at the school.

At this time, I was writing out Scripture in my own paraphrases. Looking at God's promises was a source of great comfort and hope for me.

God's Timing – Trusting God, I was to wait and to base my faith on God's purpose and goal. Habakkuk 2:3 "For the revelation awaits *an appointed time*...though it linger, wait for it." In Chuck Swindoll's study book on Habakkuk I learned that God can handle all our questions, but He answers only a few. Waiting strengthens our patience and deepens our perspective. The bottom line of our faith is not to silence all our doubts but to make us depend upon God.

"Though the fig tree does not bud and there are no grapes on the vines, though the olive crop fails and the fields produce no food, though there are no sheep in the pen and no cattle in the stalls, yet I will rejoice in the Lord, I will be joyful in God my Savior. The Sovereign Lord is my strength; he makes my feet like the feet of a deer, he enables me to tread on the heights (Habakkuk 3:17-19)."

> While I wait – I glorify God. While I trust – I glorify God.
> While I accept the fact that He has me on a holding pattern –
> I glorify God!

I was beginning to realize that in a crisis, my belief in God was challenged and I was being tempted to think my prayers were ineffective. I didn't deny God's power, but I began to fear that though it worked for others, it wasn't working for me. I was in bewilderment, and my faith was being tested. The Savior patiently showed me how important it was to spend time alone with Him instead of wallowing in despair. God doesn't mock His children. He was still there, and His faithfulness did not waver. I was being invited into an ever increasingly close fellowship with Him.

From our prayer letter, dated October 1983: "Using horse and buggy methods in the jet age! This is how one missionary couple described it, and the same could be said of our Bible translation efforts to date. In our last letter, we shared with you that the Niger field has asked us to head up the translation ministry upon our return. For years, our missionaries and nationals have been faithfully laboring over their manual typewriters translating, typing, and re-typing the books of the Bible in Zarma, sometimes with three or four carbons to boot (horse and buggy method). They accomplished much. Now, however, we wish to enter the jet age!"

Heath was asked to raise funds and purchase a good quality word processor (computer) to increase our speed and efficiency in producing the Zarma manuscript for the whole Bible. We did not have or know about e-mail in 1983. The World Wide Web didn't come into existence until 1991.

The Niger field and our mission board approved the raising of $15,000 to purchase the word processor and equipment, hopefully by the end of the year. With these funds we hoped to purchase the terminal, a dot matrix printer, a daisywheel printer, a sealed Winchester drive unit, the related software and supplies needed, and pay for the transport of all to Niger. It was recommended that we purchase a high quality Digital Equipment Corporation (DEC) word processor which other mission organizations were using in West Africa.

Our prayer letter stated, "A Zarma person has yet to hold in his hands a copy of the whole Bible in his own language. Our goal is to make that possible!"

In our December 1983 prayer letter, Heath wrote, "In answer to your prayers, gifts are coming in for the word processor fund! How we thank God for the love and interest of so many – from a college student who gave $5 to a check for $2,340 from Southgate Baptist Church's Fall Ingathering offering – bringing the funds we have received to date to $4,553. Please pray in the remaining $10,477 this month." Included in the $15,000 cost was memory storage capacity, backup tapes for the text of the whole Bible, ribbons, paper supplies, and expensive electrical equipment to assist and safeguard the use of the equipment in Africa. Besides the fierce heat and dust storms in Niger, electrical power surges and blackouts occurred unexpectedly. We also wrote, "We do want to thank you for praying especially for our family this year. Our son Alan has come to live with us at least temporarily, and we are glad to have him home once again."

In the spring of 1984, Heath went to the headquarters of JAARS in Waxhaw, North Carolina, to take an intensive two-week course. With only $10,000 of the needed $15,000 in hand, by faith Heath placed the order at JAARS for the word processor, equipment, and supplies. Unknown to us was the fact that Bible Baptist Church in Shiremanstown, Pennsylvania, had been especially burdened about this need. Heath spoke there on March 21. Our astonishment was great when they presented us with a check for $5,000 that evening! Our God is so amazing, and He truly keeps His promises to supply "all our needs according to His riches in glory by Christ Jesus."

But this was not the whole story. We were invited to speak at Bill Ford's home Bible study one evening to present the work of Bible translation. Two members of that Bible study came to us a few weeks later to tell us, "We believe God wants us to contribute whatever is lacking when the bills come due!" We hadn't thought about the possibility of being charged customs at that time. Word came from Niger that we would be required to get an import permit and the possibility of customs charges being as much as 60 percent.

Heath and Sherry Adams went to Taylor University in Upland, Indiana, for a special eight-week course titled "Basic Computer Concepts and Linguistic Applications."

In June 1984, we were asking prayer for the import permit to take the word processor into Niger and the funds needed to pay customs or that it would be exempt, according to God's will. Heath and Nathan would be leaving with the twenty-five boxes of computer materials in August, while Alan and I would stay behind until he started classes at Cedarville College.

Southgate Pastor Greening wrote a letter to the Church members communicating appreciation and confidence in us as servants of the Lord. We were so touched by the loving care of the church in Springfield during that two-year furlough.

From my journal, dated August 21, 1984: "Lord, I'm like that little butterfly – scared, fluttering each time the monkey grabs at me...Heath and Nathan are to leave in five days for Africa. I'm concerned that Alan's life isn't ready for Cedarville, our house is not rented, I grieve over being separated from Nathan his senior year, and we have no insurance on the computer for travel." I cried out, "Father, time is running out; nothing is happening…" He replied, "Trust in the Lord with all of your heart. Do not lean on your own understanding. In all your ways acknowledge me and I will make your paths straight…Rejoice in the Lord always. Don't worry about anything! In everything, pray and petition with thanksgiving. My peace, beyond understanding, will guard your heart and mind in Christ Jesus."

"Peace is the ability to wait patiently in spite of panic brought on by uncertainty." – Anonymous

On August 26, 1984, Heath and Nathan left for Africa.

Our house was rented.

Jon and Judy came to help us clean and move out of the house.

EBM insured the word processor for travel.

TWA took all twenty-six pieces of boxes and luggage.

Heath called two days later, saying all boxes arrived safely.

On September 21, Heath informed me that the Niger government wanted $5,000 for custom charges. Oh, me of little faith! Again, I felt sick with panic. This amount was astronomical to me. Roger Storer from Springfield had told us to be sure and let him and Ed Patton know about this need, but it was so hard for me to tell Roger it was $5,000. Very calmly Roger said, "Well, I can pay it all, but I will let Ed know too. I think he would feel badly if I didn't let him pay half of it!" These precious brothers in Christ did just that! God provided through them.

Alan moved into the Cedarville dorm on September 22 and on September 23, I left for Niger. My hand carry-on was heavy (with ham and cheese)! I arrived in Paris the next day to find that UTA airline was on strike and no hotel voucher was provided for my overnight. EBM missionaries Steve and Rowena Barnes, who were ministering in nearby Saint Dennis, came to my rescue. I spent the night in their home on a cot in the room where their church met. It was very cold but wrapped in Steve's woolen robe, I got along fine.

I arrived in Niger on September 25, 1984, and the temperature was 102 degrees. When this was announced just prior to landing, an audible groan went up from all the passengers, and the Frenchman sitting next to me began to peel off his sweater and long-sleeved shirt while exclaiming, over and over, *"Oh là làààà!"*

Employees at the Paris airport had evidently opened my luggage while it was there overnight and stole all the Christmas candy I had purchased for Nathan. I hope they enjoyed it. (But I also hoped they felt guilty for stealing!)

Chapter 24
Zarma Bible Translation and Revision
September 1984 to August 1988

"They read from the Book of the Law of God, making it clear and giving the meaning so that the people understood what was being read... Then all the people went away to eat...and to celebrate with great joy, because they now understood the words that had been made known to them."
Nehemiah 8:8, 12

What a surprise it was when a bearded Heath met me at the Niamey airport! During the month he had been in Niger ahead of me, he not only got our things from Dosso cleaned and moved into the house on the Yantala station, but he also didn't shave! He was only 54, but his beard was totally white, just as his hair was. It was fun to see what he looked like with a beard! The house looked so nice and a large sign greeted me when I entered our house: "Welcome home, Honey!"

Pastor Luc came to welcome us back with the thrilling report that twenty-seven souls had come to Christ during that past year in the villages of Torodi and Makalondi!

We wrote thanking all who had prayed and brought the dream of the word processor and equipment to a reality. Now we were asking that they continue to pray 1) for the translation work, 2) for the programming of the Zarma Bible, and 3) that the equipment would function well. We were certain that Satan would be attacking this project, not wanting the Bible to be translated into the heart language of the Zarma people. Heath had been warned about Satan's subtle ways of attacking translation work while he was in the JAARS classes at Taylor University. One of the teachers had said, "I don't believe Christians can be possessed by demons, but I don't know about computers!"

We began preparing a room in the Riverside House for the computer, wanting to make the room as tight as possible to escape the Sahara dust storms that could be very bad for the computer. We had windows tightly shut, plastic taped over the windows, the shutters closed, curtains covering the windows, and an air-conditioner installed. (In spite of this, bad dust storms produced a light layer of dust on things in the computer room!) We also had a battery backup that would keep the computer running for several minutes when the city electricity went off without warning. This happened fairly often. That gave us time enough to save the texts we were working on and not lose them.

Another prayer request was for a car. There was $3,000 in our car fund, which a coworker suggested might be enough to buy a donkey and cart!

However, the Lord led us to a retired African man, Alhadji Oumarou, who had been in government services in Arabic countries for many years. He had a palatial home on the other side of the Niger River and was getting into the very profitable business of growing strawberries. He wanted to sell his 1981 Peugeot 504 with 42,000 kilometers on it so he could buy a pickup truck. We bought his Peugeot and were grateful to the Lord for leading us to find it. Although a strong Muslim, Alhadji listened politely to Heath's words of testimony and accepted an Arabic New Testament Heath gave him. He promised to read it.

We visited the Gourma work out in Makalondi Village and were so blessed. The people had built a larger mud church. Our hearts were touched by these people who had so little, and yet they brought us gifts of okra, chickens, and eggs to show their pleasure in our visit.

Proverbs 11:16 says, "A kindhearted woman gains honor." My prayer: "My Father, the African Christians have so little, and yet they challenge me by their thankfulness – to You for restored health, provision of their needs, and so forth. Help me to show Your love and to be known as a kindhearted woman. Please bless Pastor Baléja, use him, protect his wife, and give her a safe delivery."

When Nathan arrived home from Ivory Coast Academy for Christmas vacation, we wondered what he would think of our car, but he was very happy because it had bucket seats in front. He had always wanted a car with bucket seats!

For Christmas, the Zarma church had a good program, and we all ate together at noon. Rebecca had secretly sent money to Julie Nunemaker to buy grapes, apples, and cheese for our Christmas present, imported from France and sold at the expensive French grocery store, Score. This was another special treat and so thoughtful of our daughter!

While he was home, Nathan wrote a letter to our supporting churches, telling them what his vacation at home was like. "There has been plenty to keep me busy here. I have put up a ceiling in the word processor room, painted at home, cleaned the sand and bat dirt out of our storage room, and reorganized it. It was filthy! Besides that, Mom is putting me to work at home helping her! I am glad though to be back and have some of my mom's cooking! The rains were poor last rainy season, so the dust blows constantly. It drives Mom crazy because there is no way to keep it out of the house. Although there is plenty of food along the river here in

Niamey, Niger is having a severe famine in the bush areas where people depend upon grain for food. We are helping distribute grain with our mission famine relief fund. School is coming along all right, and my grades were good. My hardest subject is chemistry. The two outreach ministries I was involved in at school in Ivory Coast went well too. On prison outreach, we held meetings with all the convicts, and I even met one that was from Niger and was getting out. On our building outreach, we roofed a church that was 45-by-90 feet. We worked from sunup to sundown, and out of that time, I was on the roof for eleven hours. I had my shirt off, so you can imagine what my back looked like (fried chicken). It was lots of fun though and real neat to watch the expressions on the nationals' faces as they saw their church being completed. Love in Christ, Nathan"

On January 6, 1985, Nathan left to finish his senior year at Ivory Coast Academy. Empty nest for us again. Two days later, grandson Ryan Richard Ahlgrim was born in Houston, Texas! Rebecca and Judy were always so good about sending us pictures of the grandchildren as they grew up. What a blessing that was to grandparents so far away!

Before long, it was evident that neither of the two short-term ladies would be coming to help key in the Zarma Bible. I was scared to death of the computer, using the excuse that at my age (fifty-two) and being a grandmother, I could never learn to operate one. Heath begged me to come over to the computer room for some lessons. He was confident that I could learn to do it. Finally, I agreed to try. He showed me how to boot up the computer and sign in. Immediately I saw a message on the screen that said, "Hi, Honey! You're doing great!" My dear husband had rigged the computer to be friendly! Slowly, I learned to give the commands that were necessary for keying in, doing word checks, making backups, and printing, so I then became enthusiastic about the work the Lord had dropped into my lap.

We named our DEC computer "Baruch" after Jeremiah's scribe. Baruch only wrote what Jeremiah told him to and he did it faithfully (Jeremiah 36:4, 18). This computer was state of the art at that time. It had a hard drive with ten megabytes! This was the first computer that ever was brought to our EBM Niger field. God provided a local man in Niamey who had completed DEC training in the States so he knew how to clean Baruch or repair him. Perhaps there was never a computer more prayed for than Baruch was.

Baruch never went down during all the time he was faithfully "writing down" all that the language committee "spoke to him!" On our next furlough as I was thanking a ladies group for their prayers, telling them our computer never crashed and that we attributed this to prayer warriors praying for "him," one of the ladies said, "Oh my goodness! I work at the local K-Mart, and our computer seems to go down every week!" What a wonderful God we serve! No request is too big or too small to bring to Him!

Having the computer in an air-conditioned room was a real incentive to go to work, even during rest hours! I learned to type in Zarma at a good speed, including the special letters, the "ng," the tildi, and the circumflex. It was a blessing to me to read the wording of the Bible in Zarma. Sometimes I was a little surprised by what I read, so I had to do some research. For instance, when typing Song of Solomon 7:5, I read (in Zarma), "Your neck is like a long elephant's tooth!" Sure enough, in English I read, "Your neck is like an ivory tower." The word for ivory in Zarma is "an elephant's tooth." Loose translation of the whole verse reads, "Your neck is like a long building made of elephant's tooth." ("Your neck is like an ivory tower.")

We had software that verified verse and chapter numbers were right, in case I accidentally didn't type the numbers consecutively. Another program checked to see that parentheses had a beginning and ending and that quotation marks were properly noted at the beginning and ending of a quotation. Baruch searched through completed books to make lists of the words to see that our spelling was always consistent.

Each morning, Heath worked with the translation committee, a mixture of nationals and missionaries, while I was keying in the Bible books and printing them for the committee to go over again and again. Spread out on a large table before the committee were Greek, Hebrew, French, and English Bibles. In the afternoons, Heath was in the computer room putting in the corrections the translation committee had decided on during their morning sessions.

In February 1985, we learned that Alan was no longer at Cedarville College. We were saddened, yet were learning to trust the Lord, believe He heard our prayers, and that in God's timing Alan would truly come back to His Savior. I wish I could say my faith was always strong, but there were times when I was in despair, fearing that my prayers were ineffective.

Lamentations 2:19 says, "...pour out your heart like water in the presence of the Lord. Lift up your hands to him for the lives of your children..."

Lamentations 3:21-26 says, "Yet this I call to mind and therefore I have hope: Because of the LORD's great love we are not consumed, for His compassions never fail. They are new every morning; great is Your faithfulness. I say to myself, 'The LORD is my portion; therefore, I will wait for Him.' The Lord is good to those whose hope is in Him, to the one who seeks him; it is good to wait quietly for the salvation of the LORD."

Pastor Luc Souantieba was our dear friend and a godly man. He not only preached and evangelized all around Niamey, but he made trips out to bush villages where many came to Christ and where Gourma churches were planted.

At one of the churches that Pastor Luc had planted near Makalondi, Pastor Balédja asked Heath to come and assist in the baptism of twenty-two new believers in that area.

This baptistery was a deep rainy season puddle. In the bush villages, there were small creeks that only flowed during the rainy season, so that is when baptisms were scheduled. As Heath and Pastor Balédja were baptizing, it was not unusual to see all kinds of things floating by, such as branches, old broken enamel vessels…and cow pies! However, nothing lessened the rejoicing of all of us at these happy occasions when believers followed their Savior in the obedience of baptism. We rejoiced greatly in our Lord's work among the Gourma people.

We've often reminisced about the places where Heath has baptized believers: in church baptisteries, Waneta Lake, the Niger River, rainy season creeks, a water cistern, and a big bathtub in Bosnia!

From our prayer letter, dated February 1985: "The church is made of millet stalks, and you can see the blue African sky through the roof. The benches we sit on are 4-by-4 boards placed so close together that the knees of the people in the row behind you touch the backs of those in front of them. There are 130 people gathered in this building to worship the Lord Jesus Christ.

"That morning, as we bumped over the dirt path to reach this bush village, which is about two hours from Niamey, we asked Pastor Luc how he had ever heard about this remote village to begin a work there. This is the story that he related to us:

"Ounteni, a man from this village, often came to Niamey and stayed with Luc and his family for days at a time. Pastor Luc faithfully presented God's Word to him and showed him his need of Christ, but Ounteni was not interested. In fact, because he knew some wealthy *alhadjis*, he was thinking of becoming a Muslim.

"Some time later, Ounteni went to a sorcerer to ask about his future. The sorcerer threw out sand in certain patterns on the ground and informed Ounteni, 'This year you will die.' Highly dissatisfied with this dire report, Ounteni went to a distant village and sought out another sorcerer. The prediction was the same!

"He began to reason, 'For a long time now, I have heard God's Word but rejected it. If I am going to die this coming year, I'd better receive Jesus Christ as my Savior and be ready!' Quickly he went out to the main road and got a ride to Niamey. You can imagine Pastor Luc's joy to have Ounteni walk into his compound and ask, 'What must I do to be saved?'

"Luc discipled him for several weeks, and he attended the Gourma church in Niamey. Ounteni returned home and started having his family meet on Sundays in his compound. Luc went to help the new group as often as he could. Soon another couple was won to Christ. Later the crowd increased until they built the millet stalk church. Now they are making mud bricks for a more permanent structure.

"We tell you this story to *ask your prayers* for this little church near Torodi. They now have over thirty baptized believers.

"P.S. It has now been four years since Ounteni received Christ, and he is still alive!"

I had never played tennis before, but some missionary women invited me to come down to the EBM school tennis/volleyball court on Thursday mornings to learn. We had such fun times, laughing, chasing the ball, and catching up on girlie talk. These were a couple of hours of relaxation from our busy schedules each week when possible. Sue was from England, Carol and Robyn were from Australia, and Mars was from Canada. Vicki, Julie, and I were the Americans.

March 7, 1985, was an exciting day for all Americans in Niger when Vice President and Mrs. George Herbert Walker Bush came for a visit. They were accompanied by a retinue of almost 200 people.

Shortly before Vice President Bush's arrival, Mariama received a message that she was to report to the Niger protocol office immediately. Of course, any summons to a government office is stressful, making you wonder what you had done wrong. The message to Mariama was, "You are appointed to be 'lady in waiting' for Barbara Bush during their visit. You will be her interpreter, and you will be with her from the time she gets up in the morning until she goes to bed at night!" Mariama protested that she didn't have the clothes for such a prestigious job (but she did). Protocol seemed to know all about her and how well she spoke English.

When she voiced her fears to me, I comforted her saying, "You remember what a sweet white-haired woman Aunt Cecelia Dillon was. Barbara Bush also has white hair, and you will find her to be a kind and sweet woman too." Mariama had a good time with Mrs. Bush. When Vice President and Mrs. Bush returned to Washington, they sent Mariama a lovely picture of her with the Vice President.

On March 9, we met Vice President and Mrs. Bush at the American ambassador's residence! We got our names on the list ahead of time, and we had to show our passports to get in between 7:50 and 8:20. After that, the gates were closed. The Bushes walked around and tried to talk to everyone. He was surprised to learn we had been in Niger for twenty-five years and after he asked what our work was, he remarked, "It's a lifetime commitment, isn't it? I have great respect for your work."

By March of 1985 I had keyed in Genesis, Exodus, Leviticus, Numbers, Deuteronomy, Joshua, Judges, Ruth, I and II Chronicles, 2 Kings and more – totaling 350 chapters. I loved that work. What a privilege! Heath really enjoyed the day-by-day, tedious, verse-by-verse translation and revision too. We learned so much and were blessed beyond measure. Someone compared the accurate translation of the Hebrew and Greek Bible into a local language to "unloading a ship into a canoe!" What a responsibility!

Trip to Tapoa Game Park

One of our favorite things to do when our children came home from school for Easter break was to take a trip to a game park, looking for animals in the wild and staying overnight in a rustic motel in the park. When Nathan got home for Easter break we packed overnight things, lots of water, and food for the trip. It was a hot time of year, but by then the tall grasses had dried up, making it easier to spot the wild animals. In the rainy season, the park closed because many of the dirt roads and gullies became impassable. Mariama was able to go with us this time, along with the Brock and Curtis families.

There was much fun and laughter during our trips. On this trip, Nathan and Danny Brock decided to ride on top of Jim's jeep so they could see better. It wasn't often that we saw lions because they tended to not move around in the heat of the day but usually laid quietly in the sparse shade of trees until darkness fell. This time we all saw lions, and they were not very far away. Nathan and Dan came down off the top of the jeep, through the windows, and inside in record time!

At the park motel, there was a small swimming pool, so everyone was glad to get into the cool water for a swim after supper. Just the week before, Heath had to have stitches in his finger from an accident when he was trying to move a fan so we would benefit more from the moving air. Wanting to benefit from the cool water of the swimming pool, he walked around in the water, submerged to his shoulders while holding his bandaged finger high to keep it dry. Jim Brock called out loudly to all in the pool, "Anyone who has to go to the bathroom, hold up one finger!"

Of course, everyone else made sure their hands were under the water, but Heath couldn't! That caused more gales of laughter.

We celebrated our thirtieth wedding anniversary by spending one night in the lovely Gaweye Hotel. We had been introduced to the African manager, Mr. Ego, who was a Christian. Not only did he give us a discounted price, he gave us a suite of two rooms instead of one room. What a treat the meals, the coolness, and peace and quiet of air-conditioned rooms was! We had supper out on the terrace by the swimming pool where we were entertained by local folk dancers. One girl did her whole performance with pink plastic curlers decorating her hair! That reminded me of the times Niger lady friends came to call on me when I had rollers in my hair. They thought the curlers were such lovely decorations and chided me when I removed them to comb out my hair!

June 26, 1985, was an exciting day for us because Jonathan arrived to visit for a few days before we all traveled to Ivory Coast for Nathan's high school graduation. Jonathan treated all of the GSO Africans who had worked for him when he stayed out an extra year after graduation to lunch. They had a favorite African dish of his and theirs – *fufu*!

On July 1, Jon, Heath, and I left at 5:30 a.m. for Abidjan, Ivory Coast. Jon sat in economy with his dad and let me sit in his business class section. Very nice! The plane landed at Lomé, Togo, on the way, and we were urged to get off of the plane for restroom facilities or cold drinks. I was so surprised as I went downstairs in the airport to use the bathroom to find a woman standing at the entrance of the rest room with a roll of toilet paper. She was doling out a few sheets of TP (your allotment) as you were on your way to the stalls. Heath said the woman at the men's room not only doled out your allotment of TP, but when you came out of the stall, she went over and turned on the water for you to wash your hands! We've never encountered this again in any other country. Of course, we were expected to tip her for these services!

There was a very nice senior reception in the chapel. Nathan was given The Most Inspiring Player Award by Coach Grudda. Dear Miss Jan also let Nathan take her car and drive to Yamoussoukro to see some of his friends. She surely was good to the ICA kids.

Nathan's graduation was on July 4, 1985. He wrote to our supporting churches, "A lot of tears were shed as I said goodbye to friends, many of whom I may never see again." I was struck with the thought that all our children were through high school then and fought the feeling that my life was over, that I wasn't needed anymore. I never realized how wrapped up I was in being a mother. The Lord saw me through that time of discouragement when I surely wasn't thinking straight.

On July 5, we said goodbye to Jon as he left for the States. On July 6 and 7, we continued helping the Curtises get the boys dorm cleaned and ready to close for the summer. Harold and Charlene were leaving from Bouaké for a three-month furlough and had asked us to drive their car back to Niamey for them. During the approximately 1,000-mile, three-day trip through Cote d'Ivoire, Burkina Faso, and Niger we were stopped forty-four times by police and gendarme checkpoints. It made us appreciate traveling in the States!

On the final leg of our journey home to Niamey, just before leaving Burkina Faso, we picked up Phillippe and Poinyagu's two school-aged children. Cholera was rampant at that time so, at the Niger border we were required to take sulfa pills before entering. Also, the police were emptying all the bush taxis so they could spray the interiors with disinfectant. Thankfully they did not require this of us. We arrived home to our house on Yantala station...exhausted! "Father, thank You for your watch care and protection over all the kilometers we traveled. Thank You that we met no robbers, we had no accidents, and the car held up."

Friends left their miniature dachshund, Peewee, for us to keep after their two-year short-term ministry in Bénin. Miniature dachshunds are very affectionate, and they are lap dogs. Every time one of us sat down, Peewee jumped onto our lap. It was new to us after we had Hunter, our German shepherd, for such a long time, but we surely enjoyed her. Missionary friends in Togo had first brought a male and female dachshund out to the field, and they eventually populated many missionary homes in West Africa with their puppies.

We arranged for Peewee to meet a French family's brown dachshund who was named Kiwi. Peewee's little tummy almost dragged on the floor late in her pregnancy! She could no longer jump up on my lap or go up and down steep stairs, so we had to lift her. She gave birth to seven puppies, all living, and she successfully nursed them too. They were so cute. At birth they didn't have those long noses, but the noses soon began to grow.

For the dogs' food, I usually cooked brown market rice and scraps of market meat (which Charlene Curtis had aptly named "gorp") along with some vegetables. I cooked enough for four or five days and kept the pan in the bottom of our refrigerator until it was used up.

One day I had cooked Peewee's food, this time with macaroni because I was out of rice, and left it covered on the stove to cool. Often, if I was working in the computer room through the noon hour and the rest hour, there would be some leftovers in our refrigerator for Heath to fix his own lunch and take his rest hour before I got back. When I came home later that afternoon, I saw that quite a bit of Peewee's food was gone so I thanked Heath for going ahead and feeding Peewee. When he said he hadn't fed Peewee, there was nothing for us to do but to laugh because he had eaten a good portion of Peewee's food for his lunch! (He said it wasn't bad!)

In mid-July, Heath preached to over 300 people at the dedication of the newly constructed Gourma adobe church in Torodi. Some of the people from the Makalondi church walked eighteen miles to be at this joyous celebration. Pastor Luc was praising the Lord for what He was doing in bringing souls to Himself. Ounteini was beaming! We asked prayer for these believers and their growth in Christ.

Throughout July, I was programming Proverbs into the computer. The language informants were reviewing the translation of the book of Job, one of the most difficult books in the Old Testament to translate. We could sense the prayers of God's people for us, and our hearts were so grateful.

Another drought was causing a famine. One day, a man came to our house asking for grain. His lips were dry and parched, and he really looked bad. Compassion filled our hearts as we went to get a sack of grain for him to take home.

The next morning when we arose, there was a great crowd of people sitting on the sand all around our house. Word had gotten out that one man got grain! It then dawned on us that it was the month of Ramadan when no one eats from sunup until sundown. They want to look pitiful with strained looks, parched lips, and so forth so others will see that they are fasting and suffering! We found out that many in this group had a good supply of grain from the year before, but they couldn't resist pretending to be in need to get free grain! An American friend who worked for USAID said, "God help us know the difference between those truly in need and those who are not!"

On Wednesday afternoons, we ladies had started a calling program to Muslim women. The believers were excited about this. From my journal, "Last Wednesday was the end of Ramadan (the month of daylight fasting). Kano presented the Gospel through the story of Noah to twenty-five ladies. Almost all were busy braiding and fixing each other's hair for the big Muslim holiday, but they listened."

After high school graduation, Nathan started working at the American embassy. He worked for two months in the personnel office, but then his boss decided that his ability to speak three languages could be put to better use at the reception desk. He did a good job and was well liked by everyone, but he didn't enjoy that position. He endured for four months, bored and missing his friends at ICA very much.

Jonathan called to tell us that Joel Nathan Bobbett was born on July 22, 1985. We thanked God for another healthy grandson!

A young Ethiopian man, Asghedom, employed by the United Nations, arrived in Niger that fall. Asghedom immediately sought fellowship with other believers in our Sunday evening English services and came out for our Saturday night volleyball games. He was from Eritrea and had gone through fearful times during the unrest in that country. He was able to bring his two small children, a son and a daughter, with him to Niger but his wife, Hedat, was in England studying for her master's degree. We enjoyed wonderful fellowship with them. Their children came to my English Sunday school. Asghedom was so happy when Hedat finished her schooling and joined him in Niger.

In their home, we had our first taste of *injera*, and we loved it. In both Ethiopia and Eritrea, this spongy, slightly sour flatbread was used both as a scoop for the meat and vegetable stews and as a lining on a tray on which the stews are served and where it soaks up the juices. Asghedom and Hedat told us, "When this edible plate is eaten (last), the meal is over." *Injera* is made with *teff*, a tiny, nutritious, round grain that grows in the highlands of Ethiopia. We loved trying foods from different countries and learning about other cultures.

Translation Challenges

Heath and the language committee were challenged with some words that did not exist in Zarma. The translation work of the entire Bible into the Zarma language was an eight-year process. A large committee met together regularly and was made up of missionaries, African believers, a linguist, and some Greek and Hebrew professors from the States. There was so much more to translation work than I ever realized!

They ran into a problem over Isaiah 1:18, "'Come now, and let us reason together,' says the Lord. 'Though your sins are like scarlet, they shall be as white as snow.'"

Well, how do you translate "snow" into the Zarma language? The Zarma people, living on the edge of the Sahara Desert, have never had snow, and consequently there is no word for it. Whereas the Bible compares whiteness to snow (your sins shall be "white as snow"), the Zarmas use the expression "as white as cotton." Cotton is the whitest thing they knew of. In other African countries, they say "white as milk." Should we use the Zarma expression "as white as cotton?" Then what do we do with Old Testament passages that speak of a literal snow on a literal mountain?

Here's the solution used by the Zarma Bible translation committee. French is the official language of the Niger. More and more people are coming to understand it. They have seen snow on television and have had relatives who have studied in Europe or the States. The word for snow in French is *neige*. The Zarma people often use a French word inserted into their language for a word they don't have, but they change the pronunciation slightly. Some Zarmas had been using the word *neezu* for snow. We ended up using *neezu* when it is referring to literal snow and when it is a comparison. We have put a footnote of explanation in the glossary, explaining what snow is.

Our Ethiopian friend Hedat had never seen snow until she was sent to study in England. In her country, the expression was "as white as milk." She said, "Now I know why the Bible says, 'as white as snow.' There is nothing whiter than snow!"

In December 1985, we wrote, "Our hearts rejoice in the combined ministries of our missionary team in this Muslim country and for the evidence that God is working. We have sensed a hunger for Bible studies among new Christians. Please pray for these believers. Rejoice with us that at this point we have 80 percent of the Zarma Bible programmed in! There are still thousands of hours of translation, editing, correcting, and perfecting to do, but by His grace and with the help of your prayers, we press on!"

Nathan decided to quit his embassy job and to go work with Uncle Jim Brock in the village of Guéné, Bénin. It was very hard for us to see Nathan go, but we loved bush ministry ourselves, so we understood his heart. While in Bénin, Nathan was involved in preaching, teaching, and evangelism besides the hard physical work of painting, maintenance, mechanics, welding, farming, and construction. Hauling concrete, sand, and rock was lots of work, and Nathan lost a lot of weight. He claimed that working in that sun rendered him "half as dark as the nationals!" Nathan's time in Bénin was good for him, and he learned a lot.

During the Bénin Dendi Christian conference in March, the African society asked Nathan to preach at one session. He was pretty nervous but honored that they asked him. Pastor Luc reported that Nathan's message was great.

Nathan had decided to go to Cedarville College in the fall. He had gone to three different schools during high school and could hardly believe he could look forward to spending four college years at the same school!

Another Hot Season!

In April, I wrote to Mother Bobbett, "We bought a used refrigerator last week, but it isn't working very well so I don't know what we will do. It is about 107 degrees in our kitchen, so maybe that has something to do with it. It is amazing the amount of filtered water we go through every day. It seems to go into our stomachs and right out our pores!"

Our coworkers left on their regular furlough in June, and that meant Heath had to be field director again during their year's absence while continuing the full-time translation work too. Heath wrote, "Being field director again, I thought I would have to curtail my days of meeting with the translation committee. However, other than having to be gone for short periods of time or giving everyone an extra long coffee break, I am grateful to the Lord that we still have been able to continue meeting each morning. We have accomplished about 76 percent of the revision of the Zarma Bible. It is sometimes very difficult, usually very interesting, and never lacks a challenge!"

Missionary Dropouts

A new missionary couple arrived in July after their time of language study in France. Everyone was glad to have some new reinforcements in reaching the Zarma people for Christ. They seemed so mature and sure of their call to Niger. We thought they would be a great addition to our field, but alas, they didn't really buckle down to learn the language. After only a few months on the field, they returned to the States for a medical problem and never came back. It was always sad to think about the Lord's money that was invested in new candidates for their support, a year of language study in France, and passage to and from the field.

On July 11, 1986, the offices of Evangelical Baptist Missions in Kokomo, Indiana, were destroyed by fire when lightning struck. David Marshall wrote "Estimated replacement cost of the contents of the building is in excess of $185,000. We were insured to $80,000. God's people have been very generous, and several sizable gifts have been received to help with replacement. Our building was insured for $250,000, and we hope, with the help of some volunteer labor, we will be able to reconstruct within that limit." We did not have to ask for bank loans because God's people did indeed come to the aid of EBM!"

Norma Bobbett

Tragedy Averted

Heath, Pastor Luc, and Gourma deacon Yabidi went to the bush church near Makalondi for the baptism of ten new believers. Heath was suffering from a hard cold and was taking an antihistamine. On the way back to Niamey, Luc noticed that Heath was veering into the left lane and that a semi-truck was coming toward them. Then the car went back to the right lane, which Luc thought meant Heath was getting back on the right side because of the approaching semi. The car continued to the right and off the pavement into the brush and sand. At this moment, Heath woke up! They all could have been killed, but God protected them by His power. Much of that road is built up like a dike, and if Heath had gone off where there was a sharp drop down, the car would surely have rolled over, perhaps many times. I was just waking up from rest hour when Heath got home to tell me shakily that he could have been killed that day.

In September 1986, Nathan settled into Cedarville College for the beginning of his freshman year. That summer, Rebecca, Jon, Alan, and Nathan attended an ICA reunion near Chicago. It was the first time all four of our children had been together in four years!

I was busy translating Christmas programs for the Zarma ladies group and for the Zarma Sunday school. We were rejoicing in seeing more young people coming to the Zarma church.

At our Sunday evening English services, we ladies took turns teaching a children's story, which the adults enjoyed as much as the children did. One Catholic Peace Corps fellow who always attended English service when he was in town said, "That's my favorite part of the service!" I was particularly thrilled when one of our MKs told me that she really understood that she needed to be saved after a story I taught and that she had decided to give her heart to the Lord Jesus.

Nouhou, a blind man who had done Braille schooling in Nigeria, asked if he could teach the children's story one Sunday evening. He told the story of a very rich woman who called an artist and asked if he would come to paint her picture. She kept saying, "Now when you paint my picture, I want justice! This is very important that you do me justice in your painting." The artist agreed, but when he went to her house he found her to be the ugliest woman he had ever seen in his life. "Madame," he said, "You don't want justice! What you want is mercy!" Needless to say, Nouhou then spoke about the difference between justice and mercy! Great illustration!

It was good to have Sherry Adams with us for Christmas. Sherry wrote in her prayer letter, "It was such a joy to be back with my first 'African family,' the Bobbetts. I was treated like royalty by friends in both Niamey and Dosso. My Nigerien friends reminded me of how much Zarma I had forgotten, and it was wonderful to be removed from telephones and typewriters." We missed our children terribly, but hearing Jon, Rebecca, Alan, and Nathan's voices on the phone for Christmas was very special.

The big market of Niamey, which was destroyed by fire in 1982, was finally rebuilt and opened five years later. For the grand opening and ten days afterward, we set up a display of our Bible bookstore materials. The crowds on opening day were dense and quite unmanageable. Heath went in early to be there for the official opening when the government officials were present, and I tried to join him later after teaching Sunday school. It was more than unnerving to be swept in with the mob until I could finally break free by taking refuge inside someone's display booth. I almost lost my shoes in the crush! That was one of those heart-stopping experiences I hoped I'd never have again! Some of the government ministers came into our Bible store display, and we were able to give them some Gospel literature. We gave out many tracts during the opening celebration and made many good contacts.

Nathan was enjoying his time at Cedarville College and was happy that he was given the responsibility of being class chaplain for the five hundred freshmen there. He was planning to lead some fellow students out to Niger in June to serve in MIS (Missionary Internship Service). We were joyfully looking forward to having Nathan with us and planning work for these students in various ministries.

On Easter Sunday, we attended the Goudel Baptist Church. The Zarma youth group presented a good pageant, basing it on the disciples traveling the Emmaus Road. They were getting involved in an excellent Bible study at the Saturday youth meetings, and we were praying that they would see the need of total personal commitment to the Lord Jesus Christ. That summer, four people were in the Goudel church baptismal classes, and two others, already baptized, were applying for membership.

In June the Korean ambassador to Niger called to ask Heath if he would perform the wedding of two Ghanaians who were working at their embassy. Heath set up counseling sessions with Jacob and Edna and, of course, wanted to find out if they were Christians. Their first answer was,

"Yes, we've been baptized." He was Catholic, and she was Methodist. Heath spent time explaining the Gospel to them and what it is to be born again. The happy ending was that on the fourth counseling session, they opened their hearts to receive the Lord Jesus Christ as their Savior! They were faithful to our English services, and we had discipleship classes with them. They had a lovely wedding at the Korean embassy. Since embassy property is technically the sovereign territory of that country, we always teased them saying they got married in Korea!

On June 11, Nathan and three other Cedarville students arrived. The team helped with crafts and sports in DVBS, prepared many materials for the translation committee, bound Zarma song books, and helped in our audiovisual center. Tim and Nathan helped in the extensive remodeling of our Bible store reading room while Angie and Laurel repaired and bound the books in the lending library. We kept them busy, and they even had time enough to go out to the SIM bush hospital in Galmi for a couple of days. Angie and Laurel, nursing students, helped on the wards while Tim and Nathan roofed the ulcer treatment room. Their music and testimonies blessed our hearts. Interspersed were trips to the market where they bought and made several Touareg souvenir salesmen very happy.

Their stay was appreciated by both missionaries and African believers. The rainy season was late in arriving, and although the students' time with us was very hot and humid, the Lord kept them well. Nathan had taught them some songs in French and Zarma. When they sang in the Zarma church, many thought they already knew the languages! One of the Dosso church ladies said their singing was "a little taste of heaven!"

We fed them one typical African meal of corn mush with okra and meat sauce. Nathan was the only one who balked at sitting on a mat on the floor while the girls ate out of one bowl (with their fingers) and the boys out of another bowl. Nathan did finally sit down to eat with the others but grinned broadly as he whipped a big spoon out of his back pocket so he wouldn't have to eat with his hands! Kano's daughters gave the girls a typical tight, tiny-braid hairdo. Angie held on to the end, but the pulling and pain were so bad that Laurel asked the girls to stop after a while.

The students had camel rides and their pictures taken in front of an ant hill that was twice their height. Fulani friend Jofo poled them in his leaky dugout canoe out to his village on an island in the Niger River for a visit, and they saw the donkey and camel parking lots at Belliara market. The African children fell in love with Laurel and Angie. Our little neighbors were so sad when the students left. Nathan preached in both Zarma and English during their time with us.

Nathan went home to Michigan with Tim where they were able to find work in a blueberry warehouse. While Nathan was in Niger, he told us he wanted to go out to California to attend the wedding of a good friend of his from ICA. We were very much against this, telling him that he needed to work and save his money for college that fall. He said he probably wouldn't go to California but was not happy because when he graduated from ICA, his friends were scattered all over the States and he didn't know when he would get to see them again. Jon and Judy were living in California at that time too.

A few weeks later, we got a call from Jonathan, and he said there was someone there who wanted to speak to us. It was Nathan! When we asked him what he was doing in California, his reply was amazing. He and Tim had attended a meeting at a camp in Michigan where Josh McDowell was speaking. Josh asked if there was anyone in the audience who would be willing to drive his van back to California. His wife collected antiques, the van was full, and he had to go on to speak at other meetings. He said, "If a couple of people can drive it out for me, I will pay for the gas and also pay their airfare back to Michigan!" Nathan and Tim volunteered, and *voilà*, Nathan got his expenses paid to go out to California to attend his friend's wedding after all!

In August, we welcomed Colleen McGarvey to be a replacement for our mission bookkeeper Vicki Burry, who was on home assignment. This was Colleen's first trip out of the United States. She was very mature, loved the Lord, and her testimony of how she came to know Christ while in university was thrilling. Although she did not speak Zarma or French, she immediately began to reach out evangelistically to an English-speaking woman from Ghana.

Heath was the only man on our field that summer and was exhausted from heading up the translation work and then doing the work of field director. He was having trouble with a continual pain in his side that he hoped would go away. After three weeks with no relief, he decided to go to the SIM mission hospital two hundred miles away in Galmi. There Dr. Jim Ceton discovered that Heath needed double hernia surgery. Heath was hoping they would do the surgery there, but the doctors said they didn't do that type of surgery in their primitive bush hospital unless it was an emergency or a strangulated hernia. They recommended a return to the States.

About a month after Heath's surgery in Ohio Jonathan sent us tickets to fly to California to visit the whole family as well as meet our newest granddaughter, baby Laura.

Arriving back in Niger, we found our mud house had been invaded by some unwelcome intruders called *dusey* (termites). Our bedroom closet was just an alcove in our bedroom, with a curtain across the opening. *Dusey* were always present in the thick mud walls. While our house was empty, these little creatures had appeared in our bedroom closet, removed the mud from the wall, and made a mound over six feet tall on the floor, munching away on the wooden shelf overhead and eating the side of a garment bag. Our house helper told us he had to haul out over two wheelbarrows full of mud before he could reach in and spray Raid in the six-inch-by-two-foot hole they had made in the wall!

Continuing Translation Work

To make more rapid translation progress, the translation committee was then divided into two groups meeting in separate rooms. One group was working on revising the New Testament books, and the other was working on the books of the Old Testament. Hours and hours were spent each afternoon checking references to see if proper names had been spelled the same in different passages. We were so grateful for the daily intercession of God's people who supported us back in the States. We asked them to pray for accurate translation and for His protection for the committee. We were not unmindful of Satan's opposition to the Word of God being made available to the Zarma people and of his subtle attacks. We were seeing committee members being hit by a variety of illnesses, family problems, and car accidents.

Lieutenant Colonel Seyni Kountché had been president of Niger since the military coup in 1974. He was a good leader, wanting no nonsense from government employees. He was respected and feared by the people and never seemed to be a president who padded his own pockets with the country's money. Government employees never knew when he would show up to check on them. On rainy mornings, employees often used that excuse to stay home or to arrive very late in their offices. What a shock and embarrassment it was to them when the president showed up at their workplaces on rainy mornings before they did!

President Kountché was making trips to France for his health, but the public was always assured that he was fine. Actually, he had developed a brain tumor, and surgical intervention did not help him. He died in a Paris hospital on November 10, 1987.

I was asked to write an article for our mission publication *The Gleaner* about God's Word in heart language. I told the story of visiting my dear friend Kano who was flat in bed with back problems and had gone through other physical trials and persecution for her faith. She told me how blessed she had been by our mimeographed copy of the Book of Psalms as she quoted from Psalm 23. "The man who wrote those words surely understood suffering, and God uses him to comfort us even today," she related. She was anxiously awaiting the day when she could hold the whole Zarma Bible in her hands.

Our children had helped Pastor Luc purchase a motorbike to use as he so faithfully went out to bush villages with the Good News to the Gourma people. Luc loved our children and prayed faithfully for them.

Our Home in the Hands of Renters When We Returned to Africa

When we asked a Realtor if she would be responsible for overseeing the rental of our Ohio house, she refused, saying, "What? You want to go overseas and leave your most valuable asset in the hands of strangers? That's crazy!" Evidently, she had some experiences in such situations. We rented our home at much lower than market value, and neighbors who went to our church agreed to accept the renters' checks each month to deposit them.

After a few months, the checks began to bounce. When we got our bank statements a month later, we were charged for the deposit of bad checks! The renters would apologize and pay, only to repeat this a few months later. It was very frustrating (as the Realtor told us it would be) to be so far away when these things were happening.

Although the renters had signed a no pets agreement, our neighbors let us know there was a large dog in the backyard and inside our screened-in patio. When the renters moved out without paying their last three months' rent, Jonathan confronted them about these things. The husband had many lame excuses and wouldn't meet with Jon face to face. He said his sister was having a hard time and he had to keep her dog for her and he also had to pay her rent. Meanwhile, both the renter and his wife had bought new vehicles! Jonathan told him, "You didn't pay your sister's rent. My parents paid her rent!"

We were saddened by all the damage done and the extensive repairs that were needed at the house. The dog had ripped screens on our back porch and left deep scratch marks on the sliding door, a kitchen window was broken and not replaced, a hole was kicked through the inside paneling of the front door, and someone had put a fist hole through the family room paneling. Added to all these damages, their children had been allowed to play in the bathtub with water overflowing onto the carpet, so the floor was rotted in a large portion and needed to be replaced. When Jon threatened legal action to collect the last three months' rent and damages, the renters got nervous and promised to pay by the end of the year. Our house sat empty for months until we came home.

Other missionary colleagues shared their horror stories of renting their homes while overseas too. Renters in Mississippi plowed up their front lawn and planted a vegetable garden. Other missionaries from North

Carolina said the renters got into their things stored in the attic and used them, although they knew they weren't supposed to!

March 1988 prayer letter: "We had to walk far down into the river bed to reach water deep enough for a baptismal service for believers from the Goudel village church. The Niger sun in all of the hot season intensity was beating upon us, but the occasion was a joyous one! To see seven Zarmas and one Fulani follow the Lord in the obedience of baptism filled our hearts with praise to the Savior. They have a great zeal in Bible study, learning verses, and sharing the Gospel message with others. One elderly deacon gave this testimony, "Once while preaching at the church many children and young people began to throw stones at me and the village men watched but never reprimanded the stone throwers. I prayed ever since that time that God would allow me to see the day when there would be a young people from this village who would know Jesus Christ and follow him. I also prayed for many years that God would raise up a pastor from this village who would preach to them. Praise God that today I have seen these two prayers answered!" (Pastor Kommi admitted he had been one of those throwing stones all those years ago.)

For Christians in a Muslim society, not only is there verbal abuse, but they are subjected to social ostracism. Africans have warm social groups, and their family ties are very important. When your family does not want to eat with you or refuses to feed you because you are an infidel (Christian), it is a very hurtful situation.

The rainy season began on June 8, 1988, with a noon dust storm that blotted out the sun and turned Niamey as black as midnight. It was silent and eerie outdoors. A friend videotaped the storm and the ensuing darkness and made a copy for us. All we could think was surely this was what it was like when Jesus hung on the cross.

"The Muslim fasting month of Ramadan has just ended here. It is a time of celebration with gifts exchanged and new clothing worn. We heard a Muslim teacher on the radio broadcasting assurances that their 'good work' of fasting meant their sins of the past year were forgiven. Oh, that they would come to the truth of Jesus Christ."

"Some have written assuring us of their prayers for the translation team. We are most grateful. It was a disappointment when we lost two of our African helpers, but God has provided two others in answer to your prayers. They seem to be working well. We are gradually rereading all of the finished books and checking word lists for spelling and typing errors. It is time-consuming, meticulous work. Again we thank you for keeping us before the throne of grace.

"Serving Him in Niger, Heath and Norma"

Chapter 25
Seventh Furlough
September 1988 to September 1989

The Lord had delightful surprises for us at our departure from the Niamey airport for furlough. On August 28, 1988, we arrived at the airport at 9:30 p.m. with thirty kilos of luggage each. Heath was carrying the diskettes of the entire Zarma Bible. He took out the diskettes, and a policeman kept them and our films from going through the X-rays. An old Muslim Zarma porter friend took our bags to the customs officer and had him mark them without opening them. Our Christian Ethiopian friend had a pass and helped us out to the plane. Just before we left the terminal, our Jewish friend Sue was there to see us off too. Saibou, who worked for Sabena Airlines, was telling Sue there were some empty business class seats that he could bump some travelers up to. Sue said, "Why not do it for our friends the Bobbetts?" He grinned and said he didn't know if that was possible, but after we got on the plane and were settling into our economy seats, a stewardess came to take us up to business class! Afterward, we marveled that we were assisted by a Muslim friend, a Christian friend, and a Jewish friend! We never expected such help when we got to the airport that night. What a privilege God gave us during our years in Niger to have so many international friends!

Arriving home in Springfield we found our house needed cleaning, painting, window and screen replacement, and serious plumbing work in the bathroom. Also, we needed to get our furniture out of storage. Nathan was a great help to us and he painted many rooms with his dad. Our dear godly friend, Bill Ford, did the plumbing work in our bathroom, and he and Heath redid the flooring. Bill wouldn't charge us, only allowing us to buy the parts and materials needed. It was a big job getting our house cleaned, repaired, and ready for occupancy. On September 8, we were finally able to move in.

Furlough number seven had begun! The Bible translation committee (three nationals and two missionaries) in Niger was still functioning, and we were reminding supporters to keep praying for them. The work remaining to be done on the Zarma Bible included the glossary, the maps, a small concordance, and the references of approximately five hundred words to be checked for consistency in translation from the Hebrew and Greek. Did we say in 1982 that "We hope to finish this project in about two years?" We must have been uninformed optimists!

Nathan and six other guys had decided to rent a house together just across the street from the Cedarville campus. Whoever the landlord was, he surely was brave to let seven college men rent his house! However, one of the guys was an excellent organizer. He made lists with each guy's duties posted for the week on it: loading and unloading the dishwasher, vacuuming, cleaning bathrooms, and so forth. The house interior looked pretty good in spite of its multiple tenants.

Alan had given Nathan a Burmese python, which he named Boots. He was only about two feet long at the beginning, but he was growing! Uncle Mickey helped Nathan build a glass aquarium that was big enough to accommodate Boots as he grew. All the guys thought owning a snake was really cool.

Heath went back to Niger temporarily on November 25, 1988, to work with the translation team. That day we left early to take Heath to the airport because he wanted to stop by and see a used, fleet-owned 1988 Ford Taurus that was for sale in New Carlisle, marked down to $9,788. Nathan had confidently said he knew his dad wouldn't buy a car on the spur of the moment because "Dad always thought things over and made a decision later."

We went for a tryout ride with the salesman and me in the back seat. Heath was checking all the knobs and indicators on the dashboard, the radio, and so forth. He had just asked the salesman a question about the car as he turned on the radio and the commercial song for Ford sang out, "Have you driven a Ford laaately?" We all burst into laughter, and Heath did decide to buy that car "on the spur of the moment" on his way to the airport, much to Nathan's astonishment.

Heath arrived in Niger on November 27, 1988. The "computer difference program" enabled him to see everything the committee had done in his absence. His days there were intense and busy as he worked with the committee on the Zarma Bible before returning home.

We met Judy and the children when they flew in from California before Christmas. It was very cold at that time, and they were coming from a warm climate. We had brought warm coats and hats for them, which they gladly donned after the cold walk from the airport terminal to our car. Laura, an adorable toddler, had never had winter clothes on before, so she stood stiffly not knowing if she could move or not, causing us more laughter.

Our house was full wall-to-wall with people once all our family arrived, and it was a wonderful family gathering. Our grandchildren were still small and so much fun. I bought some big red wax lips for all of them, and we marched into the living room, dancing and singing, causing peals of laughter from the adults.

The grandchildren were so much fun. Laura had heard her older brothers telling knock-knock jokes, so she wanted to tell them too. She would come up to me and say, "Na-na." When I asked, "Who's there?" she would just say some gibberish and then start laughing because she knew we all would burst into laughter too. What a precious little gift from God she was (and is).

During the first half of 1989, many weeks were spent at Bibles International in Grand Rapids, Michigan, as camera-ready copies of each book of the Zarma Bible were prepared for the printers. From January to June, we put more than 13,000 miles on our car, visiting and reporting to our supporting churches, and we still had meetings scheduled until August.

Nathan completed his junior year at Cedarville and it was great to have him nearby. I wrote that "his college friends are really neat kids who love the Lord and are a delight to have around." At honors chapel in May 1989, Nathan was surprised to receive the John W. Bickett scholarship award "for outstanding preparation for and commitment to professional Christian service."

That spring, we had found a serious problem with the foundation of our home on Wabash Drive. One corner in the basement was splitting apart, and we could see out through it! I happened to run into the man who made his fortune constructing the all-brick homes in Northridge. When I told him our problem, he said, "No, that couldn't happen!" What? When I said it did happen and asked what he could suggest that we do about it, he looked a little defeated and said, "I don't know!"

Isn't it wonderful that our loving God always knows the solutions to our problems? We often stand puzzled, not knowing which way to turn or what to do, but our Father is never puzzled, and He knows exactly what to do. Someone has said when we have problems, we shouldn't say, "God, here is my problem," but we should say, "Problem, here is my God!"

Ernie Overholser, a godly man at Southgate Baptist Church, was in construction all his adult life. He assembled a team of men volunteers from the church to help us. They dug all the way down on that open corner of our house and sealed it with cement. Then they built two strong buttresses inside the basement so the wall was well supported.

The next Saturday, Ernie was there with another Southgate men's team to reroof our house! All we had to buy was the materials. The Saturday before, they had all brought their packed lunches, but this time I made a large recipe of couscous and sauce for them to enjoy. For many it was the first time they had ever eaten couscous. I think they liked it! Both of those weekends, Heath was away in scheduled meetings, so he couldn't participate. After their work, we wrote a thank-you note to the men:

"How can we ever adequately express how very much we appreciate all the work Ernie Overholser and his great teams of Southgate men did on the two Saturday workdays at our house? It was hard work in African-type heat, and you gave us the precious gifts of your time and energy. We thank you from the bottom of our hearts. You will be much in our thoughts and prayers as we return to Niger in September.

"With sincere gratitude, Heath and Norma Bobbett"

In August 1989, Jane and Homer hosted a Bobbett family reunion at their home in Cazenovia, New York. All of Heath, Shirley, and Jane's families were there for this happy weekend. There were all kinds of activities, great food, and fun family times.

We were scheduled to return to Niger on September 14. By June, our monthly support had been promised, and we were looking to the Lord for our passage and equipment needs to come in that summer. We asked prayer for:

- strength to get all the packing done
- grace in saying goodbye to our family and friends
- our adjustment to living on the edge of the Sahara again
- and above all that we will be good ambassadors for the Lord Jesus

One big prayer request we had was for renters for our home in Springfield, especially after our former renters had been irresponsible and caused us much grief. At almost the last minute, the Lord graciously brought Jim and Betty to us. They were new to the area and didn't want to buy right away so were hunting for a house to rent. They were wonderful renters, taking good care of our home and even doing repairs or upgrades. We were so thankful to the Lord for them.

In our August 14, 1989, prayer letter, we wrote, "We are anxious to get back and settled into the work. We return with the assurance of His calling and enabling. We can do nothing in our own strength. We value the prayers of God's people, that we will walk close to Him every day and be used for His glory among the people of Niger. Please pray for the soon-to-be-published Zarma Bible."

General Director David Marshall's September 1989 letter stated, "Our main station in Niger has been devastated by torrential rains, and many of our buildings are in danger of collapsing from erosion at the foundations. We have no men on the field at this time, and our four single ladies have worked hard and long in supervising African help in sandbagging to try to divert water away from the buildings. Several hundred feet of walls have been washed out. We estimate that it will require $30,000 to $40,000 to make repairs and put in a new drainage system. Pray for funds that are needed in order to save the complex, which includes a primary school for nearly four hundred African children, several residences, guest facilities, field offices, radio studio, audiovisual center, the Zarma church building, another primary school building, as well as several storage areas."

This was the situation facing Heath, who would be the only man on the field when we got back. I sensed my dear husband's confidence in the Lord's help and the calmness that kept him looking forward in faith.

EBM'S annual conference was held in New York, from September 9 to 13, but we weren't planning to attend because it was so close to the date of our departure for Niger. EBM President Dave Marshall urged us to be attend. On Monday evening, Heath was asked to give a ten-minute testimony on the Niger and our translation work. Then I was called to the platform as well. What a surprise it was to be presented a lovely plaque from the mission for our thirty-two years of service in Niger!

Back in Indianapolis for departure on September 14, Heath, and Jon took our eight boxes and four suitcases to the airport. Both Jon and Rebecca lived in Indianapolis at that time as well as all six of our grandchildren. It was so very hard to say goodbye to all of them. However, we were ready, with the Lord's help, to begin our eighth term in Niger.

433

Chapter 26
Eighth Term in Niger
September 1989 to December 1992

"Then Samuel took a stone and set it up...He named it Ebenezer, saying, 'Thus far the Lord has helped us.'" 1 Samuel 7:12
Ebenezer is from two Hebrew words pronounced together, "Even Haazer, or Stone of Help. It was a reminder to the Israelites of God's faithfulness and might.

Arriving back in Niger on September 15, 1989, I wrote, "All our luggage came through, and we passed through *douane* (customs) with no problems. Many African friends and missionaries met us at the airport. The rain damage at the mission is unbelievable!" If this huge challenge had been facing me, I would have collapsed in tears. However, my dear godly husband had his confidence in our mighty and wise heavenly Father and believed his Savior was up to the challenges before him. A huge gully, sometimes twenty feet deep and wide, ran down the property by our house and another was over near the French school. The rushing waters from the one-hundred-year rain almost took the corner off of the mission's French elementary school.

Our four single lady colleagues were so occupied with the flood damage that they were unable to get our house ready before our arrival. We were put in our old apartment, with only a bed and chairs there from the guest house because they were in the process of taking out windows in the old mud house to put in thief bars. The screened windows and doors of bygone days were no longer all missionaries needed because crime and thievery were increasing.

We waded through dust and dirt, out a window to go over to the guest house side to make breakfast each morning. It was rather depressing. There was no way we could unpack our things and settle in until the thief bars were installed, the windows put back, and the walls painted. There were no mosquito nets on our beds, so mosquitoes were feasting on our blood each night. The thought of malaria crossed my mind, but I was more concerned for Heath. I had nursed him through malarial attacks when the chills he had were so violent he shook the whole bed! I had nursed our children through malaria and spiking fevers that brought on febrile convulsions. I had given African friends chloroquine and aspirin that brought them through attacks. Up until that time, taking more antimalarials as soon as I felt symptoms seemed to work for me in warding it off.

We received lots of hugs and greetings at the Zarma Church on Sunday morning and again at the evening English service. While we were still living half in our house and half in the adjoining guest house, we were so grateful that friends invited us out for dinner each evening.

From our October 1989 prayer letter:

"You know you are back in Niger when…

- You hear the Muslim call to prayer ringing out from the mosques in the stillness of the early morning hours.
- You reach for the hot water faucet in the shower, and there isn't any!
- You see billboards telling you to "protect yourself from malaria."
- Students let you know they are anxious for the Evening Baptist Bible Institute classes to begin.
- You say "Fill it up, please" at the gas station and then pay $40 for fourteen gallons of gas.
- Friends bring you "welcome back gifts" of eggs or onions or live guinea hens.
- Other expatriates make trips out to the EBM station to see the 'grand canyon' gully and other washouts from a heavy rainy season.
- You note the brave smiles of your coworkers who are exhausted as each of them is trying to do the work of two…or three.
- You must get used to bargaining again to buy your vegetables or fruits laid out in little piles on the ground.
- Your African friends express their concern for whether there will be a harvest after the rains came too late and then were too abundant.
- A sandstorm hits just as you leave for Sunday morning church, and no amount of spitting gets that grit out of your mouth!
- You hear of victories won and revival kindled in one of the local churches.
- A young man expresses discouragement because he has no employment and his Muslim family refuses to give him food unless he recants his faith.
- A deacon shakes your hand and says, 'We thank God for your safe arrival. We have heard reports about airplane crashes.'
- You avoid looking at the pictures of your grandchildren because, for some reason, your cheeks get wet!

- All the great fellowship you had with friends and family during your year on furlough travels is now only a warm memory.
- Pastor Kommi's wife gives you a big hug and says, 'Welcome home!'

"On Him we have set our hope...as you help us by your prayers (2 Corinthians 1:10-11)."

We had added frustrations and waiting before we could begin to settle into our mud home. The carpenter wasn't showing up to build some kitchen cabinets for us, and Joe, the builder, didn't show up to get the work finished on the windows. Heath got our stove, refrigerator, and washing machine going and was trying to get our Peugeot running. He was finally able to purchase a car battery, and our good friend and Peugeot mechanic, Boubacar, sent one of his employees to bring the car into his shop. It was great to have wheels again! The carpenter finally came late one afternoon and at least took measurements for the cabinets. Joe eventually came with his helper and two welders. Marou, the painter, showed up sick, so Heath took him home! *"Kala Suuru!"* ("Patience is needed!")

On September 24, we were invited, along with several others, to a meal at the American Ambassador's home. An American chaplain for Europe and West Africa was visiting from Stuttgart. This is the evening we met Pat and Joyce Lewellyn, retired teachers who came to work with the Southern Baptist mission. Joyce was teaching at the American school, and Pat was the pastor of the morning English church that a former IMB missionary had started. We soon became close friends with Joyce and Pat, who were about our age and a delightful couple. After a busy week, we often got together on Friday evenings for fun and relaxation in the years we were in Niger together.

Twelve days after we arrived back, I wrote, "Electricity has gone off five times today, sometimes for five minutes and sometimes an hour. Heath and I worked on the Zarma Bible in the computer room for three hours, doing chapter and verse checks (for correct numbering), and we also worked on the glossary."

As our French school opened, I was asked to help in the school office to collect tuition. The tuition fees seemed small compared to what parents pay to put their children in Christian schools in the States, but it was not always easy for Nigeriens. However, even though all our teachers were Christians and began their classes each morning with a Bible lesson and songs, a great number of Muslim families wanted their children in our school because of its excellent reputation and good teachers.

In between times, we were slowly getting our suitcases and boxes out of the store room and into our house as soon as the carpenter finished the cupboards. The windows and the painting were still not finished.

Severe Attack of Malaria!

In the mid-afternoon of October 8, I began to ache all over and had a high fever and chills. It was a miserable day for me, but I took three Flavoquine and Anacin. The fever finally broke at 9:30 p.m. October 9 was Heath's fifty-ninth birthday. I gave him Chuck Swindoll's book *Rise and Shine* and a can of mixed nuts, which he always liked. I felt weak all day but continued taking Nivaquine (chloroquine) and kept going.

On Tuesday, October 10, I was in a sweat all morning but worked at getting more things unpacked from barrels and put away. At noon, the malarial headache in the back of my head started again. I took more Flavoquine and shivered under a quilt all afternoon, aching all over. It was ninety-two degrees in the house, but I was shivering because my temperature was 102.5 degrees. Arlene Spurlock came and gave me a Quinimax injection, so my fever finally broke by 9:00 p.m. I felt like a wrung-out dish cloth with no appetite, no thirst.

Our mission nurse, Arlene, gave me another Quinimax shot. I was sweating constantly and so tired with no energy. On the next day, my fever started up again at 4:00 a.m. I just thought I couldn't bear the aching and distress again in my weakened condition. I started taking Fansidar, and Arlene gave me a third Quinimax shot. The fever didn't go as high that day, and I was thankful. On October 13, I had no energy but no fever either! PTL! It took several days of recuperation after this to get my energy back.

After going through those two episodes with malaria and aching so badly I was moaning in pain, I remember telling Heath, "If I ever get such a bad malaria attack again and if I survive, I am going home to America for good!"

A Farewell to Mariama

On November 3, 1989, we had a birthday farewell lasagna dinner for Mariama who was leaving for England on a scholarship to work on her doctorate.

Just a month later, we were awakened at 2:00 a.m. by Daouda standing outside the screened window at the head of our bed. He told us the shocking news that Mimi, one of Cecelia Dillon's orphan children who grew up in the orphanage, had just died. We got up quickly, dressed, and went to Kano in the village of Goudel. Kano had been the only real mother the orphans had known since Cecelia died in the auto accident twelve years before, and she was taking the news very hard.

Mimi had seemed fine, watching TV with others in the courtyard the evening before then suddenly began having chest pains and swooning. He went to Kano's side and said, "Mama, I am so sick!" They had a hard time getting a car to take him to the Niamey dispensary, where they were told to take him directly to the hospital. They had just gotten him to the hospital, and as he was being given an injection, he died in Kano's arms. Nurse Arlene Spurlock thought he must have had an aneurysm near the heart. We sat with Kano for part of the night and then went home again.

Pastor Kommi conducted the funeral at 3:30 p.m. that day, clearly presenting the Gospel and the assurance believers have that they are forgiven and will go directly to heaven. Muslim belief is that you must do all the good works you can and hope they outweigh your bad deeds. No one but their Allah knows who will go to heaven. Even Mohammed didn't know about his eternal destiny. Niger custom is that only the men go to the cemetery for the burial. We women stayed at the house with Kano.

Heath was the teacher and director of the Evening Baptist Bible Institute that year (Institute Biblique Baptiste du Soir) and really enjoyed teaching the men each week. I always made a big container of Kool-Aid for them to have during the class. They called it *l'eau coloré* (colored water) and usually drank the whole full Igloo before the evening was over, especially in the hot season. The Christmas party we had for them with couscous and sauce, cake, and soft drinks as well as some fun games was a real hit.

Kay, Ron, Ann, Melissa, and Bradly Washer were there for the party too, besides Sherry. Our dear mentor-colleague Dal Washer had died on May 25 of that year in Togo, West Africa. His son, Ron, didn't want his mom to spend Christmas at Kpalimé, Togo, that year, so they came to Niamey to see areas where they had served in previous years. Kay had told her daughter-in-law, Ann, how they used to get a large thorn bush at Christmas, set it in a bucket of sand, and decorate it for Christmas in their early days in Niger, so they did that again in the guest house living room. We really enjoyed having the Washers with us. Our car wasn't adequate to take them all to Téra, the station Dal and Kay had opened back in the late 1950s, but IBM missionary, Don Bolls, very kindly volunteered to drive them.

From Sherry Adams' January 1990 prayer letter: "During my school vacation, I was able to return to Niger and spend two weeks in my first African home in Niamey. Heath and Norma Bobbett are the perfect host and hostess, and it was great to be with them. I don't think I've laughed as hard in months as in a single evening of watching Heath laugh! My time with them and other missionaries…helped wreak havoc with three months of dieting! Somehow seeing God's work in Niger always reminds me of Psalm 65:8: 'Those living far away fear your wonders; where morning dawns and evening fades You call forth songs of joy.' I appreciate His reminder that His love and offer of salvation are not just for me, my family, my culture but for 'whosoever will.'"

Progress on Repairing the Flood Damage

The city of Niamey had begun helping fill in the huge gully by our house by dumping truckloads of collected city trash into it. When the wind was blowing toward our house, the garbage odors were quite pervasive! Later, the mayor of the commune sent its bulldozer to push the city garbage dumped in our compound down into the gully so we could cover it and prepare a solid foundation for the dike. He also sent forty-five truckloads of laterite dirt for the unbelievably low price of 1,000 CFA (about $4) per load! The Lord was working through this sympathetic Muslim mayor to help us. Two American friends with engineering degrees, consulted with us regarding repairing the flood damage too. We were so thankful for Barry Rand's and Ray Norman's advice and assessments of the damages. It was recommended that a dike be constructed that would carry the rain waters past the French school and down toward the Niger River. It seemed like a huge mountain of work to me, and it was, but Heath plugged along calmly, and we saw God provide time after time.

In the November/December Yantala station report, Heath wrote, "The major event of the past year, as far as the physical station is concerned, was the devastation wrought by the serious storm of this past rainy season, which destroyed our drainage system by the French school, resulting in the undermining and collapse of a good eighty-five meters of wall around the compound. The storm created a very serious gully which wiped out the newly finished road on the east side of the property and endangered the workshop area…It will probably cost between $75,000 and $100,000 to make the necessary repairs and to solve the water drainage problems in such a way that we will not face such a situation again. We still have a long way to go. Days, weeks, and months of seemingly endless hours have been spent seeking out professional advice, making various contacts, getting estimates from various construction companies, seeking the help of the mayor, and so forth."

The next months continued to be very busy for us. We were looking forward to a volunteer team from the States (eight men and three wives) who would help with the repairs from January 17 to March 5, 1990.

February 1, 1990, marked the thirtieth anniversary of our first arrival in Niger. On February 15, grandson Ryan Heath Bobbett was born to Alan and his wife, Shelley. Alan sent us pictures of himself holding this precious little son.

False cults were beginning to arrive in Niger. Sadly, they made our believers the target of their outreach, offering them jobs, clothing, and other enticements. One group went out to some of our church plants near the Burkina Faso border, telling them they were sent by Christians in Niamey. Next, they showed the folks pictures of beautiful churches their group had in Europe and the States, saying, "Just pick out which church building you like, and we'll build it for you!" When our national pastors got word of this, they went right out to let the believers know these people were false teachers and were not sent out by them.

Planting churches in Muslim lands is a slow and difficult work, very discouraging at times. When we heard that there had been a church split in the SIM Hausa work, it was sad for us. Then the same thing happened in Pastor Luc's Gourma Church in Niamey. There was a cantankerous man who moved to Niamey and was part of that church. He could be nice when he wanted to and had a following. One day, he went to Pastor Luc and told him he could leave now, he was no longer needed! Pastor Luc, a godly man and a soul-winner, told him that God had called him to that work and he couldn't leave until God told him to.

This man caused a split in the Gourma church and started another one on the other side of the Niger River. When I was expressing my sorrow and disappointment over this, Pastor Luc said, "Madame, don't feel badly. I have had it far too easy for a long time, and this trial is good for me to teach me more about being a good disciple of Christ." Pastor Luc continued to visit the people who left his church, loving them and helping them in any way he could. We could not detect any animosity in him toward the man who split the church or toward the people who left his church. What a godly example he was to all of us!

The work on translating the Bible into Zarma was nearing completion, and we were hoping Bibles International would soon choose a publisher so that the first copies would arrive by the planned September dedication.

We were able to take a six-week vacation to the states that summer. This trip was very special too as we could attend Nathan's graduation from Cedarville College on June 2, 1990. There were 402 graduates. Campus Pastor Harold Green let us in on the secret that Nathan had been chosen

With Jesus Leading the Way

to receive the President's Trophy "for Christian character, grade point average, and Christian service." The person who announces the award goes through a long list of details about the winner, only announcing his name at the end. It was fun watching Nathan's face go from puzzlement to wonder to astonishment! He was totally clueless that he had been chosen. What a surprise for him, and what an honor! His fellow graduates in communication arts stood up and cheered for him! We were so proud of Nathan and thankful for what the Lord had done in his heart. Two days later, on June 4, Nathan left for Romania as part of Cedarville's MIS program.

We spent a few more days with family in Indiana. Rebecca surprised us with a cake and small party to celebrate our thirty-fifth wedding anniversary.

We returned to Niger on June 17. During our flight I was dozing and Heath woke me up saying, "The plane is going around and around!" After a few astonished seconds, I realized he was telling me he was having another attack of Ménière's disease when the room feels like it is spinning, making him sick to his stomach.

Thankfully, we had a long layover in Paris and stayed at the Arcade Hotel at the train station, in a tiny, sparse room. I went alone down to their restaurant for supper. It was Guadeloupe night, and the waitresses were dressed in Caribbean-style dresses. They served me plain rice and a small fish head for $13! When I told her I didn't eat fish head, she took it back and brought me (no kidding!) a fish tail! I'll forever wonder who got the middle part! I fixed Cup-a-Soup for Heath in

441

the room with some bread. We arrived back in Niger at 4:00 a.m. on June 20th.

End-of-Year Program for the Evening Baptist Bible Institute

At the end of the year for the Evening Baptist Bible Institute, each of the men testified of their thankfulness for all they had learned that year and requested prayer for their walk and growth in Christ. Through our Bible bookstore, we were able to present each man with Scofield Reference Bibles in French for their studies the following year. Prizes were given for highest grade averages and perfect attendance. Out of a possible score for the year of 209 points, one young man scored 208! The students were strengthened in their love for the Lord and for each other. We asked for prayer for Heath and Steve Nunemaker as they prepared for the classes to be taught the next school year.

Our camp that summer was a study of life of Daniel. The young people were blessed and challenged to lives of purity as they studied Daniel together. What a lively place the camp, held at our French elementary school, was! The campers declared it "the best camp ever!" (They said that every year!) It was a blessed time for them away from Muslim neighbors as they studied God's Word and had fellowship with other believers.

Zarma Bible Dedication

September 15, 1990, was a day of great rejoicing when we held a dedication for the first published Zarma Bible! How thankful we were for the prayers and gifts of God's people that brought us through the years of Bible translation. What a task it was for the translators as they tried to be as accurate as possible in getting the original Greek and Hebrew into the heart language of the Zarma people.

The dedication was held in the Palais des Congrès Grand Hall in Niamey with over 300 people attending. Some Niger dignitaries were there and also our American ambassador. An old Zarma deacon said he thought he would never see the complete Bible translated into Zarma in his lifetime and how happy he was for this wonderful occasion!

We were so grateful for the missionaries and nationals who had worked with much diligence in the past on translating books from the Bible into Zarma.

After the dedication, we invited the translators and families (thirty people) to a *méchoui* on the volleyball court. This whole roasted sheep stuffed with couscous was done to perfection. I was busy serving the guests, and by the time I was ready to enjoy some food, everything was gone. The guests had taken it all, even the bones!

At church the next day, a member of the translation committee told us, "My heart was so full of happiness last night that I couldn't sleep. I read my Bible all night!"

That fall, Heath began working as a consultant with the Bénin translation team on the Dendi New Testament.

At Christmas 1990, for the first time The Jesus Film was shown on national television! We wrote this article for our London, Ontario, supporting church:

"If you were born in a Muslim country, what would you believe about Jesus? You would believe He was a prophet, but that Mohammed was the last and greatest of the prophets. You would believe that Jesus was born of a virgin but would vehemently deny that He was the Son of God. You would believe that Jesus never died on the cross or rose again. You would believe that Jesus is coming again…to convert the world to Islam!

"The Niger Republic in West Africa claims to be 95 percent Muslim, but God has kept the doors open to the preaching of the Gospel. One method our mission has used for many years is a fifteen-minute Gospel broadcast on the national radio station each Sunday. The Word is given out in the Zarma, French, and Hausa languages. In the 1980s, when Niger opened their first television station, we began to pray that we would be granted time on national television too. Last year this possibility looked very hopeful, but then it seemed to be somehow blocked. Nevertheless, as Christmas approached, we decided to ask if we might at least have some time on that holiday to show a part of The Jesus Film.

"How great was our excitement when the station manager phoned to say they liked the preview we had sent of the film and wanted to give us two full hours on Christmas Eve to show the entire Jesus Film! There was only one channel on Niger television at that time, so every household who had their television on that evening saw the story of Jesus according to the Gospel of Luke. Many people who owned televisions put their sets out in their courtyard where it is cooler, and all the neighbors came to watch.

"Many questions are being asked since The Jesus Film was shown, and the Christians in Niger are using them as springboards for witnessing. Please pray with us for their witness and for further openings to share God's Word by the medium of television."

University and High School Student Unrest

On February 25, 1991, Niger experienced university and high school unrest. The student demonstrators attacked stores, the American Cultural Center, Sabena Airline offices, the French consulate, and other places, breaking plate glass windows and throwing Molotov cocktails. They burned the cars of the American Cultural Center director and the French minister. A missionary was caught up in one of the student marches, and the back window of his car was shattered. One of our single ladies, in a small French car, also was trapped among marchers, and they began to rock her car back and forth like they were going to turn it over. That was frightening. There was suspicion that these riots were sponsored by outsiders. Similar things were going on in other African countries. The students wanted an increase in their monthly allowances of money from the government for going to school, among other things. The next day, the government closed the university and all *lycées* (high schools). Eventually the government agreed to allow a multi-party system in Niger.

In March 1991, I noted that we were rejoicing as we saw answers to prayer in the work. The Goudel Zarma church was now too small, so some people had to sit in the windows during Sunday services. They began to use what little money they had to make bricks for a future building. The youth were encouraged to go out witnessing, which they did with great fear and found God had prepared hearts so that many questions were asked. One young man even publicly prayed to receive Christ as his Savior! After all our years of planting and watering, it was a great encouragement to see some fruit being harvested!

By spring, I had put the first drafts of the entire Dendi New Testament into the computer and printed them for the team to work with. Arlene Spurlock and I did the proofreading of all the drafts I typed into the computer. It was close enough to Zarma that we could usually understand it. What a laugh we got when we read the Dendi word for gossip! They called it *mê tossi* (mouth poop)! In actuality, that is not a bad translation, is it? However, not wanting to put those words in the New Testament, the African translators came up with less vulgar words that could be used in their place!

The Dosso church asked Heath to come back to preach one Sunday and conduct a baptismal. What a joy it was to baptize seven new believers!

Military unrest continued, and the American embassy asked all Americans to lay low. The government was in financial crisis and unable to pay the soldiers.

April was a brutal and exhausting month heat-wise. April 24 was the hottest on record and we were quite exhausted.

The fall of 1991 continued to be unsettled in Niger. The national conference that had been convened in July went on and on for ninety-eight days! They desired a multi-party system which resulted in seventeen political parties being formed, each promoting whom they wanted to be next president. Many wanted the Niger to be declared an Islamic state, but those for democracy won out for freedom of religion. We thanked the Lord for continued open doors for the preaching of the Gospel.

The French schools started a month late that year and the school year would be extended an extra month the next summer. We wondered how that would affect our summer youth camp. There were strikes by hospital staff, students, teachers, police, and the postal and telecommunications systems as well as road blocks by transporters on strike.

A day of mourning was observed because of tribal conflict between the Hausas and the Fulani in East Niger. The herders (Fulani) and farmers (Hausa) are always at odds because the farmers say the herders let their cattle into their field to eat their crops. A Fulani man had killed a Hausa man, so in retaliation, the Hausas killed nine Fulanis. While they were attacking the Fulani men, the Fulani women and children ran to their chief's compound for protection. The houses and fences were constructed of dried grass and were set on fire. Over eighty women and children died. It was very sad.

In contrast, we saw the unity that knowing Christ made in our churches among different tribes. When people are born into God's family and have the same Father, they love each other, no matter what ethnic background they have.

That fall semester, the Evening Bible Institute men were assigned practice preaching. They were nervous about this but did quite well. Heath had had a number of contacts with the mayor and was able to give him a Gospel tract and a Bible. We wrote, "We feel God is really working here in so many ways. One evidence of this is that Satan seems to be trying to wreak havoc, trying to cause divisions and discouragement among believers. May we be ever mindful of our shield of faith and use it!"

Our annual conference was held in January with Dr. Ben Strohben as our main speaker. On Saturday, Mrs. Strohben spoke to all the ladies present. I wrote, "What tremendous blessings we have received from the ministered Word!"

One day, I took Mrs. Strohben with me to the open market where I bought fresh vegetables, fruit, and meat. It was difficult for her to see the piles of fruits and vegetables neatly laid out in piles on the ground and that I had to bargain for each purchase. Bargaining is such a part of Africans' lives, and they really enjoy it.

As I was heading for the part of the meat market where I could buy chunks of meat by the kilo, I had to go through the section where animal entrails, feet, heads, and piles of chopped up bones and meat were laid out for sale. The vendors were continually trying to chase the flies away. I didn't realize what a shock that was for Mrs. Strohben until she told me later, "All the way through there, I was saying over and over, 'Thank you, Lord, for my supermarket at home!'" When living in third-world countries, it helps to have a sense of humor and no sense of smell!

On Sunday, January 12, 1991, a volunteer team arrived to begin building a new Zarma Church. These dear folks took three weeks off from their busy schedules and paid their own way to Niger. We knew they were sent from the Lord for they were such a blessing and help to the Zarma Christians as well as to our missionary force. On Monday morning, Pastor Kommi and the Goudel church folks came to pray with the team as they got started. What a thrill it was to see the footers laid and the walls going up! We enjoyed praying together in the evenings and sharing testimonies with the team

Beth McGeehee, Julie Nunemaker, and I were the cooks for the team. Beth had come down with vomiting less than twenty-four hours after they arrived and was in bed! We usually expected new recruits to be there for about two weeks before they came down with an illness. Getting used to new foods, new water, antimalarial medications, and a myriad of new germs were often the causes.

January 12 was a very frustrating day for Heath as he carried on with all the duties of being field director. He had all kinds of problems with the computer as he tried to enter his Bible institute lessons and homework for the students. It erased about three hours of his work, and he had to redo it. He felt he was under satanic opposition as he was under a lot of busy stress preparing for Evening Baptist Bible Institute, preaching the next Sunday, and renewing a number of residence permits for our coworkers. Then our kitchen faucet broke and wouldn't turn off, so he had to search in the housing storeroom for a faucet to install temporarily. The door on the driver's side of our car stopped working, and we had to crawl in from the passenger side to drive it. Whew! On days like that, one is tempted to ask, "What next?!"

When Beth recovered from her illness, I took her with me to the village to call on my friend, Assibi. The women always welcomed my Bible pictures and stories. Assibi listened so well, and about a dozen children also gathered around to listen. Assibi's baby boy, Jean, was not well and he threw up three times as I was teaching.

After we got back home and I was preparing a couscous dinner for the church builder volunteers, Assibi came to my door in tears and said Jean was getting worse. We gave her money and sent her to the government hospital where Jean was hospitalized immediately.

The next day, I went to the hospital and searched the large pediatrics wards looking for her. It was difficult to see so many seriously ill children. Their moms had mats laid on the floor beside their beds to be there caring for them day and night. The smells in the hospital wards were overpowering. Finally, I found Assibi and Jean. He was in isolation because he had spinal meningitis along with pneumonia. The other ladies in that eight-bed ward told me Assibi and the nurse had a big disagreement because Assibi refused to allow them to give Jean oxygen. The nurse had said, "Okay. If you refuse this, we just won't treat your baby!" The problem was that Assibi was afraid. She had just seen them give oxygen to two children who had died.

I tried my best to explain to Assibi in Zarma what oxygen was and that it was needful. I begged her to go and apologize to the nurse, which she did, and the nurse then agreed to treat baby Jean.

In Niger, those who die are buried quickly. There is no embalming, and because of the heat, the body begins to deteriorate very quickly. The other patients in isolation told me that a little girl was diagnosed as dead, so the nurses told the father to carry her down to the building that served

Norma Bobbett

as the morgue. As they laid her down on the table at the morgue, she woke up and was still alive after all! If this little one hadn't revived when she did, she would have been buried alive. Many wondered if that happened from time to time when the time between death and burial is so short.

The time for the volunteer team working on the Zarma Church building came to an end. Julie Nunemaker's dad, Jim Roberts, flew home and was looking forward to joining his wife, Lois, in Florida. Jim was not feeling well as he started the drive south from New York, and he became critically ill upon arriving in Florida. Jim was hospitalized and treated for over a week for the flu before the doctors realized he had contacted chloroquine-resistant malaria in Niger. The malaria had affected his liver, kidneys, and brain stem. He next developed the complications of blackwater fever (the passage of dark red or black urine and the shutdown of the kidneys). Heath was able to get Julie on a flight to the States the next day. We were reminded that it wasn't good to become complacent about malaria attacks even though we lived with them all the time. Malaria can indeed be a killer.

On February 27, Jim was ushered into the presence of his Savior. This had been Jim's third trip to Niger, and he had endeared himself to all of us. Our hearts grieved for the wife and family of that servant of Christ who were left behind.

I started discipleship classes with Edna, a friend from Ghana whom Heath had led to the Lord, along with her fiancé, Jacob. She was an eager student and a joy to work with. How sad I was one day to find her little son, Martin, with badly burned arms. He had tripped and fallen, walking too close to his mother's cooking fire, resulting in his tipping over the contents and burning his arms. Edna had taken him to the dispensary for treatment and kept a long piece of cloth tied around his neck which draped over his arms to protect them from dirt and from flies. With prayer, Martin amazingly healed well over a period of time, without infection in the burns. Much credit was due Edna who kept his wounds clean and covered.

Easter Sunday, April 19, 1992, was Alan's twenty-ninth birthday. We had been praying for our beloved son for ten years. There seemed to be nothing to be encouraged about, but our loving Father was hearing us and working in ways not visible to us. He was teaching us many things day by day as we cried out to Him for Alan.

"God blessed me with two prodigals. I say blessed because they are a gift, just like every child. Prodigals are an especially precious gift because they teach us much, including patience, the depth of our own need for forgiveness, and continual dependence on God in prayer. When our children bring us to our knees, we're in the best position for God to help us." – Ruth Bell Graham

With Jesus Leading the Way

On Easter, we joined with many expatriates at the amphitheater of our French school for an excellent sunrise service. From there, we went to the Zarma Church service, then walked down to the riverside to see "Tall" Hama baptized. He gave a thrilling and clear testimony about his salvation. In my journal, I wrote, "Lord, please help Hama. The Zarma believers are so alone. Encourage him, I pray, and may the believers rally around him for support."

My dear friend Kano came to tell me that her father had died in their bush village of Touro Bon. As she wept, she said, "I told him the Gospel many times and he always said, *'A ga boori'* ('It's good'), but he never confessed Christ. If he didn't receive Jesus, then I'll never see him again." What heartbreak. All I could do was tell her that only God knows the heart and whether he did believe without her knowledge.

That day, I also had to apologize to a coworker for insensitivity in a matter and hurting her feelings. She was very gracious and thanked me. In my journal, I wrote, "How loving and forgiving my heavenly Father is when I fail. I want to walk in unbroken fellowship with You, Lord, and to be a growing Christian until my life's end. Help me to recognize tendencies toward becoming stagnant and cold! Believing in grace is one thing; living it is another!"

For some time, we had opened an audiovisual center on the field, and we missionaries had pooled our resources, picture Bible stories, flannelgraph materials (which the children loved but were hard for me to use in open air meetings because the wind lifted things off my easel!), records, Braille Bible materials, and so forth. We could check out things we needed for our classes, and the mission's French school teachers used things from the audiovisual center for their daily Bible classes. I was busy translating Biblavision lessons and illustrated Bible lessons into Zarma and enjoyed it very much. An African coworker, "Tall" Hama, went over each lesson I translated to do corrections and add the touches needed by a national before I did the final printouts for our audiovisual center. Even though I was fluent in Zarma, I was aware that I would continue to learn it all the rest of my life! I worked on lessons then used them in my Thursday Bible club.

I was asked by new IMB friends Don and Teresa to help them learn Zarma. They became dear friends to us through the years also. Their single worker also asked me to come to their center to start a weekly children's Bible class. It was so nice to have the children indoors for that class, which often was very large. They loved to sing the Bible songs and listened well to the Bible stories. Almost all were from Muslim homes. We prayed that the Lord would bring in children who would hear and understand about the true God and His Son, Jesus.

Norma Bobbett

As I was traveling to the hospital to call on Assibi and baby Jean, I couldn't get through because the whole hospital intersection (traffic circle) was blocked by police and national guards. I had no choice but to head for home without making the hospital visit. I found out later it was because the unemployed were marching, demanding that all who were from other countries and had jobs be dismissed so that only Niger people could have them.

Beth McGeehee and I did get into the hospital isolation unit the next day, but we found baby Jean much worse, with his head drawn back, eyes glazed from the meningitis. Assibi said he hadn't nursed for the last twenty-four hours. They had him on oxygen and were giving him hydration fluids. We went to a pharmacy and got a prescription filled for him. The next day, Jean was safely in the arms of Jesus. Assibi, like all African women, was stoic about his death. They lose so many infant children and must submit to the will of Allah without complaint.

Jonathan called at the end of January with news about Alan. The years were going by as we cried out in prayer, longing to see our son turn back to the Lord. I knew Satan's fiery darts were aimed at me. "Doubt God...He doesn't answer prayer. He doesn't care." I prayed, "Dear Father, help me to raise the shield of faith! Your Word is true...All things work together for good...Nothing is impossible with You."

Heath woke up about 4:45 one morning and saw a thief with a club or a crow bar outside our bedroom window, about three feet from our heads. The jalousie window was open, and the thief had removed the whole screen frame. The night guard came running when he heard our whistle and followed the footprints in the dirt with his flashlight. He saw where the thief had joined two others and run away. Through the years we had very little problem with thieves, even though we only had flimsy window screens and screen doors or were sleeping outside.

Our second semester class of the Evening Baptist Bible Institute started with Heath teaching a class on personal evangelism. After the basics and Scripture memorization, he lined up African pastors to come and help teach. He figured no one knows better how to reach their people than they do. One night he invited a

Touareg Bible school senior, Ibrahim, and Pastor Nook from Timbuktu to speak to his class. They were in town for a conference. Ibrahim gave his testimony, telling that he used to be in a dance band in Niamey and was brought to Christ by another Touareg named Zeda. Pastor Nook gave the students suggestions for soul winning. They took most of the class time, but Heath and the students really enjoyed them.

More missions and several cults continued to move into Niger. The cults seemed to pursue Christians especially. Because unemployment was such a problem, they lured people with money and jobs. We lost a fine young man because one group paid his way to Rwanda to attend their school and then gave him a job when he returned, selling and distributing their literature. A very legalistic, charismatic church and Jehovah's Witnesses were also pursuing the believers. We asked prayer that the believers would stand firm and search the Scriptures about these various teachings.

Kola Nuts

We encountered the kola nut from day one in Niger. The first senior missionary who gave us many insights into African culture told us that many of her colleagues thought kola nuts were sinful and Christians should refuse them. With tongue in cheek, she also said that these same individuals wouldn't give up their coffee, which had similar effects!

According to Wikipedia, "The kola nut has a bitter flavor and contains caffeine. It is chewed in many West African cultures, individually or in a group setting. It is often used ceremonially, presented to tribal chiefs or presented to guests. It is preferred among African Muslims, who are forbidden to drink alcohol. Chewing kola nut can ease hunger pangs. Frequent chewing of the kola nut can also lead to stained teeth. Among the urban youth of West Africa, kola nut is becoming less popular."

I translated the following from a French newspaper in Niger: "No other commodity exceeds it as a part of West African culture. The kola nut (about the size of a walnut or apricot) is used in many of their ceremonies and is a symbol in Africa. In Niger, it is used to seal social peace among humans and is used at baby naming ceremonies, circumcisions, and marriages. All manifestations punctuating a child's life from birth to death are preceded by distributing kola nuts to friends and neighbors. They are used on the third and fortieth days after a death or after a Koran reading. Kola nuts are used to knot a friendship or renew old sentiments after a falling out of two friends and in reconciliations.

In late February 1992, we heard sporadic gunfire in the night and thought another coup was in progress but learned it was a military mutiny. Their number one complaint was that they hadn't been paid in two months (neither had teachers and many others). They spent the next two days driving amok around the city and shooting into the air.

The airport had reopened so we went ahead and had our Sunday evening English service in town. Not a good idea! The continuing gunfire was especially noisy, and we were all anxious to get home and off the streets.

After the third day of this activity, the unions called for two days of *opération ville morte* (dead city operations). Everything came to a total standstill as offices, schools, markets, transportation, and so forth ceased to function. It was eerie to "hear" the silence of a dead city. Finally, the army returned to their barracks and negotiations began. The situation was fragile at best for the transitional government with its acute financial distress, and we didn't know who would go on strike next.

My dear friend Joyce Lewellyn had started a Bible study in her home for English speaking women. We had women from the States, Canada, Nigeria, Ghana, and Mexico attending. These times together were precious to me. In Africa, I especially loved praying with the African women, whether it was in English, French, or Zarma. They talked to the Lord knowing He was right before them on His throne. Many of the attendees were diplomats' wives or had husbands who worked for the American embassy and USAID. I loved studying and discussing God's Word with those ladies.

The message below is one I have given many times about all the ways the African ladies used their *pagnes*, or *zaaras*, which were two-meter lengths of cloth used as a wrap. They are beautiful illustrations of how the Lord meets our needs also:

Lessons from an African Woman's Cloth Wrapper

Before holidays in Niger, how important it is for the women and girls to have a new outfit for the occasion. The cloth sellers are happy, and business is booming for the tailors who often are found in a shady spot with their treadle machines. Many times, the tailors are up all night sewing to get their items done in time for the ladies.

Before I went to Niger, I had never heard of the wrappers, and yet a wrapper is something that is extremely useful and practical. The Zarmas call this two-meter length of cloth a *zaara*, the French call them a *pagne*, and the Hausa call it a *zane*. African women use them every day of their lives, and its uses are more than I can number.

When I was "mother" accompanying a dear African friend to the maternity for the birth of her baby, the midwife asked me to bring her a *zaara*. She wrapped the baby's placenta in it to give to me. I was told that tradition says if you bury this in the mother's yard, the child will never move far away when he grows up. (Some of us would probably have done this if we thought it would work!) Also it was important the placenta be buried with the cord up and not on the underside. Otherwise the mother will become sterile and have no more children.

Zaaras are used at birth when they are wrapped around newborns in place of a receiving blanket or a swaddling cloth. *Zaaras* are used in death when the body is washed and wrapped for burial.

In thinking about the many uses for a *zaara*, I see in it a beautiful illustration of the Word of God, both the written and the living Word. As we now meditate on a few uses for the *zaara* today, I hope it will make you think of the Lord Jesus Christ and of His Word.

As a garment. The *zaara* is wrapped around a lady for her dress or garment. It is cool and practical. Arrayed in Jesus Christ, I am fitted for service. "I delight greatly in the Lord; my soul rejoices in my God. For he has clothed me with garments of salvation and arrayed me in a robe of his righteousness… (Isaiah 61:10)." Praise God, we can come boldly into His presence, robed in the righteousness of Christ!

As a girdle or belt. In Bible times, they tied up their long robes so they could go into battle or to be able to run unhindered. Zarma ladies do this when they are ready to run or address a difficult task too. Ephesians 6:14 says, "For we wrestle not against flesh and blood, but against principalities, against powers, and against the rulers of the darkness of this world…" Isaiah 11:5 says, "Righteousness will be his belt and faithfulness the sash around his waist." We must go to battle belted with the Word of God and in the righteousness and faithfulness of our Savior.

As a carrier for the baby. It serves as a crib, stroller, and high chair! Mother's breast is there for instant food for a baby (I Peter 2:1). Babies sleep contentedly on their mothers' backs (Psalm 127:2, Isaiah 26:3). Mother lays Baby down on a *zaara* to protect him from dirt and germs. Pull the *zaara* over him as he sleeps to protect him from flies and mosquitos (Psalm 119:11). The Word protects us from the disease and filth of sin.

As a cover at night. Protection from cold or from mosquitos (difficult circumstances). Psalm 20:7 says, "Some trust in chariots and some in horses, but we trust in the name of the Lord our God." We may not understand our circumstances, but we know we are wrapped in His love and care.

As a pillow. Psalm 4:8 says, "In peace I will lie down and sleep, for you alone, O Lord, will keep me safe."

To carry your money (by tying it in a corner). Philippians 4:19 says, "But my God shall supply all your need according to his riches in glory by Christ Jesus."

To carry a load on your head. (Illustration of Boulie and me at her farm.) Psalm 55:22a says, "Cast your cares on the Lord and He will sustain you…" One reason Jesus could say "My burden is light" was because He helps us carry it.

As a bridal canopy. When the bride is taken to her husband, they keep a canopy of a *zaara* over her head. We are the bride of Christ (Revelation 21:2).

The list could go on and on. I hope these have given you some ideas and that in the future when you see a *zaara* being used in one of its many ways, you will think about the Word of God, both written and living, and all God does for us.

During the cool season (late November to early March), the local people grew vegetable gardens along the Niger River in Niamey. I canned a lot of tomatoes and froze carrots and green beans. My shopping day often involved going to the lower market for vegetables, meat, and fruit, then to the European store, Score, for some select things and canned goods. After I stopped at the post office in town to pick up everyone's mail, I went to our Bible bookstore, the "tin shack" (prices for milk and canned goods were lower there than in Score), and last of all to Vultures' Corner. I don't know who gave it that name, but surely it was because of all the sales people there who surrounded us like vultures, urging us to buy from them. Besides fruit, vegetables, and bread, there were many souvenir sales people on that corner too, and they added their aggressive selling techniques to all the other confusion! No matter where I shopped, I was accosted by beggars who made their living in that way.

Going to market in the rainy season was especially challenging. The ground became slippery, slimy, and stinky! In fact, it smelled like a pig pen! Ugh! There were small drainage paths for the rain, but all kinds of things were dropped in there. I'm thankful I never accidentally stepped in one; however, since I usually wore flip flops, there was an occasional situation when I walked where the black mud oozed between my toes! Double ugh!

Another difficult time in the market was during the Muslim celebration of Ramadan, one of the greatest religious observances in Islam. For one lunar month, Muslims do not eat or drink after the predawn prayer call until darkness falls in the evening and the evening call to prayer is given. They are not even supposed to swallow their saliva because this would count as breaking the fast. The result is that they are spitting all day long. More than once, spittle has landed on me and other missionaries in the market, and we never knew when it was an accident or when they were expressing their disgust at seeing an infidel (Christian).

With Jesus Leading the Way

Invitation to a Special Home Celebration at the Birth of a Baby

This was a fun afternoon for me, immersed in the local culture. That afternoon, I picked up the Goudel dispensary major's wife, Hawa. We went to see Aminatou who had a new four-day old son. Aminatou came regularly to the open-air children's classes I had at École Zongo when she was just a child. Now she had five children and was employed as a cashier in a European store in Niamey. She still called me Joie-Joie and introduced me to her friends with that name.

There were about fifty women in the house. The noise of their high-spirited conversations was almost deafening. I was invited with all of Aminatou's coworkers to go into her bedroom. We all ate bread with delicious meat sauce out of two common bowls. Then we drank *jeje*, which consisted of milk, millet, sugar, vanilla, and red pepper. This fourth-day celebration is called Tonka Nwaari (red pepper food) and is for women only. It is to help the new mother regain her strength. They want the new mother to drink and drink it until she perspires! The drink was quite good. I felt so at home among these women as they accepted me and were very friendly. Speaking their language always made a big difference. Along with a baby gift, I gave Aminatou some of the new tracts, "Help from Above" that we had recently translated into Zarma.

New Missionaries in Niger from Nigeria

An indigenous Nigerian organization called Calvary Ministries began working in Niger in the 1980s. This was a new and wonderful experience for us, to have Nigerian young people coming to Niger as missionaries. Calvary Ministries (also called CAPRO) began in Zaria, Nigeria, with a burden to reach out to Muslim people. Melrose was the first young woman to come to Niamey, then others followed. It was interesting for us to see these new missionaries start out with many of the same cultural and language adjustments as we did, although they were Africans. They did not dress the same as the people in Niger, nor did they have the same culture. They had to learn French and Zarma, just as we did. They had been educated in English at the universities they attended. We continued to be good friends with some very special ones who served before our retirement, Melrose and Joseph; George and Flora; and Diji Ladigi.

These young people called us Dad and Mum and thanked us for the foundation our mission's pioneers had constructed for them to build on. They were especially excited about our translating the Bible into the Zarma language. They attended our English services on Sunday evenings and became very dear to us.

Heath was asked to speak at a Calvary Ministries conference on spiritual warfare. When he asked how long his message should be, they replied, "One and a half hours, unless you need more time!" How many preachers would like to be given that much time to speak! He gave an excellent message on "The Warfare, The Warriors, and The Weapons."

When we came in from a bush station, attending the English services on Sunday evenings often brought tears to our eyes. We had truly missed the privilege of singing English hymns and enjoying the fellowship. Except in our home, there were almost no occasions to speak English in Gaya and Dosso.

I continued with my open-air children's Bible club at Zongo primary school on Thursdays. I noted once that the children's ages were from three months old to fifteen years old! One week, we were under a log-framed support that kept all the stacks of animal food high enough that the animals couldn't reach them. It was cool there, and it was a shelter from the heat. After we had sung the last song and the children left, the whole thing collapsed! How we thanked the Lord for keeping it up while all the children were there. They could have been seriously hurt or even smothered under the load that fell.

The ministry and everyday duties kept us very busy. Heath came down with another attack of Ménière's disease. The dizziness, nausea, and vomiting always put him flat in bed until the attack was over. I don't know how he kept going after those attacks. It seemed that this was going to be something he would have to deal with all of his life.

Jofo, the faithful Fulani gardener for many years on the Yantala-Goudel station, came to tell us that a hippopotamus had killed a man on the Niger River that ran behind our house. Two men were returning home in their dugout canoe at night when the hippo broke their boat in two. The men tried to escape in different directions, but the hippo followed one. The next day, his horribly mangled body was found at the small dam behind our house. The island people asked the forestry ministry to kill the hippo, but they weren't been able to find it. Jofo was concerned because he thought it might be at the water pumping station where he parked his dugout canoe each morning as he came to work.

Speaking of Jofo, a sweet mild-mannered man who never gave any trouble to any of the missionaries…we were told by missionaries who preceded us in Niger that he made a profession of faith in Christ many years before when he was a young man. When his Muslim family found out, they beat him severely and told him he could not be a Christian. We hoped and prayed that Jofo sincerely knew Christ. He always listened and agreed when we talked to him about the Lord, and we never ever saw him saying Muslim prayers.

We will never forget the time during my absence that our pretty, long-haired white cat, Frosty, disappeared. Jofo helped Heath look everywhere

– in the house, in our storeroom – but she never responded to their calls or was found. A couple of days later, our neighbor came to tell Heath that the cat was on top of their metal roof. Evidently, she had climbed a tree, dropped down on the roof, then was unable to reach the tree again to descend. Jofo got a ladder to rescue her. Heath said she was so dehydrated from two days on that hot roof with no water that she almost buried her head in her water dish, drinking and drinking! Jofo seemed as happy as Heath was at finding Frosty.

A policeman came to Heath one Sunday evening after our English service, wanting 7,000 francs. He said he took a government service car out of the city (which is illegal), had a flat, and ruined a tire he must replace. Heath told him he had no money, but if he would come the next day he could give him a used tire we had.

In the middle of the night, Heath again became very ill with Ménière's disease. He was incapacitated and unable to hold down any food or water all the next day. The policeman came and was angry that Heath was sick and couldn't see him. Although the whole eastern sky, from high up and down to the horizon, looked threatening and I could tell a sandstorm was coming, I left at 6:30 p.m. to go to the Yantala pharmacy to see if I could get some suppositories to stop Heath's nausea and vomiting. That small pharmacy had no suppositories, and because of the threatening sky, the workers were anxious to close up.

The wind struck with force, and the blowing sand stung my arms and legs as I ran for the car. Within thirty seconds, it was as black as midnight. Animals were confused and crying. I sat in the car, rocked by the high wind for ten minutes and then foolishly decided to drive home in the blackness. Headlights, on bright or dim, were of no help. Though I thought I was on the road, some dips and ruts made me realize I was not, so I finally stopped and waited. When the sandstorm began to abate, I saw I was off the road and would soon have plunged down into an open culvert had I continued in the blackness! Surely the Lord had His angels watching over me! As the road slowly became visible, I inched my way home slowly while thanking the Lord for His amazing watch care. News reports that evening said there were some serious accidents.

Traditional Healers Called "Bone-Setters"

Segdi had broken his leg, so the doctors at the hospital put him in a cast. He sent his wife to us, asking for food. I gave her 1,000 francs, then during the rest hour, Jofo and I went to the market to buy five kilos of rice and a twenty-five-kilo bag of millet to take to them. The hospital staff had to take his cast off because his leg was swelling and draining. Segdi decided to see a traditional bone-setter. A few days later, his wife came to thank us for the food and money. She said the African bone-setter already had Segdi on his feet, walking with canes! These bone-setters are quite actually quite good. The bones might not always heal straight, but they healed quickly. The bone-setters often had the patient up and walking long before the medical doctors did.

I was asked to teach the Bible lessons to 129 first- and second-graders (my favorite age group) during Bible week at the close of our French school's VBS. We met under a shade tree, and the children were surprisingly attentive. My lessons were about Jesus and the children, Onesimus and Philemon, and Naaman and the little slave girl.

June 16, 1992, was our thirty-seventh wedding anniversary. Heath was very involved that week working with the Dendi Bible translation and also preparing a message to preach the next Sunday. So instead of going out to eat, we treated ourselves to two fresh artichokes from Score. We hadn't had them in years, and they were delicious! They came from France to Niger and were not only large but expensive. We have never found those big yummy artichokes in the States.

On the Fourth of July in Niger, we were usually invited to a more formal reception at the American ambassador's residence the night before with African diplomats and Niger government ministers. At that reception, a man came over to introduce himself to us. It was Joseph Diatta, the *douanier's* (customs officer's) son from Gaya. He remembered coming to our Thursday Bible club and also playing volleyball in our yard! Now he held a high government position. In later years, Joseph was appointed Niger's ambassador to Washington and to the United Nations! We called him once to chat, and he still remembered us from his childhood in Gaya.

On July 10, Assibi told me she had accepted Jesus Christ as her Savior after I told her the Gospel story! *Maadalla!* Praise God! I prayed for her to understand clearly and that I could help her grow in Christ and learn to read. She tried hard in the literacy classes I had with her, always interjecting the comment, "Madame, you must be patient with me. Remember I am just a bush girl!" Then she would smile her beautiful smile. She had had such a hard life. After each reading lesson, I had a Bible study with her. One Sunday, she said to me, "Madame, thank you for showing me the way to Jesus. You've put me on the good path!" These were precious words to my heart.

Encouragement from the Word

"'Not by might nor by power, but by my Spirit' says the Lord Almighty (Zechariah 4:6)." This mountain shall be removed.

"If your task is to trust God to do an impossible construction job in your life, your family, your job, or some other demolished area, *remember*, God delights in rolling up His sleeves for just such projects because 'He is able to do exceedingly abundantly beyond all that we ask or think, according to the power that works in us.'" – Anonymous

Unrest continued in Niger. The government was broke and three months behind in paying their workers. Fanatical Muslims were stirring up trouble. Bands of young men sometimes grabbed African women and girls in public places, ripping their clothes off and beating them, saying the rains weren't coming because women were wearing short skirts, plaiting false hair into their own, and so forth.

Two Peace Corps volunteers were mugged in the museum parking lot in broad daylight by five thugs with knives. They took the volunteers' backpacks, jewelry they had just bought to take back to the States, and money. When one fellow tried to resist them, his hands were cut by the knives. A SIM missionary was attacked in broad daylight in Niamey too. Five guys cut his trouser pocket with a knife, removed his wallet, and left. There was a rebel attack between Arlit and Agadez, and the village chief was killed. Two large trucks, loaded with grain, were burned. We had never known of crime and insecurity to be so bad before in Niger.

The American embassy warned all Americans to be especially cautious because of the political uncertainties in Niger. They said to never walk within the radius of the Kennedy Bridge, Damsi Restaurant, or the upper or lower markets. However, I wasn't afraid of going to the lower market, believing my friends there would come to my defense if anything happened. Many times, I was probably the only "European" in the lower market.

In September 1990, we were very happy to welcome missionary colleagues Harold and Charlene Curtis back to Niger. They had remained in the States for five years to spend time with their children during the important teen years. They were planning to reopen the Filingué station that had been closed for years. Since there were more Hausa people than Zarmas in Filingué, they planned to study and learn Hausa too.

I had fun teasing Charlene. They had gone to France for language study with two small children, Andy and Caryn. While they were studying French, Charlene became pregnant with Timothy. Soon after they arrived in Niger to study Zarma, she became pregnant with Jonathan and declared, "I'm not learning any more languages because every time I do, I get pregnant!" Now she was willing to learn a new language because she was beyond childbearing years!

Attendance was running about 150 again at Pastor Luc's Gourma church. Pastor Luc said, "God has wiped away our tears!" The next Sunday, we took Harold and Charlene to the Dosso church where they had spent a number of years. How thrilled we were to see the church full! One little boy who had been so active and disruptive in my children's classes, was an adult and teaching children's Sunday school! May the Lord help us to see the potential that is there in the little ones we teach.

September 16 was Rebecca's thirty-sixth birthday. Heath called his mother who was ninety-two that day. Lena Bobbett was in amazing health, taking no prescription medications and only a vitamin each day!

A Peace Corps girl, Deborah, spent four days with us in October. She was in Niger to help in the nutritional care of children at Torodi, Niger, and was going through some difficult times of adjustment. One evening, we took her out to enjoy brochettes and fries on the terrace of the Damsi Restaurant. During our conversation, she asked me to tell her how I became a Christian! This was a fantastic opportunity and an answer to prayer. I prayed that my words would be used by the Holy Spirit to bring Deborah to Himself. What a thrill that she was ready a few weeks later, and our good friend Pat Lewellyn led her to Christ!

A new missionary couple arrived in October with their four small children, ages nine down to six weeks. It was a busy time for us getting their apartment ready and helping them to adapt to life in Africa. It had been thirty-two years since we were new missionaries being oriented by our field director, Bob Richards. However, we did our best to remember to teach them how to shop and bargain in the open market, washing all fruits and vegetables in soapy Clorox water, brushing their teeth with filtered water, sleeping under mosquito nets, "flaming" their French bread over a burner since it had been handled many times in the market and had no wrapper, and so forth. After that initial time, I began regular classes with them to teach them Zarma.

In November, our good friend, Sue Rosenfeld, asked if I would come and speak to her class of Boston University students who were to be in Niger for a semester. They were to study French and Hausa as well as other subjects. This was a social studies class on expatriates in Niger. Sue talked about the embassy, USAID, Peace Corps, and so forth. I talked about missionaries and what they do. It was scary because I didn't know how the class of two guys and ten girls would react.

Actually, they were quite respectful and curious! I took along a copy of our Bible translated into Zarma that they passed around to look at. In the time of taking questions, one girl asked me what my main reason for being in Niger was, and I said, "to win people to Christ." One of their local professors from Goudel was also present. He was interested in the Zarma Bible, and I later got one to give to him.

Often our days were made up of constant interruptions. It was easy to become frustrated, but then I needed to be reminded of Jesus, who when interrupted looked on them with compassion and welcomed them. One day, a blind friend, Seydou, asked me to write a thank-you letter for him, Laya's aged aunt came from Tondi Biya wanting clothes, and Amina came wanting milk for her baby. The list of folks continued, and it seemed I couldn't get anything else accomplished that day. How important it is to commit each moment of our day to our heavenly Father. Then we won't have disruptions, but we will have opportunities!

1 Samuel 7:12 says, "Then Samuel took a stone and set it up between Mizpah and Shen. He named it Ebenezer (Stone of Help), saying 'Thus far the Lord has helped us.'" How important it was for me to live by the Ebenezer principle, storing up memories of past mercies whenever reassurance about God's help is concerned!

One of Evangelist Cecekoy's daughters, Rahilla, had married a wonderful Christian man, Issaya, and we were so pleased with their stand for the Lord. We were saddened when he was killed in a car accident after a tire blew out. Some of our missionaries as well as the Zarma Pastor and his wife went with Heath to break this sad news to Rahilla's parents.

Custom dictated that Rahilla had to stay with her in-laws for forty days, then they came to her house and took everything they wanted of Issaya's things. It was always hard for us to understand why the widow didn't get those things.

From October 13 to 15, there was a postal and telecommunications strike. We had no phone, fax, telex, or mail. (We hadn't even heard of e-mail back in those days.) We felt cut off from the rest of the world.

I had sixty children that week in children's JOY Club. There was a good number of older boys and girls (fourteen to sixteen years old). Since I didn't know if they would be there the next week, I felt I should try to make the way of salvation very clear. They were extremely quiet and attentive. How I prayed that my heavenly Father would speak to their hearts and that some from these classes would spend eternity with us in heaven.

One day as I was shopping in a store in Niamey, two women greeted me with big smiles and called me "Joie-Joie". By that greeting, I always knew they had attended my Thursday open-air children's classes at Yenurou's compound when they were young. They made me happy when they said, "Please come back and teach our children!"

We had no idea of the marvelous experience the Lord was preparing for us when we arrived back in the States in December for a short break. How good of our God to often only reveal the next step for us to take by faith. What we know for sure is that He is always with us, and He works all things together for His glory and for our good.

I AM
by Helen Mallicoat

I was regretting the past and fearing the future.
Suddenly my Lord was speaking: "My name is I AM.
When you live in the past, with its mistakes and regrets,
it is hard. I am not there. My name is not I Was.
When you live in the future, with its problems and fears,
it is hard. I am not there. My name is not I Will Be.
When you live in this moment, it is not hard.
I am here. My name is I AM."

Chapter 27
Answered Prayer and Continued Ministry
December 1992 to December 1993

"Bring the fattened calf and kill it. Let us have a feast and celebrate, for this son of mine was dead and is alive again; he was lost and is found!"
Luke 15:23-24

"For I know the plans I have for you," declares the LORD, "plans to prosper you and not to harm you, plans to give you hope and a future."
Jeremiah 29:11

How excited we were to return to the States for a short break, to take care of dental needs and medical appointments, but most of all to be with our children and grandchildren.

We knew Alan was living in Indianapolis, and we wanted to see him while we were home. For eleven years, we had been crying out to God for our beloved son. So many times, when I was overwhelmed by discouragement and even despair, Heath would encourage me to continue to trust God and to believe He was hearing our prayers. Other times, when Heath was discouraged, I was able to help him with words from the Lord.

Family Christmas was held at Rebecca's that year. Alan came for a few hours on Christmas Day. It meant so much to me and his dad, to hug him and hold him in our arms for a few seconds. He was so thin and looked much older than his twenty-nine years. Our hearts were desperately praying, "Lord Jesus, please bring our son back to You!"

After Christmas, I talked to Alan again and told him how much we wanted to see him once more before we headed back to Niger in January. He promised us he would come to see us on New Year's Day, but much to our disappointment, he didn't show up.

God's Networking!

Heath's sister Shirley called us on New Year's Day to wish us a happy New Year. When she asked if we had seen Alan and how he was, I shared with her how discouraged I was. Shirley said, "Well, I just wanted to tell you something to encourage you. It's about my best friend's son Paul. He is about Alan's age and had the same problems. He got into a program called Dunklin in Florida and is doing very well. He has even continued there as a cook after he finished the six-month program." I thanked Shirley for telling me those encouraging words about Paul.

What is Dunklin? Dunklin Memorial Camp was founded by Mickey and Laura Maye Evans in 1962 in a wilderness area of Martin County, Florida, for the purpose of building a "city" for the spiritual, emotional, and physical regeneration of alcoholics and drug addicts. The Webster dictionary defines "refuge" as a shelter or protection from danger or distress. The "City of Refuge" concept was born out of the vision from God.

According to Dunklin's website, "Our belief is that the Christian approach to alcoholism and drug addiction produces the most effective and enduring results. As seeds are planted they begin to take root and are nurtured until they begin to bear fruit.

"Men started arriving at the camp with the goal of sobriety and found that they could achieve more than just a sober lifestyle. They soon found a permanent, lasting relationship with God. They were no longer considered 'the problem' but now a solution to that problem.

"We saw that the families of the men in the program needed healing too, and we encouraged them to participate in groups and Biblical counseling sessions every weekend. Each member of the family receives guidance and spiritual instruction in the rebuilding of family life.

"As a result, Dunklin Memorial Camp has become a growing recovery community with a thriving local church body and ministry training center. The idea is being replicated in the U.S. and overseas."

On January 2, 1993, Alan called us, and we talked and talked. I could sense that he was not anxious to hang up, so finally I asked, "Alan, would you like for Dad and me to come to see you now?"

"Yes," he replied!

We rushed to where he was living, and we found our son very sober and subdued. I began to tell him about Dunklin and that I had only heard about it the day before. We asked him if he would consider going there, to which he answered, "I'll go." We knew this had to be a God thing!

Roadblock!

When Alan called Dunklin, they said they had a long waiting list and weren't even able to take in all who were applying in Florida, let alone another state. Our hearts sank. Would God bring Alan to this point knowing the door would be closed? When we called Arlene Rox to tell her, she replied, "Honey, just get him down there! If he shows up on their doorstep, they won't send him away!"

Jonathan said he would fly down with Alan. Our time in the States was drawing to a close, and our tickets were non-refundable. We had to reluctantly say goodbye to our family and leave for Niger on January 11, 1993. As we put our arms around Alan, he said, "The next time you see me, I will be a new man." We left with hearts full of thankfulness to the Lord for what He was doing in Alan's life.

Alan and Jonathan flew to West Palm Beach, Florida, and drove to isolated Dunklin in the swamps near Lake Okeechobee. There Alan was interviewed by Director Hugh Morrow, who had lived on the streets of Atlanta, Georgia, as an addict before God turned his life around. Jonathan said Hugh's questioning of Alan was so severe it brought Alan to tears.

Alan had been very honest in filling out the papers for getting into Dunklin. One of the questions was, "Are there any outstanding warrants for your arrest?" Alan had two DWIs. Hugh said Dunklin was not a place to hide from the law. But then he put his arms around Alan and said, "Son, you go back to Indiana and take care of these problems with the law, then you can come back and begin our program. I will do everything I can to help you."

When Alan and Jon arrived back in Indiana, Alan turned himself in and was put in jail. Jon, ever the lover of his family and compassionate helper, contacted a lawyer. Alan appeared before two different judges to face charges for those DWIs. In both cases, the judges agreed to release him if he was sincerely going to enroll in the Dunklin program! Off Alan went again to Florida and began the program!

We saw again that nothing is too difficult for the Lord! How much better it would have been for me if I had just trusted our powerful God when seemingly insurmountable circumstances came up. Instead of my distress and worry, I should have said, "Father, I just can't wait to see what You are going to do with Alan's situation!"

"Even when nothing is happening, with God something is happening!" Jesus said in John 5:17, "My Father has been working until now, and I have been working."

We were back in Niger, cherishing every letter we got from Alan and praying, praying, praying for God to accomplish His good work in every area of his life.

Heath was continuing to have difficult problems with the Ménière's disease in his ear. There was lots of stress involved in being field director, and it was really sad to see him down with the room spinning, unable to walk because of the vertigo, and then overpowered by nausea. The disease was destroying more and more of the hearing in his left ear. As soon as an attack was over, he went right back to his heavy work schedule.

I was busy creating lessons and helping our newest missionaries learn the Zarma language. So often we have noted that women get the languages quicker than the men, and the men can become quite discouraged. Dr. Hutchings had told me years earlier that little girls talk much earlier than boys also. I tried to encourage the men in language study to hang in there because they would catch up with their wives later.

My open-air children's classes in Yenourou and Yabidi's yard was running between forty and fifty in attendance. A friend had written from the States, saying she had noticed in a picture that most of my JOY club consisted of boys, so she was praying we would have more girls. This year the class was made up of about half boys and half girls! The effectual fervent prayers of God's people accomplish great things!

I was also kept busy managing our mission guest house, not only seeing that the rooms were cleaned and ready for the next occupants but also keeping the guest house books. With guests coming and going, there was never a dull moment – and often never a rest hour either, which was so needful in desert climates.

Daouda, whom we had kept and nursed back to health when he was brought to us in 1964 as a month-old baby weighing only four pounds, was becoming very ill. He was hospitalized experiencing shingles, joint pain, diarrhea, and a high fever. AIDS (SIDA in French) was almost unknown in Niger at that time, but men who traveled to other coastal countries were coming back with it and giving it to their wives. Soon it was being diagnosed in people who had never been out of the country. Daouda had spent time in Cameroons and was not living for the Lord. While he was in the hospital he was diagnosed with AIDS. We received word that he was dying. The hospital patients or their families had to buy their own medications. It was heartbreaking for us to see him reduced to skin and bones. We went to the pharmacy with his prescription to get IV feedings for him. The hospital employees even had to ask Heath to buy the tubes for the IV.

Kano was so faithful in caring for Daouda, reading Scriptures to him – which he wanted – and talking to him about the Lord. He said he was a believer in Jesus Christ, so she told him no one who had seen the way he had been living lately would have known. He replied, "If I get well, everyone will see my life and then know I am a Christian." We hoped and prayed that was true.

Daouda died at the age of 29. After Pastor Kommi preached the funeral service for Daouda in Kano and Soumana's compound, we ladies stayed with Kano while the men took the body to be buried. I read Psalm

23 and Psalm 91 in Zarma. Kano had a marvelous testimony in the way she cared for Daouda, even with all she had been going through. She loved the Lord and clung to Him. We prayed for the Lord to comfort, help, and strengthen her.

In March Nadine and I drove two carloads of women to Dosso for our ladies' retreat. I wrote, "The conference was wonderful! We received a warm welcome from the Dosso Church ladies, and the fellowship and food were very special. I was asked to translate from Zarma to English for three English high school teachers who were there.

We had been thrilled that the government television station (only one channel broadcasting just in the evening hours at the beginning) had allowed us to air the Hausa and the French versions of The Jesus Film on Easter and Christmas Eve. Heath began to be burdened to have The Jesus Film be produced in the Zarma language, and he started the ball rolling for this to become a reality. He found out that a large sum of money was needed to have this done, and as he brought the idea to our field council, we realized we would need help to raise these funds. What a thrill it was when both the SIM and IMB missions agreed to help us raise these funds.

Our retirement from Niger came before the process of producing the Zarma version started, but Steve Nunemaker and others continued the work and brought it to completion. When Steve brought home a copy of the DVD for us and we heard Jesus speaking Zarma, we could not hold back the tears of joy! Probably more Nigeriens heard the Gospel through this project that Heath had spearheaded than through any other evangelization effort up to that time.

Looking back on my activities each day makes me shake my head and wonder how I ever did it! April 15, 1993, I said, "Whew, another full day! I ran errands for Heath in the morning, came home, baked a "scratch" cake, had a visiting missionary for lunch, taught a Zarma language class, had class for a missionary who want to learn Zarma greetings and numbers, went to the American Women's Club tea, then finished preparing for my language class the next day!"

Heath was asked to accompany Pastor Luc to Dosso for a wedding. Luc performed the ceremony, and Heath gave the message for the new couple. We decided to stay, for the first time, in Dosso's only hotel, Hotel Djerma. It was very old and in need of much repair. I took our own linens and pillows and lots of bug spray! One of the glass panels in the door was broken and missing, so it was rather useless to lock it. There was an old air-conditioner in the room, but about all it accomplished was noise!

The church was packed for the wedding, with many market women who knew Dieyabidi and Kwampwa. They would never have entered the church for any other reason. When Heath preached in the Sunday morning service the attendance was over one hundred! When we thought of the small group that were there when the Curtises and we first worked in Dosso, we could only say, "The Lord hath done great things for us whereof we are glad!"

Jon and Judy called for Mother's Day and let us know they had taken over temporary custody of three-year-old Ryan Bobbett, Alan's son. They weren't sure where his mother Shelley was, but she had left Ryan with a friend and then left town. Shelley's parents had called from Canada, asking that someone take Ryan away from this woman. When we expressed concern for Judy taking on this large responsibility, she came on the line and said she was very willing, wanting Ryan to be where he will hear the Gospel. Alan called and wept as he thanked them for doing this. He was still doing well in the program at Dunklin.

Jon had visited Alan at Dunklin the Sunday before and reported that Alan had gained weight, and he had never seen Alan so relaxed before. Of the sixteen men who entered Dunklin with Alan, only nine were still in the program. We praised and thanked the Lord for what He was doing.

It was an occasion of great joy when over one hundred were present for our Bible Institute graduation of Rabo and Hama.

For months I had been suffering much tooth pain and taking a lot of ibuprofen. The dentist in Niger told me the problems were beyond her ability to care for and told me I must go to the States. She gave me antibiotics and more pain pills to take on the plane in case things got worse. What a mess Dr. Richard Gillum found, with badly positioned crowns, decay underneath and also under a bridge, all done by the dentist in DeWitt, New York years earlier. I spent hours in the dentist's chair in Indianapolis during our time home so he could do root canals and new crowns and pull my last wisdom tooth. I also needed to see a dermatologist about a suspicious spot on my face.

Alan's Graduation from Dunklin

Jon drove us to Dunklin in Florida where we found Alan, smiling, healthy, and in love with his Lord. I'll never forget little Ryan running into his Daddy's arms and the happiness on both their faces. The testimonies of many of the men at Dunklin during the graduation were a real blessing. Alan told them, "If you have a praying mother and grandmother, you might as well give up and surrender to God. He hears their prayers!" I'm sure he knew that he also had a godly praying dad who wept many tears over him. We enjoyed a few days celebrating at Disney World. Little Ryan's eyes were constantly on his daddy and he wanted to be carried all the time.

Back in Indianapolis when the dermatologist's biopsy of a spot on my eyelid turned out to be basal cell carcinoma, he sent me to a plastic surgeon for the delicate surgery. My children then teased me about having a "facelift!"

That summer of 1993 Nathan went on a short-term mission trip to Odessa, Ukraine. As singles pastor at Community Church of Greenwood, he didn't feel he should date any of the girls in the group, but there were a number of them who had crushes on him! God wanted him still single for a while longer!

Heath was hospitalized from August 29 to September 3. He hadn't been feeling well for several days, having fever, chills, and aching. We treated him for malaria, but he didn't get better. At the Community Hospital ER they diagnosed him immediately with a bladder infection and hospitalized him. The medical staff said in a man of his age a UTI could move quickly into the kidneys and become life threatening. He was put on intravenous antibiotics, but it took five days for his fever to come down.

September 5, 1993, was our beautiful little granddaughter Laura's sixth birthday. Alan and Ryan were living with Jon and Judy at the time. Ryan, at three-and-a-half and Laura were both protective of their own toys. We all laughed one day as Laura eyed a toy of Ryan's and he said, "Don't even fink (think) about it!"

None of us knew where Shelley, Ryan's mother, was during the time we were in the States. When we arrived back in Niamey there was a message from Rebecca telling us to call home. It was a shock to hear that not long after we left Indianapolis, the family had received the news that Shelley had died suddenly while she was living in Memphis, Tennessee.

Our hearts went out to little Ryan. He had suffered so many challenges and insecurities already in his short life.

Daniel Rands

We became acquainted with Barry and Janine Rands when they were serving with World Vision in Mali. Barry then took a job with USAID, and they were stationed in Niamey. After many years of being married with no children, Janine was treated and became pregnant. She returned to the States for the birth of their sweet, adorable son, Daniel. We were so happy for them, and when they returned, I got to be his "grandma" in Niger since his grandparents were far away in the States. I can honestly say I have never met a more adorable, well behaved little fellow in my life. Soon after he was walking and beginning to talk, he always greeted me with "Hi, Gamma!"

Barry and Janine were blessed with another baby boy, Timothy, before Daniel was two. On October 27, 1993, we had a lovely evening of dinner and fellowship at their home. Six days later, we learned that Daniel was being rushed to the Gamkalley Clinic after falling unnoticed into the Rands's' swimming pool. We rushed down to the clinic to be with Barry and Janine as the medical personnel worked gallantly to try to revive Daniel, but it was to no avail. He was already gone. I will never forget hearing Barry's sobs. It was heartbreaking, and we all wept with him and Janine. It was so hard trying to understand why the Lord had only "loaned" Daniel to them for such a short time.

Daniel's memorial service was held on November 4 on the American ambassador's back lawn. Heath had the opportunity to give the Gospel to about three hundred people of many different nationalities. Barry and Janine held up wonderfully, and we knew so many were praying for them. Barry wrote such a touching poem for Daniel. They asked others to speak about Daniel and what he meant to us.

The American embassy arranged to send Daniel's body back home to Salem, Oregon, and asked them to choose someone to accompany them. Barry and Janine asked if I would go with them. Our plane left Niamey at noon on November 6. We had an overnight in Paris on our way to the States and were housed in the Paris airport's Sofitel Hotel. The next morning, Barry shared with us that his Bible reading that morning was about Jesus and his parents in the temple. What impressed him was that Joseph and Mary also went through the anguish of not knowing where their son was for a time. It was such a short time that Daniel escaped the watchful eyes of his parents and friends.

The United Airlines staff were so very kind to us. They seated Barry and Janine in first class and me nearby in business class so I could help with baby Timothy. I walked the plane aisles carrying the baby to keep him content and to give Barry and Janine time alone. In Portland we were met by Janine's dad, Willard Kennel, who drove us to Salem. I was immediately drawn to Janine's mom, Mae Etta Kennel, a lovely, motherly woman who still wore the sheer cap of the Mennonite women.

After Daniel's funeral Barry and Janine didn't think baby Timothy should go to the cemetery because of the wind and cold so I stayed at the church with him. The next day, Barry and Janine drove me out to see Daniel's gravesite on a hillside. When people used to ask Daniel how old he was, he would say, "Two old years!" Barry ordered the marker to say:

Daniel William Rands
October 26, 1991 – November 2, 1993
Two old years – Full of joy

How do you comfort and help parents who have gone through such a tragedy? There are no words that could help, and often it is just best to go and sit with the parents, sharing their grief and tears. An excellent book was recommended by Focus on the Family: *Sunrise Tomorrow* by Elizabeth B. Brown. I borrowed it, read it, and took many notes in my 1993 journal.

Barry and Janine stayed in the States until after Thanksgiving. I visited our children before returning to Niger. At that time, Nathan was studying for his master's degree at Trinity Evangelical School of Divinity near Chicago. Rebecca, Jon and Alan were all living in the Indianapolis area.

On my flight back to Niger I carried a frozen turkey in my hand luggage to have on hand for when Rebecca, Nansie, Sarah, and Ryan came at Christmas. We were really excited about their upcoming visit! As my hand luggage went through the X-ray machine on the conveyor belt, the man stopped the belt and moved it back to look again. A lady inspector came to look too, then declared with a laugh, "Yep, she's got a turkey in there!" They let me go through!

It was so good to be back with Heath again in Niger. I didn't like traveling alone, and he didn't like staying home alone! On Thanksgiving Day, we had twenty-two people together in our old dormitory/guest house for dinner. We had a great time and played games in the afternoon and then watched two videos. Earlier in the day, Heath had been asked by the ambassador's wife, Jacqueline Cundiff, to speak at the ambassador's residence celebration. We heard later that some embassy folks objected to his giving the Gospel, saying that missionaries try to cram their religion down people's throats. Heath was determined not to compromise the Bible message whenever he was asked to preach.

Check Fraud!

Heath had been constantly running to the notaries and lawyers, trying to finalize our mission's legal documents in order to turn over mission property to the Gourma Church and others. He called me at 6:30 p.m. on December 6 to say he was delayed and still waiting at the lawyer's office and also to inform me that he got our November bank statement from Bank One in the States and learned that someone had forged a fake check for $3,000 on our account!

Heath called Jonathan's office and also sent a fax to the bank saying, "*Urgent! Fraudulent check,*" with a photocopy of the check and information. Jonathan called back the next night (midnight our time). The check had been made out to a mail order place called Computek. The forger had sent a $10,000 check from someone else's account and another from our account for $7,000. That one bounced! He had ordered seventeen computers to be sent to Nigeria, and they were at the airport to be shipped. Interpol and the FBI were investigating. We hoped they caught the thief.

No one in Niger had access to our checkbook, but we did write four checks in April to a departing American for things she sold to us. She said she could cash them at the American embassy. We figured the crook probably was an African employee in the finance department there who had washed our checks and made them out anew. We were very thankful that the bank did not hold us liable. They closed our account and opened a new one for us.

Visitors from the States!

On Sunday, December 19, at 5:00 a.m., we welcomed Rebecca, Nansie, Sarah, and Ryan to Niger. It was like a dream to have them with us! We let them sleep until noon, then we all went to the American Recreational Center so they could see the annual tradition of Santa Claus arriving on a camel. (Santa was usually played by one of the American Marines stationed in Niger.) Our Sunday evening English service included lots of special music for Christmas, and we all enjoyed it.

Rebecca had been absent from Niger for seventeen years, so she was surprised when her French came back to her on the Air France flight and her Zarma when she got to Niger.

They had quite an adventure during their layover in Paris! I'll let Rebecca narrate this in her own words: "We had about an eleven-hour layover in Paris, so we wanted to see it all. We checked into a hotel (after flying all night) and slept for a couple hours, then headed out to see the city. We left our luggage and extra bags locked up and took a cab to all the famous sights.

"We walked up the Champs-Elysées and saw the Arc de Triomphe then dashed over to the Eiffel Tower and all the way to the top! The kids mostly climbed the stairs while I rode the elevator (and were their calves ever sore the next day)! After that, we went to Notre-Dame Cathedral. Then it was lunchtime, so we found a little café next to the Seine River. I did not have a lot of cash with me, but I decided to get a really good lunch, thinking I would just use a credit card.

"After our meal, I reached for my credit card only to find that I had left it in our bags at the hotel! Oh dear, what in the world was I going to do? I tried to explain the situation to the owner of the café. I told him I would return in about an hour with my credit card, and I left my camera with him as security.

"My problem then was that I didn't have enough cash for all four of us to ride the subway back and forth and still be able to afford the bus tickets to get us all back to the airport to catch our flight to Niger. So we hurried back to the hotel, grabbed all our stuff and took the bus to the airport. I gave the kids their tickets and said 'If I don't come back, just get on the plane and go to Grandma. That way at least I will know that you are safe!'

"I can't describe the feeling I had when the bus drove away from the airport and I left my children behind. I rode the bus back to town and got dropped off near Notre-Dame to try to find the café again. The owner still had my camera. I paid for our meal, thanked him profusely, and dashed out to the subway because at this point I didn't have enough money to ride the bus again. I was all alone and scared to death! So I sang hymns and quoted Bible verses out loud in English, hoping everyone on the subway would think I was crazy and leave me alone.

"It seemed to work, and I made it safely back to the area where the airport shuttles were. Don't ask me how I figured out where I was going each time I got on a bus or subway. It had to be the Lord who was looking out for me. I finally made it back to the airport with about forty-five minutes to spare before we had to board our flight for Niger.

"I was so relieved to see all three kids standing and waiting for me where all the airport shuttles parked. Nansie was fourteen, so I knew I could trust her to take care of her brother and sister. I am sure they were relieved to see me too. I later learned they had watched five or six other shuttles arrive and were starting to worry about me too. I certainly was in tears when we were finally all together again. How could I have planned so poorly and put my children and myself in that position? I felt terrible and thanked God over and over again for taking care of us even when I had made some very poor decisions and had not planned very well."

Norma Bobbett

I had made a list of things we hoped to do during Rebecca and the children's visit:
- Trip to Dosso
- Visit the big market
- Christmas at the Zarma Church
- New Year's celebration
- Going out to see the giraffe (The Lewellyns took us in their four-wheel drive car.) Ryan was thrilled to ride on top of the car with the guide.
- A camel ride (The camel owner was very nice and patient with the kids. He wanted to be in all the pictures too!)
- Visit the zoo and museum (The children encountered a lion cub to pet!)
- Visit Kano, Mariama Moussa, and Yacouba
- A picnic overlooking the Niger River with EBM and other missions' friends
- Souvenir shopping
- Damsi Restaurant
- Trio sing in English service
- Buy *chechenas* (bean cakes) and *doundou* (yams) from ladies selling on the street
- Eat *Kolkolti Hawru* (corn mush with okra gravy)
- A trip to the river

We were able to do all these things, except the trip to the river!

On the day we took them to the Niger Museum and Zoo, we were surprised to see a growing lion cub just lying in the shade out in the open. Evidently, he had been raised in someone's home and was being brought back to the zoo. He was so cute, docile, and very friendly. We got some good pictures of the kids petting him, especially one of Nansie almost nose-to-nose with him as she caressed his head.

On December 23, Rebecca wanted Ryan and Sarah to experience what it was like for her growing up to sleep outdoors under a mosquito net, so we got them all bedded down on the terrace outside. I was concerned all night that they might get an arm or a leg up against the net so that mosquitos could feast on them. When I went out to check on them in the morning, they were covered up and away from the edges, but to my horror there were all kinds of mosquitos inside their nets. Evidently as they moved in their sleep, the twin beds came apart so the nasty insects had come up from underneath and gotten inside their nets. I began killing as many as I could that were trapped in the nets and saw that some were Anopheles. All were bloody when I killed them. Horrors! Were my grandchildren going to come down with malaria during their visit to Niger? The Peace Corps doctor suggested we buy the antimalarial Fansadar to have on hand. The incubation period for malaria could be eight to fourteen days.

We allowed the children to open their gifts on Christmas Eve, and they liked that. We knew Christmas Day would be very busy.

For Christmas morning I made my traditional Swedish tea ring and scrambled eggs for breakfast, then we were at the Zarma church by 9:00 a.m. for the children's program. Then Deacon Cecekoy preached for an hour! The women had been up since 6:00 a.m. to start the cooking, and the sheep had been roasted to perfection over an open pit of hot coals. We had a great time of visiting and fellowshipping under the shade trees as we ate. In the evening, we went to Steve and Julie Nunemaker's for games and more goodies to eat. It was a lovely day and so good to have family with us.

The next day, there was a baptism down at the river after the morning service, but Heath was having trouble with the Ménière's disease (dizziness and nausea), so he couldn't go. Rebecca and Nansie went and took some pictures. We invited four Nigerian Calvary Ministries missionaries for dinner and enjoyed the turkey I had hand-carried back from the States! Rebecca sang a beautiful song in the evening English service, while Sarah and Nansie joined her for a second one. The next Sunday (January 2, 1994) we drove to Dosso so Rebecca could see Dieyabidi and family. They had a joyous reunion. Rebecca and the children left at midnight on January 3, 1994. What a joy it had been for us to have them with us that Christmas.

Norma Bobbett

It was hard to see them go. What a year 1993 proved to be! There were many joys and also some deep sorrows: Alan's life turned around, Daouda's death, returning to the States for Alan's graduation from Dunklin, Daniel Rands' tragic drowning, Rebecca and her children spending Christmas with us. It was quite a roller coaster ride! There were just a few weeks remaining of our final term in Niger. This had been our home for many years, and we never imagined how difficult it would be to leave it for the last time. But it wasn't the last time after all! We didn't know God still had work for us to do, not only back in Niger but also in many other countries.

Chapter 28
Final Months in Niger
January to March 1994

A few days after Rebecca and the children left, there were more problems with the Niamey university and high school students. Things were tense in Niamey. Students were refusing to go to class and were milling around in different locations in the city. They broke plate glass windows and windshields, burned vehicles, and so forth. The American embassy called the mission in the late morning, telling us to stay home and keep a low profile. From 9:00 p.m. until midnight, we heard gunfire and explosions from the university on the other side of the river. We were told that it was Nigerien authorities using tear gas plus water cannons to scatter the demonstrators.

Further complicating matters, the CFA, West African money based on the French franc, was devalued by 50 percent on January 12.

In the fall, a coworker and I had been approached by a young man as we were out for our evening walk. Alzouma wanted me to help him learn English, so he began coming to our house one or two times a week. I started out with reading and conversation, then had him reading Bible stories, which he seemed to like. He was very open to the Gospel, and I was anxious that someone continue teaching him after I left in March. I gave him a French and English Bible and got him started on a French Bible correspondence course. My good IMB friend Joyce Lewellyn continued teaching him after we left and not long after I returned to the States, Alzouma trusted Jesus Christ as his Savior!

At the close of January 1994, I realized we only had thirty-eight more days before we would be leaving Niger. Reflecting on God's faithfulness to us all through the years, I was thanking Him for:

- All the prayer warrior friends who had held us up in prayer through the years. We knew that anything that was accomplished was through their intercessions.
- Our long list of friendships with so many great African people. "Our hearts are bound to them because of Calvary. We love them and could never forget them."
- Our children – Rebecca, Jon, Alan, Nathan, and Mariama. I wrote, "I am so thankful for the children You gave us, Father. I'm thankful You have left us here on earth this long to pray for them. Lord, You love them even more than we do. You know each one's cares,

burdens, joys, fears. O Dear Father, thank You for loving them and caring for them. Our prayer is that they will think about You today in their busy schedules and that they will comprehend more about who You are. You love and care for each one of them individually. Help each of our children to love You and appreciate You and lean on You. Help Heath and me to serve You and love You all the days left to us on earth."

We were beginning to sort, pack, give away, and prepare things to sell. We set our prices very low and were glad that our beds, living room furniture, car, and other large items were being taken by other missionaries.

We had a lovely surprise on February 13 when Malam Kano (Zarma evangelist in Nigeria that we had known for years), his wife, and brother came to visit us! Malam Kano had preached for us in Gaya, Goudel, and Dosso over the many years we knew him. He was seventy-five years old then, and how good the Lord was to allow us to see him and his wife one more time on earth! He came from a Muslim family of sixteen children (same father, different mothers). Only he and his youngest brother were Christians, and they were the only two in the family still living!

Tanda Nya was a very old Zarma woman who visited me from time to time. Once when I asked her if she was really eighty years old, as her son had told me, she said, "Yes, and next year I will be ninety years old!" She had no concept of counting. I tried to share the Good News about Jesus with her in simple Zarma, praying she would understand. When I came home one day from shopping for fresh produce at Vultures' Corner, she was at our house with a grandson and a little niece. I bought some lunch for her and asked her to sit in the shade while I washed the fruits and vegetables and got some lunch for Heath. She and the children listened so well as I told them the Gospel story. When I told her that Jesus died for our sins and paid the debt we owed, she kept saying, *"Fondagoy, Irikoy."* ("Thank You, God, for Your work.") I told her I hoped I'd meet her again in heaven and that I would if she accepted Jesus. She said, "Yes, I do believe." O what a joy it will be for me if I do meet her in heaven. The average lifespan for Zarma women at that time was about forty-five years; she had long passed that life expectancy even in her poverty and many difficulties in life.

Friends were beginning to come to say goodbye to us and inviting us for a meal before we left. Our night guard, Hassan, brought a letter to us that he had a friend write for him, saying how much he liked us and how sorry he was that we were leaving. This was the man whom Heath often found sleeping when he got up in the night to check on him. Heath then took his spear home, and he had to come to sheepishly ask for it back the next morning! Here's a cultural thing that many Americans don't understand: Hassan always came to greet Heath each evening before he started his night guard duties, and Heath took the time to greet him and visit with him each time. He told us, "I know Alfa Bobbett really likes us because he takes time to talk to us while many aren't interested." His conclusion: "They don't like us!" Hassan also said that his son wanted to become a Christian, and he wouldn't prevent him. A few days later, Heath had the joy of leading Hama to Christ and giving him a Zarma Bible.

What a thrill it was later, just before we left, when Hassan told Heath that he would follow Jesus! We worked to put him and his son in contact with missionaries and other believers who could mentor them after our departure.

That evening, the Hausa Church pastor, Barajé, and family came to visit us, so Heath asked Barajé to talk to Hama too, making sure he understood what was involved in becoming a believer. Pastor Barajé's 3 children had been sick. Little Ibro barfed all over the floor! In spite of all, we had a good visit and prayer together.

Barajé was telling us about a debate that was held that week at the university, sponsored by the Groupe Biblique Universitaire (Intervarsity). There were over two hundred people to debate Jesus as prophet and Savior, and although the meeting went from 9:00 p.m. until 1:00 a.m., they didn't get finished. Barajé said the Lord gave them answers and helped them in that one of the main Muslim antagonists ended up taking their part and asking for calm. He said, "We are here to learn." One of the first things a Muslim said was, "There are over 5,000 errors in the Bible." Barajé said, "Oh really? Can you tell me one of them?" The man, of course, couldn't even name one.

They also said we had corrupted and changed the original Gospels. Barajé asked how could they know that? Did they have an old original they could compare it with and show where it had been changed?!

On February 21, 1994, a lovely farewell reception was held for us on the mission volleyball court. Everyone enjoyed the delicious couscous and sauce prepared by Pastor Kommi's wife, Gambi, and a whole roasted sheep. A number of African churches were represented and several other missions' personnel, plus our colleagues and other friends. Many kind words were said about us, and we thought again of all the precious friends we had made over the years and how much we were going to miss them.

We went to visit some African Calvary Ministries missionary friends, Oumarou and Chi. Their little Ronald was such a sweet baby. Chi kept urging us to write a book of our experiences to help and encourage young missionaries. She said she was praying about it too! Their motorbike had broken down the night before, and they weren't able to come to our farewell gathering. Chi also wrote a letter to our mission board, telling them that we were faithful servants of God and were appreciated for bringing the Gospel to the people in Africa.

Our house was slowly emptying out as we threw away, gave away, and sold our household goods. I went to say goodbye to my friend Assibi and prayed with her. She said, "Maybe I won't see you again on earth, but we will meet in heaven!" Assibi was the one who excitedly proclaimed, "Jesus speaks my language!" after seeing the Hausa version of The Jesus Film on Niger television.

In March 1994, we went to Dosso for our last Sunday in Niger, and to say our goodbyes to our loved ones at the church. They had so many kind things to say about us and then presented us with a beautiful locally woven blanket as a farewell gift. We stayed for communion. What precious memories we had of the Dosso believers and the years we had spent there with them.

Our last English service that evening in Niamey was led by our dear IMB friend Tony Lynn. Tony had a very big surprise for me! He said he knew when he left his ministry as a pastor in Flint, Michigan, his wife needed to say her farewell too. So he said, "I'm asking Norma to come up and say a few words with Heath standing by her side." I had no time to think over what I would say but just gave a testimony of God's leading in our life and marriage and His wonderful faithfulness to us over the years. MK Shelley Nunemaker sang a special song, "Thank You for Giving to the Lord," that she "dedicated to Uncle Heath and Aunt Norma." What a sweet gift. She sang with tears rolling down her face, and we couldn't keep our tears from flowing either. It was an emotional service, followed by all the goodbyes. Melrose from Calvary Ministries put her arms around me and just sobbed. She was the first of their mission to come to Niamey to open their work and was like a daughter to us.

The farewells weren't finished yet. The next night, March 8, the Gourma Church in Niamey invited us to a farewell they hosted. It was a sweet time of fellowship with delicious African cuisine. These dear friends presented us with beautiful Gourma outfits made from colorful homespun weaving as farewell gifts.

We were constantly being invited to friends' homes for meals. Francis and Eli, Evening Baptist Bible Institute students Heath had taught, brought us gifts from the students – a lovely African leather purse for me and a beautifully decorated leather briefcase for Heath. Francis became tearful as he made his farewell speech to us. The many goodbyes from beloved friends who had served with us in reaching those without Christ in Niger tugged at our heartstrings tremendously. How privileged we were to know each one of them.

SIM West African director and good friend Jim Longworth came to pray with us and say goodbye too. He stated that he really was saddened to see veteran missionaries like us leave. He praised the Lord for our long-term commitment and lamented that so many of the newer missionaries just came for short-term ministries and didn't stay for the long haul.

Leaving Niger

A large crowd was at the Niamey airport to see us off on Friday, March 12, 1994. Again, more tears and hugs. We arrived in Paris at 5:55 p.m. and because we had economy tickets, the airline provided no overnight hotel for us. We stayed at the Ibis Hotel near the airport, which was quite spartan and less expensive (though not inexpensive)!

After a nice buffet breakfast at the Ibis Hotel, we headed for the Charles de Gaulle airport. Through the years, Heath had a custom of buying Chanel No. 5 for me at the duty-free airport shops when we passed through on our furloughs. We figured this would be the last time he could ever do that!

We were met at the Indianapolis airport by our children and grandchildren with the exception of Jon, who had taken Joel to a Pacers game! Mariama was also in the States for some R&R after working hard on her doctorate in England. She was exhausted physically and emotionally.

Alan and little Ryan were installed in a nice mobile home on U.S. 31 south of Greenwood, and we stayed with them. Alan'sn Pane Away Commercial Window-washing Service was going well. Jon and Judy loaned us their Volvo for transportation.

A couple of days later, we drove to our home in Springfield, Ohio, to begin some unpacking. We were so grateful to the Lord for the wonderful renters we had during this last term. They were so kind and thoughtful, and they cared for our home just as if it was their own. They moved to their own home before we returned but still left curtains up so our house looked inhabited, raked leaves, and had our neighbors drive in and out of our driveway when there was snow so it looked like someone was living there. Alan and Nathan were a tremendous help when they came to get our things out of storage. We made arrangements to get our utilities connected then returned to Indianapolis.

Jon and Heath found a car for us. It was a nice white Buick LeSabre, and that was the first time Heath ever owned a new car in the States! All we had to pay was $4,000 plus the Ohio taxes. Jon took over the monthly payments. What a tremendous gift to us! When we were thanking him, he said, "Dad and Mom, I get more joy out of doing this than you do receiving it!" That afternoon we drove the car back to Ohio.

Sunday, March 27, was our first time back to our home church in Dayton, and we received a warm welcome from the dear saints there! They even had a food shower for us, packing our car full of groceries and paper products.

Being back in the States meant we were available to have our grandchildren come for visits. We enjoyed taking them to the Air Force Museum in Dayton, the IMAX theater, Young's Dairy, Ohio Caverns, Sea World and especially an outdoor play in Xenia called "Blue Jacket." They loved the drama and action of the Native Americans who lived in that area in the past, especially the horses, gunfights, and flaming arrows!

We weren't really retired yet, officially. Heath had another year and seven months before he was sixty-five and eligible for social security. He was still busy working on the Zarma Bible concordance and reporting to our supporting churches during those months. What would the Lord have before us in this new and strange upcoming thing called retirement? We still wanted to be actively serving Him as long as He gave us life. Even at this stage of life, our plea to the Lord was, "Here am I. Send me." What did He have for us in the days ahead?

Chapter 29
First Years Back in the States
April 1994 to January 1995

When we returned to the States, we had reverse culture shock, and adjusting was very difficult for us. The language and lack of morality on television programs were shocking and depressing. There were so many ways that we did not feel that we fit into our own culture anymore. We continued to be very busy with work on the Zarma concordance as well as reporting to our supporting churches and individuals. We had very warm relationships with our prayer and financial supporters who enabled us to serve in Niger through the years. Missionaries are blessed beyond measure by the prayer warriors who minister right along with us on their knees! They are the ones who "stayed by the stuff," and we know they will be rewarded equally for any and all that was accomplished for our Savior in Niger.

Mariama's scholarship for working on her doctorate had expired, and she was trying to get an extension so she could go back to England to try again, but it wasn't happening. She spent many months with us during this time of great discouragement for her. It was of great concern to us that she wasn't taking her diabetes seriously in following a correct diet, but we knew she was really down because of the hard work she had done and that the British professors heading the doctoral program seemed determined not to allow her to succeed. She stayed for rest and recuperation in our home when we left on a home assignment reporting trip in New York and Pennsylvania.

It had still been summer like when we left Ohio, but we found New York State to be very cold, and we didn't have warm clothing. While Heath was speaking at a men's breakfast on Saturday, a friend and I went to garage sales and thrift stores looking for sweaters for him. We found two for only $10. That evening, the pastor said we were going to their youth group's progressive supper. We had sandwiches and drinks at the first home, then were taken to the church for dessert. Surprise! The entire church family was there to have a birthday party for us! They had cake, drinks, and gifts of toiletries and food for us. The next day as we spoke in both the morning and evening at First Baptist of East Syracuse, the folks had also heard Heath needed sweaters, so they brought some too. How he did appreciate those sweaters!

With Jesus Leading the Way

It was a blessed time for us, with Heath speaking to our New York supporting churches. I spoke to several Sunday school classes and at ladies' missionary fellowship groups or teas. The children were quiet and attentive, loving the stories of Kano and others. The ladies groups were warm and interested. What a blessing it was to be in each and every church.

Many missionaries have told us they stay in motels, but we almost always were extended hospitality in homes of the church folks. It was wonderful to visit with them, learning about each family and how they had come to Christ, their prayer requests, and then answering their questions about missions and life in Niger.

Seeing Our First Gorgeous Fall Foliage in Five Years

Heath was napping as I drove from Harrisburg, Pennsylvania, up Route 81 to Vestal, New York, for our next church meeting. The leaves were at their gorgeous peak of beauty. The combination of the nice classical music playing on our car radio and the beauty of the scenery was exhilarating! Enraptured, I worshipped our gracious Creator and Lord in thanksgiving and praise. I was glad Heath woke up to see that beauty too.

We headed to Horseheads, New York to visit Norm and Gladys (Truax) Carpenter. Gladys, age ninety-one, had been in the Elmira County Nursing Home for three and a half years, no longer able to walk because of her severe arthritis. She was my role model and mentor for many years. The presence of Christ radiated in her room, and she was still ministering, although confined to a bed. She could no longer walk but her mind, sight, and hearing were still good. She continued to knit baby gifts. The nurses loved her and came to her with their problems and prayer requests. She had neither a television nor a radio in her room. I asked her if she would like to have a radio so she could listen to Christian music during the lonely evening hours. Her reply was, "Oh, I have a wonderful time here each evening. First, I go through all the books of the Bible and say the verses I've learned from each book. Then I go through the hymnal (in my mind) and sing all the songs I can remember (not out loud)! After that I spend some time in prayer then go to sleep." She really didn't have time to listen to radio programs! She continued to lift us up in prayer, and her prayers were powerful. She also wrote many poems. One of my favorites was written after she was confined to a bed in the nursing home:

Four Walls
by Gladys Truax Carpenter

Four walls do not a prison make!
My mind and spirit can soar

Norma Bobbett

> To heights I had not attained
> Nor dreamed of heretofore!
> By faith I can reach out my hand
> To the One Who dwells with me
> And feel His loving caring touch
> Though His form I cannot see.
> Within these walls with the world shut out
> I have much time to pray
> For those around me whom I love
> And those who are far away.
> So I am content to dwell here
> For He brought me to this place
> And I wait for the time He calls me
> And I shall see Him face to face!

On October 17, 1994, we returned to Ohio and three days later we headed to Indianapolis for a missions conference at First Baptist Church of Beech Grove. The missionaries in the conference were Ron Washer (Togo), Don Worch (Baptist Children's Home), David Crandall (Gospel Literature Services), Dave and Nancy Brower (Brazil), and us. All of the missionaries had lunch with the church's teenagers on Sunday. Pastor Tom Strong had all of us fill out questions to show something about ourselves as teenagers so that their youth would see that missionaries are just common folks too. Then he read some of our facts, asking the youth to try to guess which missionary this was about! These brought lots of laughter!

- loved horses, class valedictorian, traveled all over Europe at age nineteen (David Crandall)
- loved sports; played soccer, football; went to Boys State (Dave Brower)
- Cedarville homecoming queen, grew up in Brazil, didn't want to go to the mission field (Nancy Brower)
- loved sports, girls, and dancing (Heath Bobbett)
- rebellious, loved sports and girls (Ron Washer)
- grew up in the country, loved the outdoors, played trumpet in high school band (Norma Bobbett)

Trip to Michigan Churches and Fire in Our House

Shelley Nunemaker, Jon Curtis, and his friend came to spend the weekend with Mariama on her birthday, November 5. We left for meetings in Michigan. Soon after we arrived in Reed City, we got a call from our son Jonathan. Our hot water tank had caught on fire that day. We were so thankful Mariama and the kids were there! Mariama was preparing an African meal in the kitchen, and Jon Curtis was in the shower. The girls smelled smoke and screamed when they saw it coming from the water heater. The thermostat had melted down. Jon Curtis came running and put the fire out with a wet towel. The house filled with smoke and soot, especially in our basement. Mariama called 911, and everyone got out of the house because it was a gas water heater. The firemen came, took care of the gas shutoff, opened the basement windows, and put big fans in the upstairs to pull out all the smoke!

We decided to stay in Michigan for our meetings. How we thanked the Lord that Mariama and the other MKs were at our house during our absence. If no one had been there, our whole house would probably have burned. Heath called our insurance agent in and he came out to do an inspection. The pastor at Reed City First Baptist Church surprised us when he asked the congregation for an offering to help cover our deductible, and those dear folks gave $177 to help us! When we got home, our insurance company offered good and paid to have our home professionally cleaned. Our furniture didn't smell of smoke so we were grateful for that.

Thanksgiving 1994

All of our family was with us for Thanksgiving. That was very special for us, and my only regret was that I didn't take more pictures. I made a treasure hunt for the grandchildren. We celebrated Nathan's Master of Divinity degree from Trinity by laughingly giving him the little red wagon he said he never had when he was little, plus cards and money to build his library. I made a congratulatory cake, and we had cards for Alan to celebrate his engagement to a lovely woman named Angie.

Heath and I were faithful in getting up at 6:00 a.m. each day to walk two miles or more before breakfast. On December 1, 1994, the temperature was nineteen degrees. We walked anyway but decided that was the absolute lowest temperature we would walk outdoors in the future!

Christmas 1994

Jon, Judy, Stephen, Joel, and Laura came on December 23 and 24 for our Christmas dinner and gift exchange. We went to see the Christmas lights at Ramar Estates and Clifton Mill then had supper at Young's Dairy. Our grandchildren always loved going to this famous dairy farm. They could feed the goats, watch cows being milked, play miniature golf, and then have their choice of Young's wonderful ice cream flavors. On December 27, Becca, Rick, and family came for dinner and a gift exchange.

Rick got Heath's new printer hooked up to his computer. Our gifts to Nansie, Sarah, and Ryan were big posters showing the special things they experienced in Niger – Nansie with a lion cub, Ryan on a camel ride, and Sarah cuddling an African baby.

We traveled to Indiana to spend New Year's Eve with Jon and Judy. On New Year's Day, Judy had a lovely luncheon to celebrate Alan and Angie's marriage. We took little Ryan Bobbett back to Ohio with us for three days. From my journal: "Ryan B. is with us for three days. He entertains himself so well playing alone – a real sweetheart! He beat me twice in playing Memory. I asked him how he did that, and he said, 'I fink (think)!' Good answer! We took him back to Greenwood on January 5, 1995. He was tearful when we left for Florida and wanted to go with us. I prayed, 'Lord, please help this precious little guy. He has gone through so much in his five years. Please help us all to give him love and a sense of security, but above all I pray he will come to know You at a young age. May he know how much You love him and are his security."

On January 5, we said goodbye to Mariama who was returning to Leeds, England, then hurried off down the road to Florida. We were trying to outrun a fierce ice storm that was coming. We got all the way to Montgomery, Alabama, and the storm stopped just north of there, so we were safe! This trip we would report to four supporting churches in Florida and visit many friends.

While in Florida we received the heartbreaking news that Emmanuel Baptist Church's pastor was dismissed because of moral failure. After thirty-five years of godly, Bible-centered, evangelistic preaching by beloved Pastor Nile Fisher, the people had welcomed the next pastor with open arms, but he failed. The church had to relieve him of the pastorate and rescind his ordination. What a sad ending of ministry in the life of a promising young preacher. The whole church family was hurting over this man's dismissal.

The godly assistant pastor at Emmanuel, Lenny Miller, held things together through the change of pastors. We can't say enough good things about Lenny. He was a good teacher and visitation pastor (always there at the hospital or in a home when needed). He was a man who made everyone feel like they were his best friend. My, how he could sing and bless our hearts! He had been the perfect assistant to Pastor Fisher but did not feel he was called to be a preacher. He excelled in soul-winning, visitation, teaching, singing, and loving all of God's children. There was never a better team of two than Pastor Fisher and Lenny Miller.

Lord, What Does Our Future Hold?

In 1995, we continued busily reporting to supporting churches and speaking in missionary conferences but looming ahead that year was Heath's sixty-fifth birthday when we were required by the mission to retire. We were really struggling with the idea of retirement. We still were fit and energetic and didn't feel ready to be "put out to pasture." We didn't see anything in Scriptures about retirement but were reminded of Jesus' words, "Occupy until I come." There was much talk about seniors not retiring but being retreaded for more service. We liked to tell people who asked us when we were going to retire, "We retire every evening when we go to bed!"

As we wrestled with these thoughts of what we would do next, good friends came to visit us. They had served in Bénin but then returned to the States to be EBM's western representatives several years before. We told them of our unhappiness about not returning to Niger, feeling as though we were losing our identity after all the years spent as missionaries. They counseled us, saying, "You just have to submit to the Lord for this new phase of your life since He now has placed you back in the States and realize that this is what the Lord has for you at this time." This was hard news for us to hear, and tears came to our eyes.

However, we realized this counsel was exactly on target. We had to get on our knees and confess our discontent, saying, "Lord we are Your servants, and we want to be totally yielded to You for whatever You have for us in the days ahead. Not our will, Lord, but Yours." What peace He shed on our hearts as we yielded to Him for whatever He, our sovereign God, had for us in the days ahead.

From my journal: "Father, we know You called us into Your service and to Africa many years ago. You were with us all along the way, never failing us. Now, whatever ministry You have for us, be it staying home and praying, encouraging, teaching, or going somewhere else to minister, help us, Lord, to discern Your will.

God had blessed me with my best friend and dear husband, Heath. We never had any doubt that the Lord had made us for each other. How good the Lord has been to give us that assurance as we walked together through life, in good times and hard times, in blessings and in disappointments, in joys and in trials, in sickness and in health. All glory and praise goes to God alone!

We were excited to open our hearts to whatever the Lord had for us in the days ahead. There is joy in serving Jesus, and we had no idea of the exciting adventures He had planned for us.

Chapter 30
Work's End or Second Wind?
January 1995 to December 1996

My perspective must be that I am here on earth as a pilgrim and sojourner for a limited time, and during that span, all my energies and activities should be directed toward accomplishing God's plans and purposes for me. Therefore, I may retire from a particular occupation or vocation, but it would not be to live a life of ease for the rest of my days. Rather, it would be because God had called me to another activity, ministry, or vocation for His purposes. – Ron Blue

A new chapter is like a new scene in a play. As the curtain is drawn up in this chapter, we are now residents of our home country again. The scene is no longer the edge of the Sahara Desert in an adobe house, with camels, goats, cows, sheep, motorbikes, and pedestrians passing by but in the lovely home the Lord provided for us in Springfield, Ohio. My beautiful and warm African lady friends were far away, and I was greatly missing them. However, I was blessed anew in the sweet fellowship of old and new friends in the churches as we traveled reporting in our homeland.

It was a blessing to fellowship in the churches and homes of those who had prayed faithfully for us in Niger as well as supported us financially. They were very important partners on our team. The travel and speaking continued all of 1995. We did not take lightly these privileges and prayed that we would be able to communicate to all what a wonderful God we serve.

Mariama Moussa

I wrote a dialogue testimony of a Muslim woman in Niger that I presented many times in Zarma dress. I spoke in the first person, "My name is Mariama Moussa…" It was well received wherever I presented it. At a ladies retreat at Camp Patmos, Ohio, a friend told me it was the best presentation she had ever heard in helping her understand women in Muslim countries. All my illustrations of Mariama Moussa's life were taken from actual experiences of the women I knew in Niger. Something humorous happened a couple of times. Heath had been speaking in a missionary conference in Michigan. When the conference was almost over, he asked me to come up to participate by appearing as Mariama Moussa.

When I spoke in the first person about how my Muslim husband treated me and his other wives, some of the children began to look daggers at Heath! Hasty explanations had to be made that I was speaking as Mariama Moussa and not as Mrs. Bobbett!

When I began writing these memoirs, I thought I would end with our return to the States. Our careers in Niger had ended and we thought we would just be put "out to pasture" in retirement, although that was not what we wanted. We were still eager for His work, feeling we in no way wanted to cease joyfully serving the Lord. We had the health, the stamina, and the deep desire to continue serving.

I wonder if the Lord was looking down from heaven at us with an all-knowing smile? We had no idea of the wonderful adventures He had before us once we opened our hearts in submission to Him, to do whatever He had for us in the future!

After our friends had counseled and encouraged us to accept being in the States and being totally open to God's will for our days ahead, we saw our Savior open the first door of short-term ministry He had for us.

"I will praise the LORD, who counsels me; even at night my heart instructs me." (Psalm 16:7)

"Every life we touch is a field. Everything we do and all the words we speak are seed. What will the harvest be?" – Rowland

Steve and Julie Nunemaker, on home leave from Niger in the summer of 1995, stayed overnight with us when they came to pick up their daughter Shelley at Cedarville College. They arrived at supper time and we talked almost non-stop until 11:00 p.m.

This was it! The Lord opened the first door of short-term ministry for us! Steve asked Heath if he would be willing to return to Niger in January 1996 to teach a ten-week modular course at the Evening Baptist Bible Institute! Almost all of the men attending the institute had daytime jobs and were self-supporting. They had a hunger and desire to learn more of God's Word and be used of Him. Heath had taught courses to these fine men during past years in Niger and enjoyed it immensely.

Heath's teaching at IBBS would free Steve of that responsibility so he could begin construction of a radio and television building. Steve was a multi-talented missionary, excellent in French because he was born in and grew up in Niger, a builder, an electrician, and so forth. He could not build the radio-television building and still put in all the time required to study, prepare, and teach IBBS.

Were we excited about returning to Niger on a short-term basis? Oh, yes, we were! Our hearts swelled with praise to our heavenly Father for opening this wonderful opportunity for us to return and serve in the country that had been our home for so many years!

We received a letter from some of our "children," Nigerian missionaries who had come to Niger to work, including this one:

"Dear Mom and Pa Bobbett,

"We are so excited about seeing you once again and are praying that God will prosper your stay here, especially as you will be renewing many contacts with those who, over the years, have been touched by your ministry. It is wonderful how the Lord is working...He will surely continue to overthrow the wicked schemes of the enemy and bring the harvest."

As we neared the end of 1995, we were excitedly gathering things and packing suitcases to return to Niger. We were thankful that we were returning in Niger's cool season and would be back in the States before the intense hot season came in full force. Churches and friends contributed to our passage and support through our mission. On our last Sunday at our sending church, in Dayton, the pastor called us to the front of the church so that veteran missionary Carson Fremont could pray for us as we went to serve once more in Niger. Our hearts were so touched and thankful because we knew the beloved saints at Emmanuel would be holding us up in prayer every day.

We were at Rebecca and Rick's for Christmas Day: "The snow was coming down in huge flakes as we opened gifts this morning! Outside was being covered with the beautiful white flakes. Granddaughter Nansie and I just had to go outside for a little while to watch and see the silent transformation of our surroundings before Rebecca served Christmas dinner. Afterward we enjoyed playing games and watching videos with our grandchildren.

On Our Way Back for Short-Term Service in Niger

From my journal, dated December 30, 1995: "House all clean, plants watered, goodbyes said, four suitcases, one box, and two hand luggage all packed, we were ready when Mickey and Geneva came at 10:00 a.m. to pick us up for the Vandalia airport. The car was so heavily loaded that Mickey said it felt like he was driving a Cadillac! Springfield had a beautiful six-inch layer of snow, and temperatures were below freezing. Not wanting to be bothered with winter coats, I wore a heavy sweater and Heath wore a light jacket. We were a little concerned that we would be very cold in New York when we had to lug our heavy hand luggage out to catch a bus from US Air terminal to Air France, but it wasn't as bad as we feared.

During our long wait in the Paris terminal for our flight down to Niger, it was delightful to encounter SIL, SIM, and IBM missionaries, who were friends of ours, also on their way back to Niger. Visiting with them helped us stay awake because we hadn't been to bed in twenty-four hours!

Looking down over the Sahara Desert during our daylight flight was fantastic. When the plane circled at Niamey for our 6:00 p.m. landing, we could see so many familiar sights, even the mission at Goudel where we would be lodged. Customs and police were very kind to us and didn't even open our luggage. Steve Nunemaker was there to meet us and drop us off at the mission guest house before he hurried back to the evening English service at the Niamey church. We were invited to a New Year's party at the Nunemaker home later. After we unpacked, we joined them and their guests at 9:30 p.m. However, after some good food and fellowship, plus one game, we began to wilt, so we went back up the hill to bed!

As Heath crawled into bed after midnight, realizing it was New Year's Day 1996, he said, "This is the first day of my retirement. What am I doing back in Niger?" Both of our hearts were smiling.

Shelley Nunemaker was living with us in Springfield during her senior year at Cedarville College. She was in Niger when we got there though, visiting her parents over the Christmas holidays. It was good to know she would be at our house during our ten-week absence.

The Blizzard of the Century in the United States

Washington, D.C., and New York City were paralyzed as new records of snowfall were recorded! Philadelphia had thirty inches. Airports at Boston, New York, Philadelphia, Washington, D.C., and Atlanta were closed. When Shelley got back to Ohio, she found four feet of snow piled up against our front door and had to get a neighbor's help to get in the house!

We wrote to the Emmanuel Church folks back in Dayton, Ohio: "Greetings from sunny Niger! It looks like we've missed that blizzard back in the States. It is so good to be back 'home' again and seems like we've never been away. We have gotten lots of welcoming hugs from our African friends. Many said, 'We thought we'd never see you again until we meet in heaven.' We've been out on visitation and especially wanted to contact those who received Christ just before we left. They are coming along in the Lord, praise His name! Pray we will have significant input into their spiritual lives during our time here. Tonight, Heath's Bible institute classes begin. He is excited about that. He has already been asked to preach at the Gourma church next week, so undoubtedly, he will have opportunities to preach in Zarma, French, and English also while we are here. We sense the prayers of God's people and are so grateful for you. We are six hours ahead of you here…so when we pray for you in the morning we can picture you all, still snuggled down and sleeping soundly. We miss you all, are thankful for you, and praying for you. In His name, Heath and Norma"

From my journal, dated January 4, 1996: "Oh the dust! I had forgotten how it permeates and layers itself on everything in the house. During our years in Niger, we got so used to it, but now, after two years in the States, I was seeing it through American eyes and culture. The first day here, I took down all the curtains and washed them, thinking we could then breathe better. The dirt on my dishcloth when I wiped off the table or refrigerator was disgusting. We had to remove all the 'clean' dishes out of the cupboards and wash the dust off of them."

We were housed in the EBM guest house apartment next to where we lived our last term in Niger. Pete Wing was so kind and helpful. He crawled up in the bat-dirt encrusted ceiling over our apartment to attach a cable from the audiovisual TV we were borrowing to his antenna so we could get the American Forces Network. We thought back to the contrast with our first two terms in Gaya where we had no electricity. Back then we listened to the astronauts' first orbit of the earth on our battery-powered shortwave radio. Now we could watch Headline News in our guest house apartment! The office also was able to get e-mail on a limited basis through another mission's internet connection. We thought we had come full cycle!

God's Provision of a Car
Mariama's cousin Amadou Seydou, was the ambassador from Niger to the United States and the United Nations. He had bought Vicki Burry's Peugeot 504 when she left Niger, and it was just sitting, awaiting his return to Niger. Nam so kindly allowed us to activate the insurance, put in a new battery, and use it while we were there.

Part of my responsibility while we were back in Niger was to visit and have literacy classes with blind Jofo's wife, Halima. Their house was hard to find, but after going down a wrong dirt street, past potholes, people, animals, trash piles, and sellers, I finally found the right one!

It was wonderful to be greeted and welcomed by old friends at church, on the street, and in stores. I ran into a diplomat's wife, Vicki, who invited me to the international English Bible study I had attended before. I was reminded again of what a blessing it is to pray with African women. You really know the Lord is present as they talk to Him!

A Zarma friend came to talk to me about the difficult life she was having with her husband who had gone back to Islam after professing Christianity (while he had a mission job). He was so mean to her, and she lived with constant disharmony in the home. My heart ached for her. "Lord, she is Your child. She has stayed true to You over the years, even when she had no income for food. Please counsel her through me or circumstances in her life…and Lord, especially through Your Word and prayer. I know You love her, and You have promised to care for Your own. Please show her what to do or what not to do."

How the Lord answered that prayer! This friend came to me a few days later, saying she told her problems to an African pastor who was visiting from another part of Africa. He urged her to totally change her behavior toward her husband, to ask his forgiveness, greet him warmly when he came home, prepare food for him, and serve it to him on bended knee. She began to do this. At first, her sullen husband was speechless as he regarded her with suspicion. But after a while he began to warm up, and communication was slowly opening for them in the weeks that followed.

We had been back in Niger for three weeks. At 11:00 p.m., Heath used our little guest house bathroom, showered, and hopped into bed. After using the toilet, I was preparing to get in the shower when I noticed what looked like a piece of rubber seal or something hanging down inside the rim of the toilet. "Is it a gasket or rubber seal coming apart? It couldn't be a snake in the toilet, could it? Nah!" Then it moved! I got my glasses, looked again, and then called Heath. He came quickly and sure enough, a two-and-a-half-foot small spitting cobra was in our toilet bowl! The only instrument we had to attack it with was a narrow rod that was used as a curtain rod. Heath tugged at the snake to bring it down into the bowl, but the rod wasn't so good to attack it with. He kept hitting it as it tried to squirm out of the slippery bowl. I rushed to the kitchen to fill a teakettle and put it on to boil. The snake tried to go down the toilet head first, but Heath had wounded him and he could only go so far. We could still see his tail. When I brought the boiling water to finish him off, that also flushed him down.

Later, we crawled into bed and had prayer, thanking the Lord for showing us the snake and for those who were praying for us. It was hard to get to sleep after all that excitement!

From my journal, dated Saturday, January 27, 1996: "What a day this has been! We made a trip in town this morning to get gas and groceries for our trip to Dosso tomorrow and so I could prepare dinner for the Nunemakers and a new missionary couple on a one-week pre-field visit. I was preparing peanut butter gravy when I realized I had forgotten to buy some ground red pepper (cayenne) and bread. My friend Edna came with a dress she had made for me, so I offered to take her home and accomplish my errands at the same time.

"We couldn't find any ground pepper at the Yantala open market, so Edna bought whole dried peppers and said she would pound them to make freshly ground cayenne for me. At her house, I watched her pound and sift the peppers. At the same time, the neighbor girls were cleaning the intestines from a freshly killed goat. I should have had a video camera with me!

"The Lord watched over me and saw to it that I got back home around 2:00 p.m. because shortly thereafter I might have been stuck in the village at Edna's house without Heath knowing where I was. We began to hear some loud booms. When we had heard these in the days before, we were assured that it was the police flushing rebellious students out of the closed university campus or political groups out of a building, sometimes with tear gas.

"But the firing of arms continued. We heard what sounded like howitzers, machine gun fire, and small arms. We began to realize this was more serious than we had thought. All traffic on the road ceased, and the city became still. The men working at the radio-television construction site were stunned and frightened, so Steve allowed them to go home. The head mason, Joe, came from town and said the shots began near the Palais des Congrès where the president, Mahamane Ousmane, was in meetings. Then they were moving to the presidential home in the military camp, about one mile from us.

"We gathered with Steve and Julie and the new missionary couple at the Nunemakers' house for prayer, then Heath and I went back up the hill to our guest house apartment. After the Nunemakers heard a shot down by the river and heard a ricocheting bullet hit a tree, they all came up to our house because they felt safer inside the eighteen-inch-thick mud walls than they did in a house of cement blocks! Fearing water and electricity might be shut off, we began to put aside buckets of water and filtered extra water for drinking. I continued preparing supper for all of us, and we listened to the local radio station, but they continued with their regular programing, music, interviews, and even the Hausa soap opera! The gunfire continued until 6:00 p.m., and then the radio began to play military music, interspersed with dance music! ("April Showers"!?)

"After dinner, as I was rinsing dishes and putting away leftovers, the announcement came on the radio: A military coup! Colonel Ibrahim Baré Maïnassara spoke, saying that President Ousmane was under house arrest and the other officials had also been arrested. Colonel Maïnassara declared himself the new head of government, dissolved the National Assembly, and suspended the constitution. A curfew was proclaimed from 9:30 p.m. to 5:30 a.m. However, it was Ramadan, and people weren't going to follow those rules, so the curfew was changed to be from 10:00 p.m. to 5:00 a.m."

God was working so that we could continue with the Evening Bible Institute classes in spite of the government overthrow! Almost all the Bible school students had jobs, so classes were held in the evening. Other years, the curfews were usually longer, but this one happened during Ramadan, so the change in curfew hours worked perfectly for our students also. The men came to the Bible classes and were still able to get home before curfew. Later, they even extended the evening curfew to 11:00 p.m.!

We were disappointed that we weren't able to go to Dosso the next day as planned. We longed to see all our dear friends, and Heath was to preach for them. Steve and Heath tried to go to the Niamey church in the morning but returned within five minutes because the streets were blocked off by soldiers. The official report was that only five people lost their lives in the overthrow, but many thought that with all the gunfire there must have been more. Our gardener friend, Jofo, said that when he visited his daughter in the hospital the next day, he saw much activity going to the morgue and soldiers guarding the wounded in a special section of the hospital. The father of some of our French day school students, a *garde républicain*, was killed, so there was grieving at the school also.

Interesting folk medicine anecdote: I was having tummy problems, and Pepto-Bismol wasn't working. I had some French *intétrix* but it had expired a year before. I finally tried an American friend's remedy of a chopped up fresh clove of garlic, washed it down with water like small pills! By late afternoon, I had no more diarrhea!

Our ten weeks in Niger were going by so rapidly with every day filled. Our African friends were coming to visit us, and we also were calling on many. We were so warmly welcomed by both Christian and Muslim friends. How good the Lord was to allow us to go back to Niger for another time of service! Besides the literacy classes with Halima, I was recording study books for blind Jofo who was working on his master's degree at Liberty University.

It was amazing the number of missions coming into Niger to work with the Zarmas. For all the preceding years, it was only EBM missionaries reaching out to Zarmas. The Lord knew, back when we were working on the Zarma Bible translation, what an outreach it would eventually have!

I was enjoying the little Bible study of English-speaking African ladies again and was asked to lead one week. Vicki, a Ghanaian woman whose husband worked for an agricultural study and project, invited me to tea one day at her beautiful home. Her husband had his doctorate from

Cornell in Ithaca, New York. The day before was her fortieth birthday, but she still looked like she was twenty-five. Vicki had also invited Adun, a pharmacist from Nigeria who also was in our Bible study, and Jay, the wife of the deputy regional director, who was a Muslim from the Gambia. We had a nice visit, and then things got on spiritual topics. It was beautiful and thrilling to see the way Adun and Vicki witnessed to her. Jay knew the Koran well. Everything stayed on a friendly tone. They are used to bantering and teasing each other, but they also got the Gospel message across.

On Sunday, February 25, we got up at 5:00 a.m. (yawn!) to be ready to leave for Dosso. What a great day it was. The morning service lasted two hours! Pastor Luc preached, and there was a communion service after a baptismal service. We got hugs and warm greetings from all the folks at this station where we had served. What a joy to see that the church was coming along well and growing. Ladi made a delicious dinner for us. Before we left at 2:00 p.m., Dieyabidi hugged Heath three different times, thanked us for all we had done for him, and asked for prayer.

Dieyabidi had moved to Gaya with the Frenchman he was working for. This boss was not a nice man, and it was hard for Dieyabidi to be separated from his family, but at the same time, the Lord was using him there as he shared the preaching with another man at the Gaya Church. Dieyabidi told us about all the snakes and scorpions he had killed in Gaya. One scorpion had even crawled up his pant leg, but he was able to shake it out and wasn't stung, praise the Lord!

We were all praying for the young man, Joseph, who came to Christ and was baptized by Heath during our time serving in Dosso. He was in love with a young girl named Grace, and they wanted to be married.

However, she was under the jurisdiction of her Uncle. Although he pretended to want to help them as a go-between with her family in Nigeria, he wasn't doing anything. Some of the non-Christians told Joseph, "Just get her pregnant, then her family will have to let you marry her." Joseph refused to ruin his testimony in that way and continued to trust that God would act on his behalf, and He did! Joseph preserved his good testimony and saw God's faithfulness through it all. God was preparing Joseph to one day be the pastor of the Dosso Evangelical Baptist Church!

On March 1, Mariama picked us up for dinner at her brother Hama's house in Goudel. Hama worked in the prime minister's office, and his wife, Fati, was the first woman judge in Niger. I wrote, "What a lovely home they have built right in the center of Goudel!" Fati served a delicious meal and we enjoyed our time with them. With all the delicious meals we were given, it is no wonder we didn't lose any weight!

Heath continued his teaching, and we enjoyed fellowship with the many who were inviting us for meals. It was great to fellowship over a delicious African meal at Hausa Pastor Barajé and Dijé's house. I remembered when Dijé was just a young teenager, interested in knowing about Christianity. Since Hausa was her first language, I took her to the Hausa church and dear friend Nellie Germaine led Dijé to Christ. She and Barajé were married in our church in Dosso, and we found them to be faithful servants of the Lord together. We also called on many friends to let them know we would soon be leaving for the States.

On March 8, two of our French school teachers, Abraham and Marc, were honored at a ceremony and given plaques, with the Niger director of private schools present. Abraham had taught first grade for thirty-five years and was an incredible teacher. He had a sense of humor that wouldn't quit! We always enjoyed visiting with him. One year we were plagued with swarms of tiny gnats. People walking along the road in front of our house were comical as they busily and constantly kept their hands swishing around their heads, so they could see and breathe without the gnats getting in their eyes and noses. Abraham came to us and said, "I think we need to ask Pharaoh to please let the children of Israel go!"

The morning before we left, I went back to the Score *supermarché* because my friend Amina told me she just had to see me one more time before I left. How surprised I was when she presented me with a beautiful woven Zarma blanket! We went to say goodbye to Pastor Luc and found out he had gone to our house to say goodbye. We stopped also at our old station guard's house, but he was off helping a friend build a new grass hut. His wife assured us they would all be coming to our house later to say goodbye.

Back at our house, Salamatou was there to visit. She complained about her rheumatism, not having any clothes that weren't just rags, and lamented that maybe she wouldn't be alive the next time we came back to Niger. I reminded her that those who belong to Jesus will someday have a new body and that if she truly belonged to the Lord Jesus Christ we will meet again in heaven.

Hassan's wife, Mariama, and her sister came to see us. They enjoyed hearing Salamatou reminisce about old times. The three ladies teased and bantered because one was of the Songhai tribe and the other two were Bellas. When Mariama and her sister decided they would go home, the sun was brutally hot, so I told them I would drive them all home in our borrowed car. Salamatou said she was going to stay longer. I said, "But our daughter Mariama and Heath will be taking the car away to put it back at the owner's sister's house." She replied, "I'll walk." When she finally was ready to go home, I gave her the rice, onions, and garlic I had left, two of my dresses, Tylenol for her joint pains, a two-yard piece of cloth I had, and my *teeta* (little stool). She was very pleased.

The desert sand was blowing about our home, and the temperature was going up over 106, making us aware that the hot season was arriving in Niger.

Day of our Departure from Niamey

On March 10, I wanted to try to finish reading and recording the book on cults for blind Jofo, but I woke up with a terrific headache. We had slept with the window open for some air, but the dusty Harmattan winds had been blowing all night. This is bad for the sinuses! People were continuing to bring us piles of letters to mail for them in the States. Pete Wing said of all the people he had seen going through, none ever got so many people bringing mail as we did!

Our flight didn't leave the Niamey airport until midnight. Even though we urged our friends not to make that tiring trip in the night, they came anyway to say goodbye and give us one last hug. What a joy and blessing it had been to us to return to Niger again. We hoped that this was the beginning of short-term ministries the Lord would open for us in the days ahead.

Our flight from Paris to New York was eight hours. While hurrying to change from the Air France terminal to US Air, I put Heath's heavy hand luggage on my cart to help him. But as we rushed to go up a narrow escalator, the cart caught at the bottom. My feet were going up – but my hand on the cart was pulling me backwards! I tried to go backwards, then fell off the escalator onto the floor! How embarrassing! Heath ran back down the up escalator to help me! Afterward, I was so thankful that I only had a sore knee and slightly swollen ankle. A friend in Florida had recently fallen on an escalator, broke his knee, and had internal bleeding. He had to spend twenty-three days in the hospital.

About two weeks after we returned home, we were setting up a display table at Cedarville College to participate in their student missions' conference. We found the students to be friendly, with open hearts toward missions. Many missions were represented.

I remember my mother, with tears in her eyes, telling me that her mother heart didn't want me to go to Africa, but God dealt with her and she reached the place where she told Him she was willing to give me to Him to serve in Africa. I had never thought about my mother struggling with my call, but in 1996, I was to experience this myself. Nathan was planning to go to war-torn Lebanon. It was such a beautiful country and at one time was almost half Christian and half Muslim. However, because of the wars and Muslim persecution, more and more Christians were fleeing to other countries. I pleaded and prayed over and over, "Dear Lord, please don't let Nathan go to Lebanon unless it is absolutely Your will." I was so afraid he would be killed there.

In June 1996, Nathan left for Lebanon with Frontiers Mission. Later, I realized how hard it was for him to go as a single man. He was almost thirty, and although he had dated some wonderful godly women, God had not given him the green light about marrying any of them. The loneliness he experienced in Lebanon was extremely difficult, but he threw himself into the Gospel ministry there, living in a mountain village, making friends with the people, and studying the difficult Arabic language.

We heard from Nathan often. God was using him with many opportunities to witness in English and French while he was learning Arabic. We were really surprised at the journalistic abilities the Lord had given him. He wrote well and was very descriptive as he shared with us what God was doing and what was in his own heart. We were thrilled that Nathan was able to come home for Christmas and for the wedding of one of his best friends.

In our prayer letter, Heath wrote, "On July 14, 1996, I said goodbye to Norma at the Dayton airport on the first leg of my trip to Bénin for work with the Dendi Bible translation team. However, bad weather kept me from arriving at JFK Airport in New York on time to catch my overseas flight. The result was that our flights were rescheduled, and we left for Bénin on July 17 at 11:00 p.m., just three hours after TWA Flight 800 had crashed in the waters off of New York City. We did not learn of this, however until the next evening in Africa.

"I made the trip with Dr. Hantz Bernard, consultant with Bibles International. Our main task was to go over the Dendi translation of Genesis and Exodus with the translation team. We had a very busy and profitable nine days there…Even after all that hard work, they invited Hantz and me to return next year!"

I was home alone when the announcement came on television about the crash of TWA 800. We had flown out several times on that very TWA flight in the past. The announcement was barely over on television when our phone rang. It was Jonathan asking, "Where is Dad?" I could hear the fear in his voice as he asked, and I was thankful to be able to assure him that his Dad's flight was with another airline.

In our October 1996 prayer letter, we announced that Pastor Luc was promoted to Glory. "He was our beloved coworker since 1968. Many of you have prayed for Pastor Luc Souantieba over the years. We remember…

"Pastor Luc came to Niamey from Burkina Faso (formerly called Upper Volta) almost at the same time we came there from the bush station of Gaya in Niger. He had been asked to come for special evangelistic meetings with the small assembly of about twenty-five Gourma people who were meeting in a grass hut on the banks of the Niger River. When he went out in the afternoon to witness to Muslim men gathered in the shade, they told him that if they weren't afraid of what the police would do to them, they would have killed him for preaching that Jesus was the Son of God and only Savior. This was a real shock to Luc who came from pagan territory where people were much more open to the Gospel. He was looking forward to returning to his home country to work, but when he sensed God was calling him to Niger, he obeyed his Savior's voice. He left his friends and his country and was as much a missionary to Niger as we were.

"Soon after Luc moved to Niamey with his wife, Oukano, and baby daughter, Martha, tragedy struck. Baby Malata was stricken with typhoid and died. We'll never forget the heart-wrenching sight of seeing him tenderly lay her little body in the grave as we conducted the graveside service.

"A year later, Luc arrived on our porch early one morning with a big smile on his face to tell us God had blessed their home with twin boys! We rushed to the maternity to see Oukano and the babies. To our sorrow, Oukano was unconscious with toxemia. On our knees, we pled with the heavenly Father to touch her and heal her so she could raise the babies. God answered, and she recovered!

"Through the years, we had the joy of preaching, praying, and baptizing with Luc. He was zealous in evangelistic outreach. We have seen him preach with tears streaming down his cheeks. He started several churches in the bush, and his flock in Niamey began to grow. They moved out of the grass hut by the river to a more central location behind our Bible bookstore, and eventually a large church was built there.

"He was always there to pray for us and encourage us. Our children were prayed for daily by Luc too. He named their next daughter Rebecca, after our daughter. Oukano labored faithfully by his side, a godly pastor's wife.

"Luc lived with pain and physical problems. In recent years, an accident on his motorbike had so badly twisted his knee that he had constant back pain, limped, and walked with a cane. He told us the story of his childhood. His father was a powerful witch doctor with ten wives. When Luc contracted leprosy as a young teenager, his father wouldn't help him get treatment. Since his father had so many other children, Luc wasn't that important to him. Luc's mother scraped together a few francs to give him, and then he walked over one hundred miles to a Catholic leprosarium where he could be treated. When the leprosy was arrested a few years later, he returned home and had converted to Catholicism. God had been working in his home village during his absence though. One of his brothers had heard the Gospel and was born again. Luc didn't want to listen to his brother or the local evangelist at all. They continued to pray and witness, but he told us he was sometimes even rude to them. Nevertheless, they went out to the fields with him and helped with the back-breaking hand-farming of his land. His heart began to soften, and then came the glorious day when he opened his heart to receive Jesus Christ as his Savior. He then worked to help support his brother as he went through Bible school. After his brother graduated, he turned around and did the same thing for Luc so he could obtain his Bible training!

"The last letter we had from Luc this summer included a report of all the villages he and his men had been in to show The Jesus Film. On the report was the name of each village, the date of the showing, how many came to see the film, and how many accepted Christ. He wrote us, 'If we only had more workers to put in key nearby places to help disciple them! We're doing the best we can to follow up.'

"On October 22, a phone call from Niger informed us that the doctors had discovered cancerous tumors on Luc's liver and said there was nothing more they could do for him. Friends and deacons of his church took him back to his home village. We thought of all the years Luc had labored in a body ravaged by pain. Our prayer was, 'Lord, if it isn't Your will to heal him, please take him quickly and don't allow him to linger and suffer.' God, in His love and mercy, granted our request. Less than three days after Luc was taken to his home village, he was ushered into the presence of his Lord and Savior, Jesus Christ.

"Coworker Steve Nunemaker was able to be at Luc's funeral. He wrote us that the entire service was a very moving experience. Many testified to Luc's life of service and faithfulness, and others said he was their spiritual father. Steve said, 'What stood out more than anything was the realization that he was instrumental in leading so many Gourmas to the Lord.'

"We have received e-mails and phone calls from each of our children, Rebecca, Jonathan, Alan, and Nathan, as they feel his loss as deeply as we do. Though we will miss this dear brother so very much, through our tears we also rejoice to know he is pain-free and waiting with other loved ones there in Heaven."

The following were written by our sons:

"Hi, Mom and Dad. I am still in China at my factory. It was truly sad to get the news about Pastor Luc. He labored faithfully, and I am sure he is rejoicing now. I was glad to hear he went quickly and without a long time of suffering. I will be in China for a while, but I am looking forward to seeing you at the holidays. All my love, Jonathan"

"Hi, Mom and Dad (from Lebanon). Thank you for the note about Luc. That is sad and joyful. I have so appreciated his prayers for me over the years. I don't know if you feel this at your age, but at almost thirty, I am finding death has more of a sting than it used to. I am knowing more and more people who are going to Glory, more every year. It changes your perspective. It changes your life because the people you came into the world having are slowly disappearing. You go on with the void of their absence. Guess it is part of growing up, eh? Love you, Nathan"

Alan had been the last of our children to see Luc when he went with his dad to Niger and Bénin in 1995. He wrote from Hebron Ministry in Bloomington, Indiana, "Dear Mom and Dad. I have been choked up all morning thinking of Pastor Luc and praying for his family. I have not yet unpacked my journals, but I remember journaling after sitting with Pastor Luc in the Niamey guest house (old dormitory living room). I wrote something to the effect that I had been humbled by the joy of the Lord and the peace evident in his face and demeanor. As a child, we were much more fortunate than the Africans in not only our possessions but ease of life. It became apparent to me that as a child, I thought myself superior to the African church, as though they were children to be taught. As an adult, going home to where I grew up, it became very apparent to me that I was the child and they the superior. Whereas I had spent my years away from the Lord, they had persevered in the face of hardship and persecution, and it was me that needed teaching. It was humbling and a valuable reminder of what is true and what matters in life. I pray for you both, that the Lord would become nearer and dearer at this particular time. I feel a loss; I cannot imagine the loss you feel. Truly a hero has gone home, but I know I am richer for having known him. Our prayers are with Oukano and the children. Love, Alan"

Rebecca said that she wept upon hearing the news and that her first thought was realizing that a prayer warrior who had prayed for her daily for so many years was gone. She wondered who was going to take Luc's place in lifting her and her family to the throne of grace in the days to come.

Chapter 31
International Students and Short-Term Ministries
January 1997 to December 1997

"So do not fear, for I am with you; do not be dismayed, for I am your God. I will strengthen you and help you; I will uphold you with my righteous right hand." Isaiah 41:10

Our hearts were deeply touched when we learned that although there are multitudes of international university students in the States, the great majority of them spend their four years of study and return to their homelands without ever being invited into an American home.

We asked our EBM colleague George Hatfield how we could get involved with internationals. George and Dottie were doing a fantastic work with internationals at Iowa State University. George's reply to us was, "Pack up and move to Ames, Iowa, to work with us!" We didn't think that was an option, but then George did give us ideas for how to make contacts.

We invited Baptist Mid-Missions missionaries Gary and Betty Holtz and Kay Lamb for a meal so that we could hear about their work with internationals at nearby Wright State University in Fairborn, Ohio. We were invited to participate in their annual Thanksgiving banquet. A good number of students were there that evening. Sitting at our table were a couple from Bejing, China, both working on their master's degrees. They had met shortly before when he was asked to go to the airport to pick her up when she arrived in the States. They were a little puzzled by the slices of turkey and totally baffled by the stuffing! I am not sure they tasted either one. In China, where they eat with chopsticks, all meat is in bite-sized portions, so using a knife at the table to cut your meat was something they couldn't figure out!

They had given themselves the American names of Bill and Emily, but we soon learned to say their Chinese names, Guangyong and Min. We invited them to our home. With my preconceived ideas about Chinese people, I just knew they would like tea, so I prepared some, only to find out that their drink of preference was Pepsi!

They expressed a desire to get married so the Chinese embassy told them all they needed to do was to get someone to sign a marriage certificate for them. Since Heath was an ordained pastor, they requested that he do that! He explained to them that a marriage in the States was more than just that and that he would want them to have premarital counseling. The Lord brought to our minds a Chinese church in Dayton, so we took them there for church and to meet Pastor Cheng who scheduled them for premarital counseling. I'm sure they didn't understand why he explained that if only one of them was a Christian, he couldn't perform the ceremony, but if they were both non-Christians he could marry them. The church family welcomed them heartily and decided to give them a nice church wedding! As the pastor counseled them, we prayed so sincerely that they would understand the Gospel and be saved.

A Chinese Wedding

Guangyong and Min honored us by asking that we be their "parents" for the wedding. I was escorted and seated in her mother's place, and Heath walked "daughter" Min down the aisle to respond to "Who gives this bride to be married?"

The ladies of the Chinese church dressed the bride in a beautiful white wedding gown, did her hair and makeup, and had a darling flower girl. A couple believers who were their friends were best man and maid of honor. For the reception after the church ceremony, the bride changed into a stunning red sheath dress. The Chinese bridal color is red. There was abundant Chinese food, and a lovely time was had by all.

We took them to garage sales, shopping, church, and many other places. Though they were in their late twenties, they had never seen nor held a Bible in their hands before. The second time they came to our home, Guangyong said he would be interested in studying the Bible. Heath faithfully held studies with them and clearly presented the way of salvation to them many times in the Bible studies.

This was the beginning of our outreach to international students. Before we left Niger, we were encouraged by coworkers Harold and Charlene Curtis to consider working with internationals. They had done that for five years while they stayed in the States to get their last son through high school and settled before they came back to Niger.

Harold and Charlene told us that the students would love getting to know us and being in an American home. They also told us about encouragement they learned from another who worked with internationals. He had worked with a student for all of his years in university, but that student never became a Christian. He continued to correspond with the international after he returned to his home country. Ten years later, that man wrote to him, "I have finally understood what the Gospel message is, and I want you to know I have received Jesus Christ as my Savior!" Some of us plant the seeds or water the seeds others have planted or get to reap the harvest. We need to be faithful in our work, always remembering that only God can open their hearts and bring them to Himself.

After they received their master's degrees, our Chinese friends moved to Cincinnati where he landed a very good job. They later had a son and a daughter and bought a beautiful home. We continue to keep in contact and pray for them.

In our January 1997 prayer letter, we wrote, "We have been praying that God would give us a ministry on this side of the ocean and are thrilled that He is opening up many contacts with international students. We also invited a student from Ghana from another university to our home for a meal of West African rice and peanut butter gravy. He really enjoyed that and promised that other African students would be glad to come with him the next time for such a meal!"

Bosnia-Herzegovina

In August 1997, ABWE missionary to Budapest Mark Nikitin spoke to the combined adult Sunday school classes at Southgate Baptist Church, giving a report on the work in Croatia and Bosnia-Herzegovina. Our hearts were stirred. We had been praying for our good friends Jacqui and Larry Armstrong who had been in Bosnia filling in for two months at the request of national pastors, teaching and discipling in a newly formed church in Tuzla. As we prayed for them, we also were praying for someone else to work there after they left for other duties around the world. We never dreamed we might be an answer to our own prayers for this request! As we entered the auditorium for church that morning, an usher handed us a church bulletin and said, "I just heard a wonderful job description for you folks!" Heath smiled and said, "I think we're probably too old for that!"

Great was our surprise a few days later when Mark Nikitin called to ask if we would be willing to pray about going to Tuzla in the fall of 1997! After the initial shock and getting our breath back, we sensed that our heavenly Father was giving us a green light to go there for six weeks in October and November. Tuzla was predominantly Muslim, and many of the believers came from Muslim backgrounds, so Mark and the Armstrongs felt that our background of many years living and working among Muslims would be beneficial.

What used to be Yugoslavia had been divided into six different countries along ethnic lines: Croatia, Serbia, Bosnia-Herzegovina, Macedonia, Montenegro, and Slovenia. During the years of Tito's reign in Yugoslavia, he had been able to suppress the ethnic hostilities by keeping a tight rule over the country. But once the opportunity was given, old animosities resurfaced and the civil war began. We were going to a country ravaged by that war with horrible tragedies of Serbs killing Croatians and Bosnians, Croatians killing Serbs and Bosnians, and Bosnians killing Croatians and Serbs. The atrocities were unbelievably cruel. Each group persecuted and tried to kill the minority groups in their area or force them out, then blew up their homes so that they would never come back. An uneasy peace had been brokered, but there was much anger, hurt, and bitterness among the people groups. During the hostilities, landmines had been laid in many places, and lives were still being maimed and snuffed out because of them.

On August 27, 1997, I was reading Psalm 78:70-72, which says "He chose David his servant and took him from the sheep pens; from tending the sheep he brought him to be the shepherd of his people Jacob, of Israel his inheritance. And David shepherded them with integrity of heart; with skillful hands he led them."

I wrote in my journal that morning, "Lord – for Bosnia…Just as You took David from the sheep pens, take us from being 'put out to pasture' in retirement to tenderly shepherd Your own little flock in Tuzla. Use us, Father, to be helpers, teachers, examples, encouragers. We need Your skill to do this. Lord, may we do it for Your glory, with integrity of heart."

"God delights in taking nobodies and using them for His glory." – Dwight L. Moody

One of the first things we did was to write e-mails to our four children, telling them of this and asking for their prayers. Nathan wrote back from Beirut, Lebanon, with these words, "And you thought Lebanon was dangerous?!" Rebecca's first response was, "No!" Then she relented, not wanting to be against something she knew God was calling us to do. She said, "Then pray He will give me peace about your going." At her Bible study class, she said to the ladies, "My parents are going to Bosnia. Please pray…for me!"

Alan wrote, "Dear Mom and Dad, I am in prayer with you about Bosnia, but in my heart, it feels like a foregone conclusion that you will go. I always knew that you would be unable to retire and…how do you retire from 'the Father's business' other than our true retirement at the end of our days?

"It seems that probably the most pressing need in these last days is for true Biblical education and discipling of new believers. There are not all that many willing and able to do so. I am of the opinion that the Iron Curtain is only down for a short time, but by God's hand and sovereign power, the equipping of the church there is primary and necessary and a call from God.

"I love you and know that if God calls, you will be safe there. Thanks for your willingness to serve. – Alan"

We were so thankful that all of our children rallied behind us in their full support. We were aware of our utter dependence on the Lord and being safe in the place God was calling us to. How good it was to think of the words of that old hymn, "All the way my Savior leads me, what have I to ask beside? Can I doubt His tender mercies, who through life has been my guide?" We didn't ask anyone to pray for our safety. We knew that because of all the news reports about that part of the world, people would be praying without our asking. Several wrote and said, "I will pray for you every day you are there." Pastor Eric Mounts sent us an e-mail saying, "Southgate Baptist is praying!"

We needed to raise funds for our passage and the expenses of the trip. As always, we found that His calling is His enabling! Friends and churches rallied around us, and the needed support came in. We also asked prayer in our Discovery Class that the Lord would provide someone to live in our house during our long absence. That very Sunday, a lady in the class that we barely knew came to us and said she had stayed in and cared for homes before and that she would be glad to live in and care for ours!

We soon listed three answers to prayer:
- Someone to stay in our home and care for things in our absence
- An offer from Bill and Cathy Ardle to take us and our five suitcases to the airport in Columbus, Ohio
- Through our supporting churches and friends, all of the $3,000 needed was supplied

Heath was leading the northside home Bible study and prayer group each Wednesday evening. We had such a lovely group of people, and we grew very close to them as we met each week to study the Word and pray. Not long before we left, they asked Heath to tell about the work we were going to in Bosnia, then they all gathered around us to place hands on us and pray for us as we went. One of the ladies who told us she never prayed in public even spoke out and prayed for us that evening! Just before we left, we sent postcards to all our supporting churches and friends:

"Will you please faithfully uplift us before God's throne of grace as we minister in teaching and discipling in a young Baptist church in Tuzla, Bosnia? There will be people who do not know the Lord in attendance at the services too. What a great challenge and opportunity lies before us! We know we are not adequate for this task but, praise God, He is totally adequate! We want to be His instruments, His servants in this work He has called us to.

"Jonathan Edwards said of David Brainerd: 'And having put his hand to the plow, he looked not back, but gave himself, heart, soul, and mind, and strength, to his chosen mission, with unfaltering purpose, with a historic faith that feared no danger and surmounted every obstacle and with an earnestness of mind that wrought wonders on Indian lives and whole communities.'

"'You also are helping by your prayers for us.' – Missionary Paul

"Abiding in Him, Heath and Norma"

We received an e-mail from our Chinese friends titled "Have a Wonderful Trip. In Chinese way, when a friend is leaving, we usually not say 'goodbye' but 'safety and happiness all the way.' We want to say it to you."

We flew into Budapest via Frankfort, Germany, on October 2, 1997, and stayed in the ABWE guesthouse for two days. We had a lovely view of Budapest as we crossed a bridge over the Danube. (It wasn't beautiful blue, though, and we understand it is a very contaminated and muddy-colored river.)

The retired couple from Rochester, New York, who cared for the guest house were away, so we were all alone for the night. The next day, Michael and Jo Beth Loftis, ABWE's executive director for Eastern Europe took us to a little restaurant for lunch so he could brief us on some things about the Tuzla church. They urged us to try *gyumolcsleves* (cold Hungarian fruit soup). We loved it!

That evening, we had supper with Mark and Susan Nikitin and their children. The Nikitin and Loftis children had fond memories of Nathan when he was with them as an MIS worker for two summers from Cedarville.

Newly arrived ABWE missionary Jonathan Haskell and Mark Nikitin drove us to Zagreb, Croatia, where we met Pastor Mihial Kreko (Misho) and stayed overnight. Heath preached the next morning at Misho's church, Second Baptist Church of Zagreb. In the afternoon, we attended a party for the English class students of other missionaries. They were a lively and interesting group. It was October 5, my sixty-fourth birthday. For a special celebration for me that evening, Pastor Misho took us all down to the central pedestrian square of Zagreb, named after Josip Jelacic. There was an impressive statue of Josip (Joseph) on his horse. The weather was lovely, and we topped off our walk in an ice cream shop! It was a memorable birthday for me.

The next day, we began our eight-hour drive to Tuzla, Bosnia. Driving through Croatia made me think of Kentucky, with its rolling hills and marvelous scenery. Both the Hungarians and the Croatians love flowers. Their gardens, window boxes, and flower beds were in glorious colors. A few of the trees were starting to turn colors, about like it was in Ohio.

Once we crossed from Croatia over into a part of Serbia on our way to Bosnia, the scenery changed drastically. The ravages of war were prevalent everywhere. There were bombed out and empty buildings all along the road. When we were detained for hours on the roadside waiting for a ferry because a bridge had been destroyed, Mark warned us not to wander off the road because of landmines still not discovered. Our lunch that day was Coke and a candy bar purchased at a gas station. In the major towns along the way in these former communist Yugoslavia areas, we saw many of the drab high-rise apartment buildings typical of that regime.

It was late evening when we arrived at the fourth-floor apartment of Deacon Andelko Savic and his wife, Andelina. They were the parents of Vesna Kolak, who was a key woman in the church. Vesna was out of the country, but we met her husband, Dusko, as we enjoyed a delicious meal prepared by Andelina. The church had begun in the Savics' apartment about three and a half years previously, but when they began to be too numerous in the small apartment and Muslim neighbors complained of their noise and singing, they decided to divide into two groups, with only half of the group coming each week. Imagine only being allowed to go to church every other week.

The atmosphere in Bosnia was very strongly Muslim and also anti-Serb and anti-Croatian. Andelina and Andelko were typical of what had happened over the years when there was intermarriage between the different ethnic groups. Andelko was Serb, and Andelina was Croatian. Many of the church people had been forced to send their younger children out of the country to continue their education. One family in the church had brought their children back from Croatia after the war, but their Muslim classmates threatened to kill them! Some of the parents had not seen their children for five years or more because of this situation.

The church had rented a spacious second floor apartment in the center of Tuzla. Two rooms in the apartment were used for the Baptisticka Crkva Tuzla (Tuzla Baptist Church) meetings, and we lodged in the third room, with a kitchen across the hall, a small bathroom with a sink and tub, and a closet toilet off the hallway. It was so cold in our kitchen that Jell-O got firm for me without refrigeration! Our living room/bedroom had a couch that folded down into a single bed at night and a chair made of pillows that converted into a single bed. In the tiny communist apartment buildings, many of the residents' living rooms also served as their bedrooms. We were thankful for warm, layered clothes to wear in our rooms, and often wore coats during church services. After we heated our bath water on the hot plate and put it in the tub, we rolled the little space heater into the bathroom for our baths. It was so cold in the hallway going to the closet toilet that we could see our breath in the air, and it was rather like going to an outdoor facility! (Brrr, was that seat ever cold!)

We were told that Tuzla actually means "salt" in the Turkish language. Extractions of the city's salt deposits over many decades have caused sections of the city center (where the church was located) to sink. Some structures in the sinking area had collapsed and been demolished. The building next to the church apartment building had sunk a meter (over three feet) and was cracking. Someone had tried to shore it up with large planks, but that didn't keep me from an uneasy feeling as we walked up to the entrance of our building!

We learned to live without a car, washing machine, dryer, TV, stove, and telephone, just like we did in France during language study in 1959. We did our washing by hand every morning, but it was cold and most things took more than one day to dry. We had a tiny balcony area, about three-by-five feet, only open on one side, with a clothesline zig-zagged back and forth between nails to hang our wash on. The sun, if it was shining, only hit that area for a few hours in the morning. Many of the people in Tuzla heated their homes or cooked with wood, so there was a constant smell of wood smoke on our clothes while we were there.

We were thankful for a two-burner hotplate and a tiny refrigerator that was about three feet high in the kitchen. The water ceased to come from the pipes at 8:30 in the morning until in the evening again. We learned to fill buckets and bottles for water during the few hours of the day when it came through the pipes. This reminded us of similar circumstances with water supply when we were in Dosso, Niger!

We were so sure that we were in Tuzla because the Lord wanted us there and really enjoyed the adventures of all these things, including shopping in the nearby open market. The Lord was with us, and we were so warmly received by the brothers and sisters of the Tuzla Baptist Church. After our first prayer meeting, Andelina locked arms with me as we walked out of church and said in her almost non-existent English, "Norma! My friend, my seesta!" How precious it is in Christ that no matter where we go in this world, in the body of Christ we find that we have family!

I learned to make very strong coffee in the little demi tasse cups in our apartment. It was very meaningful to the Bosnian people to drink coffee with you. They used special little hand grinders with always fresh coffee beans and hospitably would say, "I want to drink coffee with you at my house." We were offered coffee at all times of the day, and after drinking with them late afternoon or late night, we wondered if we would be unable to sleep. However, we slept very well!

The church met three times a week: Sunday morning, then Wednesday night was Bible study. On Friday nights, they had "praying meeting." (We loved that expression.) Heath preached through Philippians with Dusko translating into Bosnian.

We were anxious to learn some of the local language so we could greet people and shop in the market. I quickly memorized counting to ten *(jedan, dva, tri, cetri, pet, sest, sedam, awsom, devet, deset)*. This was helpful in the market.

Dusko came several times to give us language lessons. Since Bosnian, like French, does not have the "th" sound, they really couldn't deal with Heath's name. They called him by his first name, George, which they wrote *Dord*. *Brat* is the word for brother. I couldn't help smiling when they referred to Heath as *Brat Dord!* He was *Brat Dord*, and I was *Sestra Norma!* The Bosnian language is definitely short on vowels! Some examples are *crkva* for "church" and *dvro* for "tree."

Having lived so many years in Niger where the mosques were full at prayer times and also the sidewalks and even streets during Ramadan, we were surprised that so few in Tuzla went to the mosques. The prayer call went out five times a day over the loudspeakers, but few seemed to observe the prayer rituals or the month of fasting. We were told that being Muslim gave them their identity – different from that of the Orthodox Serbs and the Catholic Croatians. It was the first time we had heard of secular Muslims. Some didn't even believe in God. The population was being urged to become Muslim in practice as well as in profession, and they were offering young women $200 if they would start wearing the hijab covering over their hair.

In many ways, Tuzla was like being back in a third-world country. We have so much in America that we take for granted and aren't grateful for. Dula and Drago were faithful at church services. When Dula was hospitalized, seriously ill with pneumonia, water on her lungs, and high blood pressure, we went with the Savics and Kolacs to visit her in the hospital.

With Jesus Leading the Way

We were warned that we would probably be shocked at the conditions in the hospital located high on a hill on the outskirts of Tuzla. It reminded me so much of the Niamey hospital. Dula was so happy to see us that she cried. We had purchased a large bag of fruit for her. As we left the hospital, Drago told us that the only way you could get your loved one into a hospital was to pay some money under the table.

Drago had a van that he used to make a living by transporting people. It had been taken away from him during the war and used by the military. They had stripped the inside of its seats, but he finally got it back and refurbished it. As we wound our way down the hillside with a beautiful view of Tuzla, Drago took us to his apartment because he wanted to make *Bosanska kahva* for us.

Drago had feigned insanity to keep from being put into the military during the war. So because he was "insane," they gave him the pension he deserved – 90 Deutche marks every three months or about $52!

At Drago's tiny, pleasant apartment (we could see Dula's touch), we met his father, Savo. Savo lived in Serbia. Before Dula got sick, Drago had gone up to see his dad and found him sick in bed in an unheated house, so he brought him back to Tuzla. A doctor gave him penicillin, to which he had an allergic reaction. He had purple blotches and ulcer-type sores on his arms and ankles but was recovering slowly, *Bogu hvala* (praise God)!

As we enjoyed Drago's coffee in our tiny cups, he told us about his father. Drago had explained to him that Tuzla Baptist Church's believers baptize by immersion. Savo said, "That makes sense! I always thought the way the Orthodox church sprinkled babies was wrong. After all, babies can't decide or say yes or no."

Drago picked up his Bible from the coffee table and said, "From now on, I'll only believe what is in this Book!" Savo said that for the first time, he was hearing good things about Christianity. He said he was seventy-seven years old, but now in his son's apartment, this was the first time in his life he had ever seen a Bible. Andelko talked to him some, and we all invited him to come to the Tuzla Baptist Church. We bade him farewell with earnest prayers in our hearts that Savo would understand and come to know Christ.

On Wednesday, October 29, our electricity suddenly went off at 3:00 p.m. The apartment quickly got even colder, and we had no hot water. It was getting dark by 5:00 p.m. at that time of year. At 5:30 p.m., people began to arrive for Bible study. Heath waited with a flashlight at the bottom of the stairs to help folks up. I got two candles going in the church room. It was cold, but the folks took it in good spirits. At 6:00 p.m., Heath had a flashlight ready for preaching when the lights suddenly came on!

After the Bible study, we had supper then planned to walk to the Savics' at 9:00 p.m. to try e-mail.

At 8:00 p.m., the electricity was gone again! Two families, Andelko and Andelina and Drago and Dula, had offered for us to spend the night with them, but because the lights had come back on, we declined! We went to bed early to keep warm. Pajamas, long underwear, socks, blankets – we were warm and cozy! The church folks never thought of canceling the service. Sitting in the dark in a cold room was just accepted, even after they had walked to church in the cold too. Bless them!

The "Holy Bathroom"

There were four candidates for baptism during our time in Bosnia. All baptisms were done in the very large bathtub of the Savics' apartment. The first lady whom Heath baptized was Gordana, a widow with several young sons. She was really beaming with joy the next Sunday. Heath had baptized believers in baptisteries, lakes, rivers, cisterns, and rainy-season creeks, but this was his first experience baptizing in a bathtub! The candidate sat in the baptismal water while Heath knelt beside the bathtub and was able to totally immerse! The church folk were gathered in the hallway, with as many as possible also in the bathroom. They sang joyfully after each immersion. The baptismal service was on Wednesday evening, our last night in Tuzla. What a blessed way to conclude our ministry!

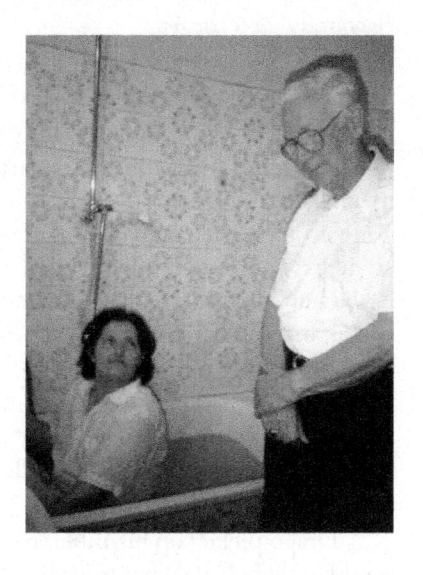

An amusing thing was that when Heath signed their baptismal certificates, he was named as the "priest". Vesna said that their word for pastor was the same as shepherd, so outsiders would be wondering why a shepherd was baptizing people!

We fell in love with the people of Tuzla Baptist Church. They had suffered so much during the war, and the peace was fragile. Although the people of Bosnia were very divided, in the church it was a different story. The church's ethnic mixture included Croatians, Bosnians, Serbs, Palestinians, and Albanians, many of whom were communists before they received Christ as Savior. Now they were one in Christ and loved one another.

Our time in Tuzla had come to an end. With reluctant hearts, we bade farewell to our brothers and sisters in Christ. They voiced their hope that we would return in the future and gave us many homemade gifts to show their love and appreciation. We left behind our sheets, blankets, some clothing, pots and pans, and food for any who needed these things at the church.

It had turned very cold when we arrived back at the ABWE guest house in Erd. There was a washing machine at the guest house, so we were able to wash our clothes to get all the smell of wood smoke out of them! The next day, we took a train into the city for a walking tour of Budapest.

When we arrived home, it looked so luxurious after seven weeks in Tuzla! We realized anew that we have so much in the States compared to those dear people of the former Yugoslavia.

We knew our praying friends were responsible for the power and presence of God during our missionary journeys. We wrote thank-you notes to our prayer warrior supporters when we returned:

"We want to say, 'Hvala' ('Thank you') again for your part in sending us to Tuzla, Bosnia, this fall. What a marvelous privilege to serve the Savior there! We fell in love with the people of Tuzla Baptist Church, and it was hard to leave. We saw God working in hearts as decisions were made. We were so busy there that we never were wondering, "What will we do today?" but rather, "How can we fit everything in today?" It was great to be busy in the Lord's work, and we thanked Him daily for the privilege of being there. Our heavenly Father watched over us, and we never missed a day of ministry because of sickness. All this, we know, was in answer to your prayers.

"We are looking forward to the holidays with our family and then will be leaving on January 1 for a month in Bénin, West Africa, working with the translation team of the Dendi Bible. Hantz Bernard (from Haiti) of Bibles International is the other consultant. We will fly to Niamey, Niger, and then proceed by road approximately two hundred miles to the bush station of Guéné in northern Bénin. Will you please pray for us – for wisdom in the translation work, for health, and that we will glorify our Savior in every aspect of the ministry He entrusts to us there."

Just before leaving for Benin, I was asked to speak to our Discovery Class on "Bosnia from the wife's perspective." I didn't expect to be asked that, but it was very interesting thinking over my perspective on our Bosnia short-term ministry and the wonderful ways God undertook for us and the church folks there.

December 27, 1997, our first grandchild, Nansie, married Kevin Whitt's in Indianapolis. Nansie was a beautiful bride. Nathan performed the wedding ceremony, and Heath gave the message.

Norma Bobbett

On our last Sunday of 1997, Heath was asked to take ten minutes in our Discovery Class to tell about Christmas in Africa and to inform the class what we would be doing in Bénin. We were already looking forward to our next short-term adventure back on the African continent!

Chapter 32
Bénin, Québec, and Haiti
January 1998 to January 2000

We were praising the Lord that we could get all our belongings in three suitcases, so we could take the sixty-pound box of French Bibles as our fourth piece of luggage, free of charge, for the Bible bookstore in Niamey. United had canceled our original reservations, and we had a seven-hour wait in Chicago for our next flight to Paris. United gave us access to their Red Carpet Club where we could relax in comfortable overstuffed chairs and have free coffee, tea, and snacks. First though, we dragged all of our hand luggage, computer, and so forth to Terminal 5 to get our Air France boarding passes. There was no one at the counter and a note said to come back at 4:45, two hours later! We dragged everything the long way back to Terminal 1 into the Red Carpet Club then left them there to go one at a time back to Terminal 5 to check in and get our boarding passes. (The more we travel, the smarter we get!)

The Harmattan that brings in dust and sandstorms was very obviously in the air when we landed in Niamey. We were thankful that the haze wasn't so bad that our plane couldn't land this time.

We were warned about men with airport badges who were coming up to debarking passengers, saying, "I am here to help you. Please sit down with a nice cold Coke while I process your papers." They then took the unsuspecting travelers' passports and health cards to the front of the lines to get them stamped by officials. (Actually, that is a free process that travelers can do for themselves.) These men then refused to return the travelers' passports and health cards until they were paid exorbitant prices.

Sure enough, as we were waiting in line, one came up to us, but when Heath spoke to him in Zarma, perhaps he was fearful we weren't good game. He went on to others. Later as we waited for our luggage at the carousel, we saw about twelve scammed people sitting dejectedly to one side, waiting for their papers! Those were expensive Cokes!

The next day, we went shopping for supplies to take to Bénin. I felt at home again, shopping at a Lebanese store, the yellow tin shack, and for fresh things along the street. From the post office in Malanville, Bénin, our missionary coworker called the Niamey mission office (no cell phones back then) to ask us to bring twenty-five pita breads and two cabbages also!

We had the weekend in Niamey while waiting for Bible consultant Hantz Bernard to join us. Many precious African friends came to greet us and welcome us back to Africa. Yenuru came for a long visit. As I told her how much we were missing Pastor Luc, she said her husband, Yabiri, had accompanied Luc back to his home village (Mahadaga, in Burkina Faso) after Luc was told he was terminally ill. Yabiri heard Luc pray, "Father, if You see that I am not going to recover, please take me quickly and don't allow me to linger." That was the exact prayer I was praying for Luc in Ohio. The Lord took him home within three days.

Yenuru also asked me to pray for two sons who weren't walking with the Lord and were causing her grief with alcohol and drugs. As we prayed together, I was thinking of Gordana, a widow in Bosnia, and her heartache with four sons to raise alone, the oldest already into drugs. "Please, Father, help her, supply her needs, give her wisdom and help her to grow, lean on You." I thought about what a friend had said when I was crying over a wayward son: "When our children are little, they step on our laps. When they are big, they step on our hearts."

Hantz's plane arrived after midnight on January 4, and by 7:30 a.m. on January 5, we were all packed and loaded into the mission truck to drive to Bénin. The Harmattan winds and dust were blowing most of the day, and sixty-five degrees, felt quite chilly!

On our way, we stopped in Dosso for a short visit with Felix and Ladi and were greeted with hugs and enthusiasm. How happy we were to see these faithful believers who were a part of the church that we helped organize during our time there. We would have loved to have seen more of the church people, but the driver was in a hurry to get us to Guéné and return home the same day. The truck wasn't really reliable, and he didn't want to be on the road at night.

Heath worked with Dr. Bernard previously but this was my first time to meet this fine man from Haiti. Many Haitians are actually descendants of slaves from Bénin, taken to Haiti by the French. Hantz was going back to some of his roots!

I was so happy to be back in Africa and interacting with the African women and children again. Guéné was much like the village of Gaya where we spent our first two terms of missionary service. One difference in Guéné was that the missionaries had installed a generator for evening electricity. We never had a generator in Gaya but relied on kerosene pressure lanterns to light our house at night.

Dust was in the air and everywhere, causing stuffed up noses and scratchy throats, especially at night when we tried to sleep. The dishes in the cupboards, the curtains and bedspreads...everything smelled of dust! And then there was the familiar smell of cockroaches in the cupboards! I sprayed our bedroom that first evening to try to rid it of malaria-carrying mosquitos, and a number of cockroaches staggered out of the closets to die!

The first evening, Hantz and I didn't have flashlights, so we were closely following Heath in the darkness as he lighted the pathway with his flashlight from the resident missionary's house to ours. We had informed Hantz that this was definitely snake country! Back at our lodgings, Heath gave Hantz a battery for his flashlight so Hantz could go out to see if anyone was playing volleyball at the court a former missionary had built.

As Hantz walked around the corner of the house, he heard leaves rustling by the wall, shined his flashlight, and saw a six-foot spitting cobra! When Zandam, heard us yelling, he came running with a long pronged stick. Mr. Cobra had slithered over into a rock pile by then, but Zandam was able to pin him and kill him. Hantz asked Zandam to save the snakeskin for him, so he could take it home and have a belt made from it! That was enough excitement for our first evening at Guéné, and once again, we were so thankful for the Lord's protection.

The first translation committee meeting began with Pastors Bagnan and Isiako and Bible school student Alassane. What they accomplished in the three weeks of hard work was amazing. In answer to prayer, they were able to check all the verses in Leviticus and Numbers! Hantz also had a session to help the committee better understand how to translate the poetical books. No one got sick or had to miss a day of work. Heath got to preach two out of the four Sundays we were in Benin.

From our prayer letter, dated February 1998: "If you can, picture in your mind the six people seated around the table each day with all kinds of Bible translations before them. Hantz is checking their translation from the Hebrew; the resident missionary and Heath are checking the Dendi and French versions; Isiako, Alassane, and Bagnan are only looking at their Dendi script. This process is called back translation. The three Dendi men took turns looking at their translated verses in Dendi and then telling what it says to them in French. Hantz, Heath, and the resident missionary could catch if any words or phrases were missing or if the thought expressed was not exactly what was said in the original text. The spirit of love and cooperation among the whole group was excellent."

We hired a young woman to help me with dishes, laundry, and other housework (especially washing the layer of dust off the cement floors and louvered windows every few days)! I was thankful for her help, and she was so happy to have employment. Most days after meal preparation and home chores, we walked together to the village on visitation or to market day on Thursdays. It was a large bush market with lots of cows, sheep, and goats for sale. I was amazed to find leaf lettuce, tomatoes (cold season only), oranges, bananas, pineapple, tiny watermelons, onions, and puffy rolls of Ghana bread.

On our way home from the market we found a Fulani lady selling eggs. She said that they were all fresh, but my African friend insisted that we needed to test them in water to see if any floated. She quickly borrowed a pan, ran to a nearby well, lowered the *loga* (container made from a truck tire inner tube) into the well, and drew out two containers of water. We tested the eggs, and they all seemed good!

The people in the market were amazed that I spoke Zarma to them. One man laughingly called me his *ay anzourey* (in-law). Haissa said this man's wife was Zarma, and he used to live in Niger.

One Saturday, we went up to the Malanville market. It had grown so much bigger than in the 1960s when we went there. I had fun shopping for kilos of loose flour and sugar weighed out on a scale, tomatoes, oranges, pineapple, carrots, and...apples! We never had bought apples in the market before. They surely didn't grow locally, so we didn't know where they came from.

Before returning to Guéné, Hantz wanted to take us out to dinner, so we went to the little Malanville hotel Rose des Sables. Sitting on the small cement terrace with a thatched roof overhead, we had tough chicken, greasy fries, and Coke. We had fun anyway, visiting together. The waitress was very nice. She brought us a pan of soapy water and a pan of clear water to wash and rinse our hands afterward.

In our prayer letter, we asked for prayer for Northern Bénin. Although Islam was progressing into Bénin, there were fewer Muslims in Northern Bénin, and the response to the Gospel among the Dendi people had been more fruitful. There were four established churches.

I didn't know if any woman had ever had children's classes or women's classes in the eight villages in the area where there were preaching points. Five missionary couples had been there in the past, but between 1990 and 1995 they had all left. The single missionary was carrying on alone, but age and health were big factors in her life. We wrote, "Please pray for a couple for Northern Bénin who will be willing to live there, love the people, learn the language, and work for God's glory. As much good as short-term workers can do, there is no substitute for lifetime commitment to missionary service." What a thrill it was to see that prayer answered just a few years later when a fine young missionary family came to Bénin!

One evening, a coworker invited us all over for supper. She had fixed a lovely meal: leg of lamb, baked potatoes, corn and cabbage salad, and apple pie! I could taste the buggy flour in the pie, so I couldn't eat the crust. Heath, on the other hand, didn't taste it. He ate his and mine too!

I wish I could say there had been no hitches or times of anxiety over the work while we were in Bénin, but that wasn't the case. The missionary we were working with was a very talented woman and accomplished great things during her years of service. She was a gifted painter, had produced primers that helped with literacy classes, wrote beautiful poetry, and at times produced mountains of work. She did love the Lord, but she also was very evidently bipolar. When her extreme mood swings came about, she was very hard on her coworkers. When one of her coworkers had suggested she seek medical help back in the States, she became angry and denied she had a problem. When she was "up" she was extremely happy, creative, and full of energy. When she had a "down" mood swing, her whole world looked bleak and she wanted to resign and go home.

Hantz shared with us that the Bénin translators had come to him on his evening walk with their concerns about her. I wrote about this in my journal: "Lord, this situation is hard. We can't handle it. We must give it to You. Please…don't allow Satan to defeat the translation of Your Word into the Dendi language. Give Hantz, Heath, and me wisdom and please speak to this troubled coworker about her actions. Help the African translation team…these young men are tender and impressionable." During this time, my heart went out to this coworker, knowing that she couldn't control her depressed moods when they came upon her.

Meanwhile the committee carried on, working hard every day. Heath and Hantz came home the next noon rejoicing that they had checked two hundred verses in Numbers that morning. Their hope was to average one hundred fifty each day, but of course, some days they weren't even able to get through one hundred.

One morning, Haissa and I walked all the way through the village, stopping at her compound to greet her family and greeting people along the way. The Dendi people were so friendly. We saw Saray and Zima. Saray had been a leader in the work when former missionaries were there, but he no longer came to church. Similar situations happened to all missionaries and were very sad for us.

It is not enough to ask the Lord for opportunities to share the Good News of our Savior, but we needed to pray also that the Lord would lead us to prepared hearts.

The translation project for this trip was wrapped up on Friday, January 24, so on Saturday afternoon we had a farewell dinner celebration for the translators and their families. I roasted two legs of lamb and one leg of goat, as did our coworker. Amina made delicious rice with sauce, and we had soft drinks. We celebrated in the *bukka*, a large round hut with a thatched roof and open sides. It was a delightful time of food and fellowship followed by enthusiastic singing of many Gospel songs.

We were wondering how to contact someone with a car to take the three of us back more than two hundred miles to Niamey for our departure. That was preferable to the three of us and our luggage piling onto a crowded and overloaded bush taxi. Dieyabidi came from Gaya to introduce us to a man he knew named Luc. Luc had an old Peugeot 504 and was happy to be our means of getting back to Niamey. Heath's observation was that the old car was a "carcass," a piece of junk, and we needed to pray it would really be able to take us to Niamey on the following Tuesday!

Heath wasn't feeling well on Monday. Two days before, he was coming out of the *bukka* and hit his head so hard that he fell down. He had a headache that wouldn't go away and felt nauseated. We were glad he was better when we left early the next day on our way back to Niamey, and we were praising the Lord that Luc's car made it all the way without breaking down!

Heath was so disappointed that there were no Zarma Bibles for sale on the shelves of our Bible bookstore. But his disappointment turned to joy when we learned that someone had come in the day before and purchased all forty-two of the Bibles, so the store manager was going to the mission storeroom to replenish!

Thursday was the holiday Mefeeri, the end of Ramadan's month of fasting. We had friends coming all day to visit us, and it was really wonderful to see them again. Our plane for Paris was to leave around midnight.

Mariama came out to have soup supper with us. I told her we were concerned about her health as we hugged her goodbye. She just clung to us as tears ran down her cheeks. She said she hadn't had good hugs like that in a long time. We prayed together. She said, "Just because I don't write doesn't mean I don't love you. Please don't give up on me!" We told her we would never do that.

We were home in Springfield by 5:00 p.m. on February 1. We had a long chat with Alan on February 3, rejoicing that he was celebrating his fifth year of being free from drugs and alcohol – all glory to the Son of God!

Four days after we got home, it began to snow. Then the snow turned to sleet. The roads were terrible, and our church prayer meeting was canceled. I wrote, "We aren't going out today at all. Our backyard and front yard look like a frozen skating rink!"

Heath resumed leading the Wednesday night home Bible studies. We had such a great group of brothers and sisters in Christ, and our group grew to over twenty people. But not everyone could be there at the same time, so we usually had at least twelve to fourteen as we met in different homes each month. Being a host family for international students continued to bring us great joy. We loved getting to know these students, and they seemed to really appreciate being invited to an American home.

At this time we learned that Jon and Judy's eighteen-year marriage was falling apart and it was heartbreaking for us. We cried out to the Lord, especially for Stephen, Joel, and Laura. We agonized in prayer constantly. The Lord, again, had much to teach us through it all. What do people do who don't have the assurance of His everlasting arms underneath them?

Trusting God in the Unpredictable

"Remember, God is God and God is good. The measure of your spirituality is seen between the time that something totally unpredictable happens and the time when you can say, 'God will take care of this.'"– Anonymous

God doesn't need any help in being God. He is very capable on His own! How important it is that I cultivate a deepening relationship with God that will satisfy, secure, and sustain me no matter what happens!

More devastating news came in March 1998 when it was discovered that Heath's sister, Jane, had pancreatic cancer. Being a nurse, she knew how serious this was, but also being a devoted follower of the Lord Jesus Christ, she stated that God was giving her peace and that she had had her "three score and ten." Jane was seventy-two.

It seemed that the summer of 1998 went by on fast forward! We were continuing to reach out to international students at Wittenberg University as well as to our Chinese friends. We remembered well what it was like to be in a foreign land and how much we appreciated those who befriended us and welcomed us into their homes. We had four students for dinner one evening from Malaysia, Ghana, Pakistan, and Tanzania. Two were Muslim, one had a Buddhist background, and one was Catholic. We wrote to our prayer warriors, "Pray we will be good testimonies to these young people and have opportunities to share the Gospel with them." The students were very dear to us, and it was great working with them. They kept us feeling young! We were delighted that some accepted our invitations to attend church with us. We invited five to an early Thanksgiving at our home. They surprised us by all coming in their national dress from their home countries, and we had a wonderful time!

Québec

From our prayer letter, dated September 1998: "Last year, we got to celebrate our October birthdays in Croatia and Bosnia. This year we will celebrate in Canada! On September 26, we will be leaving for Buckingham,

Québec, to fill in for missionaries there who will be away for some schooling and much-needed R&R. We are brushing up on our French and will appreciate your prayers that God will use us as we minister. Heath will be teaching and preaching on Sundays and Wednesdays for the month, and Norma will be teaching a Sunday school class for teenagers."

We learned that the people of Québec are not of the French (France) culture, although that is their language. They have a culture all their own, and we really had a good time learning their ways and thoughts.

The Rabbit River Baptist Church met in a beautiful little stone Anglican church. The Anglicans had a lady minister who came every other Sunday. We had to be finished with church and Sunday school and cleared out of the building by noon on the days she came.

Number one of our hurdles in Québec was that their French was very different from the French we had learned in France. The people were so friendly, but after our first home prayer meeting, I said to Heath, "I didn't understand a word they said when praying!" He said, "Neither did I!" Our prayer supporters were praying though, and our ears began to adjust!

Each Sunday, after French Sunday school and church in Buckingham, we traveled to the village of Thurso to hold an English service at the Thurso Baptist Church. This was another picturesque old building and had been a thriving English work many years before. However, the English speakers in the area were growing fewer and fewer, so there were only about twelve older ladies still attending at that time. I played the piano for the service, and Heath preached the messages in English.

From our December 1998 prayer letter: "*Joyeux Noel.* What a blessing the work in Buckingham, Québec, was to us this fall! It was great to be back in a French-speaking country. Thank you for praying for us. We praise God for the witness of this group of believers in the Rabbit River Baptist Church and the other ministries we saw in nearby towns. God is working!

"As you can imagine, the Roman Catholic Church is very strong in this French province. We learned that just forty years ago, many were arrested for preaching the Gospel in Québec. We heard of one instance where a pastor was holding an open-air meeting and a man drove his Harley-Davidson right into the midst of the crowd to break up the meeting. Suddenly the motor died and, try as he would, he could not get it started again! So, meekly, he had to push his dead cycle through the crowd and leave! Another pastor was jailed for preaching, and the jailhouse (next door to the fire station) burned down! Those are just some illustrations of the Lord's humor in letting folks know He was still in charge. But of course, there are many instances of real hardship and persecution to those who shared God's Word in Québec. We remember Hebrews 11 where it is recorded that some were spared and others were not.

"Thank you for praying that our ears would be attuned to Québecois French. We had been told, 'They will not have any trouble understanding you, but it will take a while for you to begin to understand them.' It was a surprise to us when so many English words were thrown into their French conversations. We were patient with each other and had lots of laughs together as we learned new vocabulary.

"Our friends had a hard time with our name. In France, the French always pronounced our name as 'Bo-bette.' However, the folks in Québec didn't use that name. They referred to us as 'Pastor and Madame.' Before we left, we found out that their slang name for underwear is *babettes*. We all had a good laugh when we let them know we found out why they didn't want to call us a name that was so close to underwear! Heath said, 'The Lord surely has a sense of humor in sending Pastor and Mrs. Underwear to Québec!'"

I wrote a two-person skit about our time in Québec and the cultural differences we saw. We presented the skit in churches, at our mission conference, and in missions classrooms at Cedarville University. It was humorous and really seemed to help others understand some differences.

Nathan surprised us that year by coming home from Beirut, Lebanon, for Thanksgiving, and we extended the surprise by taking him with us to Aunt Shirley Blackman's home in Sparta, New Jersey, for Heath's family Thanksgiving. It was a joy to have Heath's, Jane's, and Shirley's extended families there, but it also was very sobering because Jane was not looking well at all.

On January 3, 1999, Heath's sister Jane went home to heaven. She had requested that Heath preach her funeral in Syracuse, and that her son-in-law Dr. Dan Juster have a part too. Jane requested that "Jesus Loves Me" be sung at her funeral and the "Hallelujah Chorus" played at the conclusion. "Precious in the sight of the Lord is the death of His saints"

On January 23, 1999, we had breakfast with Becca, Alan, and Nathan in Greenwood. I wrote in my journal, "Just hearing Rebecca, Alan, and Nathan talk about the Lord and where they are in spiritual growth and ministry was such a blessing to us. Thank You, Father, for what You have done and are doing in their lives. Thank You for giving us this family time together to encourage us. Before returning to Springfield, we said goodbye to Nathan because he was preparing to return to Lebanon at the end of the month. Our prayers followed him."

We quickly were planning a second trip to Québec to minister in April 1999. Heath began working on French messages right away, and I was gearing up to teach the fourth- to sixth-graders in Sunday school as well as the women's ministry. A friend wrote that she was "praying for our French tongues and ears!"

Believing that once again "a great door was opening to us," we began our drive back to Buckingham, Québec, on March 31 and arrived on April 1. An e-mail had brought the news that the church attendance had been increasing. We looked forward to working with believers and also with those who had not yet received Christ. We wrote to our supporters, "We urge you, brothers and sisters, by our Lord Jesus Christ and by the love of the Spirit, to join strive together with us in your prayers to God for us (Romans 15:30)."

Two of the church families had a beautiful bouquet of red roses on the table, waiting to welcome us back, with a very sweet note. Then they came over in the evening for coffee and a three-hour visit. We were hearing the Québecois French much better on our second time there because God's people were praying for us.

On Sunday, we got lots of hugs and kisses (on both cheeks) at church. Heath led us in celebrating the Lord's Supper before the teachers and children left for Sunday school. I had spent many hours preparing the lessons on the tabernacle for my 10- to 12-year-olds class. What a blessing it was to see how Christ is foretold in the building of the tabernacle. The children were really sharp and were quite responsive with questions and answers.

After French church, we drove out to Thurso for the English service, but at that time they were meeting in a home because the road up to their little church on the hill hadn't been plowed yet. We had a warm welcome and hugs from the English ladies and gents too. It made us think back to our time in Tuzla, Bosnia, meeting in a house church where Heath preached from a doorway between two rooms. It was communion Sunday in the English church also. When Heath chose "I will Sing of My Redeemer" for the closing song, he noticed that the lady hosting the meeting wasn't singing and instead was thumbing through another part of the songbook, so he told her the number again. She replied very crisply, "I don't sing that song!" Oh me! Why? Well, we finished singing all the verses and closed. Afterward she said, "I never sing that song because it was my father's favorite." We then understood the emotion associated with that song and how she must miss her father.

During this time in Québec, I was asked to show our African slides at a ladies missionary meeting at the English church in Thurso. The ladies loved the slides and hearing about our work in Niger. I tried not to keep them too long, but afterward one lady said, "I would have been pleased if you had spent five minutes talking about each slide!"

With Jesus Leading the Way

My next speaking engagement was at a ladies breakfast (*déjeuner d'espoir*) in a quaint log cabin restaurant called La Maison du Steak. I had to prepare my Mariama Mousa monologue in French. The ladies were so kind, saying they really appreciated it. Heath also spoke at a men's breakfast in another restaurant.

Our prayer request was that during our time in Québec, God would do something there that only He could do. We saw Christians renew their dedications to the Lord, and at least one opened his heart to accept Jesus as his Savior. On Sunday mornings, Heath preached on spiritual maturity, and on Sunday evenings, he led a study in Romans. On Wednesday evenings, he challenged our hearts about prayer. A great blessing to us was that almost everyone prayed at the prayer meetings. There were no awkward silent pauses. These dear ones were serious about their prayer meetings, which lasted more than two hours.

At the second prayer meeting, Martin sent word that he would not be there because he felt burdened to go witnessing that evening. On Sunday, I greeted him to let him know that we had been praying for him. When I asked him how things went, he got all choked up and couldn't talk. It was noisy in the church foyer, so he asked me to come down the hall to talk to him. He was barely able to get out the words that it was his own father he went to witness to. He said he felt burdened all day at work to go talk to his dad, but when he went, his father was very rebellious and wouldn't listen to him. His father was told by the Catholic branch he belongs to that Evangelical Baptists are very bad, don't have the truth, and lead people astray. Martin said his mother had accepted the Lord but is influenced by her husband, who won't allow her to go to a good church. Our hearts ached for Martin as he wept over the unsaved condition of his father. I reminded him about the Apostle Paul and what a rebel he was, thinking even that by killing Christians he was doing God's work. But God is sovereign and His power limitless. Praise God, just a year later, we were thrilled to hear that Martin's parents had both become Christians! Our prayer request then was that they would be willing to come to church and be under the teaching of God's Word.

And then as I went outside after the morning service, a young mother, Suzanne, came up to us and told us how much the message had touched her heart. The next thing I knew, she threw her arms around me and cried on my shoulder. She said she really needed that message and wanted prayer that she would walk closer to the Lord. We felt so unworthy to be allowed to minister in Québec again. God was working as His people were praying for us.

At this time, Heath received a very interesting e-mail from our Pakistani Muslim friend, one of the students at Wittenberg for whom we were a host family. We had bonded with him in love, but we still had been praying for that opportunity to share the Gospel with him. He wrote, "What is Easter…and why are there bunny eggs?" Wow! Heath took this long-prayed-for opportunity to explain the whole Gospel message to him, about Jesus' life, death, and resurrection. And he explained to him that the Easter Bunny had nothing to do with this message! Our student friend wrote back that he hadn't expected such a thorough and long answer, but he thanked Heath just the same!

Our final prayer meeting with the church folks was such a blessed time, and it was hard for us to say goodbye. They presented us with a beautiful farewell Scripture plaque, and Nicole Sarault had baked a cake for all to share. On top she had written, *"Du fond de nos coeurs – Merci!"* ("From the bottom of our hearts – Thanks!")

We left Québec, feeling as though we were leaving a part of our hearts with those dear brothers and sisters in Christ. We had gotten to know the people even better as they shared their problems and joys with us. Once again, we found that no matter where we go in the world, in the churches we found that we had an instant family in Christ. In spite of the sadness we were rejoicing in the opportunity the Lord had opened for us to serve Him again.

In May 1999, we left Ohio for speaking engagements in the east, ending up at Mother Bobbett's home in Sparta, New Jersey, so Heath could work on her finances. At age ninety-eight-and-a-half, although quite deaf, she was doing quite well. The radiation for her cancer had caused her to lose a little weight, which she was happy about, but her appetite was still excellent.

We got home just in time to plant my garden and to teach a missions class at Cedarville College. The students were always so kind, respectful, and really interested in what we had to say.

We had a terrific summer in 1999, even though it was punctuated by Niger-like heat. We had received several requests for us to fill in for missionaries in African countries, but we didn't feel that the Lord was leading us to go overseas again at that time. Mother Bobbett was approaching her ninety-ninth birthday. We were thankful Shirley Blackman lived nearby in Sparta, New Jersey, and she did so much in caring for her mother. Shirley really wanted and needed Heath's presence and consultation, so we agreed not to go overseas for any extended ministry at that time. When we were in Québec, we were actually closer to New Jersey than we were in Ohio, so that was fine.

Heath was preaching and teaching ten different times in just the month of September, so he was spending a lot of time studying and preparing, which he always enjoyed. We also continued spending time with our international students at Wittenberg University.

The work among the Zarma people in Niger continued to have a very big place in our hearts. Missionary friends George and Flora (originally from Nigeria) wrote, "We thank God for the work that is committed into our hands. Many people are still coming and hearing the Gospel despite the efforts of the devil to stop them. Some have made decisions and have had difficulties. Their going out to the church is always in secret, and others are under threats daily to renounce Jesus."

Alan turned his commercial window-washing business, Pane Away, over to Wheeler Mission in Indianapolis and began a full-time ministry with them. The desire of his heart was to establish a work similar to the program at Dunklin where he graduated from in Florida six years before. He was working with those coming out of addictions, presenting Christ as the answer. It was beautiful to behold the love the Lord had given Alan for the men he worked with.

In a newsletter Alan explained his use of the term "regeneration" instead of "rehabilitation". "To 'rehabilitate' means to return to one's former state. Typically with addicts, this was not a great place to begin with! Regeneration involves something completely different – to become a new person from the inside out. This is not possible without the work of the Holy Spirit in our lives. Prayer, prayer, prayer. The most vital way you can be of help in this work is to faithfully pray for our group leaders and attendees."

On October 22, 1999, Mother Bobbett fell in the night and broke her hip. She had surgery that evening and came through it well. This was her first surgery in ninety-nine years! Afterward, she was placed in the nursing home where Shirley worked part time. Heath called his mother every day. When she developed a swollen thigh and a blockage, she was sent back to the hospital.

On November 29, 1999, we drove the 575 miles from Springfield, Ohio, to Shirley's home in Sparta, New Jersey, in just ten hours. The Lord watched over us on that cold day. It was snowing and blustery in the Allegheny and Pocono Mountains, but there was not a lot of snow on the ground. Shirley, Heath and I spent portions of every day sitting at his mother's bedside reading Scripture and singing. Lena Bobbett went to heaven on December 14, 1999. She was buried in a peaceful cemetery in Amber, New York, near many of her relatives.

On Christmas Day 1999, Nathan called us from an internet café in Beirut, Lebanon. It was so good to hear his voice. Our family was coming the day after Christmas, so we invited Chinese friends, Truman and Annie, for dinner on Christmas Day. They brought a new Chinese student named

Pei. Pei told us he wasn't a believer but that he was on the road to becoming one. Our hearts cried out for the Lord to open his eyes and heart to know the wonder of salvation in Christ. We asked Truman to give his testimony of how he came from an atheistic communist upbringing to Christ through the witness of an American who came to China to teach English. His story was such a blessing!

On December 26, 1999, we gathered with all of Rebecca's family as well as Judy and her children. Alan and Angie called. The big surprise was a special scrapbook that our grandchildren had made with letters from each of them to us! We cried when we looked at their pictures and read their letters. It was a wonderful gift, and we were reminded again of what a privilege God had granted us to be grandparents.

December 31, 1999, was the last day of the twentieth century! Nathan called us twice from Lebanon. Shortly before midnight, Heath and I read Psalms 90 and 91, Moses' prayer. Though written thousands of years ago, it was so appropriate that evening.

New Year's Day 2000, was called"Y2K"and had many people feeling uneasy because of the fear that computers would malfunction with possible disastrous outcomes. They predicted that electricity might fail, we might not be able to get into our bank accounts, and so forth. Sales of home generators, all kinds of batteries, food, water, camping cook stoves, and so forth were soaring. The scares never materialized! There were no major glitches in the world, in spite of the paranoia.

Haiti

On January 7, we rose at 3:50 a.m. We hadn't had much sleep, but it was time to leave for Haiti! Heath had been invited to teach a seminar to Haitian pastors and Christian workers. It was three degrees in Springfield, but we were only wearing sweaters because we didn't want to hassle with carrying winter coats in Miami or Haiti.

As we boarded the Antilles Airline plane in Miami for Port-au-Prince, Haiti, we felt like we were already in Haiti! The passengers each had three or four hand carry-ons. One man sort of pushed me aside to present his boarding pass and start down the ramp-tunnel to board. He definitely gave off an aroma indicating he hadn't had a bath in quite a while! Then, just as we started down the passage to board, there were agents we had to pass by and a nice German shepherd sniffing each bag. The dog locked his nose on this man's bag, and he was called aside by the agents for a search. So he didn't board ahead of us after all!

Arriving in Port-au-Prince airport was like arriving in Niger years ago! Customs officials waved us on by and didn't look at our things. Outside the door of the airport, there were all kinds of people wanting to carry our bags or take us to their taxis. One had a piece of paper that said, "Heath Bobbett," so we followed him to Dave Marshall's car in the parking lot.

My! Driving down the narrow streets with huge potholes was like being in Bénin again! The traffic was often bumper to bumper, and so many of the cars were dented and scraped. There were many brightly painted tap taxis with up to twenty people on board. We were told they got their name from the passengers who tap on the sides of the roof when the driver approaches the place where they want to get off. Dave very boldly pulled out into traffic at different corners, and no one seemed to get angry. Maybe it was because they knew they would need to do the same thing sooner or later on their journeys too!

A lot of the Haitian streets and roads are made of limestone rubble. Over the rubble, potholes, broken asphalt, and cement, there is a constant motion of animals, people, and dented vehicles. Dave stopped at a small grocery store. It was a little disconcerting to walk past the armed guards sitting inside the store, grimly looking us over. They are a necessity in the stores and banks because of the high crime rate.

Here is a brief history of Haiti: The French brought slaves to Haiti from Africa to work their plantations. The warrior Jean-Jacques Dessalines later led the slave rebellion that chased the French out. Haitian independence was proclaimed on January 1, 1804. At that time, all of Haiti was a tropical garden with mahogany forests. Today, it is arid and barren from all the trees cut down to make charcoal for their cooking fires. It is said that the seeds of ruin were planted by the idealistic mulatto Pétion in 1807 when he sliced up the vast private plantations and great tracts of land into small portions for homesteaders. Homesteaders could grow sufficient food with little effort. Generation to generation planted the same ground with corn or beans until the land sickened and soured. Erosion washed the rootless soil from the hills into the valleys and rivers.

Haiti has a population of nearly ten million people. It is the poorest country in the Western Hemisphere, with 80 percent of the population living under the poverty line. Most Haitians live on less than $2 a day, and more than two-thirds of the labor force does not have formal jobs.

At the time we visited, Haiti had an unemployment rate of 60 percent, a life expectancy of but 51.6 years, an illiteracy rate of 55 percent, and a birth rate of 32.5 births per 1,000. It was a trans-shipment point for the exportation of cocaine and marijuana en route to the United States and Europe.

"If there really is a third world, then Haiti is in a fourth world. It needs stability, it needs an economy and it needs a respite from voodoo politics." – Howard Kleinberg

Double Harvest, where we stayed, was started by Art van Wingerden, a prosperous Dutch-American greenhouse owner from Indiana. He purchased the two hundred acres where they developed fields and fields of vegetables, flowers, exotic plants, and so forth. An elementary school, a church, and a medical clinic were later added.

The electricity was sporadic. Electricité d'Haiti (EDH) only worked twelve to fourteen hours a day, and no one ever knew when those hours would be. It was amazing, when going through populated areas, seeing all the wires added to electrical connections so that people could pirate electricity without paying for it! Double Harvest had a generator that worked when EDH wasn't working so they could keep the irrigation pumps working. We made sure we were ready for bed by 9:30 p.m. when the lights went off. Otherwise, we only had a flashlight to use for showering and final preparations for the night.

On Sunday, Pastor Bernard picked us up for the forty-five-minute journey to his church in Port-au-Prince where Heath had been invited to preach that morning. We thought the last five kilometers out to Double Harvest was a really bad road, but Hantz said, "You haven't seen anything yet. Wait until you see the streets in the city on our way to church!" There were potholes, broken blacktop and cement, and garbage strewn all over in addition to bumper-to-bumper traffic! The church met in a large lovely home that had been given to them. Attendance was running about 250, and there was no room for more.

We saw that the Haitians took great pride in their dress. At the Berean Baptist Church, the men wore white shirts, ties, and suits. The women were in lovely dresses, and the children were immaculate and darling. The little girls had their hair done nicely, decorated with barrettes and bows, and wore beautiful "Sunday dresses" of satin and lace like I wore as a child, with patent leather shoes and lacey anklets. Heath looked nice in his shirt, tie, and summer sports coat, but he felt he wasn't dressed well enough compared to Hantz and the other men in their suits! Even among the poor, we saw men emerging from their hovel-like homes with white shirts, pressed pants, and well-polished shoes!

On Wednesday, while our husbands were busy teaching in the seminar, Sandy Clayton and I went to the nearby village of Roche Blanche with missionary Mylene. I truly felt like I was back in a Bénin bush village! The village was about half Christian and half Voodoo. Mylene said Sandy and I were her bodyguards because the week before, some young men menaced her, telling her they didn't want her there and that she couldn't park her car by their compound. We sat in the shade of a tree by a little stream flowing through the village for Mylene's children's Bible class, and thankfully, those men never came around that time.

The Créole language is a French patois, the dialect of a people who knew no French grammar or spelling and simply spoke French by the sound. Créole also includes words from other languages. Being familiar with John 1, where Mylene's Bible story was from, I could pretty much understand all that she said.

Many in Haiti still practice voodoo, which was brought there by the slaves from Dahomey (Bénin).

Heath and John Clayton taught the seminar attended by forty-nine men and two women from twenty different churches. It was a busy week, and we trusted it was also most profitable for the attendees. At the closing there was a touching program when they each received certificates of accomplishment. The men gave many testimonies of thanks to John and Heath for teaching the seminar. We will never forget the one student who sang, with a fantastic baritone voice, "Because He Lives" in Créole. I captured one verse of that on video before our battery gave out. I wonder if Bill Gaither, who wrote the song, ever heard it sung so beautifully in Créole?

On our last Sunday in Haiti, Heath preached at the church at the Double Harvest project. At noon we had lunch at the Montana Hotel. There we saw another side of Haiti! The hotel was beautiful, terraced with all kinds of exotic plants and tropical foliage, and had a marvelous view of the blue Caribbean Haitian bay and town area.

We had a delicious lunch on the terrace. Heath ordered a tropical drink made of papaya, mango, banana, and grenadine syrup that was excellent. Before leaving, we stepped into the hotel foyer to see the beautiful staircase and reception area. Elaine told us that many brides liked to have their wedding receptions at the hotel and photographs made on the staircase.

An after note from January 12, 2010: Almost ten years later to the day after we were there, a 7.0 magnitude earthquake struck Haiti. Its epicenter hit just ten miles west of Port-au-Prince and its two million inhabitants. Speaking of the lack of building standards, the mayor of Pétion-Ville estimated that about 60 percent of the buildings were shoddily built and unsafe even in normal circumstances. Thousands and thousands of people died in the earthquake.

When the earthquake hit, the Montana Hotel fell within seconds. There were three million people in need of emergency aid. We all were horrified at the television scenes of devastation and the lives lost. Port–au-Prince was in disarray with so much rubble and so many fallen buildings in the streets that aid workers could barely reach the people who so desperately needed help. The book *Unshaken* by Dan Wooley features the story of one man who was trapped for sixty-five hours in the darkness of the rubble of the Montana Hotel and survived.

On Tuesday, January 18, 2000, our goodbyes were said, and Dave took us to the airport for our 9:30 a.m. flight. We had to pay $30 each to leave Haiti and were given a receipt. We were also asked to pay 10 gourdes (Haitian money), but for that there was no receipt. Evidently that went directly into the agent's pocket!

It was seventy degrees when we left Haiti, and twenty-eight degrees when we arrived back in Springfield, Ohio, the same day! Two days later, the first major snowstorm of the year arrived in Ohio, and the temperature fell to below zero. The snow and cold continued, and the next week a huge snowstorm hit the East Coast, from the Carolinas to Maine. Major airports were closed for several hours, and even the government in Washington, D.C., shut down on January 25, costing $6 million per day! How good the Lord was to allow us to get back just before those events.

I had purchased a small book when we were up on the mountain at the Baptist Haiti Mission. The author had translated the sweet prayers of many Haitian believers. They were so frank and sincere, just like the prayers of our African friends in Niger. We put this one in our February 2000 prayer letter:

>Lord, may your missionaries
>Feel younger each day
>To distribute your Word.
>Give them zeal
>And keep them young and
>Unwrinkled in their souls.
>Although the body may get old
>The hair white, the skin wrinkled,
>Keep their souls unwrinkled.
>*Translated from Créole*

Chapter 33
Hebron Dedication, Québec, Niger, Italy, and Lebanon
February 2000 to December 2004

*"If I could see from heaven's perspective, I would know that in
The spiritual realm, when the progress seems slowest,
Kingdom movement is actually happening!
When nothing is happening, with God something is happening!
God and one believer make a majority in any problem or perplexity."*
–Dr. V. Raymond Edmond

*"I have known my Lord for fifty-seven years,
and there has never been a single day that I have failed
to get audience with the King!"* –George Mueller

September 17, 2000, was a great day of rejoicing as we were present at Camp Hunt, near Bloomington, Indiana, for the dedication of Hebron, the residential city of refuge that had recently opened! Hearing Alan's testimony, the board at Wheeler Mission in Indianapolis gave him access to this large property, with many acres of woodland and a pristine lake. How could we ever thank the Lord enough for what He had done and was doing in Alan's life? He thanked us for loving him and praying for him during his years of addictions, expressing the sorrow he felt for what he had put us through.

One of Alan's letters before the dedication said, "One of the things readily apparent in working with addictions is that it affects the whole family, not just the addict. A very strong element of our programs is that the entire family needs ministry, not just the person in recovery. We are not just responsible for the men we are accepting into the program but also for their wives and children. On weekends, we'll be working with families, guiding them through the tough steps of detachment, forgiveness, reconciliation, and more. There is no greater payday though than seeing God restore a broken family and marriage to health and wholeness."

In the opening up of the Hebron ministry, God just performed one amazing thing after another. One example was the need for water lines to be brought onto the property. There was almost no water pressure at the camp, and water lines had to be brought from the road into the property. However, when the staff was informed that it would cost up to $40,000, they were stymied. But God! The week before the dedication, a utilities vehicle came to the camp, and the gentlemen said, "We have a big problem. We need to bring a water line past here and had planned for it to be on the other side of the road from your property. However, that area is a landfill, and we don't want water to be possibly contaminated coming through there. Would you allow us to bring the water line across your property? We'll do all the work free, so all you'll need to pay for is the pipes!" Thank You, Father!

We asked our prayer supporters to lift up Alan and his staff in prayer for strength, discernment, and godly wisdom in the setup and operation of the Hebron ministry. We closed our prayer letter with the quote that Alan always put at the end of letters he wrote for Overcomers Ministry: "What are you doing of eternal value?"

What a blessing and joy it was, through the years of Alan's ministry at Hebron, to see family relationships restored, couples reunited in marriage, children brought back to their parents, and the healing of forgiveness. The men transformed and redeemed by the grace of God called themselves "jewels from the devil's junk pile!'

Back to Buckingham, Québec

On our way to Québec, we participated in two missionary conferences in New York State and also spoke in two other supporting churches. We visited many friends along the way and were always so blessed, fellowshipping with the churches and friends who so faithfully prayed for us.

It rained all day on October 6 as we drove to Buckingham. Some young men from the church helped us unload our car. On the dresser in our bedroom was a big bouquet of flowers from two of the church families to welcome us back, plus a can of maple syrup and a French book, *On the Road to Emmaus*.

Heath's seventieth birthday was to be three days after we arrived in Buckingham, Québec. So several weeks before, I secretly put out word to our friends and churches, asking that they surprise him with cards to celebrate the occasion. They were to mail the cards to André and Nicole Sarault, so they could keep them until his birthday.

We were so warmly welcomed again by the friends at the Rabbit River Baptist Church on our first Sunday back. After church, they had a celebration for Heath's birthday (cake, punch, and coffee) so he never dreamed there would be something else on Monday night, October 9.

On Monday evening, we were invited to the Sarault family's home for dinner. They have a tri-level home, so when we went in the front door, the Sarault, Bélec, and St. Amour families were all looking over the banister from the living room shouting, "Surprise!" There were balloons, streamers, wall posters with Scripture verses and, after they sang *"Bonne Fête"* to him, they all opened little bottles and blew bubbles down at us! There was lots of laughter, surprise, and joy to celebrate Heath's seventieth birthday.

After greeting everyone (a kiss on each cheek), we all sat down in the living room. Yoland was sitting so that he could look out the front picture window and see down the street. October 9 was Canadian Thanksgiving Day. A few minutes later, Yoland exclaimed, "Well, look at that! There is a mailman (*facteur*) coming down the street. I've never heard of mail being delivered on Thanksgiving Day." Then everyone in the room went over to the window to comment about what an unusual thing it was to have mail delivery on Thanksgiving. Heath and I went to look too as Yoland said, "Look! He's coming directly to this house with all that mail!"

The *facteur*, fully dressed in his nice blue uniform, rang the doorbell. Madame Sarault opened the door and exclaimed, "What a surprise that you are working today." The mailman replied, "Well, I don't normally work on Thanksgiving, but I have so much mail for Heath Bobbett that I had to work today!" By then we were all laughing. The mailman came in and handed Heath over 100 birthday cards, one at a time, until he was finished.

It turned out that the *facteur* was Nicole's brother-in-law who lived just down the street. Daniel had volunteered to do this when he heard about the celebration! He and his wife, Martine (Nicole's sister), were believers too. The surprise was so much fun, and we enjoyed the laughter as well as being able to surprise Heath.

We had a delicious turkey dinner afterward and great fellowship with those French-Canadian brothers and sisters in Christ who had become so dear to us. Their love for the Lord and evangelistic zeal for their friends and loved ones were a blessing and a challenge to us.

Heath stayed up late when we got back to the house reading all his cards. He was so touched by the notes and wishes he received.

During that time in Québec, I was loaned the book *Footprints Across Québec*, the biography of Murray Heron, pioneer missionary to Québec. When he was called by God to go to Québec in the 1940s and 1950s, there was violent opposition to the Gospel. Murray and his friends suffered greatly for preaching the Gospel on street corners. He and his coworkers were harassed, forbidden by the police to have street meetings or pass out literature, imprisoned, and so forth. Finally, the province was forced to give them freedom to do this, but they were still often attacked physically and verbally by crowds. They saw souls saved though, and that made all their suffering worthwhile.

A Key to Victory – People Pray

"There is no doubt in my mind that the Lord poured out His blessings so powerfully in Québec because a great number of people everywhere prayed for the province's 'vast spiritual needs.' Prayer enables those far from the mission field to be effective partners with missionaries on the front lines. The Scriptures are clear that God's blessing is poured out when people intercede, and little is accomplished when there is little prayer.

"This was the case when the Lord sent the children of Israel to conquer the Amalekites, as recorded in Exodus 17. Joshua was commanded to go to the battlefront with his men, but God told Moses to carry the rod of the Lord to the top of the hill and raise his arms heavenward. To me, this is a beautiful illustration of how the Lord accomplishes missionary work. Joshua and his men only had victory when Moses held his arms up. Whenever he let them down, the enemy prevailed against Joshua. The same is true of missionaries. I am convinced that it is impossible for them to be successful on the field if God's people neglect to pray." – Murray Heron

In April 2001 we returned to Québec and served in a different church and for a different ministry. We drove to Québec City, stayed with a long-time missionary friend, and held a missions conference at the Baptist Church in Charney.

We found that the believers in the Charney Baptist Church had a real heart for missions. We had never seen so much interest in our display table before. Every picture album was looked through from cover to cover, every curio or souvenir from Niger, Bosnia, Bénin, and Haiti was picked up, discussed, and many questions asked. There were two couples in the church who were very interested in missionary service. We were able to put a godly couple, Louis and Mireille Gérardin, in contact with our mission, and they went to Haiti to serve for a time.

We also met Ginette who had been led to Christ by Pastor Caron just a few days before our arrival. Her first Sunday in church was when Heath preached on "We are ambassadors for Christ." Afterward she confided, "I thought that every word he said was just for me, and I didn't want to miss anything he had to say. Is this normal to be so thirsty to hear the Word of God preached?" Heath assured her that it was a very healthy sign of what had happened in her heart! Ginette's brother had prayed for over twenty years for her to come to Christ. God blesses our perseverance in prayer!

On our way home from the missions conference near Québec City, we stopped by for a surprise visit to the church in Buckingham. Those dear friends gave us such a warm welcome! We spent time with many families and also did some serious counseling with a young friend who had grown cold toward the things of the Lord because of her involvement with a young man. Without revealing her name, we asked for prayer for her. What a relief and joy it was to hear later that she had split up with him, was walking with the Lord again, and dating a fine Christian man whom she later married.

Attendance at the Buckingham church had almost doubled, Christians were growing, and they had their own building and were no longer renting space in another church.

Back to Niger

From our prayer letter, dated February 2002: "Home again in Niger. 'Can't you come back for three years? …or at least for three months?' We were asked this question by Niger friends when we were with them in January. Now, if we were just twenty or thirty years younger…we surely would want to do that! Traveling the dirt roads or the pot-holed paved ones in a truck or a spring-less taxi rattled our bones more than it used to!

"The classes in the Evening Baptist Bible Institute went well, and there were several students who were quite sharp. It was good to be teaching again, 'equipping the saints to serve.' When we weren't grading homework or studying for the two-and-a-half-hour classes each weekday evening, we were receiving visitors or going out on visitation. God is working in Niger, and it was a thrill to meet Zarmas who have come to Christ. One young teacher told us his friend gave him a Bible. After reading it over a period of five years, he understood and received Christ as his Savior! The Word is powerful, and God works in *His* time!

"An EBM colleague very kindly drove us to Dosso to visit and preach. It used to be a three-hour round trip, but now because of the deteriorating blacktop and numerous potholes, it takes at least six hours. Many times it was better to just leave the road and drive beside it in the sand or laterite. There were close to one hundred people in the service, and the church is doing well. Heath preached in French, and Joseph translated into Zarma. We remember baptizing Joseph when he was just a young boy of fourteen. Now he is married and the father of two sweet children.

"The next Sunday, Heath preached in the Gourma Church in Niamey. How great it was to renew fellowship with the believers in our churches once again! We were warmly received and welcomed with hugs and Niger-made gifts. It made us realize anew how much we miss our dear friends in the Niger and what a privilege it was to serve Him there.

"Thanks again for continuing to partner with us as we serve Him. How good He has been to us in our forty-four years with Evangelical Baptist Missions and all of our lives! – Heath and Norma"

February 2003 marked the forty-seventh year since Heath had been ordained into the Gospel ministry.

The Church on Its Own
An article from EBM's publication, The Gleaner, *about the Gourma Church that Heath helped organize in Niamey.*

What joy there is in seeing a baby born and then watching him grow, reach maturity, and go off on his own. This is a picture of church planting! When we first left our bush station of Gaya and came to Niger's capital city of Niamey in 1967, we encountered the 'baby' Gourma church. A layman named André had started the meetings in a little grass hut down by the Niger River.

They needed a pastor, but they were unable to support one. Luc Souantieba, a Burkina Faso Bible school graduate, was invited to come to hold a series of evangelistic meetings. Coming from a pagan area that was much more open to the Gospel, he was amazed at the threats and resistance he met as he witnessed to Niamey's Muslim population. According to his own testimony, he was rather happy that the church could not support him and his family. He was ready to go back to pagan country to work when missionary Heath Bobbett told him he would give him some part-time employment to supplement the church salary. As he prayed about this, Luc sensed God was calling him to work with this group.

Over the years, we saw the group growing and had the joy of participating with Pastor Luc in baptizing those coming to know Christ. After a while, the church moved from the grass hut at the river's edge to a garage behind our Bible bookstore. This was more centrally located and not such a long walk for those living in the city.

They asked Heath to help them as they organized and wrote up a church constitution.

When the church outgrew the garage, a large open-sided hangar was built. (One advantage of Niger's climate is that you have sunshine 365 days of the year – so walls aren't always necessary!) Pastor Luc's ordination was another highlight for all of us.

The congregation increased until they were able to abandon the hangar and put up the walls and roof of a church building. For several years, they met in this unfinished shell, but through the course of this past year they have finally been able to put in the floor and ceiling. The Gourma believers contributed much manpower and funds as they were able, but they could not have done it without the gifts of God's people from our Sunday evening English service and many from the homeland.

The 'baby' that we encountered in 1967 has grown, matured, and is now on its own! We give glory to God for what He has done! It is a great joy to our Niger mission family to be in the process of signing the mission property over to this local church. Praise Him for two other church groups that we have done this for also in past years. This is what missions is all about! If EBM missionaries had to suddenly leave the country at any time, these churches will remain and function until our Lord's return.

How thankful we are for the faithful who have prayed and given sacrificially over the years in order to make this possible. You prayed, we watered, *but God gave the increase.*"

Our June 2003 prayer letter began, "Well, it has happened again! Have you ever been told that when you pray about something, you should be willing to be the answer to that prayer? A few years ago, we were praying for workers to go to the Tuzla Baptist Church, and then were asked to go ourselves. That was a blessed privilege, and we will never be the same after working with the folks in Bosnia.

"Another request we had been praying for was for the International English Church plant in Torino, Italy. The ABWE missionary who began that growing ministry had to return to the States because of health problems. As they waited and prayed for a full-time couple to pastor the work, 'senior ambassador missionaries' had been asked to fill in three months at a time. Our good friends Jacqui and Larry Armstrong were there as we prayed for another couple to fill in after them."

It was with real joy that we accepted the invitation to serve in Torino (Turin), Italy. This would be the second time we filled in at an ABWE work. Larry jokingly called us ABWE adjuncts! It was a multicultural work, with a congregation made up of people from over a dozen different English-speaking countries along with some Italian folks, meeting each week to worship God around His Word.

A special bonus for us was that one-third of the assembly was Africans! Called "the Detroit of Italy," Torino was an industrial city with people coming from all over the world to work there. The English speakers sought out the church because they wanted to worship in English.

A confirmation that this was the leading of the Lord for us was the way the Lord brought in the funds from our supporting churches and friends. Our plane tickets were $822 each, and we needed approximately $2,000 per month to pay the rent and utilities for the furnished apartment in the heart of the industrial city, plus ministry and living expenses. Southgate Baptist Church in Springfield, Ohio, purchased our round-trip tickets, and many other churches and individuals sent substantial gifts for our support needs as well.

Before we left for Italy, two very special events took place. In July, our first great-grandchild, Jacob Whitt, was born to Nansie and Kevin. We made a quick trip to Indiana before our departure for Europe to hold Jacob in our arms. The next month, Waneta Lake Baptist Chapel, situated in the beautiful Finger Lakes region of New York State, celebrated its fiftieth anniversary. They invited all former pastors and friends back to rejoice with them in God's faithfulness. Heath was their first pastor. The Lord raised up a host of faithful prayer supporters for us in this church. We have such wonderful and warm memories of our times at the Chapel and the dear saints there.

Italy

On August 15, 2003, our grandson Joel Bobbett drove us to the Dayton airport. What precious grandchildren we are blessed with! Joel said he would pick us up when we return in November if we need him.

We were surprised that our four bags were over sixty pounds each. The man who examined our luggage was a Christian. He asked us about the Christian books we were taking and if Heath liked the Bible translation he was using. We were looking forward to serving in Turin (Torino) and exploring the ancient city that dated back to 2000 BC!

We were met at the Torino airport by Robert Goodwin, a warm, helpful Englishman from the Torino church. Robert was married to an Italian lady, Carmela, and he had worked in Torino for many years. He was a wonderful asset to the church family and was so kind to us. He was also full of fun! Robert took us to the fourth-floor furnished three-room apartment that the missionary fill-ins were renting.

One of the first things we were shown was where to buy tram tickets (either at a tobacco store or at the train depot), then the way on the trolley cars from our apartment to the hotel where the church services were being held. We had no car, so we did lots of walking in Torino. The faucet water was full of calcium, so almost everyone bought bottled water. We learned to grocery shop, only buying that which we could carry home in our arms! I'm sure Heath's muscles grew as he carried all the bottled water back to our apartment day after day!

We had to deposit a euro (approximately a $1 coin) in order to get a grocery cart in the supermarkets (just like Aldi in the States). Our euro was returned when we finished shopping and left the cart. We still think this is an excellent idea and wish all grocery stores required this. We learned quickly that shoppers were not to touch any of the fresh fruits or vegetables without first donning disposable plastic gloves available in the produce department. This was another excellent procedure, we thought!

There is nothing like a real cappuccino in Italy! We couldn't resist stopping at a coffee bar on our way home from grocery shopping. Although the owner spoke no English, he smiled broadly when we came, ushered us to a table, and brought the cappuccino. In Italy, it is cheaper to purchase your coffee standing up at the bar, but we were happy to sit at a table and rest a little. Once you order something to drink or eat, that table is yours and you can stay as long as you want! It is the same way in a restaurant. When you have your meal, that table is yours to sit and visit all evening if you want to. We were puzzled at first that the waitress would not bring our check unless we asked for it. Italians explained to us that it would be an insult to present your check quickly. It would be like saying, "You can pay and leave now!" When Italians go out for dinner, they and their guests sit around the table and talk the night away. The restaurants are very noisy, but it was great seeing people having such a good time!

One Saturday, Robert Goodwin came to walk with us in the large park that was near us. He treated us to a cappuccino at a little outdoor café. When the waiter brought our drinks, there was a perfect leaf pattern he had swirled in the foam on the drink. When I expressed my delight at his artistry, he smiled, stood up straight, closed his eyes, and haughtily said, "My name is Picasso!" We loved Italian humor! We were told that Italians only drink cappuccino in the mornings, never after 10:00 a.m.

We also learned that Torino (Turin) is reputed to be Italy's main center for mysticism and the supernatural. Much of the mysticism is commonly believed to have sprung from opinions about the Shroud of Turin that is kept in a church there. The occult is widespread, and there are said to be three times as many full-time consulting magicians than there are priests. It was sad to see that the cults were working fervently in Italy also. One recent census showed that there were more Jehovah's Witnesses than born-again believers in the country.

We found the Italian people to be so very friendly. Invariably, when they asked and found out we were from the States, they would say, "I have a cousin in Chicago" or "My brother lives in New York" and so forth. What amazed us was that we were so often stopped on the streets and asked for directions. We could only smile and say something like, *"Scuzi, non parla Italiano!"* We thought we surely must have looked somewhat like Italians when we were approached with those questions. Because we spoke another Romance language, French, we could pretty well read the signs in Italian. So many French words became Italian words when a vowel was added at the end. Some examples are *bonjour = buonjourno, d'accord = d'accordo, bon appétit = buon appetito.*

Riding the trolleys to church or to shop, we found the youths to be very polite, and they still got up to offer their seats to older people. Sundays seemed to be a day to dress nicely and go for a walk. The ladies were very fashionable and even walked in their best shoes and clothes. No sneakers for them!

Unfurnished apartments in Italy are really unfurnished! The renters must bring everything, including their own kitchen sinks, bathroom fixtures, light fixtures, kitchen cupboards, appliances, and so forth! We lived on the fourth floor of an apartment building, accessible by stairs or by a tiny cage-like elevator that held only two or three people. Because it was still warm, we had all the windows open and were thankful for ceiling fans. We got used to all the street noises, especially the trams that ran from 5:00 a.m. to 1:00 a.m. on the street below our bedroom window. Parking spaces were always full, and it was amazing to see how many cars parked right in the middle of the street, leaving just enough room for the trams to pass on each side of the cars.

We rode one tram from our apartment at 88 Corso Monte Grappa to center city, then another toward the hotel where the church met. When we descended from the second tram, we had about a two-block walk to a downtown hotel where the church was meeting. We really enjoyed getting to know these folks from so many different nations. (Here I will insert that Heath's messages each Sunday were excellent, and I really enjoyed sitting under his ministry again!)

Harolyn (the pianist), John, and Katie Pinson were from Michigan. Harolyn's breast cancer was discovered when they arrived in Torino, and she was under treatment by an Italian doctor. Their second-grader, Katie, was in Italian school and was already fluent in Italian. John loaned us his Pimsleur CDs for learning Italian.

With Jesus Leading the Way

One Saturday, we were invited to go with the Pinsonsby train to Aosta, Italy. This mountain village's history goes back many years before Christ. Famous for wood carvings, the last two days of January this city has a woodcarver's fair that has been going on for the last one thousand years! It is a bilingual town (French and Italian), so we could use our French.

The Valle d'Aosta (the Aosta Valley) penetrates deeply into the Italian Alps and is an historic invasion route (Napoleon passed through) into Italy from France. The valley is bounded on all sides by some of the largest and best known mountains in the world.

The Praetorian Gate to Aosta was built in 25 BC. Harolyn noted the apartments built on the walls, and we all imagined they were perhaps like those where Rahab lived!

We purchased some Christmas presents in Aosta. Most interesting was the *gorolas*. They are little round clay coffee pots with four drinking spouts. You can enjoy special coffee with friends! The little shop where I bought some also gave me the recipe for their mountain coffee for four persons: four cups of hot coffee, four small glasses of brandy, lemon or orange rind, and as much sugar according to your taste. Reheat again before serving.

Bill and Mary were another couple we got to know. They had worked several years in Germany for General Motors Corporation. In Torino, Mary still worked for them, but Bill had retired. Every once in a while, we got a call from him asking if we'd like to go sightseeing!

Our first trip with Bill was a drive up and up switchback roads, through small picturesque villages, past unique Italian cemeteries, to the small source of the Po River which runs through Torino. It was refreshingly cool up at that altitude as the heat was still pretty oppressive in Torino. We saw many campers and hikers enjoying the area. Bill took us to a small restaurant at the top where we enjoyed our first meal featuring polenta!

Our next day trip was to visit the most important monuments in the Piedmont, high up in the Alps, the Sacra di San Michele. Construction began in 998, so it is over one thousand years old. It stands at the top of Mont Pirchiriano. Crusaders stopped there on their way to the Holy Land. We both had lost about twenty pounds before we went to Torino and were so thankful to have a little less weight to carry up the hundreds of steps to the summit.

After climbing a myriad of steps to get to the entrance, we still had to climb eight to ten stories inside to the top! The steps were uneven and mostly had no handrails. The next day, the calves of my legs were screaming, but what fun it was to explore the history-rich land of Italy.

The architecture and artwork in those chapels were astounding. The view from the top was breath-taking. Bill pointed out Torino to us, in the far distance, with the "lid" of smog hovering over it!

Torino is surrounded by the beautiful snow-covered Alps, but it is also an industrial city with a thick layer of smog that obliterated the mountains from our view most days. Occasionally, after a good rain and fresh breezes, the smog cover was lifted and then we looked in awe at the scenery that was there all the time but not usually visible.

One sweet Christian woman at the church was from Finland and had a master's degree in physics from Cornell University in New York. She was married to an Italian. She mentioned more than once that her Finnish mother was an atheist, so I was curious to know how she came to Christ. She replied, "I had a very godly Christian grandmother." I have used her story to encourage grandmothers! We never know what influence we can have on our grandchildren for eternity.

On Tuesday mornings, I traveled on two trams to Betsy's apartment to meet with eight to ten ladies and teach a Bible study. I had decided to write my own lessons for Philippians. It was a lot of work but a great blessing to study and teach one of my favorite Bible books. The ladies were a delight to work with.

Exciting "Adventures" in Italy

There were many gypsies in Italy, begging, offering things for sale, playing instruments along the street, hoping you would put some money in their tin cups. We had just been warned about the devious ways, thievery, and pickpocketing schemes of groups of children who would cluster around a person, especially at train stations. One Sunday after church, I had removed my good shoes and put on sturdy walking shoes for our long walk to lunch and then to a tram stop. I was carrying a plastic bag with my Bible, my shoes, and a very expensive tour book that Bill Smith had loaned to me. We just missed a tram, so we had a while to wait for the next one. I placed my bag on the sidewalk, up against a fence in the shade. When our tram finally came, we hopped on to go to Piazza Castello where we had to get off and wait for another tram. Just before we got off at that stop, I remembered my bag that I had left behind, and my heart sank! My Bible! Bill's book! My good shoes!

Rather than crossing the street to wait for a tram going back the direction we had come from, I started running back, praying, over and over, "Lord, please have your angels watch over that bag so that I can find it right where I left it!" When we were about a half-block away, I could see my bag there. People were walking by without giving so much as a glance toward it. Was it invisible to them? Were the angels guarding it? I think they were! I was so grateful to be able to rescue the bag and take it home with us! Heath was trailing behind me and said he never saw me move so fast!

Catherine Butler, ABWE missionary to Italy, invited us to her apartment for dinner. It was a new route for us to follow, first taking a tram from our house to a certain stop where we got off and took a bus next. It was more than a little confusing, but after we got off the bus and wandered around for a while, we finally found Cat's apartment and had a lovely evening.

I'm sure we were thinking the return to our apartment would be easier, and we were careful, as warned, about pickpockets on the buses and trams. Heath had gotten something out of his wallet on the bus, but he thought he carefully put it in his pocket afterward. Soon we arrived at the stop where we were to get off the bus and get on the tram for home. We stepped of the bus and were looking across the street for our tram stop when Heath patted his pocket and exclaimed, "I don't have my wallet!" Quickly, he jumped back on the bus as the doors closed and it pulled away.

There I was, stranded at the tram with no ticket! I decided the best thing to do was sit on a bench and wait for Heath to come back. It seemed like an hour went by as I anxiously looked at each bus or tram going by, hoping to see my beloved! Finally, I decided there was nothing for me to do but get on a tram for home and hope I wasn't caught by someone checking tickets. I actually thought Heath must have gone on home without me! Oh, the relief to see him at the next tram stop, anxiously scanning each car to see if I was on it!

The happy news was that by jumping back on the bus so quickly, he saw his wallet on the floor by our seat and was able to retrieve it before someone else took it. Evidently, he had missed his pocket when he thought he was putting it away. On Sunday when Heath thanked the Lord at church, saying he lost his wallet on a bus and was able to get it back, the church folks were amazed. They said, "That is definitely a miracle God performed on your behalf!"

On our days off, we made fascinating short train trips to Venice, Pisa, and Florence. Our times in those places were really extraordinary privileges. We were awestruck by the buildings and artworks everywhere we went. What a privilege it was to serve at the church, meet so many fascinating internationals, travel in Italy during the year of my seventieth birthday!

During our time in Italy, our prayer requests were:
- That our messages and Bible studies will be in the power of the Holy Spirit.

- For several in the Torino International Church who have spouses who are not believers.
- That the Lord will soon bring a full-time pastor to this work.
- For some who are present each Sunday but who have not yet opened their hearts to the Savior for a personal relationship with Him.
- For those who have asked for prayer, recognizing needs in their spiritual lives.
- For the spiritual growth of the followers of Jesus Christ in the church.

At the end of our three months at the International Church, we thought it would be a good idea to visit the neighboring country of Austria before we headed back to our home in Ohio. We found out about a popular, no-frills, cheap airline in Europe called Ryanair. The flight from Torino, Italy, to Strasbourg, Austria was only $25! Wow! That was definitely within our price range! However, when booking, we found out that the hub of Ryanair was at an airport north of London, England, and we had to fly to the hub first, then on to Austria. This would involve an overnight in England before our flight to Austria.

We contacted good friends Stan and Paula Boelman, who had been working in church-planting in Luton, England, for many years. They were happy to meet us at the airport, keep us overnight, and show us their work. That was very enjoyable for us to see a ministry we had been praying for through the years.

With Jesus Leading the Way

Our next plane landed at night in Salzburg, Austria, and even then, as the taxi took us to our hotel, we were amazed at the neatness and cleanliness of this city. We couldn't help but compare it to the industrial city of Torino with its smog and black dust.

Salzburg is translated as "Salt-burg." Salt was mined in the area as long as 4,500 years ago. Called "white gold," it contributed to the great wealth of the prince-archbishops who ruled for hundreds of years. These men were more political than religious. The beautiful Mirabell Gardens were built by an archbishop for his mistress who bore him fifteen children! Our guide told us that Protestant missionaries who came to Salzburg were either imprisoned in the fortress and tortured or ordered out of the country without their children!

Next, we went by train to Vienna. I had met an American lady in Torino at the American Women's Club. Hearing that we were going to Vienna, she highly recommended that we write to a Kenyan lady there, Hilda. Hilda had worked in Vienna for the United Nations for twenty years. She was a special blessing to us. We went with her to visit the UN building and a vibrant Bible study that was held there weekly.

We enjoyed visiting the sights of Vienna (Wein). The Hofburg (imperial palace) was the residence of the Hapsburgs. Over six centuries, additions were built to it so that today there are eighteen wings, 2,600 rooms and nineteen courtyards! We walked through many of the rooms of the sumptuous apartments of the Hapsburgs, with huge displays of their silver, copperware, porcelains, crystal, table dishes, and centerpieces.

It was especially fascinating for me to see the apartment in the Hofburg of Empress Elisabeth (Princess Sisi). Emperor Franz Joseph fell in love with this beautiful fifteen-year-old from Bavaria and married her when she was only sixteen.

We also visited the Schönbrunn Palace, the imperial summer getaway. Construction started in 1695. This palace had 1,440 rooms! The Hapsburgs, who ruled for over six hundred years, were very wealthy and powerful. Through marrying their children to other royal families, they expanded their wealth and territories. Maria Theresa was called "the mother-in-law of Europe" through the marriages of her fifteen children. Her last daughter, Marie Antoinette, married King Louis XVI of France and was beheaded.

Humorous Incident

It was at a restroom near this summer palace that we had the most unusual bathroom experience in our lives! I had to pay to go in. When I stood up and flushed the toilet, the seat began to rise for several inches. I must admit my eyes were getting big as I had no idea what was happening.

The next thing I saw was that a handle with a sponge in it came over the seat. Then the seat rotated and was thoroughly wiped off by some sort of antiseptic sponge! Then the seat descended to its original location, ready for the next customer! When I met Heath afterward and saw the smile on his face, I knew he had the same experience in the men's restroom!

We took an overnight train from Vienna back to Torino to pick up our luggage and return to the States. Two men shared our second-class Pullman. One was a tall and very thin man from Kosovo, and the other was a personable young Israeli father who grew up in Italy. The man from Kosovo coughed all night, and I thought he probably had tuberculosis! It was more than a little disconcerting in that tiny space where we were all breathing the same air! Because of a bomb scare in Milan, our train sat on the tracks for two hours near Venice. Everything was being routed around Milan.

Tens of thousands of residents and tourists were evacuated from their homes and hotels Sunday and hundreds of trains rerouted from the central station so that explosives experts could detonate a World War II bomb found during construction work. The operation was described as the city's largest evacuation in the six decades since the war.

About 55,000 residents of 2,000 apartment buildings as well as guests in the hotels in the neighborhood near Viale Brianza were ordered to leave, starting at 8:30 a.m. Traffic police cars circulated through the neighborhood with orders to leave delivered through loudspeakers. After the bomb, dropped by an Allied airplane during the war, had been defused and removed for detonation, orders went out that it was safe to return home.

Back in Torino, we picked up our luggage and left for our return to Springfield, Ohio, arriving on November 24, 2003. As promised, our grandson Joel Bobbett was there to take us home when we came back. That was very special care from a loving grandson.

We wrote in our Christmas prayer letter, "We loved every minute of our three months in Italy. How conscious we were of the prayers of God's people for us! The days were very full and busy, but we never missed even one day because of illness. We praise Him too for His care as we walked many miles each week, crossing streets, running for trams, and dodging scooters. He kept us from harm or accidents. The people in the International Church were delightful, and the Lord gave us unparalleled opportunities to share the Gospel with those who did not know Christ. We saw Christians hungering for the Word and growing. Because of your prayers, God worked in hearts. To God be the glory, great things *He* hath done!"

With Jesus Leading the Way

Beirut, Lebanon

In our 2004 Christmas newsletter we wrote, "Our Christmas greetings are coming to you early this year because as you read this, we will be out of the country. We have been provided with tickets to visit our son Nathan in the Middle Eastern country where he is serving...It will be great to see firsthand the work we pray for...Pray our trip will be productive and that we will be a blessing and encouragement for the team. On our way back home, Heath will be preaching in the International Church of Torino, Italy, where we were serving at this time last year. We praise the Lord that the International Church continues to grow..."

It was a busy and special time for us with Nathan in Lebanon, visiting in the homes of believers and unbelievers, meeting his team members and their language teachers. Our hearts were touched to see Nathan's love for the people and theirs for him. Nathan had us lodged in a furnished apartment because his tenth-floor apartment was totally unfurnished at the time. He was sleeping on a mattress on the floor and had a couple of lawn chairs in his living room! We were there for his birthday, which was also Thanksgiving Day.

I had another frightening experience in Beirut. As we parked and crossed the street, it was amazing to see the fast-moving traffic come to a halt when a pedestrian stepped off the curb to cross the street. I had courage to do this when walking with Nathan, but one day he and Heath got across the busy street before I did. Looking back across at me, Nathan kept saying, "Mom, just step down off the curb and the traffic will halt for you." I felt like I would be instantly run over and just couldn't do it, even though Nathan and Heath were urging me from the other side of the street. Finally, Nathan crossed back to accompany me, and sure enough, as soon as we stepped down from the curb, all the busy traffic halted for us to cross!

We planned our trip home from Lebanon to pass through Torino, Italy, to visit our friends and the International Church. They were happy to have Heath there to preach that Sunday. It was great to see old friends and meet new ones and to see the International Church continuing and growing.

Chapter 34
He's Been Faithful to Me
2005 to 2015

He's been faithful, faithful to me. Looking back on His loving mercy I see.
Though in my heart I have questioned, even failed to believe,
yet He's been faithful, faithful to me.
Faithful, You are faithful. I worship you. – Carol Cymbala

If we could isolate just our tears and follow their trail over time,
we would find that they have consistently led us closer to God.
– David Jeremiah

It has been with profound thankfulness and joy that I have written about Jesus leading the way in our lives.

Fiftieth Wedding Anniversary

June 16, 2005, was our fiftieth wedding anniversary celebration. For this momentous occasion, Mariama Salifou and Dieyabidi Lompo came from Niger to celebrate with all our family. Jonathan picked them up at the Boston airport on June 11 and called us as they were driving up to Rye, New Hampshire. Dieyabidi, seeing the States for the first time, said, "Your country is so beautiful – like Jerusalem!" (Although he had never seen Jerusalem!) On the way to Ohio they stopped to see Niagara Falls. Dieyabidi's comment there was, "When I saw the falls and all that water power, I thought of Jesus and how He could calm the wind and waves."

I had supper ready for them when they arrived at our home in Springfield, Ohio, on June 15. We ate on our screened-in terrace that was so lovely, surrounded by our flaming bush plants and roses.

With Jesus Leading the Way

Rooms were reserved for all our family on June 16 and 17 at Spring Mill Inn, south of Bloomington, Indiana. Heath's sister Shirley Blackman flew in to Indianapolis to join us.

There were lots of joyous greetings and hugs from our children for Dieyabidi and Mariama that afternoon, and we enjoyed a lovely barbeque dinner. Nathan arrived with his beautiful fiancée, Jamie Noles. We all fell in love with Jamie immediately! The story of Nathan's proposal to her on the shore of the Mediterranean Sea in Beirut, Lebanon, was wonderfully romantic!

On Friday, June 17, we all ate breakfast together. Then it was fun time – some swam in the indoor pool, some hiked, some went to explore caves, and some visited the Pioneer Village or the Gus Grissom Memorial Museum. Some of us hiked down to the creek and toured some caves with Native American carvings on the walls.

I had a white dress for the occasion, and Heath had rented a white dinner jacket – reminiscent of our white wedding garb in 1955. Heath looked so handsome! I again thanked the Lord for the dear husband he had blessed me with for the past fifty years. Heath is handsome inside and out!

At 5:30 p.m., we renewed our wedding vows in the Oak Room, which was beautifully decorated with flowers. Rebecca had recently modeled my wedding dress for a Mother's Day event at her church, so it was freshly pressed and displayed on a mannequin. It was still as beautiful as it was fifty years before! Rebecca was my "maid of honor," Jon was Heath's "best man," and sons Alan and Nathan performed the renewal of vows ceremony. Our sons were so handsome, and Rebecca was so pretty! We were tremendously grateful to the Lord for allowing us the privilege of being their parents.

After a delicious dinner we cut the wedding cake Rebecca had brought. It was decorated with our wedding colors, pink and white. Next, our children reminisced about their childhood, and there were lots of laughs. I read a poem I had written, titled "Our Four MKs." Rebecca presented us with a very special picture album she had compiled with pictures of each of our children, grandchildren, and their spouses, and love notes written by each of them to us.

Blessings were pronounced by Heath on each of our four children. He had spent a lot of time composing those blessings and got all choked up reading them to Rebecca, Jonathan, Alan, and Nathan and they were weeping as well.

Leaving Ohio

We really liked the ranch home with finished basement that God had led us to in 1982 on Wabash Drive in Springfield, Ohio. Heath had put a lot of extras in improvements to the house and in landscaping. He kept the yard beautifully, and I really enjoyed my vegetable garden. Jon helped us build a nice low deck over the uneven cement screened-in patio in the back. We had lovely neighbors, which was an added bonus.

The yard work and snow shoveling were getting to be more difficult for Heath as were the stairs for me. When we mentioned to our children that we were starting to look at condos, they felt we should move closer to them. With our children scattered all over, this was a little more difficult to think about! Nathan was in Beirut, Lebanon, and moving to Waco, Texas. Jonathan was in New Hampshire. Rebecca was near Indianapolis. And Alan was in Bloomington, Indiana. Since two of our children were in Indiana, we began to look at condos there. The Epcon community with the Canterbury floor plan was very appealing to us but we left the search for a condo in Indiana aside for a while.

Our new international student that year was a Buddhist-Shinto girl from Japan. Noriko was such a pretty girl and so sweet. We felt inadequate to work with a Buddhist because we really didn't know what her background was like. One Saturday, we picked up Noriko and her Japanese friend, Yuki, at Wittenberg's Hanley Hall, took them shopping at the mall, drove around Springfield, up to the reservoir, ate supper at Wendy's, and ended up at Young's Dairy for ice cream. The girls were so cute. Our hearts yearned for them to know the truth of the Gospel. More than once as we drove around, they asked, "What is that building?" They were churches, and it seemed they had never seen church buildings before.

It was also at this time our soldier grandson, Ryan Ahlgrim, was deployed to Iraq. I had such fears that he would be killed there or come home maimed for life. We cried out to God for his protection, and had our Discovery Class, our Wednesday Bible study group, and our prayer warriors praying for him too.

Noriko was very willing to go to church with us. She was intrigued that the whole congregation sang because she said in their ceremonies, only the monk sings (chants?). Then her comment about our Pastor Eric Mounts' sermon was, "Do you have a long lecture like that every Sunday?!

We had to share that with Eric, and he thought it was hilarious too! He was such a good speaker that his "lectures" never seemed long to us.

God was working in a wonderful way. A friend who worked at Cedarville University, told us there was a sweet Japanese student at the university who had been raised Buddhist. We arranged for Aya and Noriko to meet at Southgate Baptist Church one Sunday morning. As the girls sat together before the service began, they began to converse excitedly and happily in Japanese. They quickly discovered that their homes were only about one half hour apart in Japan! They became fast friends, and Aya was able to share her testimony with Noriko, take her to her church, have her visit Cedarville University, and stay with her in the dormitory. Aya also visited Wittenberg with Noriko.

Noriko told Aya she had never thought about God before she met us and Aya, but she was beginning to think about Him! Aya's own testimony was that it was because she wanted to learn English that she was brought into contact with missionaries in Japan, and then the Holy Spirit began to show her need of Christ. We continued to pray for Noriko's enlightenment by the Holy Spirit.

Nathan's Wedding

On October 22, 2005, Nathan married Jamie Lynn Noles in Norman, Oklahoma. It was a beautiful God-honoring wedding, and Jamie looked absolutely gorgeous. All four of our children and many of our grandchildren were there for this joyous occasion.

Since Nathan had already set up the home he and Jamie were buying, and she also had house furnishings, they asked that instead of friends and relatives buying wedding presents for them, contributions be made for building homes in Sri Lanka that had been devastated by a recent tsunami. Over $14,000 was given to this cause! What a thoughtful and generous gesture!

We were still planning to move to Indiana and had put down a deposit on a condo that was to be built in Mooresville, Indiana. The developers assured us they would start building in just a few months.

Jonathan had told us he was giving us a trip to Israel for our fiftieth anniversary. When we thanked him at our fiftieth celebration, he so generously replied, "It's from all your children."

We wanted to go in November 2005, so Heath began looking for a Christian group to go with. By chance (God directed), he called Dallas Theological Seminary. One of their professors, Stephen Bramer, had taken several groups to Israel before and was planning another trip in November! Most people in the group were from the church Dr. Bramer pastored. We didn't want to go with a large group of several buses, and this was ideal because there would only be one bus load. We were to fly from Ohio to Newark and then on Israel Airlines to meet the rest of the group in Tel Aviv. How excited we were about going to the Holy Land!

We never dreamed that the sad news would come that my fifty-five-year-old nephew, Bob Christmas, had suddenly died of a massive heart attack on November 15, 2005. Bob had been under a lot of stress. His business partner in the funeral home was giving him much grief, so he finally retired early to get out of the situation. Also, Bob's wife had left him and their four children for another man. Bob worked hard to hold on to the home the children had grown up in to keep it for them.

Just the night before, Bob and I had a long conversation on the telephone, and I was so thankful for that. He had gotten his life straightened out spiritually and was back in church attendance. We talked about my brother Carl who wasn't a Christian. Carl and Carol had no children of their own, so they were very close to their nephew Bob. He visited them as often as possible in Arizona, and they had appointed him to have their power of attorney should anything happen to them. Carl had recently spoken to Bob about the possibility of his demise and jokingly said, "Then I'll find out if I'll go up (to heaven) or down (to hell)." Bob broke down and wept as he told me what Carl had said.

Will the Circle Be Unbroken?
Lyrics by Ada R. Habershon

There are loved ones in the glory
Whose dear forms you often miss.
When you close your earthly story,
Will you join them in their bliss?

In the joyous days of childhood
Oft they told of wondrous love
Pointed to the dying Savior;
Now they dwell with Him above.

You remember songs of heaven
Which you sang with childish voice.

> Do you love the hymns they taught you,
> Or are songs of earth your choice?
>
> You can picture happy gath'rings
> Round the fireside long ago,
> And you think of tearful partings
> When they left you here below.
>
> One by one their seats were emptied.
> One by one they went away.
> Now the family is parted.
> Will it be complete one day?
>
> *Chorus:* Will the circle be unbroken
> By and by, by and by?
> Is a better home awaiting
> In the sky, in the sky?

Mickey and I had prayed for over sixty years for Carl to be saved, but he wouldn't yield. I thought often of an old song that I heard as a child, "Will the Circle Be Unbroken?" Each time I thought of those words, my eyes filled with tears. In my family of six, Mom, Dad, Evelyn, Mickey, and I were all born-again Christians. I loved Carl dearly and wept for the broken circle caused by his unwillingness to repent and come to Christ. Mickey and I were the only ones of our family still living, praying for Carl.

It was difficult for us that all our bookings for Israel were already made and couldn't be changed, so we departed for Israel on the day of Bob Christmas' funeral and couldn't be there. We stopped on our way to the airport to spend some time with Mickey and Geneva. Bob had donated his eyes and any other organs that could be harvested to those in need. He had grown up in New Carlisle and successfully served as part-owner of the only funeral home there for many years, so he was very well known. Over 1,000 people came to his viewing. How thankful we were that Bob was with His Savior and Lord for eternity, and we know we will see him again. For the believer, death is swallowed up in victory. "Where, O death, is your victory? Where, O death, where is your sting (I Corinthians 15:55)?"

Israel

On November 17, 2005, we had a long wait in the Newark airport for our El-Al plane to Israel. What a surprise to see the Dalai Lama walking down the hall, surrounded by his secret service men! There was a very talkative American Jewish lady sitting beside me as I waited for our plane.

She was going to visit her son and daughter-in-law who had immigrated to Israel to live, married there, and had her grandchildren there. She was so friendly until I mentioned that we would be seeing our niece and husband who lived in Israel, Patty and Dan Juster. As soon as I said they were Messianic Jews, she grew cold and stated, "Well, they aren't really Jews!"

Dan and Patty met us at the Tel Aviv airport, and we had a short time together to visit. Our tour group had not arrived, but we were met by the Israel tourist agency, who explained that the group's flight was delayed because a tire blew out on the plane when they were about to take off. They would not arrive until the next day.

A very nice driver picked us up at the airport and drove us to the hotel in Caesarea. We did not realize that the Israel tour group was run by Messianic Jews! On our way to Caesarea, I asked the driver what the populations of Jews and Arabs were in Israel. He gave me the statistics for Jews, Arabs, *and* Messianic Jews!" What a thrill. Before long, we heard his testimony of how he had come to Christ. At first, his wife was opposed, and she told him not to tell anyone else. It wasn't long before she too realized that Jesus was the long-promised Messiah and became a believer. He showed us a picture of them being baptized in the Mediterranean Sea. What a joy and thrill it was to meet believing Jews in Israel.

We stayed one night in Caesarea, three nights in Tiberius (Galilee region), one night at the Dead Sea, and three nights in Jerusalem. Every accommodation was lovely, but we felt the Scots Hotel in Tiberius was the most outstanding.

It was on the old steps to the temple that we realized we were actually walking where Jesus had walked when He was on earth. For us, it was a dream come true. Some tour guides seemed to repeat over and over that "Jesus actually walked here" with no such proof. Dr. Bramer never did that. I like what Chuck Swindoll says about the Sea of Galilee: "This is one location where we can know for sure Jesus actually walked!"

I made a scrapbook of our wonderful time in Israel, trying to remember every thrilling moment. It really made the Old Testament come alive for me. One person said, "After you have been to Israel, it is like reading your Bible in 3-D!" Dr. Stephen Bramer gave great Bible and history lectures at each site. We enjoyed the wonderful fellowship of the busload of Texans from his church. Ronnie Cohen, our Israel guide, shared his testimony with us at the garden tomb of his recent journey to believe Jesus was the Messiah and receive Him as his Savior.

Our last days of the tour were spent in Jerusalem. As we were nearing Jerusalem, night had fallen and we could see the lights of the city beginning to shine. Our bus driver, Munir (an Arabic believer), played a CD, and we all sang "Jerusalem! Jerusalem! Lift up your hearts and sing. Hosanna, in the highest, hosanna to our King!" I sang with tears streaming down my cheeks! Going to Jerusalem was a dream come true!

When we arrived back home, I wrote in my journal, "Arrived home from Israel – forever changed! I want to read the whole Bible through again now that I have actually been in the cities, towns, and locations mentioned!" Thank you, Father!

2006

As we entered this year, my brother Carl's health was deteriorating rapidly. The diagnosis then was prostate cancer, which had spread into his bones. He also had pain in his legs and feet from poor circulation (neuropathy). I called him often to talk and see how he was doing. After Carl and Carol's retirement they had moved to Lake Havasu City in Arizona. That was a long way from Springfield, Ohio.

When I spoke to Carol on the phone and asked if we should make a trip out to be of help to them, she would say, "Oh no. Carl is not that bad, and I am able to care for him." Twice he had fallen in the shower, and she had to call a squad to come and get him up. We began to realize that Carol was suffering from dementia along with other problems.

When I asked Carl if he would like for us to come out, he said he knew our schedule was always busy and he was afraid to ask, but he really wanted us to come. Mickey and Geneva urged us to go too. Jon arranged plane tickets and motel reservations for us. The Lord saw to it that we could clear off our schedule and go! The best and least expensive route for us to go was to fly to Las Vegas, Nevada, rent a car, and drive to Lake Havasu City.

On March 1, 2006, as we were getting off the plane in Las Vegas near midnight, my heart was so heavy as I thought of my beloved eighty-four-year-old brother Carl nearing death and not a believer. Then something happened that I can't explain, except that it was the gracious love of God, but a peace swept over my heart and I knew God was going to do something.

Carol and Carl both did not look well. I doubt that Carol weighed even one hundred pounds. They both seemed relieved and so happy that we had come. Carol's thoughts were scattered, and she didn't seem to be able to concentrate on one thing if there was any noise or distraction. She talked constantly. Carl was on pain medication, and not always clear in his thinking either.

The Hampton Inn was about ten minutes away and was a very nice place for us to stay. We had our breakfast there, and I often took some of the good things up to Carl for his breakfast. We were glad to sleep away from their house. Carol's cigarette smoke odors in the house really bothered Heath.

Hospice ladies had been coming for quite some time, and by then, they had Carl in a hospital bed with a catheter so he would not continue to get out of bed and fall. He was so happy to see us. The next day when the hospice nurses came and Carol was out of earshot, they thanked us profusely for coming, saying that Carol was totally unable to care for him. I was glad to be able to shop and cook some nutritious meals or order them in for Carl and Carol. Carl still had a pretty good appetite and was able to sit up in a wheelchair for meals.

We began putting in twelve- to sixteen-hour days with all that needed to be done for Carl's care – loads of washing, cooking, business affairs. In spite of her deafness and the beginnings of dementia, Carol's spirits lifted after we were there. They both expressed their gratitude that we had come to help them. We were giving both of them lots of hugs. Carol wanted to pray at our first meal together and said, "Thank you for this wonderful family who have helped us so much."

There Was Rejoicing in the Presence of the Angels in Heaven!

March 5, 2006, was a Sunday morning. Heath took Carol to church so I could be home alone with Carl, who was bedfast. As I sat by him, with much prayer in my heart, I asked, "Carl, how is it between you and the Lord?" He answered, "Not good." I reminded him of God's love and told him if he was the only person in the world, Jesus would have come to die for him...As I write this, my eyes well up with tears, remembering the presence of God's Holy Spirit working in Carl's heart that morning. Later, using the computer in the motel's business room, I wrote:

"Dear family,

"We just want to let you know that today Uncle Carl opened his heart to accept the Lord Jesus Christ as his Savior! Thank you for your prayers. Our hearts are just crying out to our wonderful God who has heard and answered our prayers over many, many years!

"Dad took Carol to church this morning. He has had some good talks with her as they ride in the car together. As Uncle Carl is pretty much bedfast and can't be left alone, it was my privilege to stay with him while they were gone. I prayed that the Lord would give him clarity of thought as we talked. He is on so much medication for pain and other things so is sometimes disoriented or sleepy. The Lord answered prayer here too. He was very open to my speaking to him and talking to him about what Jesus had done to give him assurance of sins forgiven and eternal life. When I asked him if he was ready to accept the Gospel message he said, 'Yes.'

"We prayed together, and he mentioned a song that he remembered from about sixty years ago, 'Lord, I'm Coming Home.' God's presence was wonderfully there with us. I remembered all the words to that great hymn and sang it to him. His face lit up in a smile. Then I sang 'Just As I Am,' and once again he smiled, saying those were his favorite hymns.

"We have been staying at the Hampton Inn at night, unless he calls in the middle of the night (once so far) needing us. Aunt Carol is very deaf and often can't hear when he calls for help. We go out to the house in the morning and are with them until 7:00 or 8:00 p.m., trying to help in every way we can with his care and chauffeuring Carol for needed things, banking, groceries, and medicines.

"Before we leave them at night, we pray with them. Tonight after Dad prayed, Carl's blue eyes filled with tears. He said, 'I want everybody to know that I have accepted Jesus Christ as my Savior, and if anything happens to me, I know I will go to heaven.'

"Oh thank You, thank You, my precious Father in heaven! My heart is so full of praise to You for Your grace, mercy, compassion, power, and love. Be encouraged! God hears and answers our prayers. Never give up!

"With love to all of you, Mom and Dad (or) Grandma and Grandpa"

The next day, Heath again took Carol out for five hours and got much accomplished. He took her to the BMV for her identification card, visited the funeral home they had chosen and checked on arrangements, took her to lunch at China Buffet, and got new batteries for her hearing aids.

Carl and I had a good time together. I fixed lunch at home and spent time talking to Him about his new life in Christ. I started reading the Gospel of John to him. He listened and then said, "Normie, you are my Sunday school teacher!" He again expressed how happy he was that we had come out to Arizona to help them. He was convinced that because we were there, he didn't have a stroke.

We spoke of our mother, Lena Christmas, and what a godly wonderful mother she was. He was still sorry for the anguish he had caused her when he was a teenager! Mom had been in heaven with the Lord for some forty-six years, and yet God, in His sovereign time, was still answering her prayers! Carl asked me questions about guardian angels and asked if I believed there were such beings. I told him I did! He said he was in so many tight and dangerous places as a soldier in World War II and thought angels had to be involved in keeping him from being killed, but he never saw one. I told him that I thought it was very possible, when his time came to go to be with the Lord, that he would see the angels coming to escort him to heaven. We both smiled at that thought.

A day later, Carl showed his repentant heart again when he got choked up, saying, "I don't see how the Lord could forgive me. I rejected him for so long." What a joy it was for me to tell him that God had removed his sins from him as far as the east is from the west and that once we accept Christ, He remembers our sins no more! That brought a smile to Carl's face again.

Rebecca and Jonathan called us every day to see how things were going. They too loved Uncle Carl dearly. Jon had been in meetings in Las Vegas, Nevada. On Tuesday, March 7, he flew to Modesto, California, rented a car, and came down to visit his Uncle Carl. He stayed from 11:00 a.m. until 8:00 p.m. Carl and Jon had a great visit, talking about Grandpa (Papaw) Christmas, fishing, airplanes, and other things. Jon ordered a special dinner brought in that evening to celebrate Carl and Carol's sixty-first wedding anniversary, which was coming up on March 15. Jon was a special encouragement to us all. Afterward, we realized that the Lord brought Jon on that day, which turned out to be Carl's last good day.

Carl was weakening and going downhill rapidly the next day. His hands were shaking, and he no longer was able to feed himself. He also was not communicating much. We were able to get him into a nursing home on Thursday, March 8. His pain medications were taken orally, so my greatest fear was that he would not be able to take the medications and would be in pain. The nursing home had nursing aids and no one to do IVs or injections. The pain meds were changed to liquids, and he seemed to get them down. I asked him over and over if he was in pain, and he always murmured, "No." (Thank You, Lord!)

On Saturday, March 11, Carl was sleeping or staring into space. I knew he could hear everything I said as I prayed with him and then reminded him of some humorous things from our childhood. Carol didn't realize that he was hearing what she said and distressed me sometimes with discouraging words in front of him. I didn't want to leave him that night because I knew the end was drawing near, but when I said I would stay with him that night, she said she would stay too! I knew that wouldn't be good, and she was also worn out. So we made him as comfortable as we could and left him in the care of the nursing home ladies.

On Sunday, March 12, 2006, Carl was promoted to heaven in the early morning hours. A hospice worker went to Carol's house to tell her and take her to Prestige nursing home to see him before Lietz-Fraze Funeral Home took him away. They called us at the motel, so we hurriedly dressed and went there too. I was sad that his body had already been taken away when we got there, but the next day when I took Carol to the funeral home for final arrangements, they asked if we wanted to see him one last time before he was cremated. Carl was lying on a gurney, covered with a pretty quilt. He looked so peaceful, and I was so thankful I got to see him that last time. Carol chose the box for cremation and the urn, which was later placed at a cemetery memorial. They had arranged for Carol's ashes to be put there too. Their names were already on the memorial. Carol died on August 29, 2006, just over five months later.

Selling Our Home in Ohio

The housing market was just beginning to decline at that time, and prices were going down. It would soon become a buyer's market and not good for sellers. But the Lord was so good to us, as usual! We thought we would try to sell our house ourselves. Professional people could be contracted to stage your house, but some of their starting prices were over $1,000! My brilliant (really!) idea was to get a book from the library (free) and do my own staging. We got rid of our coffee table (no longer in style), set the table with our best tablecloth and dishes, got new towels for the bathrooms and tied decorative bows around them, removed all personal family pictures, and decluttered everywhere. We bought a big cinnamon roll-fragranced candle to burn in the kitchen and so forth. Everything really looked lovely when we had our Sunday afternoon open house. Since folks would be wandering all through the house, including the finished basement, our friend Jim Kearney sat in our basement family room to keep a watch on strangers to see that nothing disappeared. One lady came to us and asked, "Do you realize there is a man sitting in your basement family room?" Smile!

We had talked to one Realtor, and she really tried to discourage us from selling our home ourselves. She said there were lots of legal problems we might get involved in and so forth. She said, "I have someone who will buy your home if you let me sell it. I'll reduce my commission from 6 percent to 4 percent." We still thought we should try, but when she called again and said, "If you'll let my son sell your house, we'll reduce the commission to 3 percent. I definitely have someone who is looking for a house like yours," we decided to say yes! So our home sold within two weeks!

An interesting situation arose when the inspector that our buyers obtained came to inspect our home. He kept exclaiming about what a beautiful home they were getting. He was so impressed by the deck that Jonathan had put on and many other things. It was almost like he was there to help us sell our home! The only thing he found wrong was one place of wiring in the attic that could have caused a fire. Our new buyers said, "Oh, our relative is an electrician. He can take care of that!"

We moved out of our house the first of August 2006 after the closing. Our new condo was supposed to be ready for occupancy by end of the year. So with our possessions put into storage, we visited Jonathan in New Hampshire for a month, then a month with Rebecca. They were very gracious, but we didn't want to burden them by staying longer. Next, we went to Maranatha Village in Sebring, Florida, for ten weeks. A widow friend very graciously allowed us to live in the mobile home she had there. She only occupied it two winter months each year, and the other ten months it was empty. We were hoping every month that we would be receiving the news that our condo in Mooresville was going to be built, but month after month, they were not able to begin building it. The housing market was going downhill rapidly. People who wanted to buy couldn't because they could not sell the homes they were presently living in.

Technically, we had been homeless for several months, so with much prayer, we were wondering what God had for us. We asked our mission's administrative assistant if she knew of anyone in her church on the north side of Indianapolis who needed someone to housesit for them. She wrote us quickly that there was a couple in her church who had a house they had fixed up and furnished for their mother. However, after the mother had her cancer treatment and went into remission, she wanted to return to her home in Florida and never lived in that house on Lafayette Road.

What a blessing and provision from the Lord Dave and Ellen Smitson were to us! We moved into their lovely little house on January 1, 2007, thinking surely the Mooresville Epcon home we were planning to have would be built within the next few months. We ended up living in the Smitsons' home for a whole year! Our hearts will always be grateful to the Smitsons. Their love for the Lord, His work, and His children were a great blessing to us and countless others.

Finding a Church in Indianapolis

It was difficult for us to leave our church in Ohio, but we knew God was leading us to come to Indiana. We began attending a small church plant, Indianapolis International Baptist Church, in a storefront location only a few minutes from where we were living and were a part of that work for the next seven years. We loved meeting the Africans there, speaking French with those from Ivory Coast and English with folks from Ghana and Liberia. The French-speakers were so happy to have someone to talk to in French as they struggled to learn English.

Meeting People from Niger in Indianapolis

We had heard there were a large number of people from Niger in Indianapolis. Heath wanted to meet them and was instructed to go to a barber shop on Michigan Road and 71st Street. When Heath walked in, Omar, the barber, was busy cutting hair. But when Heath said, *"Boro fo go ne kan ga maa Zarma ciine, wala?"* ("Is there anyone here who speaks Zarma?") Omar's mouth dropped open. He came over, gave Heath a big hug, then called into the back room, *"Kaa ka di anasara kan ga maa Zarma ciine!"* ("Come and see a white person who speaks Zarma!")

Omar told us to come back on Saturday afternoon when many of the Niger people weren't working, and we would find that many came then to visit with each other. We went and were warmly welcomed by everyone who was there. They even presented us with two beautiful leather *pouffes* (footstools) from Niger. And thus, the Lord had put us where we could continue to reach out to Zarmas and Hausas from Niger living in the States. Most of them were very warm and friendly, thrilled that we spoke their language, and willing to accept the Jesus DVDs we gave out in Zarma, Hausa, French, and English as well as good Gospel literature. We were invited to baby-naming ceremonies, a wedding, picnics, and soccer games.

It was a joy for us to be surrounded once again by African friends. It was especially nostalgic for me to sit with the women as they conversed, laughed, and played with their babies. It was almost like being back in a

Niger village again with dear friends. They accepted us as friends, even though they realized we had served as missionaries in their country.

Moving to a Condo

We had waited over a year for our condo to be built in Mooresville but construction had not even begun, so we decided to look again at another Epcon Community on Stop 11 Road in Indianapolis. We sensed God's peace as we looked at a mostly finished Canterbury on Lifestyle Drive. We closed on the new condo and moved in on January 1, 2008. We will always be thankful to Rick and Rebecca who graciously put up with all our belongings being stored for months in their basement.

In June 2009, Jonathan hosted a family reunion at his home in Rye, New Hampshire. It was a thrill to have all five of our children together again.

My brother Melvin Lee Christmas (Mickey) went home to be with his Lord and Savior in November 2009, so I am the only one of our Christmas family of six to still be living. I miss my loved ones so very much, but what a comfort it is to know they are in heaven, redeemed by the blood of the Lord Jesus Christ, and I will see them again!

We began volunteering as conversation partners for international students who needed to perfect their English so they could apply to universities in the States. Many of the students were from countries that are totally closed to the Gospel, and we are thankful for the opportunities we have had to be able to share the Gospel with them.

Sixtieth Anniversary Celebration

In June 2015, Heath and I celebrated our sixtieth wedding anniversary. Jonathan and Rebecca hosted a wonderful party for us in Indianapolis. Family came from all over the world to celebrate with us.

I would like to conclude my memoirs with a statement from Billy Graham: "When I think about God's love, I tend to dwell upon all the good things He has done for me. But then I must stop and realize that even when circumstances have been hard or the way unclear, God has still surrounded me with His love. God's love is just as real and just as powerful in the darkness as it is in the light. And that is *why we can have hope!*"

Please know that originally my sole purpose in writing these memoirs was to leave a record for our children and grandchildren to see what a great and faithful God we serve. All glory and praise goes only to Him. A friend once said, "Don't put missionaries on a pedestal. They get hurt when they fall off!" As Jim Elliot once wrote, "Missionaries are very human folks just doing what they are asked. Simply a bunch of nobodies trying to exalt Somebody."

So much has happened in the ensuing years. Heath and I are now octogenarians. The Lord has allowed us to live to see our children's children's children! At the time of this writing we have sixteen grandchildren and sixteen great-grandchildren! How precious each one is to us! "Children's children are a crown to the aged (Proverbs 17:6a)!" To God be the glory! Great things He has done!

Norma Bobbett

Epilogue

God has blessed me with my best friend and dear husband, Heath. We never had any doubt that the Lord had made us for each other. How good the Lord has been to give us that assurance as we walked together through life, in good times and hard times, in blessings and in disappointments, in joys and in trials, in sickness and in health. All glory and praise go to Him alone!

After thirty-five years, we left Niger and our ministry there. So often we missionaries meet people who think we are superhuman because we have given up so much to be obedient to the Lord in missionary service. They are convinced that our rewards will be much greater than others in heaven because of all our sacrifice and work. I have to tell them how wrong they are.

I truly believe that when rewards are given, we missionaries will be lost in the crowd in the back of the room while our African brothers and sisters will be called right up front. They put us to shame with their love, sacrifice, and total devotion to their Savior! We were so privileged to know them and to work alongside them.

It has been with profound thankfulness and joy that I have written about Jesus leading the way in our lives.

"An adventure is only an inconvenience rightly considered. An inconvenience is only an adventure wrongly considered."

"The Christian ideal has not been tried and found wanting. It has been found difficult and left untried." – *G.K. Chesterton*

Norma Bobbett, May 2018

Final Tribute

As my wife brings her memoirs to a close, I want to add a word of thanks to the Lord for bringing our paths together and for the wonderful helpmate she has always been to me.

I also want to congratulate her and thank her for her perseverance – for the many, many hours (hundreds really) she has spent reading through her journals, reading our prayer letters (dating from the late 1950s), researching various historical facts, and sitting at the computer to write these memoirs for our family.

In 2015, we celebrated our sixtieth wedding anniversary. We hope to celebrate many more. It would be wonderful if we are still alive to hear the trumpet sound together (whenever that will be) as the Lord returns to take us Home to be with Himself (I Thessalonians 4:13-18).

Our favorite hymn is "Great Is Thy Faithfulness," and these memoirs serve as a testimony to that great truth. He has been faithful to us over all of these years, and we know He will continue to be so until He comes again.

Heath Bobbett, May 2018

Find Us Faithful
Lyrics by Jon Mohr

We're pilgrims on the journey
Of the narrow road,
And those who've gone before us line the way,
Cheering on the faithful, encouraging the weary,
Their lives a stirring testament to God's sustaining grace.

Surrounded by so great a cloud of witnesses,
Let us run the race not only for the prize
But as those who've gone before us.
Let us leave to those behind us
The heritage of faithfulness
Passed on through godly lives.

Oh may all who come behind us find us faithful.
May the fire of our devotion light their way.
May the footprints that we leave
Lead them to believe
And the lives we live inspire them to obey.
Oh may all who come behind us find us faithful.

After all our hopes and dreams have come and gone
And our children sift through all we've left behind,
May the clues that they discover
And the memories they uncover
Become the light that leads them
To the road we each must find.

Oh may all who come behind us find us faithful.
May the fire of our devotion light their way.
May the footprints that we leave
Lead them to believe
And the lives we live inspire them to obey.
Oh may all who come behind us find us faithful.

Norma Bobbett

Some of Norma's Favorite Quotes

I could fill page after page with favorite quotes, but here are a few:

Prayer is weakness leaning on Omnipotence.

Prayer can gain access to the proud spirit, the hardened heart, to the unbelieving mind. There are no walls too thick or too high for God to breach. So pray God's will and watch lives change – especially your own!" – *Charles Stanley*

Learn to take your blessings to God in thanksgiving and your burdens to Him in petitions.

We have to pray with our eyes on God, not on the difficulties. – *Oswald Chambers*. "In the fear of the LORD **there is strong confidence** and His children will have a place of refuge" (Proverbs 14:26).

"For with God, nothing shall be impossible" (Luke 1:37). An elderly woman past childbearing age gave birth to a son, as did an unmarried virgin girl. In both cases they were told that nothing is impossible for God. (Genesis 18:14, Luke 1:37). Christ wants not nibblers of the possible, but grabbers of the impossible.– *C.T. Studd*

No one is so poor as an individual for whom not a single soul is praying and has no one to take him or her persistently and personally to the Throne of Grace.

We must carve out a time so that prayer is a priority to us. The pressures we face every day will threaten to crowd out our time with God. We are connecting with a God who loves, grieves, laughs, and hears! Prayer is the conductor that keeps our focus on God.– *Zig Ziglar*

Sometimes God lets us fall to the rock bottom to discover He is the **Rock**.

Prayer is an effective source of power for me. That is why Satan tries to keep me from it.

Father, remind me daily that I am loved and empowered by the One who brought the universe into existence with the mere sound of His voice (**Nothing** and no one is impossible with Him!) and that "the Spirit of Him who raised Jesus from the dead" dwells in me (Romans 8:1). I am to "be strong in the power of His might" (Ephesians 6:10).

I am to accept trials as part of God's good plan for me. Hezekiah said, "Surely it was for my benefit that I suffered such anguish." Romans 8:28 – All things work together for good," not by inherent force, not by fate or chance, but by Divine control.– *Charles R Erdman*. "He works all things according to the counsel of His will" (Ephesians 1:11).

Trust God's timing and wait with patience. "Those who wait for the LORD will gain new strength" (Isaiah 40:31).

They [prodigals] are a gift to me, as all children are – especially precious gifts because they teach me much: patience, the depth of my own need for forgiveness, my need of continual dependence upon my Heavenly Father in prayer. When our children bring us to our knees, we are in the best position for God to help us.– *Ruth Graham*

It is squarely a matter of believing that God will do what only He can do. – *Jim Cymbala*

The key to stabilizing faith lies in choosing to believe God, regardless of the situation. Only then will it be possible to bring natural feelings of doubt, anxiety, fear, and anger or confusion into submission to what we know to be true – that the Lord is faithful and will see us through every situation. – *Dr. Charles Stanley*

Joyful Journey
By Henry Van Dyke

...So let the way wind up the hill or down;
Though rough or smooth, the journey will be joy,
Still seeking what I sought when but a boy:
New friendship, high adventure, and a crown!
I shall grow old, but never lose life's zest,
Because the road's last turn will be the best.

Appendix
The Niger Republic

In 1922, France took over Niger, putting the Zarmas and other tribes under colonial rule. French became the official language for schools and offices. Although coming from different language groups, the educated speak the common language of French. After forty-eight years of colonial rule, Niger gained its independence the year we arrived (1960).

Niger, one of the world's poorest countries, is located in the southwestern part of the Sahara Desert. The landlocked country is hot, dry, and dusty a good portion of the year and has been named as one of the hottest countries in the world! Predominately Sahara Desert, the territory is sandy with scrubby vegetation. When we arrived, the main exports were peanuts and hides. Later uranium and some other natural resources were found.

Most of the people are sustenance farmers, meaning they need to grow enough grain during the rainy season (June to October) to feed themselves for the next year. When the rains are insufficient, famines occur. Harvests are also complicated by increasing population, soil erosion, overgrazing of animals, deforestation (getting wood for cooking), and the advancing of the Sahara Desert each year.

Statistics say there are 3,300,000 Zarmas, and the biggest population is in Niger. The literacy rate (those over age fifteen who can read and write) is 19.1 percent.

Although they adopted the Islamic religion centuries ago, Zarmas also retain many animistic beliefs and practices. These beliefs are seen in wearing charms and consulting demon-possessed mediums and local imams. Many people feel there is magic in the verses of the Koran. The imam writes verses from the Koran on wooden boards then washes them off, catching the inky water for the people to drink. Also verses from the Koran are put into leather amulets to be worn on the body.

The Zarma people are friendly and wonderfully hospitable. Evangelical Baptist Mission came to Niamey in 1929 and was the first protestant mission to work among the Zarmas. EBM was the only one in that ministry until the 1970s. EBM missionaries were the ones who reduced the language to writing and translated the Bible into the Zarma language. In recent years, several other missions have come to Niger to work among various tribes. Most work from the capital city of Niamey.

Made in the USA
Middletown, DE
29 March 2019